QuickBooks® Pro 2014:
Comprehensive

TRISHA CONLON

LABYRINTH
LEARNING™

Berkeley, CA

QuickBooks Pro 2014: Comprehensive
by Trisha Conlon

Copyright © 2014 by Labyrinth Learning

LABYRINTH
LEARNING™

Labyrinth Learning
2560 9th Street, Suite 320
Berkeley, California 94710
800.522.9746
On the web at lablearning.com

President:
Brian Favro

Product Manager:
Jason Favro

Development Manager:
Laura Popelka

Senior Editor:
Susan Scharf

Production Manager:
Rad Proctor

Editorial Assistant:
Alexandria Henderson

Production Assistant:
Andrew Kenower

eLearning Production Manager:
Arl S. Nadel

Indexing:
Joanne Sprott

Cover Design:
Mick Koller, SuperLab Design

Interior Design:
Mark Ong, Side-by-Side Studio

eBOOK ITEM:1-59136-731-X
ISBN-13: 978-1-59136-731-4

PRINT ITEM: 1-59136-686-0
ISBN-13: 978-1-59136-686-7

Manufactured in the United States of America.

10 9 8 7 6 5 4 3 2 1

Contents in Brief

Table of Contents

UNIT 3: ADDITIONAL SKILLS

Quick Reference Tables

Preface

QuickBooks® Pro 2014: Comprehensive provides essential coverage of QuickBooks 2014 software. Topics covered include basic accounting principles, backing up files, creating companies, working with vendors, working with customers, banking with QuickBooks, customizing QuickBooks, classes, the accounting cycle, physical inventory, payroll, estimates and time tracking, balance sheet accounts, budgets, closing the books, adjusting entries, and more.

For almost two decades, Labyrinth Learning has been publishing easy-to-use textbooks that empower educators to teach complex subjects quickly and effectively, while enabling students to gain confidence, develop practical skills, and compete in a demanding job market. We add comprehensive support materials, assessment and learning management tools, and eLearning components to create true learning solutions for a wide variety of instructor-led, self-paced, and online courses.

Our textbooks follow the *Labyrinth Instruction Design*, our unique and proven approach that makes learning easy and effective for every learner. Our books begin with fundamental concepts and build through a systematic progression of exercises. Quick Reference Tables, precise callouts on screen captures, carefully selected illustrations, and minimal distraction combine to create a learning solution that is highly efficient and effective for both students and instructors.

This course is supported with *comprehensive instructor support* materials that include printable solution guides for side-by-side comparisons, test banks, customizable assessments, customizable PowerPoint presentations, detailed lesson plans, preformatted files for integration to leading learning management system, and more.

This book meets the objectives for the Intuit QuickBooks Certified User (QBCU) exam offered through Certiport.

Visual Conventions

This book uses many visual and typographic cues to guide students through the lessons. This page provides examples and describes the function of each cue.

`Type this text`	Anything you should type at the keyboard is printed in this typeface.
	Tips, Notes, and Warnings are used to draw attention to certain topics.
Command→ Command→ Command, etc.	This convention indicates a Ribbon path. The commands are written: Ribbon Tab→Command Group→Command→Subcommand.

FROM THE KEYBOARD
Ctrl + S to save

These margin notes indicate shortcut keys for executing a task described in the text.

 NEW! 2014

Features new to this edition of the software are indicated with this icon.

Visualize!

If there is an Intuit video related to the QuickBooks topic being discussed, this convention will point you to it.

 2 LAB QUICK GRADER

New automatic grading available for selected assignments displaying this icon.

Exercise Progression

The exercises in this book build in complexity as students work through a lesson toward mastery of the skills taught.

- **Develop Your Skills** exercises are introduced immediately after concept discussions. They provide detailed, step-by-step tutorials.
- **Reinforce Your Skills** exercises provide additional hands-on practice with moderate assistance.
- **Apply Your Skills** exercises test students' skills by describing the correct results without providing specific instructions on how to achieve them.
- **Extend Your Skills** exercises are the most challenging. They provide generic instructions, allowing students to use their skills and creativity to achieve the results they envision.

Acknowledgements

We are grateful to the instructors who have used Labyrinth titles and suggested improvements to us over the many years we have been writing and publishing books. This book has benefited greatly from the reviews and suggestions of the following instructors.

Jennifer Adkins, *North Central State College*

Marcia Bagnall, *Chemeketa Community College*

Elaine Barnwell, *Bevill State Community College*

Errol Belt, *San Juan Unified School District*

Ed Bonner, *National Career Skills Institute*

Kevin Bradford, *Somerset Community College*

David Campbell, *Northern Virginia Community College*

Margo Chaney Adkins, *Carroll Community College*

Marilyn Ciolino, *Delgado Community College*

Catherine Combs, *College of Applied Technology at Morristown*

Martha Cranford, *Rowan Cabarrus Community College*

Julie Dailey, *Central Virginia Community College*

Kerry Dolan, *Great Falls College MSU*

Dr. Vicky Dominguez, *College of Southern Nevada*

Gregory Drakulich, *Miami Jacobs Career College*

Sandra Dragoo, *Ivy Tech Community College Lafayette*

Susan Draper, *Williston State College*

Patricia Dukeman, *College of Central Florida*

Toiya Evans, *South Piedmont Community College*

Michael Fagan, *Raritan Valley Community College*

Connie Galvin, *Delta Montrose Technical College*

Janet Garver, *Mid-Michigan Community College*

Mahnaz Ghaffarian, *Southwest Tennessee Community College*

Sharron Glover, *Black Chamber of Commerce, Metro OKC*

Yvette Gonzalez-Smith, *Savannah Technical College*

Nancy Gromen, *Eastern Oregon University*

Diane Hageman, *San Mateo Adult School*

Helen Hall, *College of Southern Maryland*

Diann Hammon, *JF Drake Community and Technical College*

Michele Hand, *Dickinson Lifelong Learning Center*

Sherry Harris, *University of Arkansas at Monticello*

Patricia Hartley, *Chaffey College*

Nancy Heinlein, *Nashua Adult Learning Center*

Rebecca Holden, *Southeastern Community College*

Peter Holland, *Napa Valley College*

Meredith Jackson, *Snead State Community College*

Stacie Jacobsen, *Pikes Peak Community College*

Carol Jensen, *City College of San Francisco*

Dr. Melanie S. Jones, *Mohave Community College*

Shawn Kendall, *Knox County Career Center*

Linda Kohnen, *North Central Technical College*

Dawn Krause, *Macomb Community College*

Denise Lawson, *Southern Westchester Board of Cooperative Educational Services*

Sue Lobner, *Nicolet Area Technical College*

Leonard Long, *Quincy College*

Diana Marquez, *Atlantic Technical Center*

Leslie Martin, *Gaston College*

Debbie McClanahan, *Balanced Books*

Autumn Matzat, *Alhambra Unified School District*

Vanessa May, *South Louisiana Community College*

Nancy Nibley, *Simi Valley Adult School and Career Institute*

Micki Nickla, *Ivy Tech Community College*

Susan Noble, *MiraCosta College*

Terry Mullin, *Cabrillo College*

John Oppenheim, *Dig-in Enterprises*

Arleen Orland, *Santa Clarita Technology & Career Development Center*

Carleen Powell, *Tri-County Adult Career Center*

Kathryn Quisenberry-Boyd, *Vista Adult School*

Kristina Rabius, *Pima Community College*

Traven Reed, *Canadore College*

Crystal Rhoades, *Wake Tech Community College*

William Simmons, *Austin Community College*

Sheila Smith, *Northwest Arkansas Community College*

Zachary Smulski, *South Seattle Community College*

Eric Stadnik, *Santa Rosa Junior College*

Traci Edmiston Thacker, *Texas State Technical College*

Mark Triller, *Blackhawk Technical College*

Laura Way, *Fortis College in Ravenna*

Sheree White, *Jupiter High School*

Diane Williams, *Colby Community College*

Alfred Worthy, *Rust College*

Peter F. Young, *San Jose State University*

Dora Zandarski, *Trumbull Career and Technical Center, Adult Training*

UNIT 1

UNIT OUTLINE

Essential Skills

Quick Books is an Intuit software program designed to help small- and medium-sized businesses keep their books easily and accurately. In this unit, we'll introduce you to the software and to basic file management tasks. You'll learn how to properly set up a company file, as well as how to work with customers, deal with vendors, and use banking tasks in QuickBooks.

1

Introducing QuickBooks Pro

CHAPTER OBJECTIVES

After studying this chapter, you will be able to:

- Discuss basic accounting concepts
- Determine if QuickBooks is right for your business
- Navigate the QuickBooks window
- Manage basic QuickBooks files
- Open a portable company file
- Back up a company file

QuickBooks has become the software of choice for many owners of small and medium-sized businesses. No doubt, this is due to the many functions and features that the software offers the smaller company. In this chapter, you will explore the various editions of QuickBooks and determine which is right for you. You will also examine what goes on behind the scenes and why it is so important for you to have a basic understanding of accounting. Finally, you will be introduced to some QuickBooks basics that are vital to your success as a QuickBooks user, and you will learn how to access valuable supplemental training tools right in your QuickBooks software.

Discovering What's New in QuickBooks 2014

Each year, Intuit introduces a new version of QuickBooks with new-and-improved features. As you work through this book, you will see these new aspects of the software called to your attention with a special icon.

 This is how you will be able to identify new or improved QuickBooks features.

The following list outlines some of the new QuickBooks 2014 features as well as the chapter in which each is introduced:

- The main color of the interface has changed from gray to blue (seen throughout the book)
- Alert and reminder links are located at the far right of the menu bar (Chapter 1, Introducing QuickBooks Pro)
- Income Tracker allows you to easily access income transactions from the Customer Center (Chapter 3, Working with Customers)
- Handling of bounced checks is dealt with in (Chapter 5, Banking with QuickBooks)
- Custom fields and Add Sales Rep can be added to purchase forms (Chapter 5, Banking with QuickBooks)
- Bank Feeds Center improves the online experience (Chapter 5, Banking with QuickBooks)
- Multiple attachments can be sent in a single email from transaction windows (Chapter 9, Working with Estimates and Time Tracking)
- Tax time categorization tools are available (Chapter 12, Reporting, Adjusting Entries, and Closing the Books)
- You can create color schemes for each company file with which you work (Chapter 12, Reporting, Adjusting Entries, and Closing the Books)

 Later in this chapter you will learn about the video tutorials available through the QuickBooks Learning Center. Once you have learned how to access tutorials, you will have a chance to view the "What's New in 2014" tutorial.

Presenting QuickBooks Pro

QuickBooks is a software program that allows companies to:

- Keep track of customers, vendors, employees, and other important entities
- Process sales transactions and cash receipts
- Process purchase transactions and payments to vendors
- Run payroll
- Track and sell inventory
- Run end-of-period financial reports
- Track assets (what you own) and liabilities (what you owe)
- Keep track of bank accounts
- Collaborate with accountants easily and efficiently

Types of Companies That Use QuickBooks Pro

QuickBooks Pro works well for different types of companies in a variety of industries. Ideally, your company should not have more than twenty employees and $1 million in annual revenue if you plan to use QuickBooks Pro (these are not strict rules, but guidelines). If your company is larger, you may want to consider using QuickBooks Enterprise Solutions. One type of business that QuickBooks Pro is not suited for is manufacturing, but Intuit has produced both Premier and Enterprise editions of QuickBooks especially for the manufacturing industry.

Aside from these issues, QuickBooks Pro can be customized and works well for many businesses, including not-for-profit organizations.

Editions of QuickBooks

Before you purchase your copy of QuickBooks, you should evaluate what you need QuickBooks to do for you. There are several editions of QuickBooks, all of which perform the basic tasks required for small-business bookkeeping. This book requires at the minimum the use of QuickBooks Pro, but it can be used with the Premier edition as well. If you are using a different edition, your screen may look a little bit different from what is displayed throughout this book.

Intuit also creates a QuickBooks edition for Mac users, which is similar to the Windows-based version in functions yet looks different because of the differences in the two platforms. The downloadable files associated with this book are *not* compatible with the Mac or International versions of QuickBooks.

Versions, as Compared to Editions

Now, don't let yourself become confused by the difference between editions and versions of QuickBooks. Intuit creates a new version of QuickBooks each year (such as QuickBooks 2012, 2013, or 2014). Each new version provides additional features that are new for that year. This book is designed for QuickBooks 2014, but once you learn how to use the features QuickBooks offers, it will be easy to switch between versions.

With each version, Intuit creates many editions from which a company may choose (such as QuickBooks Simple Start, QuickBooks Pro, QuickBooks Premier, and QuickBooks Enterprise Solutions). There are also online editions of QuickBooks available that, for a monthly fee, allow you to access your company's QuickBooks file via the Internet. Take a look at the Student Resource Center for this book to determine which edition will work best for your company.

Other Tools from Intuit

Intuit creates other tools that are a part of the "Quicken family" and are used by small businesses. You may find that software such as Quicken Home & Business or Quicken Rental Property Manager might be a better tool to track your small business' finances. To learn more about these other options produced by Intuit, browse the company's website at http://www.intuit.com.

The Online Editions of QuickBooks

Many companies are now using the online editions (Simple Start, Essentials, and Plus) of QuickBooks. The online versions look very similar to the traditional desktop editions but have some unique features, such as:

- The ability to access QuickBooks from any computer with Internet access, as well as from many popular smart phones
- A way for users in multiple or remote locations to easily utilize a single file
- Automatic online backups as all of your data is stored "in the cloud"

In addition, there is no need to worry about technological problems associated with desktop product installation and support when using QuickBooks online.

All of the users of a company file can access it through the web with a username and password, and all users work with the same up-to-date company file. It is recommended that you have a high-speed Internet connection to utilize these editions. The online editions, as with the desktop editions, allow you to set up users and determine the access level for each one.

The online interface is very similar to that of QuickBooks Pro, so once you learn the basics of the program from studying this book, you will be able to transfer your knowledge to the online editions. It is similar to learning to drive a Ford and then driving a Toyota—you will just need to familiarize yourself with the differences before you take off! You also have the ability to import your company data from a desktop edition of QuickBooks into your online account. You do not purchase software for an online edition but, instead, pay a monthly fee. Not all features are available in the online editions, though, so it is best to compare the different editions on the Intuit website in order to determine which is best-suited for your company's needs. You can find a link to the online edition comparison as well as current pricing in the Student Resource Center for this book.

QuickBooks App Center

The QuickBooks App Center is a web-based resource with tools to help you manage your business more effectively.

This link leads to the web page for the full App Center.

This is the window that appears when you click the Web and Mobile Apps task icon in the Company area of the Home page.

Types of Tasks

There are many types of tasks you can perform with QuickBooks. The tasks can be broken down into two main categories: those that affect the accounting behind the scenes (activities and company setup) and those that do not (lists and reporting). The following table lists the four basic types of tasks covered in this book.

QUICKBOOKS TASKS AND THEIR FUNCTIONS	
Task	**Function**
list (database)	Lists allow you to store information about customers, vendors, employees, and other data important to your business.
Activities	Activities affect what happens behind the scenes. They can be entered easily on forms such as invoices or bills.
Company Setup	This feature takes you through the steps necessary to set up a new company in QuickBooks.
Reports	QuickBooks provides many preset reports and graphs that are easily customizable to meet your needs.

Understanding Basic Accounting

Many business owners use QuickBooks to keep their own books and attempt to just learn the software. QuickBooks is quite intuitive, but you will find yourself running into problems if you don't understand the accounting basics on which QuickBooks is based. If you want to make sure you have a more solid understanding of accounting, you may wish to consider the book, *Accounting Basics: An Introduction for Non-Accounting Majors*, also published by Labyrinth Learning.

An Accountant's Worst Nightmare (or Greatest Dream?)

Picture yourself as an accountant who has just received a QuickBooks file from a client. The client has no idea how accounting works and, to him, debit and credit are just types of plastic cards he carries in his wallet. In his file you find duplicate accounts in the Chart of Accounts, accounts created as the wrong type, items posted to incorrect accounts, accounts payable inaccuracies, and payroll inaccuracies (to name just a few problems).

Now, as an accountant, you can consider this a nightmare because you will have to run numerous diagnostics to find all the mistakes (which could have been easily avoided if your client learned how to use QuickBooks properly in the first place) or a dream because your billable hours will increase at a rapid rate.

This scenario is exactly the reason why you, as the client, need to learn what happens behind the scenes in QuickBooks, as well as how to use the day-to-day functions of the software. By having a better understanding of the accounting and how to do things properly in the program, you will reduce the number of hours your accountant will have to spend and, thereby, save yourself the accountant fees in the end!

What's Up with GAAP?

GAAP stands for Generally Accepted Accounting Principles (GAAP). These are accounting rules used in the United States to prepare, present, and report financial statements for a wide variety of entities. The organization that creates the rules is called the FASB (Financial Accounting Standards Board). Publicly owned companies need to follow these rules unless they can show that doing so would produce information that is misleading. It is wise for the small-business owner to adhere to GAAP. These rules work to make taxation fair as it affects small-business owners.

As GAAP attempt to achieve basic objectives, they have several basic assumptions, principles, and constraints (described below). Throughout the book you will see reminders of how GAAP apply to tasks that you are completing in QuickBooks via the "Flashback to the GAAP" feature.

GENERALLY ACCEPTED ACCOUNTING PRINCIPLES (GAAP)	
Principle	**Description**
Business entity principle	The business is separate from the owners and from other businesses. Revenues and expenses of the business should be kept separate from the personal expenses of the business owner.
The assumption of the going concern	The business will be in operation indefinitely.

GENERALLY ACCEPTED ACCOUNTING PRINCIPLES (GAAP) (continued)

Principle	Description
Monetary unit principle	A stable currency is going to be the unit of record.
Time-period principle	The activities of the business can be divided into time periods.
Cost principle	When a company purchases assets, it should record them at cost, not fair market value. For example, an item worth $750 bought for $100 is recorded at $100.
Revenue principle	Publicly traded companies (not always sole proprietorships) record when the revenue is realized and earned, not when cash is received (accrual basis of accounting).
Matching principle	Expenses need to be matched with revenues. If a contractor buys a specific sink for a specific bathroom, it is matched to the cost of remodeling the bathroom. Otherwise, the cost may be charged as project expense. This principle allows a better evaluation of the profitability and performance (how much did you spend to earn the revenue?).
Objectivity principle	The statements of a company should be based on objectivity.
Materiality principle	When an item is reported, its significance should be considered. An item is considered significant when it would affect the decision made regarding its use.
Consistency principle	The company uses the same accounting principles and methods from year to year.
Prudence principle	When choosing between two solutions, the one that will be least likely to overstate assets and income should be selected.

INTRODUCING "BEHIND THE SCENES"

Throughout this book you will see a special section called "Behind the Scenes" whenever you are learning about an activity performed within QuickBooks. This section will go over the accounting that QuickBooks performs for you when you record a transaction. Please note that the account names used in this feature use QuickBooks, rather than traditional accounting, nomenclature.

Accrual vs. Cash Basis Accounting

There are two ways that companies can choose to keep the books. The method you choose to implement depends on the nature of your business. QuickBooks makes it easy for you to produce reports utilizing either method, and your data entry will be the same regardless of which method you choose. Talk to your accountant or tax advisor to determine which method you have been using (for an existing business) or should use (for a new business).

Accrual Basis

In the accrual basis of accounting, income is recorded when the sale is made and expenses recorded when accrued. This method is often used by firms and businesses with large inventories. As you just learned from the GAAP table, this is the basis you need to use for publicly traded corporations.

Cash Basis

In the cash basis of accounting, income is recorded when cash is received and expenses recorded when cash is paid. This method is commonly used by small businesses and professionals involved in occupations that are not publicly traded.

Where to Find More Help

You can learn more about accounting fundamentals in Appendix A, Need to Know Accounting, at the back of this book. It provides some basic definitions, theories, and a link to a web page with online resources. More in-depth coverage of accounting concepts can be found in the Labyrinth Learning book, *Accounting Basics: An Introduction for Non-Accounting Majors*.

In Appendix A, Need to Know Accounting, you will find information on:

■ The accounting equation

■ Debits and credits

■ Types of accounts and normal balances

Introducing the Integrative Case Studies

For the Develop Your Skills exercises, you will explore the operations of a company called Average Guy Designs. This company was started by Guy Marshall, a graphic arts and QuickBooks student from a community college, and provides production and design services to clients. In the second unit of the book, Guy will begin to sell his work and the work of other artists at his store.

You will further hone your QuickBooks skills with Reinforce Your Skills exercises that deal with Quality-Built Construction, a contractor specializing in home remodel and construction, and with Apply Your Skills exercises that deal with Wet Noses Veterinary Clinic. The Develop Your Skills exercises focus on using the Home page to perform tasks, while the Reinforce Your Skills exercises primarily use the menu bar since that is a preference for some QuickBooks users. Once you are on your own with QuickBooks, you should use whichever method(s) you prefer.

The exercises that you will complete for Average Guy Designs and Quality-Built Construction are set in the time frame of December 2014 through March 2015, and Wet Noses is set in the time frame of May through August 2014. Each exercise step that includes a date will have you set the correct date within these time frames. Tackle the Tasks exercises allow you to solidify your skills using the Develop Your Skills company file.

At the end of each chapter there are also Extend Your Skills exercises that will challenge you further. Sort Through the Stack exercises sit you down in the office of a not-for-profit organization. You will "look through" all of the papers at her desk and make the necessary entries into QuickBooks. Be Your Own Boss will allow you to create a company file for a business of your choice and then work with it throughout the entire book, and the culminating WebQuests send you to the Internet to learn more about QuickBooks and accounting.

How to Use This Book and the Student Files

You may be curious about the large number of student exercise files that come with this book and how using this book as a learning tool compares to working with your own company file. The following questions and answers should help to set you in the right direction!

Why is there a different company file for each exercise?

When you are learning QuickBooks, it is much easier to follow the instructions if your screen matches the illustrations in the book (or your instructor's screen). Having a fresh file at the beginning of each chapter helps to ensure that mistakes naturally made by students learning new material do not compound and cause a disconnect between student files and the example illustrations.

A fresh company file for each chapter also means that the chapters in this book can be completed in any order.

What if I want to use one file that continues from chapter to chapter?

You also have the option to use a file that continues from chapter to chapter. You can use each of the exercise files this way from Chapter 3 onward. This means that once you complete the Develop Your Skills exercise in Chapter 3, you can then use the file for Chapters 4–12 in order. The same is true for the Reinforce Your Skills and Apply Your Skills exercises. Note that, to use the same company file for the Develop Your Skill exercises from Chapter 3 onward, you must also complete the "Tackle the Tasks" exercise before continuing to the next chapter.

Is this how I will work in QuickBooks in "real life?"

No, using a separate file for each type of task (e.g., working with vendors, customers, inventory, etc.) is *not* how you will operate in "real life." In the real world, you will have *one* company file only. The multiple company files are for training purposes only.

Do I have to complete the chapters in the order presented in the book?

No, this book is entirely modular, and you can approach the chapters in any order you choose. For instance, some people feel that the discussion of how to create a company should come after a full discussion of the basics of the software (i.e., after Chapter 5), rather than where it is placed in this book. Chapters may be worked through in any order. Fresh company files provided for each chapter make this possible.

Why do portable company files take so long to restore? What can I do while waiting for a file to restore?

Portable company files are compressed files that QuickBooks must "inflate" before you can use them. Think of the "space bags" you may have seen on an infomercial. Using a vacuum to remove all of the air from a space bag, you can fit some thirty sweaters into a shoebox. (Okay, this is a stretch, but hopefully you get the idea!) This is akin to QuickBooks creating a portable company file. Opening the seal and letting the air back in is like what happens when you restore a portable company file. It takes time for QuickBooks to prepare the portable company files just as it takes time for air to seep back into a space bag so the sweaters can return to their normal volume. If you are using an old computer system or a USB drive, the process will take longer than it will if you have a newer system.

Many users are not happy about waiting for the restore process to occur, but it is a necessity if you have chosen this file option. You may want to begin a chapter by restoring the portable company file first so you can read the concepts discussions while it restores.

What if I want to work with "real" company files rather than portable company files?

You can download either company files or portable company files for this course. Remember that company files will take longer to download and will use more space on your storage drive. On the plus side, you need not restore them in order to use them. For every portable company file there is also a regular company file—except for the Develop Your Skills exercise in Chapter 1, as the first task teaches you how to restore a portable company file.

Follow the exercise directions based on the file type you are using.

How do I save as a PDF?

Many instructors request students to save reports as PDF files. This makes it easier to submit your work and saves paper. To save a report as a PDF, first create and display the report. Next, click the Print button on the report toolbar and choose to Save As PDF.

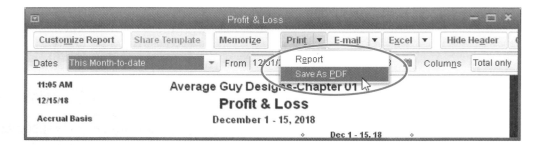

Managing Basic QuickBooks Files

Before you can begin working with a QuickBooks file, you need to understand some basic file-management operations. This section will cover how to launch the program, store files, and restore QuickBooks portable company files.

Launching the Program

There is more than one way to do just about everything on a computer, and launching QuickBooks is no exception. Each computer is set up a little differently and may have different options for launching the program depending on shortcuts that have been created. Ask your instructor how he wishes for you to launch QuickBooks in your computer lab. Depending on the version of Windows you are running, QuickBooks will be found in the All Programs or Programs menu accessed via the Start button or on the Windows 8 Start screen. In addition, there may be a shortcut to QuickBooks on the Windows Desktop.

"There is more than one way to do just about everything on a computer" is not meant to confuse you! You will be introduced to various ways to perform tasks in QuickBooks. Choose whichever methods work best for you.

Types of QuickBooks Files

There are three different types of files in which you can store your QuickBooks data: company files, backup files, and portable company files. The type of file that you will utilize when working with your business is the company file. A backup file is used to store a copy of your data in case your main file becomes corrupted and needs to be restored. A portable company file is much smaller than both company and backup files and is a convenient way to send your company information by email.

There are two other QuickBooks file types that play important support roles for your company data. A network data file has a file extension of .nd, and it contains important configuration data. A transaction log has a file extension of .tlg, and it can help you to recover any data entered after the last backup operation you have performed.

Your company file can be stored anywhere on your computer. The QuickBooks default storage location is the QuickBooks folder for the current version you are using.

Backup and portable company files contain all data stored from the company file—just compressed. These files are substantially smaller than company files, and portable company files are great for sending by email. The other "auxiliary" files do not store company data, but they do have important support functions.

WARNING Even though .nd and .tlg. files do not allow you to work with your company information, do *not* delete them. This can affect the integrity of your company data.

Opening and Restoring QuickBooks Files

In order to open a QuickBooks company file, or to restore either a backup or portable company file, you access the command via the File menu. QuickBooks doesn't save files as other applications like word-processing programs do. When you enter transactions, they are saved automatically to the QuickBooks file. To save a QuickBooks file for backup purposes, you create a compressed file—either a backup or portable company file. The act of decompressing a backup or portable company file for use is called restoring.

When you open or restore a company file from the File menu, you must choose the file type you are accessing.

QUICK REFERENCE	OPENING AND RESTORING QUICKBOOKS DATA FILES
Task	Procedure
Open a QuickBooks company file	■ Choose File→Open or Restore Company. ■ Choose Open a company file; click Next. ■ Navigate to and select the desired file; click Open.
Restore a backup file	■ Choose File→Open or Restore Company. ■ Choose Restore a backup copy; click Next. ■ Navigate to the desired backup copy, either locally or online; click Next. ■ Locate the backup copy you wish to restore; click Open. ■ Click Next, choose the save-to location, and then click Save.
Restore a portable company file	■ Choose File→Open or Restore Company. ■ Choose Restore a portable file; click Next. ■ Navigate to the portable file you wish to restore; click Open. ■ Click Next, choose the save-to location, and then click Save. ■ Be patient as the file restores! Click OK to acknowledge the successful restoration.

DEVELOP YOUR SKILLS 1-1
Restore a Portable Company File

In this exercise, you will restore a QuickBooks portable company file.

Before You Begin: Navigate to the Student Resource Center to download the student exercise files for this book. Two versions of the files are available from which you must choose—portable company files and company files.

Even if you choose to download the company files, you will use a portable company file for this exercise.

1. If necessary, start your computer.

2. Follow the steps for your version of Windows:

You may see one of two editions of QuickBooks installed on your computer: Pro or Premier. This book works with both of these editions, so choose whichever edition is installed. Make sure to correct the operating system you are using.

Windows 7

- Click the **Start** 🔘 button at the left edge of the taskbar and choose **All Programs**.
- Choose **QuickBooks,** and then choose **QuickBooks 2014** from the menu.

Windows 8

- Locate the **QuickBooks 2014** tile.
- Click the tile to start **QuickBooks**.

A "splash screen" displays the version of QuickBooks you are launching and opens the program window. If this is the first time you have used the QuickBooks installation on this computer, you will see a QuickBooks Setup window.

 Intuit provides maintenance releases throughout the lifetime of the product. These updates may require you to update your student exercise files before you begin working with them. Please follow the prompts on the screen if you are asked to update your company file to the latest QuickBooks release.

3. Choose **File**, and then choose the **Open or Restore Company** command.

 In the future, a menu bar command like this will be written as Choose File→Open or Restore Company.

QuickBooks displays the Open or Restore Company window.

4. Click in the circle to the left of **Restore a portable file**.

Restore a portable file
- Re-create a company file that was stored as a portable file (.qbm)

5. Click **Next**.

6. Follow these steps to restore your file:

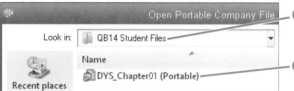

Ⓐ Navigate to the location of the downloaded student files.

Ⓑ Click to select the **DYS_ Chapter01 (Portable)** file.

Ⓒ Click the **Open** button.

7. Click **Next**, and then follow these steps to determine where the resulting company file will be located:

Ⓐ Navigate to your file storage location.

Ⓑ Add your last name and first initial to the end of the filename (e.g., the author's filename would be **DYS_Chapter01_ConlonT**).

Ⓒ Click the **Save** button.

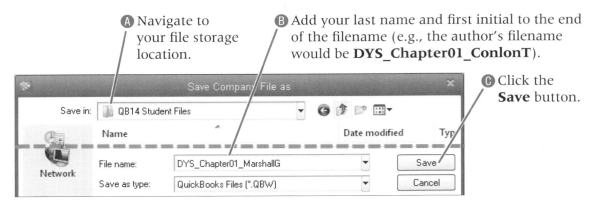

It may take a few moments for the portable company file to open. The QuickBooks window opens with the Average Guy Designs company file ready to go. Leave this window open for the next exercise.

8. Click **OK** to close the QuickBooks Information window.

9. Click **No** in the Set Up External Accountant User window, if necessary.

10. Close the **Accountant Center** window, if necessary.

For the rest of the Develop Your Skills exercises in this book, you can restore a portable company file or open a company file. This exercise showed you how to restore a portable company file. Use this process as applicable moving forward.

Working with the QuickBooks Window

There are many screen elements with which you are probably familiar if you have ever worked with a Windows-based PC. Many of the elements remain similar regardless of the program in which you are operating. The elements in common are the title bar and quick-sizing buttons. In addition, many programs utilize menu, toolbar, and Icon bars as well as a Ribbon and tabs that you will see in QuickBooks.

Viewing the QuickBooks Window

The QuickBooks window features many components designed to help you complete all of the tasks necessary to manage your business effectively.

Click a button on the menu bar to see a drop-down menu of options specific to that button.

The title bar shows the company name and the QuickBooks version/edition you are using.

Alerts and reminders can be easily accessed from the far right of the menu bar.

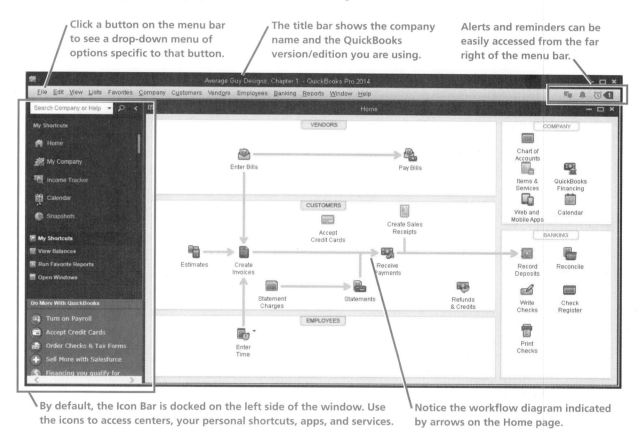

By default, the Icon Bar is docked on the left side of the window. Use the icons to access centers, your personal shortcuts, apps, and services.

Notice the workflow diagram indicated by arrows on the Home page.

Flowing Through the Home Page

The workflow diagram on the Home page is indicated by arrows going from one task icon to another. It is important to follow the diagram so as not to run into trouble. Some instances of trouble that you may encounter are listed below:

■ If you write a check rather than pay a bill (for which a bill has been entered), you will overstate expenses.

■ If you make a deposit rather than receive a payment for an invoiced amount, you will overstate income.

Sales tax errors can also occur by not following the proper flow outlined on the Home page.

The QuickBooks Icon Bar

The Icon Bar provides a quick way to access QuickBooks centers, snapshots, shortcuts, apps, and services. It is docked on the left side of the QuickBooks window by default, but you can move it to the top of the window or hide it altogether.

All commands accessible on the Icon Bar and Home page can be found through the menu bar, but the opposite is not also true. (They would be a bit too crowded!)

QuickBooks Calendar

The QuickBooks Calendar allows you to keep up with deadlines. This feature also integrates a to-do list so you can keep track of your calendar and tasks in one handy place. The calendar can be accessed via the Company area of the Home page or via the Icon Bar.

The to-do list is displayed to the right of the calendar.

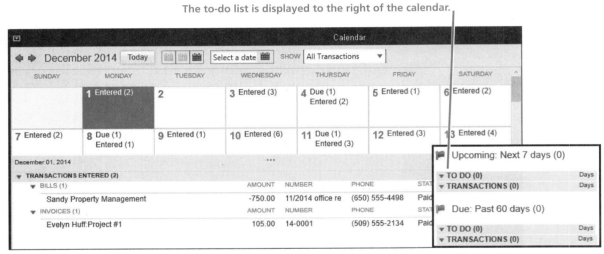

The calendar shows you how many transactions have been entered and are due on a specific day. When a date is selected, you can view details of what took place on that day in the panel at the bottom of the window.

Controlling the QuickBooks Display

If you cannot see the Icon Bar, you can turn it on through the View menu. To show or hide the Icon Bar, choose View from the menu bar.

The Icon Bar is docked to the left side of the screen.

Note where you can go to customize the Icon Bar.

To single-click or double-click—that is the question. Always single-click first; double-click only if the single-click doesn't work. Most students are "happy double-clickers," and this can get you into trouble (especially if you double-click a toggle button, which is like flipping a light switch up and down and then wondering why the light doesn't stay on). Remember, always single-click a button and a hyperlink!

The Open Window List

You may wish to display the Open Window List at the top of the Icon Bar in order to keep track of all of the windows you have open. The active window will always appear at the top of the list.

Customizing the Home Page

QuickBooks allows users to customize the Home page based on their preferences and how they use the software. The task icons displayed on the Home page will change when a user makes changes to certain preferences. For instance, if a user decides to track inventory in QuickBooks and so turns on the "Inventory and purchase orders are active" preference, additional task icons will be added to the Vendor area of the Home page to assist with the inventory-related tasks. You will learn how to change this preference in Chapter 6, Dealing with Physical Inventory. Changes to other preferences that result in changes to the Home page will be dealt with throughout this book as well.

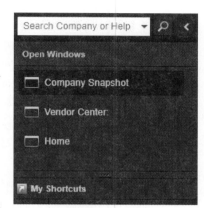

Pictured is the Icon Bar with the Open Window List displayed. Note that the Company Snapshot is the active window.

When you change a preference that will alter the content of the Home page, QuickBooks displays a warning message first.

In addition, you can choose to not display some of the task icons that you may not use as often. The commands will still be available through the menu, just not accessible via a task icon on the Home page.

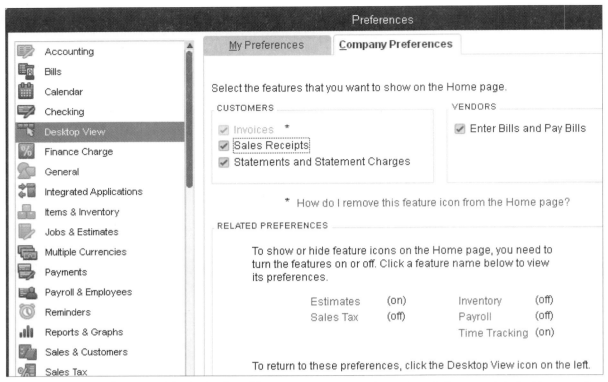

On the Company Preferences tab in the Desktop View category, you can choose to not display certain task icons on the Home page. Add them back at any time by returning to the Preferences window and reselecting the option.

Maximized vs. Restored Down Windows

Some QuickBooks users prefer to work with windows maximized and others with them restored down. This is based entirely on user preference! In this book, we will work with windows "restored down;" however, your instructor may choose to display them as maximized. It will only look different; all functions will be the same.

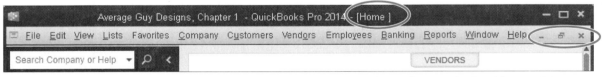

When you work with all windows maximized, the name of the active window will appear in the Title Bar of the QuickBooks window in square brackets and the quick-sizing buttons will be a part of the menu bar.

If you choose to work with windows restored down, you will see separate windows for each open window, and each will have its own Title Bar and quick-sizing buttons.

Exiting QuickBooks

When you are finished working with QuickBooks, you will need to close the company file and the program. This can be accomplished by clicking the Close button at the top-right corner of the QuickBooks window or by selecting File→Exit.

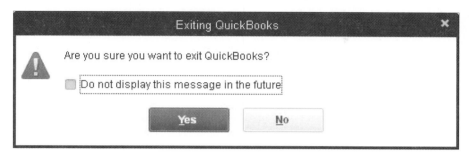

QuickBooks displays a warning message when you click the Close button at the top-right corner of the window. Notice that you can choose to not have this message appear again.

Close All Windows with One Command

If you have a lot of windows open and wish to close them all simultaneously, QuickBooks makes it easy with the Close All command. This command can be accessed by choosing Windows from the menu bar.

Task Icon ToolTips

There are many task icons on the Home page. As you customize your QuickBooks file, you may see more or fewer appear, depending on how you use the program. If you are not sure what a certain task item is used for, simply "mouse over" it (place your mouse pointer over the icon and hold it still, without clicking), and a ToolTip that explains what the task will accomplish for you will appear.

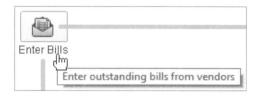

Notice that when you "mouse over" the Enter Bills task icon, a ToolTip appears to explain what task you can accomplish if you click the icon.

QuickBooks Learning Center Tutorials

Sure to be a valuable resource during your study is the QuickBooks Learning Center. It features a large number of instructional QuickBooks videos that are great learning tools for many students. You will find yourself directed to these tutorials through the "Visualize!" element in this book. Develop Your Skills 1-2 includes steps to show you how to access a video. In this book you will see a special icon and text whenever a QuickBooks Learning Center tutorial is available (see below).

Visualize! **Tab:** Thank you for upgrading
Topic: What's New in 2014

In addition, QuickBooks provides help for some topics that are not in video format. When you choose one of these topics in the Learning Center, a web page with more information will open.

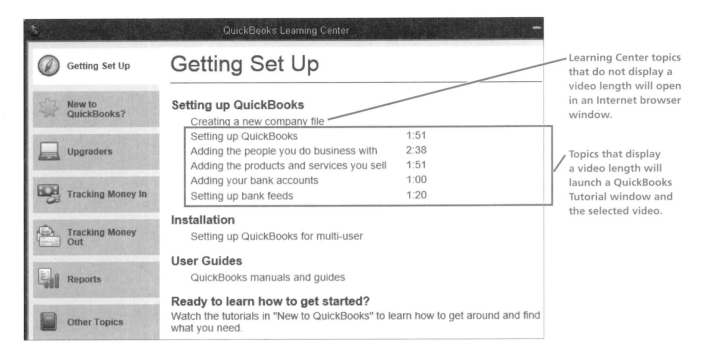

Learning Center topics that do not display a video length will open in an Internet browser window.

Topics that display a video length will launch a QuickBooks Tutorial window and the selected video.

Explore the QuickBooks Window

In this exercise, you will have a chance to explore the QuickBooks window.

1. Click the **Vendors** button on the Home page.

   The Vendor Center will open, from where you can work with the vendors on your list, manage various vendor transactions, and create new vendors.

2. Choose **Lists→Chart of Accounts**.

   The Chart of Accounts window opens. This is an example of a list in QuickBooks. It lists the various accounts this company utilizes.

3. Click the **Snapshots** icon on the Icon Bar, scrolling down if necessary.

   The Company Snapshot window opens.

4. Choose **Window**.

   Notice that all four of the open windows are listed.

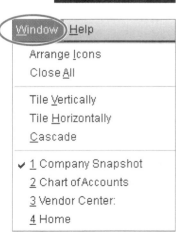

5. Click the **Chart of Accounts** item.

   The Chart of Accounts window appears on top of the other windows and is active. Look at the windows you have opened within QuickBooks and notice that each one is restored down and has its own set of quick-sizing buttons (Close, Restore/Maximize, Minimize), which you can use to control the display of each window within the QuickBooks program window.

6. Click the **Close** ☒ button for the Chart of Accounts window.

7. Choose **View→Open Window List**.

    QuickBooks will display the Open Window List at the top of the Icon Bar.

8. Choose **Window→Close All**.

    This command will close all open windows for you so you don't have to go chasing "Xs" around the screen! Notice that the Home page is closed since it is a window, but that the Open Window List/Icon Bar is still displayed since it is not.

9. Open the Home page by choosing **Company→Home page**.

10. Choose **View→Hide Icon Bar**.

    QuickBooks no longer displays the Icon Bar.

Exit and Reopen QuickBooks

11. Choose **File→Exit**.

12. Click **No** in the Automatic Backup window, if necessary.

    The QuickBooks window closes.

13. Open QuickBooks, based on the version of Windows you are using.

    Notice that QuickBooks opens the file that you were last working on and that the Icon Bar is not visible.

14. Click **No** in the Set Up an External Accountant User window, if necessary.

15. Close the **Accountant Center** window, if necessary.

16. Maximize the QuickBooks program window, if necessary.

17. Choose **View→Left Icon Bar**.

    The Icon Bar reappears.

Mouse Around the Home Page

18. Mouse over the task icon for the following tasks on the Home page, and then write the ToolTips in the spaces provided.

19. If you do not wish to write in the book, print the Mouse Around the Home Page worksheet from the Student Resource Center.

  ▦ Chart of Accounts

  _____

  _____

  ▦ Create Invoices

  _____

  _____

  ▦ Pay Bills

  _____

  _____

  ▦ Reconcile

  _____

  _____

20. Submit your responses to step 19 based on the guidelines provided by your instructor.

Explore the QuickBooks Learning Center

Throughout this book, the "Visualize!" feature will point you to QuickBooks video tutorials. These steps will show you how to access these tutorials.

21. Choose **Help→Learning Center Tutorials**.

22. Follow these steps to view a tutorial that will show you how to get around in QuickBooks:

Ⓐ Click **New to QuickBooks?**.

Ⓑ Click **Getting around in QuickBooks**. The QuickBooks Tutorial window will launch, and the video will begin.

Ⓒ Watch the tutorial and then click the **Close** button on the tutorial window.

23. Click the Go to QuickBooks button.

Leave QuickBooks open with the Home page displayed for the next exercise.

In the future, you will see text and an icon like the following to direct you to available videos.

Visualize! **Tab:** New to QuickBooks?
Topic: Getting Around in QuickBooks

Backing Up and Updating Your Company File

You have already learned how to restore a portable company file. Now you will learn how to create a backup file. If you have ever lost a file or had your computer "crash" on you, you surely can understand the importance of backing up your data!

When working in QuickBooks, you cannot save your file as you may be used to doing in programs such as Microsoft® Word. Transactions are automatically saved to your company file as you enter them, so the backup operation will back up the entire file.

How often you back up your file is up to you, but you should not let too much time go between backups. If you lose your company file and are forced to restore the backup copy, you will have to enter all of the transactions since your last backup.

Backup Location

Do not back up your company file to your hard drive or where your main company file is stored. Choose an alternate backup location such as a network drive, USB drive, external hard drive, cloud storage, or the QuickBooks' online backup option. If you back up your file to a USB drive or some other removable media, make sure to store the backup copy someplace other than where the original file is physically located. For instance, do not set the backup media on the PC where the original file is, just in case something such as fire or water damage occurs at the physical location.

Protecting Your Data Online

To ensure the security of your QuickBooks data in the event of human error, natural disaster, or a computer crash, you may wish to use Intuit Data Protect. This online service allows you to recover your data in the event you lose your working company file. Data is encrypted and backed-up automatically each day to secure servers. You can also use the service to back up other important files, such as reports and contracts, or personal items, such as valuable photos. Learn more about Intuit Data Protect through the File menu bar command.

There is a fee associated with this service.

If your data is not backed up properly, Intuit Data Protect cannot help you. Make sure to back up your data properly!

When to Save a Backup Copy

In QuickBooks, you can choose when to back up your company file. QuickBooks allows you to choose among three options:

- Save it now
- Save it now and schedule future backups
- Only schedule future backups

The future backup options make it easy to back up your company file on a regular basis without having to remember to physically issue the command. If you choose scheduled backups, make sure the backup location is available to QuickBooks at the scheduled times. For instance, ensure that you have your USB flash drive available if that is your backup location.

Updating Your QuickBooks Company File

Earlier in this chapter you learned about the different editions of QuickBooks that are available for purchase each year. In addition, Intuit releases free updates for your QuickBooks software throughout the life of the version. (At some point, Intuit will announce that they will no longer support each version of QuickBooks based on the length of time since it was released.) These updates are available for download over the Internet and may include such things as a new service, a maintenance release, a new feature, or something else relevant to your company.

The easiest way to stay abreast of these updates is to have QuickBooks automatically check for and download them for you through the Automatic Update feature.

Verifying the QuickBooks Release Number

You can easily find out which release number you are working with for your current version of QuickBooks by tapping the [F2] key. This will launch a Product Information window that displays not just the release number, but also a lot of other information about your QuickBooks file such as your license and product numbers. In addition, if you choose to open the Update QuickBooks window from the Help menu, you can also find your release number displayed at the top of that window.

FROM THE KEYBOARD
Tap [F2] to display the QuickBooks Product Information window

QUICK REFERENCE	BACKING UP AND UPDATING A QUICKBOOKS FILE
Task	**Procedure**
Create a portable company file	■ Choose File→Create Copy. ■ Choose Portable company file; click Next. ■ Choose your file storage location; click Save. ■ Click OK to allow QuickBooks to close and reopen your file. ■ Click OK to acknowledge the portable company file creation.
Create a backup file	■ Choose File→Back Up Company→Create Backup. ■ Choose to create a local or online backup; click Next. ■ Choose your file storage location; click OK. ■ Choose when you wish to create the backup copy; click Next. ■ Ensure the location for the backup file is correct; click Save. ■ Click OK to acknowledge the backup file creation.

QUICK REFERENCE	BACKING UP AND UPDATING A QUICKBOOKS FILE (continued)
Task	**Procedure**
Start Intuit Data Protect	■ Choose File→Back Up Company→Setup/Activate Online Backup. ■ View the web page with information about Intuit Data Protect that opens.
Set up QuickBooks to update automatically	■ Choose Help→Update QuickBooks. ■ Click the Options tab; choose Yes to automatically update your QuickBooks file. ■ Click Close.
Update QuickBooks manually	■ Choose Help→Update QuickBooks. ■ Click the Update Now tab; click to select/deselect the updates you wish to receive. ■ Click Get Updates.
Determine the release number of QuickBooks	■ Choose Help→Update QuickBooks. ■ With the Overview tab displayed, look at the upper-right area of the Update QuickBooks window for the release number; tap F2 to view the full Production Information window.

DEVELOP YOUR SKILLS 1-3

Back Up Your QuickBooks Data File

In this exercise, you will create a backup copy of your company file. Ask your instructor where he wants you to back up your file. A cloud storage option in the form of Dropbox is used in this example.

1. Choose **File→Back Up Company→Create Local Backup**.

2. Verify that **Local Backup** is selected, and then click **Next**.

3. Click the **Browse** button.

4. Choose your file storage location in the **Browse for Folder** window. (The drive or folder name will probably be different from the one shown here.)

If you are not sure where to save your backup copy, ask your instructor.

5. Click the **OK** button two times.

If you have chosen to save the file to the same drive on which the company file is stored, QuickBooks will display a warning window.

6. Read the information in the QuickBooks window, and then click the **Use this location** option, if necessary.

7. Ensure **Save it now**, and then click **Next** again.

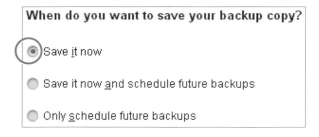

A Save Backup Copy window will appear and should display the file storage location you chose in step 4.

8. Ensure that the correct file storage location is displayed, and then click **Save**.

QuickBooks will first verify that your file is not corrupted and will then create a backup copy in the location you specified.

9. Click **OK** to acknowledge the information window that tells you a backup file has been created.

10. Choose the appropriate option for your situation:
    - If you will continue working, leave QuickBooks open.
    - If you are finished working in QuickBooks for now, choose **File→Exit**.

Concepts Review

To check your knowledge of the key concepts introduced in this chapter, complete the Concepts Review quiz on the Student Resource Center or in your eLab course.

Reinforce Your Skills

In all of the Reinforce Your Skills exercises, you will be working with a company called Quality-Built Construction. This business is an S corporation that builds and remodels homes. Angela Stevens is the proprietor of the business. You will assist Angela in a variety of QuickBooks tasks as you work your way through this book.

REINFORCE YOUR SKILLS 1-1
Find Your Way Around QuickBooks

In this exercise, you will take a look at Angela's QuickBooks company file. You will begin by opening a portable company file.

1. Start **QuickBooks**, if necessary.

2. Choose **File→Open or Restore Company**.

3. Choose to **Restore a portable file**, and then click **Next**.

4. Follow these steps to select the file to restore:

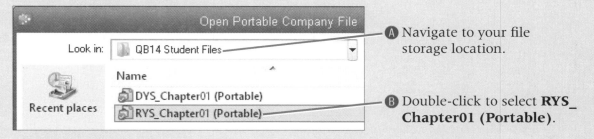

Ⓐ Navigate to your file storage location.

Ⓑ Double-click to select **RYS_Chapter01 (Portable)**.

Double-clicking the filename works the same as if you had single-clicked the filename and then clicked the Open button.

5. Click **Next** to move to the next screen.

6. Follow these steps to choose where to locate your new company file:

Ⓐ Navigate to your file storage location.   Ⓑ Here, type your last name and first initial.

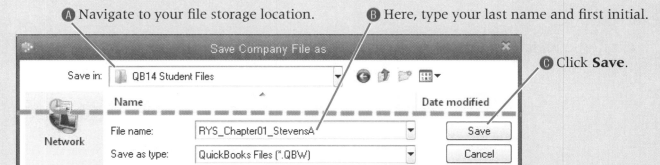

Ⓒ Click **Save**.

There is a long pause as QuickBooks opens the portable company file.

7. Click **OK** in the QuickBooks Information window, if necessary.

QuickBooks opens the company file and displays the Home page.

Navigate in the Company File

Now you will explore the QuickBooks window.

8. Click the **Items & Services** task icon in the Company area of the Home page.

   QuickBooks displays the Item List window.

9. Click the **Calendar** button on the Icon Bar.

10. Choose **Vendors→Enter Bills**.

    QuickBooks displays the Enter Bills window, ready for you to enter a bill from a vendor.

11. Choose **Company→Lead Center**.

12. Choose **Window→Item List**.

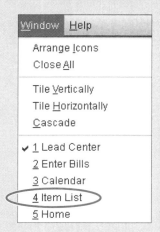

The Item List window appears on top of the other open windows. Notice that all open windows are listed at the bottom of the Window menu list. Clicking on one of them will make that window active.

13. Choose **Window→Close All**.

    The Close All command closes all open windows, including the Home page.

14. Click the **Home** icon on the Icon Bar.

    QuickBooks displays the Home page.

 Tab: New to QuickBooks?
Topic: Using the Home Page

Get to Know QuickBooks Better

15. Complete the **Get to Know QuickBooks Better** worksheet.

    Print or save the worksheet from the Student Resource Center.

16. Submit your worksheet based on the guidelines provided by your instructor.

17. Choose the appropriate option for your situation:

    ■ If you will continue working, leave QuickBooks open.

    ■ If you are finished working in QuickBooks for now, choose **File→Exit**.

REINFORCE YOUR SKILLS 1-2

Work with T-Accounts

In this exercise, you will use your accounting knowledge. Refer to Appendix A, Need to Know Accounting if you need assistance. You can either write directly in the book or download the Work with T-Accounts worksheet from the Student Resource Center.

1. Below or on your printed worksheet, write the following account names at the tops of the T-charts:
   - Bank Service Charges
   - Construction Income
   - Company Checking Account
   - Loans Payable
   - Machinery & Equipment
   - Common Stock

2. Next to each account, write the account type (asset, liability, equity, income, or expense).

3. Label the debit and credit side of each T.

4. Place an **NB** on the appropriate side of the T to indicate the normal balance of each account.

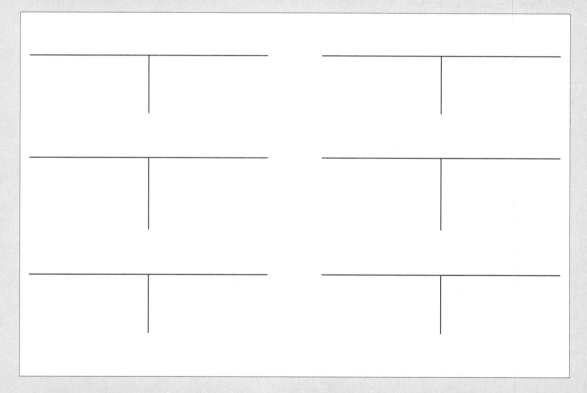

5. Submit your work based on the guidelines provided by your instructor.

Apply Your Skills

In all of the Apply Your Skills exercises, you will be working with a company called *Wet Noses Veterinary Clinic* run by Dr. Sadie James, DVM. She is a small-animal veterinarian specializing in dogs and cats.

APPLY YOUR SKILLS 1-1

Restore a Portable Company File and Explore QuickBooks

In this exercise, you will restore a portable company file and take a look at Dr. Sadie James' QuickBooks company file.

1. Start **QuickBooks**.

2. Restore the **AYS_Chapter01 (Portable)** backup company file. Name the restored company file **AYS_Chapter01_LastNameFirstInitial**.

3. Open the following windows using any of the methods described in this chapter:
   - Create Invoice
   - Item List
   - Customer Center
   - Chart of Accounts
   - Pay Bills
   - Company Snapshot

4. Display the **Item List** window above the other open windows.

   Next you will create a screen capture to submit to your instructor. Two options are presented. Use the option as directed by your instructor.

Option 1: Capture Your Work Using Microsoft Word

5. Tap PrtScn, and then launch **Microsoft Word**.

   Your screen capture is automatically copied to the Window's Clipboard, ready for pasting.

6. Display a blank document, and then press Ctrl + v.

   Your screen capture is pasted into the Word document.

7. Save your Word document as **AYS_Chapter01_Capture_LastnameFirstIntial** and submit it according to the guidelines provided by your instructor.

8. Choose the appropriate option for your situation:
   - If you will continue working, leave QuickBooks open.
   - If you are finished working in QuickBooks for now, choose **File→Exit**.

Option 2: Complete a Worksheet to Capture Your Work

9. Print or save the **Capture Your Work** worksheet from the Student Resource Center.

10. Complete and then submit the worksheet according to the guidelines provided by your instructor.

11. Choose the appropriate option for your situation:
- If you will continue working, leave QuickBooks open.
- If you are finished working in QuickBooks for now, choose **File→Exit**.

Get a Grasp on Accounting Principles

In this exercise, you will use your accounting knowledge to brainstorm the accounts that would be required for the business that you will be working with in the Apply Your Skills exercises throughout the rest of this book.

You can either write directly in the book or download the Get a Grasp on Accounting Principles worksheet from the Student Resource Center.

1. Think about a veterinary practice. On the printed worksheet or in the following space, list the accounts that you feel would be required on the business's Chart of Accounts.

2. In the second column, list the type of account for each.

3. In the third column, state whether the normal balance for the account would be a debit or a credit.

ACCOUNT NAME	ACCOUNT TYPE (ASSET, LIABILITY, EQUITY, INCOME, EXPENSE)	NORMAL BALANCE (DR/CR)

4. Submit your work based on the guidelines provided by your instructor.

Extend Your Skills

1-1 Sort Through the Stack

You have been hired by Arlaine Cervantes to help her with her organization's books. She is the founder of Niños del Lago, a nonprofit organization that provides impoverished Guatemalan children with an engaging educational camp experience. You will begin your work with Ninos del Lago in Chapter 2.

1-2 Be Your Own Boss

In this exercise, and throughout the entire book, you will be working with a company file that you create from scratch. The company should either be based on your own company or a company you would like to own or manage someday. In this first chapter you will determine what edition of QuickBooks is best for your company as well as the name and type of business formation.

Download the EYS_Chapter01 Word file from the Student Resource Center to complete this exercise. Save the completed file as **EYS2_Chapter01_LastnameFirstInitial** and submit it to your instructor based on the instructions provided.

1-3 Use the Web as a Learning Tool

Throughout this book, you will be provided with an opportunity to use the Internet as a learning tool by completing WebQuests. According to the original creators of WebQuests, as described on their website (http://WebQuest.org), a WebQuest is "an inquiry-oriented activity in which most or all of the information used by learners is drawn from the web." To complete the WebQuest projects in this book, navigate to the Student Resource Center and choose the WebQuest for the chapter on which you are working. The subject of each WebQuest will be relevant to the material found in the chapter.

WebQuest Subject: Learn more about QuickBooks versions and determine which one is most appropriate for your business

Creating a Company

CHAPTER OBJECTIVES

After studying this chapter, you will be able to:

- Plan and create a company
- Edit your QuickBooks preferences and customize a company file
- Enter opening balances and historical transactions
- Run list reports and find help for QuickBooks
- Set up QuickBooks users
- Close the books "QuickBooks style"

Now that you have had a chance to explore the QuickBooks window and learn about how to work with QuickBooks files, it is time to create a company file. By taking the knowledge that you gain from this chapter and coupling it with what you will learn in the rest of the book, you will be ready at the end of your QuickBooks studies to create a file for your own company.

Average Guy Designs

Guy Marshall is a community college student who is completing his degree in visual communications. He began his own graphic design business a year ago and has chosen to start using QuickBooks as the tool to track his business finances. Guy just took a class that focused on the business of graphic arts, and he learned that there is some important information that he needs to gather before setting up his new QuickBooks company.

Average Guy Designs
Checklist for New QuickBooks Company

Company Name	Average Guy Designs	Need from accountant	Chart of accounts, what should I use for items?
Address	110 Sampson Way, Bayshore, CA 91547	Vendors	need names, addresses, account numbers, and payment terms for each
Office	(650) 555-5555	Customers	need names and contact information, payment terms, and account numbering system
Cell	(650) 555-4455		
Fax	(650) 555-5252		
Start date	11/30/2014	Accounting basis	Cash
Fiscal year	January	Email	averageguydesigns@outlook.com
EIN	94-4555555	Website	averageguydesigns.wordpress.com
Income Tax Form	1040 (Sole Proprietor)		

Guy has written out the information he needs to have handy to start his new company file.

Planning and Creating a Company

Before you begin to set up your QuickBooks company, it is important to do careful planning. You must think about the information you want to get from QuickBooks before you begin. As with many situations, garbage in will equal garbage out!

Choosing Your Start Date

Choosing the start date that is right for you is important. Very ambitious people may think they want to start their QuickBooks file the day they started their company. This is a nice idea, but not very practical for a busy or cost-conscious entrepreneur.

Keep in mind that you must enter all transactions for your company (invoices, checks, bills paid, etc.) from the start date forward. If you choose a date too far in the past, this process will take a long time to complete.

You should strive to start your QuickBooks company file at the beginning of a month, a quarter, or your fiscal year. You may want to discuss this matter with your accountant to help determine the best and most practical starting date for your business. The actual start date should be the last day of the prior period rather than the first day of the current period; for example, we will use 11/30/18 rather than 12/1/18.

The Five Ps

Sit down and think about what you want QuickBooks to do for you. It is difficult to go back and add a new field for every customer or change every transaction! A little planning at the beginning can save you a lot of time in the future. Think about the five Ps (Prior Planning Prevents Poor Performance) as you get ready to start your company and take into account the needs of all of the stakeholders involved. What type of information will each stakeholder need to be able to interact efficiently with your business? Potential stakeholders may include your accountant, customers, vendors, employees, stockholders, partners, etc.

How Many Companies Should You Create?

Generally, the best guideline is to set up a separate QuickBooks company file for each tax return you will file.

FLASHBACK TO GAAP: BUSINESS ENTITY

Remember that the business is separate from the owners and from other businesses. Revenues and expenses of the business should be kept separate from the personal expenses of the business owner. Also, revenues and expenses for separate companies must be kept separate from the other companies that may be operated by the same owner.

Creating a New QuickBooks File

There are several ways you can go about creating your new QuickBooks file. Look at the following list to determine which one will work best for your situation:

- Create a company from scratch
- Upgrade from a previous version of QuickBooks
- Convert from a different QuickBooks edition
- Convert a Quicken file
- Convert a file from other accounting software

Choosing a Setup Path

When creating a new company, QuickBooks makes it easy for you to select from a variety of options. Express Start is the easiest method; use the Detailed Start method if you wish to fine-tune your company file as you set it up.

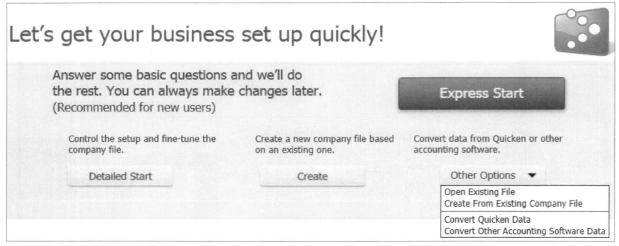

In this window, choose the method for creating a company that works best for you.

Express Start

The Express Start option for company setup allows you to provide a minimum amount of information and get started with QuickBooks right away. Once you have entered the Express Start information and your company file is created, QuickBooks helps you to set up the rest of the information needed to run your business. You will use this method in the Develop Your Skills exercises in this chapter.

Detailed Start (EasyStep Interview)

A click of the Detailed Start button takes you to the EasyStep Interview window. Here you provide more information when creating your company file. You will use this method in a Reinforce Your Skills exercise at the end of the chapter.

Using an Old QuickBooks File as a Template for a New File

If you wish to create your new company file based on an older one, QuickBooks will allow you to keep the lists and preferences from the old file while removing the old, unneeded transactions. Some QuickBooks users prefer to keep a separate company file for each fiscal year of the business, and being able to keep preferences and list data while removing transactions makes this easy.

To complete this task, you must clean up your company data from the old file using the Clean Up Company Wizard. Be sure you have a large window of time available before you start this process, as it can take some time to clean up a large file. QuickBooks will create a backup and archive copy of your file as a part of this process, as well as verify file integrity. You will work with the cleanup process in Chapter 12, Reporting, Adjusting Entries, and Closing the Books, as it is also used by many companies to clean up a company file after closing the books.

Converting Data to Start a New Company File

An additional option available to you when creating a new company file is to convert an existing file from Quicken or other accounting software data.

A Setup Checklist

There are some items that you should gather before you begin to set up your company. Review the checklist of items to collect in the Student Resource Center for this book.

A Quick Payroll Primer

You will be introduced to running payroll in QuickBooks in Chapter 8, Using QuickBooks for Payroll. If you choose to create your new company using the Detailed Start method, you need to understand a bit about how QuickBooks deals with payroll first.

If you wish to include an addition or deduction on an employee's paycheck, you must first set it up as a payroll item. During the EasyStep interview you will have an opportunity to create payroll items. If you will be using QuickBooks for payroll and wish to set it up during the setup process (you can also set this up after the fact if you choose, and that process will be covered in Chapter 8), you will need to have the following information ready:

- Information for each employee: name, address, social security number, and withholding information (from their W-4 forms)
- All "additions" that will be found on a paycheck, such as salaries, hourly wages, and bonuses
- All payroll taxes the employees are required to pay
- All payroll taxes you, as the employer, are required to pay
- Any additional deductions you will be withholding from paychecks, such as investment plan contributions or child support payments

Your Starter Chart of Accounts

During the setup process, QuickBooks will ask you to search for the business type that your company most closely resembles. QuickBooks will use your choice to create a Starter Chart of Accounts close to what you need. (It will take you less time to edit it to fit your unique business than to start from scratch.) QuickBooks will also create profile lists based on your selection. You will work with the customer and vendor profile lists in Chapter 10, Customizing and Integrating in QuickBooks. Choose carefully here, as you cannot go back and change the business type option.

In order to ensure your books are set up properly, you should talk to your accountant to make sure that your Chart of Accounts is set up correctly. A quick conversation and small bill now can prevent a large bill in the future.

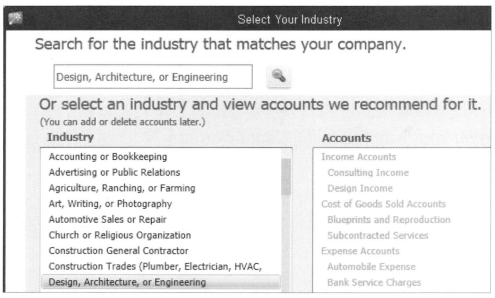

QuickBooks has several predefined company Chart of Accounts for specific industries that will help users in those or similar industries to streamline their setup processes.

 Once you select a business type during the setup process, you cannot change it later. You can edit and delete accounts and list entries, though.

Account Beginning Balances

If you have an existing company for which you are setting up QuickBooks, you should enter the balances of all asset and liability accounts during the setup process (although you can also enter them in the registers later). These account beginning balances are termed "opening balances" in QuickBooks. You will learn more about entering and editing these balances later in the chapter.

After you create your first balance sheet account, QuickBooks will create an Opening Balance Equity account, in which the account beginning balances you enter will be placed. Asset beginning balances credit the account, while liability beginning balances debit it. This account is created so you can have a balance sheet that is accurate from the start even if you haven't entered all assets and liabilities for your company.

TYPES OF ACCOUNTS IN QUICKBOOKS

Account Type	Example	Normal Balance
Bank	Checking Account	Debit
Accounts Receivable	Accounts Receivable	Debit
Other Current Asset	Prepaid Rent	Debit
Fixed Asset	Machinery	Debit
Other Asset	Long Term Notes Receivable	Debit
Accounts Payable	Accounts Payable	Credit
Credit Card	Silver Falls Bank Visa	Credit
Other Current Liability	Short Term Loan	Credit
Long Term Liability	Auto Loan	Credit
Equity	Opening Balance Equity	Credit
Income	Sales	Credit
Cost of Goods Sold	Cost of Goods Sold	Debit
Expense	Telephone Expense	Debit
Other Income*	Interest Income	Credit
Other Expense*	Corporate Taxes	Debit

*Other Income and Other Expense accounts are used to track income and expenses that are not the result of normal day-to-day business operations.

QUICK REFERENCE — CREATING A NEW COMPANY FILE

Task	Procedure
Create a new company in QuickBooks	<ul><li>Review the checklist to make sure you have all necessary information.</li><li>Plan what you want QuickBooks to do for you.</li><li>Choose File→New Company.</li><li>Choose a method set up your company file.</li></ul>
Edit information for a new company	<ul><li>Choose Company→Company Information.</li><li>Edit the information in the Company Information window.</li></ul>
Create a new company file based on a prior one, keeping list data and preferences	<ul><li>Choose File→Utilities→Clean Up Company Data.</li><li>Choose to remove all transactions as of a specific date or all transactions in the file.</li><li>Continue through the wizard screens.</li><li>Click Begin Cleanup.</li><li>Click OK to close the "message;" click Create Back Up.</li></ul>

Create a New Company

In this exercise, you will use Express Start to set up the company for Average Guy Designs.

1. Launch **QuickBooks**.
2. Choose **File→New Company**.
3. Click the **Express Start** button.

4. Follow these steps to enter the first set of company data:

Ⓐ Type **Average Guy Designs**.　　Ⓑ Tap [Tab], and then type **design**.

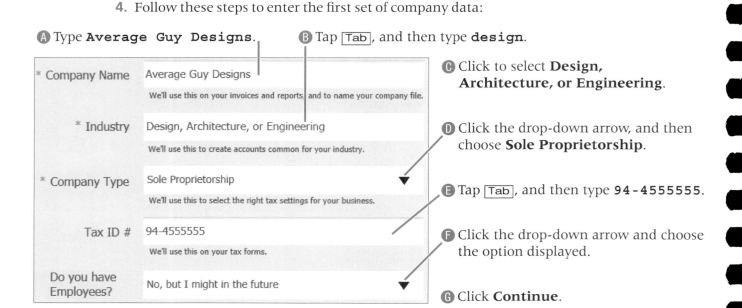

Ⓒ Click to select **Design, Architecture, or Engineering**.

Ⓓ Click the drop-down arrow, and then choose **Sole Proprietorship**.

Ⓔ Tap [Tab], and then type **94-4555555**.

Ⓕ Click the drop-down arrow and choose the option displayed.

Ⓖ Click **Continue**.

5. Follow these steps to enter your business contact information:

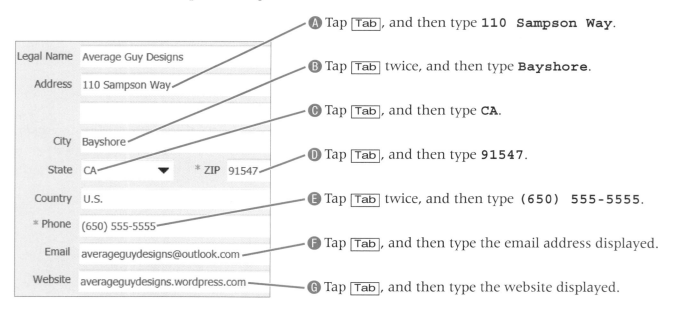

Ⓐ Tap [Tab], and then type **110 Sampson Way**.

Ⓑ Tap [Tab] twice, and then type **Bayshore**.

Ⓒ Tap [Tab], and then type **CA**.

Ⓓ Tap [Tab], and then type **91547**.

Ⓔ Tap [Tab] twice, and then type **(650) 555-5555**.

Ⓕ Tap [Tab], and then type the email address displayed.

Ⓖ Tap [Tab], and then type the website displayed.

In this window, you will need to type the phone number and address just as you wish them to appear on forms—including punctuation such as parentheses, dashes, or periods. Take care to spell everything correctly when entering this company information. Imagine how embarrassing it would be to send out invoices, bills, and other correspondence with your own company name and information incorrect!

6. Click **Preview Your Settings**.

   `Preview Your Settings`

   QuickBooks will open the Preview Your Company Settings window, where you can choose where to save your file.

7. Click the **Company File Location** tab, and then click **Change Location**.

   `Change Location`

8. Choose your file storage location in the **Browse For Folder** window, and then click **OK**.

9. Click **OK** again, and then click **Create Company File**.

   QuickBooks creates your new company file, which will take a minute or so. Once the file is created, the QuickBooks Setup window will appear.

10. Click **Start Working**.

    `Start Working`

    We will be adding information in the next several chapters, but not right now.

    The Quick Start Center, which is designed to help you perform basic tasks, will appear. We will be working from the QuickBooks Home page as we progress through this book, so this window is not necessary.

11. Close the **Accountant Center** window, if necessary.

12. Click the **Close** button at the top-right corner of the Quick Start Center window.

    The QuickBooks Home page for your new company file will be displayed. Leave it open and continue to the next topic.

Editing Your QuickBooks Preferences

The way you interact with QuickBooks is controlled by the preferences you select. The Preferences window has twenty-three categories of preferences you can set or modify so QuickBooks can work more efficiently for your company.

Here are twenty-one of the twenty-three preference categories.

Use these tabs to switch between company and personal preferences with a click of the mouse.

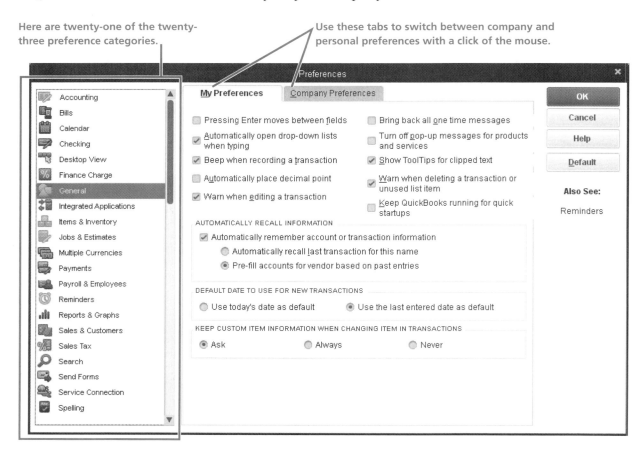

 Visualize! **Tab:** Getting Set Up
Topic: Setting up QuickBooks

Company vs. Personal Preferences

Each category has two tabs on which changes to preferences can be set: the Company Preferences tab and the My Preferences (personal) tab. Company preferences are controlled by the administrator. They determine how the entire company interacts with QuickBooks. Personal preferences are controlled by each individual user. They dictate interactions between QuickBooks and that one user only.

The following illustrations show an example of a company and a personal preference.

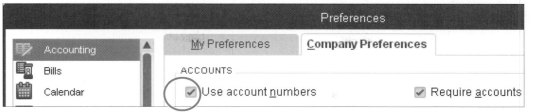

Changes made by an administrator affect all users. Here, an administrator turned on the preference to use account numbers. In the Chart of Accounts, there would then be an account number associated with each account.

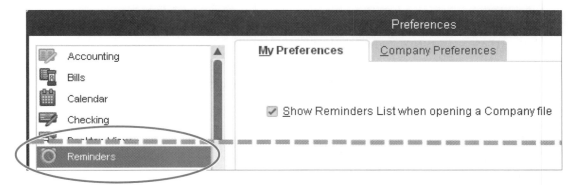

Here, a user can change the setting for the Reminder List to be shown on the My Preferences tab that will affect only her individual QuickBooks user login.

Setting a Company Preference: Account Numbers

Many businesses use account numbers for the accounts in their Chart of Accounts. You will be using account numbers as you work with the company file for Average Guy Designs. Account numbers are somewhat standard within the accounting world. "Somewhat" means that each account type begins with the same number, but the accounts listed within the account type are not universally numbered. Examine the following table to understand how account numbers work. Note that account numbers have a minimum of four characters, and you can use five or six. For instance, a Checking account (which is an asset) could be numbered 1000, 10000, or 100000.

ACCOUNT TYPES AND NUMBERS		
Account number starts with:	**Type of account**	**Example**
1	Asset	Checking Account
2	Liability	Accounts Payable
3	Equity	Retained Earnings
4	Income	Retail Product Sales
5	Cost of Goods Sold	Purchases – Resale Items
6	Expenses	Utilities Expense
7	Other Income	Interest Income
8	Other Expense	Sales Tax Penalty

Setting a Personal Preference: Show Reminders List

In many of the Preferences categories, an individual user can choose from a variety of options. In the following exercise, you will choose to show the Reminders List when starting your QuickBooks file.

QUICK REFERENCE	EDITING BASIC QUICKBOOKS PREFERENCES
Task	**Procedure**
Edit QuickBooks file preferences	■ Choose Edit→Preferences.
	■ Click the category (on the left side of the window) in which you wish to make a change.
	■ Choose the Company Preferences or My Preferences tab.
	■ Make any necessary changes.
	■ Click OK to save the new preferences.

DEVELOP YOUR SKILLS 2-2
Change Your Preferences

In this exercise, you will turn on the account number preference for the company and choose for the Reminders List to be displayed when opening QuickBooks.

Whether to turn on the use of account numbers is a company preference, is set by the company administrator, and cannot be changed by other users.

1. Choose **Edit→Preferences**.

2. Follow these steps to turn on the account numbers preference:

Ⓐ Click **Accounting**.

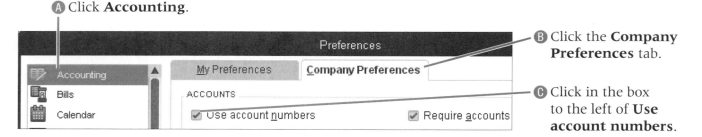

Ⓑ Click the **Company Preferences** tab.

Ⓒ Click in the box to the left of **Use account numbers**.

The Show lowest subaccount only preference will be introduced in Chapter 6, Dealing with Physical Inventory.

3. Click **OK** to accept the new preference.

Change a Desktop View Personal Preference
Now, you will turn on the Reminder List.

4. Choose **Edit→Preferences**.

5. Follow these steps to choose to have the Reminders List displayed when you open your company file:

Ⓐ Click **Reminders**.   Ⓑ Ensure that the **My Preferences** tab is displayed.

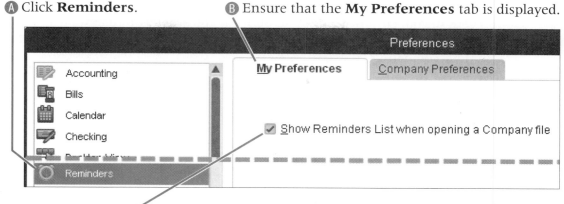

Ⓒ Click to place a checkmark in the box to **Show Reminders List**.

6. Click **OK** to accept the new preference.

   Leave the QuickBooks window open and continue with the next topic.

Customizing a Company File

During the setup process, QuickBooks allows you to choose a business type similar to your own. It is up to you to take this generic file and customize it to fit your company.

Modifying the Lists in a New File

You will need to look at several lists after you set up your new QuickBooks company to ensure they are correct. If any of them are incorrect or incomplete, you will need to edit, delete, or add entries to them. These lists include the following:

- The Chart of Accounts
- The Customers & Jobs List
- The Vendor List
- The Item List
- Customer & Vendor Profile Lists

- The Fixed Asset Item List
- The Employees List
- The Payroll Items List
- The Price Level List

Entries in these lists can be created during the EasyStep interview. If you choose to skip the interview, you will need to populate these lists once the company has been created.

The Chart of Accounts

The Chart of Accounts is composed of all of the asset, liability, equity, income, and expense accounts your company utilizes. You use the Chart of Accounts list window to create new accounts, edit existing accounts, and delete unused accounts.

Customizing the Chart of Accounts

The first task you have with your new company file is to fine-tune your Chart of Accounts. If you are using QuickBooks for an existing business, you will want to talk to your accountant and get a copy of your current Chart of Accounts. If you are starting a new business, you may also want to contact your accountant for guidance on how best to set up your Chart of Accounts for your unique company.

Adding Accounts

When you add an account to the Chart of Accounts, make sure to select the correct account type, as this is one of the most prevalent errors accountants find in their clients' QuickBooks files. Keep in mind that your "behind the scenes" action will be incorrect if the wrong account type is selected.

To Edit or Delete—That Is the Question...

The generic Chart of Accounts that QuickBooks provides will have some accounts you probably won't need for your unique business. You can choose to either rename (edit) these accounts or delete them. Renaming an account is appropriate if you are working with the same account type. Deleting is appropriate if you no longer need additional accounts of the same type.

Moving and Sorting Accounts Within the List

You can change the order in which accounts appear within your Chart of Accounts. By default, QuickBooks alphabetizes accounts by type. The Chart of Accounts is structured so that assets are listed first, liabilities second, equity accounts third, income accounts fourth, cost of goods sold accounts fifth, and expense accounts last. This structure must remain intact; you can only move accounts around within their own type.

Moving list items works the same way in the various lists in QuickBooks—by clicking and dragging the diamond to the left of the list entry.

If you move your accounts and later decide you want them alphabetized by type once again, QuickBooks allows you to re-sort the list. Re-sorting the list restores the QuickBooks default.

Subaccounts

To keep precise records, you may wish to use QuickBooks subaccounts. For instance, to keep the number of expense accounts within reason, you are likely to utilize only one telephone expense account for all of your telephone lines. To track expenses more closely, though, you may want to have separate accounts for your office phone, office fax, and cellular phone. Subaccounts are a great way to track these separate expenses while keeping the number of expense accounts down.

When you run Profit & Loss reports and budgets, you have the option to expand the report (show subaccounts) to show detail or collapse the report (show only main accounts) for brevity.

Using Classes in QuickBooks

In Chapter 11, Introducing the Accounting Cycle and Using Classes, you will go into depth in regard to using classes in QuickBooks. Classes allow you to track income and expenses for one specific aspect of your company, and they are not tied to any particular customer, job, vendor, or item. For right now, understand that if you choose to use classes for your own business, the best option is to set them up when you create your new company file.

QUICK REFERENCE	CUSTOMIZING THE CHART OF ACCOUNTS
Task	**Procedure**
Add an account	■ Click the Account menu button; choose New. ■ Choose the correct account type; click Continue. ■ Enter all necessary information. ■ Click Save & Close or Save & New.
Edit an account	■ Single-click the account you wish to edit. ■ Click the Account menu button; choose Edit. ■ Make any necessary changes; then click Save & Close.
Delete an account	■ Single-click the account you wish to delete. ■ Click the Account menu button and choose Delete; click OK.
Create a subaccount	■ Click the main account for which you wish to create a subaccount. ■ Click the Account menu button; choose New. ■ Choose the correct account type; click Continue. ■ Type the subaccount name; click in the box for Subaccount of. ■ Click the drop-down arrow, click the main account from the list, and then click OK.
Move an account	■ Click the account to move. ■ Place the mouse pointer over the diamond to the left of the account name so the four-way arrow appears. ■ Click and drag the account to the new location within the same account type.
Re-sort accounts	■ Click the Account menu button; choose Re-sort.

DEVELOP YOUR SKILLS 2-3
Make the File Fit Your Business

In this exercise, you will take the generic Chart of Accounts created for Average Guy Designs and make it fit the needs of the company. The first task is to add an account that Guy needs but that was not provided in the generic Chart of Accounts, Checking.

FROM THE KEYBOARD
Ctrl+a to open the Chart of Accounts

1. Click the **Chart of Accounts** task icon in the Company area of the Home page.

   QuickBooks opens the generic Chart of Accounts created for you. Notice the account numbers that you turned on in the previous exercise.

Chart of Accounts

2. Follow these steps to create the new account:

FROM THE KEYBOARD

Ctrl+n to create a new account

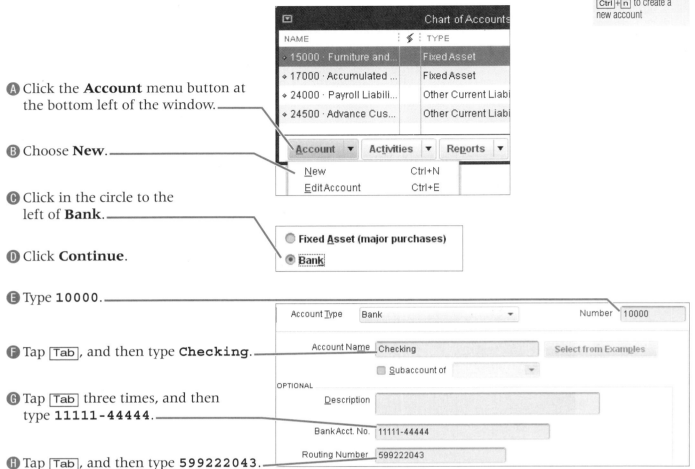

Ⓐ Click the **Account** menu button at the bottom left of the window.

Ⓑ Choose **New**.

Ⓒ Click in the circle to the left of **Bank**.

Ⓓ Click **Continue**.

Ⓔ Type **10000**.

Ⓕ Tap Tab, and then type **Checking**.

Ⓖ Tap Tab three times, and then type **11111-44444**.

Ⓗ Tap Tab, and then type **599222043**.

3. Click **Save & Close**.

4. Click **No** in the Set Up Bank Feed window.

   Take a look at your Chart of Accounts window and notice the new Checking account at the top of the list.

Edit an Account

In Chapter 3, Working with Customers, you will learn how to create items and route them to the proper account in the Chart of Accounts. For now, you will rename one of the income accounts.

5. Scroll down the Chart of Accounts, if necessary, and then single-click the **Consulting Income** account.

6. Click the **Account** menu button, and then choose **Edit Account**.

FROM THE KEYBOARD

Ctrl+e to edit the selected account

7. Follow these steps to rename the account:

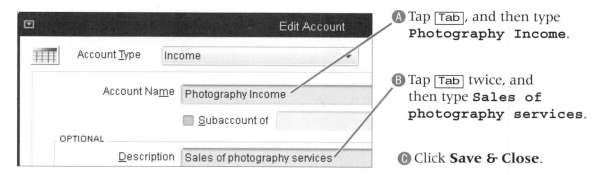

Ⓐ Tap `Tab`, and then type **`Photography Income`**.

Ⓑ Tap `Tab` twice, and then type **`Sales of photography services`**.

Ⓒ Click **Save & Close**.

Delete an Account

8. Scroll to the bottom of the Chart of Accounts window, and then single-click the **Ask My Accountant** account.

9. Click the **Account** menu button, and then choose **Delete Account**.

10. Click **OK** in the Delete Account window.

    Since you cannot undo an account deletion, QuickBooks verifies your choice.

FROM THE KEYBOARD
`Ctrl`+`d` to delete the selected account

Create Subaccounts

Guy wants to track his telephone expenses more carefully, so he has decided to use subaccounts.

11. Single-click **Telephone Expense** in the Chart of Accounts.

12. Click the **Account** menu button, and then choose **New**.

13. Follow these steps to create your new subaccount:

Ⓐ Click in the circle to the left of **Expense**.

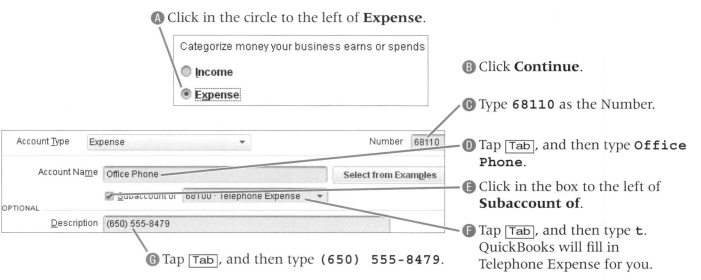

Ⓑ Click **Continue**.

Ⓒ Type **68110** as the Number.

Ⓓ Tap `Tab`, and then type **Office Phone**.

Ⓔ Click in the box to the left of **Subaccount of**.

Ⓕ Tap `Tab`, and then type **t**. QuickBooks will fill in Telephone Expense for you.

Ⓖ Tap `Tab`, and then type **(650) 555-8479**.

14. Click **Save & New** to add your new subaccount and leave the window open to add another one.

15. Follow step 13 C–G to add the following additional subaccounts for Telephone Expense, clicking **Save & New** after creating the first additional subaccount.

Account Number	Subaccount Name	Description
68120	Fax Line	(650) 555-4015
68130	Cell Phone	(650) 555-1011

16. Click **Save & Close** to create the last new subaccount and close the window.

17. Close the **Chart of Accounts** window.

Working with Opening Balances and Historical Transactions

If you chose a start date for your company that was not the first day you were in business, it is important to enter all of the historical transactions and opening balances in your file.

Entering and Editing Account Opening Balances

You need to make sure that you have the correct opening balances in QuickBooks for all of your accounts. There are five methods by which you can enter opening balances. The type of account that you are dealing with determines which method, or combination of methods, will work the best. The five methods available are:

■ EasyStep Interview (for bank accounts only)
■ Journal entries
■ Forms (for individual transactions)
■ Registers
■ Lists (lump sums can be entered when creating entries)

Editing a Beginning Balance

If you need to correct a beginning balance that you entered, you will not be able to do it through the EasyStep Interview or the Edit Account window. In order to accomplish this task, you need to use either the account register or a journal entry (journal entries will be covered in Chapter 12, Reporting, Adjusting Entries, and Closing the Books). For example, if you incorrectly entered $15,000 as the opening balance for the Savings account when you created it, you will need to open the Savings account register by double-clicking the account in the Chart of Accounts and change the amount in that window.

Entering Historical Transactions for an Account

There are two ways that you can enter historical transactions into your QuickBooks file. Transactions can be entered either individually or in a summary journal entry.

Entering Historical Transactions Individually

If you wish to enter your transactions individually, you must have all of the data for each one. It is very important that you enter them in the correct order. Check out the following illustration to see the correct order for historical transaction entry.

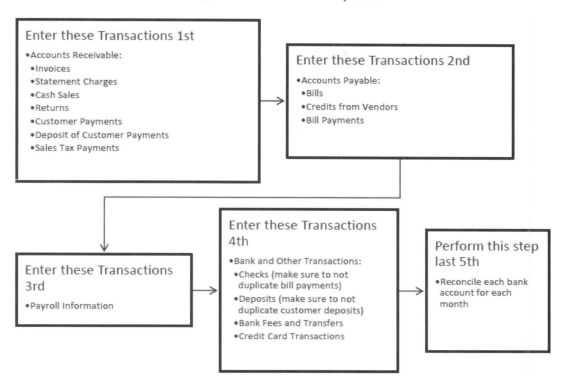

Making a Summary Journal Entry

In a summary journal entry, you will not enter the details of individual transactions; you will only enter the total amounts. In this chapter, you will edit an opening balance in a register.

QUICK REFERENCE	ENTERING HISTORICAL TRANSACTIONS
Task	**Procedure**
Edit an account opening balance	▪ Open the register for the account. ▪ Drag to select the opening amount. ▪ Type the correct amount; click Record.
Enter historical transactions individually	▪ Gather the information for all of the historical transactions. ▪ Enter all accounts receivable transactions and then accounts payable transactions using the proper QuickBooks forms. (Follow the order shown above.) ▪ Enter outstanding payroll information. ▪ Enter outstanding "bank and other" transactions. (Follow the order shown above.) ▪ Reconcile each bank account for each month chronologically.

QUICK REFERENCE	ENTERING HISTORICAL TRANSACTIONS (continued)
Task	**Procedure**
Make a summary journal entry to account for historical transactions	■ Gather the information for all historical transactions.
	■ Determine each account that is affected, whether the net effect is a debit or a credit, and the total amount.
	■ Choose Company→Make General Journal Entries.
	■ Enter each of the affected accounts and the amount of the debit/credit.
	■ Ensure that debits equal credits. (QuickBooks will not allow you to record the journal entry until they do!)
	■ Record the journal entry.

DEVELOP YOUR SKILLS 2-4

Deal with an Opening Balance

In this exercise, you will work with a register to deal with an adjustment to the opening balance for the Checking account, since it was not entered when you created the account. The account you will credit in this transaction is 30000•Open Balance Equity (the whole account name is cut off due to the size of the field).

1. Click the **Check Register** task icon in the Banking area of the Home page.

   There is only one bank account at this time, so the Checking register will open automatically for you.

Check Register

2. Follow these steps to enter the opening balance for the Checking account:

   ⓐ Type **113014** in the Date field.   ⓑ Tap ⎡Tab⎤ five times, and then type **5432.67** in the Deposit field.

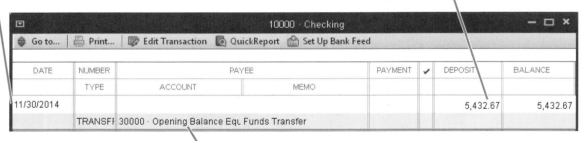

   ⓒ Tap ⎡Tab⎤, type **3**, and then tap ⎡Tab⎤ again. QuickBooks will fill in the rest of the account for you.

   The Memo will fill in automatically when you record the transaction.

3. Click the **Record** button at the bottom of the register window.

4. Click **Yes** in the Future Transactions window, if necessary.

5. Close the **Checking** register window.

Finding Help in QuickBooks

There will be times when you will need to be able to find answers to questions you have about QuickBooks on your own. QuickBooks has a built-in help feature as well as a "coaching" feature that can come to your rescue in these circumstances.

The "Have a Question?" Window

The "Have a Question?" window is a separate window you can launch to search for help. This window is contextual, which means its contents change depending on the active window. For instance, if you choose to launch it while you have the Chart of Accounts window open, the results will relate to that window.

Type keywords here and then view the topics below. In this case, no words were necessary as the window was launched when the Chart of Accounts was the active window.

Suggested answers are presented in two categories (Answers in Help and Answers from Community).

If you click this link, you will have an options to get help by: asking a community of experts, finding a ProAdvisor, finding training, or contacting Intuit.

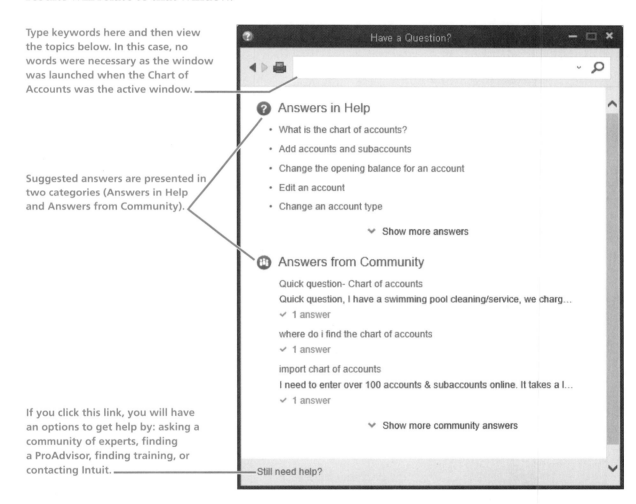

The Persistent Search Bar

The persistent search bar, which is a feature on the Icon Bar, allows you to search the company file (the results will be displayed in a Search window) or to search through help topics (the results will be displayed in the "Have a Question?" window). You will learn how to use the Search window in more detail in Chapter 3, Working with Customers.

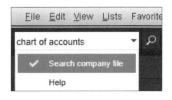

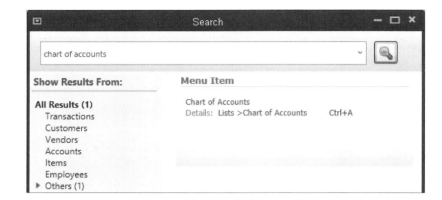

If you choose to search the company file, a Search window will show the results of the search.

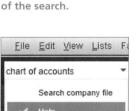

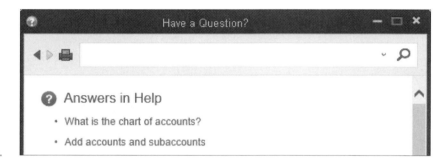

If you choose to search for help, the "Have a Question?" window will display the results.

The Quick Start Center

Earlier in this chapter, you closed the Quick Start Center window that appeared after you created your new company file. This feature is available to you whenever you need it. The command to launch it can be found on the Help menu. This center helps you to perform basic tasks and is another place to access the "Visualize!" tutorials to help you learn more about working in QuickBooks.

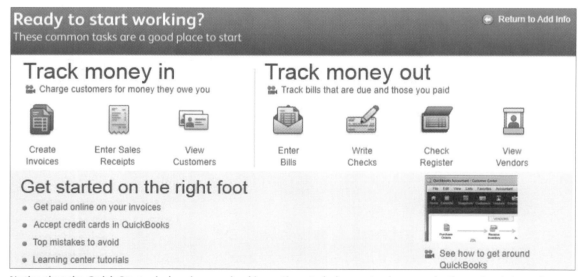

Notice that the Quick Start window is organized in sections to help you track money both coming into and leaving your business. It also features ways to start your QuickBooks experience right and to get more from the software once you are up and running.

QUICK REFERENCE — FINDING HELP FOR QUICKBOOKS

Task	Procedure
Search for help with the "Have a Question?" window	■ Choose Help→QuickBooks Help. ■ Type the relevant keyword(s); click Search. ■ Click the desired result displayed in a Help Article window.
Search for help with the persistent search bar	■ Click in the persistent search bar; type the relevant keyword(s). ■ Choose to search for Help; click Search. ■ Click the desired result in a Help Article window.
Search your QuickBooks file with the persistent search bar	■ Click in the persistent search bar; type the relevant keyword(s). ■ Choose to Search company file; click Search.
Ask a question of another QuickBooks user	■ Choose Help→QuickBooks Help. ■ Click the Ask Community link. (An Internet browser will launch.) ■ Type your question and click Ask. ■ If you feel up to the challenge, answer a question for another user!
Print a help topic	■ Search for the desired topic; click to display it in the Help Article window. ■ Click the Print Topic button. ■ Set your printer and print options; click Print.
Open the Quick Start Center window to view a tutorial	■ Choose Help→Quick Start Center. ■ Click the hyperlink to the desired tutorial.

DEVELOP YOUR SKILLS 2-5

Search for Help

In this exercise, you will use the help feature in QuickBooks.

FROM THE KEYBOARD
F1 to open the "Have a Question?" window

1. Choose **Help→QuickBooks Help**.

   The "Have a Question?" and Help Article windows will display.

2. Follow these steps to search for a help topic:

   Ⓐ Click here, and then type **user access**.

   Ⓑ Click the **Search** button.

user access
Results in Help
❓ How To
○ Add users and give them access

   Ⓒ Click this topic.

   Your chosen topic will be displayed in the Have a Question window.

3. Scroll down to read the full article.

4. Close the **"Have a Question?"** window.

Setting Up Users

When your company grows, and you hire additional employees, you may decide that you need to allow certain employees access to your QuickBooks file.

Administrators and Users

Before you can set up any users for your QuickBooks file, you must set up an administrator who will control the access of all users. You can assign a password for each person with access to your file. The administrator controls all company preferences in the Preferences window. Users have the ability to change only their own personal preferences. QuickBooks allows you to set up unlimited users for your company file, although the number that can access the file at any one time depends on your QuickBooks license agreement.

The External Accountant user has access to all areas of QuickBooks except those that contain confidential customer information. An External Accountant can conduct reviews of your file and make changes separate from those of other users. Only an administrator can create an External Accountant user.

Restricting Access

When you decide to give employees access to your QuickBooks company file, you may not want them to see all of your company's financial information. You can choose to restrict each individual user's access to specific areas of QuickBooks.

There are nine areas for which you can give access rights to a user. Guy has asked Allison to help out at Average Guy Designs with sales and product ordering, so he will need to set

Access for user: Allison

This user has the following access rights. Click the Leave button to return.

AREA	CREATE	PRINT	REP...
Sales and Accounts Receivable	Y	Y	Y
Purchases and Accounts Payable	Y	N	N
Checking and Credit Cards	N	N	n/a
Time Tracking	N	N	N
Payroll and Employees	N	N	N
Sensitive Accounting Activities	N	N	N
Sensitive Financial Reports	N	N	n/a

her up as a user with limited access. This illustration displays those areas. In this example, Allison has access to all areas of sales and accounts receivable (creating new transactions, printing forms, and running reports) and can create new purchase and accounts payable transactions.

Setting Passwords

It is very important to make sure you have a password that is not easy for others to guess and yet that is easy for you to remember. Once you set your username and password, the Change QuickBooks Password window allows you to change your password whenever you wish (recommended every 90 days) and to set or change your secret "challenge question" that will allow you to retrieve a forgotten password. This challenge question should not have an answer with which others are familiar.

Working with QuickBooks in a Multi-User Environment

QuickBooks provides a way for more than one user to access a company file at the same time. In QuickBooks Pro and Premier, up to five users can have simultaneous access to the file. Most tasks that you usually do can be completed in multi-user mode, but there are some that must be performed in single-user mode.

You *cannot* do the following in multi-user mode:

- Create a new company file
- Set or edit a closing date
- Rebuild, clean up, or verify the file
- Create or work with accountant's copies
- Merge, delete, and sort list information
- Change company preferences
- Export and import data

Visualize!

Tab: Getting Set Up
Topic: Set up QuickBooks for multi-user

QUICK REFERENCE	SETTING UP USERS AND PASSWORDS
Task	**Procedure**
Set up an administrator name and password	■ Choose Company→Set Up Users and Passwords→Set Up Users. ■ Select Admin; click Edit User. ■ Type the username and password, entering the password twice to verify. ■ Set the challenge question and answer, if desired; click OK.
Change an administrator password	■ Choose Company→Set Up Users and Passwords→Change your password. ■ Type a complex password; retype it to verify you did it correctly. ■ Set the challenge question and answer, if desired; click OK.
Set up users	■ Choose Company→Set Up Users and Passwords→Set Up Users. ■ Click Add User. ■ Type the username and password; click Next. ■ Follow the steps in the "Set up user password and access" screens to customize the access for the user. ■ View the new user's access rights; click Finish.
Switch between multi-user/single-user modes	If you are in single-user mode and wish to switch to multi-user mode: ■ Choose File→Switch to Multi-user Mode. If you are in multi-user mode and wish to switch to single-user mode: ■ Choose File→Switch to Single-user Mode.

DEVELOP YOUR SKILLS 2-6
Set Up Users for a Company

In this exercise, you will help Guy to set up Allison as a user for the Average Guy Designs' company file. The first step is to set his own password as the administrator.

1. Choose **Company→Set Up Users and Passwords→Set Up Users**.

2. Click **Edit User**.

3. Follow these steps to set up Guy's administrator account and password:

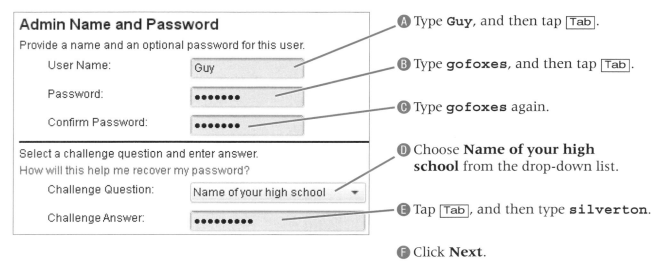

Ⓐ Type **Guy**, and then tap Tab.

Ⓑ Type **gofoxes**, and then tap Tab.

Ⓒ Type **gofoxes** again.

Ⓓ Choose **Name of your high school** from the drop-down list.

Ⓔ Tap Tab, and then type **silverton**.

Ⓕ Click **Next**.

4. Click **Finish**.

   Notice that you do not need to change the access areas for the administrator. He has access to everything in the company file!

Add a User

Now that the administrator is set up, you can set up individual users.

5. Click the **Add User** button in the User List window; then follow these steps to add Allison as a user:

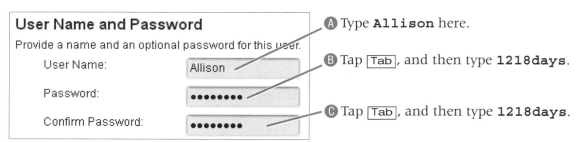

Ⓐ Type **Allison** here.

Ⓑ Tap Tab, and then type **1218days**.

Ⓒ Tap Tab, and then type **1218days**.

6. Click **Next** twice.

   Each time you click Next as you move through the "Set up user password and access" screens, you can change the access for the user in one of nine areas.

7. Click to choose **Full Access** for the Sales and Accounts Receivable option; click **Next**.

8. Click in the circle to the left of **Selective Access** for Purchases and Accounts Payable.

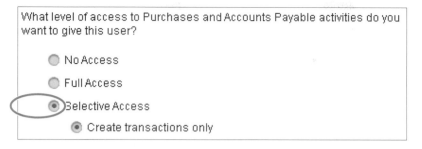

The Create transactions only option will be automatically selected.

9. Click **Finish**.

Notice that Allison has been added to the User List.

10. Click **View User**.

You will see a summary of the access you have given to Allison. You can change this at any time by opening the User List, clicking on Allison, and then clicking the Edit User button.

11. Click the **Leave** button in the View User access window.

12. Close the **User List**.

Closing the Books and Running List Reports

You will not actually close the books yet, but it is important to understand how QuickBooks deals with this task, so it will be covered now. You will, however, find the need to produce list reports early on in your QuickBooks experience. For instance, your accountant may wish to see a list of the accounts you have set up for your business to ensure all is well before you get too far down the road.

QuickBooks reports can provide you with a wealth of information about your company. You will learn a lot more about how to use these reports in Chapter 12, Reporting, Adjusting Entries, and Closing the Books.

Keeping the End in Mind

You are not required to "close the books" in QuickBooks, but you can choose to if you like. When you close the books, QuickBooks:

■ Transfers the net income or net loss to Retained Earnings

■ Restricts access to transactions prior to the closing date by requiring a password

■ Allows you to clean up your data

Only the company file administrator can set a closing date and allow or restrict access to prior-period transactions by a user. You will have an opportunity to close the books and complete the full accounting cycle in Chapter 12, Reporting, Adjusting Entries, and Closing the Books. For now, it is important for you to keep in mind how QuickBooks operates at the end of an accounting period.

The Report Center

There are many preset reports available for you to use in QuickBooks. They are broken into three main categories: list, summary, and transaction. The Report Center is a tool in QuickBooks that allows you to learn about different types of reports without having to create them by trial and error. It includes sample reports and descriptions of the type of information each report provides.

Contributed Reports

Contributed reports are specialized reports submitted by users that are integrated into the Report Center. You can search for specialized reports by your industry type, and you can even rate a report for other users to see how valuable it is to you.

These tabs let you view standard QuickBooks reports; your memorized, favorite, and recently displayed reports; and reports contributed by other users.

These three buttons let you change how you view Report Center information.

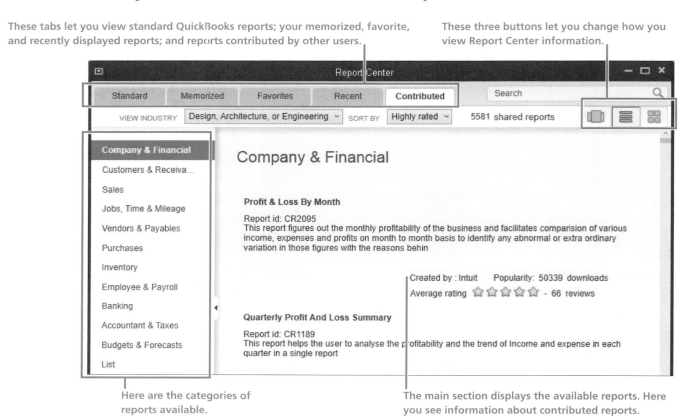

Here are the categories of reports available.

The main section displays the available reports. Here you see information about contributed reports.

 **Tab:** Reports
Topic: Reports

List Reports in QuickBooks

One category of reports that you can access contains list reports. They simply display the information that is found in your various QuickBooks lists in an easy-to-read format.

When you view the Report Center in List View, you will see a question that the report will answer below the name of the report. This will come in handy when you are completing the Apply Your Skills exercises, where you will be expected to "answer questions with reports!"

Viewing Sample Report Images

An additional feature available in the Report Center is the ability to view what a report will look like without having to actually produce the report.

When you click the Info button for a report, a sample of what the report will look like is displayed.

Email Functionality in Reports

QuickBooks allows you to email reports from any report window. You have a chance to choose whether the recipient will receive the report as an Adobe Acrobat (PDF) or Microsoft Excel file. The report will appear the same as it would if you printed it from QuickBooks.

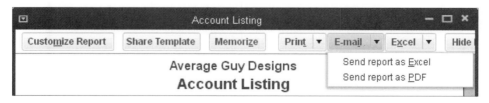

When you click the Email button on the toolbar, you can choose the type of file that will be attached to your email message.

Task	Procedure
Display an Account Listing report	■ Choose Reports→Report Center. ■ Choose List as the report category. ■ Scroll down; click Account Listing. ■ Click the Run report button.
Email a report from QuickBooks	■ Produce the report you wish to email. ■ Click the Email button and choose to send it as a PDF or an Excel file. ■ Using your email program, enter the recipients, and make any desired modifications to the message. ■ Send the email.

DEVELOP YOUR SKILLS 2-7

Produce a List Report

In this exercise, you will create and email a report for Guy's accountant that displays the accounts in his Chart of Accounts.

1. Choose **Reports→Report Center**.

2. Follow these steps to display the report:

Ⓐ Click the **List View** button.

Ⓓ Click the **Run** button.

Ⓒ Scroll down until **Account Listing** is visible in the main section.   Ⓑ Click **List**.

A report displaying all of the accounts in the Chart of Accounts is displayed.

3. Close the **Account Listing** report and **Report Center** windows.

4. Choose the appropriate option for your situation:
   ■ If you will continue working, leave QuickBooks open.
   ■ If you are finished working in QuickBooks for now, choose **File→Exit**.

FROM THE KEYBOARD
Alt + F4 to exit from QuickBooks

Tackle the Tasks

Now is your chance to work a little more with Average Guy Designs and apply the skills that you have learned in this chapter to accomplish additional tasks. You will use the same company file you just created to complete the following tasks.

(If you need to reopen the file, remember that the username is "Guy" and the password for the file is "gofoxes"!)

Add Accounts	Add the following bank account: 10200•Savings
	Add the following income account: 48800•Print Layout Services
	Add the following expense account: 61500•Job Materials
Add Subaccounts	Add the following subaccounts to the Utilities account: 68610•Gas & Electric, 68620•Water
Change Account Opening Balance	Change the Savings account opening balance to $7,382.35, as of 11/30/14
Search for Help	Use the QuickBooks help feature to learn how to enter a bill from a vendor
Change Preferences	Choose to change the color scheme to Orange (hint: Desktop View/My Preferences)
	Turn off the two date warnings (hint: Accounting/Company Preferences)
Create a List Report	Create a list report that shows all of the Terms available (these list entries were automatically added when you created the company)

Concepts Review

To check your knowledge of the key concepts introduced in this chapter, complete the Concepts Review quiz on the Student Resource Center or in your eLab course.

Reinforce Your Skills

Set Up a New QuickBooks Company

In this exercise, you will use Detailed Start to set up the company for Quality-Built Construction.

1. If necessary, launch **QuickBooks**.

2. Choose **File→New Company**.

3. Click the **Detailed Start** button in the QuickBooks Setup window.
   The EasyStep Interview window displays.

4. Refer to the information in the table below to complete the EasyStep Interview for Angela.

EASYSTEP INTERVIEW INFORMATION	
Field	**Data**
Company/Legal Name	`Quality-Built Construction`
Tax ID (Federal Employee Identification Number)	`99-9999999`
Address	`316 Maple Street` `Silverton, OR 97381`
Phone	`(503) 555-3759`
Fax	`(503) 555-3758`
Email	`qualitybuilt@samplename.com`
Industry Type	Construction General Contractor
Company Organization	S Corporation
First Month of Fiscal Year	January
Administrator Password	`Build2014` (remember that passwords are case-sensitive)
File Name	`RYS_Chapter02_[LastnameFirstinitial]` (e.g. RYS_Chapter02_StevensA)
What Is Sold?	Services Only
Sales Tax	No
Estimates	No
Billing Statements	Yes
Invoices	Yes
Progress Invoicing	No
Bill Tracking	Yes
Time Tracking	No
Employees	No
Multiple Currencies	No (this option is not available in all versions)
Start Date	`11-30-2014`
Income & Expense Accounts	Start with the accounts provided

5. Once the information is entered, click **Go to Setup** to complete the interview.

   The "You've got a company file!" screen appears in the QuickBooks Setup window.

6. Click **Start working**.

7. Click the **Close** button on the Quick Start Center window.

Change Preferences

In this exercise, you will change two preferences in the file you just created for Quality-Built Construction. You will begin by turning on the account number preference so that when you create and edit accounts, you can enter the numbers.

Before You Begin: Make sure you have completed Reinforce Your Skills 2-1.

1. Choose **Edit→Preferences**.

2. Choose the **Accounting** category.

3. Click the **Company Preferences** tab.

4. Click in the box to turn on the **Use account numbers** preference.

5. Click **OK**.

Display Additional Task Icons on the Home Page

Angela would like to be able to create sales receipts in QuickBooks, so you will make the Create Sales Receipts task icon visible on the Home page.

6. Choose **Edit→Preferences**.

7. Choose the **Desktop View** category.

8. Click the **Company Preferences** tab.

9. Click in the box to the left of **Sales Receipts** in the Customers area of the window.

10. Click **OK** to change the preference, and then click **OK** again to close the window.

Work with the Chart of Accounts

In this exercise, you will add, edit, and delete accounts as well as add subaccounts in the Chart of Accounts.

Add New Accounts

Angela wants to add her company's checking account.

1. Choose **Lists→Chart of Accounts**.

2. Click the **Account** menu button, and then choose **New**.

   The account menu button can be found in the bottom-left of the Chart of Accounts window.

3. Choose **Bank** as the account type; click **Continue**.

4. Type **10000** in the Number field, tap ⎟Tab⎟, and then type **Checking** as the Name.

5. Click **Save & New**; click **No** in the Set Up Online Services window, if necessary.

6. Choose **Income** as the account type.

7. Type **42700** in the Number field, tap ⎟Tab⎟, and then type **Remodel Income** as the Name.

8. Click **Save & Close**.

Edit an Account

Angela wants to change the name of the Construction Income account.

9. Scroll, if necessary, and right-click on the **42600•Construction Income** account; then choose **Edit Account** from the shortcut menu.

10. Change the name of the account to **New Construction Income**, and then click **Save & Close**.

Delete an Account

Angela has decided that she doesn't want the Ask My Accountant account, so you will delete it for her.

11. Scroll down, if necessary, and single-click on account **80000•Ask My Accountant**.

12. Click the **Account** menu button, and then choose **Delete Account**.

13. Click **OK** to confirm the deletion.

Add Subaccounts

You will now add two subaccounts for the Utilities account: Gas & Electric and Water.

14. Click the **Account** menu button, and then choose **New**.

15. Choose **Expense** as the account type; click **Continue**.

16. Enter **68610** as the Number and **Gas & Electric** as the Name.

17. Make it a subaccount of **68600•Utilities**.

18. Click **Save & New**, and then create one additional subaccount for Utilities: **68620•Water**.

19. Click **Save & Close**; then close the **Chart of Accounts** window.

Produce a List Report

In this exercise, you will create an Account Listing report for Angela to show her the work that you have completed on her Chart of Accounts.

1. Choose **Reports→List→Account Listing**.

2. Take a look at the report and make sure that all of the **Chart of Accounts** work you did in the last exercise is correct.

3. Either print the report or save it as a PDF, based on your instructor's direction.

4. Submit the report based on the guidelines provided by your instructor.

5. Close the **Account Listing** report.

6. Choose the appropriate option for your situation:

   - If you will continue working, leave QuickBooks open.
   - If you are finished working in QuickBooks for now, choose **File→Exit**.

Apply Your Skills

APPLY YOUR SKILLS 2-1

Create and Customize a New Company File

In this exercise, you will create a QuickBooks company file for Dr. Sadie James, DVM. You should use the Express Start method to set up the company.

1. Use the following information to set up a new company file for Dr. James. Save the file in your default file location, naming it **AYS_Chapter02_ [LastnameFirstinitial]** (e.g. AYS_Chapter02_JamesS).

Company/Legal Name	Wet Noses Veterinary Clinic
Tax ID Number	99-9999999
Address	589 Retriever Drive Bothell, WA 98011
Phone	(425) 555-2939
Company Type	LLP
Fiscal Year first month	January
Industry	Medical, Dental, or Health Service
Employees	No employees yet—will have in future

Remember that with this method of new company setup, QuickBooks will automatically save the file to the default location with the default name unless you choose to change it by previewing your settings.

2. Click **Start Working** in the QuickBooks Setup window.

3. Close the **Quick Start Center** and **Accountant Center** windows.

APPLY YOUR SKILLS 2-2

Change Account Preferences

In this exercise, you will set preferences for Wet Noses. You will not turn on account number preferences for this company, as you will operate this company without using them.

1. Open the **Preferences** window.

2. Choose to turn off **Beep when recording a transaction**. (Hint: Look in the General category.)

3. Choose to have QuickBooks show a full list of the **To Do Notes** when you open the company file.

   Hint: Look in the Reminders category.

4. Choose to turn off **date warnings**.

   Hint: Look in the Accounting category.

5. Close the **Preferences** window.

Modify the Chart of Accounts

In this exercise, you will modify the Chart of Accounts for the company you just created.

1. Open the **Chart of Accounts**.

2. Add two new **Bank** accounts: **Checking** and **Savings**.

3. Add a new **income** account: **Boarding Income**.

4. Add a new **expense** account: **Boarding Food and Supplies**.

5. Change the name of the Vaccines and Medicines account to **Pharmaceuticals**.

6. Add two **subaccounts** for Pharmaceuticals: **Vaccines** and **Medicines**.

7. Delete the **Uniforms** account.

Answer Questions with Reports

In this exercise, you will answer questions for Dr. James by running reports. You may wish to display the Report Center in List View to help you answer the questions. Ask your instructor if you should print the reports, print (save) them as PDF files, export them to Excel, or simply display them on the screen.

1. Dr. James' accountant has asked if the Chart of Accounts has been set up correctly. Produce a report that will show all of the accounts that have been set up for the company.

2. Before Dr. James begins working with customers and vendors, her accountant asks if the proper terms have been set up for her to use on invoices and bills. Display a report that will show her what terms are currently set up for the company.

3. Submit your reports based on the guidelines provided by your instructor.

4. Choose the appropriate option for your situation:
   - If you will continue working, leave QuickBooks open.
   - If you are finished working in QuickBooks for now, choose **File→Exit**.

Extend Your Skills

In the course of working through the Extend Your Skills exercises, you will utilize various skills taught in this and previous chapters. Take your time and think carefully about the tasks presented to you. Turn back to the chapter content if you need assistance.

2-1 Sort Through the Stack

You have been hired by Arlaine Cervantes to help her with her organization's books. She is the founder of Niños del Lago, a nonprofit organization that provides impoverished Guatemalan children with an engaging educational camp experience. You have just sat down at your desk and opened a large envelope from her with a variety of documents and noticed that you have several emails from her as well. It is your job to sort through the papers and emails and make sense of what you find, entering information into QuickBooks whenever appropriate and answering any other questions in a word-processing document saved as **EYS1_Chapter02_ LastnameFirstinitial**. Remember, you are digging through papers you just dumped out of an envelope and addressing random emails from Arlaine, so it is up to you to determine the correct order in which to complete the tasks.

- An email from her accountant: Set up Chart of Accounts, use Nonprofit as industry type, and add Grant Revenue as an income account.
- A bank statement from Salem First National Bank dated 6/30/2014. Checking account #21375-01, ending balance $5,462.11; Savings account #21375-20, ending balance $18,203.54.
- A handwritten sticky note: Need for three volunteers (Bill, Karel, and Chris) to have access to entering donor revenue. How can I make sure they can do this but don't have access to other areas in QuickBooks? Will I need a password or something?
- A scrap of paper with the following written on it: Fiscal year July-June.
- A scribbled phone message from Arlaine's accountant: Make sure to use account numbers when you set up in QuickBooks.
- The following message on a sticky note: Is there a reminders list to keep me on track???
- Another email from Arlaine's accountant: Make sure to not have the starting date the day you started the organization…would be too much information to enter. How about 6/30/2014 instead since it is the end of the fiscal year?
- A copy of last year's taxes: Form 990, Federal EIN 99-9999999.
- A piece of company letterhead found is posted on the Student Resource Center.

2-2 Be Your Own Boss

Before You Begin: Complete Extend Your Skills 1-2 before starting this exercise.

In this exercise, you will create the company file that you outlined in the previous chapter. Using the information identified in Extend Your Skills 1-2 and what you have learned in this chapter, create a new company file for your business. Save the new company file as **EYS2_Chapter02_ LastnameFirstinitial** and submit it to your instructor based on the instructions provided.

2-3 Use the Web as a Learning Tool

Throughout this book, you will be provided with an opportunity to use the Internet as a learning tool by completing WebQuests. According to the original creators of WebQuests, as described on their website (http://WebQuest.org), a WebQuest is "an inquiry-oriented activity in which most or all of the information used by learners is drawn from the web." To complete the WebQuest projects in this book, navigate to the Student Resource Center and choose the WebQuest for the chapter on which you are working. The subject of each WebQuest will be relevant to the material found in the chapter.

WebQuest Subject: Working with QuickBooks in a multi-user environment

Working with Customers

Let's face it. The best part of being in business is creating and developing relationships with customers. Intuit describes a customer as "any person, business, or group that buys or pays for the services or products that your business or organization sells or provides." When working with QuickBooks, you can consider a customer anyone who pays you funds. This simple definition will help you if you have a unique business, such as a not-for-profit organization that doesn't normally use the term "customer." The job feature is an optional aspect of QuickBooks, but the feature can be extremely helpful if you have more than one project for a customer. In this chapter, you will examine QuickBooks' lists, activities, and reports that allow you to deal with customers effectively.

CHAPTER OUTLINE

CHAPTER OBJECTIVES

After studying this chapter, you will be able to:

- Use the Customer Center and Customers & Jobs List
- Create service and non-inventory items
- Create invoices and receive payment on them
- Enter sales receipts
- Correct errors in customer transactions
- Work with customer-related reports

Average Guy Designs

Guy has learned from his colleague Allison that the next step he needs to complete is to set up his company to track customers and sales transactions. He will begin by working on the Customers & Jobs List, which is a part of the Customer Center. Once his customers have been entered, he will be able to create transactions for them. In order to create sales transactions such as invoices and sales receipts, though, he must first create items that will be used to direct income into the proper accounts behind the scenes. Finally, Guy will create reports that will tell him about his customer-related transactions.

Guy can access the Customers & Jobs List, and all of the transactions concerning a customer, from the Customer Center. The following illustration shows the Customer Center with Evelyn Huff selected.

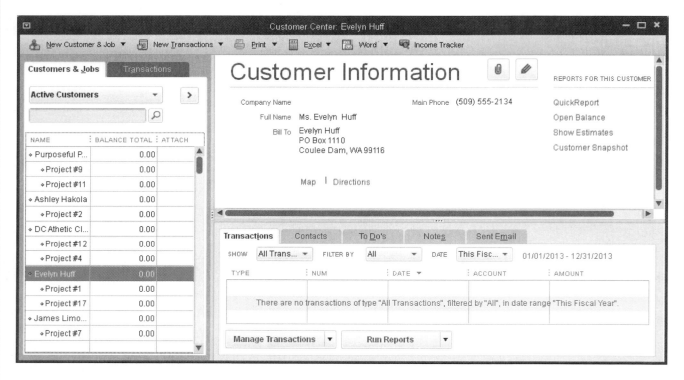

In this chapter, you will also help Guy to fix errors made when entering customer transactions.

 Tab: Tracking Money In
Topic: Sales overview; Building blocks of sales

Working with the Customer Center

When opened, the Customer Center gives you a quick look at all of your customers. If you recall from the introduction, a customer is anyone who pays you funds. This general definition is useful because it applies to all types of organizations, even those that do not have "customers" in the traditional sense, such as not-for-profits.

QuickBooks uses lists to organize your company's information. Lists allow you to store information that you can easily fill into forms by using drop-down arrows or by starting to type the entry and letting QuickBooks fill in the rest. Lists comprise the database aspect of QuickBooks. As an option, the Customers & Jobs List can be exported to contact management software such as Microsoft Outlook.

The Customer Center window provides you with the following information:

- The name of each customer and any jobs that have been created
- The balance that each customer owes
- Information for the selected customer or job
- Transactions affecting the selected customer or job

These tabs help to track information for each customer.

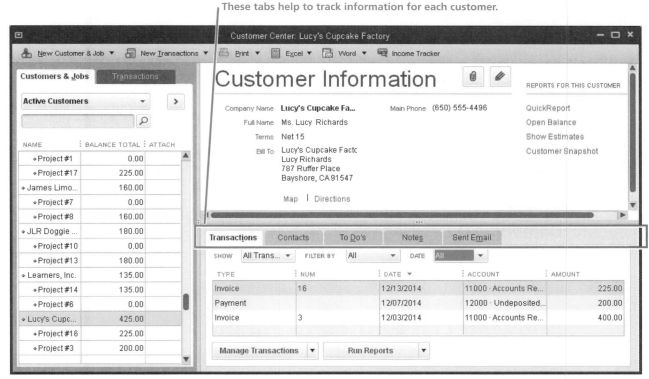

The Customer Information section displayed to the right of the Customers & Jobs List relates to the selected customer record, in this case, Lucy's Cupcake Factory.

The Customers & Jobs List tracks a lot of information for each customer and each job. This information is organized onto five tabs: Address Info, Payment Settings, Sales Tax Settings, Additional Info, and Job Info. If you have jobs assigned to a customer, you will see only four tabs. You will manage the jobs in the separate job records. If you want to track information that does not already have a field, you can create Custom Fields to customize QuickBooks for your unique business, which you will learn more about in Chapter 10, Customizing and Integrating in QuickBooks. Remember, the more information you enter for each customer, the more flexibility you will have later when you learn how to customize reports. When you utilize fields, you can sort, group, and filter your reports using those fields. You can access the Customers & Jobs List through the Customer Center.

Managing the Customers & Jobs List

List-management tasks are performed similarly for the various lists in QuickBooks. The exact procedure that you follow will depend on whether the list is integrated into a QuickBooks center (Customers & Jobs, Vendors, and Employees) or is accessible via the List option on the menu bar. The lists that are integrated into a center are not accessible separately via the menu bar.

 Centralized Info in the Customer Center

Creating a New Customer

To enter customer transactions, you must first enter your customers into the Customers & Jobs List. Customers can be entered at any time and can even be entered "on the fly" into the customer field on forms such as Create Invoices and Enter Sales Receipts; you will then have to select Quick Add or Setup from the pop-up window. Once you have added a customer to the list, you can create individual jobs for that customer.

Editing an Existing Customer

Once you have created a customer, you can always go back and edit that customer through the Customer Center. The one item that cannot be edited after you have created and saved a new customer is the opening balance (it must be adjusted through the customer register). When you change the information for a customer, including the customer's name, it will be reflected in both future and past transactions.

Deleting a Customer

You can delete a customer or job from the Customers & Jobs List *as long as you have not used it in a transaction*. If you have used it in a transaction, you can make it inactive, but you cannot delete it until after you close the books for a period and clean up your company's data.

Allowing List Entries to Fill In

When your insertion point is in a field that draws from a list, you can simply begin to type the entry that you want to choose from the list. QuickBooks will search down the list and fill in the entry for you. This fill-in feature is not case-sensitive, so you can type in lowercase even though the list entry will fill in with the proper capitalization (if you entered it with proper capitalization in the list).

Adding/Editing Multiple List Entries

You can manage the customer, vendor, and item lists all in one location. You can also choose to type the list entries or paste them from Microsoft Excel. In this chapter, you will add one entry at a time in the Customers & Jobs List. In Chapter 6, Dealing with Physical Inventory, you will work with the Add/Edit Multiple List Entries feature.

The Income Tracker

 The Income Tracker is a new feature in QuickBooks 2014 that allows you to view all of your customer-related transactions in one convenient place.

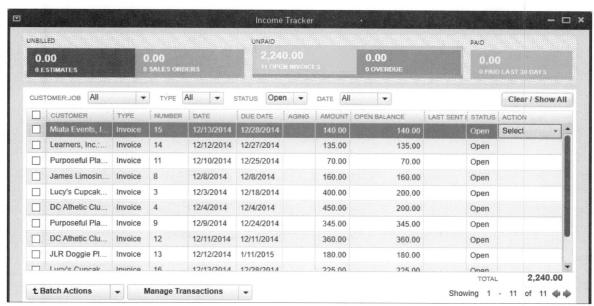

In the Income Tracker, you can easily see and manage all customer-related transactions. You can also perform actions on transactions in batches from this window.

The QuickBooks Lead Center

The QuickBooks Lead Center is a feature that provides you with a tool to track potential sales leads. Within the Lead Center, you can track outstanding tasks, contact information for the leads, location information, and notes related to your interactions and knowledge of the sales lead.

Working with Nonprofit Organizations

You use QuickBooks to work with nonprofit organizations just as you do with for-profit companies. Intuit also offers a specialized QuickBooks Premier edition designed especially for nonprofits. In this book you have been and will continue to work with a nonprofit organization, Niños del Lago, in the Extend Your Skills exercises.

When working with nonprofits in QuickBooks, take care with the term "customer." QuickBooks defines a customer as anyone who pays you funds. So, with a nonprofit, donors are customers.

They should be entered in the Customers & Jobs List. You can also use the customer and vendor profile lists in creative ways to track aspects of a nonprofit organization.

QUICK REFERENCE	MANAGING THE CUSTOMERS & JOBS LIST
Task	**Procedure**
Edit an existing customer/job	■ Open the Customer Center; double-click the desired customer or job. ■ Make the change(s) in the field(s); click OK.
Add a new customer	■ Open the Customer Center; click the New Customer & Job button, and then choose New Customer. ■ Enter all of the customer's information; click OK.
Add a new job	■ Open the Customer Center; single-click the desired customer. ■ Click the New Customer & Job button, and then choose Add Job. ■ Enter all of the information for the job; click OK.
Delete a customer/job	■ Open the Customer Center; single-click the desired customer/job. ■ Choose Edit→Delete Customer:Job; click OK to confirm.
Make a list entry inactive	■ Open the center in which the list entry is located. ■ Right-click the desired list entry, and then choose Make Inactive.
Merge list entries	■ Open the center in which the list entries are located. ■ Double-click the list entry you wish to merge with another. ■ Change the name of the entry to exactly match the entry into which you wish to merge; click OK.
Access the Income Tracker	■ Choose Customers→Income Tracker.
Access the Lead Center	■ Choose Customers→Lead Center.

Manage the Customers & Jobs List

In this exercise, you will manage the Customers & Jobs List. The first step is to open QuickBooks, and then either open a company file or restore a portable company file.

Intuit provides maintenance releases throughout the lifetime of the product. These updates may require you to update your student exercise files before you work with them. Please follow the prompts on the screen if you are asked to update your company file to the latest QuickBooks release.

1. Start **QuickBooks 2014**.

   If you downloaded the student exercise files in the portable company file *format, follow Option 1 below. If you downloaded the files in the* company file *format, follow Option 2.*

Option 1: Restore a Portable Company File

2. Choose **File→Open or Restore Company**.

3. Restore the **DYS_Chapter03 (Portable)** portable company file from your file storage location, placing your last name and first initial at the end of the filename (e.g., DYS_Chapter03_MarshallG).

   It may take a few moments for the portable company file to open. Once it does, continue with step 5.

Option 2: Open a Company File

2. Choose **File→Open or Restore Company**, ensure that **Open a regular company file** is selected, and then open the **Average Guy Designs** company file for this chapter from your file storage location.

   The QuickBooks company file will open.

3. Click **OK** to close the QuickBooks Information window. Click **No** in the Set Up External Accountant User window, if necessary.

4. Close the **Reminders** window.

Edit an Existing Customer

The first step in performing any Customers & Jobs list management task is to open the Customer Center.

FROM THE KEYBOARD

Ctrl+J to open the Customer Center

5. Click the **Customers** button located in the Customers area of the Home page.

CUSTOMERS

6. Single-click to select **DC Athetic Club LLC** in the Customers & Jobs List.

   You must first select the customer you wish to edit, and yes, it is spelled incorrectly—you will be fixing it!

7. Click the **Edit Customer** button in the Customer Information area of the Customer Center.

The Edit Customer window will open for the selected customer.

8. Correct the name to read **DC Athletic Club LLC**.

   You will need to correct this in four separate places in the Edit Customer window.

In QuickBooks, you can use the same text editing techniques you use in word-processing programs. Simply select the text to be replaced by clicking and dragging the mouse pointer over it and then type the replacement. You can also use the Delete or Backspace keys on your keyboard.

9. Click **OK** to accept the change.

Add a New Customer

Now you will add a new customer to the Customers & Jobs List.

10. Click the **New Customer & Job** button, and then choose **New Customer**.

11. Follow these steps to fill in the information on the Address Info tab:

ⓐ Type **Dance a Little**.   ⓑ Tap ⟨Tab⟩ three times, and then type **Dance a Little** again.

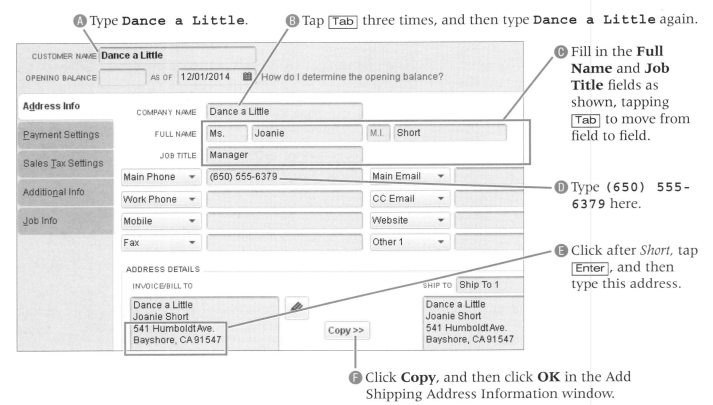

ⓒ Fill in the **Full Name** and **Job Title** fields as shown, tapping ⟨Tab⟩ to move from field to field.

ⓓ Type **(650) 555-6379** here.

ⓔ Click after *Short,* tap ⟨Enter⟩, and then type this address.

ⓕ Click **Copy**, and then click **OK** in the Add Shipping Address Information window.

Since you are not entering an opening balance, you do not need to worry about the date displayed for it.

12. Click the **Payment Settings** tab, and then follow these steps to add information:

ⓐ Type **GD-54** here.

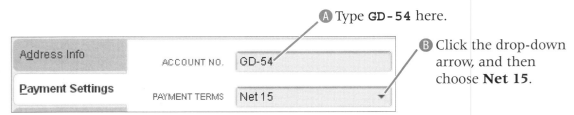

ⓑ Click the drop-down arrow, and then choose **Net 15**.

13. Click the **Additional Info** tab.

14. Click the Customer Type drop-down arrow and choose **From advertisement**.

15. Click **OK** to complete the new customer record.

Add a Job

16. Ensure **Dance a Little** is selected, click the New Customer & Job button, and then choose **Add Job**.

17. Type **Project #19** as the Job Name; click **OK**.

In the next step, you will close the Customer Center window within QuickBooks. Do not click the Close button for the QuickBooks window, as it will exit the program rather than simply close the center window!

18. Close the **Customer Center** window.

Understanding and Creating Items

Before you can create an invoice, you must create items to be included on the invoice. You will now learn how to create items for service and non-inventory items. An item is defined in QuickBooks as something that a company buys, sells, or resells in the course of business.

When you create a new item, you need to provide QuickBooks with very important information. When an item is sold, it directs the sales to the proper income account based on the information you entered when you created the item. The Item List will be studied in more depth in Chapter 6, Dealing with Physical Inventory, when you begin to work with inventory. In this chapter, you will access the Item List through the Home page.

This search feature can come in handy if you have many items through which you may need to look to find a specific item.

This column shows the item names. This is what you will enter into a form to choose the item.

TYPES OF ITEMS	
Item Type	**Description**
Service	For services you charge for or purchase (e.g., specialized labor, consulting hours, or professional fees)
Non-inventory Part	For goods you buy but don't track (e.g., office supplies) or materials for a specific job that you charge back to the customer
Inventory Part	For goods you purchase, track as inventory, and resell
Other Charge	For miscellaneous labor, material, or part charges (e.g., delivery charges, setup fees, or service charges)
Subtotal	Totals all items above it on a form up to the last subtotal; to apply a percentage discount or surcharge to many items
Group	Quickly enters a group of individual items on an invoice
Discount	Subtracts a percentage or fixed amount from a total or subtotal; do not use for an early payment discount
Payment	Records a partial payment at the time of sale; reduces the amount owed on an invoice
Sales Tax Item	Calculates a single sales tax at a specific rate that you pay to a single tax agency
Sales Tax Group	Calculates and individually tracks two or more sales tax items that apply to the same sale; customer sees only the total sales tax

Service Items

Service items are used in QuickBooks to track services that you both sell to others and purchase from them. They can be used to track time that employees spend on a certain customer's project and then be easily passed on to a customer using the QuickBooks time tracking feature. This use of service items will be covered in Chapter 9, Working with Estimates and Time Tracking.

Non-Inventory Items

Non-inventory part items are for things that a business buys but doesn't stock as inventory. You can use purchase orders to obtain non-inventory items if you wish to track items that are used in your business but not resold to customers, such as papers and printer ink. You will learn more about purchase orders in Chapter 6, Dealing with Physical Inventory. You can also purchase non-inventory items through the Enter Bills window by utilizing the Items tab. In order to track both purchase and sales information for an item, you need to identify that the item is "used in assemblies or is purchased for a specific customer: job" in the New or Edit Item window.

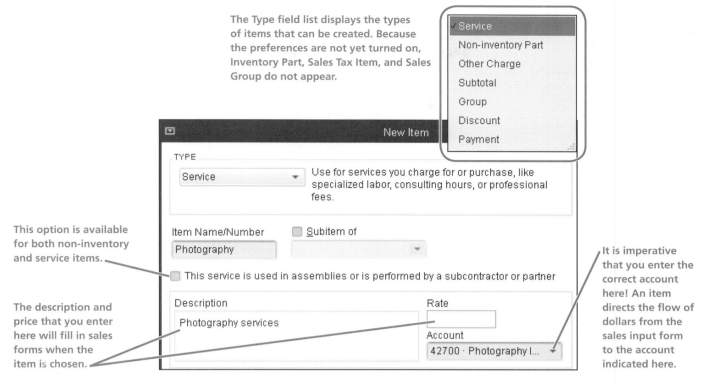

The Type field list displays the types of items that can be created. Because the preferences are not yet turned on, Inventory Part, Sales Tax Item, and Sales Group do not appear.

This option is available for both non-inventory and service items.

The description and price that you enter here will fill in sales forms when the item is chosen.

It is imperative that you enter the correct account here! An item directs the flow of dollars from the sales input form to the account indicated here.

When you enter an item on a QuickBooks form, you can override the price that you have recorded in the Item List. If you don't have standard pricing and find that you enter specialized pricing more than you use a default price, you may wish to leave the Price field blank in the Item List and fill it in on each form created.

Introducing Sales Tax Items

In some states, sales tax is collected on services provided. However, this is the exception rather than the rule. In this book, dealing with sales tax will be introduced in Chapter 6, Dealing with Physical Inventory, when you begin to work with the inventory tracking and product resale. In order to charge sales tax on a sales form, it must first be set up as an item.

Make sure that when you deal with sales tax, you take some time to learn about how the sales tax laws are set up in your jurisdiction. Some states do not collect sales tax at all. For states that do, there is variation among what is taxed. What it comes down to is that you must know the sales tax laws where you do business before you set up sales tax for your company.

Using Subitems

If you wish to track your items in a more detailed fashion, you can use subitems. They can be created for any item on your Item List and can be useful on reports to determine aspects of your business such as profitability. You might use subitems in your company file to:

- Differentiate between broad categories of products and services and individual items within them
- Manage pricing levels for volume discounts
- Differentiate between measurements (see the following figure)
- Track multiple vendors for an item

When using subitems, you state an item with no price for the main item, and then list prices for the subitems beneath it.

 Tab: Getting Set Up
Topic: Add the products and services you sell

QUICK REFERENCE	CREATING ITEMS
Task	**Procedure**
Create a new item	■ Open the Item List.
	■ Click the item menu button, choose New, and then choose the desired item type.
	■ Enter an item name, description, and price.
	■ Select the account (income for a service item, expense, or cost of goods sold for a non-inventory item) to which you want the purchase of the item directed.
Turn on the QuickBooks sales tax feature	■ Choose Edit→Preferences.
	■ Click the Sales Tax category; click the Company Preferences tab.
	■ Click in the circle to the left of Yes in the "Do you charge sales tax?" section.
	■ Select your most common sales tax item. If necessary, create the sales tax item.
	■ Select when you owe sales tax and how often you must pay it; click OK.
Create a sales tax item	■ Open the Item List, click the Item menu button, and then click New.
	■ Choose Sales Tax Item as the type of item (the sales tax preference must be set up first).
	■ Type the name and description for the item.
	■ Set the tax rate and agency to which you pay the tax; click OK.

DEVELOP YOUR SKILLS 3-2

Create Items

In this exercise, you will create both a service and a non-inventory item.

1. Click the **Items & Services** task icon in the Company area of the Home page.

2. Click the **Item** menu button and choose **New**.

3. Tap [Tab], and the default service item type, **Service**, is chosen automatically.

Items & Services

FROM THE KEYBOARD

[Ctrl]+[n] to open a New Item window from the Item List

4. Follow these steps to create a new service item:

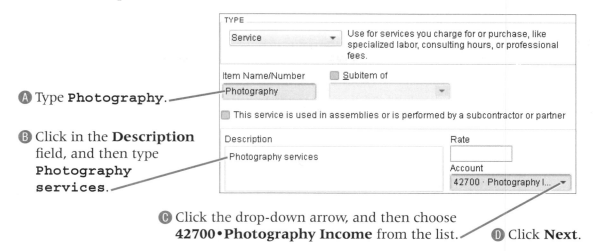

Ⓐ Type **Photography**.

Ⓑ Click in the **Description** field, and then type **Photography services**.

Ⓒ Click the drop-down arrow, and then choose **42700•Photography Income** from the list.

Ⓓ Click **Next**.

The new item will be added to the Item List, and the New Item window will remain open so you can create another item. You have left the rate field blank as you will enter the price on each sales form based on what you quoted to your customers.

Set Up a Non-Inventory Item

5. Follow these steps to create a new non-inventory part:

Ⓐ Click the drop-down arrow, and then choose **Non-inventory Part**.

Ⓑ Tap Tab, and then type **Paper**.

Ⓒ Click in the **Description** field, and then type **Specialty paper**.

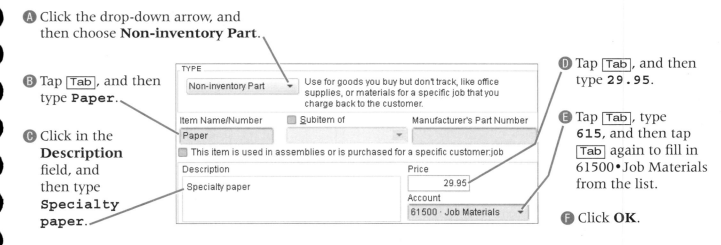

Ⓓ Tap Tab, and then type **29.95**.

Ⓔ Tap Tab, type **615**, and then tap Tab again to fill in 61500•Job Materials from the list.

Ⓕ Click **OK**.

6. Close the **Item List** window.

Creating Invoices

Once you have set up your initial Customers & Jobs List, you can begin to enter sales transactions. In this section, you will learn to create invoices and use Accounts Receivable, which is the account debited when invoices are created. When you create an invoice, you *must* specify a customer because Accounts Receivable (along with the customer's individual sub-register) will be debited by the transaction.

Invoicing a customer is also known as a customer making a purchase "on account."

After you select your customer from the drop-down list at the top of the form, all of the relevant information you entered in that customer's record will fill into the appropriate fields on the Create Invoices window.

This menu shows all entries in the Customers & Jobs list from which you may choose.

This menu shows the available invoice templates. You can customize the existing templates or create your own templates from scratch.

This column section of the invoice deals specifically with the items the customer purchases.

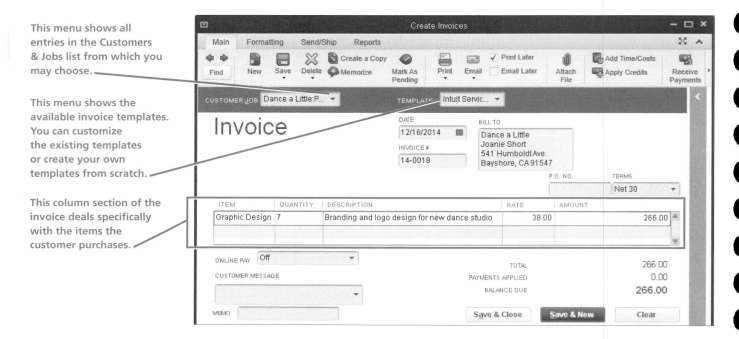

 Tab: Tracking Money In
Topic: Create an invoice

When you created your customer records, you entered a lot of information about each customer that will automatically fill into invoices when the customer is chosen. You have the option of changing that information when you create an invoice, though. If you change a customer's information in the Create Invoices window, QuickBooks will ask if you want to make the change permanent before recording the transaction.

If you click Yes, QuickBooks will change the customer information in the Customers & Jobs List.

If you click No, the new information will appear on the current invoice, but the Customers & Jobs List record will remain unchanged.

If you click Cancel, QuickBooks will return you to the Create Invoices window.

Information Changed

You have changed: Dance a Little:Project #19

Terms

Would you like to have this new information appear next time?

Yes   No   Cancel

Entering Customers Not Already on the Customers & Jobs List

When you type a new entry into a field that draws from a list, QuickBooks gives you the opportunity to add the record to the list. You can choose to Quick Add the new record (the name will be entered into the list without accompanying information, which you can add at a later date) or to complete a full setup (a New Customer window appears in which you can type all of the relevant information).

Visualize!

Tab: New to QuickBooks?
Topic: Using forms

Understanding Payment Terms

Payment terms dictate an agreement between buyer and seller as to when and how much is to be paid for a product or service. In the case of "Net 30" payment terms, the net (or entire) amount of the invoice is due in thirty days. There are also discount payment terms (discussed in Chapter 6, Dealing with Physical Inventory) that allow for a discount to be taken if the invoice is paid quickly. For instance, 2% 10 Net 30 means that the buyer can take a 2 percent discount off of the total amount of the invoice if it is paid within 10 days, or the net amount is due to the seller in 30 days.

By default, if payment terms are not stated for a customer or on an invoice, QuickBooks will set the payment due date to be ten days from the date of sale.

Emailing Invoices

For the majority of companies, email is one of the primary ways they do business nowadays. QuickBooks allows you to easily email invoices to customers, rather than having to send them via "snail mail" or fax. To indicate that you wish to send invoices and other forms to your customers via email, use the Additional Info tab of either the New or Edit Customer window. If you choose to email an invoice to a customer, that customer will receive it as a PDF file attached to the email along with a message that you set in the Preferences window.

Customer Send Method

The customer send method is the way that you primarily send invoices and other forms to a customer. You can change this on each transaction for the customer if it is not always the same method. In the Preferences window, you can customize both personal and company preferences for this feature.

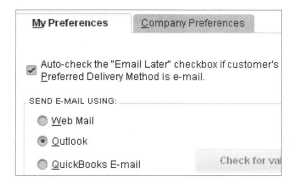

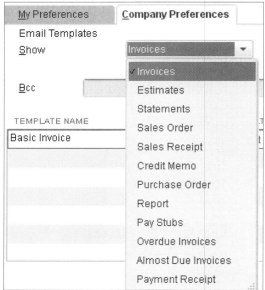

In the Send Forms category of the Preferences window, you can set preferences for both yourself and the company (if you are the administrator). The administrator controls how the email message sent with the invoice (or other type of form) to customers will appear.

Form Templates

When you first install QuickBooks, Intuit provides you with various templates, such as the Intuit Service Invoice, Intuit Product Invoice, Intuit Professional Invoice, and Intuit Packing Slip. You can continue to use these invoices as they are, create custom invoices to meet your specific needs, or download templates from the QuickBooks website. In this section, you will work with one of the default invoice forms—the Intuit Service Invoice. The creation and customization of form templates will be covered in Chapter 10, Customizing and Integrating in QuickBooks.

Going Behind the Scenes

If you recall in Chapter 1, Introducing QuickBooks Pro, there is a special feature in this book that allows you to take a peek at the accounting that QuickBooks is doing for you when you enter information into forms. In the following illustration, you will find the first instance of the "Behind the Scenes" feature. Remember that the names used in this feature are the account names QuickBooks uses, not traditional accounting nomenclature. If you would like to learn more about basic accounting principles and what the "behind the scenes stuff" is all about, you may want to check out another Labyrinth Learning book, *Accounting Basics: An Introduction for Non-Accounting Majors*.

When creating invoices, QuickBooks takes care of all of the accounting for you. Following is an illustration of the accounting that goes on behind the scenes for the first invoice you will create in the following exercise.

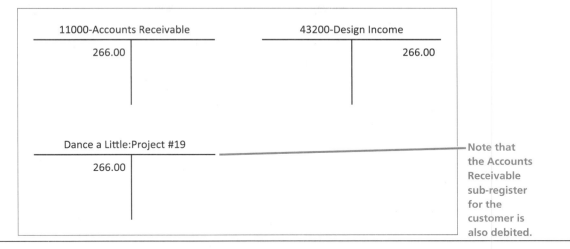

11000-Accounts Receivable	43200-Design Income
266.00	266.00

Dance a Little:Project #19	Note that the Accounts Receivable sub-register for the customer is also debited.
266.00	

Behind the Scenes (BTS) Brief

This book includes an additional feature to help you further understand the accounting that occurs behind the scenes. Labeled "BTS Brief," these accounting notes will appear within Develop Your Skills exercises. As an example (though not associated with an exercise), the BTS Brief for the transaction described in the Behind the Scenes table above is shown here.

BTS BRIEF

11000•Accounts Receivable DR 270.00; **43200•Design Income CR <270.00>**

In this feature, DR indicates a debit and CR indicates a credit. CR amounts display with brackets.

QUICK REFERENCE	CREATING INVOICES
Task	**Procedure**
Create an invoice	▪ Open the Create Invoices window.
	▪ Choose an existing customer or type a new customer.
	▪ Choose the correct date and terms.
	▪ Fill in the item(s) for which you wish to bill your customer, including the correct quantity for each item.
	▪ Choose a customer message, if desired; click Save & Close or Save & New.

Create Invoices

Joanie Short has just emailed you to ask you to do a job for her company, Dance a Little. You have agreed to a rate of $38/hour and to grant her terms of "Net 30," which means that her bill will be due in 30 days. In this exercise, you will create invoices for customers.

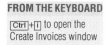

FROM THE KEYBOARD

Ctrl+I to open the Create Invoices window

1. Click the **Create Invoices** task icon in the Customers area of the Home page.

2. Click the **Customer:Job** field drop-down arrow at the top of the window, and then choose **Dance a Little:Project #19** from the Customers & Jobs List.

Create Invoices

Notice that the customer's address and terms fill in for you from the underlying list.

3. Tap ⟨Tab⟩ two times, type **121614**, and then tap ⟨Tab⟩.

When you type in a date field, you do not need to include the slash marks. QuickBooks will format the date properly for you once you move to the next field.

4. Type **14-0018** as the Invoice #.

5. Follow these steps to complete the invoice:

ⓐ Click the drop-down arrow, and then choose **Net 30**.

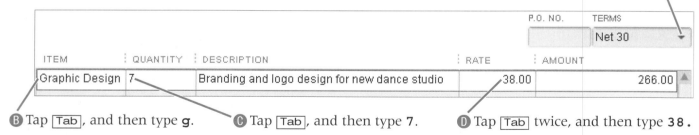

ⓑ Tap ⟨Tab⟩, and then type **g**.   ⓒ Tap ⟨Tab⟩, and then type **7**.   ⓓ Tap ⟨Tab⟩ twice, and then type **38.**

Once you select the item, the description, rate, and amount information fill in for you from the Item List. QuickBooks automatically calculates the total amount by multiplying the quantity by the rate. In this case, you had to type in the rate since it was not entered in the Item List. QuickBooks recalculates the amount once you move your insertion point to another field on the invoice form after changing the rate.

BTS BRIEF

11000•Accounts Receivable DR 266.00; **43200•Design Income CR <266.00>**

6. Click the **Save & New** button; click **Yes** in the Name Information Changed window.

A Name Information Changed window appeared since you changed the terms for the customer.

Create an Invoice for a New Customer

A new customer, Mary Jones, has stopped by Average Guy Designs' new office to pick up a project you just completed for her. You will add her as a new customer "on the fly" while creating the invoice for her. Your insertion point should be in the Customer:Job field at the top of a new invoice. If this is not the case, choose Customers→Create Invoices.

7. Type **Mary Jones**, and then tap Tab.

   The Customer:Job Not Found window will be displayed.

8. Click **Quick Add** in the Customer:Job Not Found window.

9. Tap Tab to go to the Date field, and then tap + until the date reads **12/18/2014**.

FROM THE KEYBOARD

+ to increase the date by one day at a time

- to decrease the date by one day at a time

t in a Date field to enter today's date

10. Follow these steps to complete the invoice:

Ⓐ Click the drop-down arrow and choose **Net 15**.

Ⓑ Click in the **Item** column, and then type **art** to choose **Art Work** from the list.

Ⓒ Tap Tab, and then type **6**.

Ⓓ Tap Tab again, and then type **45**.

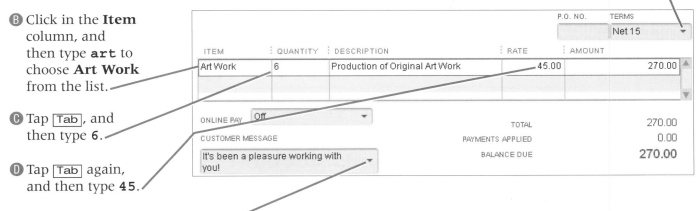

Ⓔ Tap Alt + m, and then type **i**.

TIP When you see a field name that has an underlined letter, you can tap the Alt key as well as the underlined letter to move to that field quickly.

FROM THE KEYBOARD

Alt + m to move to the Customer Message field

BTS BRIEF

11000•Accounts Receivable DR 270.00; **43200•Design Income CR <270.00>**

11. Click **Save & Close**; click **Yes** in the Name Information Changed window.

Receiving Payments

Once you have created invoices, you need to be able to accept the payments on them from your customers. In QuickBooks, you will use the Receive Payments window to credit Accounts Receivable and the appropriate customer sub-register. The other half of the equation (the account that will be debited) depends on how you treat the payments you receive.

It is very important to use the payments received window to enter payments received from invoiced customers. If you don't, the invoices will remain open, and your income and the amounts in accounts receivable will be overstated.

Options for Accepting Payments

There are many different customer payment types that you can record in QuickBooks, just as you will likely allow your customers multiple ways to pay you.

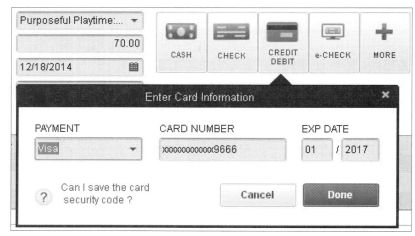

In the Receive Payments window, you can choose from a variety of popular payment methods, or choose to set up your own.

The Undeposited Funds Account

If you typically collect payments from more than one source before making a deposit, you will want to choose to group all payments in QuickBooks using the Undeposited Funds account. QuickBooks automatically creates this Other Current Asset account for you.

The default setting is for all payments received and cash sales to be placed in the Undeposited Funds account. You can change this preference in the Payments category of the Edit Preferences window.

Once you are ready to make a deposit to the bank, you will use the Make Deposit window, where you can select the payments in the Undeposited Funds account that you wish to deposit. You will learn about making deposits in QuickBooks in the next chapter.

Tab: Tracking Money In
Topic: Receiving and depositing payments

BEHIND THE SCENES

Let's look at accounting scenarios that result when you receive payments.

11000-Accounts Receivable		12000-Undeposited Funds	
Bal. 2,485.00	70.00	70.00	
2,415.00			

Purposeful Playtime:Project #11	
	70.00

Using the Undeposited Funds account when receiving a customer payment

11000-Accounts Receivable		10000-Checking	
Bal. 2,485.00	70.00	70.00	
2,415.00			

Receiving a customer payment directly into a bank account

QUICK REFERENCE	RECEIVING PAYMENTS
Task	**Procedure**
Receive a payment	■ Open the Receive Payments window.
	■ Choose the customer from whom you are receiving a payment.
	■ Enter the correct date and the amount received.
	■ Choose the correct payment method and enter any reference or check number information.
	■ Apply the payment to the correct invoice(s).
	■ Click Save & Close or Save & New.

Receive Payments

In this exercise, you will deal with payments received from invoiced customers. You have just received a credit card payment from Purposeful Playtime for Project #11.

1. Click the **Receive Payments** task icon in the Customers area of the Home page.

   The Receive Payments window opens with the insertion point in the Received From field.

2. Follow these steps to enter a customer payment:

A Click the drop-down arrow and choose **Purposeful Playtime:Project #11**.

B Tap Tab, and then type **70**.

C Tap Tab, and then type **121814** as the Date.

D Click the **Credit Debit** button.

E Choose **Visa**, tap Tab, and then type **8977554621339666**.

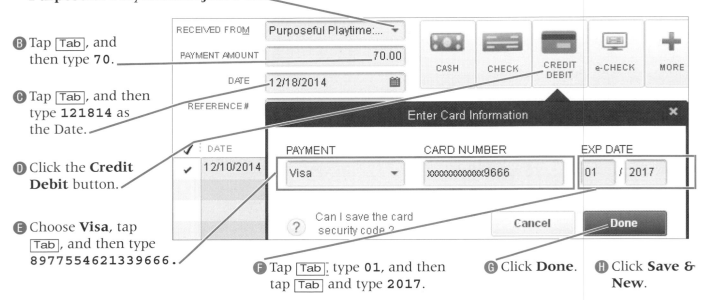

F Tap Tab, type **01**, and then tap Tab and type **2017**.

G Click **Done**.

H Click **Save & New**.

Notice that when you typed the amount, QuickBooks automatically applied it to the invoice listed. If you had multiple invoices displayed, QuickBooks would first apply the payment to the invoice that was for the exact amount. If no invoices matched the amount, it would be applied to invoice(s) beginning with the oldest one.

BTS BRIEF

12000•Undeposited Funds DR 70.00; 11000•Accounts Receivable CR <70.00>

Receive a Partial Payment

Guy just received a check from Lucy's Cupcake Factory for $100 to apply to the outstanding invoice for Project #16. You will receive this payment.

3. Choose **Lucy's Cupcake Factory:Project #16**, and then tap Tab.

4. Follow these steps to complete the payment receipt:

Ⓐ Type **100** in the **Payment Amount** field.

Ⓑ Tap ⌈Tab⌋, and then tap ⊞ to change the date to 12/19/14.

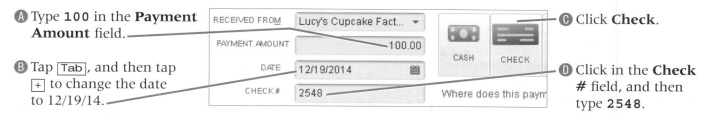

Ⓒ Click **Check**.

Ⓓ Click in the **Check # field**, and then type **2548**.

QuickBooks applies the payment to the outstanding invoice. The next time you select Lucy's Cupcake Factory:Project #16 as the customer in the Receive Payments window, QuickBooks will show that there is a balance due of $125.00. Notice that QuickBooks gives you an option as to how to deal with underpayments on invoices while you're still in the Receive Payments window.

BTS BRIEF

12000•Undeposited Funds DR 100.00; **11000•Accounts Receivable CR <100.00>**

5. Click **Save & Close** once you have ensured that you have entered all information correctly.

Entering Sales Receipts

As discussed earlier, you can use either of two forms to enter sales transactions. You have already learned how to create invoices and about the effect that they have behind the scenes. Now you will learn how to enter sales when payment is received up front.

A company does not have to choose one method of recording sales transactions and stick with it. Both forms can be used for the same company, depending on the situation at hand. When entering a sales receipt, you do not have to enter a customer (as accounts receivable is not affected) although you may want to enter customers to produce more meaningful sales reports. You have the option of adding a customer "on the fly" in the Enter Sales Receipts window just as you do when creating invoices.

As with the Receive Payments window, you can set a preference in order to be able to choose whether to group your payment with other funds waiting to be deposited or directly deposit it in the bank. The default option is to place all payments in the Undeposited Funds account. If you change the preference, you will need to choose into which account to deposit each payment.

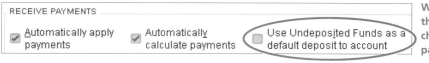

When this option is deselected in the Preferences window, you can choose which asset account the payment will go to.

You should notice how the Enter Sales Receipt form differs from the Create Invoices form and is essentially a combination of the Create Invoices and Receive Payments windows.

 Visualize!

Tab: Tracking Money In
Topic: Sales receipts

Choosing the Correct Form

In a previous section, you learned about invoices. There are other ways of recording customer sales and charges. The following table describes the three main forms you can use.

COMPARING CUSTOMER FORMS	
Form	**When to Use**
Invoices	Use this when a customer does not make a payment at the time of service and/or receipt of product. The invoice amount is held in Accounts Receivable.
Sales Receipts	Use this when a customer makes a payment at the time of service and/or receipt of product. Accounts Receivable is not affected. You will learn more about sales receipts later in this chapter.
Statements	Use this to leave a balance in the customer's Accounts Receivable account without creating an invoice. For example, if you have a customer for whom you do multiple jobs throughout the month, you can gather the charges and send one statement for all of them. You will learn more about statements in Chapter 10, Customizing and Integrating in QuickBooks.

"JIT" Customer and Transaction History

There are two tabs on the history panel that allow you to view information about the active transaction. The history panel allows you to view information just when you need it ("just in time"), without your having to leave the transaction and go to the Customer or Vendor Center to find it.

The Customer tab displays information specific to the active customer only.

You can hide the history panel by clicking this button.

The Transaction tab displays information specific to the active transaction only.

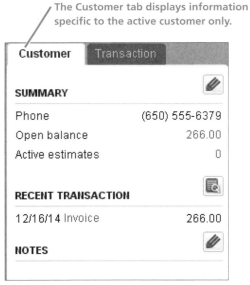

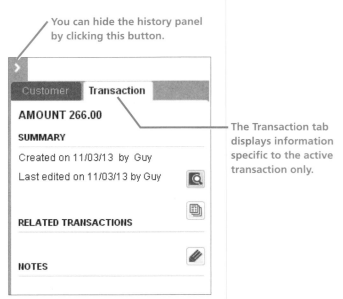

These are the two tabs of the history panel for Invoice #14-0018 associated with Lucy's Cupcake Factory. They allow you to view information quickly or "just in time" without your having to search through your company file. You can use the hyperlinks to view a transaction, edit a list entry, enter a note, or create a report.

BEHIND THE SCENES

The behind the scenes accounting that occurs when you enter cash sales is a hybrid of the two previous transactions (Creating Invoices and Receiving Payments) with the elimination of the middleman—Accounts Receivable.

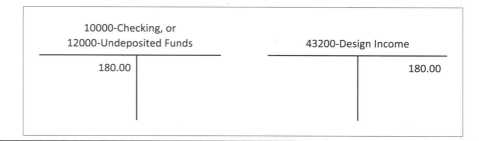

10000-Checking, or 12000-Undeposited Funds		43200-Design Income	
180.00			180.00

QUICK REFERENCE	ENTERING CASH SALES
Task	**Procedure**
Enter a cash sale	■ Open the Enter Sales Receipts window and choose a customer, if desired.
	■ Enter the date of the transaction, payment method, and reference/check number.
	■ Enter the items and quantity sold.
	■ Select a message for the customer, if desired.
	■ Click Save & Close or Save & New.

DEVELOP YOUR SKILLS 3-5
Enter Cash Sales

In this exercise, you will receive payment at the time of the sale. Ashley was in the area so she stopped by your office to pick up the art work you created for her. Since she is prepared to pay with cash, you will enter a sales receipt instead of an invoice.

1. Click the **Create Sales Receipts** task icon in the Customers area of the Home page.

   The Enter Sales Receipts window opens with the insertion point in the Customer:Job field.

Create Sales Receipts

2. Follow these steps to complete the sale:

Ⓐ Choose **Ashley Hakloa:Project #18**.

Ⓑ Click in the **Date** field, and then use ⊞ to change the date to **12/20/14**.

Ⓒ Click the **Cash** button.

Ⓓ Click in the **Item** column, and then type **art**.

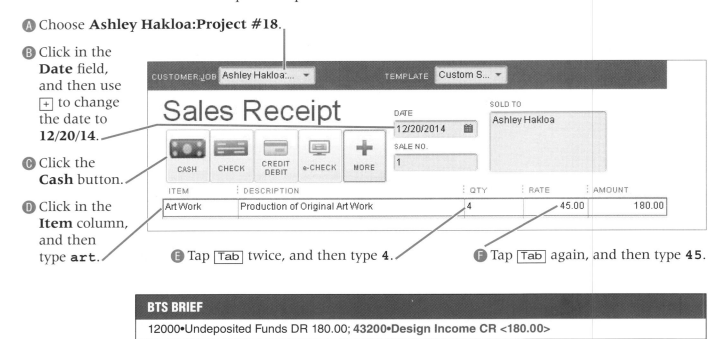

Ⓔ Tap ⎡Tab⎤ twice, and then type **4**.

Ⓕ Tap ⎡Tab⎤ again, and then type **45**.

BTS BRIEF

12000•Undeposited Funds DR 180.00; 43200•Design Income CR <180.00>

3. Click **Save & New**.

   Your insertion point should be in the Customer:Job field of a new Enter Sales Receipt window.

Record a Sales Receipt Without a Specified Customer

Since Accounts Receivable is not affected when you enter a cash sale, you can create a sales receipt without choosing a customer. This may come in handy if you sell something to someone just once and don't need that customer listed in your Customers & Jobs List or if you provide services in a different capacity. In this exercise, Guy worked with another photographer to take photos at a Christmas party.

4. Click in the date field and tap ⊞ until the date reads **12/22/2014**.

5. Follow these steps to complete the sales receipt:

Ⓐ Click the **Check** button.

Ⓑ Click in the **Check No.** field, and then type **1894**.

Ⓒ Tap ⎡Tab⎤, and then type **ph**.

Ⓓ Tap ⎡Tab⎤ three times, and then type **200**.

Ⓔ Click **Save & Close**.

This transaction will debit Undeposited Funds and credit Photography Income, but there will be no customer tracked. The purpose of selecting a customer for a sales receipt is to ensure that you can produce meaningful customer reports, such as Sales by Customer Summary, if they are important to your business.

Dealing with Oops in Customer Transactions

It is inevitable that you will need to deal with either errors or modifications to transactions in QuickBooks. It is very important that you do this properly to ensure that everything behind the scenes is correct.

Editing an Existing Transaction

To edit an existing transaction in QuickBooks, you simply open the window where the transaction is recorded and make the changes. You do need to think about the implications of any modifications that you make, though. Many transactions are tied to others, and a change to one can affect another. For instance, if an invoice has been paid, both the invoice and the payment are linked in QuickBooks.

Voiding vs. Deleting Transactions

QuickBooks allows you to either void or delete a transaction you no longer need recorded. In most cases, you will want to void a transaction so that you can keep a record of it. This will remove everything from behind the scenes and yet leave evidence that the transaction existed.

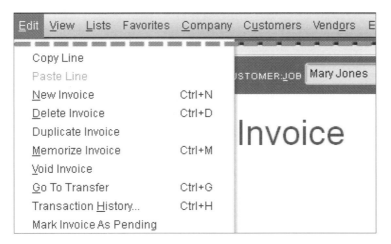

The Edit menu on the Create Invoices window provides options that allow you to work with the currently active transaction (in this case, an invoice for Mary Jones).

Locating Transactions in QuickBooks

QuickBooks provides two methods for you to choose from in order to locate transactions in your company file.

QuickBooks Find Feature

QuickBooks provides a Find feature that helps you to locate a transaction if you don't know all of the information about it. This can save you a lot of time when you have a company file with a large number of transactions. The two options within Find are:

> **FROM THE KEYBOARD**
> `Ctrl`+`f` to open the Find window

- **Simple** to perform basic searches
- **Advanced** to perform more complex searches, utilizing filters to help to sort through all of your data

QuickBooks Search Feature

With QuickBooks, you have the ability to perform searches based on text you enter throughout your company file and the menu commands. This feature is much more powerful than the Find feature and is similar to a search that you might perform on the Internet with any search engine. QuickBooks allows you to search for the following types of information:

- Forms/transactions (invoices, estimates, and so on)
- People and companies (customers, vendors, employees, and other names)
- List entries (items, tax items, and so on)
- Amounts and dates
- Menu commands (QuickBooks opens the menu and highlights the command for you)
- Specific text within notes, descriptions, memos, and transactions

You learned about the search feature and how to access it through the persistent search bar in Chapter 2, Creating a Company. You will explore it more in this chapter, and you will use it to locate a transaction to edit.

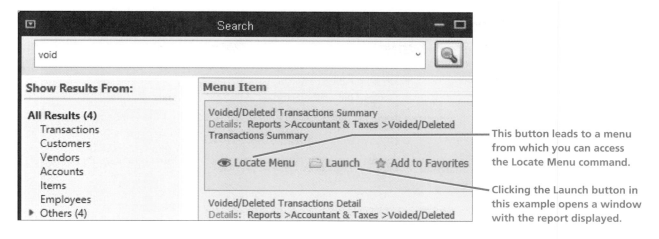

This button leads to a menu from which you can access the Locate Menu command.

Clicking the Launch button in this example opens a window with the report displayed.

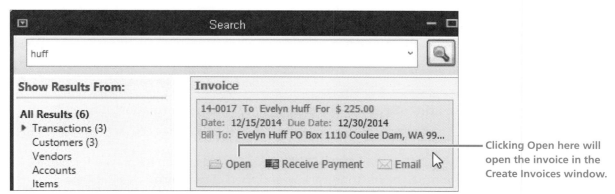

Clicking Open here will open the invoice in the Create Invoices window.

A search on *void* brings up menu items (one displayed here). A search on *huff* brings up the entry in the Customers & Jobs List and the customer invoices. The buttons below the invoice and menu items appear when you move your mouse pointer over the entries.

Fixing Errors

The following table outlines a common customer-related error, the effects of the error behind the scenes, and how to correct the error. You will see a similar table throughout the book when dealing with errors in other areas of QuickBooks.

A COMMON ERROR AND ITS FIX		
Error	**Effect Behind the Scenes**	**The Fix**
An invoice is entered but the Receive Payments window is not used when the payment is deposited	Your income will be double-stated and Accounts Receivable for the customer is not "cleared out"	Delete the deposit and then enter the transaction properly using the Receive Payments window

FLASHBACK TO GAAP: PRUDENCE
Remember that if you need to choose between two solutions, pick the one that is less likely to overstate assets and income.

Task	Procedure
Find a transaction in QuickBooks	■ Choose Edit→Find. ■ Choose either the Simple or the Advanced tab. ■ Enter as much information as possible about the transaction; click Find.
Search for text in the QuickBooks file and menu commands	■ Choose Edit→Search. ■ Type in the keyword on which you wish to base your search; tap ⌷Enter⌷.

DEVELOP YOUR SKILLS 3-6

Correct Customer Transactions

In this exercise, you will search for and edit an invoice. You will also collect a customer payment incorrectly and then fix it. First, you will help Guy to edit an invoice on which he charged a customer the wrong hourly rate.

1. Choose **Edit→Search**; choose to update search information, if necessary.

FROM THE KEYBOARD
⌷F3⌷ to launch the Search feature

2. Type **joanie**, and then tap ⌷Enter⌷.

3. Move your mouse pointer over the invoice transaction displayed for **Dance a Little** until the buttons appear, and then click **Open**.

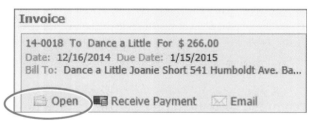

4. Change the rate for the graphic design work to **35**.

5. Click **Save & Close**; click **Yes** to record the transaction with the changes.

6. Close the **Search** window.

Do It the Wrong Way – Receive Payment for an Invoice

Guy has just received a check from Mary Jones for $270. Now you will enter the payment incorrectly for the purpose of learning how to fix the error and do it correctly.

7. Choose **Banking→Make Deposits**.

8. Close the **Payments to Deposit** window.

   You will learn how to work with this window in Chapter 5, Banking with QuickBooks.

9. Follow these steps to enter the check:

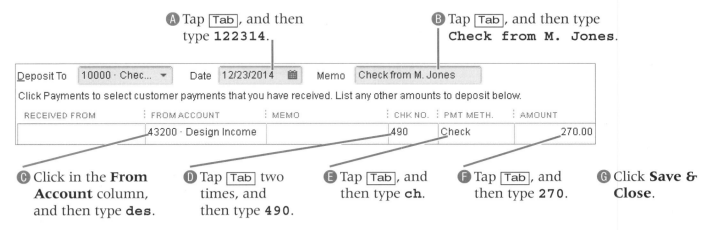

Ⓐ Tap ⎡Tab⎤, and then type **122314**.

Ⓑ Tap ⎡Tab⎤, and then type **Check from M. Jones**.

Ⓒ Click in the **From Account** column, and then type **des**.

Ⓓ Tap ⎡Tab⎤ two times, and then type **490**.

Ⓔ Tap ⎡Tab⎤, and then type **ch**.

Ⓕ Tap ⎡Tab⎤, and then type **270**.

Ⓖ Click **Save & Close**.

Think about this transaction. What is wrong with it? By entering the check for an invoice in the Make Deposits window, you have stated income twice and have not cleared the amount from Accounts Receivable.

BTS BRIEF

10000•Checking DR 270.00; 43200•Design Income CR <270.00>

Do It the Right Way – Receive Payment for an Invoice

To fix the deposit that was handled improperly, you must delete it and reenter the payment using the Receive Payments window.

10. Choose **Banking→Make Deposits**; close the **Payments to Deposit** window.

11. Click the **Previous** button until the deposit you just made is displayed.

You can look for a transaction by using the Previous and Next buttons, if you believe the transaction to be easy to locate. If not, use the Find or Search feature.

12. Choose **Edit→Delete Deposit**; click **OK** in the Delete Transaction window.

FROM THE KEYBOARD
⎡Ctrl⎤+⎡d⎤ to delete the selected transaction

13. Close the **Make Deposits** window.

14. Click the **Receive Payments** task icon in the Customers area of the Home page.

15. Follow these steps to enter the payment correctly:

Ⓐ Type **m** for QuickBooks to fill **Mary Jones** in for you.

Ⓑ Tap [Tab], and then type **270**.

Ⓒ Tap [Tab], and then type **122314**, if necessary.

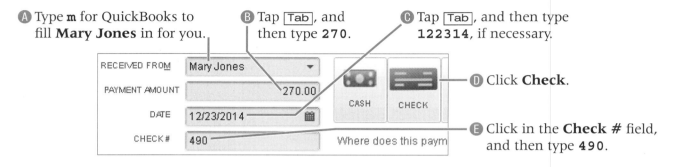

Ⓓ Click **Check**.

Ⓔ Click in the **Check #** field, and then type **490**.

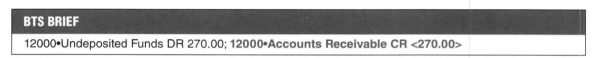

BTS BRIEF

12000•Undeposited Funds DR 270.00; **12000•Accounts Receivable CR <270.00>**

16. Click **Save & Close**.

Before moving on, think about what you have just completed and make sure you understand the "why" behind it. You have deleted the overstated income by deleting the deposit and have "cleared out" Accounts Receivable by receiving the payment correctly.

Working with Customer-Related Reports

You learned in the last chapter that there are many preset reports you can run to display QuickBooks company information. Now we will look at reports related to customer- and company-related transactions.

The Report Window Toolbar

When viewing other reports, you may also see additional buttons specific to certain reports.

Some of the basic functions that the toolbar buttons allow you to do include:

- Change and memorize the settings for the report
- Print or email the report; clicking the Print button will also allow you to choose to preview how the report will appear in printed form before you issue the command to print it
- Export the report to Microsoft Excel
- Share the report with other users as a template

QuickReports

A QuickReport can be run from the various center windows. They show all transactions recorded in QuickBooks for a particular list record. You will use this report to get a quick snapshot of all customer transactions for James Limousine Service in the Develop Your Skills exercise.

Essential Skills

FLASHBACK TO GAAP: TIME PERIOD
Remember that it is implied that the activities of the business can be divided into time periods.

QUICK REFERENCE	PRODUCING CUSTOMER AND QUICKREPORTS
Task	**Procedure**
Produce a customer-related report using the Report Center	▪ Choose Reports→Report Center. ▪ Choose Customers & Receivables as the report category. ▪ Click on the report you wish to produce in the main section of the Report Center. ▪ Click the Display report button.
Produce a QuickReport	▪ Open the center with the record on which you wish to run the report. ▪ Click the list entry. ▪ Click the QuickReport link at the right of the center window. ▪ Set the correct date range.

DEVELOP YOUR SKILLS 3-7
Produce Customer-Related Reports

In this exercise, you will help Guy to create customer reports. QuickBooks provides a report for you that displays all unpaid invoices. You will produce this for Average Guy Designs, but first you will produce a QuickReport for Dance a Little.

1. Click the **Customers** button on the Icon Bar.

2. Single-click **James Limousine Service** to select it.

You must always select the list item on which you wish to run a QuickReport.

3. Click the **QuickReport** link at the right of the Customer Center window.

If you cannot see the QuickReport link, use the sizing arrows to make the window wider.

4. Change the date range to **All** by typing **a** to select All from the Dates list.

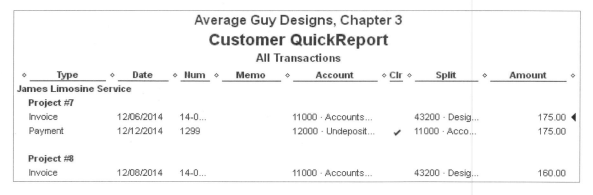

A customer QuickReport will display all transactions for a selected customer within a designated date range.

When you first display a report, the Dates field is selected. Typing *a* chooses All from the Dates list.

5. Close the **QuickReport** and the **Customer Center** windows.

Create an Open Invoices Report

6. Choose **Reports→Report Center**.

7. Follow these steps to create an Open Invoices report:

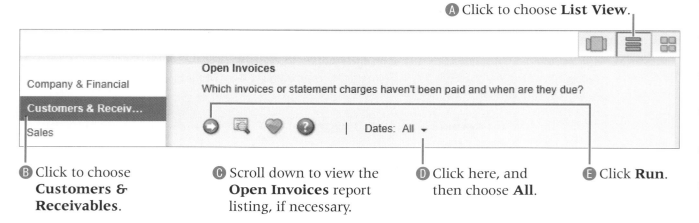

Ⓐ Click to choose **List View**.

Ⓑ Click to choose **Customers & Receivables**.

Ⓒ Scroll down to view the **Open Invoices** report listing, if necessary.

Ⓓ Click here, and then choose **All**.

Ⓔ Click **Run**.

QuickBooks will display the Open Invoices report, which shows all unpaid invoices.

8. Close the **Open Invoices** report and the **Report Center**.

9. Choose the appropriate option for your situation:
   - If you will continue working, leave QuickBooks open.
   - If you are finished working in QuickBooks for now, choose **File→Exit**.

Tackle the Tasks

Now is your chance to work a little more with Average Guy Designs and apply the skills that you have learned in this chapter to accomplish additional tasks. You will use the same company file you used in the Develop Your Skills exercises throughout this chapter. Enter the following tasks, referring back to the concepts in the chapter as necessary.

Add Customers	Add the following customers:
	Olivia York, 1021 Miller St., Medford, OR 97504 • 541-555-8921 • Referral • Due on Receipt • Job: Project #20
	Masters Manufacturing, James McDonald, 575 Industrial Way, Eureka, CA 95501 • 707-555-6722 • From Advertisement • Net 15 • Job: Project #21
	Tim's BBQ Palooza, Tim Laughlin, 8 College Drive, Berkeley, CA 94608 • 510-555-4419 • Referral • Net 30 • Job: Project #22
Create Items	Service item: Print • Print Layout Services • $40 • 48800•Print Layout Income.
	Service item: Video • Basic Video Editing Services • $55 • 48900•Video Editing Income (you will need to set up a new account).
	Service item: Adv Video • Advanced Video Editing Services • $75 • 48900•Video Editing Income.
	Service item: Branding • Comprehensive Branding Plan • $400 • 43200•Design Income.
Create Invoices	Olivia York:Project #20 • 12/23/14 • 5 hours of Print Layout Services
	Masters Manufacturing:Project #21 • 12/26/14 • 8 hours of Basic Video Editing Services
	Tim's BBQ Palooza:Project #22 • 12/27/14 • Comprehensive Branding Plan
Receive Payments (remember to choose the correct job)	Receive full payment for invoice #14-0018 from Joanie Short of Dance a Little, Check #1632, 12/27/14
	Receive full payment for invoice #14-0013 from JLR Doggie Playhouse, Check #872, 12/29/14
	Receive $200 payment for invoice #14-0003 from Lucy's Cupcake Factory, Check #341, 12/29/14
	Receive $50 payment for invoice #14-0014 from Learners, Inc., MasterCard # 9565332412894455, exp 03/2015, 12/30/14
Generate Reports	Create a report that will show the contact information for all of your customers.

Concepts Review

To check your knowledge of the key concepts introduced in this chapter, complete the Concepts Review quiz on the Student Resource Center or in your eLab course.

Reinforce Your Skills

Angela Stevens has just relocated her company, Quality-Built Construction, from California to Silverton, Oregon. You will be working with a QuickBooks Sample Company File in this exercise as it will allow you to run full payroll in a future chapter without having to purchase a payroll subscription.

Before you begin the Reinforce Your Skills exercises, complete one of these options:

■ Open **RYS_Chapter03** from your file storage location.

■ Restore **RYS_Chapter03 (Portable)** from your file storage location. For a reminder of how to restore a portable company file, see Develop Your Skills 3-1. Add your last name and first initial to the end of the filename.

REINFORCE YOUR SKILLS 3-1

Manage Your Customers & Jobs List

In this exercise, you will create, edit, and delete Customers & Jobs List entries for Angela.

1. Choose **Customers→Customer Center**.

2. Double-click **Campbell, Heather** to open it for editing.

3. Change the customer's name to `Escalona, Heather`.

   You will have to change the name in five separate locations. You can use the Copy button to copy the Bill to Address to the Ship to Address field. This customer's name will change in all of the transactions that Heather was involved in, as well as in all of her future transactions.

4. Click **OK** to accept the change.

Add a New Customer

5. Click the **New Customer & Job** button, and then choose **New Customer**.

6. Use the following information to set up the new customer, making sure to select the correct tab to enter each piece of information.

Name	Hector Ramirez
Mailing Address	PO Box 7762, Mt. Angel, OR 97362
Shipping Address	1738 Church Avenue, Mt. Angel, OR 97362
Phone	(503) 555-4431
Type	Referral
Terms	Net 15

7. Click **OK** to accept the new record.

Add a Job to a Customer

8. Single-click the new customer you just created, **Hector Ramirez** to select it.

9. Choose **Edit→Add Job**.

10. Type **New Home** as the name of the job; click **OK**.

11. Close the **Customer Center** window.

REINFORCE YOUR SKILLS 3-2
Create a New Service Item

In this exercise, you will create a subitem for an existing service item so you can use it on a sales form.

1. Choose **Lists→Item List**.

2. Click on **01 Plans & Permits,** and then choose **Edit→New Item**.

3. Use this figure to create a new service subitem:

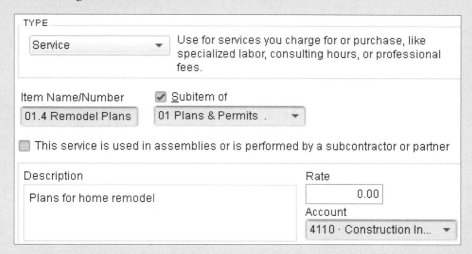

4. Click **OK** to accept the new item and close the window.

5. Close the **Item List**.

REINFORCE YOUR SKILLS 3-3
Enter Sales Transactions

In this exercise, you will create invoices for Quality-Built Construction.

1. Choose **Customers→Create Invoices**.

2. Choose **Ramirez, Hector:New Home** as the Customer: Job.

3. Set the date to read **12/16/2018,** and then choose to use the **Intuit Service Invoice Template**.

4. Click in the **Item** column of the invoice and choose **01.1 Plans** as the item.

5. Tap `Tab`, type **15**, tap `Tab` again, and type **New Home** in front of "Plans."

6. Tab `Tab`, and then type **80** in the **Rate** column.

7. Select **We appreciate your prompt payment** in the Customer Message field.

8. Click **Save & Close** to record the transaction and close the **Create Invoices** window.

Enter a Job "On the Fly" for a Customer in an Invoice

Now you will enter a new job for a customer while creating an invoice.

9. Choose **Customers→Create Invoices**.

10. Type **Escalona, Heather:Remodel** in the Customer: Job field; choose to Quick Add the new job.

11. Set the date to read **12/18/2018**.

12. Click the **Item** column of the invoice and choose **01.4 Remodel Plans** as the item.

13. Enter **9** as the quantity and **$80** as the rate.

14. Click **Save & Close** to record the transaction and close the Create Invoices window.

REINFORCE YOUR SKILLS 3-4

Receive Payments

In this exercise, you will receive the payment for the invoice you created earlier.

1. Choose **Customers→Receive Payments**.

2. Choose **Ramirez, Hector:New Home** from the Received From field.

3. Enter **1200** for the amount.

4. Set the date to read **12/24/2018**.

5. The payment was submitted by check number **1574**.

6. Click **Save & Close**.

REINFORCE YOUR SKILLS 3-5

Find and Edit a Transaction

Angela realized that the number of hours recorded on the invoice for Heather Escalona was incorrect, and she needs to edit the transaction. In this exercise, you will use the QuickBooks Find feature to locate the transaction.

1. Choose **Edit→Find**.
2. Choose **Invoice** as the Transaction Type, and **Escalona, Heather** as the Customer:Job.
   All of the invoices for the customer will be displayed in the bottom of the window. Note that previous invoices created for Heather Campbell have been updated with the new name.
3. Double-click the invoice dated **12/18/2018** in the bottom portion of the window.
   The Create Invoices window will open; leave it open for the next step.

Edit a Transaction

4. Change the quantity on the invoice to **8**.
5. Save and close the transaction; close the **Find** window.

REINFORCE YOUR SKILLS 3-6

Run Customer-Related Reports

In this exercise, you will run three reports for Angela, beginning with a QuickReport.

1. Open the **Customer Center**.
2. Single-click **Ramirez, Hector** to select it.
3. Click the **QuickReport** link at the far right of the window.
4. Set the date range to **All**.
   You will see a report that shows all of the transactions for Hector Ramirez.
5. Choose **Window→Close All**.

Create a List Report and Edit a Customer Record

6. Choose **Reports→Customers & Receivables→Customer Phone List**.
7. Double-click **Ramirez, Hector**.
   QuickBooks will open an Edit Customer window, from where you can make any changes to the customer's information.
8. Change Hector's phone number to **(503) 555-8037**; click **OK**.
9. Choose **Window→Close All**.
10. Choose the appropriate option for your situation:
    - If you will continue working, leave QuickBooks open.
    - If you are finished working in QuickBooks for now, choose **File→Exit**.

Apply Your Skills

Before you begin the Apply Your Skills exercises, complete one of these options:

- Open **AYS_Chapter03** from your file storage location.

- Restore **AYS_Chapter03 (Portable)** from your file storage location. For a reminder of how to restore a portable company file, see Develop Your Skills 3-1. Add your last name and first initial to the end of the filename.

APPLY YOUR SKILLS 3-1

Set Up a Customers & Jobs List

In this exercise, you will work on the Customers & Jobs List for Wet Noses. If you wish, you may explore the Add/Edit Multiple List Entries feature and use it to complete this exercise. It will be introduced fully in Chapter 6, Dealing with Physical Inventory.

1. Open the **Customer Center**.

2. Set up the following customers for Wet Noses Veterinary Clinic:

Name	Edison York	LaShonda Reeves	Ellie Sanders
Address	7931 NE 176th St. Bothell, WA 98011	11908 100th Pl. NE Kirkland, WA 98034	302 Northshore Blvd. Bothell, WA 98011
Phone	425-555-4401	425-555-3953	425-555-7731
Type	From advertisement	Referral	From advertisement
Terms	Due on receipt	Due on receipt	Due on receipt
Account Number	D22	C94	D34

3. Close the **Customer Center**.

APPLY YOUR SKILLS 3-2

Set Up Items

In this exercise, you will set up service and non-inventory items.

1. Set up the following service items:

Item Name	Boarding	Dental
Description	Overnight Boarding	Dental Cleaning
Rate	35.00	45.00
Account	Nonmedical Income	Fee for Service Income

2. Set up the following non-inventory item:

Item Name	Treats
Description	Treats for patients—by the box
Rate	18.43
Account	Boarding Food & Supplies

3. Close the **Item List** window.

APPLY YOUR SKILLS 3-3

Work with Customer Transactions

In this exercise, you will complete sales transactions and receive payments for Wet Noses' customers.

Record Sales Transactions

You will start by helping Dr. James to record invoices and cash sales. Enter the sales information and update the Additional Info tab for the job to capture the custom field information for each pet.

1. On 6/1/14, Emily Dallas brought her dog, Cowboy, in for an Exam, Vaccine Injection Fee, and Rabies Vaccine. Invoice her for these services. Terms are Net 15; choose to save the new terms for the customer.

2. On 6/2/14, Kimberly Wurn brought her cat, Princess, in for a New Patient Exam, Vaccine Injection Fee, Feline DHC, and FIV/FeLV. She paid cash, so you will need to create a sales receipt for her.

3. On 6/3/14, Becky Todd brought her dog, Jedi, in for an Exam requiring Venipuncture, ACTH Stimulation Test, CBC Chem, and a Kennel fee. Create an invoice for her.

4. On 6/4/14, Millie Schumann brought her kitten, Smelly, in for an Exam and Pre-A Blood Work. She paid cash, so create a sales receipt for her.

Accept Customer Payments

You will now receive the payments for customer invoices that have been recorded.

5. On 6/7/14, you received check #773 for $56.90 from Emily Dallas as payment for invoice #173.

6. On 6/8/14, you received check #2310 for $284.21 from the County Animal Shelter as payment for invoice #163.

Answer Questions with Reports

In this exercise, you will answer questions for Dr. James by running reports. You may wish to display the Report Center in List View to help you to answer the questions. Ask your instructor if you should print the reports, print (save) them as PDF files, export them to Excel, or simply display them on the screen.

1. Are there any unpaid invoices and, if so, when are they due?

2. Would you please provide a summarized list of all customers with a balance?

3. What transactions has Wet Noses had with each customer during June 2014?

4. Would you please produce a report that lists the contact information and current balance for each customer?

5. What are the prices for each item?
   Hint: One report will show them all.

6. Submit your reports based on the guidelines provided by your instructor.

7. Choose the appropriate option for your situation:
   - If you will continue working, leave QuickBooks open.
   - If you are finished working in QuickBooks for now, choose **File→Exit**.

Extend Your Skills

In the course of working through the following Extend Your Skills exercises, you will be utilizing various skills taught in this and previous chapter(s). Take your time and think carefully about the tasks presented to you. Turn back to the chapter content if you need assistance.

3-1 Sort Through the Stack

Before You Begin: Restore the EYS1_Chapter03 (Portable) file or open the EYS1_Chapter03 company file from your storage location.

You have been hired by Arlaine Cervantes to help her with her organization's books. She is the founder of Niños del Lago, a nonprofit organization that provides impoverished Guatemalan children with an engaging educational camp experience. You have just sat down at your desk and opened a large envelope from her with a variety of documents and noticed that you have several emails from her as well. It is your job to sort through the papers and emails and make sense of what you find, entering information into QuickBooks whenever appropriate and answering any other questions in a word-processing document saved as **EYS1_Chapter03_ LastnameFirstinitial**. Remember, you are digging through papers you just dumped out of an envelope and addressing random emails from Arlaine, so it is up to you to determine the correct order in which to complete the tasks.

- Sticky note: We now also receive donations from the Hanson Family Trust. Would we set them up as a customer? The information for the trust is 900 SE Commercial St., Salem, OR 97306; (503) 555-9331; contact, Richard Hanson.

- A handwritten note: We will be providing cultural competency training to schools and organizations to raise additional funds for the organization. Can we set up a service item directed to 47250•Service to Outside Orgs? (You will need to set this account up as a subaccount for 47200•Program Income.) Set the amount to zero as it will be entered at the time of "sale."

- Note: How would we set up the students who participate in our program? They don't pay us money, so are they customers or is there another list we can include them on? Enter the following students when you find an answer: Diego Margarita, Maria Prentice, Felipe Valdez, and Rosa Batres.

- Scribbled on a scrap of paper: Provided a Cultural Competency 3-day workshop on 7/9/2014 at St. Martin's Catholic School, received check #3821 for $4,500. Can we enter this receipt of cash into QuickBooks?

- A letter from the House Foundation: They will be providing a $5,000 grant (not yet received) to the organization to complete construction on the dormitories. Set up the new customer, who is located at 552 Sheridan Avenue, Macon, GA 31205.

- Handwritten invoice dated 7/10/2014: Cultural competency workshop to be held at Lakeside Christian School on 7/27/2014 for $1,500. Due Net 15. (They have agreed to pay 50% upfront.)

- Scribbled note from Arlaine: Can you produce a report for me that shows all of the donors and customers for Niños del Lago?

- Photocopy of check #1826 from Lakeside Christian School for $750 (50% deposit for upcoming training), with a note of "deposited into checking account on 7/15/2014."
- A handwritten question: I don't have customers, but I do have donors and grants… How do I set them up if QuickBooks just has customers?

3-2 Be Your Own Boss

Before You Begin: Complete Extend Your Skills 2-2 before starting this exercise.

In this exercise, you will build on the company file that you outlined and created in previous chapters. If you have created a file for your actual business, enter your customers and customer transactions that have occurred since your start date. If you are creating a fictitious company, enter fifteen customers and at least one transaction for each customer. You will make up the names and information for this exercise.

Create Customer Transaction List and Transaction List by Customer reports and submit them to your instructor based on the instructions provided.

Open the company file you created in Extend Your Skills 2-2 and complete the tasks outlined above. When you are finished, save it as a portable company file, naming it as **EYS2_ Chapter03_LastnameFirstinitial (Portable)**, and submit it to your instructor based on the instructions provided.

3-3 Use the Web as a Learning Tool

Throughout this book, you will be provided with an opportunity to use the Internet as a learning tool by completing WebQuests. According to the original creators of WebQuests, as described on their website (http://WebQuest.org), a WebQuest is "an inquiry-oriented activity in which most or all of the information used by learners is drawn from the web." To complete the WebQuest projects in this book, navigate to the Student Resource Center and choose the WebQuest for the chapter on which you are working. The subject of each WebQuest will be relevant to the material found in the chapter.

WebQuest Subject: Charging sales tax for services and different types of payment receipt options

Working with Vendors

Tracking expenses properly is very important for your financial statements as well as for keeping your vendors happy! A vendor is essentially anyone to whom you pay money. However, this does not include employees. A vendor could be the electric company, the organization to which you pay taxes, a merchandise supplier, or subcontractors you pay to do work for your customers. QuickBooks allows you to produce 1099 tax forms for subcontractors at the end of the year. In this chapter, you will examine the QuickBooks lists, activities, and reports that allow you to effectively deal with vendors.

CHAPTER OUTLINE

Exploring the Vendor Center
Entering Bills
Paying Bills
Writing and Printing Checks
Dealing with Oops in Vendor Transactions
Producing Vendor and P&L Reports
Working with QuickBooks Graphs
Tackle the Tasks
Concepts Review
Reinforce Your Skills
Apply Your Skills
Extend Your Skills

CHAPTER OBJECTIVES

After studying this chapter, you will be able to:

- Work with the Vendor Center and List
- Enter and pay bills
- Write and print checks
- Correct errors in vendor transactions
- Produce vendor and profit & loss reports and QuickBooks graphs

Average Guy Designs

Now that Guy Marshall has set up his customers and entered transactions related to them, he needs to set up the Vendor List for Average Guy Designs before he can track his expenses by entering bills, paying bills, and writing checks. Once he has established the list of vendors, he will be able to choose them from drop-down lists in the various vendor forms. Guy will also learn how to produce reports that will provide relevant vendor information as well as a profit & loss report.

Guy can access the Vendor List and activities (entering and paying bills) from the Vendor Center, pictured below. In total, there are four centers: Customer, Vendor, Employee, and Report. As you saw in the last chapter, centers allow you to view a snapshot of information; in this case, it's an all-in-one look at an individual vendor's information, bills, and payments. You can also initiate a new transaction for the selected vendor from the center.

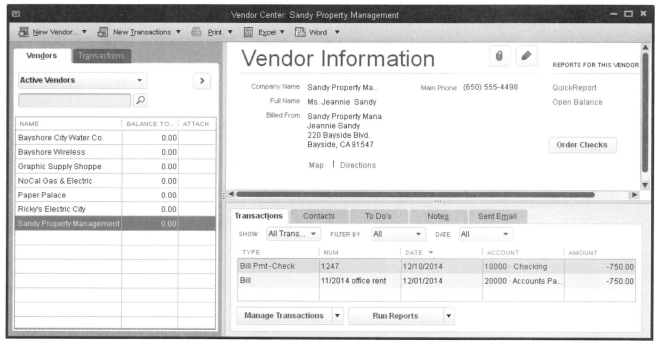

The Vendor Center window displays the Vendor List as well as a snapshot view of the selected vendor.

Exploring the Vendor Center

In Chapter 1, Introducing QuickBooks Pro, you were introduced to the four types of tasks you will work with in QuickBooks throughout this book (lists, activities, company setup, and reports). Information is stored in QuickBooks through the use of lists. Lists allow you to store information that can easily be filled into forms by using drop-down arrows or by beginning to type the entry and letting QuickBooks fill in the rest. Lists comprise the database aspect of QuickBooks; the Vendor List can even be exported to contact management software such as Microsoft® Outlook.

 Tab: Tracking Money Out
Topic: Expenses overview; Building blocks of recording expenses

Each individual vendor record tracks information organized into five tabs: Address Info, Payment Settings, Tax Settings, Account Settings, and Additional Info. In addition, you can customize eight different contact fields. Keep in mind that the more information you enter for each vendor, the better prepared you will be later when you learn how to customize reports because you can sort, group, and filter your reports using the information in the vendor records.

Here you can add vendors to the list. | Here you can create transactions for the selected vendor. | The Attach button lets you attach files to the selected vendor record. | This button opens the Edit Vendor window so you can modify information.

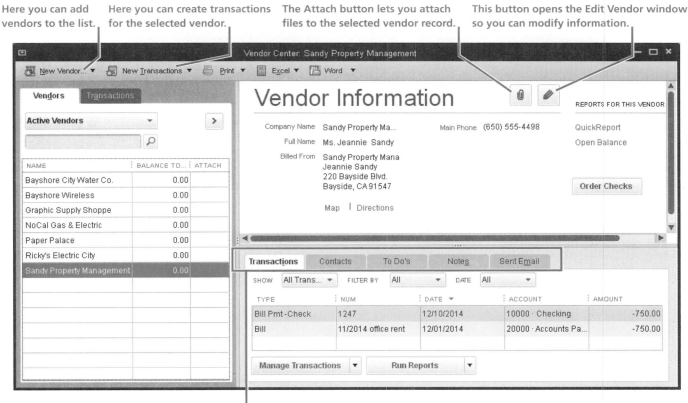

The tabs allow you to see transactions, contacts, to do's, and notes from the main vendor center window.

 Tab: New to QuickBooks?
Topic: Using Centers

Managing the Vendor List

The list management techniques that you learned about in Chapter 3, Working with Customers are very similar for the Vendors List as well as the Employees List. The next three concepts will serve as a review of creating, editing, and deleting Customers & Jobs, Vendors, and Employees List entries.

Creating a New Vendor

To start entering vendor transactions, you must first enter your vendors into the Vendor List. You can enter vendors directly into the list in the Add/Edit Multiple List Entries window (which you will learn more about in Chapter 6, Dealing with Physical Inventory) or "on the fly" in forms such as Enter Bills and Write Checks and then select Quick Add or Setup from the pop-up window. Remember that subcontractors should be set up as vendors, not as employees.

Editing an Existing Vendor

Once created, the vendor can always be edited through the Vendor Center. The only item that cannot be edited after you have created and saved a new vendor is the opening balance (it must be adjusted through the accounts payable register). When you change the information for a vendor, including the vendor's name, it will be reflected in both future and past transactions.

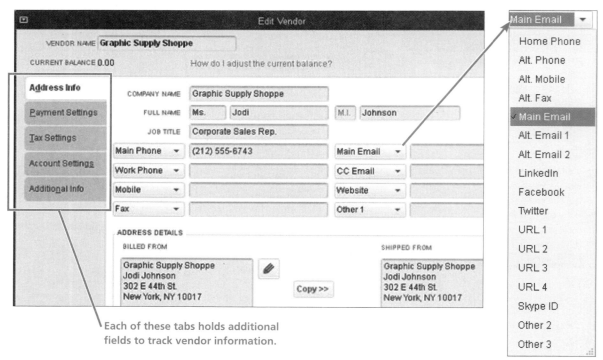

Each of these tabs holds additional fields to track vendor information.

The Edit Vendor window allows you to enter a large amount of information for an individual vendor. The eight contact fields are highly customizable by simply clicking the drop-down arrow, as seen by the list displayed.

Deleting a Vendor

You can delete a vendor from the Vendor List *as long as you have not used it in a transaction*. If you have used it in a transaction, you can make it inactive, but you cannot delete it until after you close the books for a period and clean up your company's data.

Making a List Entry Inactive

If you have a customer, vendor, or employee with whom you are no longer working, you cannot delete him from the associated list if he has been involved in any transactions. What you can do is make him inactive. The benefit of making list entries inactive is that they will no longer clutter your lists. If you find you need a list entry again, you can reactivate it.

Merging List Entries

Occasionally, you may find that you have two records created for the same list entry. QuickBooks allows you to merge these duplicated entries into one. You perform the merge by editing one of the entries and changing its name to match the other exactly. The two entries will permanently become one once you complete the merge. All prior transactions with the merged list entry will reflect the change in name.

WARNING

Merging list entries *cannot* be undone!

Visualize!

Tab: Getting Set Up
Topic: Add the people you do business with

QUICK REFERENCE	MANAGING THE VENDOR LIST
Task	**Procedure**
Edit an existing vendor	▪ Open the Vendor Center. ▪ Double-click the vendor you need to edit. ▪ Make the desired changes; click OK.
Add a new vendor	▪ Open the Vendor Center. ▪ Click the New Vendor button on the toolbar. ▪ Enter the necessary information; click OK.
Delete a vendor	▪ Open the Vendor Center. ▪ Click the vendor you wish to delete. ▪ Choose Edit→Delete Vendor; click OK.

DEVELOP YOUR SKILLS 4-1
Manage the Vendor List

In this exercise, you will manage the Vendor List for Average Guy Designs. The first step is to open QuickBooks, and then either open a company file or restore a portable company file.

1. Start **QuickBooks 2014**.

   If you downloaded the student exercise files in the portable company file *format, follow Option 1 below. If you downloaded the files in the* company file *format, follow Option 2 below.*

Option 1: Restore a Portable Company File

2. Choose **File→Open or Restore Company**.

3. Restore the **DYS_Chapter04 (Portable)** portable file for this chapter from your file storage location, placing your last name and first initial at the end of the filename (e.g., DYS_Chapter04_MarshallG).

   It may take a few moments for the portable company file to open. Once it does, continue with step 4.

Option 2: Open a Company File

2. Choose **File→Open or Restore Company**, ensure that **Open a regular company file** is selected, and then open the **DYS_Chapter04** company file from your file storage location.

   The QuickBooks company file will open.

3. Click **OK** to close the QuickBooks Information window. If necessary, click **No** in the Set Up External Accountant User window.

Edit an Existing Vendor

The first step in modifying a vendor record is to open the Vendor Center so you can view the Vendor List. You did not enter the address and phone number for Graphic Supply Shoppe when you created the vendor, so you will add it now.

FROM THE KEYBOARD

Ctrl + e to open the selected list item to edit

4. Click the **Vendors** button in the Vendors area of the Home page.

5. Double-click **Graphic Supply Shoppe** to open it for editing.

When you double-click a record on the Vendor List, QuickBooks opens it for editing. You could also single-click the vendor you wish to open and then click the Edit Vendor button.

6. Follow these steps to edit the vendor information:

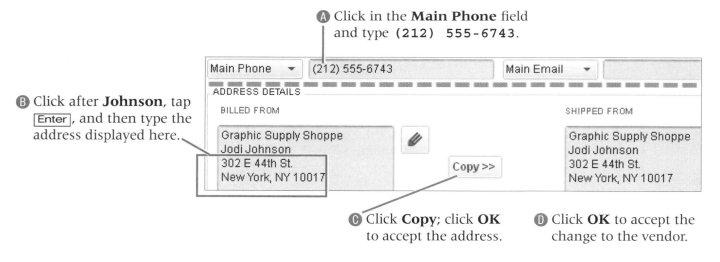

ⓐ Click in the **Main Phone** field and type **(212) 555-6743**.

ⓑ Click after **Johnson**, tap Enter, and then type the address displayed here.

ⓒ Click **Copy**; click **OK** to accept the address.

ⓓ Click **OK** to accept the change to the vendor.

Add a New Vendor

Next you will help Guy to add a new vendor to the list.

7. Click the **New Vendor** button on the toolbar, and then choose **New Vendor** from the menu.

8. Follow these steps to enter the information for the vendor:

You will not need to change the Opening Balance date unless you enter an amount for the opening balance, as the information is used only when accompanied by an amount.

Ⓐ Type **Popelka Broadband**.　Ⓑ Tap ⌜Tab⌝ three times, and then type **Popelka Broadband**.

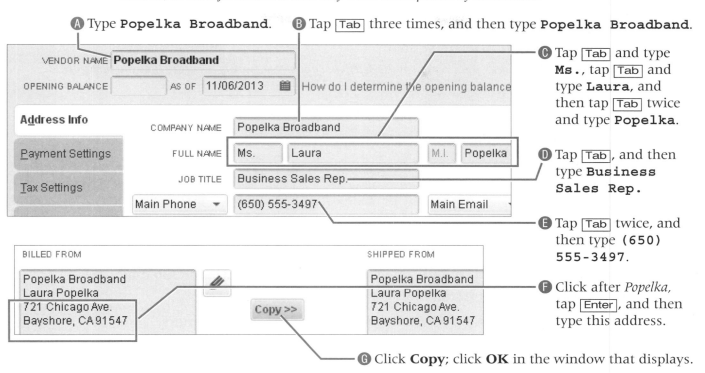

Ⓒ Tap ⌜Tab⌝ and type **Ms.**, tap ⌜Tab⌝ and type **Laura**, and then tap ⌜Tab⌝ twice and type **Popelka**.

Ⓓ Tap ⌜Tab⌝, and then type **Business Sales Rep.**

Ⓔ Tap ⌜Tab⌝ twice, and then type **(650) 555-3497**.

Ⓕ Click after *Popelka,* tap ⌜Enter⌝, and then type this address.

Ⓖ Click **Copy**; click **OK** in the window that displays.

Tapping ⌜Enter⌝ in a field with multiple lines (such as the Billed From Address field) takes you to the next line. Tapping ⌜Enter⌝ while working in a single line field (such as Name or Phone) is equivalent to clicking the default button in the window (the blue button)—in this case, the OK button.

9. Follow these steps to add the additional vendor information:

Ⓐ Click the **Payment Settings** tab.

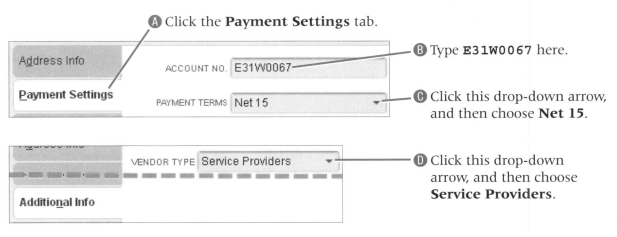

Ⓑ Type **E31W0067** here.

Ⓒ Click this drop-down arrow, and then choose **Net 15**.

Ⓓ Click this drop-down arrow, and then choose **Service Providers**.

10. Click **OK** to complete the new vendor record.

Delete a Vendor

Guy has not purchased anything from Paper Palace yet, and the company has just gone out of business. You will now delete this company from the Vendor List.

11. Single-click the **Paper Palace** record in the Vendor List to select it.

12. Choose **Edit→Delete Vendor**.

    QuickBooks asks you to confirm the deletion. QuickBooks wants to ensure that you don't delete anything by accident; it will always ask you to confirm deletions.

13. Click **OK** to confirm the deletion.

14. Close the **Vendor Center** window.

Make a List Entry Inactive

Customer Mary Jones was a "one time" customer with whom you do not believe you will do business again. You can make her inactive so her name will no longer appear in the Customers & Jobs List (unless you choose to show the customers who are inactive).

15. Choose **Customers→Customer Center**.

16. Right-click on **Mary Jones**, and then choose **Make Customer:Job Inactive**.

    You will no longer see Mary displayed on the Customers & Jobs List.

17. Click the **View** drop-down arrow, and then choose **All Customers**.

    Notice that when you choose to view all customers, you see the inactive customers listed with an "X" next to their names and jobs.

18. Click the **View** drop-down arrow again, and then choose **Active Customers**.

Merge List Entries

Customer Ashley Hakola has been entered twice by mistake. You will now help Guy to merge the two list entries into one. The problem you will encounter, however, is that a job has been created under the incorrect name. You will need to move the job to the correct customer first, and then merge the list entry.

19. Follow these steps to move the Job to another customer:

    Ⓐ Place your mouse pointer over the diamond to the left of **Project #18** until you see a move pointer.

    Ⓑ Click and drag down until you see the two-way arrow below **Project #2** and release.

◦ Ashley Hakloa	0.00
⊕ Project #18	0.00
◦ Purposeful Playti...	345.00
◦ Project #9	345.00
◦ Project #11	0.00
◦ Ashley Hakola	0.00
◦ Project #2	0.00
◦ DC Athletic Club L...	560.00

20. Double-click the list entry for **Ashley Hakloa**.

    You must always open the incorrect entry (or the one that is "going away") for editing when you are merging list entries.

21. Type **Ashley Hakola** in the Customer Name field.

    You must type the name exactly as it appears in the list or it will not merge into the other entry! You only need to change the name in the Customer Name field, not elsewhere in the Edit Customer window in order to perform the merge (however, you will want to correct the rest of the information as well for your company file).

22. Click **OK**.

    QuickBooks displays a message asking if you would like to merge the duplicate list entries. Remember, clicking Yes is a permanent action! If you did not receive the Merge pop-up window, check your spelling. You must enter the name you want it to merge into perfectly.

23. Click **Yes** to permanently merge the two entries

    Ashley Hakloa will no longer be displayed on the Customers & Jobs List, and any transactions for her will appear with Ashley Hakola displayed as the customer.

24. Close the **Customer Center**, leaving the Home page displayed.

Entering Bills

Once you have set up your initial Vendor List, you can begin to enter spending transactions. In this section, you will learn to enter bills and use accounts payable, which is the account credited when bills are entered. When you enter a bill, you *must* specify a vendor because accounts payable will be credited by the transaction.

Entering Vendor Information on Bills

After you select your vendor from the drop-down list at the top of the form, QuickBooks automatically fills the relevant information for that vendor into the appropriate fields on the Enter Bills window. If you wish to enter a bill for a new vendor not yet entered into the Vendor List, QuickBooks will allow you to create the new record "on the fly," just as you did for customers.

When entering bills, you need to decide if the expenditure is for an expense or items that you will add to your inventory. The following illustration displays the primary features of the Enter Bills window.

In this chapter you will deal only with expenses. You will learn about QuickBooks' inventory features in Chapter 6, Dealing with Physical Inventory.

The Ribbon provides you with a variety of commands related to the window within which you are working.

On the right side of the Enter Bills window is a snapshot of information for the selected vendor.

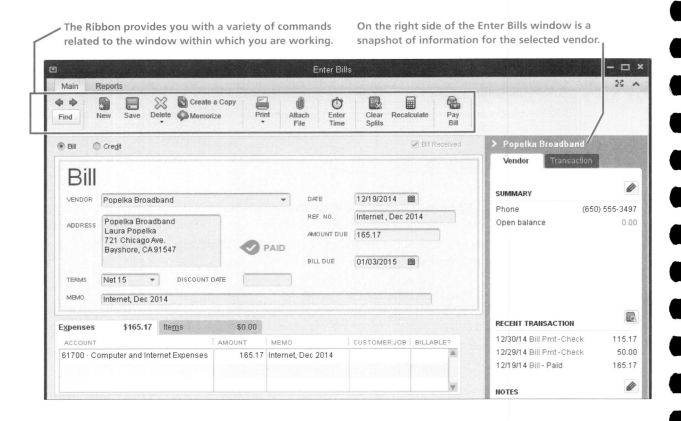

Importance of Entering Reference Numbers and Memos

When entering a bill, it is very important to enter reference information or the bill number in the Ref. No. field and notes in the Memo fields. This information displays in reports and can aid you if you are looking for a duplicate bill number.

Making Changes to Vendor Information on Forms

Whenever you make a change to a vendor's information on a form such as the Enter Bills window, QuickBooks asks if you want to make that change permanent. If you choose Yes, QuickBooks will change the vendor's record. If you choose No, the new information will appear only on the current form; the permanent record remains unchanged.

Entering a Vendor "On the Fly"

You can enter customers "on the fly" in sales forms just as you did with vendors in the last chapter by simply typing them into the Vendor field. Once you enter the customer that is not in the Vendors List, you will have an option to Quick Add or Setup the new vendor before completing the rest of the form.

Choosing Accounts to Prefill Information

In QuickBooks, when you set up a vendor, you have the option to choose up to three expense accounts for which information will fill in when you make a payment. By setting up expense account information to be prefilled, you can make tracking expenses easier and faster.

When you enter a vendor's name in the Enter Bills, Write Checks, or Enter Credit Card Charges windows, QuickBooks fills in the expense account names for you. This allows you to then enter the amounts to be debited to each expense account. By prefilling information, you can make sure that you use the same expense account(s) each time you use a particular vendor. You can always choose to override the default accounts that are filled in by changing them in the individual transaction window. If there are fewer than three expense accounts for a vendor, just leave the additional account prefill fields blank.

Editing a Vendor Record from a Form

You do not have to return to the Vendor Center (or Customer Center if you are dealing with a customer-related transaction) in order to make a change to a vendor's record. In the history pane there is an edit button that will allow you to go directly to an Edit Vendor window so that you can make any necessary changes.

Notice the Edit button in the history panel of the Enter Bills window.

Passing On Expenses to Customers

When you enter a bill, you may be purchasing equipment or supplies for which you wish to pass on the expense to the customer. QuickBooks allows you to easily indicate which expenses are to be billed to a customer by providing a "Billable?" column in the Enter Bills window. Simply ensure that there is a checkmark in the column; it will be easy to create a customer invoice for the item(s).

The Cost of Goods Sold comprises expenses that are directly related to the manufacture of products or services that the company sells. Some expenses that might be considered Cost of Goods Sold are labor, raw materials, depreciation, and overhead. You cannot pass on the Cost of Goods Sold to a customer (it is instead incorporated into the final price of the product), so make sure that you use the proper type of account (expense) if the costs are to be billed to your customer. You will have an opportunity to create an invoice for billable costs later in this lesson.

FLASHBACK TO GAAP: COST

Remember that when a company purchases assets, it should record them at cost, not fair market value. For example, if you bought an item worth $750 for $100, the item should be recorded at $100.

QUICK REFERENCE	ENTERING BILLS
Task	**Procedure**
Enter a bill for an existing vendor	■ Open the Enter Bills window; select a vendor. ■ Enter the amount of the bill; ensure that the terms are correct. ■ Expense the bill. ■ If desired, select a customer to whom you wish to pass on the expense; click OK.
Enter a bill for a vendor not on the Vendor List	■ Open the Enter Bills window, fill in the Vendor field, and choose to Quick Add or Set Up. ■ Enter the amount of the bill and the terms for the vendor. ■ Expense the bill. ■ If desired, select a customer to whom you wish to pass on the expense; click OK.

DEVELOP YOUR SKILLS 4-2
Enter Bills

In this exercise, you will enter bills and track expenses. First you will enter the broadband internet bill that Guy just received into QuickBooks.

1. Click the **Enter Bills** task icon in the Vendors area of the Home page.

Enter Bills

2. Click the **Vendor** drop-down button, and then choose **Popelka Broadband**.

Look at the form and notice that the vendor's terms fill in for you from the underlying list and that the due date is calculated.

3. Tap $\boxed{\text{Tab}}$ to move to the date field, and then follow these steps to create a bill for Popelka Broadband:

Ⓐ Type **121914** here.

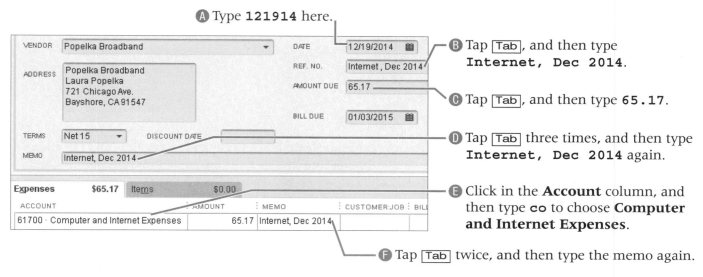

Ⓑ Tap $\boxed{\text{Tab}}$, and then type **Internet, Dec 2014**.

Ⓒ Tap $\boxed{\text{Tab}}$, and then type **65.17**.

Ⓓ Tap $\boxed{\text{Tab}}$ three times, and then type **Internet, Dec 2014** again.

Ⓔ Click in the **Account** column, and then type **co** to choose **Computer and Internet Expenses**.

Ⓕ Tap $\boxed{\text{Tab}}$ twice, and then type the memo again.

When you typed "co," QuickBooks filled in Computer and Internet Expenses *from the underlying list for you (in this case, the Chart of Accounts).*

You know that all bills for Popelka Broadband will use the same expense account , so you will now edit the vendor and set the account pre-fills right from the Enter Bills window.

4. Click the **Edit** button in the history panel of the **Enter Bills** window.

The Edit Vendor window will be displayed.

5. Click the **Account Settings** tab, and then click the drop-down arrow and choose **61700 • Computer and Internet Expenses**.

6. Click **OK** to save the changes to the vendor record, and then click the **Save & New** button.

QuickBooks records your bill transaction by crediting Accounts Payable and debiting the expense(s) you chose in the Account column (in this case, 61700•Computer and Internet Expense). The Enter Bills window stays open for the next step.

BTS BRIEF

61700•Computer and Internet Expense DR 65.17; 20000•Accounts Payable CR <65.17>

Enter a Bill for a Vendor Not on the Vendor List

When you enter a vendor name that is not on the Vendor List, QuickBooks allows you to add it to the Vendor List.

7. Make sure the insertion point is in the Vendor field at the top of a new bill. Type **Rankin Family Insurance**, and then tap `Tab`.

A Vendor Not Found window will appear.

8. Click **Set Up**.

9. Follow these steps to create the new vendor:

Ⓐ Tap `Tab` three times, and then type **Rankin Family Insurance** again.

Ⓑ Tap `Tab`; fill in the **Full Name** and **Job Title** fields as shown, tapping `Tab` to move from field to field.

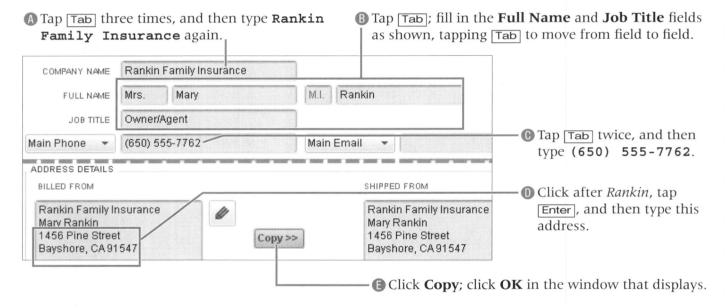

Ⓒ Tap `Tab` twice, and then type **(650) 555-7762**.

Ⓓ Click after *Rankin*, tap `Enter`, and then type this address.

Ⓔ Click **Copy**; click **OK** in the window that displays.

10. Click **OK** to accept the information for the new vendor.

You could also Quick Add the vendor, in which case you would need to return to the Vendor List later and edit the entry to include all of the vendor information in your company file.

11. Follow these steps to finish entering the bill:

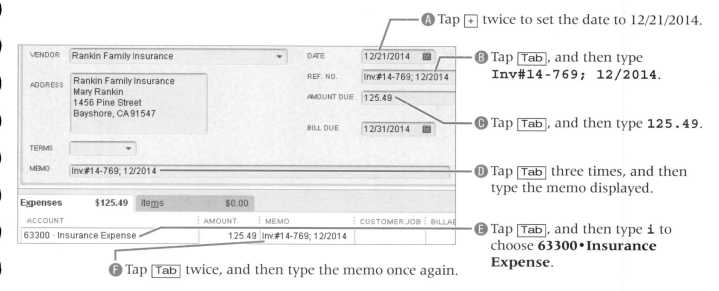

Ⓐ Tap ⊞ twice to set the date to 12/21/2014.

Ⓑ Tap Tab, and then type `Inv#14-769; 12/2014`.

Ⓒ Tap Tab, and then type `125.49`.

Ⓓ Tap Tab three times, and then type the memo displayed.

Ⓔ Tap Tab, and then type `i` to choose **63300•Insurance Expense**.

Ⓕ Tap Tab twice, and then type the memo once again.

Rather than typing the information for the reference number and memo fields three times, you can drag to select the information in the Ref. No. field, copy it, and then paste it in the two Memo fields.

BTS BRIEF
63300•Insurance Expense DR 125.49; **20000•Accounts Payable CR <125.49>**

12. Click **Save & Close** to record the bill.

Paying Bills

Once you have entered your bills, you will need to pay them in a timely manner. In QuickBooks you use the Pay Bills window to debit accounts payable. The other half of the equation (the account that will be credited) depends on the account from which you withdraw funds (or charge, in the case of bill payment by credit card). The Pay Bills window shows all bills due in chronological order by due date. If you wish, you can choose Due on or before and set a date by which to arrange the list. You also have the option to pay only a portion of what you owe on a particular bill by editing the value in the Amt. To Pay column.

When you have used the Enter Bills window, make sure you use the Pay Bills window to issue the payment—*not* the Write Checks window! If you use the Write Checks window, you will expense the purchase twice and not "clear out" the entry in the accounts payable account.

The top portion of the Pay Bills window lets you choose which bills to pay as well as notes any discount and credit information for the selected bill.

 Tab: Tracking Money Out
Topic: Entering and paying bills

Payment Details

At the bottom of the Pay Bills window, you must make three important choices regarding your payment: Payment Date, Payment Method, and Payment Account.

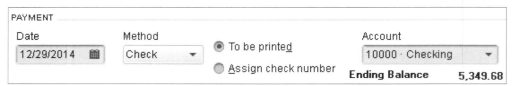

QuickBooks allows you to choose the payment options for each bill.

- **Payment Date**—Make sure you select the date you want the payment to be reflected in your bank and Accounts Payable accounts.
- **Payment Method**—You can choose how you will pay the bill. If you choose to pay by check, you must select whether you will print the check or write it by hand. You will learn how to print checks in the Writing Checks section. You can also choose to pay your bill by credit card. In order to pay by credit card, you must have a credit card account set up. Then you can choose it from the Payment Method drop-down list.
- **Payment Account**—You can select to pay the bill from any bank account you have set up. When you select an account, QuickBooks will show you the ending balance for the account so you can ensure you have enough money to pay the bill. Make sure to select the proper account, as it will be credited behind the scenes!

The Payment Summary Window

Once you have chosen to pay the selected bills in the Pay Bills window, QuickBooks will display a Payment Summary window. There are three options made available to you from this window: pay another bill, print checks, or close the window.

Making Other Forms of Payment

You can also choose to pay your bills using additional forms of payment such as by credit card or by electronic check. You will have an opportunity to pay a bill with a credit card in Chapter 5, Banking with QuickBooks. If you use electronic checks to pay your bills, it will be treated similar to a debit card, which you will also have a chance to work with in the next chapter.

BEHIND THE SCENES

Let's look at the accounting scenario that results when you pay bills.

20000-Accounts Payable		10000-Checking	
125.49	Bal. 290.66		125.49
	Bal. 165.17		

Rankin Family Insurance		QuickBooks debits the sub-register for the vendor along with Accounts Payable.
125.49		

QUICK REFERENCE	PAYING BILLS
Task	**Procedure**
Pay a bill	▪ Open the Pay Bills window; select the desired bill.
	▪ Select the account from which you wish to make the payment, along with the payment method and date.
	▪ Click Pay & Close or Pay & New.
Pay a partial amount on a bill	▪ Open the Pay Bills window; select the desired bill.
	▪ Enter the bill amount in the Amt. To Pay column.
	▪ Select the account from which you wish to make the payment, along with the payment method and date.
	▪ Click Pay & Close or Pay & New.

Pay Bills

In this exercise, you will pay bills that have been entered into QuickBooks.

Guy is ready to pay his bills and will pay the bills that were entered in the last exercise, although he will enter a partial payment for one of them. He will complete this task by using the Pay Bills window because the bills were originally entered in the Enter Bills window and, therefore, are "sitting" in Accounts Payable.

1. Click the **Pay Bills** task icon on the Home page.

   The Pay Bills window opens with the Show All Bills option selected at the top of the window.

2. Follow these steps to pay the insurance bill:

Ⓐ Click in the box beside the bill due for **Rankin Family Insurance**.

Ⓑ Click the calendar button in the Payment Date field, and then click to choose **12/29/2014**.

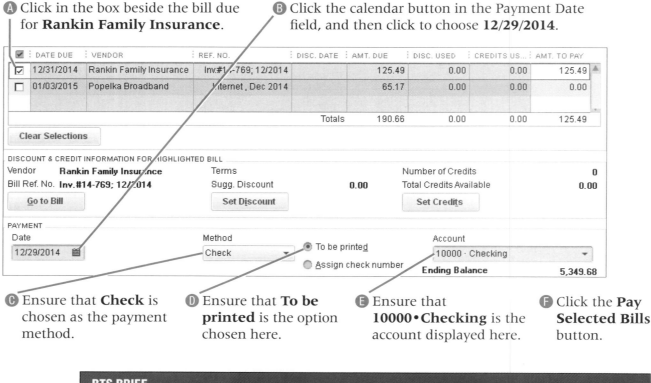

Ⓒ Ensure that **Check** is chosen as the payment method.

Ⓓ Ensure that **To be printed** is the option chosen here.

Ⓔ Ensure that **10000•Checking** is the account displayed here.

Ⓕ Click the **Pay Selected Bills** button.

BTS BRIEF

20000•Accounts Payable DR 125.49; **10000•Checking CR <125.49>**

---

3. Click **Pay More Bills** in the Payment Summary window.

Pay a Partial Amount on a Bill

You will now help Guy to pay a partial amount of a bill due.

4. Follow these steps to pay a portion of the Popelka Broadband bill:

   Ⓐ Click to place a checkmark for the **Popelka Broadband** bill.   Ⓑ Drag to select the total amount in the **Amt. To Pay** column and type **50**.

	DATE DUE	VENDOR	REF. NO.	DISC. DATE	AMT. DUE	DISC. USED	CREDITS US...	AMT. TO PAY
☑	01/03/2015	Popelka Broadband	Internet , Dec 2014		65.17	0.00	0.00	50.00

5. Click the **Pay Selected Bills** button to complete the transaction.

6. Click **Pay More Bills** in the Payment Summary window.

   Take a look at the current bills to be paid. Notice that the bill for Popelka Broadband is still on the list, but only for the remaining amount due of $15.17.

   > **BTS BRIEF**
   >
   > 20000•Accounts Payable DR 50.00; **10000•Checking CR <50.00>**

7. Close the **Pay Bills** window.

Writing and Printing Checks

If you are using the cash basis of accounting, you do not have to use the enter bills and pay bills features of QuickBooks—even though they are useful features for managing cash flow. Instead, you can simply write a check to pay for your expenditures when they are due and expense them properly.

Remember that if you use the Enter Bills feature, you must use the Pay Bills feature for the bills you have entered! If you don't, your expenses will be overstated, and you will have funds "hanging out" in Accounts Payable and getting you into trouble.

As with the Pay Bills window, you must decide from which account to issue the check and whether to print or handwrite the check.

The following illustration displays the primary features of the Write Checks window.

Notice that a check number displays if one has been assigned and the Print Later option is not checked.

You can choose from which account to write the check, if applicable.

This area looks like a typical check. The "Pay to the Order of" field will draw from all of your name lists.

On this tab you can expense your purchase just as you did in the Enter Bills window. You can also pass on expenses to customers or jobs.

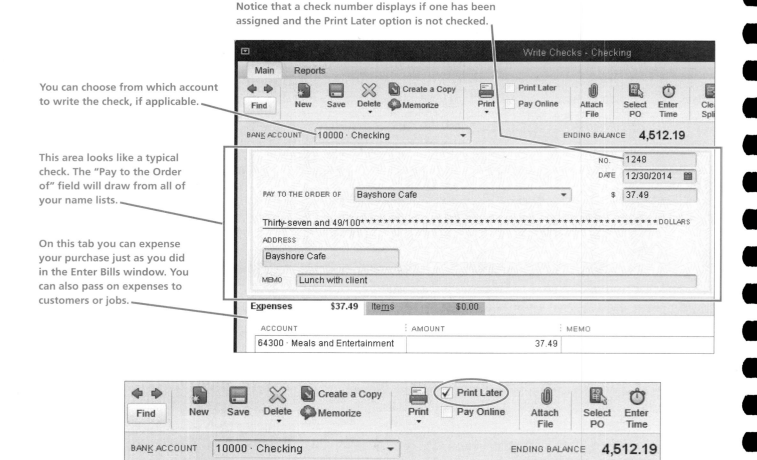

If you choose to Print Later, the check number will be set "to print."

Tab: Paying Money Out
Topic: Write checks

Printing Checks

When you choose to print your checks in the Pay Bills and Write Checks windows, QuickBooks will "hold" all of them in a queue until you are ready to print a batch of them. You can issue the command to print a batch of checks from the menu bar, or you can click the Print Checks task icon in the Banking area of the Home page.

```
                              Select Checks to Print

BankAccount   [10000 · Checking        ▼]      First Check Number   [1251]

Select Checks to print, then click OK.
There is 1 Check to print for $750.00.

  ✓ │ DATE              │ PAYEE                    │ AMOUNT
  ✓ │ 12/30/2014        │ Sandy Property Management│        750.00
```

From this window, you can choose exactly which checks from your batch to print.

BEHIND THE SCENES

The behind the scenes accounting that occurs when you write a check is a hybrid of the two previous transactions (Enter Bills and Pay Bills), with the elimination of Accounts Payable, the middle man.

67100-Rent Expense		10000-Checking	
750.00			750.00

QUICK REFERENCE	WRITING CHECKS
Task	**Procedure**
Write a check to be printed	■ Open the Write Checks window; choose the payee. ■ Type the check amount; ensure the Print Later box is checked. ■ Select the proper expense account(s) on the Expense tab; select a customer if you wish to pass on the expense. ■ Click Save & Close or Save & New.
Record a handwritten check	■ Open the Write Checks window; choose the payee. ■ Type the amount of the check; ensure there is *not* a checkmark in the Print Later box. ■ Type the check number in the "No" field at the top of the window. ■ Select the proper expense account(s) on the Expense tab; select a customer if you wish to pass on the expense. ■ Click Save & Close or Save & New.
Print a batch of checks	■ Choose File→Print Forms→Checks. ■ Select the checks you wish to print from the Select Checks to Print window; click OK. ■ Select the correct options in the Print Checks window, ensuring the correct first check number is entered; click OK.

Write and Print Checks

In this exercise, Guy will pay for expenses with both printed and handwritten checks.

1. Click the **Write Checks** task icon in the Banking area of the Home page.

2. Follow these steps to complete the check:

Ⓐ Ensure the **Print Later** box is checked.

Find New Save Delete Memorize ✓ Print Later □ Pay Online Print Attach File Select PO Enter Time	Ⓑ Tap Tab, and then type **123014** here.

DATE 12/30/2014

PAY TO THE ORDER OF   Sandy Property Management $ 750.00

Ⓒ Tap Tab, and then type **s**.

Seven hundred fifty and 00/100*** DOLLARS

ADDRESS

Sandy Property Management
Jeannie Sandy
220 Bayside Blvd.
Bayside, CA 91547

Ⓓ Tap Tab, and then type **750** here.

MEMO   Rent for January 2015

Ⓔ Tap Tab twice, and then type the memo displayed.

Expenses $750.00   Items $0.00

ACCOUNT	AMOUNT	MEMO
67100 · Rent Expense	750.00	

Ⓕ Tap Tab, and then type **r** for the account.

BTS BRIEF

67100•Rent Expense DR 750.00; **10000•Checking CR <750.00>**

---

3. Click **Save & New** to record this check and leave the Write Checks window open.

Record a Handwritten Check

You may not always be at your computer when you wish to write a check. In this situation, Guy has taken his checkbook shopping and needs to record the handwritten check.

4. Click to remove the checkmark from the **Print Later** box.

   The check number field can be edited once this checkmark is removed.

5. Follow these steps to record the handwritten check:

Ⓐ Tap ⎣Tab⎦, and then type **1248**.

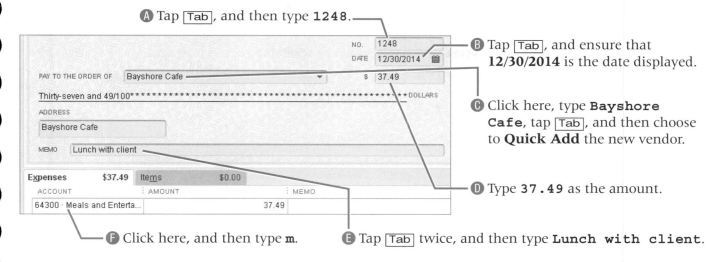

Ⓑ Tap ⎣Tab⎦, and ensure that **12/30/2014** is the date displayed.

Ⓒ Click here, type **Bayshore Cafe**, tap ⎣Tab⎦, and then choose to **Quick Add** the new vendor.

Ⓓ Type **37.49** as the amount.

Ⓕ Click here, and then type **m**.

Ⓔ Tap ⎣Tab⎦ twice, and then type **Lunch with client**.

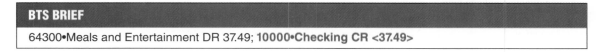

BTS BRIEF

64300•Meals and Entertainment DR 37.49; **10000•Checking CR <37.49>**

6. Click the **Save & Close** button to complete the transaction.

Print a Batch of Checks

Once you have indicated that checks are to be printed, you need to issue a separate command to print them.

7. Click the **Print Checks** task icon in the Banking area of the Home page.

 If you don't see the Print Checks task icon, use the sizing arrow to make the Home page larger or choose File→Print Forms→Checks.

8. Tap ⎣Tab⎦, and then type **1249** as the first check number.
   By default, all of the checks will be selected.

9. Click the checkmark to the left of the **Sandy Property Management** to deselect it.

| Bank Account | 10000 · Checking | ▼ | First Check Number | 1249 |

Select Checks to print, then click OK.
There are 2 Checks to print for $175.49.

✓	DATE	PAYEE	AMOUNT
✓	12/29/2014	Rankin Family Insurance	125.49
✓	12/29/2014	Popelka Broadband	50.00
	12/30/2014	Sandy Property Management	750.00

10. Click **OK**.
    The Print Checks window will appear.

If you wish to be "green," you can choose to not physically print the checks in the next step by choosing to print to PDF or to just preview how they would appear if printed.

11. Ensure that **Voucher** is chosen as the check style, and then click **Print**.

    QuickBooks will display a Print Checks - Confirmation window. Here you have the opportunity to reprint any checks that did not print correctly or to troubleshoot the order in which your checks printed.

12. Click **OK** in the Print Checks - Confirmation window.

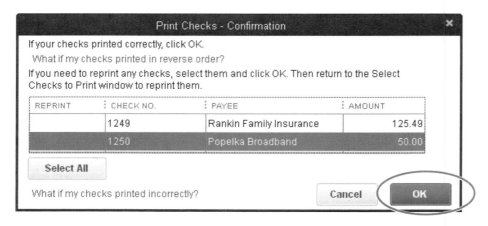

Notice that there are links to help you if your checks do not print correctly.

Dealing with Oops in Vendor Transactions

In Chapter 3, Working with Customers, you learned how to deal with errors related to customer-related transactions. Now we will look at those associated with transactions related to vendors.

QuickBooks tries very hard to make sure you don't make errors that will affect what happens behind the scenes, as shown by the Open Bills Exist window that is displayed. However, it seems that users still end up making errors that need to be corrected!

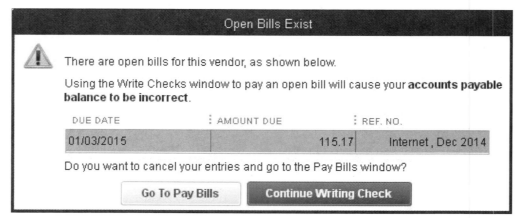

The Open Bills Exist window is displayed when you try to write a check to a vendor for whom you have an outstanding bill.

Fixing Errors

The following table outlines a common vendor-related error as well as an error that occurs in the Write Checks window, the effects of the errors behind the scenes, and how to correct them.

COMMON ERRORS AND FIXES

Error	Effect Behind the Scenes	The Fix
A bill is entered but the Pay Bills window is not used when the payment is made.	Your expenses will be double-stated and Accounts Payable for the vendor is not "cleared out".	Delete the check or credit card payment for the expense and then enter the transaction properly using the Pay Bills window.
A "regular" check was cut to pay payroll or sales tax liabilities.	The liability accounts are not cleared out; QuickBooks payroll essentially has a second set of books that are affected only when you pay the liabilities through the proper method.	Void the "regular" check and then process the payment through the proper method (Pay Payroll Liabilities or Pay Sales Tax).

FLASHBACK TO GAAP: PRUDENCE

Remember that if you need to choose between two solutions, pick the one that is less likely to overstate assets and income.

You will learn how to process liability payments properly in Chapter 7, Working with Balance Sheet Accounts and Budgets and Chapter 9, Working with Estimates and Time Tracking as they must be treated differently since QuickBooks keeps a separate set of books behind the scenes for payroll.

DEVELOP YOUR SKILLS 4-5

Correct Vendor Transactions

In this exercise, you will find and edit a bill. Then you will execute a task incorrectly and fix it.

Use the Find Feature to Edit a Bill

You will help Guy to edit the bill for Popelka Broadband, as it should have been for $165.17 rather than $65.17.

1. Choose **Edit→Find**.

2. Follow these steps to locate the bill and then go to it:

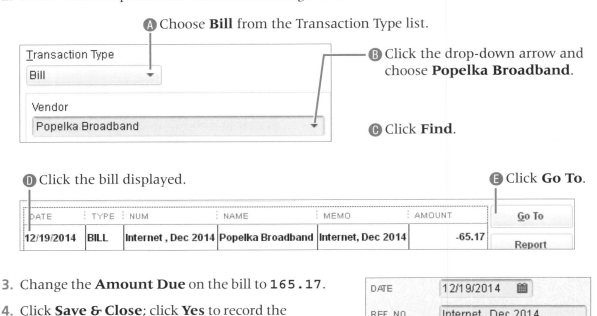

Ⓐ Choose **Bill** from the Transaction Type list.

Ⓑ Click the drop-down arrow and choose **Popelka Broadband**.

Ⓒ Click **Find**.

Ⓓ Click the bill displayed.

Ⓔ Click **Go To**.

DATE	TYPE	NUM	NAME	MEMO	AMOUNT	
12/19/2014	BILL	Internet , Dec 2014	Popelka Broadband	Internet, Dec 2014	-65.17	Go To / Report

3. Change the **Amount Due** on the bill to **165.17**.

4. Click **Save & Close**; click **Yes** to record the transaction with the changes.

5. Close the **Find** window.

DATE	12/19/2014
REF. NO.	Internet , Dec 2014
AMOUNT DUE	165.17

BTS BRIEF

61700• Computer and Internet Expense DR 100.00; 20000•Accounts Payable CR <100.00>

Do It the Wrong Way – Pay a Bill with a Check

Guy has decided to pay the bill due for Popelka Broadband. Now you will enter the payment incorrectly *for the purpose of learning how to fix the error and do it correctly.*

6. Choose **Banking→Write Checks**.

7. Follow these steps to begin to create the check:

Ⓐ Click to choose to **Print Later**.

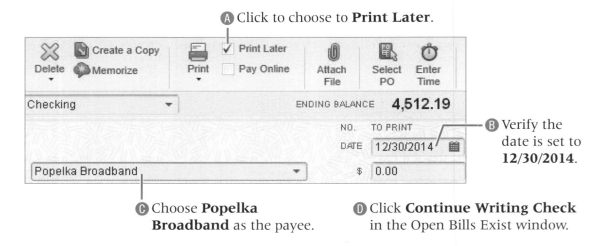

Ⓑ Verify the date is set to **12/30/2014**.

Ⓒ Choose **Popelka Broadband** as the payee.

Ⓓ Click **Continue Writing Check** in the Open Bills Exist window.

8. Tap $\boxed{\text{Tab}}$, and then type **115.17**; click **Save & Close** to record the check.

Think about this transaction. What is wrong with it? By writing a check for an outstanding bill in the Write Checks window, you have stated income twice and have not cleared the amount from Accounts Payable.

> **BTS BRIEF**
>
> 61700• Computer and Internet Expense DR 115.17; **10000•Checking CR <115.17>**

Do It the Right Way – Pay a Bill Using the Pay Bills Window

To fix the bill that was paid improperly, you must delete the check and reenter the payment using the Pay Bills window.

9. Choose **Banking→Write Checks**.

10. Click the **Previous** button until the check you just entered is displayed.

You can look for a transaction by using the Previous and Next buttons, if you believe the transaction to be easy to locate. If not, use the Find or Search feature.

11. Choose **Edit→Delete Check**; click **OK** in the Delete Transaction window.

FROM THE KEYBOARD
$\boxed{\text{Ctrl}}+\boxed{\text{d}}$ to delete the selected transaction

12. Close the **Write Checks** window.

13. Choose **Vendors→Pay Bills**.

14. Follow these steps to enter the payment correctly:

Ⓐ Click to select the **Popelka Broadband** bill.

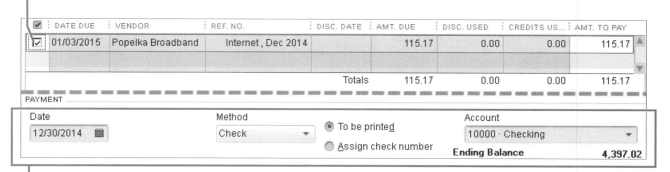

Ⓑ Ensure the payment details match what is displayed.

Ⓒ Click **Pay Selected Bills**.

> **BTS BRIEF**
>
> 10000•Checking DR 115.17; **61700•Computer and Internet Expense CR <115.17>**
>
> 20000•Accounts Payable DR 115.17; **10000•Checking CR <115.17>**

15. Click **Done** in the payment summary window.

Before moving on, think about what you have just completed and make sure you understand the "why" behind it. You have deleted the overstated expenses by deleting the check and have "cleared out" Accounts Payable for Popelka Broadband by processing the payment correctly.

Producing Vendor and P&L Reports

Once you have recorded your vendor-related transactions, QuickBooks has many reports that you can produce to view your data. In Chapter 2, Creating a Company, you learned about list reports. The other two general types of reports are listed below:

- Summary reports subtotal your data and provide a summary.
- Transaction reports show each transaction that makes up the subtotal found in a summary report.

If you wish to see all transactions grouped by vendor, there are two different reports you can run. The Vendor Balance Detail report (found in the Vendors & Payables category) shows only those transactions affecting Accounts Payable (transactions entered and paid as "bills"). The Expense by Vendor reports (both summary and detail, found in the Company & Financial category) show transactions made by all payment methods.

QuickZoom

QuickBooks has a great feature called QuickZoom. This feature allows you to zoom through underlying sub-reports until you reach the form where the data was originally entered. This can be extremely useful if you have questions as to where a figure in a report comes from. You can even edit the source transaction once you have QuickZoomed to it, if you desire.

Average Guy Designs, Chapter 4
Transaction List by Vendor
All Transactions

Type	Date	Num	Memo	Account	Clr	Split	Debit	Credit
Bayshore Cafe								
Check	12/30/2014	1248	Lunch with ...	10000 · Checking		64300 · Meal...		37.49
Graphic Supply Shoppe								
Bill	12/03/2014		Supplies for...	20000 · Accounts...		-SPLIT-		302.50
Bill Pmt -Check	12/10/2014	1245	Supplies for...	10000 · Checking		20000 · Acco...		302.50

The zoom pointer indicates that you can double-click to dive deeper into your data. The number of layers to zoom through depends on the type of report (or graph) with which you started. Here, a double click would open the Write Checks window with the transaction for Bayshore Café displayed.

The Profit & Loss Report

Now that you have recorded both income and expenses for December, you will be able to run a meaningful profit and loss (P&L) report. It is important to make sure all income and expense transactions are entered so that income is matched to expenses for the period you are reporting. A P&L is a financial report that can be found in the Company & Financial category of the Report Center window. The P&L report will reflect all transactions that have affected income and expense accounts.

> **FLASHBACK TO GAAP: MATCHING**
>
> Remember that expenses need to be matched with revenues.

Visualize! **Tab:** Reports
Topic: Profit & Loss statement

QUICK REFERENCE	CREATING VENDOR-RELATED REPORTS
Task	**Procedure**
Produce a vendor-related report using the Report Center	■ Choose Reports→Report Center. ■ Choose Vendors & Payables as the report category. ■ Click the report you wish to produce in the main section of the Report Center. ■ Click the Display report button.
Print or preview a report	■ Display the report you wish to print or preview. ■ Click the Print button on the toolbar. ■ Click Preview or Print.
Produce a profit & loss report	■ Choose Reports→Company & Financial→Profit & Loss Standard.

Produce Vendor and P&L Reports

In this exercise, you will produce a vendor summary report, a vendor detail report, and a profit & loss report.

Create a Vendor Detail Report and Use QuickZoom

You will now create a report that shows what you owe all vendors. Then you will use QuickZoom to see the details of where a balance originated.

1. Choose **Reports→Vendors & Payables→Vendor Balance Detail**.

   You can generate reports through the Report Center or the menu bar with the same result. The report will be displayed with the date range of All selected, as it is the default for this particular report.

2. Place your mouse pointer over the amount due for Popelka Broadband until you see the zoom pointer, and then double-click.

◇ Type	◇ Date	◇ Num	◇ Account	◇ Amount	◇ Balance
Popelka Broadband					
Bill	12/19/2014	Intern...	20000 · Accounts...	165.17	165.17
Bill Pmt -Check	12/29/2014	1250	20000 · Accounts...	-50.00	115.17
Bill Pmt -Check	12/30/2014	1253	20000 · Accounts...	-115.17	0.00
Total Popelka Broadband				0.00	0.00

A Customer Transaction Detail Report will be displayed that shows the transactions leading to the balance for Popelka Broadband.

3. Place your mouse pointer over the Bill date 12/19/2014 that you entered for this vendor until you see the zoom pointer, and then double-click.

◇ Type	◇ Date	◇ Num ◇	Name
▶ Bill	@19/2014	Intern...	Popelka Broadband
Bill Pmt -Check	12/29/2014	1250	Popelka Broadband
Bill Pmt -Check	12/30/2014		Popelka Broadband

The Enter Bills window will open with the bill that you entered for this vendor earlier in this chapter. If need be, you could edit the transaction at this point.

4. Choose **Window→Close All**.

Click No if asked to memorize any of the reports displayed.

Display a Vendor Summary Report

Now you will create a report that shows a summary of all expenses by vendor, regardless of payment method

5. Choose **Reports→Company & Financial→Expenses by Vendor Summary**.

6. Tap $\boxed{a}$ to set the date range to **All**.

The Expenses by Vendor Summary report will be displayed, listing the total amount ever paid or accrued for each active vendor.

7. Close the report, clicking **No** when asked if you want to memorize it.

Create a Profit and Loss Report

Guy would now like to see if the company had a net income or loss for December based on the transactions entered.

8. Choose **Reports→Company & Financial→Profit & Loss Standard**.

Remember, you can display all reports available through the Report Center via the menu bar as well.

9. Follow these steps to set the correct date range:

Ⓐ Tap $\boxed{\text{Tab}}$ to reach the **From** field, and then type **120114**.

Ⓑ Tap $\boxed{\text{Tab}}$, type **123114**, and then tap $\boxed{\text{Tab}}$ again.

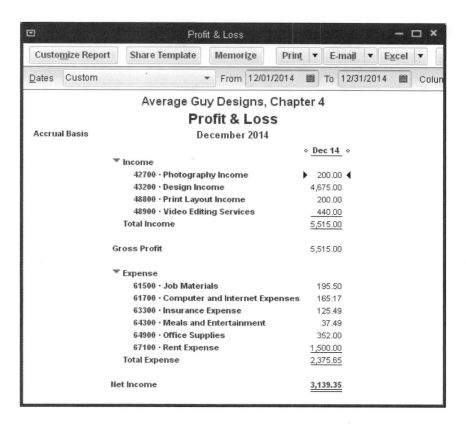

You will see a report that shows your total income and expenses for the time period along with the resulting net income (or loss). The income portion of your report should match the illustration. Notice that the date range is set to Custom on the toolbar. QuickBooks gives you the option to set the exact date range you desire in your reports.

10. Close the **Profit & Loss** report, choosing not to memorize it.

Working with QuickBooks Graphs

QuickBooks provides several graphs along with the preset reports. QuickBooks graphs are accessible through the Reports option on the menu bar or through the Report Center.

Types of QuickBooks Graphs

Following are the six graphs provided by QuickBooks. If you can't find a graph that suits your needs, you always have the option of exporting a report to Microsoft Excel and using the Excel charting features to create additional charts and graphs.

The graphs provided in QuickBooks include:

- Income and Expense
- Net Worth
- Accounts Receivable
- Sales
- Accounts Payable
- Budget vs. Actual

The Graph Toolbar

The Graph toolbar displays different buttons depending on which graph you have created. Once you have created your graph, you can use the Graph toolbar to do a variety of tasks such as:

- Customize your graph by date
- Choose how to view your data
- View your next group of information
- Print your graph
- Refresh the data contained within your graph (if you have made changes to your data since the graph was created)

For some graphs, there are also buttons at the bottom of the window that allow you to choose how to view the pie chart data at the bottom of the window (e.g., by Income or by Expense).

QuickZooming with Graphs

The QuickZoom feature you used previously in this chapter for reports is also available with graphs. You simply double-click on a portion of a graph (when you see the QuickZoom pointer) to zoom in and see where the data comes from.

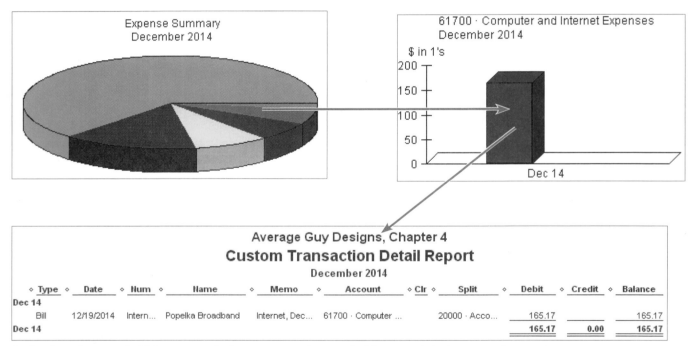

Notice that when you QuickZoom on a pie chart, you see a bar graph. When you QuickZoom on a bar graph, you see a report showing where the data originated.

QUICK REFERENCE	CREATING AN ACCOUNTS PAYABLE GRAPH
Task	**Procedure**
Produce an Accounts Payable graph	Choose Reports→Company & Financial→Income & Expense Graph.

DEVELOP YOUR SKILLS 4-7

Create QuickBooks Graphs

In this exercise, you will create a graph that will depict the information you already viewed on the profit & loss report—income and expenses. You will use QuickZoom to drill down to the source of the data for one vendor.

1. Choose **Reports→Company & Financial→Income & Expense Graph**.

2. Follow these steps to set the date for the graph:

Ⓐ Click the **Dates** button on the graph toolbar.

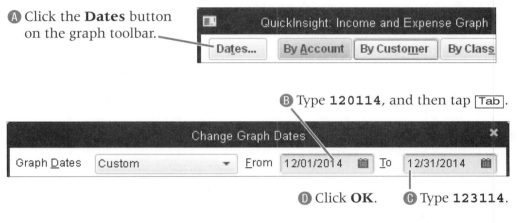

Ⓑ Type **120114**, and then tap Tab.

Ⓓ Click **OK**.   Ⓒ Type **123114**.

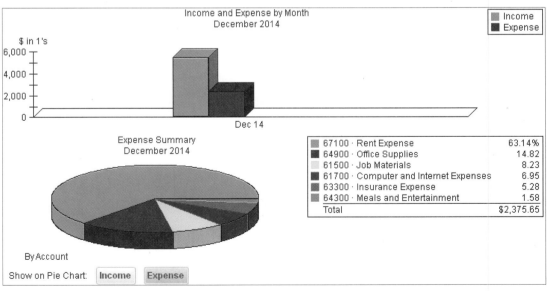

The Income & Expense graph will display data from December 2014.

3. Place your mouse pointer over the green slice that shows the rent expense, and then hold down the right mouse button.

   Holding down the mouse button allows you to see the dollar amount corresponding to the "pie slice."

4. Double-click on the pie slice for **Computer and Internet Expenses**.

   A bar graph will appear showing just the amount for the selected expense account.

5. Double-click on the bar graph showing the amount of computer and Internet expenses.

   A Custom Transaction Detail Report will be displayed.

6. Double-click on the bill dated 12/19/14 for Popelka Broadband.

   The Enter Bills window will be displayed. This is as far as QuickZoom will go!

7. Choose **Window→Close All**.

8. Choose **Company→Home Page**.

9. Choose the appropriate option for your situation:

   ▪ If you will continue working, leave QuickBooks open.

   ▪ If you are finished working in QuickBooks for now, choose **File→Exit**.

Tackle the Tasks

Now is your chance to work a little more with Average Guy Designs and apply the skills that you have learned in this chapter to accomplish additional tasks. You will use the same company file you used in the Develop Your Skills exercises throughout this chapter. Enter the following tasks, referring back to the concepts in the chapter as necessary.

Add a Vendor	Enter the following vendor: Professional Software Distributors 6439 Washington Square, Wausau, WI 54401 Contact: Abby Gibbs, Manager, (715) 555-9922 Acct #: PR203X, Type: Supplies, Terms: Net 15
Enter Bills	Enter the following bills: Professional Software Distributors; Dated: 12/31/2014; Amt. $563.27; Memo: Inv. #17-222; Acct: 61700•Computer and Internet Expenses Handyman by the Bay; Dated: 1/2/2015; Amt. $239.44; Memo: Inv. #15-001; Acct: 67200•Repairs and Maintenance NoCal Gas & Electric; Dated: 1/2/2015; Amt. $82.37; Memo: NGE Jan 2015; Acct: 68610 Gas & Electric Bayshore City Water Co.; Dated: 1/5/2015; Amt. $48.22; Memo: BC Inv. #9435D1; Due: 1/17/2015; Acct: 68620•Water
Pay Bills	Pay all bills due on or before 1/13/2015 on 1/7/2015; Acct.: Checking; checks to be printed Pay $200 towards the bill for Professional Software Distributors on 1/9/2015; Acct.: Checking; check to be printed
Write and Print Checks	Write a check on 1/3/2015 to Allen Brothers Grocery for $36.21 for Office Supplies, check #1251 Print all checks waiting in the queue on 1/9/2015, first check #1252
Display Reports	Display reports that will answer the following questions: Which bills are due? What is my company's current balance with each vendor? What is the contact information and current balance for each vendor? Did I have a profit or a loss during December?

Concepts Review

To check your knowledge of the key concepts introduced in this chapter, complete the Concepts Review quiz on the Student Resource Center or in your eLab course.

Reinforce Your Skills

Angela Stevens has just relocated her company, Quality-Built Construction, from California to Silverton, Oregon. You will be working with a QuickBooks Sample Company File in this exercise as it will allow you to run full payroll in a future chapter without having to purchase a payroll subscription.

Before you begin the Reinforce Your Skills exercises, complete one of these options:

- Open **RYS_Chapter04** from your file storage location.
- Restore **RYS_Chapter04 (Portable)** from your file storage location. For a reminder of how to restore a portable company file, see Develop Your Skills 3-1. Add your last name and first initial to the end of the filename.

REINFORCE YOUR SKILLS 4-1
Manage the Vendor List

In this exercise, you will work with the Vendor List for Quality-Built Construction. You will edit an existing vendor, create a new vendor, and delete a vendor.

To begin, Valley Insurance Company has changed its name to Vista Insurance Company. You will help Susie to make that change in QuickBooks.

1. Choose **Vendors→Vendor Center**.
2. Scroll down and double-click **Doors Galore** to open it for editing.
3. Change the vendor's name to **Coast Doors**.

   You will have to change the name in four separate places, including on the Payment Settings tab. This new name will be reflected in all transactions that deal with this vendor—past and present.

4. Click **OK** to accept the change.

Add a New Vendor

Angela has begun to purchase job supplies from a new vendor in Oregon. You will set up the company as a vendor.

5. Click the **New Vendor** button, and then choose **New Vendor**.
6. Enter the following information to create a new vendor.

Company Name	Valley Building Supply
Contact Name	Ms. Carmela Hutch, Owner
Address	525 E. Valley Road
	Salem, OR 97305
Phone	503-555-9438
Fax	503-555-9455
Type	Suppliers
Terms	Net 15
Account #	84-976

7. Click **OK** to accept the new vendor record.

Delete a Vendor

8. Click **Abercrombie Fence Co** to select it.

9. Choose **Edit→Delete Vendor**.

10. Click **OK** to confirm the deletion.

11. Close the **Vendor Center** window.

REINFORCE YOUR SKILLS 4-2

Enter and Pay Bills

In this exercise, you will enter a bill Angela just received. You will also pay all bills due by a certain date for Angela.

1. Choose **Vendors→Enter Bills**.

2. Click the drop-down arrow and choose **Ruff Postage Machines** as the Vendor.

3. Set the date to **12/19/2018**, and then enter `Postage, Dec 2018` as the memo and ref. no.

4. Type **$100.00** as the amount, and choose **6610•Postage and Delivery** as the account.

5. Click the **Save & Close** button to enter the transaction and close the window.

Pay a Bill

6. Open the Pay Bills window by choosing **Vendors→Pay Bills**.

7. Choose all bills that are due on or before **12/31/2018** (you should find one).

8. Set the date to **12/23/2018**, and choose to print the check.

9. Click **Pay Selected Bills** to record the payment and close the window.

10. Click **Done** in the Payment Summary Window.

Write and Print Checks

In this exercise, you will write a check for an expense and print the checks you have created.

1. Choose **Banking→Write Checks**.

2. Set the check to print later.

3. Set the date to **12/26/2018**.

4. Type **Marion County** into the Pay to the Order of field and choose to **Quick Add** it to the Vendor List.

5. Type **$250** as the amount and **Business License, 2019** as the memo.

6. Select **6090•Business License & Fees** as the account.

7. Click **Save & Close** to accept the transaction and close the window.

Print a Batch of Checks

8. Choose **File→Print Forms→Checks**.
   Notice that, by default, QuickBooks selects all checks; you can change this if you need to.

9. Ensure that **Checking** is the bank account and type **11353** as the first check number.

10. Click **OK** to move to the Print Checks window.
    At this point you can verify that the correct printer and check style are selected. Now, either "stay green" and print the checks to a PDF file or physically print the checks using an available printer.

11. Click **Print** once you have chosen how you will print the checks.

12. Click **OK** in the Print Checks - Confirmation window.

Find and Edit a Transaction

Angela received an adjusted amount for the December phone bill. Rather than clicking the Previous button over and over again, in this exercise, you will use the QuickBooks Find feature to locate the transaction.

1. Choose **Edit→Find**.

2. Choose **Bill** as the Transaction Type and **Western Telephone Company** as the Vendor.

3. Enter the date range as **12/1/2018** to **1/15/2019**, and then click **Find**.
   The bill you are looking for will be displayed in the bottom of the window.

4. Double-click the bill dated **1/2/2019** in the bottom portion of the window.
   The Enter Bills window will open; leave it open for the next step.

Edit a Transaction

5. Change the amount of the bill to **329.77** and choose to record the change to the transaction.

6. Save and close the transaction; close the **Find** window.

Create Vendor and P&L Reports

In this exercise, you will run vendor and profit & loss reports for Quality-Built Construction.

1. Choose **Reports→Vendors & Payables→Vendor Balance Summary**.

2. Submit the report based on the guidelines provided by your instructor.

3. Choose **Reports→Company & Financial→Profit & Loss Standard**.

4. Type **a** to set the date range to **All**.

5. Submit the report based on the guidelines provided by your instructor.

6. Choose **Window→Close All**, choosing not to memorize either.

7. Choose the appropriate option for your situation:

   - If you will continue working, leave QuickBooks open.
   - If you are finished working in QuickBooks for now, choose **File→Exit**.

Apply Your Skills

Before you begin the Apply Your Skills exercises, complete one of these options:

- *Open* **AYS_Chapter04** *from your file storage location.*

- *Restore* **AYS_Chapter04 (Portable)** *from your file storage location. For a reminder of how to restore a portable company file, see Develop Your Skills 3-1. Add your last name and first initial to the end of the filename.*

APPLY YOUR SKILLS 4-1

Work with the Vendor List

In this exercise, you will manage the Vendor List for Wet Noses.

1. Using the following information, create three new **Vendor List** entries.

Name	Casey's Consulting	Take a Walk	Billy's Van Service
Address	902 Creekview Dr. Kirkland, WA 98034	13602 75th Ave NE Seattle, WA 98132	9501 NE 182nd Pl Bothell, WA 98011
Phone	425-555-9569	206-555-9433	425-555-4477
Fax	425-555-9568	206-555-9434	425-555-4478
Contact Name	Ms. Casey Scripps	Ms. Shannon High	Mr. Billy Ranch
Job Title	Owner	Walker	President
Type	Consultant	Service Providers	Service Providers
Terms	Due on Receipt	Net 15	Net 15
Account Number	JR154	VET87	BB23

2. Edit the **Puget Sound Power Company** vendor record to display **Shaunda Jones** as the contact.

3. Add the following vendor types to the existing vendor records, adding a new entry to the **Vendor Type List** when necessary:
   - Wyland Broadband: Service Providers
   - Northshore Water Company: Utilities
   - Oberg Property Management: Service Providers
   - Puget Sound Power Company: Utilities
   - Seattle Vet Supply: Suppliers
   - Whoville Office Supplies: Supplies
   - Brian's Pet Taxi: Service Providers

Enter and Pay Bills

In this exercise, you will deal with expenses incurred by Wet Noses.

1. On 7/2/2014, Dr. James received a bill from Seattle Vet Supply for $3,813.58. It should be broken down by account as follows: $1,773.25 for medical supplies, $1,056.92 for vaccines, and $983.41 for medicines. The ref. no./memo is: Inv. #77-9-56.

2. Enter a bill received on 7/8/2014 from Northshore Water Company for **$210.67**.

3. The ref. no./memo is **Water Bill, 7/2014**.

4. On 7/18/2014, a bill was received from Puget Sound Power Company for **$241.33**.

5. The ref. no./memo is **Power Bill, 7/2014**.

6. Enter a bill received on 7/21/2014 from Wyland Broadband for **$159.44**. It should be broken down by account as follows: $55.99 for internet service and $103.45 for telephone service.

7. The ref. no./memo is **Int/Phone July 2014**.

8. On 7/21/2014, Sadie decided to sit down and pay her bills. Pay all of the bills due on or before 7/22/2014. You will print the checks later.

9. Choose **Done** in the Payment Summary window.

Write and Print Checks

In this exercise, you will write and print checks for Dr. James. You will need to use your best judgment to determine the account to use for each transaction.

1. Dr. James took all of her employees out for a working lunch at Laura's Café on 7/21/2014. The total cost was **$84.35**. She wrote a check at the restaurant, using check number 1418.

2. Sadie received a bill from Animal Lovers for an advertisement for $135.00 on 7/22/2014. Since she just paid her bills she has decided to just enter a check for the expense that she will print next.

3. Print all checks in the queue using 1419 as the first check number.

Find and Edit a Transaction

Dr. James received an adjusted amount for the bill from Patrick Janitorial Service. Rather than clicking the Previous button over and over again, in this exercise, you will use the QuickBooks Find feature to locate the transaction.

1. Using the QuickBooks Find feature, locate the **Patrick Janitorial Service** bill dated **6/30/2014**.

2. Open the bill and change the amount of it to **$505.00**.

   Since you have already paid this bill for the initial amount, this vendor will have a negative amount (debit balance) until you receive the next bill from them.

3. Save and close the transaction; close the **Find** window.

Answer Questions with Reports

In this exercise, you will answer questions for Dr. James by running reports. You may wish to display the Report Center in List View to help you answer the questions. Ask your instructor if you should print the reports, print (save) them as PDF files, export them to Excel, or simply display them on the screen.

1. Are any of the bills overdue?

2. Is there a way to see all of the transactions for each vendor for the month of July 2014?

3. I would like to have a list of the phone numbers for all of the vendors. Can you create one for me?

4. Can I see a graph of the total amount owed and the amount by vendor as of July 31, 2014?

5. Submit your reports based on the guidelines provided by your instructor.

6. Choose the appropriate option for your situation:
   - If you will continue working, leave QuickBooks open.
   - If you are finished working in QuickBooks for now, choose **File→Exit**.

Extend Your Skills

In the course of working through the following Extend Your Skills exercises, you will be utilizing various skills taught in this and previous chapter(s). Take your time and think carefully about the tasks presented to you. Turn back to the chapter content if you need assistance.

4-1 Sort Through the Stack

Before You Begin: Restore the EYS1_Chapter04 (Portable) file or open the EYS1_Chapter04 company file from your storage location.

You have been hired by Arlaine Cervantes to help her with her organization's books. She is the founder of Niños del Lago, a nonprofit organization that provides impoverished Guatemalan children with an engaging educational camp experience. You have just sat down at your desk and opened a large envelope from her with a variety of documents and noticed that you have several emails from her as well. It is your job to sort through the papers and emails and make sense of what you find, entering information into QuickBooks whenever appropriate and answering any other questions in a word-processing document saved as **EYS1_Chapter04_ LastnameFirstinitial**. Remember, you are digging through papers you just dumped out of an envelope and addressing random emails from Arlaine, so it is up to you to determine the correct order in which to complete the tasks.

- Sticky note: New source for cultural competency books—enter Woods Publishing Company as a vendor: 921 Pamela Lake Drive, Pittsburg, KS 66762; (620) 555-2211; Terms—Net 30; Contact—Pam Woods.

- Bill: From Network Links (for website hosting), dated 7/3/2014, for $34.57, due 7/13/2014.

- Canceled check: Written to USPS for stamps on 7/2/2014 for $25.10, number 1003.

- Sticky note: There are some checks that can be used with the printer. Could you please print checks for any bills that I didn't write a check for?

- Note: Would like to track employee anniversaries. How can I do that?

- Scribbled on a scrap of paper: I need a report that shows all of the bills that have been entered into QuickBooks.

- Packing slip and bill: Materials received for a cultural competency seminar; need to enter the bill for $124.32, payable to Chandler Distributors, dated 7/1/2014, terms Net 15. (Arlaine is not tracking inventory in QuickBooks.)

- Carbon copies of checks: Used to pay Network Links (#1004, 7/7/2014, for full amount) and Hernandez Catering (#1005, 7/15/2014, for full amount).

- Note: We have donors who are referred to us by a local service organization. Can we include them in the customer type list?

- Bill: From Child Play, Inc. for supplies for the camp, dated 7/5/2014, for $1,212.65, due 7/15/2014.

- Printed email message from accountant: Please send a report that shows the amount owed to each vendor as of 7/10/2014.

- Bill: From Hernandez Catering for food provided at a fundraising event in California, dated 7/8/2014, payment due on receipt, for $167.21.

4-2 Be Your Own Boss

Before You Begin: Complete Extend Your Skills 3-2 before starting this exercise.

In this exercise, you will build on the company file that you outlined and created in previous chapters. If you have created a file for your actual business, then enter your vendors and vendor-related transactions that have occurred since your start date. If you are creating a fictitious company, then enter ten vendors and at least one transaction for each vendor. You will make up the names and information for this exercise.

Create Vendor Transaction List and Transaction List by Vendor reports and submit them to your instructor based on the instructions provided.

Open the company file you worked on in Extend Your Skills 3-2 and complete the tasks outlined above. When you are done, save it as a portable company file, naming it as **EYS2_Chapter04_ LastnameFirstinitial (Portable)** and submit it to your instructor based on the instructions provided.

4-3 Use the Web as a Learning Tool

Throughout this book, you will be provided with an opportunity to use the Internet as a learning tool by completing WebQuests. According to the original creators of WebQuests, as described on their website (http://WebQuest.org), a WebQuest is "an inquiry-oriented activity in which most or all of the information used by learners is drawn from the web." To complete the WebQuest projects in this book, navigate to the Student Resource Center and choose the WebQuest for the chapter on which you are working. The subject of each WebQuest will be relevant to the material found in the chapter.

WebQuest Subject: Working with web-based vendor information

Banking with QuickBooks

CHAPTER OBJECTIVES

After studying this chapter, you will be able to:

- Create bank accounts
- Make deposits into bank accounts
- Transfer funds
- Manage debit and credit card transactions
- Reconcile accounts
- Create banking reports
- Use online banking with QuickBooks

Any business must be able to work with bank accounts and the funds contained within to be able to operate effectively. If you utilize debit and credit cards for your business, you will need to know how to work with them as well. In this chapter, you will learn all about dealing with bank and credit card accounts in QuickBooks, from creating them to running reports about them. You will also have an opportunity to explore a little about banking online with QuickBooks.

Average Guy Designs

Guy has been getting comfortable performing the basic vendor and customer transactions in QuickBooks. One of the individuals whom he often contracts with, Allison Fox, is now going to take over the books because Guy has gotten quite busy with his design work customers and marketing his new company. Allison will take over creating bank accounts, tracking banking transactions, dealing with credit card transactions, and reconciling both the bank and credit card accounts.

In addition, Allison is interested in exploring how online banking with QuickBooks works.

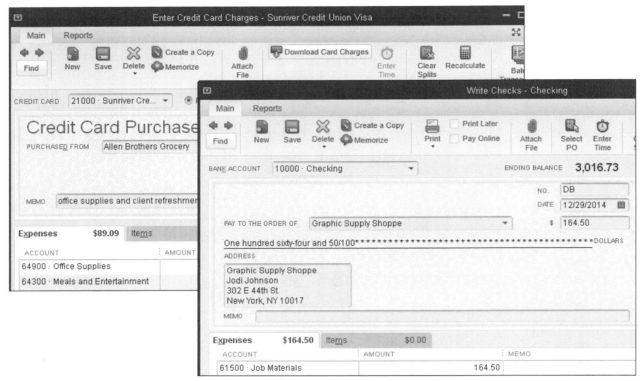

You use the Enter Credit Card Charges window to enter credit card purchases and the Write Checks or Bill Payment window to enter debit card transactions.

Creating Bank Accounts

The accounts you will work with in this chapter are assets (bank accounts) and liabilities (credit cards). There are two types of bank accounts you will deal with: Checking and Savings. petty cash accounts will be covered in Chapter 7, Working with Balance Sheet Accounts and Budgets.

Accessing Banking Activities in QuickBooks

The Banking area on the Home page displays task icons for many of the activities you will perform in this chapter. The rest of the activities can be accessed via the menu bar.

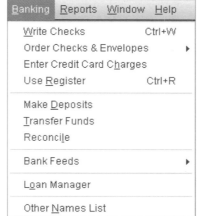

Notice that you can begin the reconciliation process by either clicking the task icon in the Banking area of the Home page or by choosing an option from the menu bar. However, to transfer funds and work with the bank feeds feature, you must use the menu bar.

The Chart of Accounts

Remember from Chapter 2, Creating a Company that the Chart of Accounts is composed of all of the asset, liability, equity, income, and expense accounts your company utilizes. In that chapter, you learned how to create new accounts, edit existing accounts, and delete unused accounts. QuickBooks responds differently when you double-click items in the Chart of Accounts, depending on the type of account, as explained in the following table.

DOUBLE-CLICKING ACCOUNTS AND QUICKBOOKS RESPONSES	
When you double-click this type of account...	**QuickBooks responds by...**
Any balance sheet account (asset, liability, or equity)	Opening an account register for that account (Exception: The Retained Earnings account, which is a specially created account without a register; you will get a QuickReport when you double-click this account)
Any income or expense account	Creating an account QuickReport

NAME	⚡	TYPE	BALANCE TOTAL	ATTACH
◈ 10000 · Checking		Bank	3,839.00	
◈ 10200 · Savings		Bank	7,382.35	
◈ 11000 · Accounts Receivable		Accounts Receivable	2,680.00	
◈ 12000 · Undeposited Funds		Other Current Asset	1,495.00	
◈ 15000 · Furniture and Equipment		Fixed Asset	0.00	
◈ 17000 · Accumulated Depreciation		Fixed Asset	0.00	
◈ 20000 · Accounts Payable		Accounts Payable	411.49	
◈ 24000 · Payroll Liabilities		Other Current Liability	0.00	
◈ 24500 · Advance Customer Payments		Other Current Liability	0.00	
◈ 30000 · Opening Balance Equity		Equity	12,815.02	
◈ 30800 · Owners Draw		Equity	0.00	
◈ 32000 · Owners Equity		Equity		
◈ 42700 · Photography Income		Income		
◈ 43200 · Design Income		Income		

The Chart of Accounts window displays all accounts for a company. It shows balances for all balance sheet accounts but not for income, cost of goods sold, and expense accounts. Accounts are listed alphabetically by type (unless you manually rearrange them). The highlighted account (Checking here) will be affected if you issue any command.

Creating and Editing Accounts

You have already learned the basics regarding creating and editing accounts in the Chart of Accounts. In this chapter, you will look specifically at the basic accounts used in banking: Bank and Credit Card. Remember that you will use the same editing techniques used in a word-processing program to edit account information.

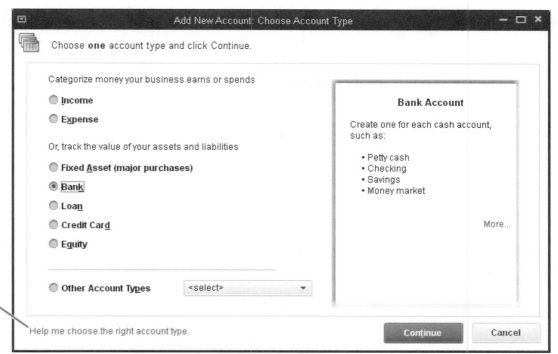

You can use this link to launch a window to assist you in choosing the correct type of account to create.

The Add New Account window will help to ensure that you choose the correct type of account when creating a new one. Notice how, when an account type is selected on the left, you see a description of how it is used on the right to assist you in choosing the correct type.

Tab: Getting Set Up
Topic: Add your bank accounts

Working with an Account Register

Each balance sheet account (except for Retained Earnings) has its own register, which is a record of all transactions pertaining to the account. A QuickBooks register looks like the check register you may already keep for your personal checking account. The running balance automatically recalculates as you record each new transaction.

When you double-click within a transaction in a register, QuickBooks takes you to the source of the transaction (similar to the QuickZoom feature). For instance, if you double-click the transaction for Handyman by the Bay in the following illustration, QuickBooks opens the Bill Payments (Check) - Checking window with all information for the transaction displayed.

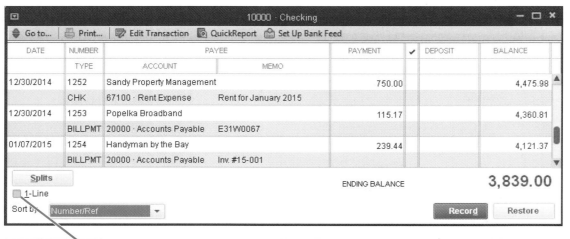

Notice that by default each transaction in the register includes two lines. The header at the top consists of two lines and describes what is found in each field.

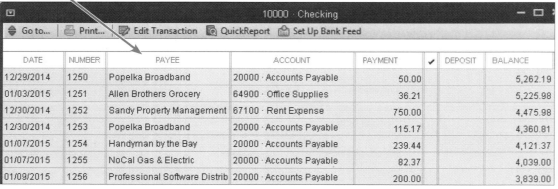

If you choose the 1-Line option, your register will be displayed in a more condensed fashion, and you will not have a Memo field available to you.

DEVELOP YOUR SKILLS 5-1

Work with Banking Accounts

In this exercise, you will help Allison to work with banking accounts and view a register. The first step is to open QuickBooks, and then either open a company file or restore a portable company file.

1. Start **QuickBooks 2014**.

   If you downloaded the student exercise files in the portable company file *format, follow Option 1 below. If you downloaded the files in the* company file *format, follow Option 2 below.*

Option 1: Restore a Portable Company File

2. Choose **File→Open or Restore Company**.

3. Restore the **DYS_Chapter05 (Portable)** portable file for this chapter from your file storage location, placing your last name and first initial at the end of the filename (e.g., DYS_Chapter05_FoxA).

   It may take a few moments for the portable company file to open. Once it does, continue with step 4.

Option 2: Open a Company File

2. Choose **File→Open or Restore Company**, ensure that **Open a regular company file** is selected, and then open the **DYS_Chapter05** company file from your file storage location. *The QuickBooks company file will open.*

3. Click **OK** to close the QuickBooks Information window. If necessary, click **No** in the Set Up External Accountant User window.

Edit an Existing Account

4. Click the **Chart of Accounts** task icon in the Company area of the Home page.

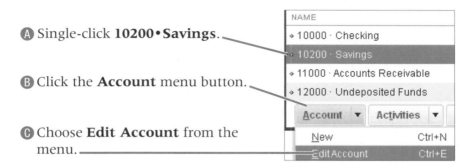

Ⓐ Single-click **10200•Savings**.

Ⓑ Click the **Account** menu button.

Ⓒ Choose **Edit Account** from the menu.

5. Follow these steps to edit the account:

Ⓓ Click in the **Bank Acct No** field and type **22222-55555**.

Ⓔ Tap **Tab**, and then type **599222043**.

Ⓕ Click **Save & Close**.

Create a New Account

You will now create a new credit card account that will be used later in this chapter. The Chart of Accounts window should still be open. If it isn't, choose Lists→Chart of Accounts.

6. Click the **Account** menu button, and then choose **New**.

7. Follow these steps to create the new credit card account:

Ⓐ Click to choose the **Credit Card** type.

Ⓑ Click **Continue**.

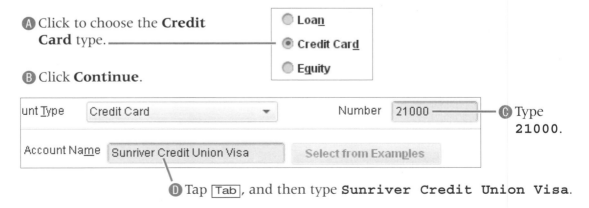

Ⓒ Type **21000**.

Ⓓ Tap **Tab**, and then type **Sunriver Credit Union Visa**.

8. Click **Save & Close**; click **No** in the Set Up Online Services window.

Open and View a Register

FROM THE KEYBOARD
Ctrl + r to open a register

9. Double-click **10000•Checking** in the Chart of Accounts window, scrolling up if necessary.

10. Scroll up, and then double-click anywhere within the two lines of the **1/7/2015 Handyman by the Bay** transaction.

DATE	NUMBER	PAYEE		PAYMENT	✔	DEPOSIT	BALANCE
	TYPE	ACCOUNT	MEMO				
12/30/2014	1253	Popelka Broadband		115.17			4,360.81
	BILLPMT	20000 · Accounts Payable	F31W0067				
01/07/2015	1254	Handyman by the Bay		239.44			4,121.37
	BILLPMT	20000 · Accounts Payable	Inv. #15-001				

QuickBooks will take you to the Bill Payments (Check) – Checking window.

11. Choose **Window→Close All**.

All QuickBooks windows will close.

Making Deposits

If you have utilized the Undeposited Funds account (as you did in Chapter 3, Working with Customers), you will need to take one more step to move your payments to your bank account. This step is accomplished through the Make Deposits window. The Make Deposits window can also be used when you make a sale and do not need a sales receipt, or when you want to deposit a lump sum that will credit an income account and debit your bank account.

Reviewing the Undeposited Funds Account

In Chapter 3, Working with Customers, you learned that funds received through the Receive Payments and Enter Sales Receipts windows are deposited into the Undeposited Funds account by default. Think of it as a "holding tank" that stores all of the funds you have collected together until you are ready to make a deposit. In this section, you will learn how to empty the Undeposited Funds account.

If you have payments sitting in your Undeposited Funds account and you click the Record Deposits task icon on the Home page, you will get the Payments to Deposit window. Here you can choose which payments you wish to deposit.

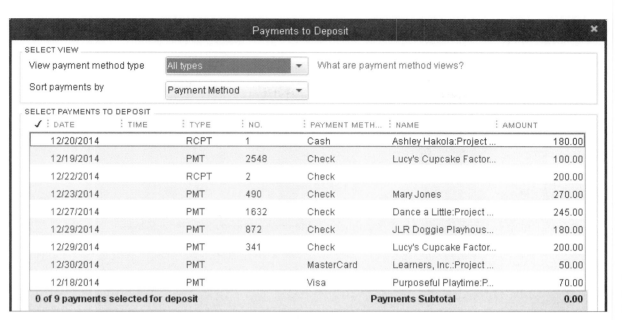

The Payments to Deposit window

TIP You can always click OK if you are not ready to deposit the payments shown in the Payments to Deposit window yet still need to work with the Make Deposits window.

By clicking this drop-down arrow, you can select any bank account that you have set up in QuickBooks.

The Memo fields are optional, but keep in mind that you can display your memos on reports.

If you wish to keep cash back from the deposit, you can indicate that here. You will learn about petty cash in Chapter 7, Working with Balance Sheet Accounts and Budgets.

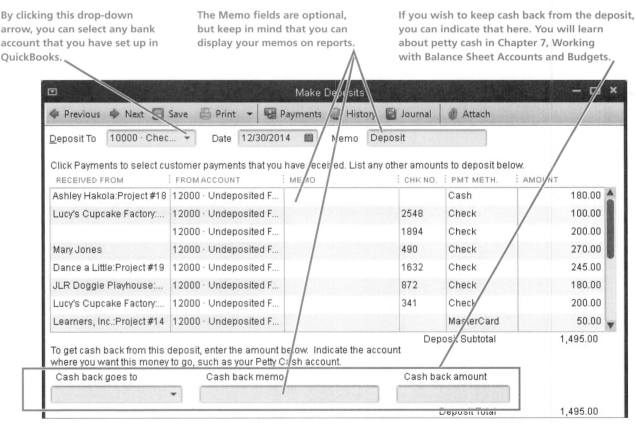

The Make Deposits window. You can click the Print button to print a detailed report of your deposits, including deposit slips if you choose to purchase and use them.

If you make deposits from your Undeposited Funds account, the following accounting will occur behind the scenes.

10000-Checking		12000-Undeposited Funds	
1,495.00			1,495.00

If you use the Make Deposits window to record sales, the accounting involved is as follows.

10000-Checking		43200-Design Income	
200.00			200.00

QUICK REFERENCE	MAKING DEPOSITS
Task	**Procedure**
Make a deposit from the Undeposited Funds account	■ Choose Banking→Make Deposits. ■ Choose the payment(s) you wish to deposit; click OK. ■ Choose the correct bank account and date for the deposit. ■ Click Save & Close or Save & New.
Make a deposit directly to a bank account	■ Choose Banking→Make Deposits; click OK if the Payments to Deposit window appears. ■ Choose the correct bank account and date for the deposit. ■ Enter all of the deposit information including the customer (if desired), account, payment method, and amount. ■ Click Save & Close or Save & New.

DEVELOP YOUR SKILLS 5-2

Use the Make Deposits Window

In this exercise, you will work with the Make Deposits window to deposit funds from the Undeposited Funds account and to make a deposit without a sales form.

1. Click the **Home** button on the Icon Bar.

2. Click the **Record Deposits** task icon in the Banking area of the Home page.

3. Click the **Select All** button; QuickBooks will place a checkmark to the left of all nine payments waiting to be deposited.

Notice that after you click the Select All button, it is grayed out. It is no longer a valid selection since all payments are already selected.

4. Click **OK** to accept the payments for deposit and move on to the Make Deposits window.

5. Click the drop-down arrow for the **Deposit To** field, and then choose **10000•Checking**; click **OK** in the Setting Default Accounts window, if necessary.

6. Tap Tab, and then type **123014** as the date.

7. Click the **Save & New** button to make the deposit to your Checking account. Leave the Make Deposits window open for the next step.

BTS BRIEF

10000•Checking DR 1,495.00; 12000•Undeposited Funds CR <1,495.00>

Your insertion point should be in the Deposit To field of a clear Make Deposits window. If it's not, choose Banking→Make Deposits.

Make a Deposit Without Specifying a Customer

Guy and Allison worked at a Quick Sketch fundraiser where people could meet with a graphic artist for 15 minutes to describe a need they have for their organization and for $15 receive a sketch and description of a possible solution to their stated need. Average Guy Designs made $5 from each of the quick consultations. Since there were multiple customers whom Guy does not want to track individually, Allison will make a deposit to Checking, directly crediting Design Income.

8. Tap Tab to move to the Date field.

9. Follow these steps to complete the deposit:

Ⓐ Tap ⊞ until the date reads **01/03/2015**.

Ⓑ Tap [Tab], and then type **Quick Sketch Event**.

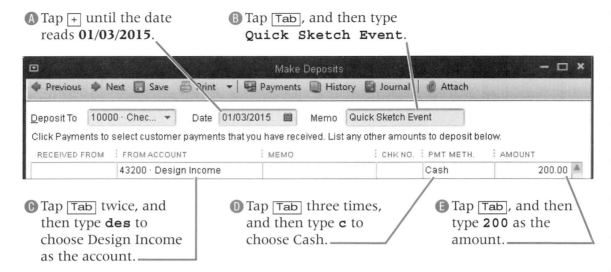

Ⓒ Tap [Tab] twice, and then type **des** to choose Design Income as the account.

Ⓓ Tap [Tab] three times, and then type **c** to choose Cash.

Ⓔ Tap [Tab], and then type **200** as the amount.

Note that you don't fill in an item in this form, but you do fill in the account. Remember that an item is used to direct funds to the underlying account. You cannot leave the From Account field blank because you must specify the account that will be credited since you will be debiting a bank account with the deposit.

BTS BRIEF

10000•Checking DR 200.00; **48800•Design Income CR <200.00>**

10. Click **Save & Close**; your deposit will be recorded, and the window will close.

Moving Funds Between Accounts

Most people have transferred money between their bank accounts. QuickBooks has a feature that allows you to record this transfer. If you use online banking, you may even be able to set QuickBooks to perform the transfer for you when you go online (if your financial institution allows it).

Since you are transferring funds between two asset accounts, you want to debit the account that is increasing and credit the account that is decreasing. Look at the following T-accounts to visualize this transaction.

FLASHBACK TO GAAP: MONETARY UNIT

Remember that it is assumed a stable currency is going to be the unit of record.

BEHIND THE SCENES

In this illustration, you are transferring funds from the Checking account to the Savings account.

10200-Savings		10000-Checking	
200.00			200.00

QUICK REFERENCE	TRANSFERRING FUNDS BETWEEN ACCOUNTS
Task	**Procedure**
Transfer funds	■ Choose Banking→Transfer Funds.
	■ Choose the account from which you wish to draw the funds.
	■ Choose the account to which you wish to send the funds.
	■ Type the amount to be transferred and, if you wish, a memo.
	■ Click Save & Close or Save & New to record the transfer.

DEVELOP YOUR SKILLS 5-3
Move Funds Between Accounts

In this exercise, Allison will transfer funds between the Checking and Savings accounts.

1. Choose **Banking→Transfer Funds**.

2. Follow these steps to complete the funds transfer:

Ⓐ Type **010315**. Ⓑ Click to choose **10000•Checking**.

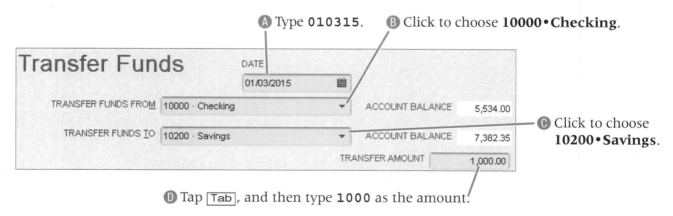

Ⓒ Click to choose **10200•Savings**.

Ⓓ Tap ⎡Tab⎤, and then type **1000** as the amount.

Notice that QuickBooks displays the account balances of the accounts involved in the transfer so you can verify sufficient funds are available.

BTS BRIEF

10200•Savings DR 1,000.00; **10000•Checking CR <1,000.00>**

3. Click **Save & Close** to record the transaction.

Managing Credit and Debit Card Transactions

Credit cards give business owners an easy way to track their expenses. QuickBooks allows you to track credit card transactions just as you track checking and savings account transactions. You can set up as many credit card accounts as you need and simply choose the account you want to work with in the Enter Credit Card Charges window.

If you use your personal credit cards occasionally for business purposes, you should *not* enter them in QuickBooks as business credit cards. Only create accounts for business credit cards.

Credit card transactions are classified as either a charge (when you make a purchase) or a credit (when you make a return). As you will use the same form for both types, you need to choose the correct type when entering transactions.

You can choose from all of your credit card accounts.

You choose to record a purchase or a refund. Purchase/Charge is selected by default when you open the window.

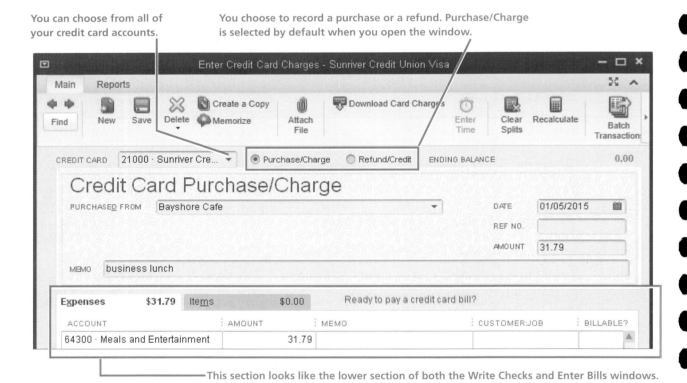

This section looks like the lower section of both the Write Checks and Enter Bills windows.

Type of Account and Normal Balance

A credit card is a liability, so its normal balance is a credit. This means you credit the account when you make a purchase (a "charge") and debit the account when you make a payment (a "credit").

The term credit is a bit confusing at this point, as you will debit your credit card account if you enter a "credit" transaction. However, if you think of it from the perspective of the merchant, it makes perfect sense!

Pay a Bill with a Credit Card

If you have entered a bill into QuickBooks, you do have the option to pay it with a credit card. Make sure that you use the Pay Bills window to accomplish the task, though, as you must remove the amount from Accounts Payable!

If you use a credit card to pay a bill that you entered through the QuickBooks Enter Bills window, you must use the Pay Bills window when you pay it—or expenses and Accounts Payable will be overstated!

Dealing with Debit Card Transactions

When you make a purchase or pay a bill with a debit card, funds are taken directly from your checking account, which is different from what occurs for credit card purchases. Use the Write Checks window to handle debit card transactions. If you use the Enter/Pay Bills windows in QuickBooks, you can continue to use them when working with debit card purchases. This means that if you have entered a bill in QuickBooks and then choose to use a debit card to pay it, you must enter that payment through the Pay Bills window. Otherwise, the expenses will be overstated, and you will leave the bill hanging out in Accounts Payable.

When you enter a debit card transaction in the Write Checks window, indicate it by entering a code such as "DB" in the No. field.

Other Types of Transactions Affecting the Checking Account

In addition to debit card transactions, you may have other ones that draw funds from the checking account as well. For instance, ATM cards and a service such as PayPal™ can withdraw funds directly from your bank account. All of these transactions will be entered using the Write Checks window; you just need to create common codes that will be used in the No. field to record each type of transaction. Common codes include DB for debit card, ATM for an ATM card transaction, and PP for a PayPal payment. You do not have to use the codes suggested here; however, you should choose one code for each type of transaction and stick with it!

BEHIND THE SCENES

A purchase credits the credit card account, as shown here.

64900-Office Supplies	64300-Meals and Entertaintment	21000-Sunriver CU Visa
57.84	31.25	89.09

A payment or refund debits the credit card account, as shown here.

64900-Office Supplies	21000-Sunriver CU Visa
10.46	10.46

When you use a credit card to pay a bill, the following occurs behind the scenes for you.

20000-Accounts Payable	21000-Sunriver CU Visa
363.27	363.27

Using a debit card to make the same bill payment as above looks like the following behind the scenes.

20000-Accounts Payable	10000-Checking
363.27	363.27

When you use a debit card to purchase office supplies, the following occurs behind the scenes for you.

64900-Office Supplies	10000-Checking
363.27	363.27

QUICK REFERENCE	RECORDING CREDIT AND DEBIT CARD TRANSACTIONS
Task	**Procedure**
Record a credit card transaction	▪ Choose Banking→Enter Credit Card Charges. ▪ Choose the account to record a purchase or refund to. ▪ Enter the transaction information. ▪ Click Save & Close or Save & New.
Record a debit card transaction	▪ Choose Banking→Write Checks. ▪ Select the bank account to which the debit card is linked. ▪ Enter "DB" or the code you have chosen in the No. field. ▪ Enter information into the payee, amount, and memo fields. ▪ Ensure the proper expense/asset accounts are indicated on the Expense and/or Item tab. ▪ Click Save & Close or Save & New.
Record a debit card transaction for a bill already entered into Accounts Payable	▪ Choose Vendors→Pay Bills. ▪ Select the bill you wish to pay by debit card. ▪ Set the date and account to which the debit card is linked. ▪ Choose to Assign check number in the Payment Method area; click Pay Selected Bills. ▪ Type your code in the Assign Check Numbers window; click OK. ▪ Click Done in the Payment Summary window.

Manage Credit Card Transactions

Guy needs to purchase some supplies for the office. He has also decided to purchase refreshments for clients who stop in. In this exercise, you will help Allison to enter a credit card purchase and a return, as well as pay a bill with a credit card.

1. Click the **Enter Credit Card Charges** task icon in the Banking area of the Home page.

    Since you have only one credit card set up at this time, the information will fill in to the Credit Card field. If you had multiple cards, you would need to choose the appropriate one before entering other information.

Enter Credit Card Charges

2. Follow these steps to record the credit card charge:

Ⓐ Tap Tab three times, and then type **a**.

Ⓑ Tap Tab, and then type **010315**.

Ⓒ Tap Tab twice, and then type **89.09**.

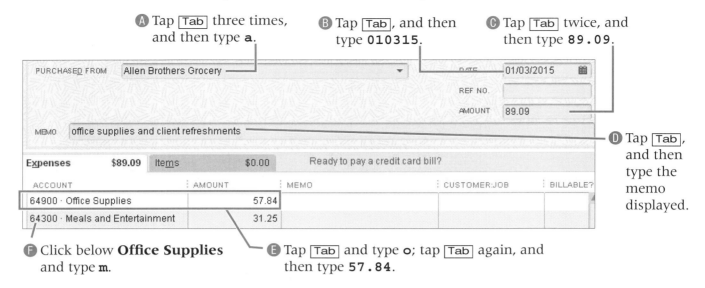

PURCHASED FROM Allen Brothers Grocery   DATE 01/03/2015

REF NO.

AMOUNT 89.09

MEMO office supplies and client refreshments

Ⓓ Tap Tab, and then type the memo displayed.

Expenses	$89.09	Items	$0.00	Ready to pay a credit card bill?		
ACCOUNT		AMOUNT	MEMO		CUSTOMER:JOB	BILLABLE?
64900 · Office Supplies		57.84				
64300 · Meals and Entertainment		31.25				

Ⓕ Click below **Office Supplies** and type **m**.

Ⓔ Tap Tab and type **o**; tap Tab again, and then type **57.84**.

The amount for the Meals and Entertainment split will automatically fill in for you.

BTS BRIEF

64900•Office Supplies DR 57.84; 64300•Meals and Entertainment DR 31.25; **21000•Sunriver Credit Union Visa CR <89.09>**

3. Click the **Save & New** button.

Record a Credit Card Return

In the next transaction, Guy returns a calculator he purchased at Allen Brothers Grocery, as he realized he didn't need it once he got back to the office.

4. Follow these steps to record the credit card refund:

Ⓐ Click to choose the **Refund/Credit** option.

Ⓑ Tap Tab, and then type **a**.

Ⓒ Tap Tab, and then use + to change the date to **1/6/15**.

Ⓓ Tap Tab twice, and then type **10.46**.

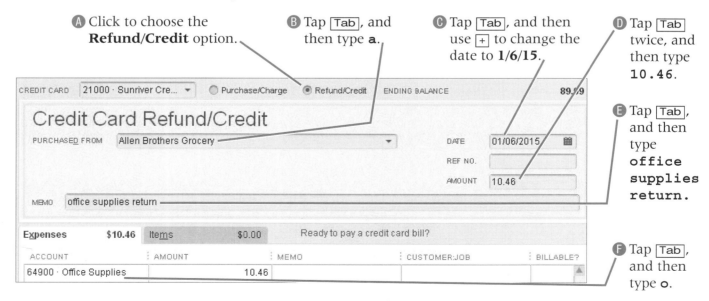

CREDIT CARD 21000 · Sunriver Cre... ○ Purchase/Charge ● Refund/Credit ENDING BALANCE 89.09

Credit Card Refund/Credit

PURCHASED FROM Allen Brothers Grocery   DATE 01/06/2015

REF NO.

AMOUNT 10.46

MEMO office supplies return

Ⓔ Tap Tab, and then type **office supplies return**.

Expenses	$10.46	Items	$0.00	Ready to pay a credit card bill?		
ACCOUNT		AMOUNT	MEMO		CUSTOMER:JOB	BILLABLE?
64900 · Office Supplies		10.46				

Ⓕ Tap Tab, and then type **o**.

5. Click the **Save & Close** button.

   QuickBooks records the transaction and closes the Enter Credit Card Charges window.

Pay a Bill with a Debit Card

You can record a bill paid by debit card in QuickBooks, although you must use the Pay Bills window in order to properly affect Accounts Payable.

6. Click the **Pay Bills** task icon in the Vendors area of the Home page.

Pay Bills

7. Follow these steps to pay a bill with a debit card:

Ⓐ Click to place a checkmark in this box.

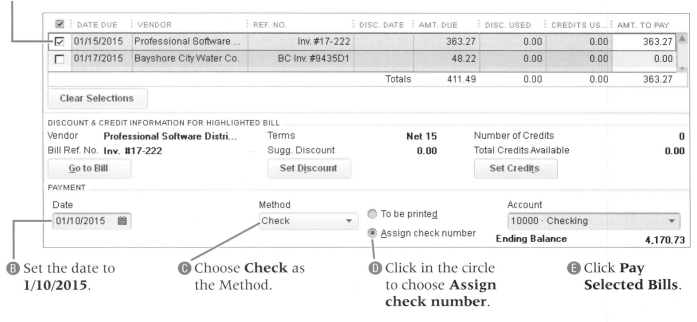

	DATE DUE	VENDOR	REF. NO.	DISC. DATE	AMT. DUE	DISC. USED	CREDITS US...	AMT. TO PAY
☑	01/15/2015	Professional Software ...	Inv. #17-222		363.27	0.00	0.00	363.27
☐	01/17/2015	Bayshore City Water Co.	BC Inv. #9435D1		48.22	0.00	0.00	0.00
				Totals	411.49	0.00	0.00	363.27

Clear Selections

DISCOUNT & CREDIT INFORMATION FOR HIGHLIGHTED BILL

Vendor	**Professional Software Distri...**	Terms	**Net 15**	Number of Credits	**0**
Bill Ref. No.	**Inv. #17-222**	Sugg. Discount	**0.00**	Total Credits Available	**0.00**

Go to Bill   **Set Discount**   **Set Credits**

PAYMENT

Date
01/10/2015 📅

Method
Check ▾

○ To be printed
◉ Assign check number

Account
10000 · Checking ▾

Ending Balance   4,170.73

Ⓑ Set the date to **1/10/2015**.

Ⓒ Choose **Check** as the Method.

Ⓓ Click in the circle to choose **Assign check number**.

Ⓔ Click **Pay Selected Bills**.

Ⓕ Click in the **Check No.** column, and then type **DB**.

	CHECK NO.	DATE	PAYEE	AMOUNT
◉ Let me assign the check numbers below.				
	DB	01/10/2015	Professional Software Distributors	363.27

Ⓖ Click **OK**.

When you pay a bill with a debit card, you are affecting the Checking account, so you will need to assign the transaction the "check number" that you use for all debit card transactions. In the scenario above, that would be "DB."

8. Click **Done** in the Payment Summary window.

   QuickBooks records the bill payment, debiting Accounts Payable and crediting Checking for you.

Dealing with Bounced Checks

Unfortunately, almost all business owners must deal with customers whose checks are returned for non-sufficient funds (NSF) at some time or another. Many people call these "bounced check," and this is the term also used in QuickBooks. This book uses the terms *NSF* and *bounced check*, though the latter is used more often because it is the term used in QuickBooks.

With the new Bounced Check feature, you can easily account for NSF checks received from invoiced customers.

With the 2014 version, QuickBooks makes it very easy to account for bounced checks right from the Receive Payments window. However, if you receive a bounced check that was originally received on a sales receipt or directly through a deposit, you will need to account for it using the alternate method described in the following Quick Reference tables.

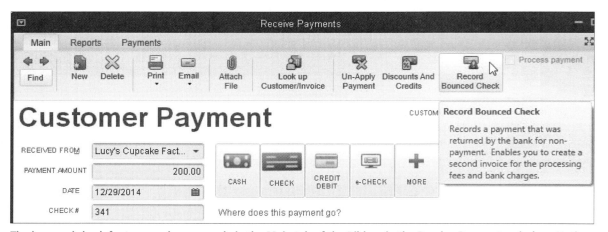

The bounced check feature can be accessed via the Main tab of the Ribbon in the Receive Payments window. Notice the ToolTip that appears when you place your mouse pointer over the Record Bounced Check button.

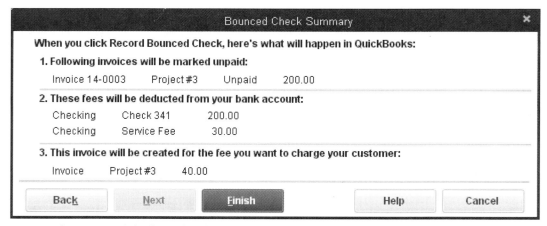

Once you have entered the fees related to the bounced check, you will see a Bounced Check Summary.

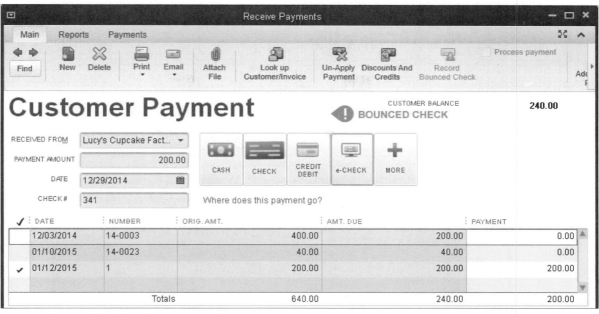

Once the bounced check has been entered for a customer payment, you will see the Bounced Check stamp displayed.

A bounced check associated with a sales receipt or a straight deposit can be dealt with by generating a statement for the customer.

The bank may charge you a lesser amount than you choose to pass on to the customer for a bounced check.

BEHIND THE SCENES

When you deal with a returned check, you will affect multiple accounts behind the scenes.

11000-Accounts Receivable		10000-Checking	
200.00			200.00
40.00			30.00

60400-Bank Service Charges		48910-Returned Check Charges	
30.00			40.00

QUICK REFERENCE	DEALING WITH BOUNCED CHECKS
Task	**Procedure**
Process a bounced check associated with an invoice	■ Open the Receive Payments window and locate the returned check. ■ Click the Record Bounced Check button. ■ Set the fees for the bounced check; click Next and then Finish.
Account for a bounced check received on a sales receipt or through the Make Deposit window	■ Create an Other Charge item for the service charge, directing it to the Other Income account. ■ Record the bank's fee in your bank account register (Bank Service Charges as account). ■ Record the check in your bank account register (customer/job as payee; Accounts Receivable as account). ■ Enter a statement charge for the customer's fee. ■ Send the customer a statement that shows the bounced check and fee.

Handle a Bounced Check

In this exercise, you will account for a check that was returned to Average Guy Designs for non-sufficient funds.

1. Click the **Receive Payments** task icon in the Customers area of the Home page.

Receive Payments

2. Click the **Previous** button two times until the payment received on check #341 from **Lucy's Cupcake Factory** is displayed.

Main

Find

3. Click the **Record Bounced Check** button on the Main tab of the Ribbon.

Record Bounced Check

4. Follow these steps to set the fees for the bounced check:

Ⓐ Type **30** as the **Bank Fee**. Ⓑ Tap Tab, and then type **011215**.

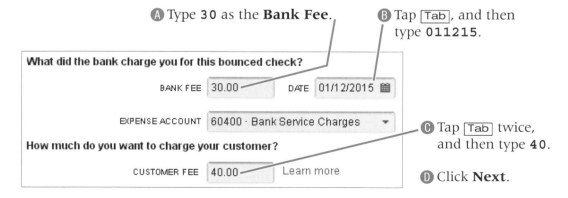

What did the bank charge you for this bounced check?

BANK FEE 30.00 DATE 01/12/2015

EXPENSE ACCOUNT 60400 · Bank Service Charges

How much do you want to charge your customer?

CUSTOMER FEE 40.00 Learn more

Ⓒ Tap Tab twice, and then type **40**.

Ⓓ Click **Next**.

A Bounced Check Summary will be displayed.

5. Click **Finish**.

The Receive Payments window will again be displayed and you will see that the check has been marked as bounced and a new invoice has been created to account for the bounced check.

BTS BRIEF

11000•Accounts Receivable DR 240.00; 60400•Bank Service Charges DR 30.00; 10000•Checking CR <230.00>; 48910•Returned Check Charges CR <40.00>

Reconciling Accounts

It is important to make sure that your account records in QuickBooks match those of the bank. The process of matching your accounts to the bank statements you receive is called reconciliation.

Clicking here will allow you to focus on transactions associated with the statement you are reconciling.

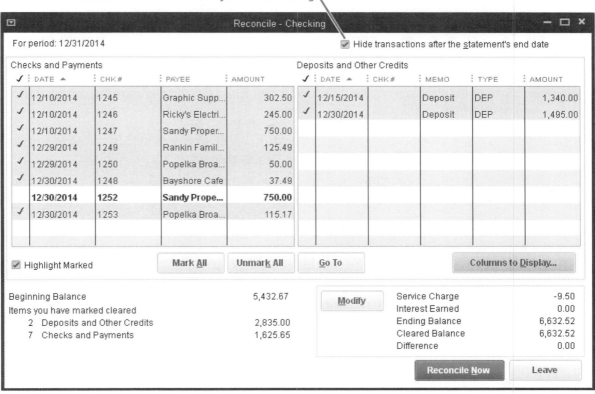

QuickBooks bank account reconciliation window

QuickBooks' Reconciliation Features

You should be aware of some important reconciliation features in QuickBooks. You can save your reconciliation reports in PDF so they are ready to send via email and are viewable with the free Adobe Reader program (also known as Acrobat Reader). In QuickBooks Pro, when you reconcile a new statement, the reconciliation report replaces the prior report with the new month's information. You should save each report as a PDF file to a storage location such as your hard drive, a cloud service, or a network drive if you are using the Pro edition. In QuickBooks Premier and Enterprise editions, QuickBooks stores all reconciliation reports as PDF files for you, and you can access them through QuickBooks at any time.

Locating Discrepancies

QuickBooks also provides a feature that helps you to locate discrepancies if there is a difference in balances during the reconciliation process. You can run a Reconciliation Discrepancy Report that lists transactions affecting the reconciliation balance. The types of transactions that can affect the balance are:

- Deleted transactions
- A change to a previously cleared amount
- Transactions that were manually un-cleared in the register
- Transactions in which the date was changed to a different statement period

When Your Accounts Don't Match

It is important to take the time when performing reconciliations to ensure there are no errors. As you clear each transaction, make sure the amounts are exactly the same. It is very frustrating when you get to the end of the transactions, and they don't balance.

Once you have cleared transactions through the reconciliation process, it is important to *not* change them. Changes may alter your starting balance for the next reconciliation. If you find yourself in such a situation, you can run a Reconciliation Discrepancy report to find the problem(s).

Problem Resolution Process

If you do find yourself in the unfavorable situation of finishing your reconciliation without balancing, consider the following suggestions:

- Look for a transaction that is exactly the same amount as the difference and ensure whether or not it should be cleared.
- Determine whether you are missing a deposit or a payment by looking at the totals of each on the bank statement and the QuickBooks reconciliation window.
- Compare the number of transactions on the bank statement to the number of cleared transactions in QuickBooks.
- Verify the individual amount of each transaction on the bank statement and compare it to the amounts you have in QuickBooks.
- Determine whether it is a bank error (the bank may have recorded a transaction for the wrong amount).
- If it is a bank error, you can create an adjustment transaction in QuickBooks, notify the bank, and then reverse the adjustment transaction after the bank corrects the error.
- Run a Reconciliation Discrepancy report to see if any changes were made to previously cleared transactions. If changes were made to previously cleared transactions, undo the last reconciliation and redo it.

Reconciling Credit Cards

You can reconcile your credit cards the same way as you reconcile your bank account, although you access the command through the Chart of Accounts.

Once you have reconciled the credit card, you have the option to pay any amount due. You can choose to either write a check or enter a bill for the payment. QuickBooks takes the balance due on the credit card and fills it in to either the Enter Bills or the Write Checks window. If you don't plan to pay the entire amount owed, you can change the amount manually. You will reconcile the credit card in the "Tackle the Tasks" section at the end of the chapter.

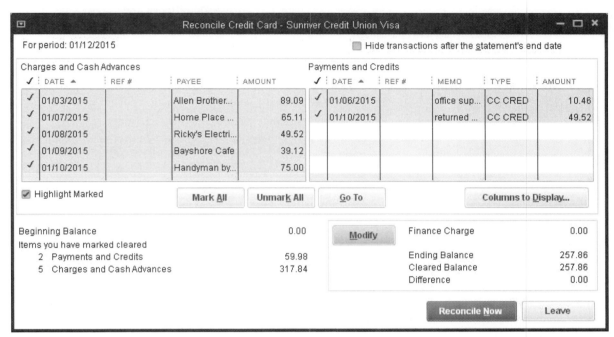

You can access the command to reconcile a credit card through the Chart of Accounts, rather than the Banking option on the menu bar. The process from there looks the same as it does when you reconcile a bank account.

After you complete the reconciliation of a credit card, you will be prompted to either write a check or enter a bill for the balance due, as displayed in the illustration.

FLASHBACK TO GAAP: ASSUMPTION OF A GOING CONCERN

Remember that it is assumed that the business will be in operation indefinitely.

QUICK REFERENCE	RECONCILING BANK AND CREDIT CARD ACCOUNTS
Task	**Procedure**
Reconcile a bank account	▪ Choose Banking→Reconcile.
	▪ Choose the account you wish to reconcile; enter the statement date and ending balance.
	▪ Enter any service or finance charges; click Continue.
	▪ Compare the QuickBooks transactions to the bank statement; mark off cleared transactions.
	▪ Once the difference between QuickBooks and the bank statement is zero, click Reconcile Now.
Reconcile a credit card	▪ Choose Lists→Chart of Accounts; single-click the desired credit card account.
	▪ Click the Activities button at the bottom of the window; choose Reconcile Credit Card.
	▪ Choose the account; enter the statement date and ending balance.
	▪ Enter any service or finance charges; click Continue.
	▪ Compare the QuickBooks transactions to the bank statement; mark off cleared transactions.
	▪ Once the difference between QuickBooks and the bank statement is zero, click Reconcile Now.

DEVELOP YOUR SKILLS 5-6
Reconcile the Checking Account

In this exercise, you will reconcile the checking account in QuickBooks. First, you will help Allison prepare to reconcile the checking account for Average Guy Designs. The bank statement for this account that you will use to complete the reconciliation is displayed here.

Before You Begin: You will be working with a bank statement. You can use the illustration shown, or you can print Develop Your Skills 5-6 from your file storage location.

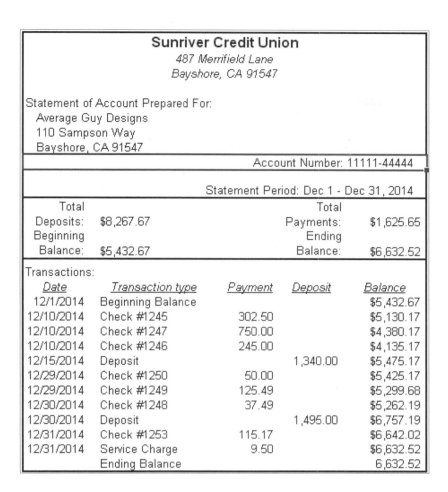

Sunriver Credit Union
487 Merrifield Lane
Bayshore, CA 91547

Statement of Account Prepared For:
Average Guy Designs
110 Sampson Way
Bayshore, CA 91547

Account Number: 11111-44444

Statement Period: Dec 1 - Dec 31, 2014

| Total Deposits: | $8,267.67 | Total Payments: | $1,625.65 |
| Beginning Balance: | $5,432.67 | Ending Balance: | $6,632.52 |

Transactions:

Date	Transaction type	Payment	Deposit	Balance
12/1/2014	Beginning Balance			$5,432.67
12/10/2014	Check #1245	302.50		$5,130.17
12/10/2014	Check #1247	750.00		$4,380.17
12/10/2014	Check #1246	245.00		$4,135.17
12/15/2014	Deposit		1,340.00	$5,475.17
12/29/2014	Check #1250	50.00		$5,425.17
12/29/2014	Check #1249	125.49		$5,299.68
12/30/2014	Check #1248	37.49		$5,262.19
12/30/2014	Deposit		1,495.00	$6,757.19
12/31/2014	Check #1253	115.17		$6,642.02
12/31/2014	Service Charge	9.50		$6,632.52
	Ending Balance			6,632.52

1. Click the **Reconcile** task icon in the Banking area of the Home page.
   QuickBooks displays the Begin Reconciliation window.

Reconcile

2. Using the illustration of the bank statement provided or the one you printed, follow these steps to prepare for reconciliation:

   Ⓐ Ensure that **10000•Checking** is the account displayed.

   Ⓑ Tap Tab, and then type **123114**.

   Ⓒ Tap Tab, and then type **6632.52**.

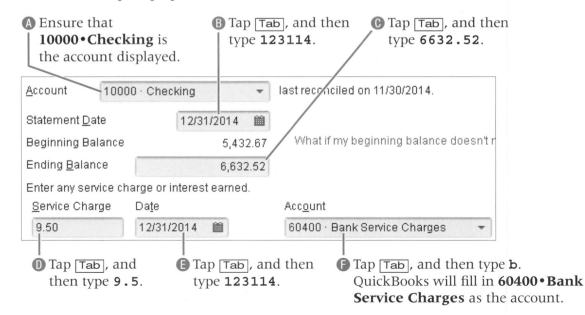

Account	10000 · Checking ▼	last reconciled on 11/30/2014.
Statement Date	12/31/2014 📅	
Beginning Balance	5,432.67	What if my beginning balance doesn't r
Ending Balance	6,632.52	

Enter any service charge or interest earned.

| Service Charge | Date | Account |
| 9.50 | 12/31/2014 📅 | 60400 · Bank Service Charges ▼ |

   Ⓓ Tap Tab, and then type **9.5**.

   Ⓔ Tap Tab, and then type **123114**.

   Ⓕ Tap Tab, and then type **b**. QuickBooks will fill in **60400•Bank Service Charges** as the account.

There will be a difference in the beginning balance between this window and the bank statement because this is the first reconciliation performed since you started your QuickBooks company file.

3. Click **Continue** to move to the Reconciliation-Checking window.

   The Reconciliation-Checking window shows all transactions waiting to be cleared.

Reconcile a Checking Account

Now that you have finished the prep work, it is time to begin the actual reconciliation.

4. Click to place a checkmark to hide all transactions after the statement's end date.

5. Click in the **Checkmark** column to the left of each transaction in QuickBooks that is also on the bank checking statement displayed above step 1.

   When you are finished, your Reconciliation-Checking window should match the following illustration.

For period: 12/31/2014   ☑ Hide transactions after the statement's end date

Checks and Payments | | | | Deposits and Other Credits | | | | |
✓	DATE ▲	CHK #	PAYEE	AMOUNT	✓	DATE ▲	CHK #	MEMO	TYPE	AMOUNT
✓	12/10/2014	1245	Graphic Supp...	302.50	✓	12/15/2014		Deposit	DEP	1,340.00
✓	12/10/2014	1246	Ricky's Electri...	245.00	✓	12/30/2014		Deposit	DEP	1,495.00
✓	12/10/2014	1247	Sandy Proper...	750.00						
✓	12/29/2014	1249	Rankin Famil...	125.49						
✓	12/29/2014	1250	Popelka Broa...	50.00						
✓	12/30/2014	1248	Bayshore Cafe	37.49						
	12/30/2014	**1252**	**Sandy Prope...**	**750.00**						
✓	12/30/2014	1253	Popelka Broa...	115.17						

6. Look at the **"Difference"** at the bottom right of the window to see if you have successfully reconciled your account.

   The goal when you perform a reconciliation is for the Difference to be 0.00. The Difference is calculated by determining the difference between the transactions on the bank statement and those that you have marked cleared in QuickBooks.

Beginning Balance	5,432.67			Service Charge	-9.50
Items you have marked cleared			**Modify**	Interest Earned	0.00
2 Deposits and Other Credits	2,835.00			Ending Balance	6,632.52
7 Checks and Payments	1,625.65			Cleared Balance	6,632.52
				Difference	(0.00)

7. Click the **Reconcile Now** button, and then click **OK** in the Information window.

   There is a pause as QuickBooks records the marked transactions as cleared.

8. Click **Close** to choose to not produce a report at this time.

   You will learn about reconciliation reports in the next section.

Dealing with Oops in Banking Transactions

It is inevitable that you will need to deal with either errors or modifications to transactions in QuickBooks. It is very important that you do this properly to ensure that everything behind the scenes is correct. You have already seen what errors dealing with customer- and vendor-transactions look like, so now we will look at possible errors when working with banking accounts.

Fixing Errors

The following table outlines an error related to the Chart of Accounts as well as an error that occurs when dealing with a debit card transaction incorrectly, the effects of the errors behind the scenes, and how to correct them.

COMMON ERRORS AND FIXES

Error	Effect Behind the Scenes	The Fix
The wrong account type was chosen when creating a new account in the Chart of Accounts	The types of accounts involved will determine what the damage will be behind the scenes (but there will be damage!)	Edit the account through the Chart of Accounts and choose the correct account type
A debit card transaction was entered in the Enter Credit Card Charges window	The wrong account is credited, and you will have an inflated amount displayed in Checking as well as the credit card account	Delete the credit card transaction and reenter it through a window that affects Checking

Correct Banking Errors

In this exercise, you will execute two tasks incorrectly and then fix them.

Do It the Wrong Way – Set the Account Type

The business has just received a Discover card that will be used for expenses. In this next example, you will set up the account incorrectly for the purpose of learning how to fix the error and do it correctly.

1. Choose **Lists→Chart of Accounts**.

2. Click the **Account** menu button, and then choose **New**.

3. Select **Expense** as the type of account, and then click **Continue**.

4. Type **62300** as the Number, tap ⎡Tab⎤, and then type **Discover Card** as the Account Name.

Essential Skills

5. Click **Save & Close**.

   No doubt you have already realized what the error is in this example! While you will be using the card to pay for expenses, you should not set it up as an expense account. This will have huge ramifications behind the scenes, so you need to fix it pronto!

Do It the Right Way – Set the Account Type

In order to fix the error of setting up an account as the wrong type, you need to open the Edit Account window. The Chart of Accounts should still be open from the last step.

6. Right-click **62300•Discover Card** in the Chart of Accounts window, and then choose **Edit Account** from the menu.

7. Follow these steps to fix the error:

   A Click the drop-down arrow, and then choose **Credit Card**.   **B** Tap Tab, and then type **23000**.

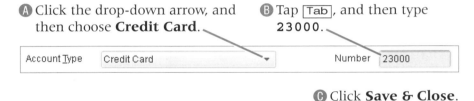

   C Click **Save & Close**.

   You must change the account number when you change the account type.

8. Close the **Chart of Accounts** window.

Do It the Wrong Way – Enter a Debit Card Transaction as a Credit Card

Allison has just received a receipt from Guy for graphic art supplies. He used his debit card, but you will enter it as a credit card transaction, incorrectly, for the purpose of learning how to fix the error and do it correctly.

9. Choose **Banking→Enter Credit Card Charges**; ensure **Sunriver Credit Union Visa** and **Purchase/Charge** are selected.

10. Follow these steps to enter the transaction:

Ⓐ Click the drop-down arrow and choose **Graphic Supply Shoppe**.

Ⓑ Tap `Tab`, and then type **122914**.

Ⓒ Tap `Tab` twice, and then type **164.50**.

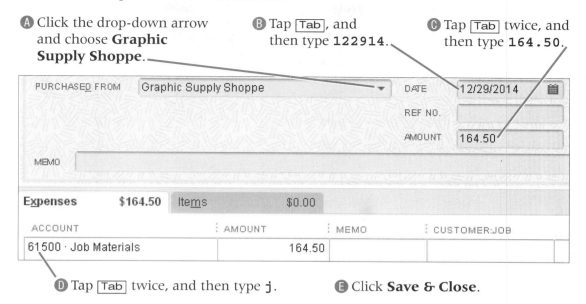

PURCHASED FROM	Graphic Supply Shoppe	DATE	12/29/2014
		REF NO.	
		AMOUNT	164.50
MEMO			

Expenses	$164.50	Items	$0.00		
ACCOUNT		AMOUNT	MEMO	CUSTOMER:JOB	
61500 · Job Materials		164.50			

Ⓓ Tap `Tab` twice, and then type **j**.

Ⓔ Click **Save & Close**.

Think about this transaction. What is wrong with it? By entering the debit card transaction in the Enter Credit Card Charges window, you have increased the balance in the credit card account and have not removed the funds from your Checking account.

BTS BRIEF

61500•Job Materials DR 164.50; **21000•Sun River Credit Union Visa CR <164.50>**

Do It the Right Way – Enter a Debit Card Transaction and Credit Checking

To fix the debit card transaction that was handled improperly, you must delete it and reenter the payment using the Write Checks window.

11. Choose **Banking→Enter Credit Card Charges**.

12. Click the **Previous** button until the transaction you just entered is displayed.

    You can look for a transaction by using the Previous and Next buttons, if you believe the transaction to be easy to locate. If not, use the Find or Search feature.

13. Choose **Edit→Delete Credit Card Charge**; click **OK** in the Delete Transaction window.

FROM THE KEYBOARD
`Ctrl`+`d` to delete the selected transaction

14. Close the **Enter Credit Card Charges** window.

15. Click the **Write Checks** task icon in the Customers area of the Home page.

Write Checks

16. Follow these steps to enter the debit card purchase correctly:

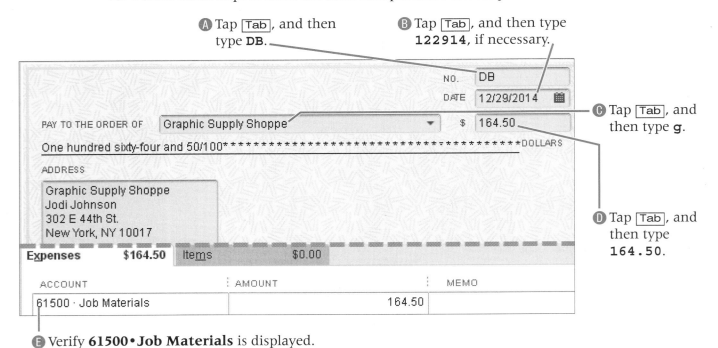

Ⓐ Tap [Tab], and then type **DB**.

Ⓑ Tap [Tab], and then type **122914**, if necessary.

Ⓒ Tap [Tab], and then type **g**.

Ⓓ Tap [Tab], and then type **164.50**.

Ⓔ Verify **61500•Job Materials** is displayed.

BTS BRIEF
21000•Sunriver Credit Union Visa DR 164.50; **61500•Job Materials CR <164.50>**
61500•Job Materials DR 164.50; **10000•Checking CR <164.50>**

17. Click **Save & Close**.

Before moving on, think about what you have just completed and make sure you understand the "why" behind it. You have ensured the balances in the Checking and credit cards accounts are now correct by recording the debit card purchase correctly.

Working with Banking and Balance Sheet Reports

In this section, you will learn about reports that can tell you stories about your banking activities in QuickBooks as well as those that display information about your balance sheet accounts (asset, liability, and equity). You will also have an opportunity to look at the snapshots available in QuickBooks. You can access snapshots relative to your payments, company, and customers.

Banking Reports

The QuickBooks banking feature comes with preset reports for you to use to get answers from your data. Banking reports deal with answers to questions such as:

- What are all of the transactions involving a specific payee?
- What checks have not cleared the bank as of the last bank statement?
- Which payments still need to be deposited?
- Where can I find a list of all transactions that affect my checking account?
- What changes in transactions may affect my next reconciliation?

Register QuickReports

Register QuickReports are run right from a register window. Once you have selected a transaction and clicked the QuickReport button, you will receive a report that shows all transactions for the payee of the selected transaction.

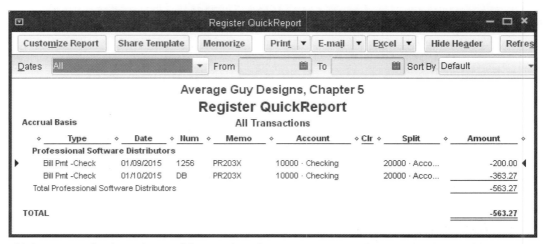

This is an example of a register QuickReport based on Average Guy Designs' transactions with Professional Software Distributors.

Reconciliation Reports

Reconciliation reports show transactions that have cleared as well as those that have yet to clear the bank. QuickBooks allows you to save reconciliation reports in a PDF format.

Average Guy Designs, Chapter 5
Reconciliation Summary
10000 · Checking, Period Ending 12/31/2014

	Dec 31, 14
Beginning Balance	5,432.67
Cleared Transactions	
Checks and Payments - 8 items	-1,635.15
Deposits and Credits - 2 items	2,835.00
Total Cleared Transactions	1,199.85
Cleared Balance	6,632.52
Uncleared Transactions	
Checks and Payments - 1 item	-750.00
Total Uncleared Transactions	-750.00
Register Balance as of 12/31/2014	5,882.52
New Transactions	
Checks and Payments - 8 items	-2,151.29
Deposits and Credits - 1 item	200.00
Total New Transactions	-1,951.29
Ending Balance	3,931.23

Take note of what a reconciliation report will display for you. In this example, you can see a Reconciliation Summary report, and you will produce a Reconciliation Detail report in the next exercise.

Alternatives to Printing Reports

Of course you can send any report to the printer. QuickBooks also gives you options for storing or working with a report:

- **Email:** QuickBooks can convert the report to PDF, which can be viewed with the free Adobe Reader program. This allows viewing of the report exactly as it would print even to those who do not have QuickBooks. When you choose to email a form or report to a customer, the form or report will be converted automatically to PDF for you.

- **Export:** QuickBooks can export the report to Microsoft Excel so you can use Excel's powerful spreadsheet features to work with your data. You will have an opportunity to work with QuickBooks reports in Excel in Chapter 10, Customizing and Integrating in QuickBooks.

Saving Reports and Forms as PDF

PDF copies of QuickBooks reports and forms make emailing forms and reports convenient for you. They are also a great way to create copies to save for your own records. You learned about printing a file to PDF in the How do I save as a PDF? section of Chapter 1 (page 12).

QUICK REFERENCE	PRODUCING BANKING REPORTS
Task	**Procedure**
Produce a register QuickReport	■ Open the register from which you wish to create the report. ■ Click within the transaction on which you wish to base the report. ■ Click QuickReport on the register toolbar.
Produce a reconciliation report	■ Choose Reports→Banking→Previous Reconciliation. ■ Choose the correct account and the statement ending date. ■ Choose whether you want a detail or summary report (or both); click Display.
Produce a reconciliation discrepancy report	■ Choose Reports→Banking→Reconciliation Discrepancy. ■ Choose the correct account; click OK.

DEVELOP YOUR SKILLS 5-8

Produce Banking Reports and a PDF Copy of a Report

In the last exercise, you reconciled the checking account for Average Guy Designs. In this exercise, you will help Allison to produce two banking reports and save one of them as a PDF file.

1. Choose **Reports→Banking→Previous Reconciliation**.

2. Ensure **10000•Checking** is displayed and that the circle to the left of Detail is selected.

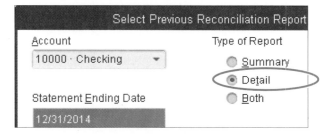

3. Click the **Display** button to produce the report.

   QuickBooks generates this report as a PDF file that can be saved, printed, or emailed.

4. Close the **Reconciliation Detail** report window.

Run a Register QuickReport

You will now create a report based on information contained within your Checking account.

5. Click the **Check Register** task icon in the Banking area of the Home page.

6. Click **OK** to choose the **10000•Checking** account.

   The Average Guy Designs Checking register will be displayed.

Check Register

7. Follow these steps to produce the register QuickReport:

Ⓐ Scroll up until the January transactions for **Professional Software Distributors** are visible; single-click anywhere within either of the transactions.

Ⓑ Click the **QuickReport** button on the toolbar.

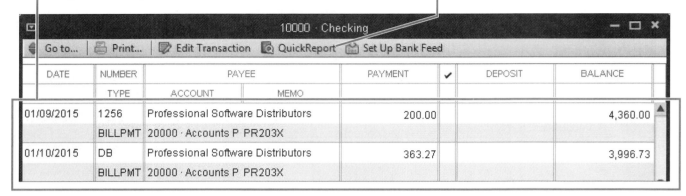

A report will be displayed that shows all of the transactions from the checking register for Professional Software Distributors. Notice the various buttons on the toolbar that you can use to print, email, export, and perform other tasks with this report. Leave this report open for the next step.

FROM THE KEYBOARD
Ctrl+q to display a QuickReport

Produce a PDF Copy of a Report

Now you will help Allison to save a PDF copy of this report. You will save it in your default file location.

8. Make sure that the QuickReport for **Professional Software Distributors** is still the active window, and then choose **File→Save as PDF** from the main QuickBooks menu bar.

A Save document as PDF window will appear.

9. Follow these steps to save a copy of the report as a PDF file:

Ⓐ Navigate to your file storage location.

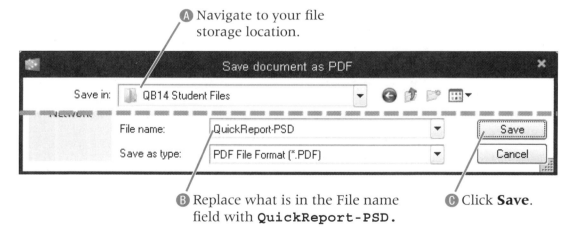

Ⓑ Replace what is in the File name field with **QuickReport-PSD.**

Ⓒ Click **Save**.

QuickBooks will process the command, saving a copy of the file to your default file location.

10. Choose **Window→Close All**.

Balance Sheet Reports

In Chapter 4, Working with Vendors, you learned how to produce one of the main company reports, Profit & Loss. In this section, you will look at another vital report, the balance sheet report. Extensive coverage of the reports produced at the end of a reporting period for a company can be found in Chapter 12, Reporting, Adjusting Entries, and Closing the Books.

Types of Accounts Displayed on a Balance Sheet Report

A balance sheet report displays all of your asset, liability, and equity accounts (hence the designation the "balance sheet accounts"). You can customize your report to show only the accounts you wish to display.

Average Guy Designs, Chapter 5		
Balance Sheet		
As of December 31, 2014		
		◇ Dec 31, 14 ◇
ASSETS		
Current Assets		
Checking/Savings		
10000 · Checking	▶	5,718.02 ◀
10200 · Savings		7,382.35
Total Checking/Savings		13,100.37
Accounts Receivable		
11000 · Accounts Receivable		2,680.00
Total Accounts Receivable		2,680.00
Total Current Assets		15,780.37
TOTAL ASSETS		**15,780.37**
LIABILITIES & EQUITY		
Liabilities		
Current Liabilities		
Accounts Payable		
20000 · Accounts Payable		563.27
Total Accounts Payable		563.27
Total Current Liabilities		563.27
Total Liabilities		563.27
Equity		
30000 · Opening Balance Equity		12,815.02
Net Income		2,402.08
Total Equity		15,217.10
TOTAL LIABILITIES & EQUITY		**15,780.37**

Average Guy Designs, Chapter 5	
Balance Sheet	
As of January 15, 2015	
	◇ Jan 15, 15 ◇
▼ ASSETS	
▼ Current Assets	
▼ Checking/Savings	
10000 · Checking ▶	3,766.73 ◀
10200 · Savings	8,382.35
Total Checking/Savings	12,149.08
▼ Accounts Receivable	
11000 · Accounts Receivable	2,920.00
Total Accounts Receivable	2,920.00
Total Current Assets	15,069.08
TOTAL ASSETS	**15,069.08**
LIABILITIES & EQUITY	
Liabilities	
Current Liabilities	
Accounts Payable	
20000 · Accounts Payable	48.22
Total Accounts Payable	48.22
Credit Cards	
21000 · Sunriver Credit Union Visa	78.63
Total Credit Cards	78.63
Total Current Liabilities	126.85
Total Liabilities	126.85
▼ Equity	
30000 · Opening Balance Equity	12,815.02
32000 · Owners Equity	2,402.08
Net Income	-274.87
Total Equity	14,942.23
TOTAL LIABILITIES & EQUITY	**15,069.08**

Note the balance sheet as of December 31, 2014 on the left compared to the one dated January 15, 2015 on the right. The Net Income has been "rolled" into Owner's Equity for you at the end of the accounting period and "starts over" at the beginning of the next one.

Visualize! **Tab:** Reports
Topic: Balance sheet

Company Snapshot

The Company Snapshot window gives you a quick view of your company's bottom line in one convenient place. You can customize it to include "at-a-glance" reports that are most important to your company. The Company Snapshot can be accessed via a button on the Icon Bar or by choosing Reports→Company Snapshot from the menu bar. The Company Snapshot will show information only within a preset date range. If you don't see anything displayed, it is likely because the date for which you are performing the exercise is past the date range available through the snapshot.

 Visualize! **Tab:** Reports
Topic: Company Snapshot

Browse for content panels to include in your Company Snapshot.

Bring back any removed panels, reset any date range changes, and remove any added panels.

These drop-down menus provide options to print, print preview, or save as an image your content panel data.

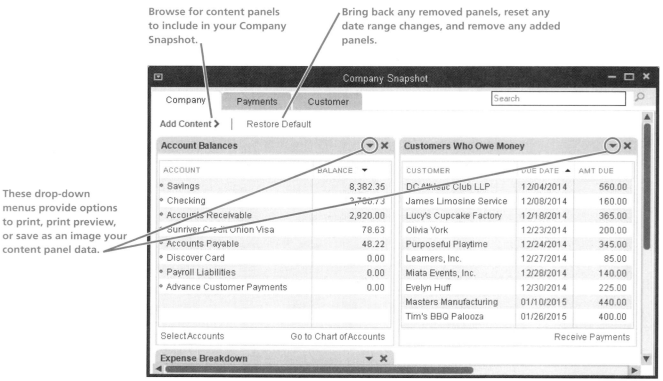

Information in the Company Snapshot is contained within content panels, each with its own Close button. You can customize the Company Snapshot to display information that is of value to you. Notice the three tabs at the top of the window that allow you to switch between the three snapshot views.

QUICK REFERENCE	WORKING WITH BALANCE SHEET REPORTS AND COMPANY SNAPSHOTS
Task	**Procedure**
Produce a balance sheet report	■ Choose Reports→Company & Financial→Balance Sheet Standard.
Produce a Company Snapshot	■ Choose Reports→Company Snapshot. ■ Customize the snapshot to meet your needs.

View a Balance Sheet Report and a Company Snapshot

In this exercise, you will create both a balance sheet report and a company snapshot for Average Guy Designs. When you create a balance sheet report, it will be based as of a certain date rather than for a period of time (as is the case for a Profit & Loss report).

1. Choose **Reports→Company & Financial→Balance Sheet Standard**.

2. Tap Tab, type **123114**, and then tap Tab again.

   QuickBooks displays a balance sheet report showing the asset, liability, and equity account balances as of December 31, 2014.

3. Close the **Balance Sheet** window, choosing not to memorize the report.

Display and Customize the Company Snapshot

You will now help Allison to customize the Company Snapshot and then restore the default.

4. Choose **Reports→Company Snapshot**.

   Depending on the actual date that you perform this exercise, you may or may not have information displayed since all of the transactions we have entered up to this point are dated in December 2014/ January 2015. Don't worry about the data displayed in the content panel for this exercise, but rather focus on how to manipulate it.

5. Follow these steps to remove a content panel from the snapshot:

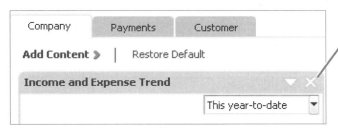

Ⓐ Click the **Close** button to remove the Income and Expense Trend panel.

Ⓑ Click **OK** in the Remove Content window.

   Notice that once you have removed the Income and Expense Trend panel, the Account Balances panel "snaps" up into the vacated space. You will now restore the default content panels to the snapshot.

6. Click the **Restore Default** link above the Account Balances panel.

7. Click **Yes** in the Restore Default window.

8. Close the **Company Snapshot** window.

9. Once you are finished learning about Banking Online with QuickBooks, choose the appropriate option for your situation:

   ■ If you will continue working, leave QuickBooks open.

   ■ If you are finished working in QuickBooks for now, choose **File→Exit**.

Working with QuickBooks Bank Feeds

There are a variety of tasks that can be carried out online with QuickBooks. With the 2014 version of QuickBooks, the online banking features have taken on a new name of "bank feeds." Bank feeds allow you to download transactions, view the transactions that have cleared your account, see your current balance, and add new transactions to QuickBooks from your financial institution. This feature allows you to save time from having to type in all your transactions, helps you to maintain better accuracy in your records, and also assists in cash flow management.

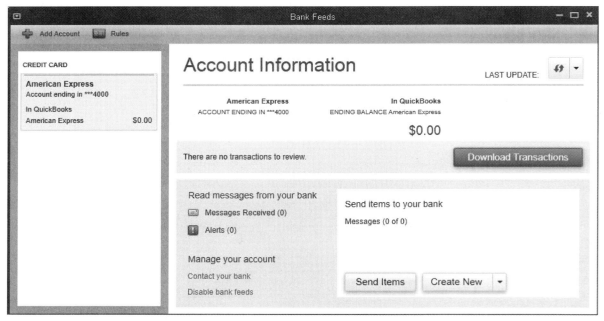

Once you have set up at least one bank feed in QuickBooks, the Bank Feeds Center will be available to you.

What you can do through bank feeds is determined by your financial institution, so you must check with it to verify what services are offered (or if any are offered at all). Also, there is no fee to use bank feeds in QuickBooks, but your financial institution may charge a fee for the service.

 Bank Feeds is a new QuickBooks feature that builds on and improves the previous online banking features.

Bank Feeds Exclusivity

In Chapter 2, Creating a Company, you learned about multi-user mode. If you do work on your company file with others, be aware that only one person at a time can be using bank feeds. The person who will be performing bank feed tasks must acquire exclusive use. If you are working in single-user mode, you do not need to acquire exclusivity as you already have it.

The Modes of Bank Feeds

You can choose how to work with your banking transactions through bank feeds as there are two different modes:

- **Express**—This mode is the new and improved QuickBooks online banking experience. In this mode, you work within the Transactions List window in order to match and add transactions, and renaming rules are created for you automatically.
- **Classic**—This mode is what was available in QuickBooks 2013 and earlier versions. In this mode, you work within account registers to match and add transactions, and you work with aliases to match names.

BANK FEEDS

View and enter downloaded transactions using:

◉ Express Mode (new in QuickBooks 2014)

    ☑ Create rules automatically
    ☑ Always ask before creating a rule

◯ Classic Mode (Register Mode)

You can choose to switch between the modes of bank feeds on the Company tab of the Checking category in the Edit Preferences window.

You do not have to choose one mode with which to work as you can switch between the two at any time. However, renaming rules from Express mode and aliases from Classic are not available in the other mode if you switch.

Bank Feeds and Reconciliation

Earlier in this chapter you learned about reconciling your QuickBooks records with the bank. When you use bank feeds you still must reconcile your accounts in the same way as you learned in this chapter. The advantage of reconciling when you use bank feeds, however, is that the majority (if not all) of your transactions have been matched already and reconciliation will be quicker. If you do have a discrepancy, then use the same problem-solving process outlined in this chapter to resolve it.

Setting Up Bank Feeds in QuickBooks

Before you can use the bank feeds feature in QuickBooks, you must complete any required applications with your financial institution(s) for your banking, credit card, or other eligible accounts. The set-up process involves four steps that QuickBooks will guide you through.

You will be able to match your bank accounts to your
QuickBooks account or create a new QuickBooks account here.

Note the four steps in the setup process.

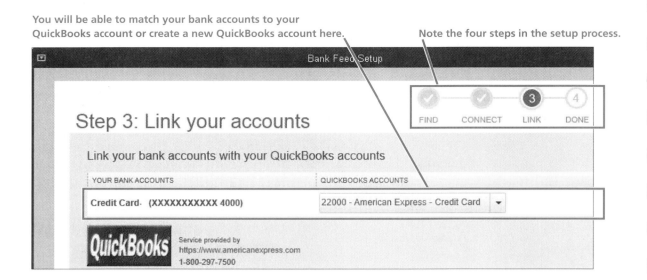

Matching and Recording Bank Feeds

Once you have set up bank feeds in QuickBooks, you will be able to download transactions from your financial institution(s), match them to transactions you have entered into QuickBooks, and properly record (remember you have to get it right behind the scenes!) new transactions that are not yet entered into QuickBooks.

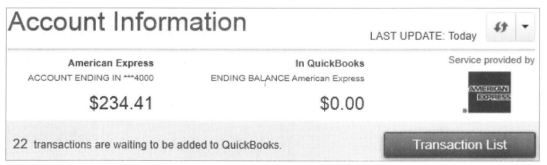

Once QuickBooks is done downloading transactions in the Bank Feeds Center, you will see a link to the Transaction List and a summary of what your next step is.

QuickBooks attempts to match transactions for you by looking at check numbers, amounts, dates, and payees. You can also choose to unmatch or manually match a transaction if QuickBooks didn't get the matching right.

Recording Deposits

Many times your bank deposits comprise more than one payment, but it is recorded as one. Once you have downloaded your bank feeds, you will need to match the individual items in your register to the downloaded information. You will learn how to do this through the WebSim exercise in this section.

Recording Expenses

In the same way that you may have downloaded a deposit that doesn't match a single transaction in your QuickBooks register, you may also have a transaction that doesn't match an expense.

Record a Credit Card Transaction

Credit card transactions are treated the same as other banking transactions when working with bank feeds. You will need to create a bank feed for your QuickBooks credit card account(s) the same as you did for your bank accounts and then follow the procedures to match and record transactions once they have downloaded.

You can also choose multiple transactions and then process all of them as a batch.

You can choose what you wish to do with each transaction that you have downloaded in the Action column.

The Transaction List window will be displayed for you to match and record downloaded transactions.

Passing Notes with Your Financial Institution

If you have a direct connection with your financial institution, you can exchange messages back and forth with it. Make sure to pay attention to messages you have received, as some require you to complete a task before they can be deleted.

Electronic Invoice Payment Processing

Another feature available in QuickBooks is that you can email invoices to your customers and then receive payment from them electronically via the Internet. You will learn more about this invoicing and payment processing feature in Chapter 6, Dealing with Physical Inventory.

Making Vendor Payments with Bank Feeds

If your bank offers the service, you can make payments to your vendors through bank feeds as well. If your institution does not offer this service, you can still pay your bills through QuickBooks by using the QuickBooks Bill Pay Service that has you work with a vendor that partners with Intuit.

QuickBooks Doc Center

The Doc Center allows you to store electronic documents on your local computer, network drive, or other storage location accessible from your computer station that can be attached to your QuickBooks transactions and customer, vendor, and employee list items for no additional fee. You will learn more about this powerful feature in Chapter 11, Introducing the Accounting Cycle and Using Classes.

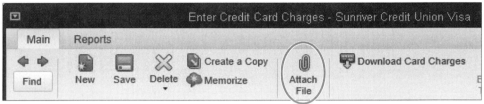

Notice the Attach buttons available in the Vendor Information area of the Vendor Center and on the toolbar of the Enter Credit Card Charges window.

QUICK REFERENCE	WORKING WITH BANK FEEDS AND THE DOC CENTER
Task	**Procedure**
Set up an account for online access	▪ Contact your financial institution and find out what services they offer; complete an application, if necessary.
	▪ Choose Banking→Bank Feeds→Setup Bank Feed for an Account.
	▪ Progress through the steps in the Bank Feeds Setup interview.
Acquire exclusive use of Bank Feeds	▪ Choose Banking→Bank Feeds→Acquire Exclusive Use.
Switch between bank feed modes	▪ Choose Edit→Preferences.
	▪ Click the Checking category, and then display the Company Preferences tab.
	▪ In the Bank Feeds section, select the mode option; click OK.
Open the Doc Center	▪ Choose Company→Documents→Doc Center.

Working with Web-based Simulations

The next exercise you will complete in this book will be a web-based simulation (WebSim) that requires you to have an Internet connection. With a WebSim, you will be working as if you were using QuickBooks; however, the exercise is actually being performed on a web page.

DEVELOP YOUR SKILLS 5-10
Work with Bank Feeds

WebSim   Work with Bank Feeds

1. Navigate to the Student Resource Center.

2. From the left navigation bar, click **Unit 1**; in the main content window, click **Chapter 5**; and then click **Develop Your Skills 5-10 Work with Bank Feeds.**

3. Follow the instructions on your screen.

Tackle the Tasks

Now is your chance to work a little more with Average Guy Designs and apply the skills that you have learned in this chapter to accomplish additional tasks. You will use the same company file you used in the Develop Your Skills exercises throughout this chapter. Enter the following tasks, referring back to the concepts in the chapter as necessary.

Create banking accounts	Use the following information to create two new accounts: 10400•Money Market; Sunriver Credit Union 22000•American Express
Make a deposit	On 1/5/15, Guy traveled to a local business and provided assistance to the owner who was trying to edit a video. He received $250 cash and chose to not enter the customer in QuickBooks. Deposit the funds from this transaction to Checking on the same day.
Transfer funds	On 1/5/15, transfer $1,000 from Checking to Money Market.
Enter credit card transactions	Enter the following Sunriver Credit Union Visa transactions: On 1/7/15, purchased a customer appreciation lunch from Home Place Pizzeria (add as a new vendor) for $65.11, using the 64300•Meals and Entertainment account. On 1/8/15, purchased a new computer mouse from Ricky's Electric City for $49.52, using 64900•Office Supplies as the account. On 1/9/15, took a new client out to lunch at Bayshore Café for $39.12, using 64300•Meals and Entertainment as the account. On 1/10/15, paid $75.00 to Handyman by the Bay for work he did to wire Allison's new workstation, using 67200•Repairs and Maintenance as the account. On 1/10/15, returned the computer mouse to Ricky's Electric City.
Reconcile a credit card	Now it is time to reconcile your Sunriver Credit Union Visa credit card. From the Student Resource Center, open the file labeled Credit Card Statement. Once you have reconciled the credit card, choose to enter a bill for payment later (QuickAdd Sunriver Credit Union as a vendor) and create a summary reconciliation report.
Produce reports	Display a summary previous reconciliation report for the Checking account. Display a balance sheet detail report as of 12/31/14.

```
┌─────────────────────────────────────────────────────────┐
│               Sunriver Credit Union                      │
│                 487 Merrifield Lane                      │
│                  Bayshore, CA 91547                      │
│                                                          │
│  Visa Statement Prepared For:                            │
│    Average Guy Designs                                   │
│    110 Sampson Way                                       │
│    Bayshore, CA 91547                                    │
│                                                          │
│                   Account Number: XXXX XXXX XXXX 7777    │
│                                                          │
│         Statement Period: December 13, 2014 - January 12, 2015 │
├──────────────────────────┬──────────────────────────────┤
│  Total                   │      Total                    │
│  Charges:   $317.84      │      Payments:    $59.98      │
│  Beginning               │      Ending                   │
│  Balance:     $0.00      │      Balance:    $257.86      │
├──────────────────────────┴──────────────────────────────┤
│ Transactions:                                            │
│   Date          Description        Charge   Credit  Balance │
│                 Beginning Balance                   $0.00 │
│   1/3/2015      Allen Brothers Grocery  89.09       $89.09 │
│   1/6/2015      Allen Brothers Grocery         10.46  $78.63 │
│   1/7/2015      Home Place Pizzaria   65.11         $143.74 │
│   1/8/2015      Ricky's Electric City 49.52         $193.26 │
│   1/9/2015      Bayshore Café         39.12         $232.38 │
│   1/10/2015     Handyman by the Bay   75.00         $307.38 │
│   1/10/2015     Ricky's Electric City          49.52  $257.86 │
│   1/12/2015     Periodic Finance Charge   0         $257.86 │
│                 Ending Balance                      $257.86 │
└─────────────────────────────────────────────────────────┘
```

Concepts Review

To test your knowledge of the key concepts introduced in this chapter, complete the Concepts Review quiz on the Student Resource Center or in your eLab course.

Reinforce Your Skills

Angela Stevens has just relocated her company, Quality-Built Construction, from California to Silverton, Oregon. You will be working with a QuickBooks Sample Company File in this exercise as it will allow you to run full payroll in a future chapter without having to purchase a payroll subscription.

Before you begin the Reinforce Your Skills exercises, complete one of these options:

- Open **RYS_Chapter05** from your file storage location.
- Restore **RYS_Chapter05 (Portable)** from your file storage location. For a reminder of how to restore a portable company file, see Develop Your Skills 3-1. Add your last name and first initial to the end of the filename.

REINFORCE YOUR SKILLS 5-1
Work with Bank Accounts and Make a Deposit

In this exercise, you will take care of the banking tasks for Quality-Built Construction. Since Angela's business checking account does not earn interest, she has decided to open a money market account. You will begin by helping her to set up this account.

1. Choose **Lists→Chart of Accounts**.
2. Click the **Account** menu button and choose **New**.
3. Choose **Bank** as the account type, and then click **Continue**.
4. Type **Company Money Market Account** as the new account name, and **1150** as the account number.
5. Click **Save & Close**, choosing **No** in the Set Up a Bank Feed window.
6. Close the **Chart of Accounts** window.

Move Funds Between Accounts

Since the money market account earns interest, Angela has decided to transfer some funds from her checking account into it.

7. Choose **Banking→Transfer Funds**.
8. Set the date to **1/2/19**.
9. Choose **Company Checking Account** as the Transfer Funds From account.
10. Choose **Company Money Market Account** as the Transfer Funds To account.
11. Type **80000** as the transfer amount.
12. Click **Save & Close** to record the transfer and close the window.

Make Deposits

Angela did a presentation for a local organization on the steps you need to take prior to building a new home. She needs to deposit the fee she earned into her checking account along with the funds that are currently in the Undeposited Funds account. You will do this in two separate steps.

13. Choose **Banking→Make Deposits**.

14. Select all of the payments in the **Payments to Deposit** window, and then click **OK**.

15. Ensure **Checking** is the Deposit To account. Click **OK** if the default account information window appears in order to acknowledge it and move to the Make Deposits window.

16. Set the deposit date as **1/03/19**, and then click **Save & New**.

17. Change the Date for the next deposit to **1/4/19**, tap Tab, and then type **Presentation** as the memo.

18. Click in the **From Account** column, and then type **consu** to fill in **Consultation Income** as the income account.

Remember, you do not have to enter a customer, but you must enter an income account!

19. Enter the payment in the form of a check: number **753** for **$800**.

Your screen should resemble the following illustration.

20. Click **Save & Close** to record the transaction and close the window.

Reconcile a Bank Account

The bank statement has just arrived. In this exercise, you will reconcile Quality-Built Construction's Company Checking Account. You may print your own statement (Reinforce Your Skills 5-2 Bank Statement) from your file storage location or refer to the illustration shown after step 2.

1. Choose **Banking→Reconcile**.

2. Use the back statement to reconcile the Checking account for Angela.

Tradesman Credit Union

Statement of Account Prepared For:	Account Number: 555-777
Quality-Built Construction	Statement Period: December 1 - 31, 2018
Angela Stevens	
316 Maple Street	
Silverton, OR 97381	

Total Deposits:	$33,500.00		Total Payments:	$120,253.43
Beginning Balance:	$186,145.28		Ending Balance:	$99,391.85

Date	Transaction type	Payment	Deposit	Balance
	Beginning Balance			$186,145.28
12/4/2018	Check #11327	27.05		$186,118.23
12/5/2018	Check #11329	35,034.00		$151,084.23
12/5/2018	Check #11328	24,098.00		$126,986.23
12/5/2018	Check #113342	11,986.00		$115,000.23
12/5/2018	Check #11341	4,521.00		$110,479.23
12/5/2018	Check #11337	3,567.09		$106,912.14
12/5/2018	Check #11332	3,400.00		$103,512.14
12/5/2018	Check #11333	2,790.03		$100,722.11
12/5/2018	Check #11338	2,380.00		$98,342.11
12/5/2018	Check #11330	2,350.00		$95,992.11
12/5/2018	Check #11331	1,250.00		$94,742.11
12/5/2018	Check #11344	936.00		$93,806.11
12/5/2018	Check #11340	400.00		$93,406.11
12/5/2018	Check #11334	227.00		$93,179.11
12/5/2018	Check #11336	185.00		$92,994.11
12/5/2018	Check #11339	180.00		$92,814.11
12/5/2018	Check #11335	100.00		$92,714.11
12/5/2018	Check #11343	12.00		$92,702.11
12/5/2018	Transfer	6,100.00		$86,602.11
12/8/2018	Check #10769	999.42		$85,602.69
12/15/2018	Check #10768	200.00		$85,402.69
12/15/2018	Deposit		33,500.00	$118,902.69
12/15/2018	Check #11345	32.05		$118,870.64
12/18/2018	Check #11351	4,800.00		$114,070.64
12/20/2018	Check #11346	2,300.00		$111,770.64
12/20/2018	Check #11347	1,635.02		$110,135.62
12/20/2018	Check #11349	1,364.55		$108,771.07
12/20/2018	Check #11350	512.22		$108,258.85
12/20/2018	Check #11348	227.00		$108,031.85
12/20/2018	Check #11352	180.00		$107,851.85
12/22/2018	Transfer	8,100.00		$99,751.85
12/23/2018	Check #11355	100.00		$99,651.85
12/26/2018	Check #11356	250.00		$99,401.85
12/31/2018	Service Charge	10.00		$99,391.85
	Ending Balance			$99,391.85

Pay attention to the following hints when you reconcile:

- *Make sure to set the reconciliation date to 12/31/2018.*

- *In the Begin Reconciliation window, make sure to enter the ending balance and the service charge.*

- *In the Reconcile-Checking window, make sure to mark only those transactions that have cleared the bank (and are on the bank statement) and that have zero differences before you click Reconcile Now.*

- *If the difference is not zero, see the Problem Resolution Process section on page 186.*

3. Choose to not create a reconciliation report now.

REINFORCE YOUR SKILLS 5-3

Manage Credit Card Transactions

In this exercise, you will help Angela to set up and use her new Visa credit card in QuickBooks.

1. If necessary, choose **Lists→Chart of Accounts**.

2. Click the **Account** menu button and choose **New** from the context menu.

3. Choose **Credit Card** as the account type, and then click **Continue**.

4. Name the new account **2070•Marion CU Visa**.

5. Click **Save & Close** to enter the new account and close the window, choosing **No** when asked if you want to set up bank feed services.

Enter a Credit Card Charge

Angela is purchasing oil filters for the business vehicles. She is not sure of the exact filter for one of the trucks, so she will purchase two and return one of them later.

6. Choose **Banking→Enter Credit Card Charges**, and ensure that the **Marion CU Visa** is selected.

7. Tap Tab three times, and then type **Auto Supply Warehouse** as the vendor. Tap Tab again, and then choose to **Quick Add** the store as a vendor.

8. Set the date to **1/2/19**, tap Tab twice, and then type **$150** as the amount.

9. Click in the **Account** column and choose **6101•Gas and Oil** as the expense account.

10. Click **Save & New** to record the transaction.

Enter a Credit Card Credit

Now you will process the return for Angela. The Enter Credit Card Charges window should still be open from the last step; if it isn't, choose Banking→Record Credit Card Charges→Enter Credit Card Charges.

11. Choose **Auto Supply Warehouse** as the vendor.

12. Set the date to **1/4/19**.

13. Choose the **Refund/Credit** option to show it is a return.

14. Type **$30** as the amount and ensure that **6101•Gas and Oil** is the account.

15. Click **Save & Close** to record the refund and close the window.

Produce Banking and Balance Sheet Reports

Angela wants to run some banking reports to get answers from hers data. In this exercise, you will help her to do just that. Angela has already performed the reconciliation, and she asks you to print the reconciliation report.

1. Choose **Reports→Banking→Previous Reconciliation**.

2. Choose to create a **Summary** report for the reconciliation you just performed (statement ending date of 12/31/2018).

3. Click **Display** to produce the report.

4. Preview how the report will print, and then close the **Reconciliation Summary** window.

Run a Deposit Detail Report

Angela would like to see all of her bank deposits for December, so she will run a report to display them.

5. Choose **Reports→Banking→Deposit Detail**.

6. Tap [Tab], and then type **120118**; tap [Tab], and then type **123118**.

7. Click the Refresh button on the report toolbar.

   You will see a report that displays the details for each deposit in December.

If you tap [Tab] after changing the date, QuickBooks will automatically refresh the report for you, too.

8. Choose **File→Save as PDF**.

9. Choose to save a copy of the report in your default storage location, naming it **December 2018 Deposits**.

10. Close the **Deposit Details** report window, clicking **No** when asked to memorize the report.

Display a Balance Sheet Report

11. Choose **Reports→Company & Financial→Balance Sheet Standard**.

12. Tap [a] to change the date range to **All**.

13. Choose **Window→Close All**.

14. Choose the appropriate option for your situation:

    ■ If you will continue working, leave QuickBooks open.

    ■ If you are finished working in QuickBooks for now, choose **File→Exit**.

Apply Your Skills

Before you begin the Apply Your Skills exercises, complete one of these options:

- Open **AYS_Chapter05** from your file storage location.
- Restore **AYS_Chapter05 (Portable)** from your file storage location. For a reminder of how to restore a portable company file, see Develop Your Skills 3-1. Add your last name and first initial to the end of the filename.

APPLY YOUR SKILLS 5-1
Manage Banking and Deposits

In this exercise, you will help Dr. James with some basic banking tasks.

1. Open the **Chart of Accounts** and create two new accounts for Wet Noses: a bank account named **Money Market** and a credit card account named **American Express**. Choose to not set up online services for either account.

2. Open the **Make Deposits** window and choose to deposit all four payments from the Undeposited Funds account into your Checking account on 6/8/14.

3. Open the **Transfer Funds** window and transfer $30,000 from Checking to Money Market on 6/10/14.

APPLY YOUR SKILLS 5-2
Enter Credit Card Transactions

In this exercise, you will enter transactions into the credit card account you just created.

1. Open the Enter Credit Card Charges window.

2. Enter the following **American Express** charges for the month.

   Quick Add any vendors not on the Vendor List and use your best judgment in selecting an expense account.

Date	Vendor	Amount	Memo
6/1/14	Thrifty Grocery	$26.73	Bottled water and soda for office
6/4/14	Glen's Handyman Service	$108.70	Office repairs
6/4/14	Malimali Hardware Store	$43.20	Supplies for office repairs
6/8/14	Labyrinth Veterinary Publications	$94.85	Reference books
6/11/14	Thrifty Grocery	$18.49	Refreshments for office
6/14/14	Bothell Pet Supply Co.	$115.43	Boarding supplies
6/14/14	Karel's Gardening Service	$60.00	Monthly garden maintenance
6/20/14	Beezer Computer Repair	$145.00	Computer repair
6/20/14	Bothell Pet Supply Co.	-$38.29	Return-Boarding supplies
6/22/14	Laura's Café	30.21	Business lunch with partner

3. Close the **Enter Credit Card Charges** window when you are finished.

Deal with a Returned Check

In this exercise, you will help Dr. James to account for check #6666 from Mary Ann Gulch for $145.65 that was returned for non-sufficient funds.

1. Choose **Customers→Receive Payments**.

2. Click the **Previous** button until the bounced check used to pay invoice **167** is displayed.

3. Click the Record Bounced Check button.

Enter the Fee Information

4. Enter a **Bank Fee** of $25 on **6/6/2014**, using **Bank Service Charges** as the account.

5. Enter a **Customer Fee** of **$45**.

Reconcile a Credit Card Account

In this exercise, you will reconcile the American Express account.

1. Open the **Chart of Accounts** and begin the process to reconcile the **American Express** account using the following illustration.

American Express
6539 Beck Place
New York, NY 07852

Credit Card Statement Prepared For:
Wet Noses Veterinary Clinic
589 Retriever Drive
Bothell, WA 98011

Account Number: 3333-888888-55555

Statement Period: May 21 - June 20, 2014

| Total Charges: | 612.40 | | | Total Credits: | $38.29 |
| Beginning Balance: | $0.00 | | | Ending Balance: | $574.11 |

Transactions:

Date	Description	Charge	Credit	Balance
	Beginning Balance			$0.00
5/1/2014	Thrifty Grocery	26.73		$26.73
5/4/2014	Glen's Handyman	108.70		$135.43
5/4/2014	Malimali Hardware Store	43.20		$178.63
5/8/2014	Laby Vet Pub	94.85		$273.48
5/11/2014	Thrifty Grocery	18.49		$291.97
5/14/2014	Bothell Pet Supply	115.43		$407.40
5/14/2014	Murray Gardening Service	60.00		$467.40
5/20/2014	Beezer Computer	145.00		$612.40
6/20/2014	Bothell Pet Supply		38.29	$574.11
	Periodic Finance Charge	0		$574.11
	Ending Balance			$574.11

2. When you have completed the reconciliation, write a check to **American Express** for the entire amount on 6/22/2014, choosing for it to be printed later. Then, display a **summary reconciliation report**.

APPLY YOUR SKILLS 5-5

Answer Questions with Reports

In this exercise, you will answer questions for Dr. James by running reports. You may wish to display the Report Center in List View to help you answer the questions. Ask your instructor if you should print the reports, print (save) them as PDF files, export them to Excel, or simply display them on the screen.

1. What are the details of the checks that have been written during June 2014?

2. Which transactions were cleared and which were not cleared when the American Express account was reconciled?

3. Is it possible to get a detailed list of all deposits for June 2014?

4. Are there any missing or duplicate check numbers in the Checking account?

5. What is the balance of all of the balance sheet accounts as of June 22, 2014?

6. Submit your reports based on the guidelines provided by your instructor.

7. Choose the appropriate option for your situation:
   - If you will continue working, leave QuickBooks open.
   - If you are finished working in QuickBooks for now, choose **File→Exit**.

Extend Your Skills

In the course of working through the following Expand Your Skills exercises, you will be utilizing various skills taught in this and previous chapter(s). Take your time and think carefully about the tasks presented to you. Turn back to the chapter content if you need assistance.

5-1 Sort Through the Stack

Before You Begin: Restore the EYS1_Chapter05 (Portable) file or open the EYS1_Chapter05 company file from your storage location.

You have been hired by Arlaine Cervantes to help her with her organization's books. She is the founder of Niños del Lago, a non-profit organization that provides impoverished Guatemalan children with an engaging educational camp experience. You have just sat down at your desk and opened a large envelope from her with a variety of documents and noticed that you have several emails from her as well. It is your job to sort through the papers and emails and make sense of what you find, entering information into QuickBooks whenever appropriate and answering any other questions in a word-processing document saved as **EYS1_Chapter05_ LastnameFirstinitial**. Remember, you are digging through papers you just dumped out of an envelope and addressing random emails from Arlaine, so it is up to you to determine the correct order in which to complete the tasks.

- Scribbled on a scrap of paper: I looked at QuickBooks and saw money in an account called "Undeposited Funds." Why isn't it in the Checking account? Can you move it for me? I deposited those funds into the Checking account on 7/11/2014!
- New credit card document on desk: From Jasper State Bank, number 7777 2222 0000 2938, $7,500 credit limit.
- Note: Opened a new Money Market bank account at Jasper State Bank on 7/10/14. Transferred $1,000 from Savings to fund the new account. Need QuickBooks account set up.
- Bank deposit slip: Check #2323 dated 7/14/2014 for a $2,500 deposit to Checking. Handwritten message on slip reads, "From Hanson Family Trust."
- Credit card receipt: Dated 7/15/2014; for office supplies; $75.11; paid to Supplies Online.
- Note: Would you please create a report that shows all of the activity in the Checking account for July 2014 and save it as a PDF file so I can email it to the accountant?
- Bank deposit slip: Dated 7/30/2014 for $750; handwritten on slip, check #1835 from Lakeside Christian School for remaining balance due.
- Credit card receipt: Dated 7/23/2014; payable to Casey's Service Station; for auto fuel; amount of $35.61. (Hint: This is for travel to a workshop site.)
- Scribbled note from Arlaine: Can you produce a report for me that shows the balances for all of the asset, liability, and equity accounts as of 7/31/2014?

5-2 Be Your Own Boss

Before You Begin: Complete Extend Your Skills 4-2 before starting this exercise.

In this exercise, you will build on the company file that you outlined and created in previous chapters. If you have created a file for your actual business, then enter your bank and credit card accounts and deposit any funds waiting in Undeposited Funds; complete any fund transfers between accounts and enter all credit and debit card transactions; enter any bounced checks; finally, use the bank statements received from your financial institution and reconcile all accounts. If you are creating a fictitious company, then create at least two banking accounts and one credit card account. Deposit all funds received in Chapter 4 into a bank account and transfer funds between your two bank accounts; account for a bounced check. You will make up the names and information for this exercise.

Create Balance Sheet and Deposit Detail reports and submit them to your instructor based on the instructions provided.

Open the company file you worked on in Extend Your Skills 4-2 and complete the tasks outlined above. When you are done, save it as a portable company file, naming it as **EYS2_Chapter05_ LastnameFirstinitial (Portable)** and submit it to your instructor based on the instructions provided.

5-3 Use the Web as a Learning Tool

Throughout this book, you will be provided with an opportunity to use the Internet as a learning tool by completing WebQuests. According to the original creators of WebQuests, as described on their website (http://WebQuest.org), a WebQuest is "an inquiry-oriented activity in which most or all of the information used by learners is drawn from the web." To complete the WebQuest projects in this book, navigate to the Student Resource Center and choose the WebQuest for the chapter on which you are working. The subject of each WebQuest will be relevant to the material found in the chapter.

WebQuest Subject: Online banking with QuickBooks

U N I T

2

Advanced Skills

Advanced Skills

Now that you've mastered the basics, in this unit we'll dive deeper into the accounting knowledge that will help you master efficient bookkeeping. You'll learn about how QuickBooks deals with inventory, how to work with balance sheets and accounts, and how to run payroll. You'll also learn about how to work with estimates and time tracking, and how to customize a variety of QuickBooks forms and reports.

Dealing with Physical Inventory

CHAPTER OUTLINE

CHAPTER OBJECTIVES

After studying this chapter, you will be able to:

- Create and use items to track inventory
- Create purchase orders and receive items
- Adjust quantity/value on hand
- Sell items and process sales discounts and refunds
- Collect and track sales tax
- Work with reports to manage your inventory and sales

In Chapter 3, Working with Customers, you learned to create service and non-inventory items. In this chapter, you will examine the inventory features available in QuickBooks. When you turn on the inventory features, QuickBooks allows you to create inventory items and purchase orders, receive items into inventory, sell inventory items, and run inventory-related reports. QuickBooks also creates accounts that you did not need until you began tracking inventory—Inventory Assets and Cost of Goods Sold. You can also create subaccounts for each of these new accounts to track your assets and costs for individual products or product types, if you choose. In addition, you will learn how to set up and track sales tax in QuickBooks, and how to deal with customer refunds. This chapter will conclude with a look at common inventory and sales reports.

Average Guy Designs

In this chapter, you will help Guy to learn how to work with inventory items in QuickBooks as he has decided to sell items created by other designers from his shop as well as online. This will include the creation of inventory items, as well as their sales to customers. You will also learn how to set up and receive payments when sales discounts are involved. Finally, you and Allison will explore reports in QuickBooks that will help Average Guy Designs to manage inventory and report on sales.

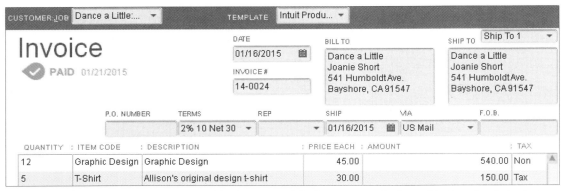

The product invoice template provides fields that are useful when you are dealing with the sale of physical inventory. You can sell inventory and service items on both the product and service invoice templates.

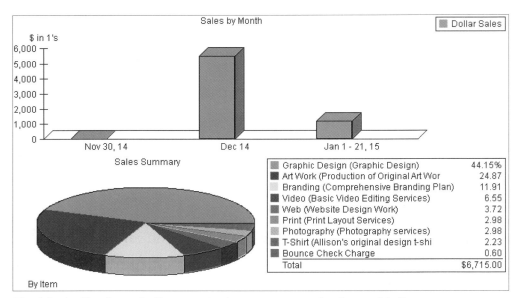

The Sales by Month graph allows you to view your company's sales graphically.

Tracking Inventory in QuickBooks

A useful feature in QuickBooks is inventory tracking. It must be turned on in the Preferences window. Once activated, it will add links to the Home page and options to the menu bar.

Should I Use QuickBooks to Track My Company's Inventory?

Not all companies are perfectly aligned to use QuickBooks to track their inventory. There are several factors that you should consider before deciding to use QuickBooks to track your company's inventory items:

- **How many types of products do I sell?** QuickBooks Pro and Premier work well for companies that have up to a few hundred items. If you have more items, you may want to consider using QuickBooks' Point-of-Sale edition.

- **Does my inventory include perishable items?** The bookkeeping for perishable items can be a bit tedious due to differences between your on-hand quantities and what you have recorded in QuickBooks.

- **Do I sell unique, one-of-a-kind products?** If you sell items such as antiques, you will have to create a new QuickBooks item for each product you sell.

- **Do I manufacture the products that I sell?** If you purchase raw materials and assemble them into products, QuickBooks Pro is not the most compatible software for your company. You may want to look at purchasing QuickBooks: Premier Manufacturing & Wholesale Edition or QuickBooks Enterprise Solutions: Manufacturing & Wholesale Edition, which address the unique needs of manufacturing businesses.

- **How fast do my inventory items become obsolete?** If this timeframe is quite short, you may find that updating your inventory in QuickBooks is tedious.

- **How do I value my inventory?** QuickBooks Pro uses the average cost method of inventory valuation. If you are using LIFO, FIFO, or another method, you may want to look at using a different tool to track your inventory.

Beginning with the Enterprise edition of QuickBooks 2012, the FIFO method of inventory valuation may be used.

Inventory Valuation

There are three inventory valuation methods allowed by GAAP:

- **Last-In, First-Out (LIFO):** With this method, the value of the last inventory brought in is used to determine the cost of goods sold (COGS), whereas the value of the inventory is based on the inventory purchased earlier in the year.

- **First-In, First-Out (FIFO):** With this method, the value of the first inventory brought in is used to determine the COGS, whereas the value of the inventory is based on the inventory purchased last (which more closely resembles the actual replacement cost).

- **Average Cost (or Weighted Average):** With this method, the value of the inventory is determined by dividing the total value of the inventory by the total number of inventory items.

QuickBooks Pro and Premier use the average cost method of inventory valuation; the Enterprise edition uses the FIFO method as well.

Inventory Center

In some Premier versions of QuickBooks, there is a feature called the Inventory Center. This center looks similar to the Customer and Vendor centers. It provides a convenient place for you to manage your inventory items.

Using Units of Measure

In the Premier and higher versions of QuickBooks, there is a feature that allows you to convert units of measure. With this feature, QuickBooks users can work with either single units of measure (e.g., buy a pound, sell a pound) or multiple units of measure (e.g., buy a yard, sell a foot).

The unit of measure feature is especially useful to companies that distribute or manufacture items. However, all companies that track inventory could find it handy if they purchase and sell in different units of measure or need to indicate units on purchase or sales forms.

Setting Up the Item List

If you want to see anything on a sales form or a purchase order, it must be set up as an item first. Before you can create an inventory item, you must turn on QuickBooks' inventory features in the Preferences window.

Inventory vs. Non-Inventory Parts

In Chapter 3, Working with Customers, you learned about non-inventory parts. Once you turn on the QuickBooks inventory feature, you'll see both inventory and non-inventory parts. Inventory parts are tracked and sold by quantity. Examples of inventory parts might be vitamins that a doctor purchases and sells to her patients or lamps that an interior decorating company buys and resells.

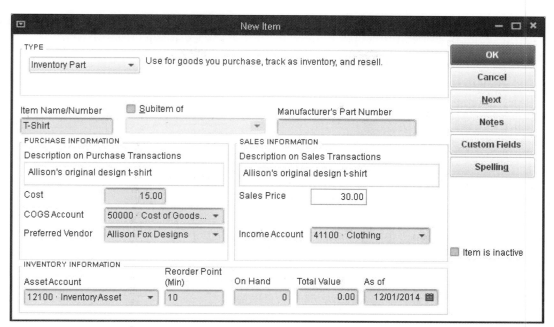

The Inventory Parts window consists of two sides: one for the purchase information and one for the sales information.

QuickBooks allows you to track non-inventory parts as well as inventory parts. Examples of items that should be created as non-inventory parts include:

- Items you don't track as inventory, such as nails used by a contractor or thread used by a seamstress
- Items you purchase for a particular customer
- Items you sell but don't first purchase, such as livestock that you breed and sell

Add/Edit Multiple List Entries

As you learned in Chapter 3, Working with Customers, there is a feature in QuickBooks that allows you to easily record multiple entries in your lists.

You can quickly update several entries in your lists by right-clicking and choosing either the Clear Column or Copy Down command.

Cost of Goods Sold

When you purchase items at wholesale to resell to your customers, the purchase price you pay is the cost of goods sold (COGS). Your profit is the difference between your sales and COGS.

Tracking Inventory Sales

You will likely need to create a new account and possibly subaccounts to track your inventory sales. In this chapter, we will be creating a new account and three subaccounts to make sure that we can track our sales effectively.

Show Lowest Subaccount Preference

It is often difficult to see the name and number of the subaccount you use in a transaction while working with the narrow account fields in the QuickBooks windows. QuickBooks has a way to help you overcome this problem by allowing you to choose to see only the lowest subaccount in these fields. For example, if you need to choose the Gas & Electric subaccount, it would normally be displayed as:

41000•Product Sales:41100•Clothing

By choosing the Show Lowest Subaccount preference, it will simply be displayed as:

41100•Clothing

QUICK REFERENCE	PREPARING TO TRACK AND SELL INVENTORY
Task	**Procedure**
Turn on QuickBooks' inventory features	■ Choose Edit→Preferences. ■ Choose the Items & Inventory category and the Company Preferences tab. ■ Click in the box to the left of Inventory and purchase orders are active; click OK.
Turn on the Show Lowest Subaccount preference	■ Choose Edit→Preferences. ■ Choose the Accounting category, and then the Company Preferences tab. ■ Click in the box to the left of the Show Lowest Subaccount Only option; click OK.
Create an inventory part item	■ Open the Item List; choose to create a new item. ■ Choose Inventory Part as the type of item. ■ Enter all required information in both the purchase and sales sides of the window; click OK to record the new item.

DEVELOP YOUR SKILLS 6-1
Prepare to Track and Sell Inventory

In this exercise, you will first confirm that inventory features are turned on. Then you will set the Show Lowest Subaccount preference and create inventory items. The first step is to open QuickBooks, and then either open a company file or restore a portable company file.

Intuit provides maintenance releases throughout the lifetime of the product. These updates may require you to update your student exercise files before you begin working with them. Please follow the prompts on the screen if you are asked to update your company file to the latest QuickBooks release.

1. Start **QuickBooks 2014**.

   If you downloaded the student exercise files in the portable company file *format, follow Option 1 below. If you downloaded the files in the* company file *format, follow Option 2.*

Option 1: Restore a Portable Company File

2. Choose **File→Open or Restore Company**.

3. Restore the **DYS_Chapter06 (Portable)** portable company file from your file storage location, placing your last name and first initial at the end of the filename (e.g., DYS_Chapter06_MarshallG).

   It may take a few moments for the portable company file to open. Once it does, continue with step 5.

Option 2: Open a Company File

2. Choose **File→Open or Restore Company**, ensure that **Open a regular company file** is selected, and then open the **Average Guy Designs** company file for this chapter from your file storage location.

The QuickBooks company file will open.

3. Click **OK** to close the QuickBooks Information window. Click **No** in the Set Up External Accountant User window, if necessary.

4. Close the **Reminders** window.

Set Preferences and Create a New Account to Track Inventory Sales

Allison believes that the QuickBooks file has been set up to track inventory, but she will open the Preferences window in order to confirm this, and while she is at it, she will set the show lowest subaccount preference.

5. Choose **Edit→Preferences**.

6. Follow these steps to turn on the inventory feature:

Ⓐ Click the **Items & Inventory** category.   Ⓑ Click the **Company Preferences** tab.

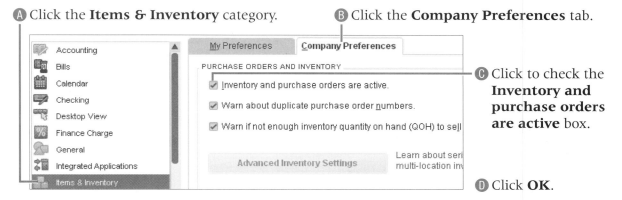

Ⓒ Click to check the **Inventory and purchase orders are active** box.

Ⓓ Click **OK**.

Before you can set the show lowest subaccount option, you must ensure that all accounts have a number assigned. While you are in the Chart of Accounts, you will also create a new account and subaccounts to track inventory sales.

7. Choose **Lists→Chart of Accounts**.

8. Scroll through the **Chart of Accounts** to see if there are any that do not have an account number assigned.

You will see that all accounts have a number assigned.

9. Click the **Account** menu button and choose **New** from the menu.

10. Choose **Income** as the type of account; click **Continue**.

11. Follow these steps to create the new account:

Ⓐ Type **41000**.

Ⓑ Tap Tab, and then type **Product Sales**.

Ⓒ Click **Save & New**.

You will now create three subaccounts to further classify your inventory sales.

12. Follow these steps to create the first subaccount:

Ⓐ Type **41100**.

Ⓑ Tap Tab, and then type **Clothing**.

Ⓒ Tap Tab twice, and then tap Space.

Ⓔ Click **Save & New**.   Ⓓ Tap Tab, and then type **pro**.

13. Repeat the previous step to add the following two additional subaccounts to **Product Sales**. Choose to **Save & Close** after the last subaccount is created.

Account Number	Account Name
41200	Accessories
41300	Home Decor

14. Close the **Chart of Accounts** window.

Set the Show Lowest Subaccount Preference

15. Choose **Edit→Preferences**.

16. Follow these steps to turn on the show lowest subaccount preference:

Ⓐ Click the **Accounting** category.   Ⓑ Click the **Company Preferences** tab.

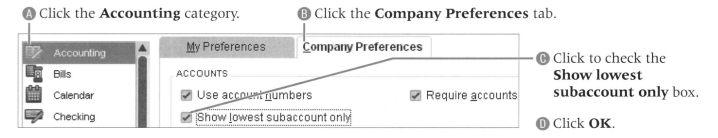

Ⓒ Click to check the **Show lowest subaccount only** box.

Ⓓ Click **OK**.

Create Multiple Inventory Items

Now you will help Allison to create inventory items for the company first by entering a single item, and then by utilizing the Add/Edit Multiple List Entries feature.

17. Click the Home button on the Icon Bar.

🏠 Home

18. Click the Item & Services task icon in the Company area of the Home page.

FROM THE KEYBOARD
Ctrl+n to open a New Item window from the Item List

19. Click the **Item** menu button and choose **New** from the menu.

20. Follow these steps to create an inventory item:

Ⓐ Choose **Inventory Part**.

Ⓑ Tap Tab, and then type **T-Shirt**.

Ⓒ Tap Tab four times, and then type this description.

Ⓓ Tap Tab and type **15**.

Ⓔ Tap Tab two times and type **Allison Fox Designs**.

Ⓕ Click here, and then type **30**.

Ⓖ Tap Tab, and then type **411**.

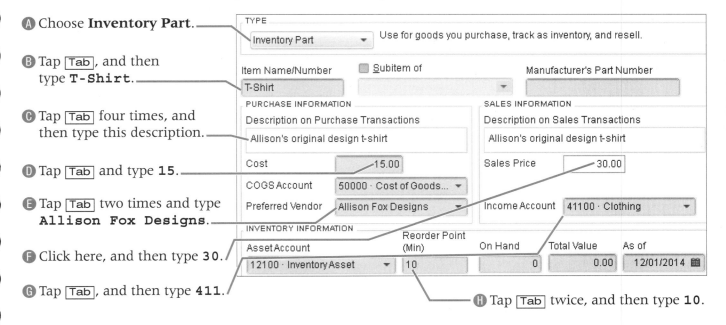

Ⓗ Tap Tab twice, and then type **10**.

21. Click **OK**, choosing to **Add** "t" as a spelling error (and correcting any errors that you may have made).

Next you will create multiple inventory items using the Add/Edit Multiple List Entries window, but first you will customize the columns that are displayed.

22. Click the **Item** menu button and choose **Add/Edit Multiple List Entries**. If the Time Saving Tip window appears, click **OK**.

23. Click the **Customize Columns** button.

Customize Columns

24. Follow these steps to set the inventory part items column:

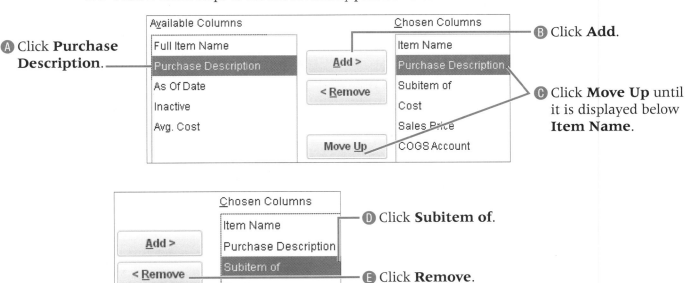

Ⓐ Click **Purchase Description**.

Ⓑ Click **Add**.

Ⓒ Click **Move Up** until it is displayed below **Item Name**.

Ⓓ Click **Subitem of**.

Ⓔ Click **Remove**.

Ⓕ Click **OK**.

25. Verify **Inventory Parts** is the **List** selected, and then follow these steps to begin creating the rest of your inventory part items:

Ⓐ Click in the Item Name column below the T-Shirt entry, and then type **LS Shirt**.

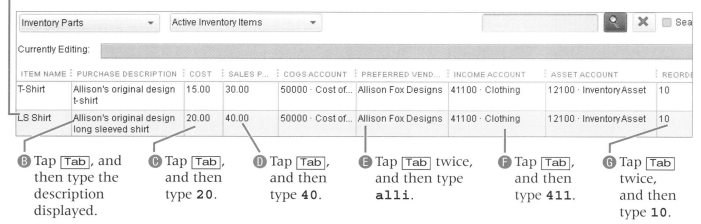

Ⓑ Tap ⌨Tab, and then type the description displayed.

Ⓒ Tap ⌨Tab, and then type **20**.

Ⓓ Tap ⌨Tab, and then type **40**.

Ⓔ Tap ⌨Tab twice, and then type **alli**.

Ⓕ Tap ⌨Tab, and then type **411**.

Ⓖ Tap ⌨Tab twice, and then type **10**.

26. Enter these inventory items, using **QuickAdd** for the new vendors.

ITEM NAME	PURCHASE DESCRIPTION	COST	SALES P...	COGS ACCOUNT	PREFERRED VENDOR	INCOME ACCOUNT	ASSET ACCOUNT	REORDER PT (MIN)
Coasters	Coaster Set	7.93	15.00	50000 · Cost of...	Hartwell Designs	41300 · Home Decor	12100 · Inventory Asset	8
Scarf	Handmade scarf	10.00	20.00	50000 · Cost of...	Knit a Bit	41200 · Accessories	12100 · Inventory Asset	12
Sm Tiles	Small hanging tile with original design	5.45	10.00	50000 · Cost of...	Hartwell Designs	41300 · Home Decor	12100 · Inventory Asset	20

27. Click the **Save Changes** button at the bottom of the window and click **OK** in the Record(s) Saved window.

28. Close the **Add/Edit Multiple Entries List** and **Item List** windows.

Dealing with Sales Tax in QuickBooks

QuickBooks makes it easy to charge and collect sales tax for items. You can also choose whether to charge tax for individual customers who resell merchandise to *their* customers and charge sales tax on the final sale rather than pay the tax to you. How you set up sales tax in QuickBooks depends entirely on which state(s) you conduct business in. There are some states that do not collect sales tax at all (yay, Oregon!), and there is variation among the others regarding what is taxed. Some states tax service that is performed, while others do not (charging sales tax on services is the exception rather than the rule). Some tax grocery food items; others do not. You must know the sales tax laws in your state before you set up sales tax for your company.

When dealing with sales tax, take some time to learn about how the sales tax laws are set up in your jurisdiction. How you display items on invoices, in both structure and whether items are stated separately or grouped together, can affect the amount of tax due on a transaction. Taking time up front can save you and your customers money and headaches in the long run.

Behind the scenes, the sales tax collected will be directed to a Sales Tax Liability account that QuickBooks automatically creates for you. The funds will be held there until you pay them to the appropriate governing authority.

Sales Tax Items and Groups

To include sales tax on a sales form, you must set up the tax as an item. An interesting situation arises, though, when you have to pay the tax collected to multiple tax agencies. QuickBooks helps you to deal with this situation by allowing you to combine multiple sales tax items into a sales tax group. This is necessary, as you can apply only one sales tax item or group to a sales form. Before you can collect sales tax, you must turn on the preference and create a sales tax item or group.

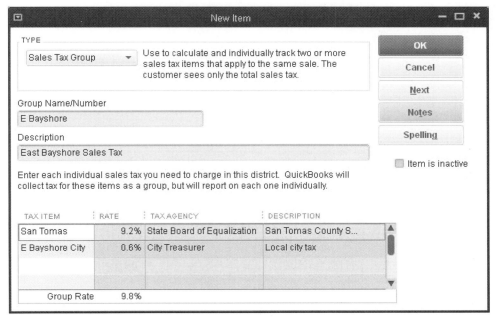

Notice that the sales tax group in this example comprises two sales tax items payable to two separate tax agencies.

Default Tax Rate

Once you have created your sales tax item(s) and group(s), you should set up a default tax rate in your preferences. This rate will appear when you create a sales form for a customer for whom a tax rate is not specified. You should choose the tax rate that you use most of the time as the default; you can change it on a sale-by-sale basis.

Dealing with Multiple Sales Tax Rates

Some companies conduct business in multiple jurisdictions. As such, the company must set up different sales tax items and/or groups with the different rates and taxing agencies. You can set one default tax rate for the company or default tax rates for each customer. Do this on the Additional Info tab of the New Customer and Edit Customer windows.

QUICK REFERENCE	SETTING UP SALES TAX IN QUICKBOOK
Task	**Procedure**
Turn on the QuickBooks sales tax feature	■ Choose Edit→Preferences.
	■ Click the Sales Tax category; click the Company Preferences tab.
	■ Click in the circle to the left of Yes in the "Do you charge sales tax?" section.
	■ Select your most common sales tax item. If necessary, create the item.
	■ Click OK to record the new preference.
Create a sales tax item	■ Open the Item List; choose to create a new item.
	■ Choose Sales Tax Item as the type of item (the sales tax preference must be set up first).
	■ Type the name and description for the item.
	■ Set the tax rate and the agency to which you pay the tax; click OK.
Create a sales tax group	■ You must first set up the items for the group following the above steps.
	■ Open the Item List and then choose to create a new item.
	■ Choose Sales Tax Group as the type.
	■ Type the group name and description.
	■ Choose each sales tax item that is to be included in the group; click OK.
Set your company's default tax rate	■ Choose Edit→Preferences.
	■ Click the Sales Tax category, and then click the Company Preferences tab.
	■ Choose your default tax rate from the "Your most common sales tax item" field drop-down button; click OK.
Set a customer's default tax rate	■ Open the Customer Center, and then double-click the customer whose default tax rate you wish to set.
	■ Choose the Additional Info tab.
	■ Choose the correct tax rate from the Tax Item field drop-down arrow; click OK.

Set Up Sales Tax

In this exercise, you will help Allison to create a sales tax item.

Before you can create any sales tax items or groups, you must have the preference turned on.

1. Choose **Edit→Preferences**.
2. Follow these steps to set the sales tax preference status and to set up your sales tax item:

Ⓐ Click the **Sales Tax** category.　　　　Ⓑ Click the **Company Preferences** tab.

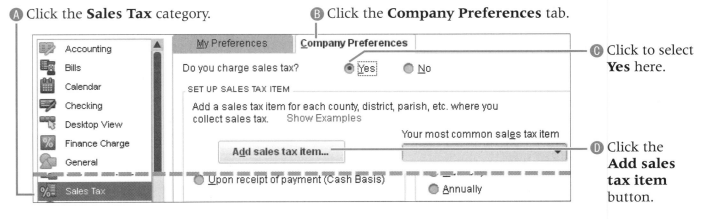

Ⓒ Click to select **Yes** here.

Ⓓ Click the **Add sales tax item** button.

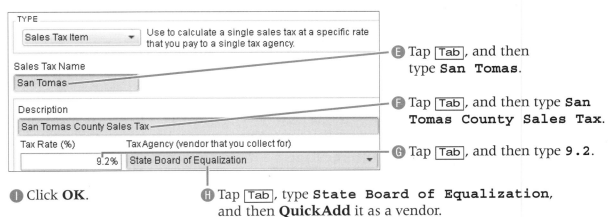

Ⓔ Tap ⎡Tab⎤, and then type **San Tomas**.

Ⓕ Tap ⎡Tab⎤, and then type **San Tomas County Sales Tax**.

Ⓖ Tap ⎡Tab⎤, and then type **9.2**.

Ⓘ Click **OK**.　　　　Ⓗ Tap ⎡Tab⎤, type **State Board of Equalization**, and then **QuickAdd** it as a vendor.

3. Click the drop-down arrow for **Your most common sales tax item**, and then choose **San Tomas**.

4. Click **OK**, and then click **OK** again in the **Updating Sales Tax** window.
5. Click **OK** in the **Warning** window.

Creating Purchase Orders

Many businesses use purchase orders for ordering items into inventory. When a purchase order is created, nothing occurs "behind the scenes," as you have done nothing yet to debit or credit an account.

Non-Posting Accounts

When you create your first purchase order, QuickBooks creates a non-posting account (an account that *does not* affect your P&L report or your balance sheet report), called Purchase Orders. Non-posting accounts appear at the end of your Chart of Accounts. By creating these accounts for you, QuickBooks allows you to create reports based on them.

QUICK REFERENCE	WORKING WITH PURCHASE ORDERS
Task	**Procedure**
Create a purchase order	■ Choose Vendors→Create Purchase Orders; choose the desired vendor. ■ Enter the items you are ordering; click Save & Close.
Produce an open purchase orders report	■ Choose Lists→Chart of Accounts; scroll to the bottom of the list. ■ Double-click the Purchase Orders account; set the correct date range for the report (if necessary).

DEVELOP YOUR SKILLS 6-3
Work with Purchase Orders

In this exercise, you will help Guy to create purchase orders for Average Guy Designs and view the purchase orders report.

1. Choose **Company→Home Page**.

2. Click the **Purchase Orders** task icon in the Vendors area of the Home page.

3. Follow these steps to create a purchase order:

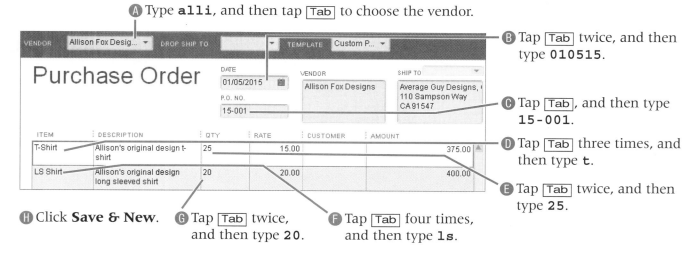

Ⓐ Type **alli**, and then tap Tab to choose the vendor.

Ⓑ Tap Tab twice, and then type **010515**.

Ⓒ Tap Tab, and then type **15-001**.

Ⓓ Tap Tab three times, and then type **t**.

Ⓔ Tap Tab twice, and then type **25**.

Ⓕ Tap Tab four times, and then type **ls**.

Ⓖ Tap Tab twice, and then type **20**.

Ⓗ Click **Save & New**.

4. Follow these steps to create the second purchase order:

Ⓐ Type **k**, and then tap Tab to choose the vendor.

Ⓑ Click in the **Item** column, and then type **s**.

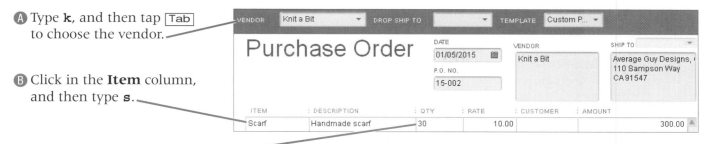

Ⓒ Tap Tab twice, and then type **30**.　　Ⓓ Click **Save & Close**.

View the Open Purchase Orders Report

Next you will take a look at the Purchase Orders non-posting account QuickBooks created for Average Guy Designs when the first purchase order was created.

Chart of Accounts

5. Click the **Chart of Accounts** task icon in the Company area of the Home page.

6. Scroll to the bottom of the list and notice the non-posting **90100•Purchase Orders** account.

7. Double-click the **Purchase Orders** account.

   QuickBooks creates a QuickReport showing open purchase orders.

8. Type **a** to set the date range to all; then, scroll to the bottom of the report to view the purchase orders you just created.

9. Choose **Window→Close All**.

Receiving Items

When you receive the items on a purchase order, you need to enter them into inventory. You can carry this transaction out in either one or two steps, depending on how your vendor delivers the accompanying bill.

The Two Methods of Receiving Items

If a vendor sends the inventory items and the bill together, you can record them as one transaction. On the other hand, if you receive the items first and the bill later, you will enter them in two separate steps.

By clicking the drop-down arrow next to the Receive Inventory link on the Home page, you can choose how to enter the receipt of your items, either with or without the bill.

If you received the inventory items and later received the bill, click the Enter Bills Against Inventory link on the Home page to enter the bill for the items at a later date.

If you will pay a bill that is attached to a purchase order with a credit card, use the Enter Credit Card Charges window so QuickBooks will prompt you to receive against open purchase orders.

When you receive the items, QuickBooks will use the Items tab rather than the Expenses tab in the Enter Bills window. If you recall from Chapter 4, Working with Vendors, the Items tab is used to enter items into an inventory asset account rather than record an expense.

Including Expenses on a Bill for Items

You may incur additional shipping and handling charges when you order inventory items. These charges should not be entered on the Items tab but rather as an expense on the Expenses tab. Once QuickBooks enters the information on the Items tab, you can click on the Expenses tab to enter any additional expenses due with the bill.

Expenses	$25.00	Items	$250.00
ACCOUNT	AMOUNT	MEMO	
67500 · Shipping Expense	25.00		

Expenses	$25.00	Items	$250.00		
ITEM	DESCRIPTION	QTY	COST	AMOUNT	
Scarf	Handmade scarf	25	10.00	250.00	

Notice how the delivery charges are displayed on the Expenses tab of the Enter Bills window while the inventory items are displayed on the Items tab.

Discount Payment Terms

Your vendors may offer you discount payment terms in an attempt to get you to pay your bills earlier, which in turn improves their cash flow. Payment terms are created in the Terms List, which is one of the Customer & Vendor Profile Lists. You can change the terms on an individual invoice as needed without permanently changing them for the customer.

You will use the payment terms of 1% 10 Net 30 when entering a bill in this section. This means that if you pay the bill within 10 days of receipt, you will receive a 1 percent discount. But if you don't pay within the first 10 days, the full bill is due in 30 days.

> **FLASHBACK TO GAAP: COST**
>
> Remember that when a company purchases assets, it should record them at cost, not fair market value. For example, if you bought an item worth $750 for $100, it should be recorded at $100.

> **BEHIND THE SCENES**
>
> Regardless the path you take, the behind-the-scenes action is the same: An Inventory Asset will be debited, and Accounts Payable will be credited.

12100-Inventory Asset		20000-Accounts Payable	
775.00			775.00

QUICK REFERENCE	RECEIVING INVENTORY
Task	**Procedure**
Receive the inventory and the bill together	■ Choose Vendors→Receive Items and Enter Bill; choose the desired vendor. ■ Click Yes in the Open PO's Exist window. ■ Click in the checkmark column to the left of the PO against which you are receiving items; click OK. ■ Make any necessary changes to the Enter Bills window; click Save & Close or Save & New.
Receive the inventory and the bill separately	Task 1: Update inventory when you receive the items: ■ Choose Vendors→Receive Items; choose the desired vendor. ■ Click Yes in the Open PO's Exist window. ■ Click in the checkmark column to the left of the PO against which you are receiving items; click OK. ■ Make any necessary changes to the Item Receipt window; click Save & Close. Task 2: Enter the bill after you receive it: ■ Choose Vendors→Enter Bill for Received Items; choose the desired vendor. ■ Click within the line of the proper item receipt; click OK. ■ Make any changes to the Enter Bills window; click Save & Close.
Include an expense on a bill for items	■ After the Item information is entered in the Enter Bills window, click the Expenses tab. ■ Choose the correct expense account in the Expense column; tap Tab. ■ Type the amount of the expense and correct the total amount due for the bill; click Save & Close.

DEVELOP YOUR SKILLS 6-4
Receive Inventory

In this exercise, you will receive the shirts and later receive the bill for them. Following the receipt of the bill for the shirts, you will receive the scarves and the bill for them together.

1. Choose **Company→Home Page**.

2. Click the **Receive Inventory drop-down arrow** in the Vendors area of the Home page, and then choose **Receive Inventory without Bill**.

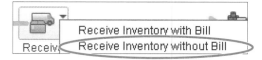

3. Type **alli**, and then tap Tab.

   QuickBooks fills in Allison Fox Designs, and the Open PO's Exist window appears.

4. Click **Yes** in the Open PO's Exist window.

5. Click to place a checkmark in the first column for PO number **15-001** dated 1/5/2015, and then click **OK**.

QuickBooks displays the Create Item Receipts window with the information from the purchase order filled in. Notice that the items appear on the Items tab at the bottom of the window, not on the Expense tab!

6. Tap ⊞ on the keyboard to change the date to **1/12/2015**.

7. Click **Save & Close** to record the item receipt.

Receive the Bill

8. Click the **Enter Bills Against Inventory** task icon in the Vendors area of the Home page.

Enter Bills Against Inventory

The shirts were entered into inventory when you received them. Now the bill for the items has arrived, and you need to enter it.

9. Follow these steps to choose the correct Item Receipt:

Ⓐ Type **alli**, and then tap ⸢Tab⸣.

Ⓑ Click anywhere within the line for the **Item Receipt** dated **1/12/2015**.

Ⓒ Click **OK**.

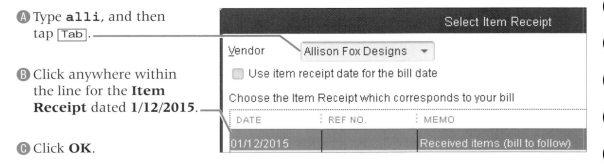

QuickBooks will display the Enter Bills window.

10. Tap ⸢Tab⸣, type **011515** as the date, and then tap ⸢Tab⸣ again.

11. Click **Save & Close** to record the new bill; click **Yes** to record your changes.

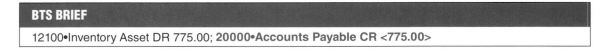

BTS BRIEF

12100•Inventory Asset DR 775.00; **20000•Accounts Payable CR <775.00>**

Receive Inventory Items with a Bill and Add an Expense to the Bill

The scarves and the bill for them arrived at the same time. The bill also included a shipping fee of $25 that must be accounted for on the bill.

12. Click the **Receive Inventory drop-down arrow** in the Vendor area of the Home page, and then choose **Receive Inventory with Bill**.

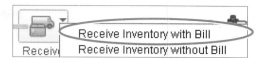

13. Type **k**, and then tap Tab.

QuickBooks fills in Knit a Bit as the vendor and the Open PO's Exist window appears.

14. Click **Yes** in the Open PO's Exist window.

15. Click to place a checkmark in the first column for PO number **15-002**.

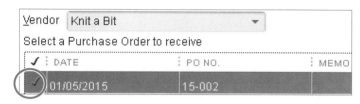

16. Click **OK** to move to the Enter Bills window; click **OK** in the Warning window.

Knit a Bit was short by five scarves for your order, so you need to record a receipt of only 25.

17. Follow these steps to complete the bill:

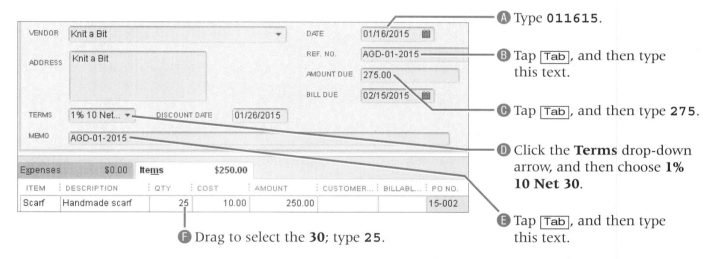

Ⓐ Type **011615**.

Ⓑ Tap Tab, and then type this text.

Ⓒ Tap Tab, and then type **275**.

Ⓓ Click the **Terms** drop-down arrow, and then choose **1% 10 Net 30**.

Ⓔ Tap Tab, and then type this text.

Ⓕ Drag to select the **30**; type **25**.

You will receive a 1 percent discount if you pay the bill by the discount date (01/26/2015).

Enter an Expense on the Bill for Inventory Items

When you received the bill for the scarves, there was also a shipping charge of $25. You will now enter that as an expense on the bill.

18. Follow these steps to enter the shipping expense:

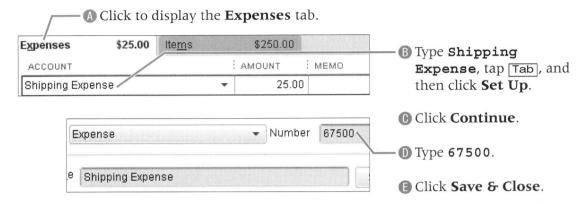

Ⓐ Click to display the **Expenses** tab.

Ⓑ Type **Shipping Expense**, tap `Tab`, and then click **Set Up**.

Ⓒ Click **Continue**.

Ⓓ Type **67500**.

Ⓔ Click **Save & Close**.

> **BTS BRIEF**
>
> 12100•Inventory Asset DR 250.00; 67500•Supplies Expense DR 25.00; **20000•Accounts Payable CR <275.00>**

19. Click **Save & Close** in the **Enter Bills** window.

20. Click **No** to reject changing the current terms for **Knit a Bit**.

Selling Inventory Items

Once you have created, ordered, and received your items, it is time to start selling them! You will use the same Create Invoices window you used in Chapter 3, Working with Customers. In the last section, you learned about discount payment terms as they relate to your payables. In this section, you will apply them to a receivable transaction.

Selling Inventory for Cash and On Account

Just as you learned about in Chapter 3, Working with Customers, you can sell inventory items using either the Create Invoices window (on account—it affects Accounts Receivable behind the scenes) or the Enter Sales Receipts window (for cash—it does *not* affect Accounts Receivable).

Batch Invoicing

The batch invoicing feature allows you to fill out the invoice just once for the customers in the "batch" and then create invoices for all of them. In order to complete this task, you should first create a billing group of the customers for whom you wish to create a batch invoice (although you can add customers one at a time as well).

NOTE

Make sure that the terms, sales tax code, and preferred delivery method are set for any customer you wish to include in the batch. You also must have an email address entered for the customers you plan to batch invoice.

On each customer record, the payment terms and preferred delivery method are on the Payment Settings tab, and the sales tax code is on the Sales Tax Settings tab. To make changes, go to Edit the Customer from the Customer Center.

Batch Invoices Summary

Once you have created a batch of invoices for customers, you will see the Batch Invoices Summary window. Here you can choose to either print or email the invoices (based on the preferred send method for each customer).

Send a Batch of Forms

You can send more than just invoices from QuickBooks. In the Preferences window, you have the ability to set the default message for twelve types of forms and reports.

When you are ready to send all of the forms and reports that you have indicated you wish to send, issue a command from the File menu that displays the Select Forms to Send window. From this window, you can choose to send any form listed in the queue. QuickBooks uses Microsoft Outlook to send emails, so it will open once you have chosen to send forms.

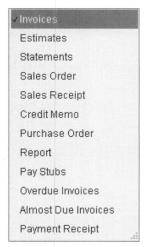

Note the types of forms and reports that you can choose to send from QuickBooks.

Producing Sales Orders

If you have the Premier or Enterprise edition of QuickBooks, there is a sales orders feature available that allows you to manage customer orders for both products and services. You can track items that have been ordered by a customer but are currently out of stock, schedule work to be done, plan costs for labor, and estimate future revenue based on the work that has been scheduled.

Benefits of Sales Orders

There are certain benefits to using the sales order feature in QuickBooks:

- You can create one invoice for multiple sales orders.
- You can create multiple invoices for one sales order if you can only partially fulfill an order.
- You can track items that are on backorder.
- You can print a Sales Order Fulfillment Worksheet, which gives you a "big picture" and allows you to determine which orders to fill with the current inventory.

Once a sales order has been created, you can print a pick list that will assist you in fulfilling the order from inventory. If the order is for a service, you can schedule the service.

Tracking Sales Orders

Sales orders will not affect what goes on behind the scenes because no money has changed hands. You can track open sales orders the same way you track open purchase orders: by creating a QuickReport from the non-posting account called 90200•Sales Orders, which is located at the bottom of the Chart of Accounts. Remember that, in order for you to complete the sale and for things to happen correctly behind the scenes, you must invoice the customer from the sales order.

BEHIND THE SCENES

The accounting that occurs for product sales is different from what occurs when you sell services. Take a look behind the scenes.

50000-Cost of Goods Sold		12100-Inventory Asset	
75.00			75.00

When an inventory item is sold, it "moves" the value of the item from the Inventory Asset account to the Cost of Goods Sold account.

11000-Accounts Receivable		25500-Sales Tax Payable	
703.80			13.80

40140-Clothing		43200-Design Income	
	150.00		540.00

Don't forget our friend sales tax... The rest of what happens behind the scenes looks similar to what happens when service items are sold. Notice that the credits (Clothing + Design Income + Sales Tax Payable) equal the debits (Accounts Receivable).

Task	Procedure
Create a batch of invoices and a new billing group	■ Choose Customers→Create Batch Invoices. ■ Click the Billing Group drop-down arrow; choose Add New. ■ Type the name of the new group; click Save. ■ Click to select a customer; click Add. Continue as necessary. ■ Click Save Group; click Next. ■ Enter the item information for the invoice and a customer message; click Next. ■ Review the list of invoices that you will create; click Create Invoices. ■ Choose to print or email invoices from the Batch Invoices Summary window.
Email an invoice from the Create Invoices window	■ Open the Create Invoices window and display the desired invoice. ■ Click the Send button drop-down arrow; choose E-mail Invoice. ■ Review the email message in your email program and make any changes. ■ Choose to send the email from your email program.
Send a batch of forms	■ Choose File→Send Forms. ■ Click to deselect any forms you do not wish to send. ■ Edit any emails you wish; click Send Now.
Create a sales order	■ Choose Customers→Create Sales Orders. ■ Fill in all relevant information; click Save & Close. ■ If the order is for a product, you can print a pick list to assist in fulfilling it. ■ If the order is for a service, you should schedule the service at this time.
Create an invoice from a sales order	■ Choose Customers→Create Invoices. ■ Choose the customer for whom you wish to create the invoice. ■ Mark the appropriate order in the Available Sales Orders window; click OK. ■ Choose whether the invoice is for all sales orders or only selected items. ■ Verify all of the information that has been filled in, adding any additional items if desired; click Save & Close.

Advanced Skills

DEVELOP YOUR SKILLS 6-5

Sell Inventory Items

In this exercise, you will first help Allison to create an invoice for a customer with discount payment terms. Then you will assist her in creating a batch of invoices for website maintenance services.

Joanie Short from Dance a Little has asked Guy to do design work to produce business cards, letterhead, flyers, and a website mock-up. She has also decided that she likes Allison's t-shirts and has purchased five of them for her staff. You will need to create a new job for the customer first.

1. Click the **Customers** button on the Icon Bar.

2. Single-click **Dance a Little** on the Customers & Jobs List.

3. Click the **New Customer & Job** button, and then choose **Add Job**.

4. Type **Project #23**, and then click **OK**.

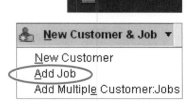

Create an Invoice with Discount Payment Terms

Now that the job has been created, you will create an invoice with discount payment terms that will be emailed. The job you just created should still be selected in the Customers & Jobs List.

5. Click the **New Transactions** button, and then choose **Invoices**.

The Create Invoices window will appear with the Customer:Job entered.

6. Follow these steps to complete the invoice for Dance a Little:

A Click the **Template** drop-down arrow and choose **Intuit Product Invoice**.

B Tap Tab, and then type **011615**.

C Click the **Ship To** drop-down arrow and choose **Ship To 1**.

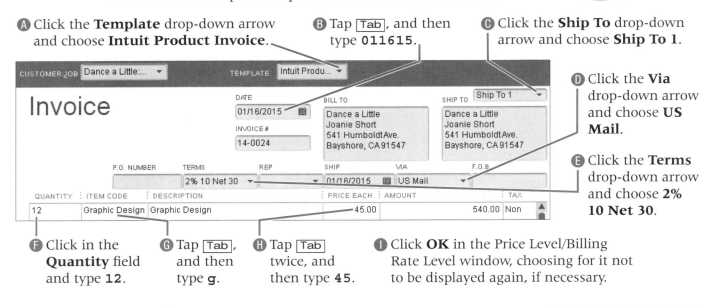

D Click the **Via** drop-down arrow and choose **US Mail**.

E Click the **Terms** drop-down arrow and choose **2% 10 Net 30**.

F Click in the **Quantity** field and type **12**.

G Tap Tab, and then type **g**.

H Tap Tab twice, and then type **45**.

I Click **OK** in the Price Level/Billing Rate Level window, choosing for it not to be displayed again, if necessary.

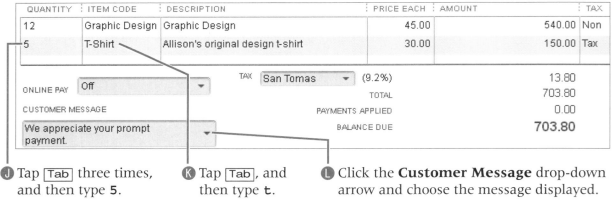

J Tap Tab three times, and then type **5**.

K Tap Tab, and then type **t**.

L Click the **Customer Message** drop-down arrow and choose the message displayed.

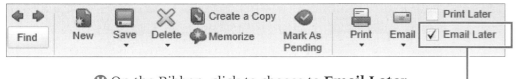

M On the Ribbon, click to choose to **Email Later**, ensuring that Print Later is not selected.

BTS BRIEF

11000•Accounts Receivable DR 703.80; **40140•Clothing CR <150.00>**; **43200•Design Income CR <540.00>**; **Sales Tax Payable CR <13.80>**; **50000•Cost of Goods Sold CR 75.00; 12100•Inventory Asset CR <75.00>**

7. Click **Save & Close**.

   An Information Missing or Invalid window will launch.

8. Type **jshort@labpub.com**; click **OK**.

9. Click **No** in the **Information Changed** window.

Create a Batch of Invoices and a New Billing Group

Guy is now offering a monthly fee for website maintenance, so you will help him to create a batch of invoices for the first two customers who subscribe to the monthly maintenance service fee. These customers pay a flat fee for the month. First, you will need to ensure that the two customers are set up correctly.

The Customer Center should still be open. If it is not, choose Customers→Customer Center.

10. Double-click **Tim's BBQ Palooza** to open it for editing.

11. Follow these steps to ensure it is set up properly for batch invoicing:

Ⓐ Click in the **Main Email** field and type **timBBQ@labpub.com**.

Ⓑ Click the **Payment Settings** tab.

Ⓒ Verify there are **Payment Terms** entered.

Ⓓ Click the drop-down arrow and choose **E-mail** here.

Ⓔ Click the **Sales Tax Settings** tab.

Ⓕ Verify that a tax code is entered.

Ⓖ Click the drop-down arrow and choose **San Tomas** here.

Ⓗ Click **OK**.

12. Double-click **Masters Manufacturing** to open it for editing.

13. Following the instructions in step 11, enter the email as **mastersm@labpub.com**, set the **Preferred Delivery Method** to **E-mail** and the **Tax Item** to **San Tomas** for **Masters Manufacturing**.

14. Close the **Customer Center**.

15. Choose **Customers→Create Batch Invoices**; click **OK** in the "Is your customer info set up correctly?" window.

   The Batch Invoice window will appear.

16. Follow these steps to create a new billing group:

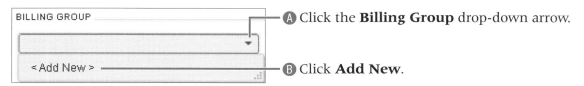

Ⓐ Click the **Billing Group** drop-down arrow.

Ⓑ Click **Add New**.

The Group Name window appears.

Ⓒ Type **Monthly Website Maintenance**.

Ⓓ Click **Save**.

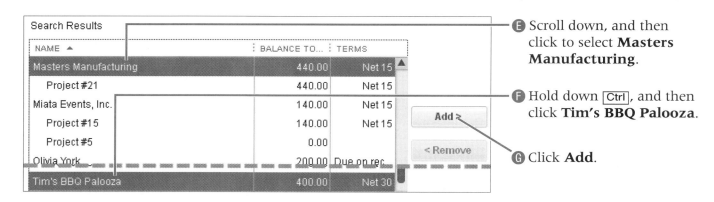

Ⓔ Scroll down, and then click to select **Masters Manufacturing**.

Ⓕ Hold down Ctrl, and then click **Tim's BBQ Palooza**.

Ⓖ Click **Add**.

After clicking Tim's BBQ Palooza, both customers should be highlighted in green so that you can add both of them to the group at the same time.

17. Click the **Save Group** button located below the Customers in This Group list, and then click **Next**.

18. Follow these steps to add a new item and set it for the invoice:

A Tap the ⊞ key until the date is displayed as **01/20/2015**.

B Choose Intuit Service Invoice as the Template.

C Click in the **Item** column, and then type **Web**.

D Click **Yes** in the Item Not Found window.

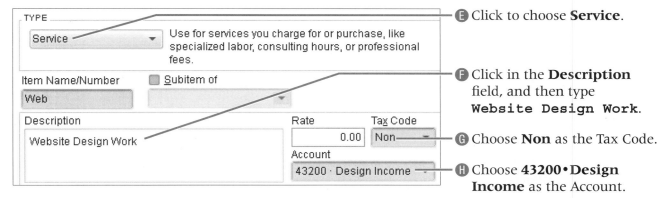

E Click to choose **Service**.

F Click in the **Description** field, and then type **Website Design Work**.

G Choose **Non** as the Tax Code.

H Choose **43200•Design Income** as the Account.

I Click **OK**, choosing to **Add Website to the dictionary** in the Spell Check window.

J Tap Tab twice, and then type **125**.

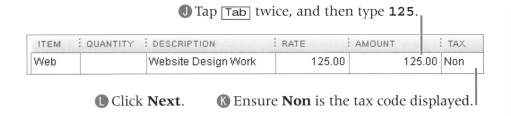

ITEM	QUANTITY	DESCRIPTION	RATE	AMOUNT	TAX
Web		Website Design Work	125.00	125.00	Non

L Click **Next**.   **K** Ensure **Non** is the tax code displayed.

19. Review the list of invoices that you are preparing to create.

Invoice Date: 01/20/2015									
SELECT	CUSTOMER	TER...	SEND METH...	AMOUNT	TAX CODE	TAX RATE	TAX	TOTAL	STATUS
✓	Masters Manufacturing	Net 15	Email	125.00	Tax	9.2%	0.00	125.00	OK
✓	Tim's BBQ Palooza	Net 30	Email	125.00	Tax	9.2%	0.00	125.00	OK

You will see a screen that shows all of the invoices to be created. If you were to choose to not create an invoice for a member of the group, you could deselect it at this step.

20. Click **Create Invoices**.

The Batch Invoice Summary window displays.

BTS BRIEF

11000•Accounts Receivable DR 250.00; **43200•Design Income CR <250.00>**

21. Close the **Batch Invoice Summary** window because you will choose to send all six of the invoices you have created in this exercise in the next few steps.

Choose to Send Forms from QuickBooks

Now you will send the invoice for Dance a Little that you marked to be sent by email as well as the two invoices you created as a batch. Since QuickBooks now sends emails utilizing Outlook, we will just look at how to initiate the action but will not actually send them since the computer you are working on may not have Outlook installed or set up.

22. Choose **File→Send Forms**.

    The Select Forms to Send window will be displayed.

23. Take a look at the three invoices selected to be emailed.

	SEND TO	TYPE	NUM	DATE	AMOUNT
☑	Project #23	INV	14-0024	01/16/2015	$703.80
☑	Masters Manuf...	INV	14-0025	01/20/2015	$125.00
☑	Tim's BBQ Palo...	INV	14-0026	01/20/2015	$125.00

Select the email(s) you want to send and click Send Now
3 of 3 Selected — 3 email(s) to Send

If you were working with your own company and had Outlook installed, this is when you would click Send Now.

24. Click **Close** in the **Send Forms** window.

Receiving Discounted and Electronic Payments

In Chapter 3, Working with Customers, you learned how to receive customer payments for the entire invoice amount. Now you will deal with a discounted customer payment. The procedure for receiving a discounted payment is almost identical to receiving a "regular" payment, except that you must identify the account to be debited for the discount amount.

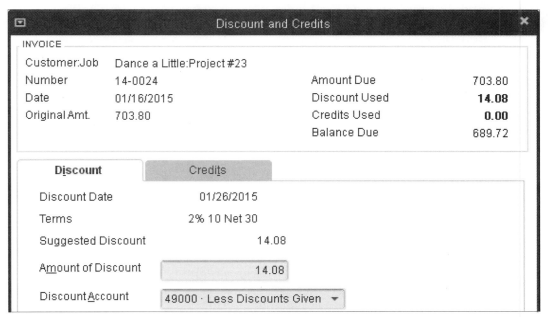

You can easily apply the discount in the QuickBooks Discount and Credits window. QuickBooks calculates the discount based on the payment terms.

Working with Electronic Customer Payments/Wire Transfers

In some instances, you may receive payments from your customers electronically. When the bank notifies you that you have received an electronic payments, you enter the receipt in the Receive Payments window, noting E-Check as the payment type. You will then be able to run reports, filtering by payment type, if you need to track electronic customer payments.

Online Customer Payments via QuickBooks

Intuit offers a Billing Solution through QuickBooks for an additional fee. Take a look at the following illustration to see what the service can do for you.

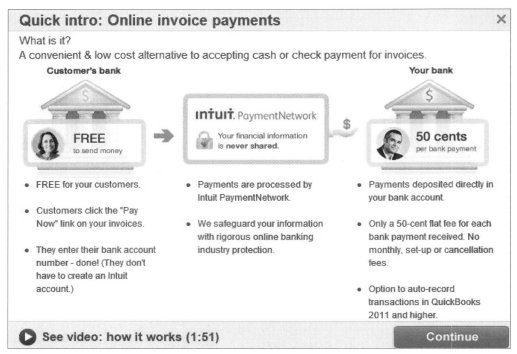

When you choose Customer→Intuit PaymentNetwork→About PaymentNetwork, you will see a window displayed that will describe the service and even be provided with a link to watch a video about the service.

The Shipping Manager

You can ship a package right from QuickBooks from both the Create Invoices and Enter Sales Receipt windows using FedEx, UPS, and now the United States Postal Service (through Stamps. com). You can use either your existing account(s) for any of these services, or you can sign up right from QuickBooks. QuickBooks will process the shipment and create a shipping label for you with the customer information that you have stored in QuickBooks. In addition, you can track your shipments from within QuickBooks.

BEHIND THE SCENES

When you receive a discounted payment, you need to credit the customer's Accounts Receivable account for the full amount even though you are not receiving the full amount in cash. The additional debit will be recorded in an expense account called 40199•Less Discounts Given.

12000-Undeposited Funds		11000-Accounts Receivable		40199-Less Discounts Given	
689.72			703.80	14.08	

QUICK REFERENCE	PROCESSING SALES DISCOUNTS AND ELECTRONIC PAYMENTS
Task	**Procedure**
Receive a discounted payment	▪ Choose Customers→Receive Payments; choose the customer/job from whom/which you received the payment.
	▪ Enter the payment information.
	▪ Click to choose the invoice to which the discount applies; click Discount & Credits.
	▪ Enter the discount amount and account.
	▪ Click Done; click Save & Close or Save & New.
Receive an electronic payment	▪ Choose Lists→Customer & Vendor Profile Lists→Payment Method List; create a new payment method called Electronic Payment.
	▪ Choose Customers→Receive Payments; choose the desired customer/job.
	▪ Enter the payment information; enter Electronic Payment as the payment type.
	▪ Click Save & Close to record the payment.
	▪ Choose Banking→Make Deposits; click to choose the electronic payment.
	▪ Click OK to move to the Make Deposits window; enter the desired account.
	▪ Enter the date of the deposit; click Save & Close.

Advanced Skills

Receive a Discounted Payment Electronically

In this exercise, you will help Allison to record a discounted payment and process an electronic payment for Average Guy Designs.

1. Click the **Receive Payments** task icon in the Customers area of the Home page.

2. Follow these steps to record the discounted payment:

A Choose **Dance a Little:Project #23** from the list.

B Tap Tab, and then type **689.72** as the amount.

C Tap Tab, and then type **012115** as the date.

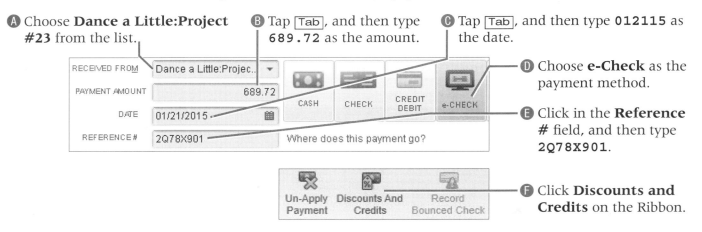

D Choose **e-Check** as the payment method.

E Click in the **Reference #** field, and then type **2Q78X901**.

F Click **Discounts and Credits** on the Ribbon.

Notice the Underpayment section of this window. Whenever you enter a payment amount that is less than the total amount due, you will see this section. You can then choose how to handle the underpayment. You will apply a discount to the invoice to take care of the underpayment in this case.

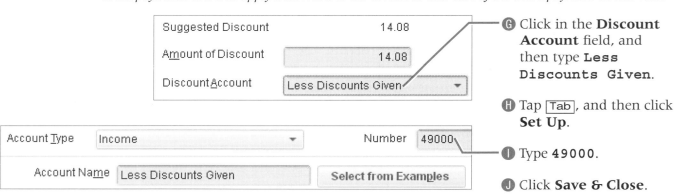

G Click in the **Discount Account** field, and then type **Less Discounts Given**.

H Tap Tab, and then click **Set Up**.

I Type **49000**.

J Click **Save & Close**.

3. Click **Done** to return to the Receive Payments window.

BTS BRIEF

12000•Undeposited Funds DR 689.72; 40199•Less Discounts Given DR 14.08; **11000•Accounts Receivable CR <703.80>**

4. Click **Save & Close** to complete the payment receipt.

Deposit an Electronic Payment

Now you will record the deposit of the electronic payment into your bank account.

5. Click the **Record Deposits** task icon in the Banking area of the Home page.
   The Payments to Deposit window will appear.

Record
Deposits

6. Click the **e-Check** you just entered to select it, and then click **OK**.

✓	DATE	TIME	TYPE	NO.	PAYMENT METHOD	NAME	AMOUNT
✓	01/21/2015		PMT	2Q78X901	E-Check	Dance a Little:Project #23	689.72

7. Tap Tab , and then verify **01/21/2015** is the date.

> **BTS BRIEF**
>
> 10100•Checking DR 689.72; **12000•Undeposited Funds CR <689.72>**

8. Click **Save & Close** to record the deposit to 10000•Checking.

Working with Refunds

There are many times when you may need to issue a refund to a customer. Once a credit memo has been created, you can choose to refund a customer by returning the payment in full, or your policy may be to issue a credit that can be applied to another purchase or to an invoice.

Issuing a Refund

There are a variety of reasons why you may wish to issue a refund to a customer, such as:

- For merchandise that has been returned
- For an order that was canceled
- To reimburse for an overpayment

If you wish to return a customer's payment, you can choose to issue a refund check or to return the funds to a credit card.

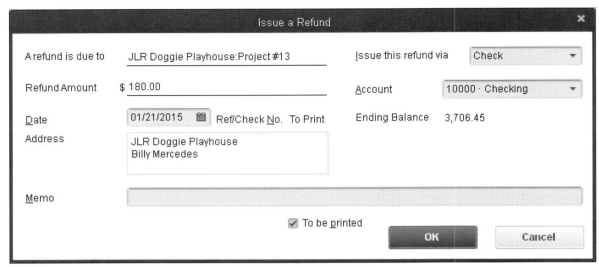

When you choose to issue a refund, the Issue a Refund window will appear. In this window, you can enter the information for the refund check.

Creating a Credit Memo

To account for returned merchandise, you may need to issue a credit memo. Once a credit memo has been created, you can choose to apply the credit to an invoice (so the customer can apply it toward a future purchase), or you can choose to issue a refund check to a customer.

One-Click Credit Memo

If you need to refund a customer for a purchase that was made on an invoice, you can use a feature in QuickBooks that allows you to convert an invoice to a credit memo with one click. This can save you time as you will not have to retype the information for the new transaction.

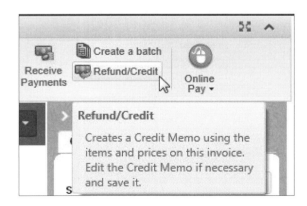

The Refund/Credit button on the Create Invoice window Ribbon allows you to easily create credit memos from invoices.

Applying a Credit as a Part of a Payment

Once a credit has been issued to a customer, you can apply it against invoices for future purchases. This is done through the Create Invoices or Receive Payments windows.

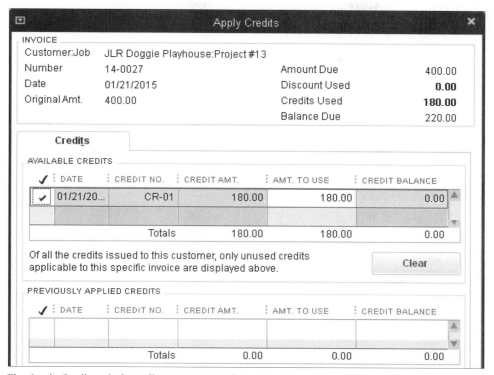

The Apply Credits window allows you to apply existing customer credits against an invoice.

Entering a Credit from a Vendor

If you are on the receiving end of a credit memo, you will need to enter it in your QuickBooks company file as well. This is easily done through the Enter Bills window. Once you have recorded the credit, you can either pass it on to a customer (if you chose to do so in the Enter Bills window when you recorded it) or use it when you pay bills to this vendor in the future.

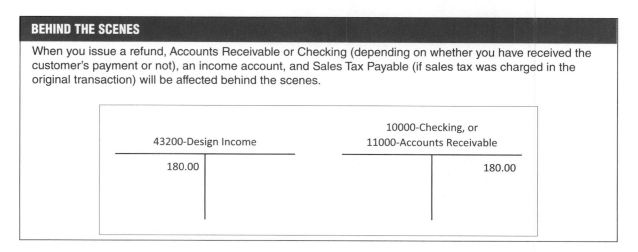

BEHIND THE SCENES

When you issue a refund, Accounts Receivable or Checking (depending on whether you have received the customer's payment or not), an income account, and Sales Tax Payable (if sales tax was charged in the original transaction) will be affected behind the scenes.

43200-Design Income		10000-Checking, or 11000-Accounts Receivable	
180.00			180.00

Task	Procedure
Create a credit memo	▪ Choose Customers→Create Credit Memos/Refunds. ▪ Select the customer and set the date; enter the credit information.
Issue a refund check for returned merchandise	▪ Choose Customers→Create Credit Memos/Refunds. ▪ Choose the desired customer. ▪ Enter the items being returned as separate line items. ▪ Click the Use Credit button; choose Give Refund. ▪ Enter a memo (optional); click OK.
Issue a refund for overpayment on an invoice	▪ Choose Customers→Receive Payments. ▪ Enter payment information. (The overpayment box will appear.) ▪ Choose to refund the amount to the customer; save the transaction. ▪ Complete the customer information in the Issue a Refund window. ▪ Enter a memo as to the purpose of the refund (optional); click OK.
Issue a refund for a canceled prepaid order/deposit	▪ Choose Banking→Write Checks. ▪ Fill in the customer information in the top portion of the window. ▪ Choose Accounts Receivable; save the check. ▪ Choose Customers→Receive Payments. ▪ Choose the correct customer at the top of the window; leave the amount as zero. ▪ Click the Discounts & Credits button. The check you just wrote should be selected. If an invoice is selected, click to remove the checkmark. ▪ Save & Close the transaction.
Enter a credit from a vendor	▪ Choose Vendors→Enter Bills. ▪ Choose Credit, choose the vendor, and enter the credit amount. ▪ In the Account column, choose the account that you use to track vendor credits. ▪ Enter the amount of the credit; indicate whether to pass the credit on to a customer. ▪ Save & Close the credit.
Create a credit memo from an invoice	▪ Open the invoice from which you wish to create the credit memo. ▪ Click the Create button on the Create Invoices window toolbar; choose Credit Memo for this Invoice. ▪ Verify the information; click Save & Close.

Create a Credit Memo and Issue a Refund

In this exercise, you will create a credit memo and then apply the credit toward a future invoice. In this example, you have told Billy Mercedes that you will refund invoice 14-0013 as he has decided to go with you for a comprehensive branding plan.

1. Choose **Customers→Customer Center**.
2. Single-click the **Project #13** job in the Customers & Jobs list.

3. Double-click the **Invoice** displayed on the Transactions tab.

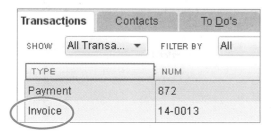

4. Click the **Refund/Credit** button on the Ribbon.

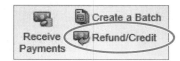

5. Follow these steps to create the credit memo for Billy:

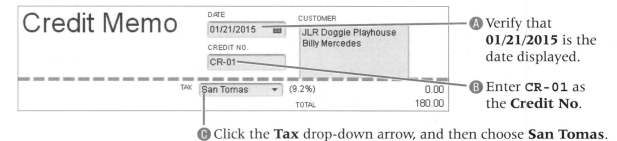

A Verify that **01/21/2015** is the date displayed.

B Enter **CR-01** as the **Credit No**.

C Click the **Tax** drop-down arrow, and then choose **San Tomas**.

Leave the Create Credit Memos/Refunds window open. You will issue the refund from it in the next step.

Apply a Credit to and Create a New Invoice

You will now choose to apply the credit to a new invoice and then create the new invoice.

6. Click the **Use credit to apply to invoice** button on the Ribbon.

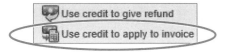

7. Click **OK** in the Warning window; click **Save & Close** to record the credit memo.

BTS BRIEF
43200•Design Income DR 180.00; **11000-Accounts Receivable CR <180.00>**

8. Click Save & New in the Create Invoices window.

9. Follow these steps to create an invoice for the branding and apply the credit to it:

A Choose the **Project #13** job for JLR Doggie Playhouse. **B** Verify the date is **01/21/2015**.

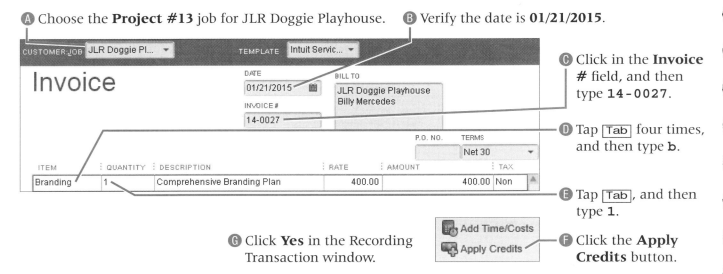

C Click in the **Invoice #** field, and then type **14-0027**.

D Tap ⟦Tab⟧ four times, and then type **b**.

E Tap ⟦Tab⟧, and then type **1**.

G Click **Yes** in the Recording Transaction window.

F Click the **Apply Credits** button.

The Apply Credits window will launch. Take a look at how the credit has been applied to the invoice, and the balance due is now $220.

10. Click **Done** in the Apply Credits window; close the **Create Invoices** window.

Producing Inventory and Sales Reports and Graphs

QuickBooks features many preset reports to help you efficiently manage inventory and sales. You will produce these reports in much the same way as you have created reports for other aspects of your business.

Physical Inventory Worksheet

Periodically, it is important to physically count your inventory items and to make sure that what is "on the books" is actually what you have in stock. Many businesses do this type of procedure annually and adjust their books accordingly. QuickBooks provides a great report that can aid in this process—the Physical Inventory Worksheet. It shows the name, description, preferred vendor, and on-hand quantity of each item you have in inventory. It also provides a column with blank lines, where you can record what you actually have during a physical inventory count.

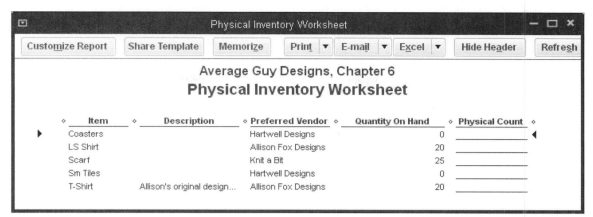

Notice that there is no Description for the inventory items entered earlier. This is because we did not enter that information in the Add/Edit Multiple List Entries window, but you can do so by going back there and adding columns or by editing in the Edit Item window.

Making Inventory Adjustments

In Chapter 12, Reporting, Adjusting Entries, and Closing the Books, you will learn how to make inventory adjustments that are necessary when there is a discrepancy between the quantity on hand (as per QuickBooks) and the physical count of an inventory item.

The following table lists many reports useful when you work with inventory items.

INVENTORY REPORTS AND THEIR PURPOSES	
Inventory Report Name	**What it will tell you...**
Inventory Valuation Summary	The value of your inventory by item
Inventory Valuation Detail	The details of the transactions that affect the value of inventory
Inventory Stock Status by Item	The inventory items you need to reorder and the current number in stock of each item
Inventory Stock Status by Vendor	Similar to the Inventory Stock Status by Item but arranged by vendor
Physical Inventory Worksheet	A printable worksheet used to count physical inventory or to compare physical quantity to the number QuickBooks has recorded

Tracking Sales

The Sales area of the Report Center features reports and graphs that help you to stay on top of your company's sales. You can choose from reports grouped by Sales by Customer, Sales by Item, and Sales by Rep (if sales reps have been set up). You can also view sales information by job if you have jobs set up for your company. The Sales Graph can graphically display your sales by item, customer, and rep.

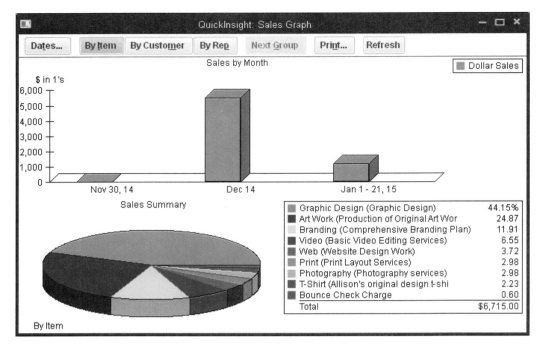

Graphs are a great way to illustrate your company's information. Here, you can see the sales by month for the fiscal year to date as well as the sales by item. Remember that if QuickBooks doesn't provide a preset graph that works for you, you can export your data to Excel and create your graphs there.

QUICK REFERENCE	PRODUCING INVENTORY, RECEIVABLES, AND SALES REPORTS AND GRAPHS
Task	**Procedure**
Display an inventory, receivable or sales report or graph	■ Open the Report Center. ■ Choose the category of the report you wish to run. ■ Click the report; click the Display button.

DEVELOP YOUR SKILLS 6-8
Create Inventory and Sales Reports

This report will show the dollar value (based on purchase price) of the company's inventory.

1. Choose **Reports→Inventory→Inventory Valuation Summary**.

2. Tap $\boxed{a}$ to set **All** as the date range for the report.
   The report will show the number of items you have in inventory as well as their asset value (cost) and retail value.

3. Close the report, choosing not to memorize it.

Determine Which Items to Reorder

This report will help Guy to determine when he needs to order additional items.

4. Choose **Reports→Inventory→Inventory Stock Status by Item**.

5. Tap a to set the date range to **All**.

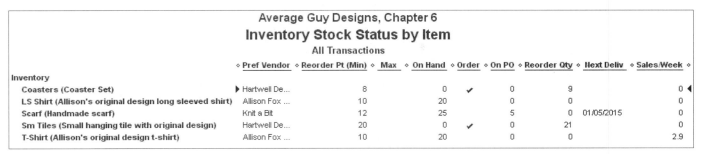

	◇ Pref Vendor	◇ Reorder Pt (Min)	◇ Max	◇ On Hand	◇ Order	◇ On PO	◇ Reorder Qty	◇ Next Deliv	◇ Sales/Week
Inventory									
Coasters (Coaster Set)	▶ Hartwell De...	8		0	✔	0	9		0 ◀
LS Shirt (Allison's original design long sleeved shirt)	Allison Fox ...	10		20		0	0		0
Scarf (Handmade scarf)	Knit a Bit	12		25		5	0	01/05/2015	0
Sm Tiles (Small hanging tile with original design)	Hartwell De...	20		0	✔	0	21		0
T-Shirt (Allison's original design t-shirt)	Allison Fox ...	10		20		0	0		2.9

Average Guy Designs, Chapter 6
Inventory Stock Status by Item
All Transactions

Notice that a checkmark appears in the Order column when it is time to place an order.

6. Close the **Inventory Stock Status by Item** window, choosing not to memorize it.

Create a Sales Graph

Finally, you will create a graph that will show you all of the sales by month and the sales by customer for the fiscal year to date.

7. Choose **Reports→Sales→Sales Graph**.

8. Click the **Dates** button on the toolbar, tap a, and then click **OK**.

9. Click the **By Customer** button on the toolbar.

Notice the sales graph in the lower area of the window by customer. There are so many customers for the company that you will have to use QuickZoom to drill down to those classified as "Other."

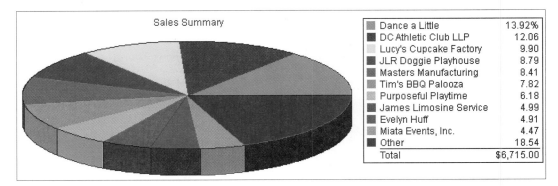

	Sales Summary	
■	Dance a Little	13.92%
■	DC Athletic Club LLP	12.06
■	Lucy's Cupcake Factory	9.90
■	JLR Doggie Playhouse	8.79
■	Masters Manufacturing	8.41
■	Tim's BBQ Palooza	7.82
■	Purposeful Playtime	6.18
■	James Limosine Service	4.99
■	Evelyn Huff	4.91
■	Miata Events, Inc.	4.47
■	Other	18.54
	Total	$6,715.00

10. Close the **Sales Graph** window.

11. Choose the appropriate option for your situation:
    - ■ If you will continue working, leave QuickBooks open.
    - ■ If you are finished working in QuickBooks for now, choose **File→Exit**.

Tackle the Tasks

Now is your chance to work a little more with Average Guy Designs and apply the skills that you have learned in this chapter to accomplish additional tasks. You will use the same company file you used in the Develop Your Skills exercises throughout this chapter. Enter the following tasks, referring back to the concepts in the chapter as necessary.

Create Inventory Item	Item Name: Earrings; Description: Designer Earrings; Cost: 19.50; Sales Amt.: 40.00; COGS: 50000•Cost of Goods Sold; Pref. Vendor: Holly's Bead Art; Income Acct: 41200•Accessories; Asset Acct.: 12100•Inventory Asset; Reorder: 15; Qty on Hand: 0.
Create Purchase Order	Create a PO to purchase 25 of the earrings you just entered as an inventory item on 1/24/15.
Receive Items	Receive the earrings with the bill on 1/30/15. Add a $15 shipping charge to the bill.
Sell Items	Sell three pairs of earrings to Chris Nelson (new customer) for his employees on 1/31/15, terms 2% 10 Net 30. Terms are only for this invoice.
Receive Payment	Receive an e-check, 758946, from Chris Nelson for the earrings on 2/4/15. Chris has taken advantage of the early payment discount. Deposit the payment to Checking on the same day.
Run Reports	Create a report that shows the inventory on hand and its value as of 1/31/15.
	Create a report that shows the total sales for January 2015.

Concepts Review

To check your knowledge of the key concepts introduced in this chapter, complete the Concepts Review quiz on the Student Resource Center or in your eLab course.

Reinforce Your Skills

Angela Stevens has just relocated her company, Quality-Built Construction, from California to Silverton, Oregon. You will be working with a QuickBooks Sample Company File in this exercise as it will allow you to run full payroll in a future chapter without having to purchase a payroll subscription.

Before you begin the Reinforce Your Skills exercises, complete one of these options:

■ Open **RYS_Chapter06** from your file storage location.

■ Restore **RYS_Chapter06 (Portable)** from your file storage location. Add your last name and first initial to the end of the filename.

Set Up Inventory and Sales Tax Items

In this exercise, you will set up sales tax and inventory items for Angela. The first step is to turn on the sales tax preference and set up a sales tax item.

It is understood that there is no sales tax in Oregon in "real life," but you will use it in this exercise in order to learn how to use the feature.

1. Choose **Edit→Preferences**.

2. Display the **Company Preferences** tab of the Sales Tax category.

3. Turn on the sales tax preference.

4. Set up a new sales tax item using this information.

Sales Tax Name	Marion County ST
Description	Marion County Sales Tax
Tax Rate	8.25%
Tax Agency	Marion County

5. Click **OK** to add the new sales tax item.

6. Choose **Marion County ST** as the most common sales tax item.

7. Click **OK** to close the Preferences window and accept the new preference.

8. Click **OK** in the Updating Sales Tax window; click **OK** to acknowledge the closing of all open windows.

Turn On Inventory Preferences

Angela wants to start offering custom-built woodworking items for sale to her customers. You will now help her to set up her QuickBooks file to deal with her inventory along with the new income and expenses involved.

9. Choose **Edit→Preferences**.

10. Click the **Items & Inventory** category, and then click the **Company Preferences** tab.

11. Click in the box to the left of **Inventory and purchase orders are active**.

12. Click **OK** to close the Preferences window; click **OK** to close the Warning window, if necessary.

Create a New Income Account

The next step for Angela to take is to set up a separate income account for the product sales.

13. Choose **Lists→Chart of Accounts**.

14. Click the **Account** menu button, and then choose **New**.

15. Choose **Income** as the account type, and then click **Continue**.

16. Type **4500**, tap Tab, type Product Sales, and then click **Save & Close**.

17. Close the **Chart of Accounts**.

Create a New Inventory Item

Now Angela needs to set up an inventory item to be able to sell her product using the sales forms.

18. Choose **Lists→Item List**, click the **Item** menu button, and then choose **New**.

19. Choose **Inventory Part** as the item type.

20. Use the following illustration to create the new item; click **OK** when you are finished.

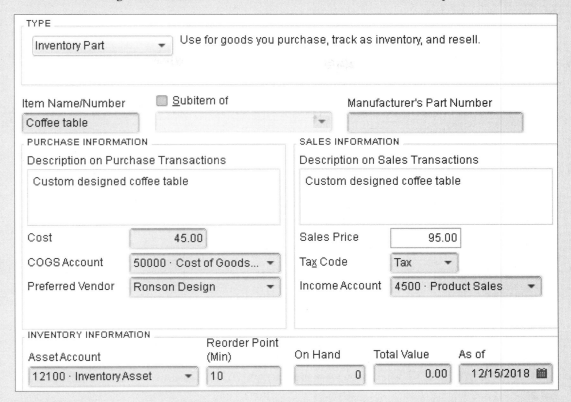

21. Close the **Item List**.

Create Purchase Orders and Receive Items

In this exercise, you will help Angela to order and receive inventory items. You will begin by creating a purchase order for the custom coffee tables.

1. Choose **Vendors→Create Purchase Orders**.

2. Use the following illustration to enter the information into the purchase order.

3. Click **Save & Close**.

Receive the Items

The coffee tables have arrived without the bill, so Angela needs to receive them into QuickBooks.

4. Choose **Vendors→Receive Items**.

5. Choose **Ronson Design** as the vendor, tap ⌷Tab⌷, and then click **Yes** to receive against an open purchase order.

6. Click in the **checkmark** column to the left of the purchase order dated 1/8/2019, and then click **OK**.

7. Change the date of the **Item Receipt** to **1/12/2019**, and then click **Save & Close**.

Receive the Bill

The bill for the coffee tables has just arrived, so it is time to enter it into QuickBooks.

8. Choose **Vendors→Enter Bill for Received Items**, and then choose **Ronson Design** as the vendor.

9. Click on the Item Receipt dated **1/12/19** to select it, and then click **OK**.

10. Tap ⌷Tab⌷, and then tap ⌷+⌷ until the date reads **1/14/19**.

11. Enter **Inv. #PCH-1** as the Ref. No. and Memo, and then enter **Net 15** as the terms.

12. Click **Save & Close**, clicking **Yes** to agree to change the transaction.

13. Click **Yes** to permanently change the information for Ronson Designs.

REINFORCE YOUR SKILLS 6-3
Sell Inventory Items

Once the products have been entered into inventory, it is time to start selling! In this exercise, you will record inventory sales.

1. Choose **Customers→Enter Sales Receipts**.

2. Choose **Ramirez, Hector:New Home** as the **Customer:Job**.

3. Use the following illustration to enter the information for the sales receipt.

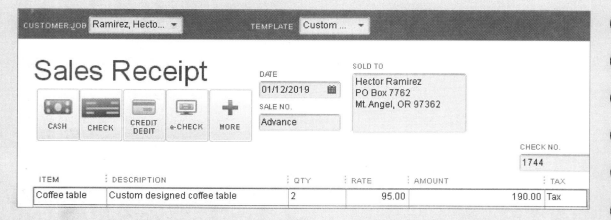

4. Click **Save & New** to record the sale.

Record Sales from a Craft Fair

Angela's daughter rented a booth at a local craft fair and sold the coffee tables. You will now help her to enter the sales.

5. Enter **1/13/2019** as the date of the sale, and then **Cash** as the Payment Method.

6. Choose **Coffee Table** as the Item, with a quantity of **5**.

7. Enter **Craft Fair Sales** as the memo.

8. Click **Save & Close** to record the sale.

REINFORCE YOUR SKILLS 6-4

Process Payments

In this exercise, you will help Angela to deposit all of the payments received into the Checking account.

1. Choose **Banking→Make Deposits**.

   The Payments to Deposit window will appear.

2. Click the **Select All** button, and then click **OK**.

3. Change the date of the deposit to **1/14/2019**, ensure that Checking is the account displayed, and then click **Save & Close**.

   All of the payments waiting in the Undeposited Funds account have now been deposited into the Checking account.

REINFORCE YOUR SKILLS 6-5

Produce Reports

In this exercise, you will create an inventory report that details the quantity and value of inventory on hand.

1. Choose **Reports→Inventory→Inventory Valuation Detail**.

2. Tap ⓐ to set the date range to **All**.

3. Using **QuickZoom**, go to the bill for the coffee tables.

4. Change the terms of the bill to **Net 30**.

5. Save the bill with the changes, choosing to have the new terms appear next time and become a permanent change to the vendor record.

6. Click **Yes** to refresh the report.

7. Close the report, choosing not to memorize it.

8. Choose the appropriate option for your situation:

   ■ If you will continue working, leave QuickBooks open.

   ■ If you are finished working in QuickBooks for now, choose **File→Exit**.

Apply Your Skills

Before you begin the Apply Your Skills exercises, complete one of these options:

■ Open **AYS_Chapter06** from your file storage location.

■ Restore **AYS_Chapter06 (Portable)** from your file storage location. Add your last name and first initial to the end of the filename.

APPLY YOUR SKILLS 6-1
Set Up Sales Tax and Inventory Items

In this exercise, you will help Sadie to set up sales tax and inventory items that she will begin selling to her customers.

1. Open the **Preferences** window and set the preference to collect sales tax.

2. Set up a new sales tax item (**King County Sales Tax** for **10%**, payable to **King County Treasurer**), and then set it as the most common sales tax item.

3. Click **OK** to close the Preferences window and accept the new preference.

4. Choose to make all existing customers taxable but not all existing non-inventory and inventory parts.

Turn On the Preference and Create a New Income Account

Before you can set up inventory items, you must turn on the preference and have an income account for the item sales to flow into.

5. Open the **Preferences** window, and then turn on the **Inventory and purchase order** feature; click OK in the Preferences window.

6. Choose **Company→Home Page**.

7. Open the **Chart of Accounts**, and then create a new income account called **Sales**. Close the **Chart of Accounts** when finished.

Create New Inventory Items

Now you will set up the new items that will be sold.

8. Using either the **Item List** or the **Add/Edit Multiple List Entries** window, create these inventory part items.

Item Name	Toothbrush	Chew Toy	Cat Collar
Purchase/Sales Description	Dog toothbrush and paste kit	The great indestructible ball!	Designer cat collar
Cost	6.49	3.71	8.00
Preferred Vendor	Seattle Vet Supply	Bothell Pet Supply Co.	Take a Walk
Sales Price	14.99	8.99	19.99
Income Account	Sales	Sales	Sales
Reorder Point	15	20	10

9. Close the **Item List** or **Add/Edit Multiple List Entries** window.

Purchase and Receive Inventory Items

In this exercise, you will help Dr. James to purchase and receive her new inventory items in order to have them in stock.

Create Purchase Orders

First you must create the purchase orders.

1. Open the **Create Purchase Orders** window.

2. Order 25 toothbrushes from Seattle Vet Supply on 7/1/14; click **Save & New**.

3. Order 40 chew toys from Bothell Pet Supply Co. on 7/2/14; click **Save & New**.

4. Order 15 cat collars from Take a Walk on 7/2/14; click **Save & Close**.

Receive the Items

You will now receive the items into inventory.

5. You received all 25 toothbrushes from Seattle Vet Supply on 7/7/2014, along with the bill. Receive the items and enter the bill, making sure to receive against the purchase order you created.

6. You received 33 of the chew toys from Bothell Pet Supply Co. The rest are on backorder, so you did not receive the bill yet. Receive these 33 items into inventory on 7/8/2014.

7. You received all 15 of the cat collars from Take a Walk on 7/12/2014, along with the bill. Included on the bill was a shipping charge of $12.95. Receive the items into inventory and enter the bill. Create a new Postage and Delivery expense account for the shipping charge.

8. On 7/14/2014, you received a bill for the chew toys you received on 7/8/2014, along with a shipping charge of $13.50 and a note stating that they would not be charging you a shipping charge for the backordered chew toys.

9. Receive the seven chew toys that were on backorder, along with the bill, on 7/25/2014.

Sell Inventory

In this exercise, you will help Sadie to process sales for the new inventory items. Jill Ann Tank came in to pick up two of the new cat collars she heard you talking about.

1. Using an **Enter Sales Receipts** window, sell Jill Ann Tank two of the new designer cat collars on 7/14/2014. She pays with cash.

Sell Inventory with Discount Payment Terms

One of the dog handlers from King County Sheriff decided to get toothbrushes and chew toys for the dogs. You will create an invoice using discount payment terms.

2. Sell seven toothbrushes and seven chew toys to King County Sheriff K-9 Unit on 7/15/2014. The Terms should be 2% 10 Net 30. Choose to not make the change in Terms permanent.

Sell Inventory with Service and Non-Inventory Items

Inventory items can be sold on invoices with any other type of item. You will create an invoice that includes service, inventory, and non-inventory items.

3. Stacy LiMarzi brought in his cat, Reagan, for a new-patient exam on 7/19/2014. Create an invoice for him for the New Patient Exam, a FIV/FeLV test, and a dose of Revolution for a cat. Stacy noticed the new cat collars in the lobby and decided to get one for Reagan as well. Only the collar is taxable.

Receive Payments for Inventory Sales

Now you will receive payment on the two invoices you just created.

4. Open the **Receive Payments** window, and then choose King County Sheriff K-9 Unit as the customer. Receive check 7796 for $180.96 to pay for invoice 176 on 7/21/2014, applying the 2 percent discount of $3.69 since the payment was received within 10 days. Create a new income account called Less Discounts Given as the Discount Account, clicking Save & New when you have entered all of the information correctly.

5. Choose Stacy LiMarzi as the customer and 7/22/2014 as the Date. Stacy has paid the entire amount of invoice 177 with check 448. **Save & Close** the transaction.

Issue a Credit and a Refund Check

In this exercise, you find Dr. James realizing that she overcharged the City of Seattle K-9 Unit on invoice 148, as Duke did not receive a nail trim. You will help her to issue a credit memo and a refund check to the city.

1. Open the **Create Credit Memos/Refunds** window, and then choose **City of Seattle K-9 Unit:Dog-Duke** as the Customer:Job.

2. Set the date to **7/14/2014**, enter **RF1** as the Credit No., and then choose **Nails** as the non-taxable Item.

3. Click **Save & Close**, and then choose to **Give a refund** in the Available Credit window.

4. Verify that the information is correct in the Issue a Refund window, making sure that the check is set to be printed, and then click **OK**.

   The refund check is now in the queue waiting to be printed.

Answer Questions with Reports

In this exercise, you will answer questions for Dr. James by running reports. You may wish to display the Report Center in List View to help you answer the questions. Ask your instructor if you should print the reports, print (save) them as PDF files, export them to Excel, or simply display them on the screen.

1. How many inventory items do we currently have in stock as of 7/31/2014?

2. How much is the inventory that we have in stock worth as of 7/31/2014?

3. What is the sales amount for each customer during the month of July 2014?

4. What item have we sold the most of during the month of July 2014?

5. What bills are still unpaid, as of 7/31/2014, including those for the inventory we purchased?

6. Submit your reports based on the guidelines provided by your instructor.

7. Choose the appropriate option for your situation:
   - If you are continuing on to the next chapter or the Extend Your Skills exercises, leave QuickBooks open.
   - If you are finished working in QuickBooks for now, choose **File→Exit**.

Extend Your Skills

In the course of working through the following Extend Your Skills exercises, you will be utilizing various skills taught in this and previous chapter(s). Take your time and think carefully about the tasks presented to you. Turn back to the chapter content if you need assistance.

6-1 Sort Through the Stack

Before You Begin: Restore the EYS1_Chapter06 (Portable) file or open the EYS1_Chapter 06 company file from your storage location.

You have been hired by Arlaine Cervantes to help her with her organization's books. She is the founder of Niños del Lago, a nonprofit organization that provides impoverished Guatemalan children with an engaging educational camp experience. You have just sat down at your desk and opened a large envelope from her with a variety of documents and noticed that you have several emails from her as well. It is your job to sort through the papers and emails and make sense of what you find, entering information into QuickBooks whenever appropriate and answering any other questions in a word-processing document saved as **EYS1_Chapter06_ LastnameFirstinitial**. Remember, you are digging through papers you just dumped out of an envelope and addressing random emails from Arlaine, so it is up to you to determine the correct order in which to complete the tasks.

- Sticky note from Arlaine: We are going to start selling items made by Guatemalan women. I would like to see if we can set them up in QuickBooks. Our accountant told me that we should use the "average cost" method to keep track of our inventory. Will we be able to track this in QuickBooks? (Explain your answer.)
- Packing slip and bill from GWAA dated 8/14/2014. You have received the rest of the scarves and cosmetic bags, and a $45 shipping charge was included on the bill.
- Note from Arlaine: A box containing traditional Guatemalan scarves was damaged in shipment to our sales rep in the U.S., and three scarves are no longer in sellable condition. Please figure out a way to take them out of inventory in QuickBooks.
- Scribbled on a scrap of paper: If we can track inventory in QuickBooks, please set up "Traditional Guatemalan Scarf" as an inventory item; the cost from Guatemalan Women's Art Alliance (GWAA) is $7.00, and the resale price is $20.00. Also, please set up two more inventory items to track "Cosmetic Bag" and "Handbag". The cost from GWAA for the cosmetic bag is $8.00 with a resale price of $18.00, and the cost for the handbag is $15.00 with a resale price is $35.00. As of 8/1/2014, order the following inventory: 50 scarves, 40 cosmetic bags, and 25 handbags.
- Handwritten invoice: 10 scarves and 5 handbags sold to Average Guy Designs, dated 8/16/2014, due 2% 10 Net 30.
- Packing slip from GWAA: Dated 8/5/2014 for receipt of 45 scarves, 30 cosmetic bags, and 25 handbags; the rest are on backorder.
- Photocopy of a check: Check 2007 from Average Guy Designs dated 8/23/2013 written for the total amount due and with a memo stating the company took advantage of the 2 percent discount.
- Scribbled note from Arlaine: Can you produce a report for me that shows the value of the inventory we currently have in stock? How about the number of each item?

6-2 Be Your Own Boss

Before You Begin: Complete Extend Your Skills 5-2 before starting this exercise.

In this exercise, throughout the entire book, you will build on the company file that you outlined and created in previous chapters. If you have created a file for your actual business, then enter your starting inventory and any purchases since your starting date. If you are creating a fictitious company, then create at least five inventory items and order and receive a reasonable quantity of each. Create at least ten invoices selling your products to either existing or new customers, ensuring that at least five of them are sold with discount payment terms. Receive the payments for the invoices, making sure to allow those with discount payment terms to take advantage of the discount. You will make up the names and information for this exercise.

Create Inventory Stock Status by Item and Transaction List by Customer reports and submit them to your instructor based on the instructions provided.

Open the company file you worked on in Extend Your Skills 5-2 and complete the tasks outlined above. When you are done, save it as a portable company file, naming it as **EYS2_Chapter06_ LastnameFirstinitial (Portable)** and submit it to your instructor based on the instructions provided.

6-3 Use the Web as a Learning Tool

Throughout this book, you will be provided with an opportunity to use the Internet as a learning tool by completing WebQuests. According to the original creators of WebQuests, as described on their website (http://WebQuest.org), a WebQuest is "an inquiry-oriented activity in which most or all of the information used by learners is drawn from the web." To complete the WebQuest projects in this book, navigate to the Student Resource Center and choose the WebQuest for the chapter on which you are working. The subject of each WebQuest will be relevant to the material found in the chapter.

WebQuest Subject: Learning about sales tax where you do business

Working with Balance Sheet Accounts and Budgets

CHAPTER OBJECTIVES

After studying this chapter, you will be able to:

- Work with current assets and transfer funds between accounts

- Track petty cash

- Work with fixed asset accounts and items

- Pay current liabilities and set up a long term liability

- Work with equity accounts

- Set up and use QuickBooks budgets and deal with receivables

In previous chapters you learned to work with banking and credit card accounts, Accounts Receivable, and Accounts Payable. In this chapter, you will tackle the other balance sheet accounts in QuickBooks: Other Current Assets, Fixed Assets, Current Liabilities, Long Term Liabilities, and Equity. These other balance sheet accounts allow you to track the various assets owned by your business, liabilities owed by your business, loans that span more than one year, prepaid expenses, and owner/shareholder investment in a company. Finally, you will learn how to use the Collections Center, receivable reports, and budgeting feature in QuickBooks.

Average Guy Designs

Average Guy Designs has been approached by the landlord who offered Guy a discount on the monthly rent amount if the company will pay six months of rent up front. Guy has decided to take advantage of this offer and has asked Allison to set QuickBooks up to track this rent prepayment. In the last chapter, sales tax was collected for the inventory sales and is being held in a current liability account, Sales Tax Payable. You will help Allison to pay the sales tax due for January in this chapter.

Guy has decided to purchase a new scooter that he will use to visit customers around town. Allison will be setting up a fixed asset item for the scooter and a long term liability to track the loan for it.

Finally, Allison will explore how to work with budgets in QuickBooks.

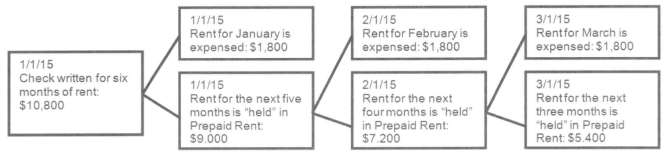

Notice how the Prepaid Insurance account "holds" funds that you have prepaid so you can expense them in the month they are actually used.

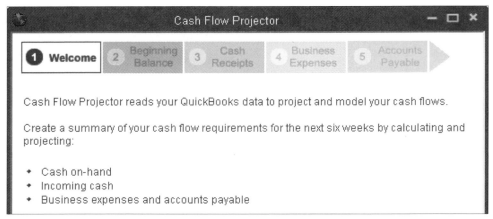

The new Cash Flow Projector feature in QuickBooks 2014 allows you to use your own data to help you to manage your company's cash flow.

Working with Other Current Assets

Companies use other current assets to help them match their expenses to income within the same reporting period. This is a particularly important aspect when you use the accrual basis of accounting. You will recall from Chapter 1, Introducing QuickBooks Pro that a company using the accrual basis of accounting records expenses when accrued, not when cash is paid. This means that even if you pay a six-month insurance policy or six months of rent up front, you must expense it during the month that it covers.

Balance Sheet Accounts

Remember, the balance sheet accounts are the asset, liability, and equity accounts. You have already learned about many balance sheet accounts: bank, credit card, Accounts Receivable, and Accounts Payable. Now you will focus on the remaining balance sheet accounts. Refer to the following table to learn more about these other accounts.

ADDITIONAL TYPES OF BALANCE SHEET ACCOUNTS

Account Type	Description	Examples
Other Current Asset	Assets you plan to either use or convert to cash within one year	■ Prepaid Insurance ■ Security Deposit
Fixed Asset	Assets you do not plan to convert to cash within one year; they are usually depreciable	■ Vehicle ■ Equipment
Other Current Liability	Funds your business owes and plans to pay within a year	■ Sales Tax Payable ■ Payroll Liabilities
Long Term Liabilities	Liabilities (loans) you do not plan to pay off within the next year	■ Mortgage ■ Auto Loan
Equity	The owner's equity in the company, whether it is a sole proprietor, a partner, or shareholders	■ Owner's Equity ■ Retained Earnings

BEHIND THE SCENES

When writing a check for six months of rent, you expense the current month's coverage and hold the rest in the Prepaid Rent account.

13200-Prepaid Rent	67100-Rent Expense	10000-Checking
3,500.00	700.00	4,200.00

QUICK REFERENCE	USING OTHER CURRENT ASSET ACCOUNTS
Task	**Procedure**
Create an Other Current Asset account	■ Choose Lists→Chart of Accounts. ■ Click the Account menu button and choose New. ■ Choose Other Account Types, select Other Current Asset from the drop-down list, and then click Continue. ■ Type the account number and the name of the new account.
Fund an Other Current Asset account	■ Choose Banking→Write Checks. ■ Choose Checking as the bank account; complete the rest of the vendor information. ■ Enter the amount for the current month as an expense and the remaining amount as a debit to the other current asset account you created to track it (such as Prepaid Rent).

DEVELOP YOUR SKILLS 7-1

Create and Fund a Prepaid Rent Account

In this exercise, you will help Allison set up QuickBooks to track the prepayment of rent for the company. The first step is to open QuickBooks, and then either open a company file or restore a portable company file.

 Intuit provides maintenance releases throughout the lifetime of the product. These updates may require you to update your student exercise files before you begin working with them. Please follow the prompts on the screen if you are asked to update your company file to the latest QuickBooks release.

1. Start **QuickBooks 2014**.

   If you downloaded the student exercise files in the portable company file *format, follow Option 1 below. If you downloaded the files in the* company file *format, follow Option 2.*

Option 1: Restore a Portable Company File

2. Choose **File→Open or Restore Company**.

3. Restore the **DYS_Chapter07 (Portable)** portable company file from your file storage location, placing your last name and first initial at the end of the filename (e.g., DYS_ Chapter07_MarshallG).

   It may take a few moments for the portable company file to open. Once it does, continue with step 5.

Option 2: Open a Company File

2. Choose **File→Open or Restore Company**, ensure that **Open a regular company file** is selected, and then open the **DYS_Chapter07** company file from your file storage location.

   The QuickBooks company file will open.

3. Click **OK** to close the QuickBooks Information window. Click **No** in the Set Up External Accountant User window, if necessary.

4. Close the **Reminders** window.

Create a Prepaid Rent Account

Now you will create a prepaid rent account.

5. Click the **Chart of Accounts** task icon in the Company area of the Home page.

6. Click the **Account** menu button, and then choose **New**.

7. Follow these steps to create the new account:

Chart of
Accounts

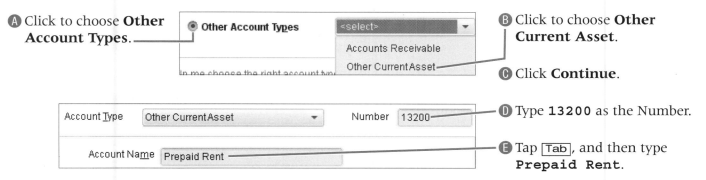

Ⓐ Click to choose **Other Account Types**.

Ⓑ Click to choose **Other Current Asset**.

Ⓒ Click **Continue**.

Ⓓ Type **13200** as the Number.

Ⓔ Tap Tab, and then type **Prepaid Rent**.

8. Click **Save & Close**; close the **Chart of Accounts** window.

Fund the Prepaid Rent Account

Allison will now write the check for the rent payment, expensing the current month and placing the rest in the prepaid rent account. However, she has realized that she will first need to transfer funds from Savings to Checking to cover the expense.

9. Choose **Banking→Transfer Funds**.

10. Transfer **$5,000** from Savings to Checking, using this illustration as a guide.

11. Close the **Transfer Funds Between Accounts** window.

12. Click the **Write Checks** task icon in the Banking area of the Home page.

Write
Checks

13. Follow these steps to write the rent check:

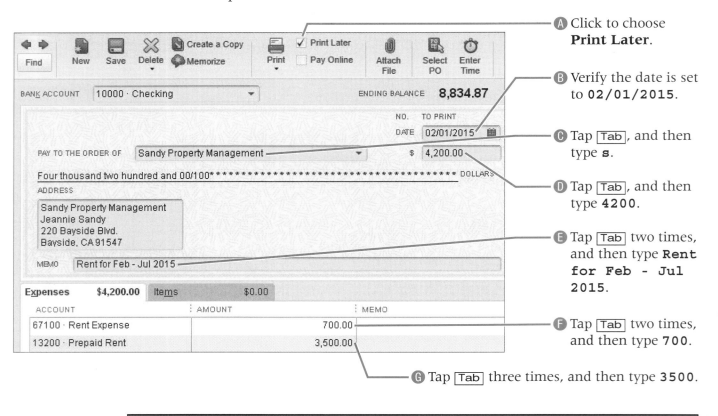

(A) Click to choose **Print Later**.

(B) Verify the date is set to **02/01/2015**.

(C) Tap ⌨Tab, and then type **s**.

(D) Tap ⌨Tab, and then type **4200**.

(E) Tap ⌨Tab two times, and then type **Rent for Feb - Jul 2015**.

(F) Tap ⌨Tab two times, and then type **700**.

(G) Tap ⌨Tab three times, and then type **3500**.

> **BTS BRIEF**
>
> 13200•Prepaid Rent DR 3,500.00; 67100•Rent Expense DR 700.00; **10000•Checking CR <4,200.00>**

14. Click **Save & Close**.

Transferring Funds Between Accounts

Once you place funds in an Other Current Asset account, you must be able to expense them when they are used. This is important, as you need to make sure to match expenses to income during the period in which they are utilized. Another term for this transfer of funds from the asset to the expense account is *amortization*. Amortization is likely familiar to you; it is simply the process of a balance decreasing over time. For instance, if you have a home mortgage, the way that the balance that you owe decreases over, say, 30 years is amortization. You can accomplish this transfer in the register window of the asset; you do not have to use a formal journal entry (which you will learn about in Chapter 12, Reporting, Adjusting Entries, and Closing the Books).

Memorizing Transactions

There are many transactions (such as the expensing of other current assets) that you have to repeat over and over again. You can choose to have

FROM THE KEYBOARD

Ctrl+t to open the Memorized Transactions List

QuickBooks memorize these transactions to increase your efficiency. When QuickBooks memorizes a transaction, you can choose:

- To be reminded about the transaction
- To not be reminded and simply have it listed on the Memorized Transaction List
- To have QuickBooks automatically enter it as frequently as you wish

By default, QuickBooks will choose for you to be reminded of the memorized transaction. You must make sure to choose one of the other options if you want the transaction to be listed or to occur automatically.

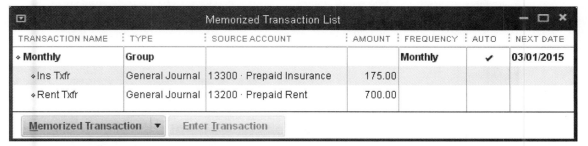

The Memorized Transaction List keeps track of all of your memorized transactions for you. Access it via the Lists option on the menu bar.

Recurring Transactions

When you are creating a new memorized transaction that you want QuickBooks to enter automatically for you, you can now group it with other transactions you have memorized.

The Enter Memorized Transactions window appears whenever you open QuickBooks and have transactions that are scheduled to be entered. This detailed list includes automatic transactions and helps you to stay on top of which transactions are slated to be entered. And, if you enter all of them, you will have a reminder of exactly what QuickBooks is doing for you behind the scenes when entering automatic transactions.

Using Memorized Transactions for Common Transactions

You can also use the Memorized Transaction List for transactions that you complete on a regular basis. For instance, if you often pay bills electronically, you can memorize a Write Checks window with BPOL (Bill Pay Online) in the check number field and then just double-click it from the Memorized Transaction List when you need to enter another online bill payment.

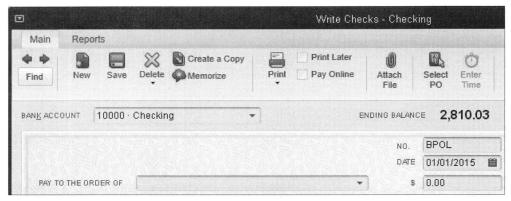

To set up a common transaction to be memorized, add the entries in the correct transaction window. Here, note that "BPOL" has been entered as the check number.

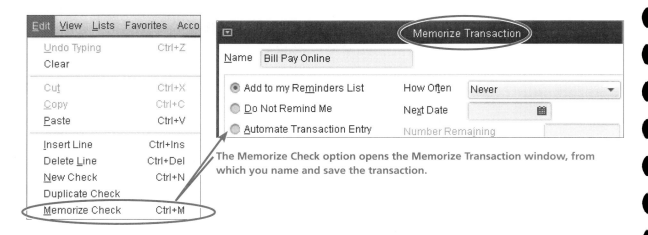

The Memorize Check option opens the Memorize Transaction window, from which you name and save the transaction.

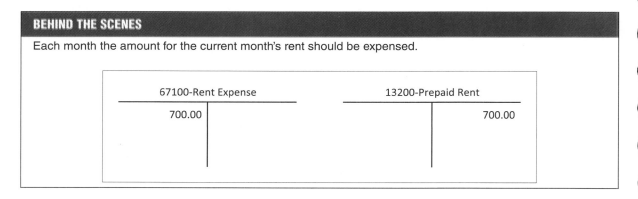

BEHIND THE SCENES

Each month the amount for the current month's rent should be expensed.

67100-Rent Expense		13200-Prepaid Rent	
700.00			700.00

Task	Procedure
Transfer funds between accounts using a register	■ Choose Lists→Chart of Accounts. ■ Double-click the desired account; enter the date and amount of the transfer. ■ Choose the desired account; record the transaction.
Memorize a transaction	■ Ensure that the desired transaction is currently displayed, and then single-click within it to select it. ■ Choose Edit→Memorize General Journal (or whatever type of transaction it is). ■ Enter the information regarding how you want QuickBooks to deal with the memorized transaction; click OK.

Advanced Skills

DEVELOP YOUR SKILLS 7-2

Make and Memorize a Transfer of Funds

In this exercise, you will help Allison to record the first transfer of funds from Prepaid Rent to Rent Expense. Once the transfer is set up, you will memorize it to occur automatically. Before you set up your first recurring monthly transaction in your Memorized Transaction List, you will create a group called "Monthly" for this list entry. You can then add new monthly transactions as they are created.

1. Choose **Lists→Memorized Transaction List**.

   The Memorized Transaction List window will appear.

2. Click the **Memorized Transaction** menu button, and then choose **New Group**.

   The New Memorized Transaction Group window will be displayed.

3. Follow these steps to create the new group:

Ⓐ Type **Monthly**.

Ⓑ Click to the left of **Automate Transaction Entry**.

Ⓒ Click the drop-down arrow and choose **Monthly**.

Ⓓ Tap ⟨Tab⟩, and then type **030115**.

4. Click **OK** to record the new memorized group.

Record Next Month's Rent Expense

5. Choose **Lists→Chart of Accounts**.

6. Double-click the **13200•Prepaid Rent** account.

   The register for the asset will open. Notice that QuickBooks has registered an increase in the Prepaid Rent account for $3,500.

7. Follow these steps to record a transfer of $700 from Prepaid Rent to the Rent expense account:

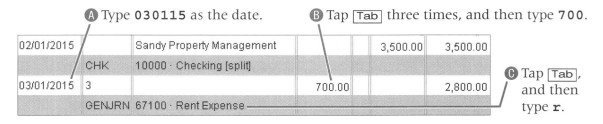

Ⓐ Type **030115** as the date.　　**Ⓑ** Tap ⌈Tab⌉ three times, and then type **700**.

02/01/2015		Sandy Property Management			3,500.00	3,500.00
	CHK	10000 · Checking [split]				
03/01/2015	3		700.00			2,800.00
	GENJRN	67100 · Rent Expense				

Ⓒ Tap ⌈Tab⌉, and then type **r**.

BTS BRIEF

67100•Rent Expense DR 700.00; **13200•Prepaid Rent CR <700.00>**

---

8. Click **Record** at the bottom-right of the register window.

Memorize the Transaction

So Allison will not have to sit down at the computer at the first of each month and record this transfer, she will memorize it and choose for QuickBooks to include it in the Enter Memorized Transactions list.

9. Click anywhere within the two lines of the transaction you just recorded.

10. Choose **Edit→Memorize General Journal**.

   This transaction is considered a general journal entry because it is a basic transfer between accounts.

11. Follow these steps to memorize the transaction in the Monthly group:

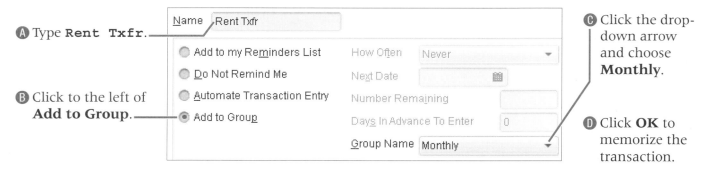

Ⓐ Type **Rent Txfr**.

Ⓑ Click to the left of **Add to Group**.

Ⓒ Click the drop-down arrow and choose **Monthly**.

Ⓓ Click **OK** to memorize the transaction.

12. Close the **Prepaid Rent** account register and the **Chart of Accounts** window.

   Take a look at the Memorized Transaction List and notice the new group and rent transfer entries.

13. Close the **Memorized Transaction List** window; close the **Chart of Accounts** window.

Tracking Petty Cash

Most businesses keep cash around for small expenditures. This is known as petty cash. In QuickBooks, you set up Petty Cash as a bank account in your Chart of Accounts. You fund it by transferring money from another account or by keeping cash back when you make a deposit.

Recording Methods

QuickBooks offers two methods to record petty cash expenditures:

- **Write Checks Method:** You can choose Petty Cash as the account and use the Write Checks window to record your petty cash expenses.
- **The Register Method:** You can enter petty cash expenditures directly into the register.

The register method allows you to enter your petty cash expenditures more quickly, as you can tab through it faster.

BEHIND THE SCENES

When you use the checking account to fund the petty cash account, you debit Petty Cash and credit Checking.

10500-Petty Cash		10000-Checking	
300.00			300.00

When you use petty cash for a purchase, you debit the expense account (in this example Shipping Expense) and credit Petty Cash.

67500-Shipping Expense		10500-Petty Cash	
18.49			18.49

QUICK REFERENCE	TRACKING PETTY CASH
Task	**Procedure**
Create a Petty Cash account	■ Choose Lists→Chart of Accounts. ■ Click the Account menu button; choose New. ■ Choose Bank as the account type; click Continue. ■ Type the account number, and then name the account Petty Cash.
Fund the Petty Cash account	■ Choose Banking→Write Checks. ■ Enter a check to cash for the amount, with Petty Cash as the account, and then record the transaction.
Enter petty cash expenditures	■ Choose Banking→Write Checks. ■ Choose Petty Cash as the Bank Account, enter the details, and then record the transaction.

DEVELOP YOUR SKILLS 7-3
Work with a Petty Cash Account

In this exercise, you will help Allison to create, fund, and use a petty cash account.

1. Choose **Lists→Chart of Accounts**.

   Note that there is not currently an account set up to track petty cash.

2. Click the **Account** menu button, and then choose **New**.

3. Choose **Bank** as the account type, and then click **Continue**.

4. Follow these steps to create the new account:

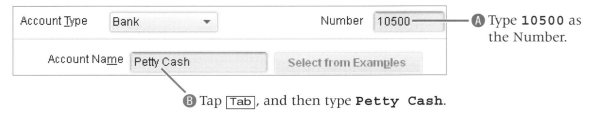

Ⓐ Type **10500** as the Number.

Ⓑ Tap Tab, and then type **Petty Cash**.

5. Click **Save & Close**; click **No** in the Set Up Bank Feeds window.

6. Close the **Chart of Accounts** window.

7. Click the **Write Checks** task icon in the Banking area of the Home page.

Write Checks

8. Tap ⎡Tab⎤ once you have ensured that Checking is the account, and then follow these steps to complete the check and fund petty cash:

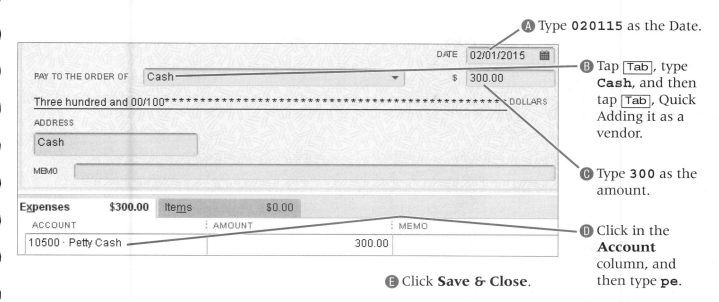

Ⓐ Type **020115** as the Date.

Ⓑ Tap ⎡Tab⎤, type **Cash**, and then tap ⎡Tab⎤, Quick Adding it as a vendor.

Ⓒ Type **300** as the amount.

Ⓓ Click in the **Account** column, and then type **pe**.

Ⓔ Click **Save & Close**.

Pay for Stamps Using the Petty Cash Register

Allison will now pay to ship a piece of art to a customer with petty cash and record the transaction in the Petty Cash register.

9. Click the **Chart of Accounts** task icon in the Company area of the Home page.

Chart of Accounts

10. Double-click the **Petty Cash** account in the Chart of Accounts window.

11. Follow these steps to record the charge to petty cash:

Ⓐ Type **020415** as the Date.

Ⓑ Tap ⎡Tab⎤, and then tap ⎡Delete⎤ to remove the check number.

Ⓒ Tap ⎡Tab⎤, type **USPS** as the Payee, and then tap ⎡Tab⎤ and Quick Add it as a vendor.

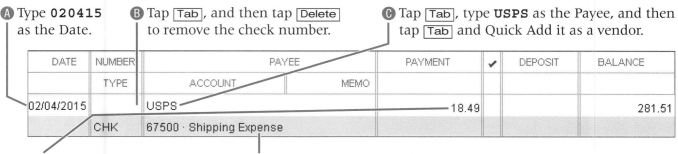

DATE	NUMBER	PAYEE		PAYMENT	✓	DEPOSIT	BALANCE
	TYPE	ACCOUNT	MEMO				
02/04/2015		USPS		18.49			281.51
	CHK	67500 · Shipping Expense					

Ⓓ Type **18.49** as the amount.

Ⓔ Tap ⎡Tab⎤, and then type **sh**.

12. Click **Record**; close the **Petty Cash** register window.

13. Close the **Chart of Accounts** window.

Advanced Skills

Writing Off Uncollectable Receivables

Virtually every business has to write off money owed as bad debt at some point or another and remove it from Accounts Receivable. QuickBooks does allow you to do this via one of two methods: treating it as a discount or using a credit memo. Your sales tax liability will not be affected if you choose to treat bad debt as a discount, whereas it will be reduced if you use the credit memo method. It is for this reason that the credit memo is recommended when sales tax is involved. Regardless of the method selected, you will need to create an expense account in which to direct the bad debt.

Example: You learn that Purposeful Playtime has gone out of business. You believe it is unlikely that you will be able to collect for the amount due. You decide that it is time to write off the amount owed by this customer as a bad debt.

FLASHBACK TO GAAP: MATERIALITY

Remember that when an item is reported, its significance should be considered.

Treating Bad Debt as a Discount

To treat bad debt as a discount (not recommended for a debt that has sales tax associated with it), you would enter it as a discount in the Receive Payments window as you learned about in Chapter 6, Dealing with Physical Inventory. Make sure, though, that you use the proper expense account for the bad debt (e.g., Bad Debt Expense). If you receive a partial payment from a customer, you can also choose to "Write off the extra amount" in the Receive Payments window if you do not expect to ever receive the remaining balance.

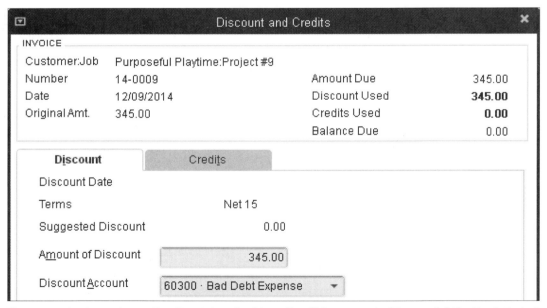

If you were to choose to use the discount method to write off the amount of Purposeful Playtime's Project #9 invoice, you would launch the Discount and Credits window from the Receive Payments window and choose 60300•Bad Debt Expense as the account.

Using a Credit Memo to Write Off a Bad Debt

In the next exercise, you will have the opportunity to create a credit memo in order to write off a bad debt. When you choose this method, you will use an Other Charge item to "route" the bad debt to the appropriate expense account (which will be debited), and Accounts Receivable will be credited. You can include both taxable and nontaxable bad debts on a single credit memo. You will finish the procedure by applying the credit memo to the original invoice.

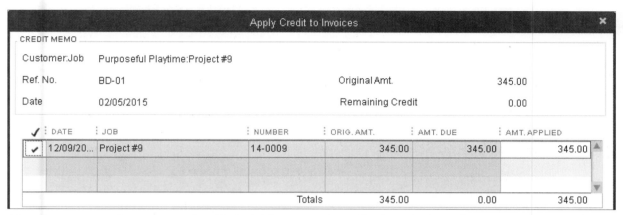

Apply Credit to Invoices	✕

CREDIT MEMO

Customer:Job	Purposeful Playtime:Project #9		
Ref. No.	BD-01	Original Amt.	345.00
Date	02/05/2015	Remaining Credit	0.00

✓	DATE	JOB	NUMBER	ORIG. AMT.	AMT. DUE	AMT. APPLIED
✓	12/09/20...	Project #9	14-0009	345.00	345.00	345.00
			Totals	345.00	0.00	345.00

After you create a credit memo to write off a bad debt, you can immediately apply the credit to the unpaid invoice(s) through the Apply Credit to Invoices window.

BEHIND THE SCENES

When you write off a bad debt, you need to credit the Accounts Receivable account and the customer sub-register (which automatically occurs when you choose the customer) and debit the expense account you created to track bad debts, in this case Bad Debt Expense.

60300-Bad Debt Expense		11000-Accounts Receivable	
345.00			345.00

QUICK REFERENCE | WRITING OFF BAD DEBT

Task	Procedure
Write off bad debt as a discount	▪ Create a new expense account called *Bad Debt Expense*. ▪ Choose Customers→Receive Payments. ▪ Select the customer and set the write-off date. ▪ Click the Discounts & Credits button. ▪ Enter the amount of the bad debt; choose Bad Debt Expense as the Discount Account. ▪ Complete the transaction.

	WRITING OFF BAD DEBT (continued)
Task	**Procedure**
Write off bad debt using a credit memo	■ Create a new expense account called *Bad Debt Expense*.
	■ Create an Other Charge item called Bad Debt that is routed to the Bad Debt Expense account.
	■ Choose Customers→Create Credit Memos/Refunds.
	■ Select the customer and set the date.
	■ Using the Bad Debt item, enter a line item for the total nontax sales you are writing off; choose Non in the Tax column.
	■ Using the Bad Debt item, enter a line item for the total taxable sales you are writing off; choose Tax in the Tax column.
	■ Click Save & Close.
	■ Choose to which invoice you wish to apply the credit (bad debt write-off).

DEVELOP YOUR SKILLS 7-4

Write Off Bad Debt

In this exercise, you will use the credit memo method to write off the amount owed by Purposeful Playtime. The first step is to create an expense account for the payment.

1. Click the **Chart of Accounts** task icon in the Company area of the Home page.

Chart of Accounts

2. Click the **Account** menu button, and then choose **New**.

3. Choose **Expense** as the account type; click **Continue**.

4. Follow these steps to create the new account:

Ⓐ Type **60300** as the **Number**.

Ⓒ Click **Save & Close**.   Ⓑ Tap [Tab], and then type **Bad Debt Expense**.

5. Close the **Chart of Accounts**.

Set Up the Bad Debt Item

The next step in writing off a bad debt using a credit memo is to create the item.

6. Click the **Items & Services** task icon in the Company area of the Home page.

7. Click the **Item** menu button, and then choose **New**.

Items & Services

8. Follow these steps to create the new item:

Ⓐ Choose **Other Charge** as the type.

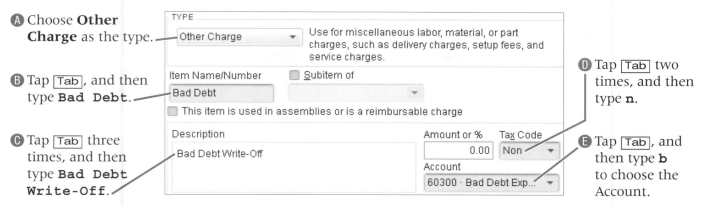

TYPE

Other Charge ▾ | Use for miscellaneous labor, material, or part charges, such as delivery charges, setup fees, and service charges.

Item Name/Number ☐ Subitem of
Bad Debt

☐ This item is used in assemblies or is a reimbursable charge

Description | Amount or % | Tax Code
Bad Debt Write-Off | 0.00 | Non ▾
Account
60300 · Bad Debt Exp... ▾

Ⓑ Tap Tab, and then type **Bad Debt**.

Ⓒ Tap Tab three times, and then type **Bad Debt Write-Off**.

Ⓓ Tap Tab two times, and then type **n**.

Ⓔ Tap Tab, and then type **b** to choose the Account.

Ⓕ Click **OK** to create the item.

The amount is left blank here so you can fill in the correct amount for each transaction. The Tax Code is set to Non so that you can set it for each receivable written off.

9. Close the **Item List** window.

Create the Credit Memo
Finally, you will create the credit memo to write off the bad debt and choose to which invoice(s) it should be applied.

10. Click the **Refunds & Credits** task icon in the Customers area of the Home page.

11. Follow these steps to complete the memo:

Ⓐ Click to remove the checkmark from this box.

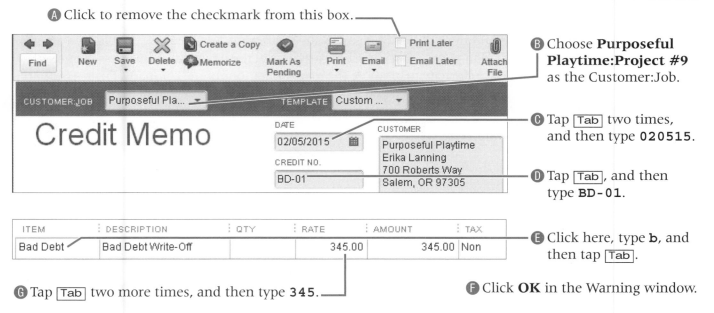

◄ ► | Find | New | Save | Delete | Create a Copy | Memorize | Mark As Pending | Print | Email | ☐ Print Later ☐ Email Later | Attach File

CUSTOMER:JOB Purposeful Pla... ▾   TEMPLATE Custom ... ▾

Credit Memo

DATE
02/05/2015 📅

CREDIT NO.
BD-01

CUSTOMER
Purposeful Playtime
Erika Lanning
700 Roberts Way
Salem, OR 97305

ITEM	DESCRIPTION	QTY	RATE	AMOUNT	TAX
Bad Debt	Bad Debt Write-Off		345.00	345.00	Non

Ⓑ Choose **Purposeful Playtime:Project #9** as the Customer:Job.

Ⓒ Tap Tab two times, and then type **020515**.

Ⓓ Tap Tab, and then type **BD-01**.

Ⓔ Click here, type **b**, and then tap Tab.

Ⓖ Tap Tab two more times, and then type **345**.

Ⓕ Click **OK** in the Warning window.

You will leave the transaction as nontaxable since the original invoice did not include tax.

Advanced Skills

12. Click **Save & Close**.

    An Available Credit window appears, from which you can decide what to do with the resulting credit.

13. Choose **Apply to an invoice**, and then click **OK**.

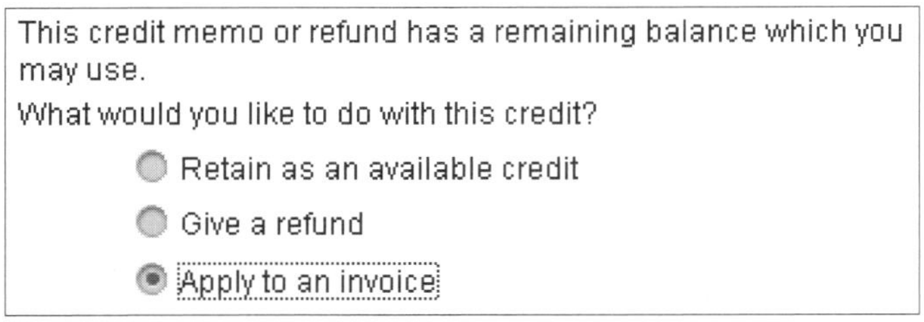

    This credit memo or refund has a remaining balance which you
    may use.
    What would you like to do with this credit?

    ○ Retain as an available credit
    ○ Give a refund
    ◉ Apply to an invoice

    The Apply Credits to Invoice window appears, listing all open invoices for the customer. QuickBooks checked both invoices to which to apply the amount from the credit memo.

14. Click **Done** in the **Apply Credits to Invoice** window.

    The total amount owed by Purposeful Playtime has now been transferred to the Bad Debt Expense account.

> **BTS BRIEF**
>
> 60300•Bad Debt Expense DR 345.00; 11000•Accounts Receivable CR <345.00>

Working with Fixed Assets

As you saw in the Additional Types of Balance Sheet Accounts table on page 279, a fixed asset is one that you don't plan to use up or turn into cash within the next year. A business uses fixed assets in a productive capacity to promote the main operations of the company. Fixed assets are also depreciable, which means that you don't expense the assets when you purchase them but rather over the useful life of the asset.

Look at the following list to see the main types of fixed assets:

- Land
- Buildings
- Leasehold Improvements
- Furniture & Equipment
- Vehicles

Setting Up Fixed Assets in QuickBooks

There are many correct ways to set up your fixed assets in QuickBooks. You should ask your accountant which method she prefers that you use. In this chapter, you will look at one method that involves creating a fixed asset account for each major type of fixed asset and then an account to track accumulated depreciation for all fixed assets. This is displayed in the following illustration.

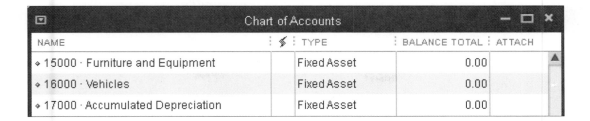

NAME	$\lightning$	TYPE	BALANCE TOTAL	ATTACH
◆ 15000 · Furniture and Equipment		Fixed Asset	0.00	
◆ 16000 · Vehicles		Fixed Asset	0.00	
◆ 17000 · Accumulated Depreciation		Fixed Asset	0.00	

Depreciation

Depreciation provides a business with a way to match income to expenses. A fixed asset is used to produce income over a period of time, and depreciation allows you to record the appropriate expense for the same period. Many small businesses record depreciation transactions just once a year, but they can be entered monthly or quarterly if the business produces financial statements for those periods. You will learn how to enter the annual depreciation transaction in Chapter 12, Reporting, Adjusting Entries, and Closing the Books.

FLASHBACK TO GAAP: MATCHING

Remember that expenses need to be matched with revenues.

Accumulated Depreciation

Each accounting period, a business records a depreciation expense for the fixed asset(s). These depreciation expenses "accumulate" in an account called Accumulated Depreciation, which is also a fixed asset account. Accumulated Depreciation is a *contra account*, which means it offsets the balance of the related fixed asset accounts by entering a negative amount so that the book value is displayed rather than the original cost on the balance sheet report.

Fixed Asset Items

Fixed asset items provide a convenient way to track your fixed assets. After creating your fixed asset account and subaccounts, you should set up the fixed asset item. These items help you to consolidate all of the important information about each fixed asset in a convenient place. In addition, your accountant can transfer the information from your Fixed Asset List to the Fixed Asset Manager, if they use that feature of QuickBooks.

In the Fixed Asset Item List QuickBooks allows you to track the following information:

- Purchase information/cost basis
- Corresponding asset account
- Warranty information

- Sales information
- Serial number
- Notes and descriptions

NAME	FAM NUMBER	PURCHASE DATE	PURCHASE DESCRIPTION	ACCOUNT	COST	ATTACH
◆ Vespa Scooter - 1		02/08/2015	2013 Used Vespa Scooter	16000 · Vehicles	4,500.00	

Item ▼ Activities ▼ Reports ▼ Attach ☐ Include inactive

The Fixed Asset Item List helps you to track your fixed assets and compile all of the essential information for them in one convenient place.

Creating Fixed Asset Items

There are two ways that a new fixed asset item can be set up:

- Create the new item when entering the purchase transaction
- Open the Fixed Asset Item List and create a new item

When you enter fixed assets upon creation of a new company, you will debit the fixed asset account and credit Opening Balance Equity. If you recall from Chapter 2, Creating a Company, this account is created by QuickBooks when the first balance sheet account is created so you have an accurate balance sheet from the beginning.

If a loan is associated with the fixed asset, the loan amount will be entered in a Long Term Liabilities account and the difference in an equity or bank account.

When you set up a fixed asset item, you indicate the account into which it has been entered. This does not enter it into the account or affect what happens behind the scenes. You must also complete the appropriate transaction to make sure and enter the fixed asset properly.

Accountant Tool: Fixed Asset Manager

If your accountant uses the Premier Accountant version of QuickBooks, he can pull the fixed asset information from your Fixed Asset Item list into the Fixed Asset Manager in order to work with your fixed assets. This tool will help him determine how to depreciate the fixed assets as well as the amount that needs to be posted back to the company file as an adjusting entry.

FLASHBACK TO GAAP: COST

Remember that when a company purchases assets, it should record them at cost, not fair market value. For example, if you bought an item worth $750 for $100, it should be recorded at $100.

DEVELOP YOUR SKILLS 7-5

Create a Fixed Asset Account and Item

In this exercise, you will help Allison to create a new fixed asset item for the new scooter that was purchased. To begin with, she will have to create a new fixed asset account for vehicles.

1. Click the **Chart of Accounts** task icon in the Company area of the Home page.

Chart of Accounts

2. Click the **Account** menu button, and then choose **New**.

3. Choose **Fixed Asset** as the account type; click **Continue**.

4. Follow these steps to create the new account:

Ⓐ Type **16000**.

Ⓒ Click **Save & Close**. Ⓑ Tap [Tab], and then type **Vehicles**.

5. Choose **Lists→Fixed Asset Item List**.

6. Click the **Item** menu button, and then choose **New**.

7. Follow these steps to create the new item:

Ⓐ Type **Vespa Scooter - 1.**

Ⓑ Click to select **Used.**

Ⓒ Tap ⬚Tab⬚, and then type **2013 Used Vespa Scooter.**

Ⓓ Tap ⬚Tab⬚, and then type **020815.**

Ⓔ Tap ⬚Tab⬚, and then type **4500.**

Ⓕ Tap ⬚Tab⬚, and then type **Bayshore Vespa.**

Ⓖ Tap ⬚Tab⬚, and then type **v.**

Ⓗ Tap ⬚Tab⬚ two times, and then type **2013 VESPA GTS 300 IE SUPER.**

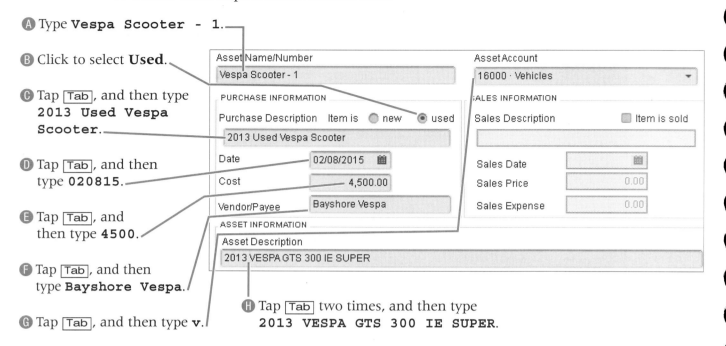

8. Click **OK**, choosing to **Add** Vespa, GTS, and IE to the dictionary.

9. Close the **Fixed Asset Item List**; close the **Chart of Accounts** window.

    You did not affect anything behind the scenes in this exercise, but in the long term liability exercise you will see how the purchase of the new fixed asset is entered behind the scenes.

Dealing with Current Liabilities

Current liabilities are funds that your company owes and expects to pay within a year. You have been collecting sales tax for your inventory sales. Now it is time to learn how to pay the collected tax (a current liability) to the appropriate tax agencies.

Sales Tax Payable

As you have seen, when you bill a customer and collect sales tax, QuickBooks holds the funds in a current liability account. These taxes are never actually the property of your business (an asset), so you have been using a liabilities payable account as a place to "store" the taxes until it is time to remit them.

When you are ready to pay your sales tax, it is *imperative* that you do so through the Pay Sales Tax window. This is to ensure that the proper liability account is affected behind the scenes when the payment is processed.

When you are ready to pay sales tax, you must use the proper procedure, or you will not "empty" the Sales Tax Payable account behind the scenes.

The Sales Tax Liability Report

You can choose to run a sales tax liability report to see what funds you are holding in your sales tax payable account. This report will give you the values you need to file your sales tax return: total sales, taxable sales, nontaxable sales, and the amount of tax collected.

The Manage Sales Tax Window

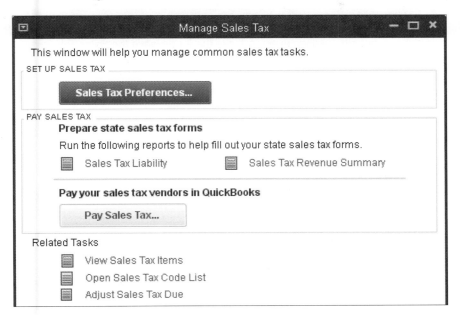

The Manage Sales Tax window helps you deal with all QuickBooks preferences, activities, and reports related to sales tax.

The Manage Sales Tax window helps you manage all of your sales tax activities and reports easily by providing links to all of the tasks you will be performing when working with sales tax, from setting it up to paying it.

Dealing with Adjustments in Sales Tax

There are many situations that could result in an incorrect amount in the Pay Sales Tax window or on the sales tax liability report. You may have charged a customer a tax rate for the wrong jurisdiction or tax may have been charged for a nontaxable item. There could also be rounding errors, penalties, or credits/discounts that you need to take into account.

You can make an adjustment to the tax owed through the Pay Sales Tax window or by choosing Adjust Sales Tax Due from the Vendors menu. Make sure that you don't use Sales Tax Payable as the "pay from account." Instead, you should use the following types of accounts:

- **For a rounding error:** You can set up a special account or use the Miscellaneous Expense. Some businesses opt to create a special income account for a negative error or a special expense account for a positive error.
- **For a credit or to apply a discount:** Use an income account such as Other Income.
- **For interest due, fines, or penalties:** Use an expense account such as Interest Expense or Non-deductible Penalties.

If you make an adjustment to the sales tax liability account, you will need to choose the adjustment the next time you pay sales tax in order to get the correct amount to pay.

Changing a Tax Jurisdiction

If a customer is charged sales tax for the wrong jurisdiction, you need to go back to the original transaction and choose the correct sales tax item or group. If you charged tax on a nontaxable item (or vice versa), you need to adjust the invoice or sales receipt where the sale was made. This may require you to issue a credit to the customer if they overpaid or reissue the invoice/receipt (or a statement) if they underpaid.

BEHIND THE SCENES

When you pay sales tax, behind the scenes you will see the funds leave the Sales Tax Payable account as a debit.

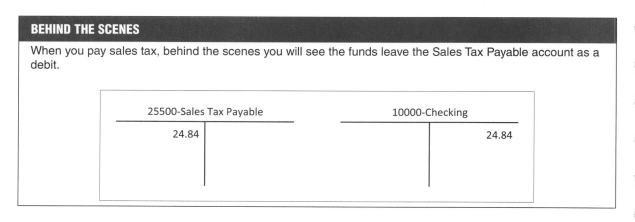

25500-Sales Tax Payable		10000-Checking	
24.84			24.84

QUICK REFERENCE	PAYING SALES TAX
Task	**Procedure**
Pay sales tax	■ Choose Vendors→Sales Tax→Pay Sales Tax.
	■ Choose the bank account from which you will be paying the taxes.
	■ Enter the date of the check and the date through which to show sales taxes.
	■ Choose which taxes to pay by clicking in the Pay column; click OK.
Run a sales tax liability report	■ Choose Reports→Vendors & Payables→Sales Tax Liability.
	■ Set the correct date range for the report.
Adjust the amount of sales tax owed	■ Choose Vendors→Sales Tax→Adjust Sales Tax Due.
	■ Enter the date, vendor, account, amount, and memo; click OK.

DEVELOP YOUR SKILLS 7-6
Pay Current Liabilities

In this exercise, you will help Allison to pay the sales tax collected in January 2015. The first step is to run a report to determine how much sales tax is owed and to whom.

1. Click the **Manage Sales Tax** task icon in the Vendors area of the Home page.

   QuickBooks displays the Manage Sales Tax window.

2. Click the **Sales Tax Liability** link in the Manage Sales Tax window.

Manage Sales Tax

Prepare state sales tax forms

Run the following reports to help fill out your state sales tax forms.

▤ Sales Tax Liability   ▤ Sales Tax Revenue Summary

3. Tap ⌜Tab⌝, type **010115**, tap ⌜Tab⌝ again, and then type **013115**.

4. Click **Refresh** on the report toolbar.

   Take a look at the information this report contains. The information you need to pay and file your taxes is in the last column, Sales Tax Payable as of Jan 31, 2015, which is $24.84.

5. Close the **Sales Tax Liability** report, choosing not to memorize it.

Pay the Sales Tax

From the report you just ran, you know that Average Guy Designs owes $24.84 as of 1/31/15 to the State Board of Equalization.

6. Click the **Pay Sales Tax** button in the Manage Sales Tax window.

7. Ensure that **10000 • Checking** is the Pay From Account.

8. Follow these steps to pay the taxes due:

Ⓐ Tap ⌜Tab⌝, and then type **013115**. Ⓑ Tap ⌜Tab⌝, and then type **013115** again.

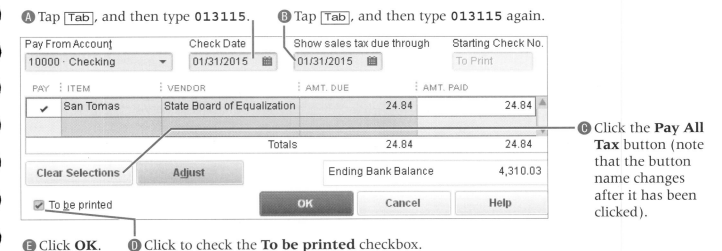

Ⓒ Click the **Pay All Tax** button (note that the button name changes after it has been clicked).

Ⓔ Click **OK**. Ⓓ Click to check the **To be printed** checkbox.

The liability check has now been entered into the queue of checks to be printed.

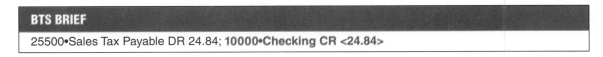

BTS BRIEF

25500•Sales Tax Payable DR 24.84; **10000•Checking CR <24.84>**

9. Close the **Manage Sales Tax** window.

Setting Up a Long Term Liability

Most companies have to take out a loan for a fixed asset (or a loan for some other purpose for a period longer than a year) at some time or another. In this section, you will create a Long Term Liability account to track the new truck loan. A company uses a Long Term Liability to track a loan that is scheduled to take longer than a year to pay off.

The QuickBooks Loan Manager

QuickBooks provides a tool for you to track your loans, similar to the Fixed Asset Item List that allows you to track your fixed assets. The Loan Manager allows you to set up loans based on information that you have entered in a long term liability or other current liability account. The Loan Manager tracks the principle and interest payments without having to set up separate amortization schedules. You can also use the Loan Manager to compare different loan scenarios. In addition, you have the opportunity to print loans from the Loan Manager.

The Loan Manager provides you with a place to track your long term liabilities. You can even click the What If Scenarios button to explore possible loan situations before you make a decision.

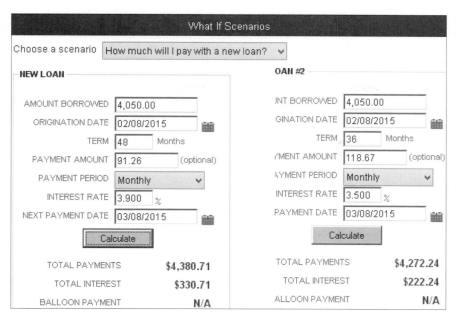

The Loan Manager also provides a "what if" tool that allows you to see if you can afford a loan and to compare multiple loan options.

Preparing to Use the Loan Manager

There are a number of items you should prepare before you set up a loan in the Loan Manager:

- **Set Up Your Accounts:** Make sure to set up any liability (i.e., 26000•Loan – Vehicles (Vespa)), expense (i.e., 63400•Interest Expense), and escrow (only if required) accounts that will be affected by the loan.

- **Set up the Vendor, if not already in your Vendor List.**

- **Check Previous Transactions:** If you are working with an existing (rather than new) loan, you will also need to confirm that all of the transactions related to it are entered into QuickBooks before setting up the loan in the Loan Manager.

- **Gather Loan Documents:** Make sure you have all of your original loan documents handy before you begin to set up the loan. It is important that you enter the opening balance and other information properly.

Once all transactions are up to date and the loan has been entered into the Loan Manager, you will be able to record future loan payments in the Set Up Payment window.

When you pay for the scooter with your new loan and down payment, the offsetting account will be the fixed asset account.

16000-Vehicles		10000-Checking		26000-Loan - Vehicles (Vespa - 1)	
4,500.00			450.00		4,050.00

Making a payment affects three accounts (unless you have a 0 percent interest loan): the loan account, the bank account, and the interest expense account.

63400-Interest Expense		26000-Loan - Vehicles (Vespa - 1)		10000-Checking	
13.16		78.10			91.26

Task	Procedure
Enter the funds for the loan	▪ Choose Lists→Chart of Accounts. ▪ Double-click the desired Long Term Liability account. ▪ Enter the transaction date and the amount. ▪ Choose the correct fixed asset to debit; click Record.
Enter a loan in the Loan Manager	▪ Gather all of your loan documents and information. ▪ Set up the liability and expense accounts required to track the loan. ▪ Choose Banking→Loan Manager; click the Add a Loan button. ▪ Enter the information on each screen, clicking Next to move through the setup screens and clicking Finish once all information has been entered.
Set up a loan payment with the Loan Manager	▪ Choose Banking→Loan Manager. ▪ Click to select the loan for which you need to set up a payment; click Set Up Payment. ▪ Make any necessary changes in the Set Up Payment window; click OK. ▪ Look over the bill or check to ensure its accuracy; click Save & Close.

Create a Long Term Liability

In this exercise, you will assist Allison with setting up the loan account for the scooter, funding the loan, and setting up the loan in the Loan Manager. First, you will create the new liability account.

1. Click the **Chart of Accounts** task icon in the Company area of the Home page.
2. Click the **Account** menu button, and then choose **New**.
3. Follow these steps to create the new Long Term Liability account:

Chart of Accounts

Ⓐ Click to choose **Other Account Types**. Ⓑ Click **Long Term Liability**.

Ⓒ Click **Continue**.

Ⓓ Type **26000** as the Number.

Ⓔ Tap ⟨Tab⟩, and then type **Loan – Vehicles (Vespa - 1)**.

4. Click **Save & Close** to record the new account.

Fund the Long Term Liability Account

Average Guy Designs has just received the scooter and the First Bank of Bayshore has issued the funds on your behalf to Bayshore Vespa. It's now time for Allison to record the starting balance for the loan and the cost of the truck.

5. Double-click the **Loan – Vehicles (Vespa - 1)** account in the Chart of Accounts window.
6. Follow these steps to record the funding of the loan:

Ⓐ Type **020815** as the Date. Ⓑ Tap ⟨Tab⟩ three times, and then type **4050** as the amount.

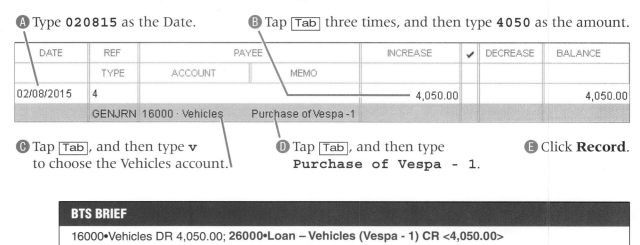

Ⓒ Tap ⟨Tab⟩, and then type **v** to choose the Vehicles account. Ⓓ Tap ⟨Tab⟩, and then type **Purchase of Vespa - 1**. Ⓔ Click **Record**.

BTS BRIEF

16000•Vehicles DR 4,050.00; **26000•Loan – Vehicles (Vespa - 1) CR <4,050.00>**

---

7. Close the register window; close the **Chart of Accounts** window.

Write a Check for the Down Payment

Guy has asked Allison to prepare a check for funds that the company put down on the new Vespa.

8. Click the **Write Checks** task icon in the Banking area of the Home page.

9. Check **Print Later** from the Ribbon, and then follow these steps to create the check for the down payment:

Ⓐ Verify the date is set to **2/8/2015**.

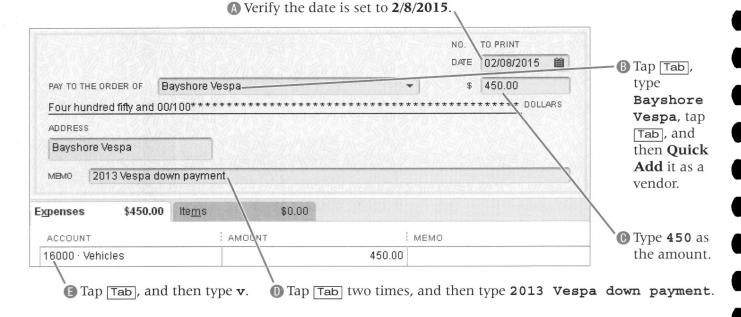

Ⓑ Tap Tab, type **Bayshore Vespa**, tap Tab, and then **Quick Add** it as a vendor.

Ⓒ Type **450** as the amount.

Ⓔ Tap Tab, and then type **v**.   Ⓓ Tap Tab two times, and then type **2013 Vespa down payment**.

BTS BRIEF

16000•Vehicles DR 450.00; 10000•Checking CR <450.00>

---

10. Click **Save & Close** to record the transaction.

The 16000•Vehicles account will be increased by the total cost of the scooter ($4,050 from the loan and $450 from the down payment).

Enter a Loan in the Loan Manager

Before you can enter the loan in the Loan Manager, you must first enter the vendor on the Vendor List.

11. Choose **Vendors→Vendor Center**.

12. Tap Ctrl + n to open a New Vendor window.

13. Type **Bank of Bayshore** as the **Vendor Name**; click **OK** to save the new vendor.

You are only entering the vendor name in this exercise in order to be able to move on to the Loan Manager. You can always go back and enter the rest of a vendor's information later. When working in your own company, you may wish to enter all of the information before continuing.

14. Close the **Vendor Center**.

15. Choose **Banking→Loan Manager**.

16. Click the Add a Loan... button.

17. Follow these steps to enter the account information for the loan:

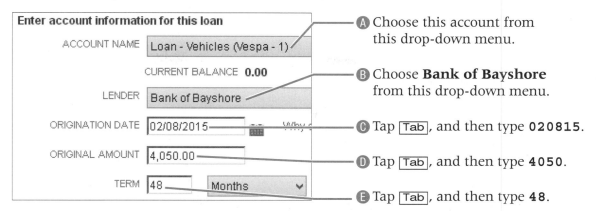

A Choose this account from this drop-down menu.

B Choose **Bank of Bayshore** from this drop-down menu.

C Tap ⎡Tab⎤, and then type **020815**.

D Tap ⎡Tab⎤, and then type **4050**.

E Tap ⎡Tab⎤, and then type **48**.

18. Click **Next**, and then follow these steps to enter the payment information:

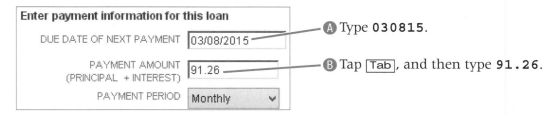

A Type **030815**.

B Tap ⎡Tab⎤, and then type **91.26**.

19. Click **Next**, and then follow these steps to enter the interest information:

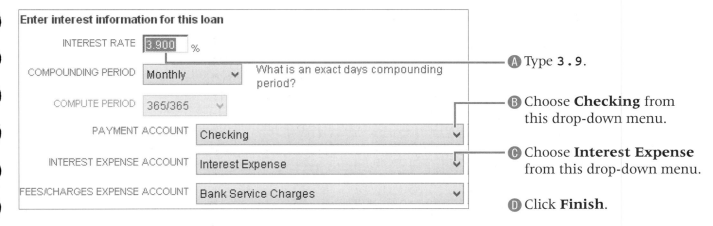

A Type **3.9**.

B Choose **Checking** from this drop-down menu.

C Choose **Interest Expense** from this drop-down menu.

D Click **Finish**.

The loan is now set up in the Loan Manager, ready for you to track.

20. Close the **Loan Manager** window.

Working with Equity Accounts

Equity accounts reflect the net worth of a company. Take another look at Appendix A, Need to Know Accounting and notice that the accounting equation teaches that the sum of the equity accounts is equal to assets (what you own) less liabilities (what you owe):

$$Equity = Assets - Liabilities$$

An equity account has a credit normal balance. It represents how viable your company is since it shows how much you would have left if you sold all of your assets and then paid off the liabilities.

Owner's Equity / Capital Stock

In a sole proprietorship, the equity is what the owner has invested in the company. In a corporation, the equity is what the shareholders have invested in the company. An owner's investment occurs when an owner deposits funds or other assets into the company or shareholders purchase stock. An owner's withdrawal of funds from the company is known as a draw; if it is a corporation you will see shareholder distributions.

Retained Earnings

At the end of the fiscal year, a business will show either a net income or a net loss. When the books are closed, this amount is transferred into the Retained Earnings account to clear out all income and expense accounts for the next year. When the fiscal year ends, QuickBooks automatically makes this transfer.

Opening Balance Equity

QuickBooks creates the Opening Balance Equity account when you first create your company. As you enter opening balances into the accounts, QuickBooks uses Opening Balance Equity as the offset account so you can have a working balance sheet right from the beginning. You may need to enter a transfer between accounts if there is a balance in the Opening Balance Equity account once all of your new accounts are entered into QuickBooks. In addition, there are other times when QuickBooks may use the Opening Balance Equity account and an adjustment must be made. For instance, when you set QuickBooks up to track inventory, such as you did in Chapter 6, Dealing with Physical Inventory and enter a beginning number of inventory items on hand, you debit 12100•Inventory Asset, and 30000•Opening Bal Equity is credited behind the scenes.

Equity transactions can be a bit tricky. You should talk to your accountant about how to deal with them for your unique company. Dealing with the transfer of funds from the Opening Balance Equity account will be covered in Chapter 12, Reporting, Adjusting Entries, and Closing the Books.

> **FLASHBACK TO GAAP: BUSINESS ENTITY**
>
> Remember that the first assumption of GAAP is that the business is separate from the owners and from other businesses. Revenues and expenses of the business should be kept separate from the personal expenses of the business owner.

Task	Procedure
Record an Owner's Investment	■ Choose Banking→Make Deposits.
	■ Choose the account into which the deposit will be made and the owner's equity account in the From Account field.
	■ Enter the payment information and amount; click Save & Close.
Record an Owner's Draw	■ Choose Banking→Write Checks.
	■ Enter the owner as the payee, as well as the date and amount of the check.
	■ Choose Owner's Draw in the Account column on the Expenses tab.
	■ Choose whether to print the check; click Save & Close.

Advanced Skills

Budgeting & Predicting in QuickBooks

QuickBooks includes a budgeting feature that allows you to create account-based budgets for Balance Sheet or Profit & Loss accounts. Budgets can be created based on a previous year's budget or from scratch—or, if you have been using QuickBooks for a year, the actual figures from the previous year.

Predicting the Future Cash Flow

In addition to budgets, QuickBooks also supplies you with a Cash Flow Projector feature that assists you with making predictions about the future; for instance, it allows you to conduct "what-if" analyses as well as look at future cash flow or revenue. Projections can be based on actual figures from the last year or from scratch.

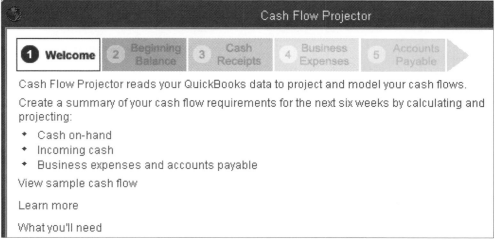

The Cash Flow Projector takes you through five steps in order to give you a cash flow report that will show you your "liquidity" over the next six weeks.

Budget Reports

Once you have created a budget, you will run a report to view the information. QuickBooks provides several reports that will allow you to use the information in your budget(s).

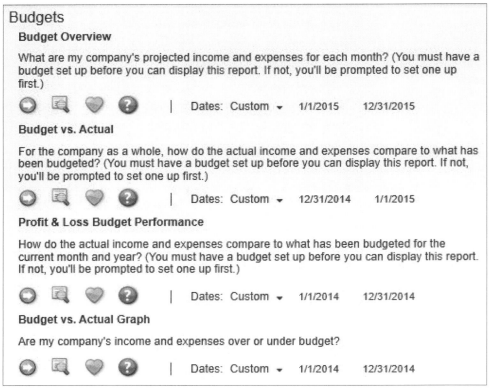

The Report Center lists all of the budget reports available for you to create.

QUICK REFERENCE	CREATING BUDGETS & FORECASTS IN QUICKBOOKS
Task	**Procedure**
Create a budget in QuickBooks	■ Choose Company→Planning & Budgeting→Set Up Budgets.
	■ Click the Create New Budget button.
	■ Choose the budget year and type; click Next.
	■ Choose to base the budget on a customer:job or class, or neither; click Next.
	■ Choose whether you wish to create the budget from scratch or by using the previous year's actual data, and then click Finish.
Create a Cash Flow Projection in QuickBooks	■ Choose Company→Planning & Budgeting→Cash Flow Projector.
	■ Click the Create New Forecast button.
	■ Choose the year for the forecast; click Next.
	■ Choose whether the forecast will use customer:job, class, or neither of them as additional criteria; click Next.
	■ Choose whether you wish to create the forecast from scratch or by using the previous year's actual data, and then click Finish.

Produce a Budget and a Budget Report

In this exercise, you will help Allison to create a budget for 2015.

1. Choose **Company→Planning & Budgeting→Set Up Budgets**.

2. Ensure that **2015** and **Profit and Loss** are selected; click **Next**.

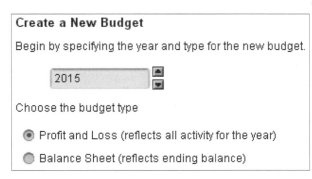

3. Ensure that **No additional criteria** is selected; click **Next**.

   Your budget will be based on all customers:jobs, so you do not need to provide additional criteria at this time.

4. Click to the left of **Create budget from scratch**; click **Finish**.

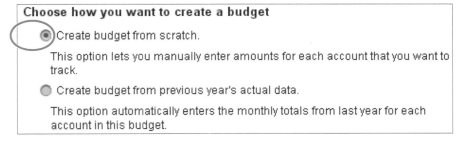

A blank budget will be displayed with all of your income and expense accounts included. In order to populate the budget, you will enter a monthly amount in the January column for each account and then copy the amount across. The amounts entered will be "averages" in this example, but when you are creating your own company's budget, you can also choose to enter a different amount for each month.

5. Follow these steps to enter the income and COGS amounts in the budget:

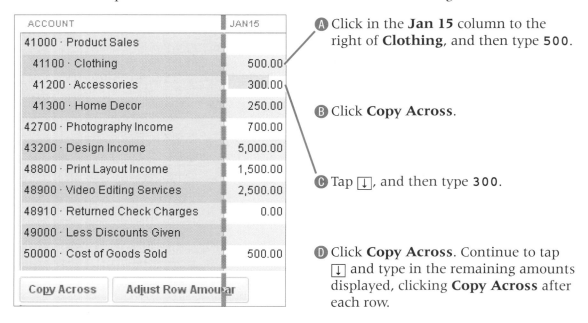

ACCOUNT	JAN15
41000 · Product Sales	
41100 · Clothing	500.00
41200 · Accessories	300.00
41300 · Home Decor	250.00
42700 · Photography Income	700.00
43200 · Design Income	5,000.00
48800 · Print Layout Income	1,500.00
48900 · Video Editing Services	2,500.00
48910 · Returned Check Charges	0.00
49000 · Less Discounts Given	
50000 · Cost of Goods Sold	500.00

| Copy Across | Adjust Row Amount |

Ⓐ Click in the **Jan 15** column to the right of **Clothing**, and then type **500**.

Ⓑ Click **Copy Across**.

Ⓒ Tap ⬇, and then type **300**.

Ⓓ Click **Copy Across**. Continue to tap ⬇ and type in the remaining amounts displayed, clicking **Copy Across** after each row.

6. Click **Save** to update the budget with what you have entered so far.

7. Enter each of the **Jan 15** expense amounts as displayed below, making sure to click **Copy Across** after each one.

ACCOUNT	JAN15
60200 · Automobile Expense	50.00
60300 · Bad Debt Expense	20.00
60400 · Bank Service Charges	25.00
61000 · Business Licenses and Per...	20.00
61500 · Job Materials	100.00
61700 · Computer and Internet Expe...	100.00
62000 · Continuing Education	50.00
62400 · Depreciation Expense	125.00
62500 · Dues and Subscriptions	25.00
63300 · Insurance Expense	200.00
63400 · Interest Expense	50.00
64300 · Meals and Entertainment	400.00

ACCOUNT	JAN15
64900 · Office Supplies	200.00
66000 · Payroll Expenses	4,000.00
66700 · Professional Fees	250.00
67100 · Rent Expense	700.00
67200 · Repairs and Maintenance	100.00
67500 · Shipping Expense	100.00
68100 · Telephone Expense	
68110 · Office Phone	40.00
68120 · Fax Line	40.00
68130 · Cell Phone	100.00
68600 · Utilities	
68610 · Gas & Electric	80.00
68620 · Water	75.00

8. Click OK when you are finished entering all budget amounts.

If you accidently leave the Set Up Budgets window, just choose Company→Planning & Budgeting→ Set Up Budgets again.

Produce a Budget Report

Now that the budget for 2015 has been produced, Guy would like to see a report showing an overview of it.

9. Choose **Reports→Budgets & Forecasts→Budget Overview**.

A Budget Report "wizard" will appear to walk you through selections that will help you create the report you desire.

10. Click **Next** two times, and then click **Finish**.

The budget for 2015 will be displayed by month.

11. Scroll down and note whether there is a Net Income or Net Loss projected for each month.

You will see that there is a $3,400 net income budgeted per month.

12. Close the budget report window.

13. Choose the appropriate option for your situation:

- If you will continue working, leave QuickBooks open.
- If you are finished working in QuickBooks for now, choose **File→Exit**.

Tackle the Tasks

Now is your chance to work a little more with Average Guy Designs and apply the skills that you have learned in this chapter to accomplish additional tasks. You will use the same company file you used in the Develop Your Skills exercises throughout this chapter. Enter the following tasks, referring back to the concepts in the chapter as necessary.

Create and fund a prepaid insurance account	Average Guy Designs has decided to prepay the insurance for the next six months. Create 13300•Prepaid Insurance as an Other Current Asset account. Write a check to be printed to Rankin Family Insurance on 2/1/15 for $1,050, expensing $175 in February to 63300•Insurance Expense, placing the rest in the Prepaid Insurance account.
Record and memorize a transfer of funds	Record a transfer of $175 from 13300•Prepaid Insurance to 63300•Insurance Expense on 3/1/15. Memorize the transaction in the Monthly group.
Make a petty cash expenditure	Use 10500•Petty Cash to purchase a birthday cake on 2/21/15 for Allison's birthday. The total amount is $33.75, payable to Jordan2 Bakery, expensed to 64300•Meals and Entertainment.
Create a new fixed asset item	Guy purchased furniture for his office on 2/14/15 for $2,639 from Pa's Custom Furniture. Create a new fixed asset item called Office Furniture – 2, and use 15000•Furniture and Equipment as the Asset Account.
Create a long term liability	Create a long term liability account for the new furniture called 28300•Loan – Office Furniture. On 2/14/15, enter the total amount of the furniture as an increase in the new liability account you just created, using 15000•Furniture and Equipment as the Account.
Use the Loan Manager	Enter the furniture loan in the Loan Manager. The interest rate is 7.25% and the loan is for 24 months. The loan is issued by Bank of Bayshore. Use the What If Scenario tool to determine the monthly payment. The Payment Account is Checking, and the Interest Expense Account is Interest Expense.
Create a budget report	Create a Budget vs. Actual report for the budget you created in the last exercise for the month of January 2015.

Concepts Review

To check your knowledge of the key concepts introduced in this chapter, complete the Concepts Review quiz on the Student Resource Center or in your eLab course.

Reinforce Your Skills

Angela Stevens has just relocated her company, Quality-Built Construction, from California to Silverton, Oregon. You will be working with a QuickBooks Sample Company File in this exercise as it will allow you to run full payroll in a future chapter without having to purchase a payroll subscription.

Before you begin the Reinforce Your Skills exercises, complete one of these options:

- Open **RYS_Chapter07** from your file storage location.
- Restore **RYS_Chapter07 (Portable)** from your file storage location. Add your last name and first initial to the end of the filename. Place your last name and first initial at the end of the filename.

REINFORCE YOUR SKILLS 7-1
Use a Prepaid Rent Account

In this exercise, you will help Angela to set up and use a Prepaid Rent account. The first step is to set up an Other Current Asset account.

1. Choose **Lists→Chart of Accounts**.
2. Click the **Account** menu button, and then choose **New**.
3. Create a new **Other Current Asset** account called `1300•Prepaid Rent`.

Write the Rent Check

The next step is to write the check for the rent.

4. Choose **Banking→Write Checks**.
5. Write a `$6900` check to `Capitol Property Services` on `1/1/19` for six months of discounted rent ($1,150/month).
6. Choose for the check to be printed later and enter a Memo of `Rent for Jan – Jun 2019`; expense the first month (`$1,150`) to Rent Expense and the rest (`$5,750`) to Prepaid Rent.
7. Save the check and close the **Write Checks** window.

Memorize a Funds Transfer

Now you will help Angela to make the first transfer from Prepaid Rent to Rent Expense. The Chart of Accounts should still be open. If it isn't, choose Lists→Chart of Accounts.

8. Double-click the **Prepaid Rent** account to open the register.
9. Record a transfer of `$1,150` to Rent Expense on `2/1/19`.
10. Click within the transaction and choose **Edit→Memorize General Journal**.
11. Create a memorized transaction called `Rent Transfer` that is a monthly automated transaction entry. The next transfer will be on `3/1/19` and there are `4` remaining.
12. Close the **Prepaid Rent** register window.

Track Petty Cash

In this exercise, you will help Angela to replenish Petty Cash and then make a purchase using it. If necessary, choose Lists→Chart of Accounts.

1. Choose **Banking→Write Checks**, and then choose **1110•Company Checking Account**.

2. Enter the next check number, **11357**, and then set the date to **1/7/19**.

3. Write the check to **Cash** (Quick Add as a vendor) for **$300**, and choose **1140•Petty Cash Account** as the account.

Make a Purchase with Petty Cash

Now that the Petty Cash account is set up, you will use it to purchase postage stamps.

4. Double-click **1140•Petty Cash Account** from the Chart of Accounts window.

5. Enter **1/9/2019** as the date, tap Tab , and then tap Delete to remove the Number.

6. Tap Tab again, and then choose **Post Office** as the **Payee**.

7. Type **$46.00** as the Payment, and then choose **6610•Postage and Delivery** as the Account.

8. Enter **stamps** as the Memo; save the transaction, and then close the **Petty Cash** window.

Deal with a New Fixed Asset Item

Angela purchased a new Mac computer system with high graphics capabilities for the office. In this exercise, you will set up this purchase as a fixed asset item in her QuickBooks company file.

1. Choose **List→Fixed Asset Item List**.

2. Create a new **Fixed Asset Item** for the equipment using the following information:
   - Asset Name: **Mac System**
   - Purchase Description: **New Mac System**
   - Date: **1/15/2019**
   - Cost: **$4,560**
   - Vendor: **Willamette Computer Sales**
   - Asset Account: 1520•Computer & Office Equipment
   - Asset Description: **Mac all-in-one system**

3. Save the new **Fixed Asset Item**; close the **Fixed Asset Item List**.

   Leave the Chart of Accounts open for the next exercise.

Pay Sales Tax and Track a Long Term Liability

Angela needs to pay the sales tax collected for the coffee tables sales as well as set up a loan for a portion of the cost of the new computer system. In this exercise, you will help her to pay sales tax, set up the Long Term Liability account, and record the purchase transaction. The Chart of Accounts window should still be open. If it is not, choose Lists→Chart of Accounts.

Pay Sales Tax

1. Choose **Vendors→Sales Tax→Pay Sales Tax**.

2. Ensure **1110•Company Checking Account** is the account from which the payment will come.

3. Set the **Check Date** and **Show sales tax due through** to **1/31/19**.

4. Choose for the check to be printed and to pay all tax due.

5. Click **OK** to send the liability check to the queue to be printed.

Create the Long Term Liability Account

6. Click the **Account** menu button, and then choose **New**.

7. Choose to create a new **Long Term Liability** account (which is an Other Account Type), and then click Continue.

8. Type **2420** as the **Number**, and **Computer Loan** as the **Account Name**.

9. Click **Save & Close**.

Enter the Down Payment Transaction

You will now enter the two transactions to account for the full purchase price of the computer system.

10. Choose **Banking→Write Checks**, and then choose **1110•Company Checking Account** as the account.

11. Choose for the check to be printed later, and then set the date to **1/25/2019**.

12. Enter **Willamette Computer Sales** as the payee, **Quick Add** it as a vendor, and enter **$1000** as the amount of the down payment.

13. Type **Computer System Down Payment** as the Memo, and then choose **1520•Computer & Office Equipment** as the Account.

14. Click **Save & Close**.

Enter the Loan Transaction

The loan has been funded, so now you need to account for it in QuickBooks. The Chart of Accounts should still be open. If it is not, choose Lists→Chart of Accounts.

15. Double-click the **2420•Computer Loan** Long Term Liability account.

    The Computer Loan register window opens.

16. Ensure that the date is set to **1/25/2019**, and then tap ⟨Tab⟩ three times.

17. Type **$3,560** as an Increase and choose **1520•Computer & Office Equipment** as the Account; record the transaction.

18. Close the **Computer Loan** and **Chart of Accounts** windows.

19. Choose the appropriate option for your situation:

    ■ If you will continue working, leave QuickBooks open.

    ■ If you are finished working in QuickBooks for now, choose **File→Exit**.

Apply Your Skills

Before you begin the Apply Your Skills exercises, complete one of these options:

- Open **AYS_Chapter07** from your file storage location.

- Restore **AYS_Chapter07 (Portable)** from your file storage location. Add your last name and first initial to the end of the filename.

APPLY YOUR SKILLS 7-1

Deal with Prepaid Web Hosting

Dr. James has decided that her business needs a website, and she has found a company to host it. She can get a deal if she pays for a year in advance, so she has decided to take that option. In this exercise, you will set up an Other Current Asset account for her to track the prepaid web hosting expense.

1. Open the **Chart of Accounts,** and then choose to create an **Other Current Asset** account.

2. Name the account **Prepaid Web Hosting**, and then save it.

Pay for the Prepaid Expense

You will now pay for the entire year, expensing one month's worth and placing the rest in the prepaid expense account you just created.

3. Open the **Write Checks** window, ensure that it is set for the check to be printed later, and then set the date to **7/22/2014**.

4. Type **Zoom Web Services** as the payee (Quick Add it as a vendor), and then **$1,068** as the amount (the deal is for $89/month).

5. Type **One year web hosting, July 2014-June 2015** as the Memo.

6. Choose to expense **$89** to Computer and Internet Expenses and the rest to Prepaid Web Hosting. Save the transaction.

Make and Memorize a Transfer of Funds

You will now enter the transfer of $89 from the other current asset account to the expense account for August and set it up to happen automatically for the rest of the 12-month period.

7. Open the **Prepaid Web Hosting** register window from the Chart of Accounts.

8. Enter **8/22/2014** as the date and **89** in the Decrease field. Set **Computer and Internet Expenses** as the Account.

9. Choose to memorize the transaction.

10. Type **Web Host Txfr** as the Name.

11. Choose to have the transaction entry automated every month, with the next transfer occurring on **9/22/2014** and **10** more remaining.

12. Save the memorized transaction and the register entry; close the **Prepaid Web Hosting** window.

   Leave the Chart of Accounts window open for the next exercise.

Track and Use Petty Cash

In this exercise, you will create a petty cash account and use it to pay for an expense.

1. Open the **Chart of Accounts**, and then create a new bank account called `Petty Cash`.
2. Write a check to fund the **Petty Cash** account on **7/8/14** for **$300**.
3. Enter the next check number, **1440**.
4. Purchase an appetizer platter for **$44.95** from Laura's Café for an office party on **7/12/14**. Use **Petty Cash** to pay for it.
5. Close the **Write Checks** or **Petty Cash** register window.

Deal with Bad Debt

Dr. James has learned that Natalie Sheehan moved out of town. You do not expect to receive payment for the two invoices (27 for $399.50 and 117 for $148.10, for a total of $547.60) she has outstanding. In this exercise, you will help Dr. James to write off the amount as bad debt using a credit memo.

1. Create a new expense account called `Bad Debt Expense`.
2. Create a new **Other Charge** item called `Bad Debt` and route it to the Bad Debt Expense account you just created. Leave the amount as zero.

Create the Credit Memo and Apply It to the Invoices

3. Open the **Create Credit Memos/Refunds** window, and then choose **Natalie Sheehan: Dog-Sandy** as the Customer:Job.

   You must choose the Customer:Job just as it appears on the invoice to which you will be applying the credit.

4. Set the date to **7/13/2014**, enter **BD1** as the Credit No., choose **Bad Debt** as the Item, and then type **547.60** as the nontax amount.
5. Choose for the credit memo to not be printed; click to **Save & Close** the window.
6. Choose to apply the amount of the credit to an invoice, and then click **OK**.
7. Click **Done** in the Apply Credit to Invoices window, ensuring both invoices are checked first.

Advanced Skills

Buy a New Ultrasound Machine (Fixed Asset)

In this exercise, you will help Sadie to enter a new ultrasound machine into the Fixed Asset Item List.

1. Open the **Fixed Asset Item List**.

2. Use the following information to create a new fixed asset item:
   - Asset Name: **Ultrasound Machine**
   - Purchase Description: **New Health Power Ultrasound Machine**
   - Date: **7/21/2014**
   - Cost: **$2,050**
   - Vendor: **Seattle Vet Supply**
   - Asset Account: **Furniture and Equipment**
   - Asset Description: **High Performance +7.5 MHz Vet Ultrasound**

3. Save the new **Fixed Asset Item**; close the **Fixed Asset Item List**.

Work with Liabilities

In this exercise, you will pay the sales tax due and use the Loan Manager to track the loan that you took out for the x-ray machine.

Pay Sales Tax

You will now help Sadie to pay the sales tax that she collected.

1. Choose **Vendors→Sales Tax→Pay Sales Tax**.

2. Set the **Check Date** and **Show sales tax due through** to **7/31/14**, ensuring that **Checking** is the payment account.

3. Choose for the check to be printed and to pay all tax due.

4. Click **OK** to send the liability check to the queue to be printed.

Create a Long Term Liability

5. Create a new long term liability account called **Ultrasound Loan**.

6. Fund the loan by entering an increase to the Ultrasound Loan account for **$2,050** on 7/22/14.

7. Open the **Loan Manager**.

8. Create a new loan using the following information:
   - Account Name: Ultrasound Loan
   - Lender: Bank of Bothell
   - Origination Date: **7/21/2014**
   - Original Amount **$2,050**
   - Term: **36** months
   - Due Date of Next Payment: **8/21/2014**
   - Payment Amount: **$64.05**
   - Payment Period: Monthly
   - Interest Rate: **7.8%**
   - Payment Account: Checking
   - Interest Expense Account: Interest Expense
   - Fees/Charges Expense Account: Bank Service Charges

9. Close the **Loan Manager** and the **Chart of Accounts**.

APPLY YOUR SKILLS 7-6
Answer Questions with Reports

In this exercise, you will answer questions for Dr. James by running reports. You may wish to display the Report Center in List View to help you answer the questions. Ask your instructor if you should print the reports, print (save) them as PDF files, export them to Excel, or simply display them on the screen.

1. Will you please print a list of all of the accounts that are set up in the Chart of Accounts for the accountant?

2. If we were to take out a five-year loan at 8.75 percent interest for a new piece of equipment for $5,000, what would the monthly payments be? (Hint: The Loan Manager has a feature that can help with this! If the Loan Manager is not working for you, go online and use a free loan calculator.)

3. Create a report that shows the entries of the Fixed Asset Item List.

4. Prepare a report that shows all transactions affecting the Prepaid Web Hosting account.

5. Could you please create a list of our memorized transactions for me?

6. Submit your reports based on the guidelines provided by your instructor.

7. Choose the appropriate option for your situation:
   - If you will continue working, leave QuickBooks open.
   - If you are finished working in QuickBooks for now, choose **File→Exit**.

Extend Your Skills

In the course of working through the following Extend Your Skills exercises, you will be utilizing various skills taught in this and previous chapter(s). Take your time and think carefully about the tasks presented to you. Turn back to the chapter content if you need assistance.

7-1 Sort Through the Stack

Before You Begin: Restore the EYS1_Chapter07 (Portable) file or open the EYS1_Chapter07 company file from your storage location.

You have been hired by Arlaine Cervantes to help her with her organization's books. She is the founder of Niños del Lago, a nonprofit organization that provides impoverished Guatemalan children with an engaging educational camp experience. You have just sat down at your desk and opened a large envelope from her with a variety of documents and noticed that you have several emails from her as well. It is your job to sort through the papers and emails and make sense of what you find, entering information into QuickBooks whenever appropriate and answering any other questions in a word-processing document saved as **EYS1_Chapter07_ LastnameFirstinitial**. Remember, you are digging through papers you just dumped out of an envelope and addressing random emails from Arlaine, so it is up to you to determine the correct order in which to complete the tasks.

- Receipt from USPS: Dated 8/15/2014, $46.00 for 100 first-class stamps, paid for with petty cash.

- Deposit slip: Check #578 for $5,000 from the House Foundation, deposited in the Checking account on 8/12/2014; $200 was kept back for petty cash.

- Bill from landlord of U.S. office for six months of rent at a discount: Arlaine wrote a note on the bill stating she wants to take advantage of a discounted rent by prepaying it for six months. The amount per month is $500, payable to Keely Amaral Properties, LLC. Pay the rent for August 2014 on 8/5/2014 and then set it up for the remaining months of rent to automatically transfer on the fifth of each month for the remainder of the six-month term.

- Note from the accountant: Need to set up account for loan for new computer equipment for U.S. office. Total financed is $3,029. Loan was funded on 8/10/2014. Please set up the equipment as a fixed asset item as well, using Furniture & Equipment as the account. Description of equipment is two new Sony desktop computers, two 21-inch dual monitors, and a new laser printer. The vendor is Lancaster Computer Sales. It was financed by Cherry City Finance.

- Scribbled note from Arlaine: I would like to set up a budget for our new fiscal year (October 2014–September 2015) based on the amounts spent and received in July and August. Is that something you could do in QuickBooks for me? If so, please create the budget for me and save it for me as a PDF file so I can send it by email.

7-2 Be Your Own Boss

Before You Begin: Complete Extend Your Skills 6-2 before starting this exercise.

In this exercise, throughout the entire book, you will build on the company file that you outlined in previous chapters. If you have created a file for your actual business, then enter any other current assets you may utilize, enter all of your fixed assets both as items and in a fixed asset account, create and fund a petty cash account, set up all long term liabilities, enter any owner investments or draws since your starting date, and create a budget. If you are creating a fictitious company, then create, fund, and expense over time a Prepaid account; create a petty cash account and make at least three purchases with it; enter at least five fixed asset items, making sure you also enter them in a fixed asset account; create a long term liability for at least three of the fixed items and enter the opening transactions; and create a budget for the next year by entering in the amounts yourself. You will make up the names and information for this exercise.

Create Account Listing, Fixed Asset Listing, Balance Sheet Standard, and Budget Overview reports and submit them to your instructor based on the instructions provided.

Open the company file you worked on in Extend Your Skills 6-2 and complete the tasks outlined above. When you are done, save it as a portable company file, naming it as **EYS2_Chapter07_ LastnameFirstinitial (Portable)** and submit it to your instructor based on the instructions provided.

7-3 Use the Web as a Learning Tool

Throughout this book, you will be provided with an opportunity to use the Internet as a learning tool by completing WebQuests. According to the original creators of WebQuests, as described on their website (http://WebQuest.org), a WebQuest is "an inquiry-oriented activity in which most or all of the information used by learners is drawn from the web." To complete the WebQuest projects in this book, navigate to the Student Resource Center and choose the WebQuest for the chapter on which you are working. The subject of each WebQuest will be relevant to the material found in the chapter.

WebQuest Subject: Learning about the depreciation of fixed assets

Using QuickBooks for Payroll

CHAPTER OBJECTIVES

After studying this chapter, you will be able to:

- Manage the Employees List
- Input information from an outside payroll service into QuickBooks
- Set up QuickBooks to run payroll
- Create paychecks
- Track and pay payroll liabilities
- Deal with payroll errors
- Process payroll forms and reports

Payroll is a very sensitive subject as it affects people's livelihoods. As an employer, you should be well-informed of all the payroll options and well-equipped to efficiently manage payroll for your business. In this chapter, you will manage the Employee List and input payroll information from an outside service. In addition, you will examine how QuickBooks deals with payroll, and you will create paychecks and track payroll liabilities. You will also learn how to process payroll forms by using a sample company file that includes a free payroll subscription.

Average Guy Designs

Average Guy Designs has been doing so well that Guy needs to hire two employees to help out, in addition to hiring Alllison officially. Allison knows that Guy has been using an outside service to run the company's payroll, so she will enter the new employees into the Employees List and then enter the information from the payroll service for them. She will also evaluate payroll options available through QuickBooks to make sure that the company is using the option that is right for it and will complete a payroll cycle with a sample company file to see how it works.

The Employees area of the Home page provides task icons that will help you with payroll and time tracking tasks.

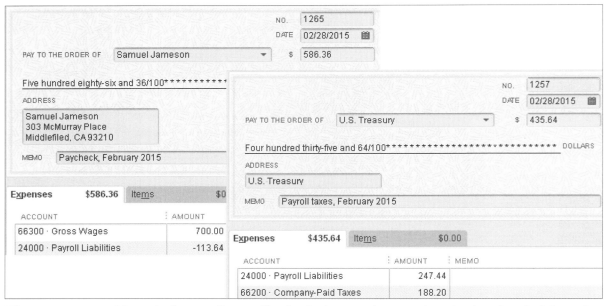

When you use an outside service for payroll, you will write checks to employees and vendors based on the information provided to you by the service.

This book teaches how to use QuickBooks to run payroll for a company using a basic service with a sample company file as well as fictitious information from an outside payroll service. You must contact your local tax agency to determine what tax laws apply to you and to whom you should submit your taxes. Do not use the specific percentages, vendors, or amounts shown, even if it is from your local jurisdiction, because tax laws change all the time! It is your responsibility to stay informed, either on your own or through a paid service (such as those offered by Intuit).

Working with Employees in QuickBooks

Just as you used the Vendor Center to track vendors and the Customer Center to track customers and jobs, you will use the Employee Center to track employees. If you recall, QuickBooks defines a customer as someone who pays you money. Well, the QuickBooks definition of an employee is someone to whom you issue a W-2 at the end of the year. Subcontractors are *not* to be entered into the Employees List; remember from Chapter 4, Working with Vendors that subcontractors are included in the Vendor List.

Managing the Employees List

Managing the Employees List is similar to managing the Customers & Jobs List and the Vendors List. You will edit, delete, and create new employees the same way you did for customers and vendors. New employees can also be set up as part of the QuickBooks Payroll Setup Interview.

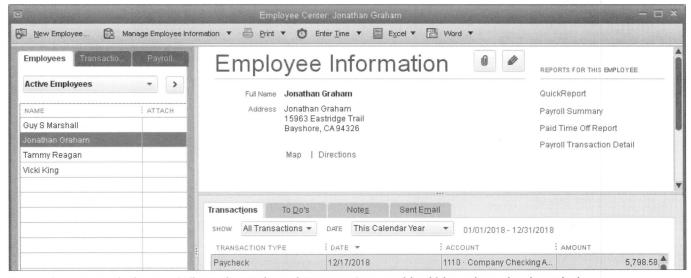

The Employee Center looks very similar to the Vendor and Customer Centers with which you have already worked.

Setting Up a New Employee

To run payroll, you need to enter important tax information for each employee. If you don't have your employees' W-4s handy, you can always add the information later—as long as it is entered before you first run payroll. (This is not optional!)

It is very important to have all of your employees' W-4 and I-9 forms filed neatly with all personnel records (or that your outside payroll service has all of them completed). Workers' Compensation companies are very thorough when they review company payroll records. Even though you do not treat independent contractors as employees in QuickBooks, it is important that you have an I-9 form on file for each contractor as well.

Gather Your Employee Information

Before you can set up employees in QuickBooks, regardless of which approach you take, you need to have certain information handy. If you don't have all of the information from the W-4 forms when you set up your employees, you will need to ensure that it is entered before you first run payroll.

Following is a list of necessary employee information required for payroll setup:

- Name
- Social security number
- Federal and state exemption information
- Address
- Birthday

Setting Employee Defaults

Before you set up your employees, you should set the employee defaults if you are using QuickBooks for payroll. These preferences will be applied to each new employee you create, and you can change them as needed. When setting employee defaults, choose the options that you assume will apply to the majority of employees you will create.

One of the default items you can set deals with how (and if) sick and vacation time is tracked for employees.

Visualize! **Tab:** Other Topics
Topic: Paying employees

QUICK REFERENCE	MANAGING THE EMPLOYEES LIST
Task	**Procedure**
Create a new employee	■ Choose Employees→Employee Center; click the New Employee button. ■ Enter all applicable information on each of the tabs; click OK.
Edit an existing employee	■ Choose Employees→Employee Center; double-click the desired employee. ■ Make any necessary changes; click OK.
Set employee defaults outside of the Payroll Setup Interview	■ Choose Employees→Employee Center; click the Manage Employee Information button at the top of the window. ■ Choose Change New Employee Default Settings, enter the new settings, and then click OK.

DEVELOP YOUR SKILLS 8-1
Set Up and Manage Employees

In this exercise, you will help Allison to set up three new employees for Average Guy Designs.

Intuit provides maintenance releases throughout the lifetime of the product. These updates may require you to update your student exercise files before you begin working with them. Please follow the prompts on the screen if you are asked to update your company file to the latest QuickBooks release.

1. Start **QuickBooks 2014**.

   If you downloaded the student exercise files in the portable company file *format, follow Option 1 below. If you downloaded the files in the* company file *format, follow Option 2.*

Option 1: Restore a Portable Company File

2. Choose **File→Open or Restore Company**.

3. Restore the **DYS_Chapter08 (Portable)** portable company file from your file storage location, placing your last name and first initial at the end of the filename (e.g., DYS_Chapter08_MarshallG).

It may take a few moments for the portable company file to open. Once it does, continue with step 5.

Option 2: Open a Company File

2. Choose **File→Open or Restore Company**, ensure that **Open a regular company file** is selected, and then open the **DYS_Chapter08** company file from your file storage location.
The QuickBooks company file will open.

3. Click **OK** to close the QuickBooks Information window. Click **No** in the Set Up External Accountant User window, if necessary.

4. Close the **Reminders** window.

Set Up a New Employee Using the Employees List

5. Click the **Employees** button in the Employees area of the Home page.
The Employee Center will be displayed.

6. Click the **New Employee** button on the Employee Center toolbar.

7. Follow these steps to set up the personal information for Stephen:

Ⓐ Type **Mr.** here.   Ⓑ Tap Tab, and then type **Stephen**.

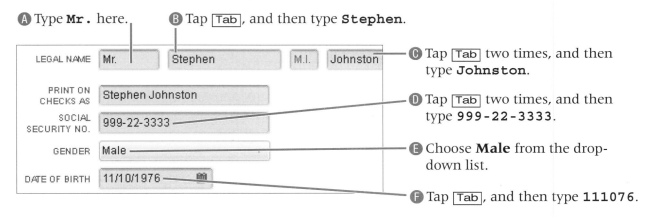

Ⓒ Tap Tab two times, and then type **Johnston**.

Ⓓ Tap Tab two times, and then type **999-22-3333**.

Ⓔ Choose **Male** from the drop-down list.

Ⓕ Tap Tab, and then type **111076**.

Ⓖ Click the **Address & Contact** tab.   Ⓗ Type **7534 Golden Pony Rd.** here.

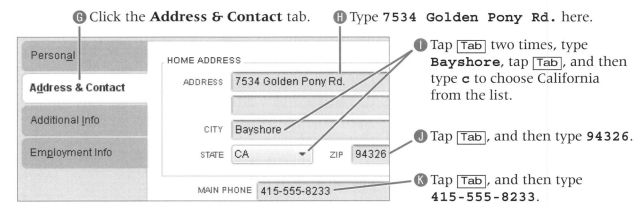

Ⓘ Tap Tab two times, type **Bayshore**, tap Tab, and then type **c** to choose California from the list.

Ⓙ Tap Tab, and then type **94326**.

Ⓚ Tap Tab, and then type **415-555-8233**.

8. Click **OK,** and then click **Leave As Is**.

Add an Additional Employee

You will now help Allison to add two more employees, Sam Jameson and herself!

9. Use the following information and the procedure outlined in the previous section to add two more employees.

Name	Mr. Samuel Jameson	Ms. Allison Fox
Address	303 McMurray Place Middlefield, CA 93210	130 Technology Way Bayshore, CA 94326
Phone	415-555-8791	415-555-7733
SS No.	999-88-7777	999-77-5555
Gender	Male	Female
Date of Birth	013078	022172

10. Close the **Employee Center**.

Working with an Outside Payroll Service

Many companies choose to go with an outside payroll service. If this is the case, you still need to enter the information into QuickBooks so you can create meaningful financial statements. The level of information you track in QuickBooks does not have to be as detailed when you use an outside service because much of the information is tracked for you.

Information to Track

You will not need to worry about setting QuickBooks up for payroll or using the payroll features of the software, since you are not tracking specific withholdings and deductions. Your intent when working with an outside service is to track expenses, cash flow, and balances being held in liability accounts so that your balance sheet, profit & loss, and cash flow reports are accurate.

Do not turn on the QuickBooks payroll features to track payroll from an outside source.

Track Employees

Enter your employees into the Employees List in QuickBooks. You will not need to enter information on the Payroll and Compensation Info tab, though, as that will be tracked by the service.

Track Expenses

To account for the payroll expenses for your company, you will need to set up an expense account, such as Payroll Expenses, and appropriate subaccounts for each type of payroll expense. Examples of subaccounts that you may wish to create are Gross Wages, Company-Paid Taxes, and Company-Paid Benefits.

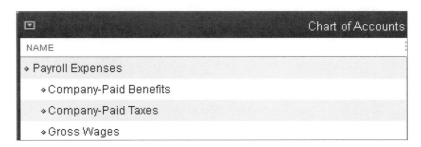

Notice the subaccounts that are set up for Payroll Expenses and used to track information from an outside payroll service.

Track Liabilities

You will still be holding deductions and withdrawals from employees that have to be paid to the appropriate agency at some time in the future. This means that you need to set up an Other Current Liability account, such as Payroll Liabilities, to track this information.

Enter Information from the Outside Service into QuickBooks

When you receive a report from the payroll service that shows the payroll activity for your company, you will need to enter it into QuickBooks. You will see payments going to employees and out to the agencies for which you are currently holding funds in the Payroll Liabilities account.

Enter Employee Paychecks

Employee paychecks should be entered in the Write Checks window since you are not worried about keeping the "other set of books" for payroll in QuickBooks (that you will learn about later in this chapter). You will enter gross wages on the first line of the Expenses tab. All deductions will be entered on the second line with a minus sign and will flow to the Payroll Liabilities account.

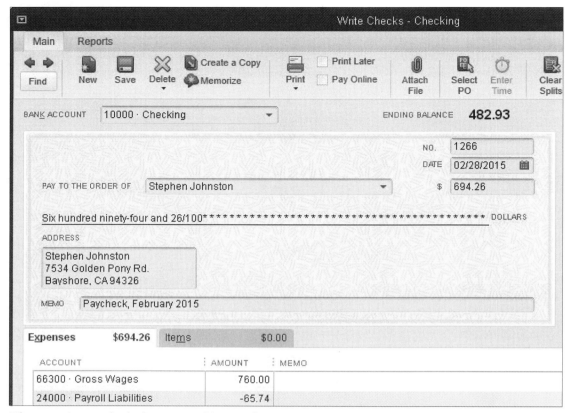

When entering paychecks from an outside payroll service, you use the Write Checks window and enter the gross wages as a positive amount and the payroll liabilities as a negative amount.

Enter Tax and Benefit Payments

When you use an outside payroll service, you will also use the Write Checks window to enter payments when you pay the payroll liabilities. On the Expense tab, you will enter the employee-paid taxes/deductions being held in Payroll Liabilities. Company-paid taxes and benefits will be entered on separate lines using the appropriate Payroll Expenses subaccounts.

Remember that, in this section, what we are talking about applies *only* when a company is using an outside payroll service! You should *never* use the Write Checks window for payroll transactions if you are completing your own payroll in QuickBooks!

When you issue paychecks from an outside service, you will credit Checking and Payroll Liabilities, while debiting the Gross Wages subaccount of Salary Expense.

66300-Gross Wages	24000-Payroll Liabilities	10000-Checking
2,460.00	272.04	2,187.96

When it is time to pay the payroll liabilities, you will debit it as well as the expense account that tracks company-paid taxes. Checking will be credited for the total amount. In the example below, only the federal taxes are being paid (hence the different amount from the example above).

66200-Company-Paid Taxes	24000-Payroll Liabilities	10000-Checking
188.20	247.44	435.64

Task	Procedure
Set up to track payroll expenses	▪ Choose Lists→Chart of Accounts. ▪ Set up the following expense account: Payroll Expenses. ▪ Set up the following subaccounts for Payroll Expenses: Gross Wages, Company-Paid Taxes, and Company-Paid Benefits.
Set up to track payroll liabilities	▪ Choose Lists→Chart of Accounts. ▪ Set up the following other current liability account: Payroll Liabilities.
Enter an employee paycheck from an outside payroll service	▪ Choose Banking→Write Checks. ▪ Set the date of the check and fill in the employee in the Pay to the Order of field. ▪ Enter the amount of the check. ▪ On the Expenses tab, enter the total wages on the first line using the Payroll Expenses:Gross Wages account. ▪ On the second line of the Expenses tab, enter the total taxes and deductions held from the employee's gross wages as a negative number using the Payroll Liabilities account.
Enter tax and benefit payments	▪ Choose Banking→Write Checks. ▪ Set the date of the check; fill in the vendor to whom you are paying the taxes or benefits in the Pay to the Order of field. ▪ Enter the amount of the check. ▪ On the Expenses tab, enter the employee deductions being paid on one line using Payroll Liabilities as the account. ▪ On a separate line of the Expenses tab, enter the company-paid portion of the taxes or benefits using the appropriate subaccount, either Payroll Expenses: Company – Paid Taxes or Payroll Expenses Company – Paid Benefits.

Advanced Skills

Enter Payroll From an Outside Service

In this exercise, you will help Allison to enter information from an outside payroll service for the first half of February 2015 (employees are paid on the 15th and last day of each month). To begin, you will turn off payroll in QuickBooks.

1. Choose **Edit→Preferences**.
2. Follow these steps to turn the QuickBooks payroll features off:

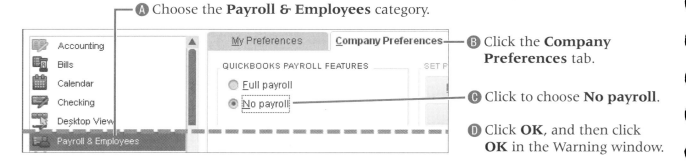

Ⓐ Choose the **Payroll & Employees** category.

Ⓑ Click the **Company Preferences** tab.

Ⓒ Click to choose **No payroll**.

Ⓓ Click **OK**, and then click **OK** in the Warning window.

Set Up Expense and Liability Accounts

3. Choose **Lists→Chart of Accounts**.
4. Scroll down to verify that **24000•Payroll Liabilities** and **66000•Payroll Expenses** are set up for you.

   You will now create the expense subaccounts to track payroll expenses.

5. Click the **Account** menu button, and then choose **New**.
6. Follow these steps to create the new account:

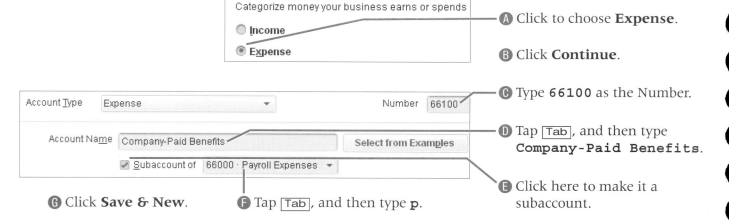

Ⓐ Click to choose **Expense**.

Ⓑ Click **Continue**.

Ⓒ Type **66100** as the Number.

Ⓓ Tap Tab, and then type **Company-Paid Benefits**.

Ⓔ Click here to make it a subaccount.

Ⓕ Tap Tab, and then type **p**.

Ⓖ Click **Save & New**.

7. Now create two more **Payroll Expenses** subaccounts with this information:
   - 66200•Company-Paid Taxes
   - 66300•Gross Wages
8. After creating the **Gross Wages** subaccount, click **Save & Close**; close the **Chart of Accounts** window.

Create Paychecks Using Data from an Outside Service

You will now help Allison to take data received from an outside payroll service and enter it into QuickBooks. The statement received from the payroll service is displayed below:

AVERAGE GUY DESIGNS FEBRUARY 2015 MONTHLY PAYROLL

Employee	Gross Wages	Employee Fed Taxes W/H	Employee State Taxes W/H	Net Pay	Company Fed Taxes Owed	Company Benefits Owed
Allison Fox	$1,000.00	$82.66	$10.00	$907.34	$76.50	$203.50
Samuel Jameson	700.00	106.64	7.00	586.36	53.56	0.00
Stephen Johnston	760.00	58.14	7.60	694.26	58.14	0.00
Totals, 2/15/15	$2,460.00	$247.44	$24.60	$2,187.96	$188.20	$203.50

9. Click the **Write Checks** task icon in the **Banking** area of the Home page.

Write Checks

10. Follow these steps to create the first paycheck for Allison:

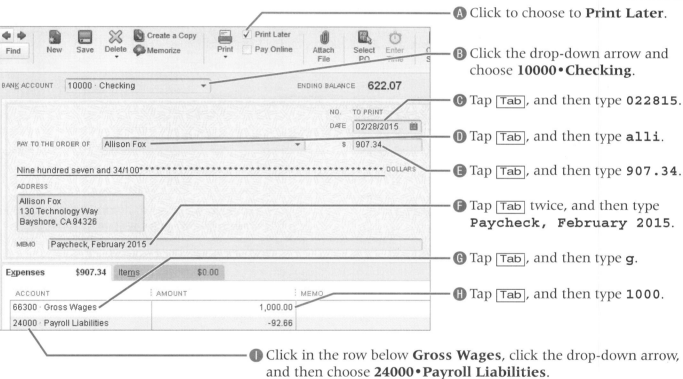

Ⓐ Click to choose to **Print Later**.

Ⓑ Click the drop-down arrow and choose **10000•Checking**.

Ⓒ Tap Tab, and then type **022815**.

Ⓓ Tap Tab, and then type **alli**.

Ⓔ Tap Tab, and then type **907.34**.

Ⓕ Tap Tab twice, and then type **Paycheck, February 2015**.

Ⓖ Tap Tab, and then type **g**.

Ⓗ Tap Tab, and then type **1000**.

Ⓘ Click in the row below **Gross Wages**, click the drop-down arrow, and then choose **24000•Payroll Liabilities**.

11. Click **Save & New**.

12. Follow these steps to record Samuel's paycheck:

Ⓐ Tap ⸢Tab⸣, and then type **s**.

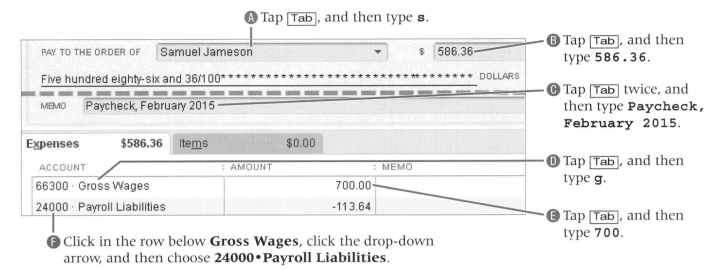

Ⓑ Tap ⸢Tab⸣, and then type **586.36**.

Ⓒ Tap ⸢Tab⸣ twice, and then type **Paycheck, February 2015**.

Ⓓ Tap ⸢Tab⸣, and then type **g**.

Ⓔ Tap ⸢Tab⸣, and then type **700**.

Ⓕ Click in the row below **Gross Wages**, click the drop-down arrow, and then choose **24000•Payroll Liabilities**.

13. Click **Save & New**.

14. Using the information in the preceding steps and the data in the monthly payroll statement, create a **February 2015** paycheck for **Stephen**.

15. Click **Save & New**.

BTS BRIEF

66300•Gross Wages DR 2,460.00; **24000•Payroll Liabilities CR <272.04>, 10000•Checking CR <2,187.96>**

You will leave the Write Checks window open.

Remember, you only use the Write Checks window to create paychecks if you use an outside payroll service. *Never* use it if you are running payroll through QuickBooks!

Pay Payroll Liabilities

Now you will use the monthly payroll statement to create a payroll liability check as well as a benefits check for February 2015. The state taxes are due quarterly, so you will not remit them at this time.

16. Follow these steps to create a liability check to the U.S. Treasury for all federal taxes owed (this includes the amount held in Payroll Liabilities as well as the amount owed by the company):

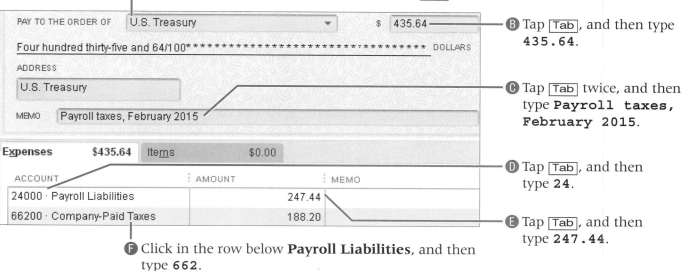

Ⓐ Tap ⎡Tab⎤ twice, type **U.S. Treasury**, tap ⎡Tab⎤, and then **Quick Add** it as a Vendor.

Ⓑ Tap ⎡Tab⎤, and then type **435.64**.

Ⓒ Tap ⎡Tab⎤ twice, and then type **Payroll taxes, February 2015**.

Ⓓ Tap ⎡Tab⎤, and then type **24**.

Ⓔ Tap ⎡Tab⎤, and then type **247.44**.

Ⓕ Click in the row below **Payroll Liabilities**, and then type **662**.

> **BTS BRIEF**
>
> 24000•Payroll Liabilities DR 247.44, 66200•Company-Paid Taxes DR 188.20; **10000•Checking CR <435.64>**

17. Click **Save & New**.

18. Follow these steps to record the benefits payment:

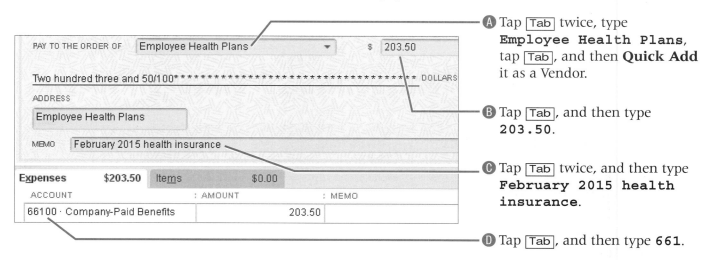

Ⓐ Tap ⎡Tab⎤ twice, type **Employee Health Plans**, tap ⎡Tab⎤, and then **Quick Add** it as a Vendor.

Ⓑ Tap ⎡Tab⎤, and then type **203.50**.

Ⓒ Tap ⎡Tab⎤ twice, and then type **February 2015 health insurance**.

Ⓓ Tap ⎡Tab⎤, and then type **661**.

19. Click **Save & Close**.

Print Paychecks and Liability Checks

The final step is to print the paycheck and liability checks. Since you have additional checks in the queue, you will go ahead and print them as well.

20. Click the **Print Checks** task icon in the **Banking** area of the Home page.

21. Click **OK** to choose to print the checks in the queue, including the paychecks and liability checks you just created.

22. Verify the information is correct in the **Print Checks** window, and then choose to either print the checks to PDF, physically print them, or click **Cancel**. (Ask your instructor what you are required to do.)

23. If you printed the checks, click **OK** in the **Print Confirmation** window.

Setting Up QuickBooks to Run Payroll

Now that you have learned about working with the Employee Center and how to enter payroll from an outside service, you will look at the payroll options in QuickBooks and learn how to set up payroll items properly.

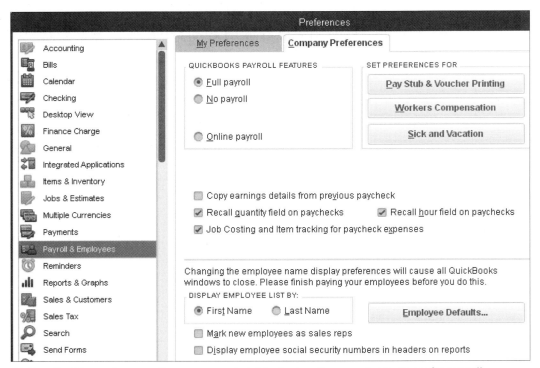

Notice all of the preferences the company administrator has the opportunity to set for payroll.

Payroll Recordkeeping in QuickBooks

To produce all of the required federal, state, and local payroll forms and reports, QuickBooks keeps a separate set of records for payroll. This separate set of records tracks payroll liabilities, paychecks (and the items listed on them), and taxes. Due to this method of payroll recordkeeping, only those transactions entered via QuickBooks' payroll features will affect payroll reporting.

Evaluating Payroll Options

QuickBooks payroll offers multiple options: Manual, Basic, Enhanced, and Full Service. In addition, there are separate services for accountants, online edition users, and those who need to process household and nanny payroll. There are also mobile payroll apps to allow you to keep up on your payroll tasks when on the go. Each option has its pros and cons, and all but the Manual option have an associated fee for the service. Intuit does not recommend the Manual option, as it requires you to stay on top of all tax law changes and there is a higher likelihood of errors and resulting penalties when you have to enter everything yourself.

If you are using QuickBooks for a Canadian company, Intuit produces a separate line of products for the Canadian market that addresses multiple currencies and Canadian payroll regulations. Find more information at http://quickbooks.ca/.

If you would like to learn more about the payroll options available through QuickBooks, check out the link on the Student Resource Center. QuickBooks can change its payroll options at any time, so it is advised that you check out the website to ensure that you are dealing with the most current information.

QuickBooks is not ideal for all companies' payroll needs. If multiple states require you run payroll for an individual employee, or you withhold a certain percentage of wages on paychecks, using QuickBooks for payroll may not be the best solution for you.

Common Mistakes When Using QuickBooks for Payroll

Two very common mistakes people make when using QuickBooks for payroll are:

- Making a payroll liabilities adjustment with a journal entry
- Paying the liabilities with a "regular check" rather than a liability check similar to what you used when paying sales tax

In both cases, the Chart of Accounts will be affected but the separate payroll records that QuickBooks keeps will not be. If you have used a regular check for payroll liabilities, you will need to make an adjustment in the Liability Adjustment window, from where you can choose for QuickBooks to not affect the Chart of Accounts.

Another very common error is for people to set up their payroll items incorrectly. If you do choose to use subaccounts and remap your payroll accounts manually, be very careful to map the payroll items correctly!

Entering Historical Amounts

If you are beginning to use the QuickBooks payroll feature for existing employees who have received at least one paycheck from you (and it is not the first day of January), you must enter the payroll history amounts. This will ensure that QuickBooks properly calculates taxes with thresholds. It also ensures that you will be able to produce accurate W-2s at the end of the year.

QuickBooks offers step-by-step help to assist you in entering the required payroll history. Before you begin setting up historical amounts, make sure you have:

- Prior-period paychecks
- Prior liability payments

Step-by-step help for this task is accessible through the QuickBooks Payroll Setup Interview. Once you have entered the information, you will have the opportunity to reconcile and verify your data to ensure it is correct.

Visualize!

Tab: Other Topics
Topic: Payroll overview

FLASHBACK TO GAAP: TIME PERIOD

Remember that the activities of the business can be divided into time periods.

QUICK REFERENCE	PREPARING TO USE QUICKBOOKS TO RUN PAYROLL
Task	**Procedure**
Turn on QuickBooks payroll preferences	▪ Choose Edit→Preferences. ▪ Click the Payroll & Employees category; click the Company Preferences tab. ▪ Click in the circle to the left of Full Payroll; click OK.
Sign up for a QuickBooks payroll service	▪ Choose Employees→Payroll Service Options→Order Payroll Service. ▪ Click the Learn More button or dial the indicated phone number.
Access the Payroll Setup Interview	▪ Choose Employees→Payroll Setup. ▪ Follow the interview to complete the process by answering questions and clicking the Continue button.
Create subaccounts for payroll accounts	▪ Choose Lists→Chart of Accounts, right-click the desired item, and then choose New Account. ▪ Create Other Current Liability subaccounts for your Payroll Liabilities account. ▪ Create Expense subaccounts for your Payroll Expenses account.
Edit payroll items	▪ Choose Lists→Payroll Item List; double-click the desired item. ▪ Follow the steps on the screen, making any necessary changes. ▪ Ensure you have the items mapped to the correct accounts.
Enter payroll year-to-date amounts	▪ Complete steps 1–4 of the QuickBooks Payroll Setup Interview. ▪ Choose Employees→Payroll Setup (if you are not still viewing the interview). ▪ Complete step 5 "Payroll History" of the interview.
Make an adjustment to a payroll liability	▪ Choose Employees→Payroll Taxes and Liabilities→Adjust Payroll Liabilities. ▪ Enter the adjustment information; click OK.

Task	Procedure
Run a payroll item listing report	■ Choose Reports→Employees & Payroll→Payroll Item Listing.

Set Up QuickBooks to Run Payroll

In this exercise, you will view how to set the payroll preference for a company. The first step is to open a QuickBooks sample file that includes a payroll service. You can either open a company file or restore a portable company file.

Option 1: Restore a Portable Company File

1. Choose **File→Open or Restore Company**.

2. Restore the **DYS_Chapter08-PR (Portable)** portable company file from your file storage location, placing your last name and first initial at the end of the filename (e.g., DYS_Chapter08-PR_MarshallG).

   It may take a few moments for the portable company file to open. Once it does, continue with step 5.

Option 2: Open a Company File

2. Choose **File→Open or Restore Company**, ensure that **Open a regular company file** is selected, and then open the **DYS_Chapter08-PR** company file from your file storage location.

   The QuickBooks company file will open.

3. Click **OK** twice to close both of the QuickBooks Information windows. Click **No** in the Set Up External Accountant User window, if necessary.

4. Close the **Reminders** window.

View the Payroll Preference

If you are setting QuickBooks up to run payroll for the first time in your company file, you will need to set the preference. In this case, you will help Allison to verify that it is set correctly.

5. Choose **Edit→Preferences**.

6. Click the **Payroll & Employees** category on the left and then the **Company Preferences** tab.

7. Notice that **Full payroll** is turned on for this company file.

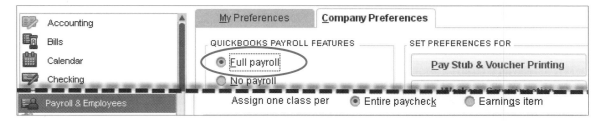

8. Click **Cancel** to close the Preferences window.

Dealing with Payroll Deductions

You have learned about two of the three main tasks associated with setting up QuickBooks to run payroll—setting up payroll items and employees. Now you will need to let QuickBooks know which taxes and deductions to collect and to whom they need to be paid. You can use the QuickBooks Payroll Setup Interview to take a quick whirl through the taxes you have set up to make sure they are correct. In addition, you can view the Payroll Item Listing report to verify that the taxes and deductions are being routed to the right expense and liability accounts as well as the actual Payroll Item List to make sure the vendors to whom you pay them are correct.

You must have your Federal Employer Identification Number (FEIN) listed in your company file in order for payroll to be processed correctly. If you did not enter this correctly or at all when you created your company file, you can make that change at any time.

The Payroll Setup Interview

To set up payroll in QuickBooks, you are provided with a Payroll Setup Interview that will walk you through all of the steps to make sure you set up taxes, compensation, and benefits correctly. After the interview leads you through the steps to set up your payroll items, it will help you to set up your employees and enter historical amounts so you can begin doing your company's payroll in QuickBooks.

Payroll Items

Anything you wish to include on a paycheck—such as wages, taxes, employee loans, and 401(k) withholdings—must first be set up as a payroll item. The majority of payroll mistakes are made because payroll items were not set up properly.

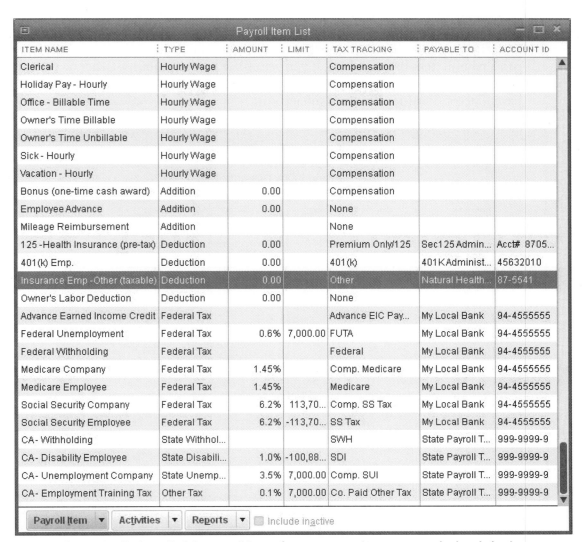

ITEM NAME	TYPE	AMOUNT	LIMIT	TAX TRACKING	PAYABLE TO	ACCOUNT ID
Clerical	Hourly Wage			Compensation		
Holiday Pay - Hourly	Hourly Wage			Compensation		
Office - Billable Time	Hourly Wage			Compensation		
Owner's Time Billable	Hourly Wage			Compensation		
Owner's Time Unbillable	Hourly Wage			Compensation		
Sick - Hourly	Hourly Wage			Compensation		
Vacation - Hourly	Hourly Wage			Compensation		
Bonus (one-time cash award)	Addition	0.00		Compensation		
Employee Advance	Addition	0.00		None		
Mileage Reimbursement	Addition			None		
125 -Health Insurance (pre-tax)	Deduction	0.00		Premium Only/125	Sec125 Admin...	Acct# 8705...
401(k) Emp.	Deduction	0.00		401(k)	401K Administ...	45632010
Insurance Emp -Other (taxable)	Deduction	0.00		Other	Natural Health...	87-5541
Owner's Labor Deduction	Deduction	0.00		None		
Advance Earned Income Credit	Federal Tax			Advance EIC Pay...	My Local Bank	94-4555555
Federal Unemployment	Federal Tax	0.6%	7,000.00	FUTA	My Local Bank	94-4555555
Federal Withholding	Federal Tax			Federal	My Local Bank	94-4555555
Medicare Company	Federal Tax	1.45%		Comp. Medicare	My Local Bank	94-4555555
Medicare Employee	Federal Tax	1.45%		Medicare	My Local Bank	94-4555555
Social Security Company	Federal Tax	6.2%	113,70...	Comp. SS Tax	My Local Bank	94-4555555
Social Security Employee	Federal Tax	6.2%	-113,70...	SS Tax	My Local Bank	94-4555555
CA- Withholding	State Withhol...			SWH	State Payroll T...	999-9999-9
CA- Disability Employee	State Disabili...	1.0%	-100,88...	SDI	State Payroll T...	999-9999-9
CA- Unemployment Company	State Unemp...	3.5%	7,000.00	Comp. SUI	State Payroll T...	999-9999-9
CA- Employment Training Tax	Other Tax	0.1%	7,000.00	Co. Paid Other Tax	State Payroll T...	999-9999-9

Payroll Item ▼   Activities ▼   Reports ▼   ☐ Include inactive

The Payroll Item List displays all of the payroll items, from compensation to taxes and other deductions.

If you need to add payroll items later, you can always return to the QuickBooks Payroll Setup Interview or access the Payroll Item List from the menu bar.

Making Payroll Data More Meaningful

When you turn on the payroll preference in QuickBooks, the payroll expense and liability accounts are created for you. QuickBooks then automatically routes payroll items set up through the QuickBooks Payroll Setup to these accounts. If you wish to provide more meaningful information in your reports and make troubleshooting more user-friendly, you may want to consider setting up subaccounts for the payroll accounts QuickBooks creates for you. Once you create these subaccounts, you must remap each payroll item to the correct one through the Payroll Item List.

Verifying Correct Payroll Item Setup

To verify that payroll items are set up correctly and mapped to the correct accounts, you need to run a payroll item listing report. If you see either Payroll Liability-Other or Payroll Expense-Other displayed on a balance sheet or P&L, you know that you have a payroll item mapped to a parent account rather than to a subaccount.

Notice that the Payroll Item Listing report shows you what happens behind the scenes with expense and liability accounts when you use a payroll item.

Workers Compensation Insurance

QuickBooks can process Workers' Compensation insurance in much the same way that it processes payroll taxes. To track this payroll expense, the preference must be turned on in QuickBooks.

The Workers Compensation button in the Set preferences for area of the Company Preferences tab of the Payroll & Employees category leads to a window that allows you to choose whether to track workers comp in QuickBooks.

Task	Procedure
Enter your company's FEIN	■ Choose Company→Company Information. ■ Click in the Federal Employer Identification No. field, and then type your FEIN. ■ If you are a sole proprietor and don't have a FEIN, click in the Social Security Number field, type your SSN, and then click OK.
Choose to track workers comp in QuickBooks	■ Choose Edit→Preferences. ■ Click the Payroll & Employees category; choose the Company Preferences tab. ■ Click the Workers Compensation button; click in the checkbox to the left of Track Workers Comp. ■ Click OK two times to set the new preference.
Create a Payroll Item Listing report	■ Choose Reports→Employees & Payroll→Payroll Item Listing.
View the Payroll Item List	■ Choose Lists→Payroll Item List.

DEVELOP YOUR SKILLS 8-4

Set Up Payroll Taxes

In this exercise, you will make sure that the FEIN is entered properly and that the company is set up correctly to account for payroll taxes and deductions.

1. Choose **Company→My Company**.

2. Verify that **94-5-4555555** is the FEIN entered for Rock Castle Construction.

3. Close the **My Company** window.

Legal Name & Address	Average Guy Designs 110 Sampson Way Bayshore CA 91547 US
EIN	94-4555555

Verify Correct Payroll Tax Setup

You will now use the QuickBooks Payroll Setup Interview as a tool to make sure the payroll taxes are set up properly. If there is an obvious error, QuickBooks will alert you and ask you to make a change.

4. Choose **Employees→Payroll Setup**.

5. Click in the box to the left of **Taxes**.

6. Click **Continue**.

   You will see a screen that lists all of the federal taxes that have been set up for you. Notice that both Medicare and Social Security have two separate entries; they are paid by both the company and employee.

7. Click **Continue**.

   On this next screen, you will see the state taxes that QuickBooks has set up for you. Remember that this book is meant to be a training tool only. You must contact your local tax agency to know how to set up taxes for your jurisdiction!

QuickBooks
Payroll Setup

- ✓ Introduction
- ☐ Company Setup
- ☐ Employee Setup
- ➡ **Taxes**
  - ☐ Federal taxes
  - ☐ State taxes
  - ☐ Schedule payments
- ☐ Year-to-Date Payrolls
- ☐ Finishing Up

8. Click **Continue**.

   A Schedule Payments window will appear as there is incorrect information entered for the state taxes. You will fix it in the next step.

9. Tap ⟨Tab⟩, and then type **999-9999-9** as the CA Employment Development Dept Employer Acct No.; click **Next**.

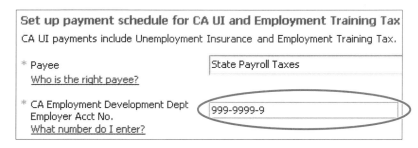

10. Tap ⟨Tab⟩, and then type **999-9999-9** as the CA Employment Development Dept Employer Acct No. again; click **Finish**.

    In this next screen, you will see how and when you pay each of your withholding taxes.

11. Click the **Finish Later** button at the bottom left of the QuickBooks Payroll Setup window; click **OK** in the Finish Later window.

    Notice that even after your payroll is set up, you can use the QuickBooks Payroll Setup feature to examine the information you have entered for it.

Create a Payroll Item Listing Report to Verify Accounts

It is important for your payroll items to link to the proper accounts in your Chart of Accounts! You will now review a report that shows how the items are linked so you can ensure you are doing payroll properly.

12. Choose **Reports→Employees & Payroll→Payroll Item Listing**.

    The Payroll Item Listing report will be displayed.

13. Note the **Expense Account** and the **Liability Account** columns.

    The expense accounts indicate the payroll expenses for your company, from salaries and benefits to employer taxes that you are required to pay. The liability accounts are where you "hold" the funds until you have to pay them to the proper taxing authority. Remember that QuickBooks keeps a separate set of records for payroll behind the scenes, so when you choose to pay your payroll liabilities with a special Liability Check window, it will "empty" these accounts properly.

14. Close the **Payroll Item Listing** window.

Verify Vendors and Edit a Payroll Item

The final step you will take to verify that your payroll taxes are set up properly is to make sure that you are paying the taxes to the proper vendors.

15. Choose **Lists→Payroll Item List**, resizing the window as necessary so you can see all columns clearly.

    Look in the Payable To column. This shows to whom you must pay each tax that you are holding in your liability accounts. Notice that there is no vendor listed for Health Insurance in the Payable to column. You will help Allison to add this information now.

16. Double-click **Insurance Emp-Other** to open it for editing.

An Edit Payroll Item window displays. You will be clicking Next to move through the screens to modify this item.

17. Click **Next** if the name for the item is correct.

18. Follow these steps to set up the vendor to whom you will pay the insurance premiums:

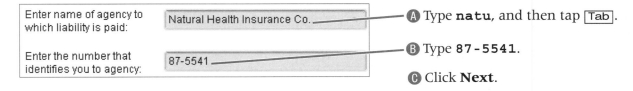

Ⓐ Type **natu**, and then tap Tab.

Ⓑ Type **87-5541**.

Ⓒ Click **Next**.

The Liability account is correct, so you do not need to edit it.

19. Type **o** in the **Tax tracking type** screen to choose **Other**; click **Next**.

20. Click **Next** in the **Taxes** screen; click **Next** in the Calculate based on quantity screen.

21. Click **Next** in the Gross vs. net window.

22. Click **Finish** in the Default rate and limit window.

You will enter the deduction amount when you set up each new employee, rather than entering a default here.

Create a Payroll Item

You will now create a new payroll item to track court-mandated child support deductions as well as payments to a charity the company has adopted, Niños del Lago. The Payroll Item List should still be displayed from the previous step, but if not, Choose Lists→Payroll Item List.

23. Click the **Payroll Item** menu button, and then choose **New**.

24. Click **Next** to choose **EZ Setup**.

25. Click in the circle to the left of **Other Deductions**, and then click **Next**.

> ○ Other Additions (Reimbursements, Company Contributions...)
> ◉ Other Deductions (Garnishments, Union Dues...)

26. Click in the boxes to the left of **Wage garnishment** and **Donation to charity**, and then click **Next**.

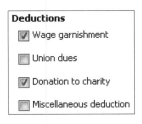

27. Follow these steps to set up the payment schedule for the charity donations:

Ⓐ Type **Ninos del Lago.**

Ⓑ Tap ⌈Tab⌉, and then type **AGD.**

Ⓒ Click in the circle to the left of **Quarterly.**

Ⓓ Click **Next.**

Payee (Vendor)	Ninos del Lago ▾ Explain
Account #	AGD
	(The number the payee uses to identify you. Example: 99-99999X)
Payment frequency	○ Weekly, on Monday ▾ for the previous week's liabilities
	○ Monthly, on the 1 ▾ day of the month for the previous month's liabilities
	⦿ **Quarterly, on the** 1 ▾ day of the month for the previous quarter's liabilities

28. Follow these steps to set up the payment schedule for the child support deductions:

Ⓐ Type **County Family Services.**

Ⓑ Tap ⌈Tab⌉, and then type **00-7904153.**

Ⓒ Click in the circle to the left of **Monthly.**

Ⓓ Click **Next.**

Payee (Vendor)	County Financial Services ▾ Explain
Account #	00-7904153
	(The number the payee uses to identify you. Example: 99-99999X)
Payment frequency	○ Weekly, on Monday ▾ for the previous week's liabilities
	⦿ **Monthly, on the** 1 ▾ day of the month for the previous month's liabilities

29. Click **Finish.**

You will now see the Payroll Item List displayed with your two new payroll items added to it. If you wish, you can rename the items from this list.

30. Close the **Payroll Item List.**

Creating Paychecks

Once you have chosen your payroll method, made sure your payroll items are set up properly, and set up your employees and payroll tax information, you can begin to create paychecks for your employees. When you first choose to pay employees, you will see an Enter Hours window displayed. Once you have entered the paycheck information for each employee, you will see all of the data displayed in the Review and Create Paychecks window.

The Pay Employees tab lets you process payroll.

The Pay Liabilities tab helps you ensure that you pay all funds you are holding in your payroll liability accounts on time.

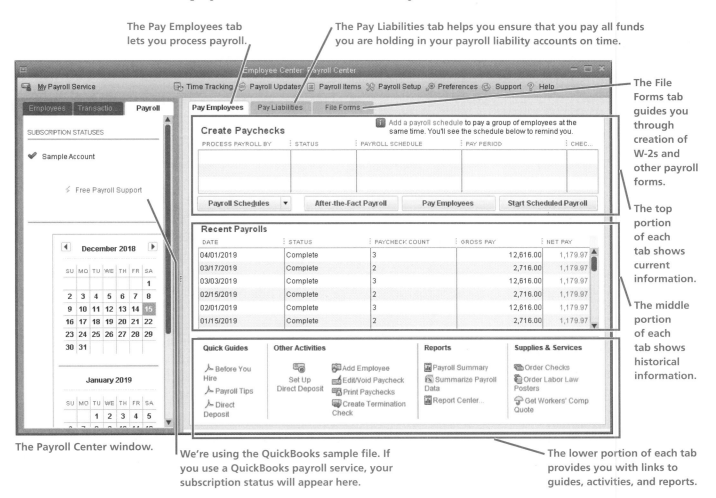

The File Forms tab guides you through creation of W-2s and other payroll forms.

The top portion of each tab shows current information.

The middle portion of each tab shows historical information.

The Payroll Center window.

We're using the QuickBooks sample file. If you use a QuickBooks payroll service, your subscription status will appear here.

The lower portion of each tab provides you with links to guides, activities, and reports.

You will have the opportunity to enter information for each employee in a Review or Change Paycheck window, moving from one employee to another using the Next and Previous buttons.

Working with Payroll Schedules

When you choose to use QuickBooks for payroll, you have the option to set up payroll schedules to more efficiently run payroll. Payroll schedules allow you to set how often you pay employees, the date on which the paycheck is due, the date on which you will run payroll, all the while taking into account holidays and weekends to ensure that you pay your employees on time. Another benefit of using scheduled payroll is that you can choose to pay your employees by group or by batch.

Advanced Skills

Payroll schedules are created from the Payroll Center after the payroll setup is complete. You will have an opportunity to run a scheduled payroll for Rock Castle Construction. In the Reinforce Your Skills exercise, you will run payroll without using a payroll schedule.

Using scheduled payroll does not limit you from creating a paycheck for an employee "off schedule." This can be completed by clicking the Unscheduled Payroll button in the Payroll Center.

In the New Payroll Schedule window, you can set the vital information that will apply to the payroll schedule being created for a group of employees.

Passing On Billable Time to Customers

In Chapter 4, Working with Vendors, you learned that it was possible to pass on expenses to customers. In this section, you will learn to pass on billable payroll expenses to customers. When you create a paycheck for an employee who has billable hours, make sure to choose the correct customer or job to which to pass on the expense.

Assigning Sick or Vacation Hours

You learned how to set QuickBooks up to track sick and vacation hours for employees previously in this chapter. To document an employee's use of "banked" paid time off, you will assign the time to payroll items that specifically track the banked time.

BEHIND THE SCENES

When you create paychecks, you will pay employees, pay taxes, and withhold taxes from employee paychecks. In this example, we will look at Jonathan Graham's paycheck, which you will create in the next exercise. You will issue a net paycheck for $1,720.88, with $779.12 of employee deductions going to the Payroll Liability subaccounts (only the parent accounts of Payroll Liabilities and Wages are shown in this example). The gross pay is $2,500.00.

6500-Wages		2100-Payroll Liabilities		1110-Company Checking	
2,500.00			779.12		1,720.88

QUICK REFERENCE	CREATING PAYCHECKS AND PAYROLL SCHEDULES
Task	**Procedure**
Create employee paychecks	■ Choose Employees→Pay Employees; set the check date and the last day of the pay period.
	■ Set the bank account and paycheck options.
	■ Click the employees for whom you wish to enter paycheck information and enter the hours for each employee in the correct field.
	■ Verify the information in the Review or Change Paycheck window; click Next.
	■ Verify that the information is correct; click Create Paychecks.
Print paychecks	■ Choose File→Print Forms→Paychecks; choose the correct bank account.
	■ Select the checks you wish to print; click OK.
	■ Select the type of checks you use; click Print.
Print pay stubs	■ Choose File→Print Forms→Pay Stubs; set the correct date range.
	■ Select the desired statements, click OK, and then click Print.
Pass billable payroll expenses on to a customer	■ Choose Customers→Create Invoices.
	■ Choose the customer to whom you will be passing on the expense.
	■ Click the Time/Costs button on the toolbar, and then click the Expenses tab.
	■ Choose the hours you wish to pass on; click OK.
	■ Finish entering invoice information; click Save & Close.
Create a payroll schedule	■ Choose Employees→Payroll Center.
	■ Click the Related Payroll Activities button; choose Add or Edit Payroll Schedules.
	■ Click the Payroll Schedule menu button; click New.
	■ Enter a name for the schedule, how often the payroll will run, and the pay period end date as well as the paycheck date; click OK.
	■ Assign the payroll schedule to all employees with the same pay frequency.
Edit a payroll schedule	■ Choose Employees→Payroll Center.
	■ Click the Related Payroll Activities button; choose Add or Edit Payroll Schedules.
	■ Click to select the payroll schedule you wish to edit.
	■ Click the Payroll Schedule menu button; click Edit.
	■ Make any desired changes; click OK.

DEVELOP YOUR SKILLS 8-5

Create Paychecks for Employees

In this exercise, you will run payroll for two employees for the period ending 06/15/2019.

1. Choose **Company→Home Page**.

2. Click the **Employees** button on the Home page.

   EMPLOYEES

3. Click the **Pay Employees** task icon in the Employee area of the Home page.
   The Employee Center: Payroll Center window opens.

Pay Employees

4. Click the **Pay Employees** button on the Pay Employees tab.

The Enter Payroll Information window displays with the Check Date field selected.

5. Follow these steps to select which employees to pay, when to pay them, and what and how many hours to pay them for:

Ⓐ Type **061519**.

Ⓑ Click to the left of **Johnathan Graham** and **Vicki King**.

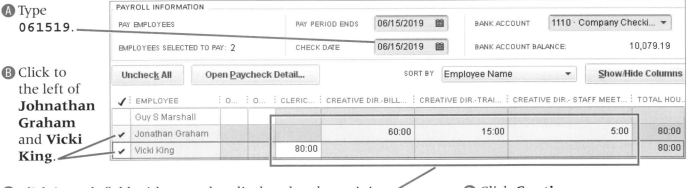

Ⓒ Click in each field with a number displayed and type it in.　　Ⓓ Click **Continue**.

The Review and Create Paychecks window will appear. When you enter the hours for each employee, QuickBooks will calculate all payroll taxes automatically for you. This will happen for you as well as long as you have subscribed to a QuickBooks payroll service. You can choose to do paychecks manually, but that will require you to enter each amount manually and to stay on top of all tax law changes. It results in a much greater chance for error.

6. Click **Create Paychecks**.

The Confirmation and Next Steps window will be displayed. Notice that this window shows you the "flow" for payroll. It provides buttons for you to make printing paychecks and pay stubs easy.

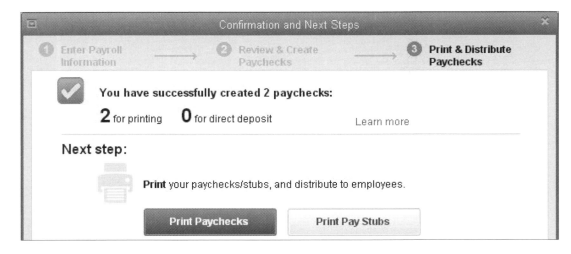

In the following BTS Brief section, the numbers reflect both paychecks. You are also viewing the "parent accounts" in this case, not the various subaccounts.

Print Paychecks and Pay Stubs

Once you have created paychecks, you need to print them. You will print the paychecks from the Confirmation and Next Steps window and then print the pay stubs using the menu bar command that is always available.

7. Click the **Print Paychecks** button in the Confirmation and Next Steps window.

   The Select Paychecks to Print window displays. At this point, you would place preprinted checks into the printer. Of course, for this exercise there are no preprinted checks. You will print them on blank sheets of paper or as a PDF file.

8. Click **OK** to choose to print both paychecks, using **5388** as the first check number.

   The Select Paychecks to Print dialog box displays. When you are dealing with your own company, look at the checks you place in the printer to verify that the first check number is correct.

9. Follow the desired step, depending on whether you wish to physically print the paychecks:

   ▪ Click **Print**. You can also choose this option if you wish to print the checks as an electronic PDF file. Click **OK** to verify that all checks printed correctly.

   ▪ Print choosing ***.pdf** as the printer, and then choose where to save the PDF file. Click **OK** to verify that all checks printed correctly.

10. Close the **Confirmation and Next Steps** window.

    Yes, you could have printed the pay stubs from that window, but it is important for you to know how to print paychecks and pay stubs from the menu bar as well!

11. Choose **File→Print Forms→Pay Stubs**.

12. Tap [Tab], type **061519**; tap [Tab], and then type **061519** again.

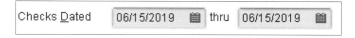

    Now only the pay stubs for the paychecks you just created display.

13. Click **Preview** to view what the employee pay stubs will look like. Close the **Print Preview** window when you are finished.

14. Close the **Select Pay Stubs** and the **Employee Center: Payroll Center** windows.

Tracking and Paying Payroll Liabilities

In Chapter 6, Dealing with Physical Inventory, you collected sales tax and held it in a current liability account until it was time to pay the tax agencies in Chapter 7, Working with Balance Sheet Accounts and Budgets. When you run payroll, you must collect taxes and other deductions and hold them in a payroll liabilities account until you are required to pay them.

Knowing How Much to Pay

QuickBooks has preset reports that you can run to determine how much you need to pay from what you hold in Payroll Liabilities. Remember that you hold taxes along with other deductions in the payroll liabilities account.

If you have your bank send in your federal payroll taxes electronically, clear the Print Later checkbox and enter EFTPS (Electronic Federal Tax Payment Service) into the check number field.

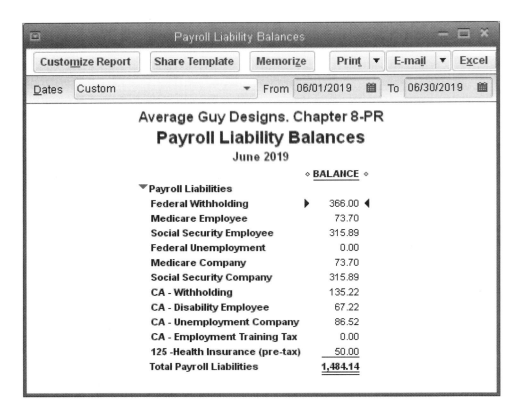

The Pay Payroll Liabilities Window

Just as you used the Pay Sales Tax window to pay your sales tax liabilities, you will use a special Pay Liabilities window to pay your payroll taxes and deductions. You should never just "write a check" for your payroll taxes because QuickBooks will not properly debit the liability accounts.

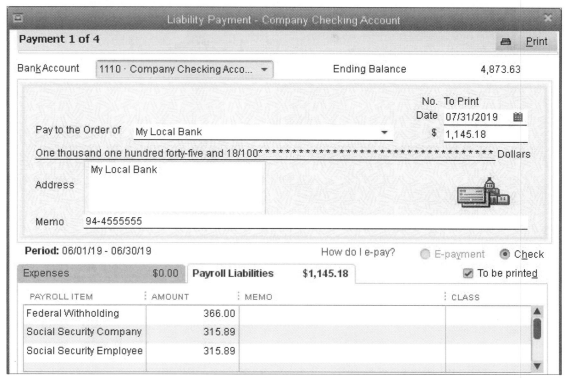

When you choose to pay payroll liabilities, they will be entered in a Liability Payment window, on a Payroll Liabilities tab.

One of the top errors made by new users is to use the Write Checks window for paying payroll liabilities rather than the QuickBooks Pay Liabilities window.

Visualize!

Tab: Other Topics
Topic: Pay taxes and other liabilities

BEHIND THE SCENES

When you pay your payroll liabilities, you decrease the amount in both your checking (by crediting) and payroll liabilities (by debiting) accounts. In the following example, you can see the result of the four liability payments ($1,145.18 + 202.44 + 50.00 + 86.52 = $1,484.14) you will make in the next exercise on 07/31/2019. Only the parent account, Payroll Liabilities, is used in this example.

2100-Payroll Liabilities		1110-Company Checking	
1,484.14			1,484.14

Task	Procedure
Run a payroll liability report	▪ Choose Reports→Employees & Payroll→Payroll Liability Balances. ▪ Set the proper date range, and then click Refresh.
Pay payroll liabilities	▪ Choose Employees→Process Payroll Liabilities→Pay Payroll Liabilities. ▪ Set the date range for the liabilities; click OK. ▪ Set the bank account and the check date. ▪ Select the payroll liabilities you need to pay; click Create.

DEVELOP YOUR SKILLS 8-6

Pay the Payroll Liabilities

In this exercise, you will pay the payroll liabilities that have been collected. In order to see exactly how much you need to pay to the various payroll vendors, you will run a report that shows all of the taxes and deductions being held in the payroll liabilities account.

1. Choose **Reports→Employees & Payroll→Payroll Liability Balances**.

2. Follow these steps to set the date range for the report:

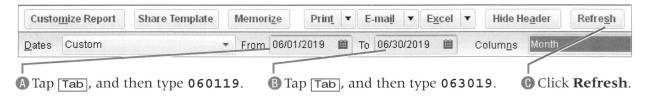

Ⓐ Tap ⌷Tab⌷, and then type **060119**.   Ⓑ Tap ⌷Tab⌷, and then type **063019**.   Ⓒ Click **Refresh**.

Your report should show a balance of $1,484.14.

3. Close the **Payroll Liability Balances** report; choose to not memorize the report.

Proceed with Paying

You are now ready to pay the payroll liabilities due in July 2019. You will pay them by using a liability check. Remember that if you are paying liabilities for your own company, you need to pay them based on the schedule that applies to your business.

4. Click the **Pay Liabilities** task icon in the Employees area of the Home page.

The Employee Center: Payroll Center will launch with the Pay Liabilities tab displayed.

Pay Liabilities

5. Follow these steps to pay the liabilities due in July:

Ⓐ Click to the left of the four payments due in July, scrolling down, if necessary.

Pay Taxes & Other Liabilities

✓	DUE DATE ▲	STATUS	PAYMENT	METHOD	PERIOD	AMOUNT DUE
✓	07/15/19	> 6 Months	Federal 941/944/943	Check	Jun 2019	1,145.18
✓	07/15/19	> 6 Months	CA Withholding and Disability Ins...	Check	Jun 2019	202.44
✓	07/20/19	> 6 Months	125 -Health Insurance (pre-tax)	Check	Q2 2019	50.00
✓	07/31/19	> 6 Months	CA UI and Employment Training T...	Check	Q2 2019	86.52

Total Selected Items: 1,484.14 **View/Pay**

Ⓑ Click **View/Pay**.

The Liability Payment – Checking window will be displayed (notice that it is not *the Write Checks window!), with the check information for the first payroll vendor filled in.*

6. Change the date on the check to **07/31/2019**, and then click **Save & Next**.

Since this is a sample company file, QuickBooks loads 12/15/2018 as the date each time you go to create a new transaction. In your own company file, the date that would be displayed is the last date you used in another transaction.

The second liability payment information displays in the window.

7. Change the date on the second payroll liability check to **07/31/2019**, and then click **Save & Next**.

8. Change the date on the third liability check to **07/31/2019**, and then click **Save & Next**.

9. Change the date on the fourth liability check to **07/31/2019**, and then click **Save & Close**.

A Payment Summary window displays. Notice that you can choose to print the checks right from this window. If you choose to print them at a later date, they will be placed in the queue of checks waiting to be printed. You can access that from the menu bar.

In the following BTS Brief section, you are viewing the "parent account" for Payroll Liabilities, not the various subaccounts.

BTS BRIEF

2100•Payroll Liabilities DR 1,484.14; **1110•Checking CR <1,484.14>**

10. Close the **Payment Summary** and **Employee Center: Payroll Center** windows.

Dealing with Errors in Payroll

When you encounter a situation that needs to be corrected in payroll, you must be very careful and ensure that you handle it in the proper manner. Remember that QuickBooks keeps a separate "set of books" for payroll, so you must make changes via the payroll features in QuickBooks.

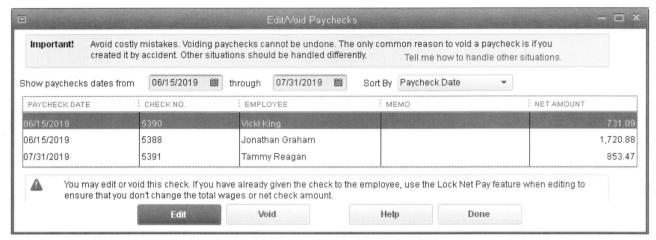

The Edit/Void Paychecks window allows you to choose which paycheck to void or edit and provides guidance. Note the important message at the top of the window regarding voiding paychecks and the message at the bottom of the window that refers to the selected paycheck (Vicki King's).

Fixing a Paycheck

It is only on rare occasions that you should void a paycheck. Two such times that it would be warranted are when you accidentally created a paycheck or when you have to correct a paycheck from a prior year.

Correcting a Paycheck Error from a Prior Year

If you need to change the date of a paycheck from one year to another, you must void the paycheck and reissue it. (In previous versions, you could change a paycheck in a prior year without re-creating it.) Voiding a paycheck is done in basically the same way as voiding any transaction in QuickBooks. Just remember that when you re-create the paycheck, you must do it through the proper method in QuickBooks. In other words, you cannot just create a new check in the Write Checks window.

Lock Net Pay Feature

If you need to make changes to a paycheck and want to make sure that you don't change the amount of the check (which would need to be dealt with in a different way), you can use the QuickBooks Lock Net Pay feature that ensures you don't change the amount of the paycheck or the total wages. When this feature is activated, you will only be able to make changes that do not affect the amount of the check, such as the Class to which it is assigned, vacation or sick time accrual, or select/deselect to use a direct deposit.

Unscheduled Payroll Checks

There may be times when you need to issue a paycheck to an employee, and it is not at the end of a pay period. For instance, you may have underpaid an employee and do not want that employee to have to wait until the next payday to receive the compensation, or you may need to issue a final paycheck. These situations can easily be dealt with in QuickBooks from the Payroll Center window by choosing either to conduct an unscheduled payroll or to create a termination check.

Notice the additional options available in the Other Activities area of the Payroll Center.

Let's take a look at how to correct some common paycheck errors that may occur.

COMMON PAYROLL ERRORS AND THEIR FIXES	
The Error	**The Fix**
You have to replace a paycheck that was lost or damaged	Reprint and reissue the check with the next check number; document the event by creating and then voiding a check
You find out that the pay period dates are wrong but still within the same calendar year	Edit the pay period dates in the Review Paycheck window and create a memo in the check register
You discover that an employee was overpaid	Correct the overpayment on the next payroll (rather than reissuing the paycheck)
You discover that an employee was underpaid	Issue an unscheduled payroll check or correct the underpayment on the next payroll
You realize that a paycheck item is incorrect and that the error will not affect the amount of the check	Edit the paycheck information while in Lock Net Pay mode

Depending on the type of payroll service you subscribe to, there may be limitations on how you will be able to correct certain payroll errors.

Making Corrections to a Payroll Liability Payment

Paying a payroll liability with a regular check rather than a liability check will create issues for you behind the scenes. To set things right, you need to void the regular check and then process the payment through the pay payroll liabilities feature in QuickBooks.

QUICK REFERENCE	DEALING WITH PAYROLL ERRORS
Task	**Procedure**
Replace a lost or damaged paycheck	**Reissue the check:**
	▪ Choose Banking→Use Register; choose the desired account.
	▪ Find the applicable check; record the check number and net pay amount.
	▪ Double-click the paycheck entry in the check register; click in the To be printed checkbox.
	▪ Click the print button at the top of the window (use the next check number).
	▪ Click Save & Close; close the register.
	Document the lost check:
	▪ Choose Banking→Write Checks.
	▪ Create a check using the same check number and day as the one that was lost, payable to the employee.
	▪ Enter the net amount from the original check; note in the memo field that this check was replaced.
	▪ Choose Payroll Expenses as the Account on the Expenses tab; click Save & Close.
	▪ Choose Banking→Use Register; choose the same account into which you just entered the check.
	▪ Right-click on the check that you just created using the lost check number and date; choose to Void Check.
Issue an unscheduled payroll check	▪ Choose Employees→Pay Employees→Unscheduled Payroll.
	▪ Choose the employees for whom you wish to create a paycheck.
	▪ Create the paycheck(s) using the same procedure you used to issue scheduled paychecks.
Void a regular check and replace it with a payroll liabilities check	▪ Open the Checking register and locate the check you wish to void.
	▪ Right-click the check; choose Void Check.
	▪ Choose Employees→Process Payroll Liabilities→Pay Payroll Liabilities.
	▪ Set the date range for the liabilities to be paid; click OK.
	▪ Set the bank account and the check date.
	▪ Select the payroll liabilities you need to pay; click Create.

DEVELOP YOUR SKILLS 8-7

Fix a Payroll Error

In this exercise, you will replace the paycheck for Vicki King.

1. Click the **Check Register** task icon in the Banking area of the Home page.

2. Click **OK** to choose **1110•Company Checking Account** as the account to use.

3. Scroll up, if necessary, and double-click anywhere within **Vicki King's paycheck, 5389** transaction.

   The Paycheck – Checking window displays.

Check Register

4. Write down the check number (5389) and net amount ($731.09) for future reference.

5. Follow these steps to reprint the check:

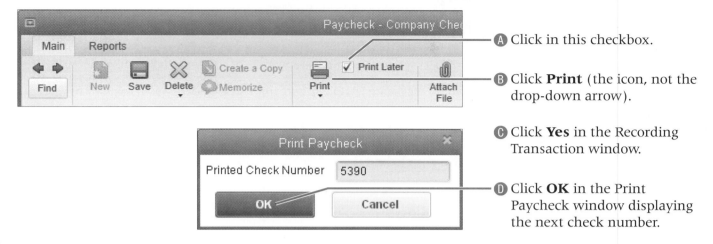

Ⓐ Click in this checkbox.

Ⓑ Click **Print** (the icon, not the drop-down arrow).

Ⓒ Click **Yes** in the Recording Transaction window.

Ⓓ Click **OK** in the Print Paycheck window displaying the next check number.

6. Ensure that the correct printer is selected (or choose to print to PDF), and then click **Print**.

7. Click **OK** in the Print Checks Confirmation window.
   This is the check you will give Vicki.

8. Click **Save & Close** in the Paycheck – Checking window.
   Leave the 1110•Company Checking Account register window open; you will need to use it again.

9. Choose **Banking→Write Checks**.

10. Ensure that the check will not be printed later.

11. Follow these steps to create a check matching the one that was lost:

Ⓐ Enter **5389** as the No.

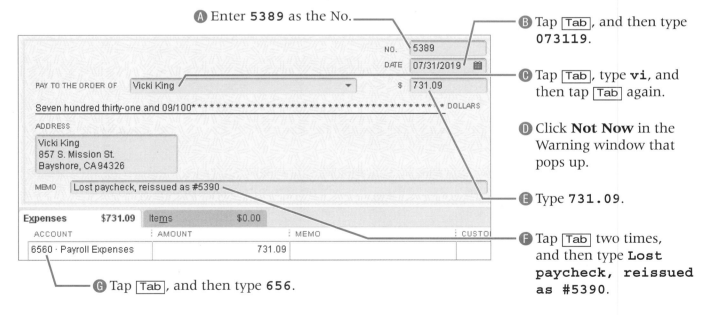

Ⓑ Tap ⸤Tab⸥, and then type **073119**.

Ⓒ Tap ⸤Tab⸥, type **vi**, and then tap ⸤Tab⸥ again.

Ⓓ Click **Not Now** in the Warning window that pops up.

Ⓔ Type **731.09**.

Ⓕ Tap ⸤Tab⸥ two times, and then type **Lost paycheck, reissued as #5390**.

Ⓖ Tap ⸤Tab⸥, and then type **656**.

12. Click **Save & Close**.

    The 1110•Company Checking Account register window should be displayed.

13. Locate the check you just created (**5389**) in the 1110•Company Checking Account window, scrolling if necessary.

14. Right-click anywhere within the two lines of the **check 5389 transaction**, and then choose **Void Check**.

    You will see VOID: preceding the memo you entered into the check, and the dollar amount will be zero.

15. Click **Record**; click **Yes** to record the transaction.

16. Click **No, just void the check**, and then close the Checking register window.

Working with 1099s and Processing Payroll Forms and Reports

The forms you are able to produce through QuickBooks depend on the payroll option you select. Look at a few basic payroll forms used in the United States and how QuickBooks supports each of them. If you live in Canada, check out www.quickbooks.ca to learn about payroll solutions and Intuit products available for the Canadian market.

W-2s and W-3s

W-2s are provided to each employee. They summarize earnings and deductions for the year. A W-3 form is what you prepare and submit to the government. It summarizes the W-2 information you provided to employees.

If you subscribe to one of the Enhanced payroll services, you can print W-2s and W-3s on blank paper right from QuickBooks. If you subscribe to the Full Service, QuickBooks will provide the completed forms to you.

940 and 941

Form 941 is the Employer's Quarterly Federal Tax Return. QuickBooks will fill in the appropriate amounts. You can edit the amounts if the IRS rules instruct you to do so.

Form 940 is the Employer's Annual Federal Unemployment (FUTA) Tax Return. QuickBooks stores forms for only one year at a time. You will need to subscribe to a payroll service to download the correct year's form. QuickBooks will fill in the appropriate amounts, which you can edit if necessary.

1099-MISC and 1096

When you have vendors to whom you subcontract work, you will report their earnings on a 1099-MISC form that is provided to them. The 1096 form is something you prepare for the federal government. It summarizes the 1099 information you provided to subcontractors.

If you subscribe to the Enhanced payroll service, you can print 1099-MISC forms for your subcontractors right from QuickBooks. If you subscribe to the Full Service, Intuit will prepare the 1099-MISC forms for you.

Before you can run 1099-MISC forms, you must turn on the preference in QuickBooks and properly set up your 1099 vendors. A wizard will walk you through 1099 and 1096 form preparation and filing.

When you choose to process payroll forms the File Forms tab of the Employee Center: Payroll Center is displayed.

Tab: Other Topics
Topic: File payroll tax forms

Other Payroll Reports

In addition to the reports you have already seen that deal with payroll, QuickBooks provides a variety of additional reports, including a number of them that can be run in Excel. All of these reports can be found in the Employees & Payroll category in the Report Center.

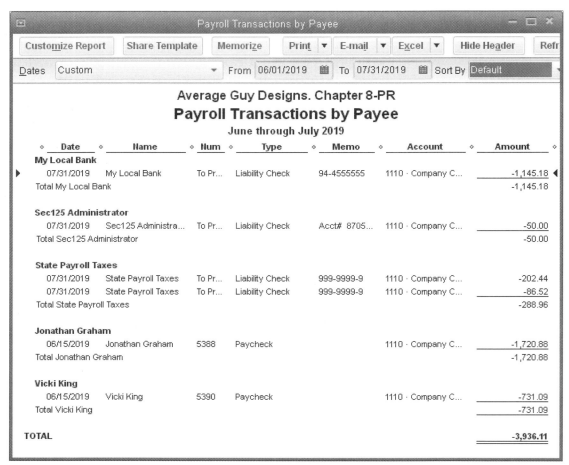

The Payroll Transactions by Payee is just one report that is available when you use QuickBooks for payroll. It shows the amount paid to all employees and vendors for a selected time period.

QUICK REFERENCE	PROCESSING PAYROLL FORMS
Task	**Procedure**
Turn on the 1099 preference	■ Choose Edit→Preferences. ■ Click the Tax: 1099 category, and then the Company Preferences tab. ■ Click to choose Yes, that you file 1099-MISC forms; click OK.
Produce annual W-2 and W-3 reports	■ Choose Employees→Payroll Tax Forms & W-2s→Process Payroll Forms. ■ Click File Form and follow the directions on the screen.
Produce 1099-MISC and 1096 forms	■ Choose Vendors→Print 1099s/1096. ■ Work through the first three steps of 1099 production. ■ Click the Print 1099s button and specify the date range; click OK. ■ Click Print 1099 and ensure your printer settings are correct; click Print. ■ Click the Print 1096 button; enter your contact information. ■ Preview how the form will print; click Print.
Produce Form 940	■ Choose Employees→Payroll Tax Forms & W-2s→Process Payroll Forms. ■ Click File Form and follow the directions on the screen.

QUICK REFERENCE	PROCESSING PAYROLL FORMS (continued)
Task	**Procedure**
Produce Form 941 and Schedule B	■ Choose Employees→Payroll Tax Forms & W-2s→Process Payroll Forms. ■ Click File Form and follow the directions on the screen.
Produce a payroll-related report	■ Choose Reports→Employees & Payroll. ■ Choose the report that will answer the question you have.

DEVELOP YOUR SKILLS 8-8

Produce Payroll Reports

In this exercise, you will produce three payroll reports available when you use QuickBooks for payroll.

1. Choose **Reports→Employees & Payroll→Payroll Transactions by Payee**.

2. Tap Tab , type **060119**, tap Tab again, and then type **073119**.
   A report will be displayed that will show all of the payroll transactions you have completed.

3. Close the **Payroll Transactions by Payee** window, choosing not to memorize it.

Produce an Employee Earnings Summary

4. Choose **Reports→Employees & Payroll→Employee Earning Summary**.

5. Tap Tab , type **010119**, tap Tab again, and then type **073119**.
   A report will be displayed that will show all of the amounts by payroll item for the time period.

6. Close the **Employee Earnings Summary** window, choosing not to memorize it.

Produce an Employee Withholding Report

7. Choose **Reports→Employees & Payroll→Employee Withholding**.
   A report will be displayed that will show all your employees and their tax withholding information.

8. Close the **Employee Withholding** window, choosing not to memorize it.

9. Choose the appropriate option for your situation:
   ■ If you will continue working, leave QuickBooks open.
   ■ If you are finished working in QuickBooks for now, choose **File→Exit**.

Advanced Skills

Tackle the Tasks

Now is your chance to work a little more with Average Guy Designs and apply the skills that you have learned in this chapter to accomplish additional tasks. You will use the same company file you used in the Develop Your Skills exercises throughout this chapter. Enter the following tasks, referring back to the concepts in the chapter as necessary.

Add an employee	Add the following new employee.
	Tammy Reagan; 14896 Highridge Estates, Bayshore, CA 91547; 415-555-4004; SS# 333-22-1111; Female; DOB 6/17/1969; Pay frequency: Semimonthly; Clerical, sick, and vacation rate $20; Holiday pay rate $30; Filing status-Single with one exemption; State—CA; 125-Health insurance $50/paycheck.
Process a paycheck	Create a paycheck for Tammy for the pay period ending 07/31/2019. Date the paycheck 07/31/2019 for 56 hours of clerical work.
Print a paycheck and pay stub	Print the paycheck you just created for Tammy; print a pay stub to go with it.
Pay liabilities	Run a Payroll Liabilities Report for August 2019 to view what is currently being held. Pay the payroll liabilities from Tammy's check on 8/31/2019.
Run a report	Create a report showing all of your employees and their withholding information.

Concepts Review

To check your knowledge of the key concepts introduced in this chapter, complete the Concepts Review quiz on the Student Resource Center or in your eLab course.

Reinforce Your Skills

Angela Stevens has just relocated her company, Quality-Built Construction, from California to Silverton, Oregon. You will be working with a QuickBooks Sample Company File in this exercise as it will allow you to run full payroll in a future chapter without having to purchase a payroll subscription.

Before you begin the Reinforce Your Skills exercises, complete one of these options:

- Open **RYS_Chapter08** from your file storage location.
- Restore **RYS_Chapter08 (Portable)** from your file storage location. Add your last name and first initial to the end of the filename. Place your last name and first initial at the end of the filename.

REINFORCE YOUR SKILLS 8-1

Turn on Payroll and Enter a New Employee

In this exercise, you will help to add a new employee that Angela just hired.

1. Choose **Edit→Preferences**.
2. Click the **Payroll & Employees** category, and then the **Company Preferences** tab.
3. Choose to turn on **Full payroll**.

Enter a New Employee

4. Choose **Employees→Employee Center**.

   The Employee Center will be displayed with seven current employees.

5. Click the **New Employee** button.
6. Use this information to set up Aiyana Harrison as a new employee.

Name	Ms. Aiyana Harrison
Address	503 Oregon Place Silverton, OR 97381
Phone	503-555-2134
SS No.	999-88-6666
Gender	Female
Date of Birth	04/13/86
Hourly/Sick/Vacation Rate	20.00
Holiday Rate	30.00
Filing Status and Allowances	Single, 0
Vacation and Sick Leave	Use defaults

7. Close the **Employee Center** window.

Create Paychecks for Employees

In this exercise, you will create a paycheck for all of the employees for the period of 12/16/18–12/31/18.

Pay Employees

1. Choose **Employees→Payroll Center**.

2. Click the **Pay Employees** button in the top area of the Payroll Center.

   No scheduled payrolls have been set up for this company, so there is no Unscheduled Payroll button. Instead, you see a Pay Employees button.

3. Set the **Check Date** and the **Pay Period Ends** date both to **12/31/2018**.

4. Enter **80** hours in the **Office** column, and then click to the left of **Aiyana Harrison** to place a checkmark to choose to pay her.

Create and Print Paychecks

You will now review the information entered for Aiyana and then create the paycheck.

5. Click **Continue**.

   The Review and Create Paychecks window will be displayed.

6. Click **Create Paychecks**.

   The Confirmation and Next Steps window will appear, showing a summary of how many paychecks were created as well as providing you with a shortcut to printing paychecks and pay stubs.

7. Click **Print Paychecks**, tap ⌷Tab⌷, and then type **497** as the First Check Number.

8. Click **OK** in the Select Paychecks to Print window, and then follow the desired step, depending on whether you wish to physically print the paycheck:

   ■ Click **Print**, and then retrieve the printout from the printer. You can also choose this option if you wish to print the checks as an electronic PDF file. Click **OK** to verify that all checks printed correctly.

   ■ Print choosing ***.pdf** as the printer, and then choose where to save the PDF file. Click **OK** to verify that all checks printed correctly.

9. Click the **Print Pay Stubs** button.

10. Tap ⌷Tab⌷, type **123118**, tap ⌷Tab⌷ again, and then type **123118** (if necessary).

11. Click **Preview** to view how the pay stubs will print, and then close the **Print Preview** window.

12. Close the **Select Pay Stubs** window and the **Confirmation and Next Steps** window.

13. Close the **Payroll Center**.

Pay the Payroll Liabilities

In this exercise, you will pay all of the payroll liabilities due in January 2015.

1. Choose **Employees→Payroll Taxes and Liabilities→Pay Scheduled Liabilities**.

2. Click to the left of all of the liability payments due in **January** to place checkmarks.

3. Click the **View/Pay** button in the Pay Scheduled Liabilities area of the Payroll Center.
   A Liability Payment – Checking window will be displayed for the first payment.

4. Change the date to **1/31/15**, enter **U.S. Treasury** as the vendor, and then click **Save & Next** to view the next payment.

5. Change the date to **1/31/15**, and then click **Save & Close** to record the liability check.

6. Close the **Payment Summary** window, and then close the **Payroll Center**.

7. Choose the appropriate option for your situation:
   - If you will continue working, leave QuickBooks open.
   - If you are finished working in QuickBooks for now, choose **File→Exit**.

Advanced Skills

Apply Your Skills

Before you begin the Apply Your Skills exercises, complete one of these options:

- Open **AYS_Chapter08** from your file storage location.
- Restore **AYS_Chapter08 (Portable)** from your file storage location. Add your last name and first initial to the end of the filename.

APPLY YOUR SKILLS 8-1

Set Up QuickBooks to Track Payroll from an Outside Service

Dr. James has been using an outside payroll service. In this exercise, you will help her to verify that the correct accounts are set up to track expenses and liabilities properly. Then you will enter a new employee. You will need to have accounts set up in your Chart of Accounts to track your payroll expenses and liabilities.

The QuickBooks payroll features should not be turned on when entering payroll from an outside source.

1. Open the **Chart of Accounts**.
2. Verify that **Payroll Liabilities** is set up as an **Other Current Liability**.
3. Scroll down, and then verify that **Payroll Expenses** is set up as an **Expense** account.

   Dr. James has learned that she should set up subaccounts for the Payroll Expenses account, so you will help her to do this now.

4. Set up three subaccounts for Payroll Expenses: `Gross Wages`, `Company-Paid Taxes`, and `Company-Paid Benefits`.

Enter a New Employee

When you are entering a new employee and using an outside payroll service, you do not need to set up tax information.

5. Create a new employee for Wet Noses using this information.

Name	Mr. Viho Locklear
Address	2611 Lake Road Kirkland, WA 98034
Phone	(425) 555-1066
SS No.	000-33-5555
Gender	Male
Date of Birth	04/24/83

6. Close the **Employee Center** window.

Create Paychecks Based on Information from an Outside Payroll Service

Dr. James has received a statement from the payroll service showing the amount to pay each employee (see below) and the amount that has been deducted. In this exercise, you will help her to create the paychecks for the employees.

WET NOSES VETERINARY CLINIC JUNE 2014 PAYROLL

Employee	Gross Wages	Employee Federal Taxes Withheld	Net Pay	Company Federal Taxes Owed	Company Benefits Owed
Bently Batson	$1,500.00	$234.62	$1,265.38	$174.55	$450.00
Carrie Jones	$2,166.00	$395.72	$1,770.28	$243.19	$450.00
Samantha Reese	$2,166.00	$324.21	$1,841.79	$228.61	$450.00
Viho Locklear	$1,000.00	$119.48	$880.52	$87.37	$225.00
Totals	$6,832.00	$1,074.03	$5,757.97	$733.72	$1,575.00

1. Create paychecks for the employees listed above dated 6/30/2014 using the Write Checks window. Look at the example below as a hint regarding how to create the checks.

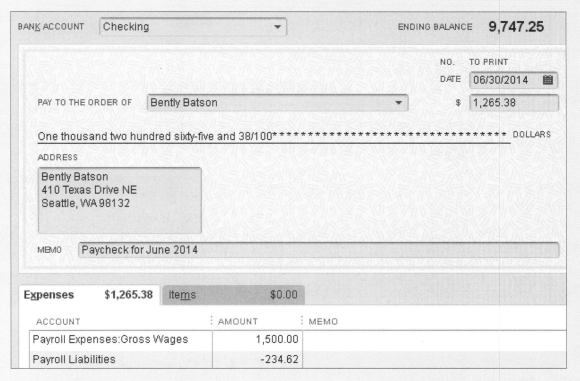

Remember, you only use the Write Checks window to create paychecks if you use an outside payroll service. *Never* use it if you are running payroll through QuickBooks!

Pay the Payroll Liabilities and Print Checks

In this exercise, you will use the information in the table shown above to create a payroll liability check for June 2014.

1. Open the Write Checks window, and then set the date to 6/30/2014.

2. Create a liability check to the U.S. Treasury (Quick Add as a vendor) for all federal taxes owed. Use this illustration as a guide.

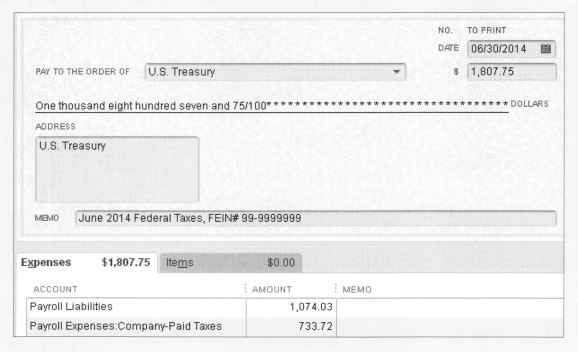

3. Create a second check dated 6/30/2014, made payable to Kellerman Insurance, for the company-paid medical benefits owed.

4. Enter **June 2014 Medical/Dental Insurance for Employees** as the Memo, and Company-Paid Benefits subaccount as the Account.

5. Choose to print all checks in the queue waiting to be printed, using 1441 as the first check number.

APPLY YOUR SKILLS 8-4

Answer Questions and Correct Information with Reports

In this exercise, you will answer questions for Dr. James by running reports. You may wish to display the Report Center in List View to help you answer the questions. Ask your instructor if you should print the reports, print (save) them as PDF files, export them to Excel, or simply display them on the screen.

1. How much has been paid in payroll to each employee? (Hint: Use a Quick Report for the Checking account, and then filter by Name, choosing All Employees.) Leave this report open for the next step.

   As you are creating this report, you realize that you just set up the Payroll Expenses subaccounts and that the 5/31/2014 payroll checks did not use the correct account. You will use QuickZoom to change the account on each of the three checks from 5/31/2014.

2. Double-click on each of the 5/31/2014 checks, using QuickZoom to open the transaction in the Write Checks window, and change the Payroll Expenses account to Payroll Expenses:Gross Wages, as indicated in the following illustration.

Expenses	$1,265.38	Items	$0.00	
ACCOUNT		AMOUNT		MEMO
Payroll Expenses:Gross Wages		1,500.00		
Payroll Liabilities		-234.62		

3. How much was paid in Gross Wages from 5/1/2014–6/30/2014?

4. Would it be possible for you to print a list of all of the employees with their name, phone number, and address? Please make sure there is no information such as social security number or birthday displayed on the list, for privacy reasons.

5. After the report is displayed, you notice that phone numbers were not entered for three employees. Using QuickZoom, add the following phone numbers to the employee records:

   - Bently Batson (206) 555-8789
   - Carrie Jones (425) 555-2052
   - Samantha Reese (425) 555-1742

6. What is the current balance of the Payroll Liabilities account?

7. Submit your reports based on the guidelines provided by your instructor.

8. Choose the appropriate option for your situation:

   - If you will continue working, leave QuickBooks open.
   - If you are finished working in QuickBooks for now, choose **File→Exit**.

Extend Your Skills

In the course of working through the following Extend Your Skills exercises, you will be utilizing various skills taught in this and previous chapter(s). Take your time and think carefully about the tasks presented to you. Turn back to the chapter content if you need assistance.

8-1 Sort Through the Stack

Before You Begin: Restore the EYS1_Chapter08 (Portable) file or open the EYS1_Chapter08 company file from your storage location.

You have been hired by Arlaine Cervantes to help her with her organization's books. She is the founder of Niños del Lago, a nonprofit organization that provides impoverished Guatemalan children with an engaging educational camp experience. You have just sat down at your desk and opened a large envelope from her with a variety of documents and noticed that you have several emails from her as well. It is your job to sort through the papers and emails and make sense of what you find, entering information into QuickBooks whenever appropriate and answering any other questions in a word-processing document saved as **EYS1_Chapter08_ LastnameFirstinitial**. Remember, you are digging through papers you just dumped out of an envelope and addressing random emails from Arlaine, so it is up to you to determine the correct order in which to complete the tasks.

- Sticky note from Arlaine: Hired two part-time employees to work at the U.S. office to raise funds and sell inventory on 8/15/2014. Will use an outside payroll service. How will we enter the payroll information into QuickBooks? (Explain your answer.)

- Completed W-4 and I-9: Chelsea Sathrum; 8213 NW College Ct., Salem, OR, 97304; 503-555-2003; SS# 999-22-3333; Female; DOB 05/21/1988.

- Sticky note from Arlaine: Please prepare a check to pay all federal payroll liabilities that are owed. The amount in Payroll Liabilities that is owed to the U.S. Treasury is $80, but don't forget to pay the company's share!

- Note from accountant: Enter the accounts and subaccounts necessary to track an outside payroll service in QuickBooks.

- Statement from payroll service, dated 8/31/2014.

MONKEY BUSINESS AUGUST 31, 2014 PAYROLL					
Employee	Gross Wages	Employee Federal & State Taxes Withheld	Net Pay	Company Federal Taxes Owed	Company Unemployment Owed
Andy Martinez	$450.00	$78.00	$372.00	$34.42	$16.28
Chelsea Sathrum	$420.00	$48.71	$371.29	$32.13	$15.35

- Completed W-4 and I-9: Andy Martinez; 16932 SE Freedom Way, Salem, OR 97306; SS# 999-22-1111; Male; DOB 07/04/1987.
- Scribbled note from Arlaine: Can you produce a report for me that shows how much has been paid in payroll for each employee?

8-2 Be Your Own Boss

Before You Begin: Complete Extend Your Skills 7-2 before starting this exercise.

In this exercise, throughout the entire book, you will build on the company file you outlined and created in previous chapters. If you have created a file for your actual business, then enter your employees into QuickBooks, enter any historical payroll information since the first of the year, and enter all payroll transactions since your company's start date, including liability payments. If you are creating a fictitious company, then enter at least four employees, enter at least one paycheck for each employee (using an outside payroll service), and then pay the liabilities as well. You will make up the names and information for this exercise.

Create an Employee Contact List report as well as a report showing how much was paid to each employee for the past month, submitting them to your instructor based on the instructions provided.

Open the company file you worked on in Extend Your Skills 7-2 and complete the tasks outlined above. When you are done, save it as a portable company file, naming it as **EYS2_Chapter08_ LastnameFirstinitial (Portable)** and submit it to your instructor based on the instructions provided.

8-3 Use the Web as a Learning Tool

Throughout this book, you will be provided with an opportunity to use the Internet as a learning tool by completing WebQuests. According to the original creators of WebQuests, as described on their website (http://WebQuest.org), a WebQuest is "an inquiry-oriented activity in which most or all of the information used by learners is drawn from the web." To complete the WebQuest projects in this book, navigate to the Student Resource Center and choose the WebQuest for the chapter on which you are working. The subject of each WebQuest will be relevant to the material found in the chapter.

WebQuest Subject: Researching payroll regulations and determining the best payroll option

Working with Estimates and Time Tracking

CHAPTER OBJECTIVES

After studying this chapter, you will be able to:

- Create an estimate for a job or customer and convert it to a progress invoice

- Apply the time tracking feature and create a paycheck based on tracked time

- Work with customer deposits on account

- Assign finance charges to overdue accounts

- Work with reports for estimates and time tracking

QuickBooks allows you to create estimates for your jobs or for your customers if you don't have jobs assigned to them. Once you are awarded a job based on an estimate, QuickBooks makes it easy to convert the estimate to an invoice, saving you the time of reentering the information. Job costing is an important aspect for many businesses. In this chapter you will learn how to use jobs in QuickBooks to track profitability by those jobs. Also covered is the time tracking feature, which allows you to track the time spent by each employee on each job. This feature allows you to track payroll expenses for each job much more accurately.

Average Guy Designs

Guy Marshall will be bidding for a job with the City of Bayshore to do a complete branding process as well as creating the new logo and business documents. Allison has been asked to create an estimate in QuickBooks to be submitted with the proposal.

Once the job is awarded, Allison will need to convert the estimate to an invoice and bill the city for a portion of the amount using QuickBooks' progress invoicing feature. Allison will receive the payment from the city and take some time to learn about how to deal with customer deposits for unearned income.

Time tracking allows a company to track employee time and create paychecks and invoices based on the data collected. You will look at how this QuickBooks feature works and help Allison to create an invoice and a paycheck using the time data.

Finally, Allison will assess finance charges for customers and produce reports that will allow Guy to analyze job costing, estimate, and time tracking data for the company.

Notice that when you create a progress invoice from an estimate, the invoice includes all items on the estimate and shows the progress in regard to how much has been billed.

Creating an Estimate for a Job

When you create an estimate, QuickBooks creates a non-posting account that allows you to track your outstanding estimates. This account is displayed at the bottom of your Chart of Accounts. The non-posting account is created because estimates, like purchase orders, do not affect anything behind the scenes and, therefore, do not affect actual QuickBooks accounts.

You can create estimates for either customers or jobs. You can also create multiple estimates for a customer or a job. If a customer has no jobs created for it, there will be a Job Info tab available in the Edit Customer window with which you can work, but if at least one job has been created for a customer, that tab is no longer available. Before you can create any estimates, you must turn on the estimates feature in your Preferences window.

Job Costing in QuickBooks

In Chapter 3, Working with Customers, you learned that job information is stored with your customer data in the Customers & Jobs List, which is a component of the Customer Center. If you have multiple projects for an individual customer, you can create separate jobs for that customer. If you will perform just one job for a customer, you can track that information in the customer's record on the Job Info tab.

For Rock Castle Construction, all customers have a job associated with them, so you must always choose a job on a form, not just the customer.

> **FLASHBACK TO GAAP: MATCHING**
>
> Remember that expenses need to be matched with revenues. If a contractor buys a specific sink for a specific bathroom, it is matched to the cost of remodeling the bathroom. If there is no connection, then the cost may be charged as an expense to the project. This principle allows a better evaluation of the profitability and performance.

Job Profitability

For companies that deal with jobs, especially businesses such as construction companies, it is important to be able to look at the profitability of each job. To conduct job costing in QuickBooks, you need to take three basic steps:

1. Set up your data in the Customers & Jobs List.
2. Enter all job revenues and expenses.
3. Use QuickBooks reports to analyze job data.

The first two steps are covered as long as you set up your customers and jobs correctly and then enter them properly on sales and purchase forms. We will look at the job costing reports available in QuickBooks later in this chapter.

QUICK REFERENCE	CREATING AN ESTIMATE IN QUICKBOOKS
Task	**Procedure**
Add a job to a customer	■ Open the Customer Center; single-click the desired customer. ■ Click the New Customers & Jobs button; click Add Job. ■ Enter the information for the job; click OK.
Turn on estimating and progress invoicing	■ Choose Edit→Preferences. ■ Click the Jobs & Estimates category, and the Company Preferences tab. ■ Choose Yes to create estimates and do progress invoicing; click OK.
Create an estimate for a job	■ Choose Customers→Create Estimates. ■ Enter all of the information for the estimate; click Save & Close.

Create an Estimate

In this exercise, you will help Allison to create an estimate for a new customer. The first step is to open QuickBooks, and then either open a company file or restore a portable company file.

Intuit provides maintenance releases throughout the lifetime of the product. These updates may require you to update your student exercise files before you begin working with them. Please follow the prompts on the screen if you are asked to update your company file to the latest QuickBooks release.

1. Start **QuickBooks 2014**.

   If you downloaded the student exercise files in the portable company file *format, follow Option 1 below. If you downloaded the files in the* company file *format, follow Option 2 below.*

Option 1: Restore a Portable Company File

2. Choose **File→Open or Restore Company**.

3. Restore the **DYS_Chapter09 (Portable)** portable company file for this chapter from your file storage location, placing your last name and first initial at the end of the filename (e.g., DYS_Chapter09_MarshallG).

   It may take a few moments for the portable company file to open. Once it does, continue with step 5.

Option 2: Open a Company File

2. Choose **File→Open or Restore Company**, ensure that **Open a regular company file** is selected, and then open the **DYS_Chapter09** company file from your file storage location.

   The QuickBooks company file will open.

3. Click **OK** to close the QuickBooks Information window. Click **No** in the Set Up External Accountant User window, if necessary.

4. Close the **Reminders** window.

Verify the Estimates and Progress Invoicing Preferences

Now you need to make sure that the preferences are set up correctly for Average Guy Designs to use estimates and progress invoicing.

5. Choose **Edit→Preferences**.

6. Follow these steps to turn on the estimates and progress invoicing features:

Ⓐ Click the **Jobs & Estimates** category.   Ⓑ Click the **Company Preferences** tab.

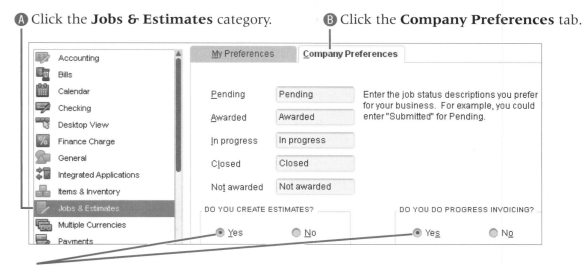

Ⓒ Verify that **Yes** is selected for both estimates and progress invoicing.   Ⓓ Click **OK**.

7. Click **OK** in the **Warning** window.

Create a New Customer

The City of Bayshore is not yet set up as a customer, so you will help Allison to create a new customer and a job for the customer.

8. Choose **Customers→Customer Center**.

9. Tap Ctrl + n to open a New Customer window.

10. Type **City of Bayshore**, and then tap Tab three times.

11. Follow these steps to create the new customer:

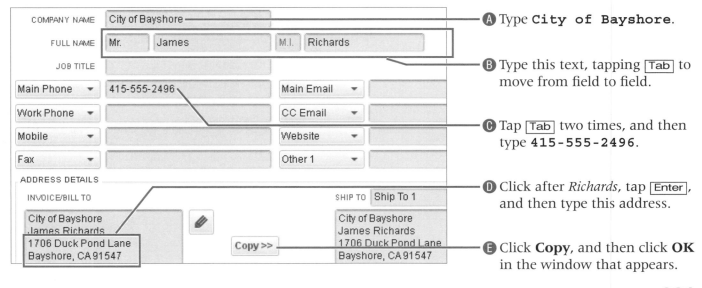

Ⓐ Type **City of Bayshore**.

Ⓑ Type this text, tapping Tab to move from field to field.

Ⓒ Tap Tab two times, and then type **415-555-2496**.

Ⓓ Click after *Richards*, tap Enter, and then type this address.

Ⓔ Click **Copy**, and then click **OK** in the window that appears.

12. Click **OK**.

You will see your new customer displayed on the list; it is selected.

Create a New Job for the Customer

13. Click the **New Customer & Job** button, and then choose **Add Job**.

14. Follow these steps to add information for the new job:

Ⓐ Type **Project #24**.

Ⓑ Click the **Job Info** tab.

Ⓒ Type **City branding project** here.

Ⓓ Choose **Pending** from the drop-down menu.

Ⓔ Click **OK** to save the new job.

Create an Estimate for a Job

The newly created job now appears in the Customers & Jobs List and is selected, ready for you to create a new transaction for it.

15. Click the **New Transactions** button, and then choose **Estimates**.

The Create Estimates window opens with the City branding project job already filled in.

16. Follow these steps to complete the estimate:

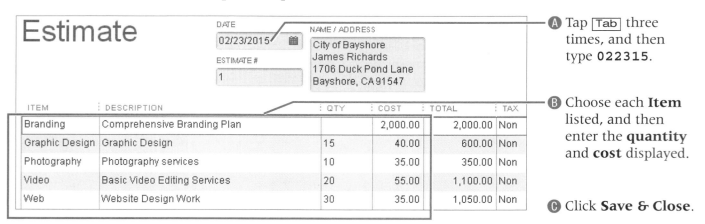

Ⓐ Tap Tab three times, and then type **022315**.

Ⓑ Choose each **Item** listed, and then enter the **quantity** and **cost** displayed.

Ⓒ Click **Save & Close**.

The estimate is created. Now you will wait to hear if you have been awarded the job before doing anything else with it. Remember that nothing happens behind the scenes here!

17. Close the **Customer Center**.

Using an Estimate to Create a Progress Invoice

QuickBooks makes it very easy for you to convert an estimate to an invoice once a job has been awarded. When you choose a customer or job with an existing estimate in the Create Invoices window, you have the opportunity to choose to create the invoice based on the estimate.

Progress Invoicing

QuickBooks allows you to invoice from an estimate in stages rather than for the entire estimate amount. You can either invoice a customer for the entire amount or for a percentage of the entire amount. You can even specify different percentages for each line item or which items to include. You must turn on the progress invoicing feature in the Preferences window before you can use it.

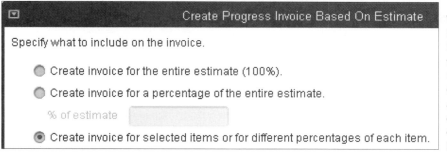

When the progress invoicing feature is turned on, you will see the Create Progress Invoice Based On Estimate window appear after you choose the estimate on which you will base an invoice.

Once you have chosen how much you wish to include on the invoice, you will see an invoice based on the Progress Invoice template. You will see new columns included on this invoice template: Est Amt, Prior Amt, and Total %.

Using Estimates for Change Orders

If you are using the contractor or accountant version of QuickBooks Premier, you can use estimates to track change orders. If you are using a different version, you can make changes to estimates, but they will not be called out as change orders. The change order feature will detail the amount of each change, exactly what changed, and the net change to the amount of the estimate. It will also document the change order for you in the description field of the estimate window.

Working with Sales Reps

For many businesses, being able to track sales by employee or representative is important, and QuickBooks provides a way to track this information by providing a Sales Rep List as one of the Customer & Vendor Profile Lists that you will learn about in Chapter 10, Customizing and Integrating in QuickBooks. Sales Reps may be employees, a partner in the business, or independent contractors to whom you issue 1099s.

You will be creating a progress invoice based on the estimate for 50 percent of the branding work that has been completed. Take a look at the following T-accounts to see what is happening behind the scenes in this transaction.

11000-Accounts Receivable		43200-Design Income	
1,000.00			1,000.00

QUICK REFERENCE	CREATING AN INVOICE FROM AN ESTIMATE
Task	**Procedure**
Use an estimate to create an invoice	■ Open the Create Invoices window; choose the desired customer/job.
	■ Select the desired estimate; choose whether to use progress invoicing.
	■ Enter any additional information, including selecting a price level if appropriate; click Save & Close.
Add a new sales rep	■ Choose Lists→Customer & Vendor Profile Lists→Sales Rep List.
	■ Click the Sales Rep menu button; choose New.
	■ Click the drop-down arrow; choose the name from the Vendors, Employees, or Other Names List.
	■ Enter the initials of the sales rep and the sales rep type; click OK.

DEVELOP YOUR SKILLS 9-2

Create a Progress Invoice Based on an Estimate

Guy has just learned that Average Guys Designs has been awarded the job with the city. In this exercise, you will update the job information and create a progress invoice based on the estimate. The first step is to open the Edit Job window for the City Branding Project and change the status of the job on the Job Info tab.

1. Choose **Customers→Customer Center**.

2. Double-click the **Project #24** job for the **City of Bayshore** to open it for editing.

3. Follow these steps to edit the job:

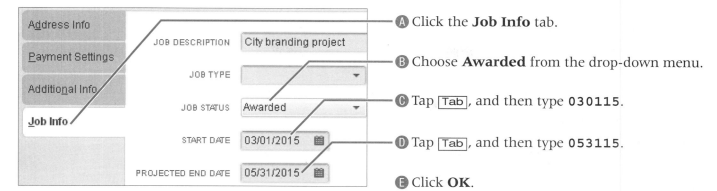

Ⓐ Click the **Job Info** tab.

Ⓑ Choose **Awarded** from the drop-down menu.

Ⓒ Tap `Tab`, and then type **030115**.

Ⓓ Tap `Tab`, and then type **053115**.

Ⓔ Click **OK**.

The Edit Job window closes after recording the changes to the job information.

4. Close the **Customer Center** window.

Create the Invoice

Now you will create a progress invoice based on the estimate. Average Guy Designs has completed 50 percent of the branding work.

5. Choose **Company→Home Page**.

6. Click the **Create Invoices** task icon in the Customers area of the Home page.

Create Invoices

7. Choose the **Project #24** job as the Customer:Job, and then tap `Tab`.

The Available Estimates window appears, displaying all of the available estimates for the job.

8. Single-click to select **Estimate 1** in the Available Estimates window, and then tap `Enter`.

The Create Progress Invoice Based on Estimate window appears.

9. Click to the left of **Create invoice for selected items or for different percentages of each item**, and then click **OK**.

The Specify Invoice Amounts for Items on Estimate window appears.

10. Follow these steps to identify what should be included on the invoice:

Ⓐ Click in the checkbox to select **Show Percentage**.

Ⓑ Enter **50** in the **Curr %** column for **Branding**.

Ⓒ Click **OK**.

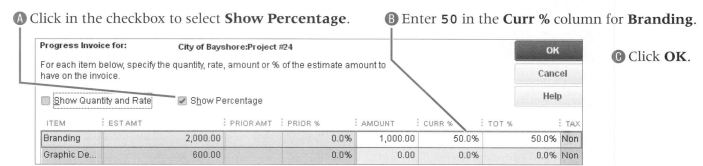

11. Click **OK** in the **Zero Amount Items** window.

The Create Invoices window displays with 50 percent of the Branding charge filled in for you.

12. Follow these steps to complete the invoice:

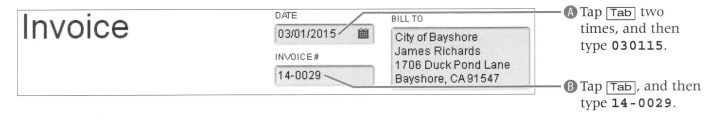

Invoice

DATE
03/01/2015

INVOICE #
14-0029

BILL TO
City of Bayshore
James Richards
1706 Duck Pond Lane
Bayshore, CA 91547

Ⓐ Tap Tab two times, and then type **030115**.

Ⓑ Tap Tab, and then type **14-0029**.

> **BTS BRIEF**
>
> 11000•Accounts Receivable DR 1,000.00; **43200•Design Income CR <1,000.00>**

13. Click **Save & Close**.

The progress invoice is recorded. The next time you choose to create an invoice based off of the estimate for the Project #24 job, the 50 percent that you just invoiced for will show as a prior amount.

Dealing with Customer Deposits

When you collect money from a customer as a deposit or sell a gift certificate, you need to record the receipt as unearned income, since no work has been performed and no product has been sold.

Unearned Income

If you receive funds before they are earned, they are considered unearned income or unearned revenue. You may also hear this called customer deposits or deferred revenue. You shouldn't credit unearned income to an income account. The proper way to deal with it is to hold it in a liability account such as Customer Deposits or Unearned Revenues. Once you have delivered the goods or performed the service, you can then decrease the liability account and credit, or increase, an income account.

Customer Deposits or Gift Certificates, Oh My!

No worries! Both customer deposits and gift certificates are tracked the same way in QuickBooks. And they both require you to go through the three steps of setting up, collecting, and recording. In this chapter, we will deal specifically with customer deposits, but you can apply the same principles if you need to account for gift certificates.

Set Up to Track Customer Deposits

The first step in dealing with unearned income is to set up an Other Current Liability account and two items (an Other Charge and a Payment type) because, by accepting a customer deposit or a payment for a gift certificate, you essentially are accepting the liability to turn the deposit into a payment or to redeem the gift certificate for goods or services. By setting up a liability account, you will be able to show that you are holding the funds in a separate account until the income becomes "earned."

Receiving a Customer Deposit

You will use an invoice to record the receipt of the deposit, but you will use the item that you created to direct the funds to a liability account. In essence, you are "liable" for doing something in return for the funds you are receiving, and you will hold onto the funds in a special account until you have done what is promised. You will not record the income until the service is performed, the product is delivered, or the gift certificate is redeemed.

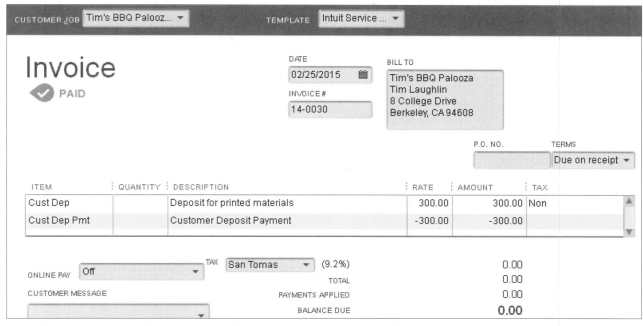

Notice the invoice created when a customer deposit is received. It does not affect an income account or Accounts Receivable (since the balance owing on the invoice is zero).

Presto! Turning a Deposit into a Payment

Once you have delivered on your promise and have traded goods or services for the deposit or gift certificate, you will use an invoice to record the income. The invoice will increase an income account and then reduce the liability account when the income becomes "earned" and you are no longer liable to perform or deliver.

BEHIND THE SCENES

When you receive the customer deposit or issue a gift certificate, you will increase both Undeposited Funds (by debiting it) and Customer Deposits (by crediting it).

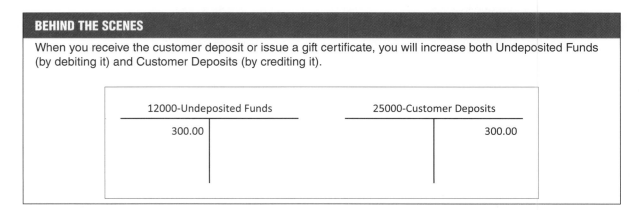

Once the gift certificate is redeemed or the goods/services are delivered, you will remove the funds from the Customer Deposits liability account and realize the earned income. In the exercise you are about to complete, the cost of the service was more than the deposit amount, so the remainder will go into Accounts Receivable.

11000-Accounts Receivable		25000-Customer Deposits	
305.00		300.00	

43200-Design Income		61500-Job Materials	
280.00			325.00

QUICK REFERENCE	WORKING WITH CUSTOMER DEPOSITS
Task	**Procedure**
Set up to track customer deposits	**Create a liability account:**
	▤ Choose Lists→Chart of Accounts.
	▤ Create a new Other Current Liability account named Customer Deposits with the proper account number (if applicable).
	Create two new items:
	▤ Choose Lists→Item List.
	▤ Create a new Other Charge item named Cust Dep.
	▤ Direct the item to Customer Deposits (amount is blank; item is nontaxable).
	▤ Create a new Payment item named Cust Dep Pmt.
Collect a customer deposit	▤ Choose Customers→Create Invoices.
	▤ Enter the Customer:Job, Date, Class, and Terms in the top area of the invoice.
	▤ First line: Enter the Cust Dep Other Charge and deposit amount; fill in the Description field.
	▤ Second line: Enter the Cust Dep Pmt item and the deposit amount.
	▤ Click Save & Close; the net amount of the invoice should be zero.
Turn a customer deposit into a payment	▤ Choose Customers→Create Invoices.
	▤ Enter the Customer:Job, Date, Class, and Terms in the top area of the invoice.
	▤ Enter all of the sales items, line by line, into the invoice.
	▤ Enter the Cust Dep Other Charge item in the next line of the invoice after the sales items. If the deposit is for more than the amount of the invoice, enter only the total invoice amount for the deposit. If the deposit is for less than the amount of the invoice, then enter the full amount of the deposit.
	▤ Click Save & Close.

Account for a Customer Deposit

In this exercise, you will assist Allison in preparing to track customer deposits, receive a deposit from a customer, and turn the deposit into a payment. Before you can even think about dealing with unearned income, you must set up the proper account and items.

1. Click the **Chart of Accounts** task icon in the Company area of the Home page.

2. Click the **Account** menu button, and then choose **New**.

Chart of Accounts

3. Follow these steps to create the new account:

Ⓐ Click in the circle for **Other Account Types**.   Ⓑ Click to choose **Other Current Liability**.

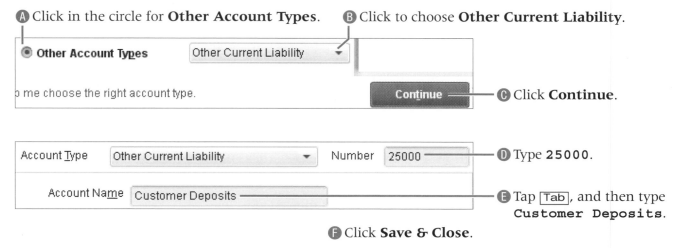

Ⓒ Click **Continue**.

Ⓓ Type **25000**.

Ⓔ Tap ⟨Tab⟩, and then type **Customer Deposits**.

Ⓕ Click **Save & Close**.

4. Close the **Chart of Accounts**.

5. Click the **Items & Services** task icon in the Company area of the Home page.

6. Click the **Item** menu button, and then choose **New**.

Items & Services

7. Follow these steps to create the first item:

Ⓐ Click to choose **Other Charge** as the type of item.

Ⓑ Tap ⟨Tab⟩, and then type **Cust Dep.**

Ⓒ Tap ⟨Tab⟩ three times, and then type **Customer Deposit.**

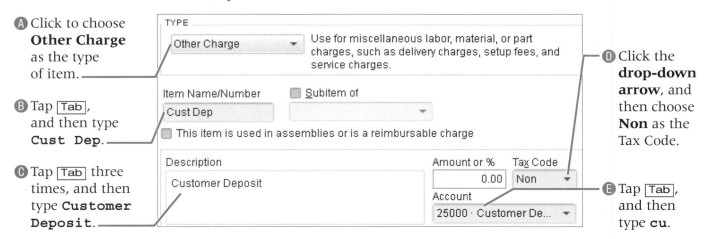

Ⓓ Click the **drop-down arrow**, and then choose **Non** as the Tax Code.

Ⓔ Tap ⟨Tab⟩, and then type **cu.**

The Amount field is left as 0.00; you will fill that in at the time of sale.

8. Click **Next**.

9. Follow these steps to create the second new item:

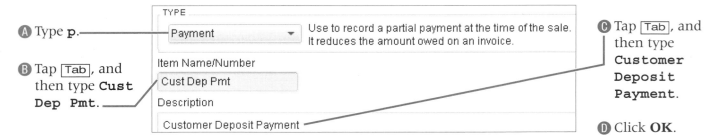

Ⓐ Type **p**.

Ⓑ Tap Tab, and then type **Cust Dep Pmt**.

TYPE

Payment ▾

Use to record a partial payment at the time of the sale. It reduces the amount owed on an invoice.

Item Name/Number

Cust Dep Pmt

Description

Customer Deposit Payment

Ⓒ Tap Tab, and then type **Customer Deposit Payment**.

Ⓓ Click **OK**.

10. Close the **Item List** window.

Collect a Customer Deposit

Tim Laughlin just called and asked Average Guy Designs to do a graphic design job that includes a large amount of printing. Guy asked for a deposit to be made before the work begins. You will help Allison to record this deposit. You will need to create a new job for this customer first.

11. Choose **Customers→Customer Center**.

12. Right-click on **Tim's BBQ Palooza**, and then choose **Add Job**.

13. Type **Project #25** as the **Job Name**, and then click OK to save the new job.

The Customer Center will still be open with the new job selected.

New Transactions ▾   🖨 Prin

 Estimates
 Sales Orders
 (Invoices)   Ctrl+I

14. Click the **New Transactions** button, and then choose **Invoices**.

15. Follow these steps to complete the invoice:

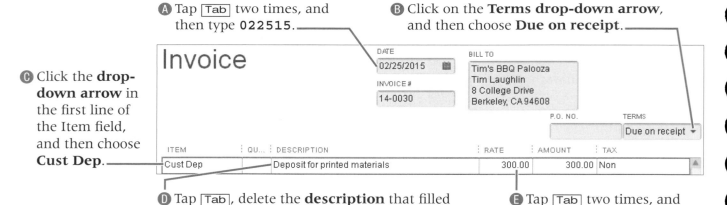

Ⓐ Tap Tab two times, and then type **022515**.

Ⓑ Click on the **Terms drop-down arrow**, and then choose **Due on receipt**.

Ⓒ Click the **drop-down arrow** in the first line of the Item field, and then choose **Cust Dep**.

Invoice

DATE
02/25/2015 📅

INVOICE #
14-0030

BILL TO
Tim's BBQ Palooza
Tim Laughlin
8 College Drive
Berkeley, CA 94608

P.O. NO. TERMS
   Due on receipt ▾

ITEM	QU...	DESCRIPTION	RATE	AMOUNT	TAX
Cust Dep		Deposit for printed materials	300.00	300.00	Non

Ⓓ Tap Tab, delete the **description** that filled in, and then **type** the description displayed.

Ⓔ Tap Tab two times, and then type **300**.

ITEM	QU...	DESCRIPTION	RATE	AMOUNT	TAX
Cust Dep		Deposit for printed materials	300.00	300.00	Non
Cust Dep Pmt		Customer Deposit Payment	-300.00	-300.00	

Ⓕ Click the **drop-down arrow** in the second line of the Item field, and then choose **Cust Dep Pmt**.

Ⓖ Tap Tab two times, and then type **-300**.

Ⓗ Click **Save & Close**.

The total due for the invoice should be 0.00 because the net effect to Accounts Receivable is 0.00. In other words, the customer doesn't owe anything as a result of the transaction. What you have accomplished behind the scenes, though, is that you collected $300 that debited Undeposited Funds and credited Customer Deposits.

> **BTS BRIEF**
>
> 12000•Undeposited Funds DR 300.00; 25000•Customer Deposits CR <300.00>

16. Click **No** in the Name Information Changed window.

    You changed the terms to Due upon receipt for this one transaction, but you want the default terms you have set for the customer to remain the same.

Pay for an Expense to Pass on to a Customer

Next you will pay for the printing that you will be passing on to the customer.

17. Choose **Banking→Enter Credit Card Charges**; ensure **Sunriver Credit Union Visa** is selected.

18. Follow these steps to enter the charge you will pass on to your customer:

    Ⓐ Tap ⌈Tab⌉ three times, type **Bayshore Printing and Graphics**, tap ⌈Tab⌉, and then **Quick Add** it as a vendor.

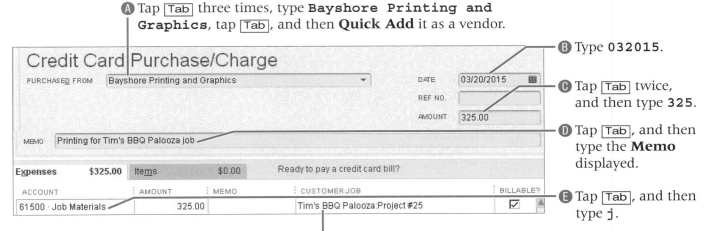

Ⓑ Type **032015**.

Ⓒ Tap ⌈Tab⌉ twice, and then type **325**.

Ⓓ Tap ⌈Tab⌉, and then type the **Memo** displayed.

Ⓔ Tap ⌈Tab⌉, and then type **j**.

Ⓕ Click and choose **Tim's BBQ Palooza:Project #25** here.

19. Click **Save & Close**.

Turn a Deposit into a Payment

The final step when working with customer deposits is to do a little magic and turn the deposit into a payment!

20. Choose **Customers→Create Invoices**.

21. Choose **Tim's BBQ Palooza:Project #25** as the **Customer:Job**.

22. Ensure the option to select outstanding billable time and costs is selected, and then click **OK**.

23. Follow these steps to select the billable cost:

Ⓐ Click the **Expenses** tab.

Ⓑ Click to the left of the **03/20/2015** expense.

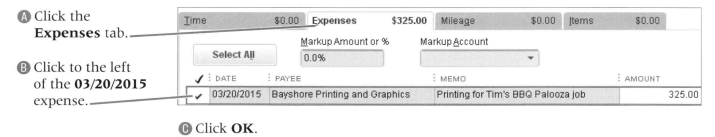

| Time | $0.00 | Expenses | $325.00 | Mileage | $0.00 | Items | $0.00 |

Markup Amount or %   Markup Account

Select All   0.0%

✓	DATE	PAYEE	MEMO	AMOUNT
✓	03/20/2015	Bayshore Printing and Graphics	Printing for Tim's BBQ Palooza job	325.00

Ⓒ Click **OK**.

24. Follow these steps to complete the invoice:

Ⓐ Tap [Tab] three times, and then type **032015**.

Ⓑ Click the **drop-down arrow** in the second line of the Item field, and then choose **Graphic Design**.

Ⓒ Tap [Tab], and then type **7**.

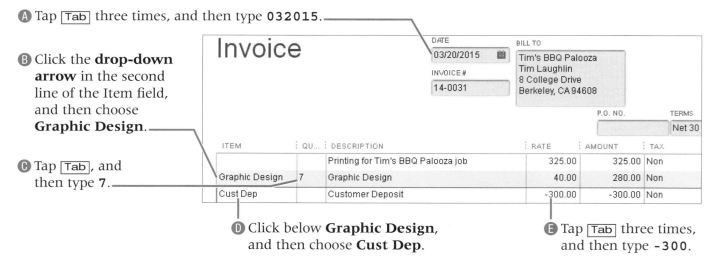

Invoice

DATE
03/20/2015

INVOICE #
14-0031

BILL TO
Tim's BBQ Palooza
Tim Laughlin
8 College Drive
Berkeley, CA 94608

P.O. NO.   TERMS
                Net 30

ITEM	QU...	DESCRIPTION	RATE	AMOUNT	TAX
		Printing for Tim's BBQ Palooza job	325.00	325.00	Non
Graphic Design	7	Graphic Design	40.00	280.00	Non
Cust Dep		Customer Deposit	-300.00	-300.00	Non

Ⓓ Click below **Graphic Design**, and then choose **Cust Dep**.

Ⓔ Tap [Tab] three times, and then type **-300**.

Note that it is up to you to type in the amount of the deposit that will apply to the invoice. In this case, the invoice was for more than the deposit, so the customer owes $305 (see the following illustration), and Accounts Receivable will be debited for this net amount owing on the invoice. If the deposit was for more than the total invoice amount, you would only enter that amount for the Customer Deposit on the invoice; the rest would remain in the liability account.

	RATE	AMOUNT	TAX
	325.00	325.00	Non
	40.00	280.00	Non
	-300.00	-300.00	Non

TAX	San Tomas (9.2%)	0.00
	TOTAL	305.00
	PAYMENTS APPLIED	0.00
	BALANCE DUE	**305.00**

BTS BRIEF

25000•Customer Deposits DR 300.00; 11000•Accounts Receivable DR 305.00; **43200•Design Income CR <280.00>; 61500•Job Materials CR <325.00>**

25. Click **Save & Close**, choose to **Add** both **BBQ** and **Palooza** to the dictionary.

The invoice is recorded. There are no longer funds on deposit in the liability account for this customer.

Assessing Finance Charges and Producing Statements

If you are invoicing customers, you will inevitably find that not all of your customers pay their invoices on time. You may wish to assess finance charges for these late-paying customers.

Lending laws vary by jurisdiction, so you will need to research those applicable to you regarding whether you can assess finance charges on overdue balances. After you've performed this research, you are ready to set your preferences in QuickBooks.

Finance charge laws are different in different locations! Do *not* use the specifics provided in this book; rather, find out the laws that apply to you and apply them to the principles you have been taught.

QuickBooks allows you to set several finance charge preferences in the Finance Charge category on the Company Preferences tab. The following illustration shows an example of the types of preferences you can control.

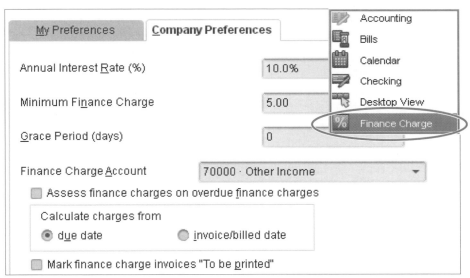

Note the preferences that you are responsible for setting in regard to finance charges. The finance charge account is an Other Income account as the income received is not the result of your normal business practices (unless you are a bank!). Before you set whether you will assess finance charges on overdue finance charges or when to calculate charges from, understand the laws where you do business.

The Assess Finance Charges Window

The Assess Finance Charges window does more than provide you with a means to determine which customers are overdue and should be charged a finance charge. It also calculates the charge due (based on the preferences set) and gives you a quick way to view the preferences and customize the finance charge invoice template.

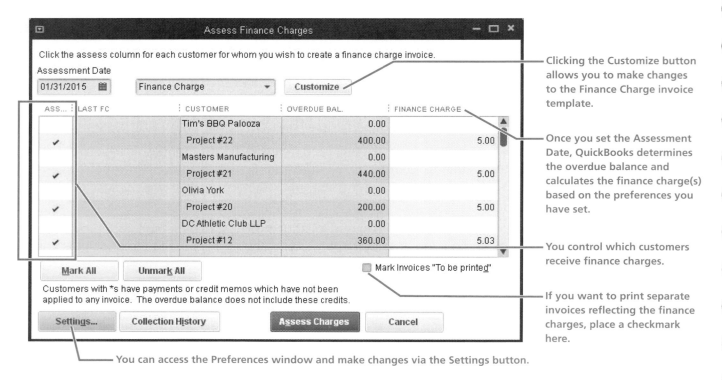

Clicking the Customize button allows you to make changes to the Finance Charge invoice template.

Once you set the Assessment Date, QuickBooks determines the overdue balance and calculates the finance charge(s) based on the preferences you have set.

You control which customers receive finance charges.

If you want to print separate invoices reflecting the finance charges, place a checkmark here.

You can access the Preferences window and make changes via the Settings button.

Once you view the Assess Finance Charges window, you may also see customers that need friendly collections calls or may need to have their balances written off as bad debt. You learned how to deal with collections and bad debt Chapter 7, Working with Balance Sheet Accounts and Budgets.

Entering Statement Charges

If you wish to enter a charge for a customer without producing an invoice, you can use the Accounts Receivable register window. It is important that you choose the correct customer to whom you wish to apply the charge. Any transactions entered in a customer's Accounts Receivable register will show up on statements that you print for them.

Creating Statements for Customers

There are many instances when you may wish to send your customer a statement rather than an invoice. For instance, you may have one customer or job for which you do multiple projects within a billing period and you wish to bill them with an itemized statement. Another example, shown in this chapter, is to create a statement to bill a customer for a finance charge. Statements can be produced for an individual customer or in a batch for multiple customers.

Using a Batch of Statements to Bill for Finance Charges

You can send an invoice reflecting assessed finance charges to your customers. To do this, you need to ensure that there is a checkmark in the "To be printed" checkbox in the Preferences window.

The more common way to alert customers to finance charges that they owe is to produce a statement that reflects the finance charge, outstanding invoices, and aging information. You can produce a statement for just one customer, if you wish, but in the following exercise, you will produce a batch of statements for multiple customers.

When you assess finance charges, you need to debit Accounts Receivable and the appropriate accounts receivable customer subregister (you can see the example for Masters Manufacturing below), as well as indicate the account credited by the charge (in this case, 70000•Other Income).

11000-Accounts Receivable		70000-Other Income	
5.00		5.00	

Masters Manufacturing	
5.00	

Task	Procedure
Set a company's finance charge preferences	▪ Choose Edit→Preferences. ▪ Click the Finance Charge category, and then the Company Preferences tab. ▪ Enter the appropriate finance charge preferences; click OK.
Assess finance charges	▪ Choose Customers→Assess Finance Charges. ▪ Set the date from which to assess the charges; choose which customers should be assessed charges. ▪ Verify and modify, if necessary, the information; click Assess Charges.
Enter statement charges	▪ Choose Customers→Enter Statement Charges. ▪ Choose the customer whose Accounts Receivable register you wish to view. ▪ Enter the information for the statement charge; record the transaction.
Create a statement to send to a customer	▪ Choose Customers→Create Statements. ▪ Choose the date range for which you wish to create statements. ▪ Choose the customer(s) for whom you wish to create statements. ▪ Choose any additional options, as desired. ▪ (Optional) Click Preview to view the statement(s). ▪ Click Print or Email to deliver the statement(s) to the customer(s).
Produce a batch of statements	▪ Choose Customers→Create Statements. ▪ Choose the appropriate date range and customers, as well as any additional options. ▪ Click Print or Email to deliver the statements.

Advanced Skills

Assess Finance Charges and Prepare Statements

In this exercise, you will help Allison to assess finance charges for any customers who have overdue balances and then send statements to affected customers.

1. Choose **Edit→Preferences**.

2. Follow these steps to set the finance charge preferences:

Ⓐ Click the **Finance Charge** category on the left.

Ⓑ Click the **Company Preferences** tab.

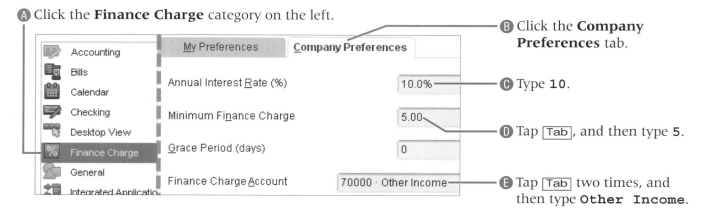

Ⓒ Type **10**.

Ⓓ Tap [Tab], and then type **5**.

Ⓔ Tap [Tab] two times, and then type **Other Income**.

A Set Up window will display since Other Income is not yet set up as an account.

Ⓕ Click **Set Up**.

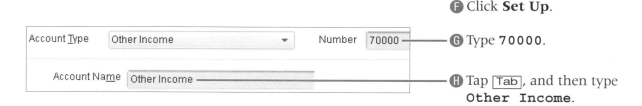

Ⓖ Type **70000**.

Ⓗ Tap [Tab], and then type **Other Income**.

3. Click **OK** to set the preferences.

Assess Finance Charges

Now that you have set the finance charge preferences, you will choose to assess finance charges on all overdue invoices.

4. Click the **Finance Charges** task icon in the Customers area of the Home page.
   The Assess Finance Charges window will be displayed.

5. Type **013115** as the Assessment Date, and then tap [Tab].
   All customers with open invoices that are past due as of January 31 display, along with the calculated finance charge.

6. Click **Assess Charges,** and then click **Yes** in the Assess Finance Charges window.
   The finance charges are now reflected in Accounts Receivable for each customer assessed.

> **BTS BRIEF**
>
> 11000•Accounts Receivable DR 55.03 (each customer's sub-register is also debited for the finance charge amount); **70000•Other Income CR <55.03>**

Enter a Statement Charge for the Customer's Fee

Due to the increased business with Tim's BBQ Palooza, you have decided to delete the finance charge assessed for it. You will do this through the customer's register.

7. Click the **Statement Charges** task icon in the Customers area of the Home page.

Statement Charges

   When you choose to enter a statement charge, you will view the Accounts Receivable register for a customer. It is important that you choose the correct customer, as is shown in the following step.

8. Click the drop-down arrow for the **Customer:Job** field and choose **Tim's BBQ Palooza:Project #22**.

   You will now be able to view the register for Project #22.

9. Right-click anywhere within the two lines of the finance charge transaction, and then choose **Delete Invoice**.

10. Click **OK** in the **Delete Transaction** window.

BTS BRIEF

70000•Other Income DR 5.00; 11000•Accounts Receivable CR <5.00>

11. Close the **Tim's BBQ Palooza:Project #22 – Accounts Receivable** window.

   Know that you can use the same procedure described in the past few steps to add a charge to a customer as well.

Produce a Batch of Statements

You will now help Allison to create statements for all customers with a balance.

Statements

12. Click the **Statements** task icon in the Customers area of the Home page.

13. Follow these steps to produce a batch of statements for all customers with a balance (including all customers for whom a finance charge was assessed):

Ⓐ Type **020115**.

Ⓑ Click to choose the **All open transactions** option.

Ⓒ Click to choose the **All Customers** option.

Ⓓ Click to choose the **with a zero balance** option.

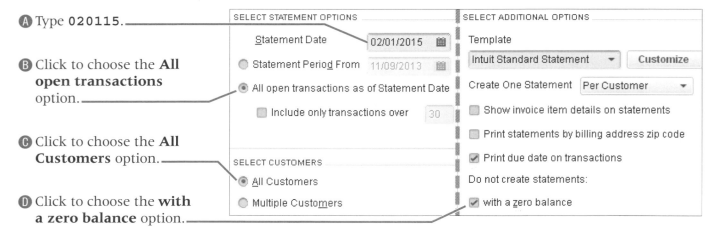

14. Click the **Preview** button at the bottom-left of the Create Statements window.

You can now see what each statement will look like printed.

15. Click the **Close** button at the top of the Print Preview window.

At this point, you would choose to print or email the statements by clicking the appropriate button at the bottom of the window.

16. Close the **Create Statements** window, unless your instructor wishes for you to print the statements for review.

Using QuickBooks' Time Tracking and Mileage Features

The Time Tracking feature allows you to create weekly timesheets so you can break down the hours by customer/job or to record single activities for a customer/job. In addition to these payroll benefits, time tracking also allows you to:

■ Invoice customers for number of hours worked

■ Automatically fill in the hours worked on paychecks

■ Track time for subcontractors by automatically filling in time data on bills and checks

■ Track payroll costs by job, class, or type of work performed

■ Track billable versus non-billable time

Once you have used time data, you can run reports such as the Time by Job Summary to view how many man-hours you are putting into each job. Time tracking also allows you to allocate the appropriate payroll costs to a job, making your job costing reports more accurate and meaningful.

Methods of Entering Time

When you enter a single activity, it is recorded on that employee's weekly timesheet. A single activity can be entered by typing in the amount of time or by using the timer feature to actually track the exact amount of time on a task. If you choose to use the timer feature, you can use it only for timed activities on the current day.

There are two methods by which you can enter time data in QuickBooks:

- **As a single activity when it occurs:** You can either type the amount of time in the single activity window or use the built-in timer to record the exact amount of time.

Notice the Timesheet button. It allows you to toggle to the Weekly Timesheet window.

The check in the Billable checkbox shows that you intend to use this time data in the future to bill a customer.

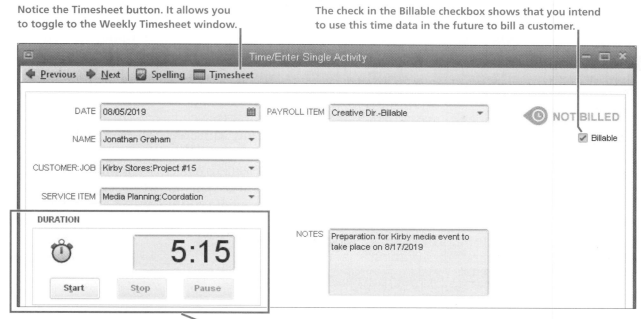

You can either type in the duration of a task or click Start to record the actual time.

- **On a weekly timesheet:** The weekly timesheet allows you to enter time data for multiple customer/jobs, service items, and payroll items for a single employee. You can use this information to create paychecks when you process payroll.

The Weekly Timesheet window allows you to enter time for each employee by job worked. Note the column to the far right, which is the "billable" column. If a checkmark is in this field, you can bill the customer for the time. If an invoice icon appears, it means the time has already been invoiced.

Fields Available in Both Time Data Entry Windows

Regardless of whether you choose to enter time as single activities or on a weekly timesheet, notice that each window provides the following fields:

- **Customer:Job:** Information entered in this field allows you to bill a customer for the time and to keep track of information required for accurate job costing.
- **Service Item:** Information entered in this field allows you to track services performed.
- **Payroll Item:** Information entered in this field allows you to create paychecks from your time data.
- **Billable:** If you choose this field, the information is made available for you to bill the customer for the time.
- **Notes:** Information entered in this field is displayed in the description field on reports and invoices.

Batch Timesheets

Some businesses may find that they have employees or vendors who work the same hours for a job, for instance, if you are a construction company with crews who work together on the same jobs each day. These businesses can create one timesheet for multiple payroll names (employees for whom you have chosen to use time data to create paychecks) or multiple non-payroll names (can be vendors and/or employees). Something to keep in mind if you choose to work with batch timesheets, though, is that all workers for whom you are creating a timesheet must have the following criteria in common: job, number of hours worked per day, payroll item(s), and service item(s).

Notice that when you go to choose a name for a weekly timesheet, you have the option to choose multiple payroll or multiple non-payroll names in order to create a batch timesheet.

Tracking Mileage

The mileage tracking feature in QuickBooks allows you to track mileage for your business vehicle—but not for the purpose of reimbursing your employees. If you do track mileage, you can use the data to bill customers for the expense or for tax reporting purposes. It will be up to you to keep on top of the IRS mileage reimbursement rates, and QuickBooks will calculate the mileage expense based on the approved rate on the specific day. To track mileage for a particular vehicle, you need to enter the vehicle into the Vehicle List first.

To view your mileage information once you have start tracking it, QuickBooks provides mileage reports from which you can choose to display your data. You can also choose to pass on the mileage expense to your customers and create reports to view the amount that has been billed.

QUICK REFERENCE	USING QUICKBOOKS TIME AND MILEAGE TRACKING FEATURES
Task	**Procedure**
Create a single time activity	■ Choose Employees→Enter Time→Time/Edit Single Activity. ■ Choose the desired Name; enter the Date, Customer:Job, Service Item, and Payroll Item information. ■ Enter the time spent, and any appropriate note; click Save & Close.
Enter hours on a weekly timesheet	■ Choose Employees→Enter Time→Use Weekly Timesheet. ■ Choose the desired Name. ■ Click the Set Date button, and then type the appropriate week; enter the Customer: Job, Service Item, and Payroll Item for each line. ■ Enter the time worked for each day; click Save & Close.
Create a batch timesheet for multiple people	■ Choose Employees→Enter Time→Use Weekly Timesheet. ■ Choose to select from either Payroll or Non-Payroll multiple names. ■ Choose the desired Names. ■ Click the Set Date button, and then type the appropriate week; enter the Customer: Job, Service Item, and Payroll Item (if appropriate) for each line. ■ Enter the time worked for each day; click Save & Close.
Enter vehicle mileage	**Enter the current mileage rate:** ■ Choose Company→Enter Vehicle Mileage. ■ Click the Mileage Rates button. ■ Type in the Effective Date and the Rate; click Close. **Add a vehicle to the list:** ■ Choose Lists→Customer & Vendor Profile Lists→Vehicle List. ■ Click the Vehicle menu button; choose New. ■ Enter the vehicle's name and description; click OK. **Add an item, if you wish to pass mileage expenses on to customers:** ■ Choose Lists→Item List. ■ Create a new service or other charge item called Mileage or Delivery Charges, leaving the rate field as zero. ■ Choose the appropriate expense account; click Save & Close. **Enter mileage:** ■ Choose Company→Enter Vehicle Mileage. ■ Choose the Vehicle; enter the start and end dates for the trip. ■ Type in the odometer readings from the start and end of the trip. ■ If passing this expense on to a customer or job, mark the Billable checkbox, choose the appropriate Customer:Job, and choose Mileage or Delivery Charges as the Item. ■ Enter any appropriate notes, if desired; click Save & Close.

Advanced Skills

Track Time for a Job

In this exercise, you will track time to be used to create paychecks for a company. The first step is to open a QuickBooks sample file that includes a payroll service. You can either open a company file or restore a portable company file.

Option 1: Restore a Portable Company File

1. Choose **File→Open or Restore Company**.

2. Restore the **DYS_Chapter09-PR (Portable)** portable company file for this chapter from your file storage location, placing your last name and first initial at the end of the filename (e.g., DYS_Chapter09-PR_MarshallG).

   It may take a few moments for the portable company file to open. Once it does, continue with step 5.

Option 2: Open a Company File

2. Choose **File→Open or Restore Company**, ensure that **Open a regular company file** is selected, and then open the **DYS_Chapter09-PR** company file from your file storage location.

   The QuickBooks company file will open.

3. Click **OK** twice to close both of the QuickBooks Information windows. Click **No** in the Set Up External Accountant User window, if necessary.

4. Close the **Reminders** window.

Enter Time for a Job

In this exercise, you will help Allison to record the time spent on the branding job for the City of Bayshore and track the mileage for the job.

5. Click the **Enter Time** task icon in the Employees area of the Home page, and then choose **Time/Enter Single Activity**.

6. Follow these steps to enter Jonathan's billable time:

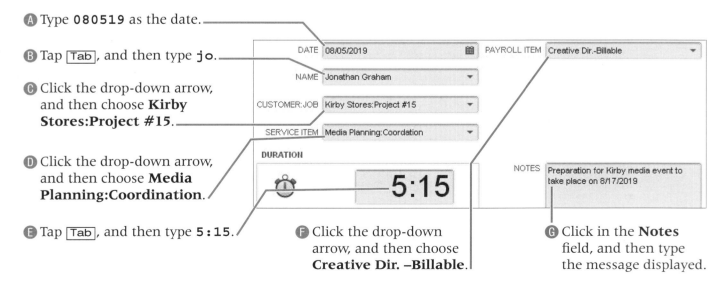

Ⓐ Type **080519** as the date.

Ⓑ Tap Tab, and then type **jo**.

Ⓒ Click the drop-down arrow, and then choose **Kirby Stores:Project #15**.

Ⓓ Click the drop-down arrow, and then choose **Media Planning:Coordination**.

Ⓔ Tap Tab, and then type **5:15**.

Ⓕ Click the drop-down arrow, and then choose **Creative Dir. –Billable**.

Ⓖ Click in the **Notes** field, and then type the message displayed.

7. Click **Save & Close**.

Enter Time Using a Weekly Timesheet

You will now enter the rest of Jonathan's time for the week.

8. Click the **Enter Time** task icon in the Employees area of the Home page, and then choose **Use Weekly Timesheet**.

9. Type **jo**, and then tap `Tab` to fill in Jonathan Graham as the Name.

10. Follow these steps to set the time frame for the timesheet:

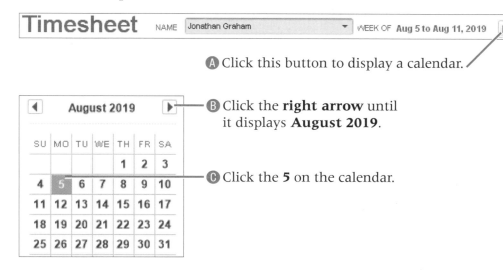

> **Timesheet** NAME Jonathan Graham ▼ WEEK OF **Aug 5 to Aug 11, 2019** 📅

Ⓐ Click this button to display a calendar.

Ⓑ Click the **right arrow** until it displays **August 2019**.

Ⓒ Click the **5** on the calendar.

QuickBooks sets the week of Aug 5 to Aug 11, 2019 as the date range for the timesheet. Notice that the time data you just entered as a single activity appears on the weekly timesheet for the week of 8/5/2019.

11. Follow these steps to enter the rest of Jonathan's time data for the week:

Ⓐ Click on the drop-down arrow in each row in this field, and then choose the correct **Customer:Job**.

CUSTOMER:JOB	SERVICE ITEM	PAYROLL ITEM	NOTES	M 5	TU 6	W 7	TH 8	F 9	SA 10	SU 11	TOTAL	BILLABL
Kirby Stores:Project #15	Media Planning:Coordation	Creative Dir.-Billable	Preparat...	5:15	3:00						8:15	☑
Peacock Research:Project #1	Film Production:Editing	Creative Dir.-Billable		3:00	6:00	8:00					17:00	☑
Kirby Stores:Project #15	Event Planning:Meetings	Creative Dir.-Billable					1:30	1:00			2:30	☑
Kirby Stores:Project #15	Event Planning:Research	Creative Dir.-Billable					4:00				4:00	☑
Kirby Stores:Project #15	Event Planning:Lay Out	Creative Dir.-Billable						7:00			7:00	☑
			Totals	8:15	9:00	8:00	5:30	8:00	0:00	0:00	38:45	

Ⓑ Click on the drop-down arrow in each row in this field, and then choose the correct **Service Item**.

Ⓒ Verify that **Creative Dir-Billable** fills in for each line.

Ⓓ Type the number of hours in each field, as displayed.

12. Click **Save & Close**.

Using Time Tracking Hours to Create a Paycheck

You can use time data for employees to create their paychecks, if you have entered it as we did in the previous exercise.

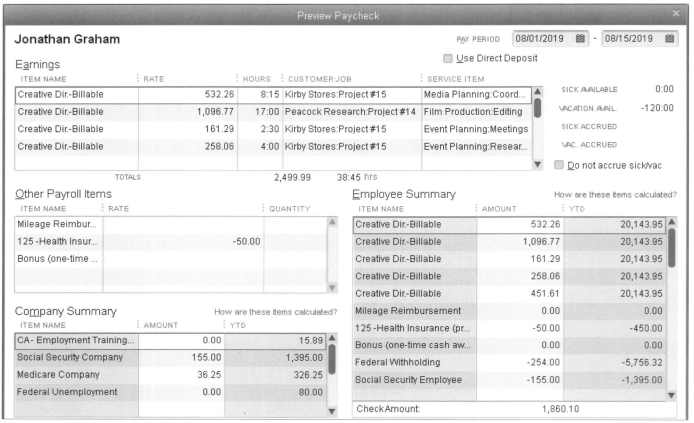

Notice how the time data easily transfers right over to Jonathan's paycheck.

Allocating Salaried Pay to an Individual Customer or Job

To accurately determine the cost of a job, you need to account for the time spent by salaried employees, too. You can record their time using the time tracking features and choosing to "use time data to create paychecks" in the Preview Paycheck window.

Invoicing a Customer for Time Spent on a Job

You can use the time tracking feature to pass on billable time to customers. In addition, you can use the same procedure to include the billable mileage. Regardless of what type of cost you are passing on to the customer, the process is virtually the same—and you can even choose to specify a markup amount for the hours.

QUICK REFERENCE	USING TIME DATA TO CREATE A PAYCHECK
Task	**Procedure**
Use time tracking to create a paycheck	■ Choose Employees→Pay Employees. ■ Enter the check date, pay period end date, and the payee; click Create. ■ Enter any Class information or modifications, if appropriate; click Create.
Create an invoice for a customer using time and mileage information	■ Choose Customers→Create Invoices. ■ Choose the Customer:Job you wish to bill; indicate that you wish to include the outstanding billable time and costs to the invoice. ■ Click the Time tab and select any time data; click the Mileage tab and select any mileage data.

DEVELOP YOUR SKILLS 9-6
Create a Paycheck and Invoice from Time Data

In this exercise, you will create a paycheck for Jonathan based on the time data that was entered, and then invoice one of the customers.

1. Click the **Pay Employees** task icon in the Employees area of the Home page.

2. Click the **Pay Employees** button in the **Employee Center: Payroll Center** window.

The Enter Payroll Information window displays. Look at the Creative Dir-Billable column for Jonathan Graham (you may have to re-size the columns to read the headers) and notice that the amount is in blue, which indicates it is for the amount of billable time that you have entered.

3. Follow these steps to choose to pay Jonathan:

Ⓐ Type **081519**.

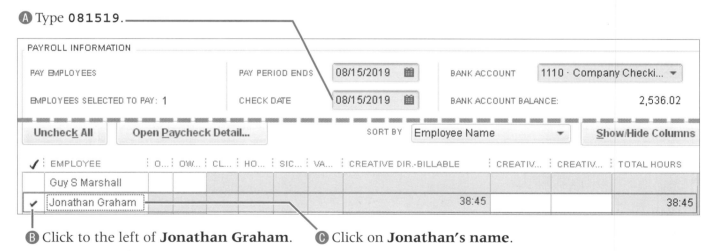

Ⓑ Click to the left of **Jonathan Graham**.   Ⓒ Click on **Jonathan's name**.

The Preview Paycheck window appears. Take a look at how the time data is used to create the paycheck.

4. Click **Save & Close**, and then click **Continue**.

5. Click **Create Paychecks**, and then close the **Confirmation and Next Steps** window as well as the **Payroll Center**.

   The following BTS Brief section shows the "parent accounts," not the various subaccounts.

> **BTS BRIEF**
>
> 6500•Wages DR 2,499.99; **2100•Payroll Liabilities CR <639.89>**; 1110•Company Checking CR <1,860.10>

Create an Invoice from Time Data

You will now create an invoice for Kirby Stores that includes the time costs for the work Jonathan completed.

6. Click the **Create Invoices** task icon in the Customers area of the Home page.

Create Invoices

7. Click the **Customer:Job** field drop-down arrow and choose the **Project #15** job for **Kirby Stores**.

   The Billable Time/Costs window appears.

8. Click **OK** in the Billable Time/Costs window to choose the default of selecting outstanding billable time and costs to add to the invoice.

   The Time tab of the Choose Billable Time and Costs window displays.

9. Click the **Select All** button, and then click **OK**.

   The Create Invoices window displays.

   Select All

10. Follow these steps to complete the invoice:

   Ⓐ Tap ⎡Tab⎤ three times, and then type **081519**.

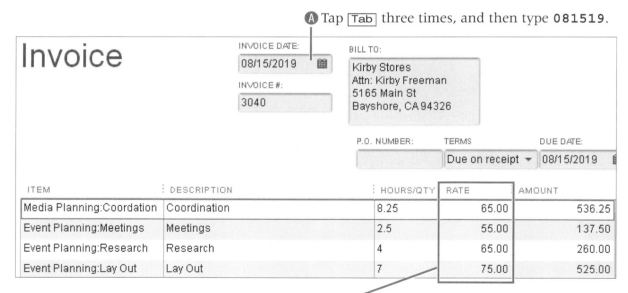

Ⓑ Enter the **Rate** for each **Item** as displayed here.

> **BTS BRIEF**
>
> 1210•Accounts Receivable DR 1,458.75; **4200•Event Income CR <1,458.75>**

11. Click **Save & Close**.

Reporting for Estimates and Time Tracking

QuickBooks' job costing, estimating, and time tracking features include many preset reports that you can run to learn more about your business. Notice in the figure below the reports available in the QuickBooks Pro version for the Jobs, Time & Mileage category on the Reports menu. Many other reports are available for your use if you use a Premier version of QuickBooks that is specialized for your type of company.

Jobs, Time & Mileage ▶
Job Profitability Summary
Job Profitability Detail
Job Estimates vs. Actuals Summary
Job Estimates vs. Actuals Detail
Job Progress Invoices vs. Estimates
Item Profitability
Item Estimates vs. Actuals
Profit & Loss by Job
Estimates by Job
Unbilled Costs by Job
Open Purchase Orders by Job
Time by Job Summary
Time by Job Detail
Time by Name
Time by Item
Mileage by Vehicle Summary
Mileage by Vehicle Detail
Mileage by Job Summary

There are a large number of standard reports available to QuickBooks users to help with tracking jobs, time, and mileage.

QUICK REFERENCE — PRODUCING REPORTS ABOUT ESTIMATES, TIME TRACKING, AND JOB COSTING

Task	Procedure
Produce a report to show the amount of an invoiced estimate	■ Choose Reports→Jobs, Time & Mileage→Job Progress Invoices vs. Estimates. ■ Set the date range.
Produce a report to show time tracked for each job	■ Choose Reports→Jobs, Time & Mileage→Time by Job Summary. ■ Set the date range.
Produce a report to show the profitability of all jobs	■ Choose Reports→Jobs, Time & Mileage→Job Profitability Summary.

Produce Job, Estimate, and Time Tracking Reports

In this exercise, you will produce a variety of reports for Average Guy Designs.

1. Choose **Reports→Jobs, Time & Mileage→Job Progress Invoices vs. Estimates**.

   The Job Progress Invoices vs. Estimates report displays.

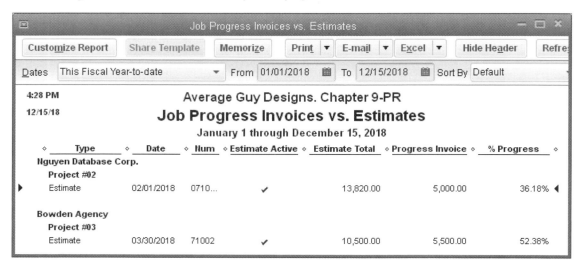

2. Close the **Job Progress Invoices vs. Estimates** window.

Report on Time Tracking

The next report will show the time spent on each job.

3. Choose **Reports→Jobs, Time & Mileage→Time by Job Summary**.

4. Tap ⓐ to set the date range to All.

   The Time by Job Summary report displays for all dates. Take a look down the report and notice the time for which you invoiced Kirby Stores for the Project #15 job, as shown in the following illustration.

Average Guy Designs. Chapter 9-PR
Time by Job Summary
All Transactions

	Aug 15, 19
▼ Kirby Stores:Project #15	
Event Planning:Contract Review	8:00
Event Planning:Coordination	24:00
Event Planning:Event Review	16:00
Event Planning:Lay Out	23:00
Event Planning:Meetings	18:30
Event Planning:Research	44:00
Media Planning:Coordation	8:15
Print Production:Coordination	36:00
Print Production:Editing	42:00
Total Kirby Stores:Project #15	219:45

5. Close the **Time by Job Summary** window.

Report on Job Costing

The third report will show the profitability of each job.

6. Choose **Reports→Jobs, Time & Mileage→Job Profitability Summary**.

   The Job Profitability Summary report displays with the default date range of all dates.

7. Take a look at the profitability so far for the Kirby Stores.

	Act. Cost	Act. Revenue	($) Diff.
Average Guy Designs. Chapter 9-PR			
Job Profitability Summary			
All Transactions			
▼ Kirby Stores			
Project #15	9,248.52	18,120.15	8,871.63
Project #09	6,724.31	28,430.50	21,706.19
Total Kirby Stores	15,972.83	46,550.65	30,577.82

8. Close the **Job Profitability Summary** window.

Tackle the Tasks

Now is your chance to work a little more with Average Guy Designs and apply the skills that you have learned in this chapter to accomplish additional tasks. You will use the same company file you used in the Develop Your Skills exercises throughout this chapter. Enter the following tasks, referring back to the concepts in the chapter as necessary.

Create an estimate for a new job	Create a new job for Chancey and Co. called Project #16, as you will be bidding on the opportunity to create a new marketing video.
	Create an estimate for the film production job on 08/15/2019 for 2 hours of contract review, 20 hours of research, 10 hours of meetings, 30 hours of coordination, 25 hours on location, and 40 hours of editing. The hourly rate for all is $45/hour.
Create a progress invoice based on an estimate	You have been awarded Project #16 for Chancey and Co., so edit the job to show this. The dates for the job will be 9/1/2019 to 12/1/2019.
	Create an invoice dated 9/1/2019 for 50 percent of the entire estimate. Set the terms for the invoice as Net 15 (do not make the change permanent).
Receive a customer deposit	Bowden Agency would like you to do some print production work for them and to print a large number of items for which you will collect a deposit up front. Receive a deposit from Bowden Agency using a new job, Project #17, on 8/17/2019 for $500 for the printing.
Apply a customer deposit as a payment	The print production for Bowden Agency is complete. Create an invoice for 10 hours of print production coordination, 40 hours of editing, and printing in the amount of $550 on 9/9/2019 for the work. Apply the $500 customer deposit to the invoice with terms of Net 10 (do not make the change in terms permanent).
Create an invoice from billable time	Create an invoice for Peacock Research for the billable time for film editing. Date the invoice 8/15/19 and charge them the three lines on the Time tab for Editing. (Hint: The total amount you are passing on is $1,445.)

Advanced Skills (side tab)

Tackle the Tasks **409**

Choose the appropriate option for your situation:

- If you are continuing on to the next chapter or to the end-of-chapter exercises, leave QuickBooks open.
- If you are finished working in QuickBooks for now, choose **File→Exit**.

Concepts Review

To check your knowledge of the key concepts introduced in this chapter, complete the Concepts Review quiz on the Student Resource Center or in your eLab course.

Reinforce Your Skills

Angela Stevens has just relocated her company, Quality-Built Construction, from California to Silverton, Oregon. You will be working with a QuickBooks Sample Company File in this exercise as it will allow you to run full payroll in a future chapter without having to purchase a payroll subscription.

Before you begin the Reinforce Your Skills exercises, complete one of these options:

■ Open **RYS_Chapter09** from your file storage location.

■ Restore **RYS_Chapter09 (Portable)** from your file storage location. Make sure to place your last name and first initial at the end of the filename (e.g., RYS_Chapter09_StevensA).

REINFORCE YOUR SKILLS 9-1
Create a Job and an Estimate for a Customer

In this exercise, you will enter a new customer and a job for the customer as they have asked you for an estimate for a remodel of their kitchen.

Before Angela can create estimates and conduct progress invoicing, the preferences must be set.

1. Choose **Edit→Preferences**.

2. Click the **Jobs & Estimates** category, and then the **Company Preferences** tab.

3. Click in the circle to the left of **Yes** to turn on both the estimate creation and progress invoicing features, and then click **OK**. Click **OK** to close all windows to set the preference.

Create a Customer and a Job

Next you will enter a new customer and job.

4. Choose **Customers→Customer Center**.

5. Click the New Customer & Job button, and then choose New Customer.

6. Type Tania Bates as the Customer Name, and then OK.

7. Click the New Customer & Job button, and then choose Add Job.

8. Type Remodel Kitchen as the Job Name.

9. Click the Job Info tab, and then use the following illustration to enter the job information.

10. Click OK to save the new job.

    The new job appears on the Customers & Jobs List; it is selected.

Create an Estimate for a Job

Now that you have a job set up for the kitchen remodel, you will create an estimate for it. The Kitchen Remodel job should still be selected.

11. Click the **New Transactions** button, and then choose **Estimates**.

12. Enter **1/7/2019** as the **Date**.

13. Using the following illustration as a guide, type the quantity and estimate cost displayed.

ITEM	DESCRIPTION	QTY	ESTIMATE	TOTAL
01 Plans & Permits .:01.4 Remodel Plans	Plans for home remodel	1	1,200.00	1,200.00
02 Site Work:02.10 Demo	Demolition	8	55.00	440.00
07 Wall Framing	Wall Framing	5	60.00	300.00
13 Windows & Trim	Windows & Trim	6	65.00	390.00
14 Plumbing	Plumbing	5	75.00	375.00
16 Electrical & Lighting	Electrical & Lighting	8	65.00	520.00
18 Interior Walls	Interior Walls	8	55.00	440.00
20 Millwork & Trim	Millwork & Trim	12	50.00	600.00
23 Floor Coverings	Floor Coverings	8	45.00	360.00
24 Paint	Painting	9	50.00	450.00
25 Cleanup	Cleanup & Restoration	10	45.00	450.00

14. Click **Save & Close** for the estimate.

15. Close the **Customer Center**.

Create a Progress Invoice Based on an Estimate

In this exercise, you will change the status of the job for Tania Bates, and then you will create a progress invoice to charge for the remodel plans that have been completed.

1. Choose **Customers→Create Invoices**, and then choose **Tania Bates: Remodel Kitchen** as the Customer:Job.

2. Click the estimate for **1/7/2019** in the **Available Estimates** window, and then click **OK**.

3. Click to choose to create the invoice for selected items or for different percentages of each item, and then click **OK**.

Specify what to include on the invoice.

- ○ Create invoice for the entire estimate (100%).
- ○ Create invoice for a percentage of the entire estimate.
    - % of estimate
- ◉ Create invoice for selected items or for different percentages of each item.

4. Click OK in the **Zero Amount Items** window

5. Click to deselect the options to **Show Quantity and Rate** and **Show Percentage**; type in 1200 as the **Amount** for the first line, **01.4 Remodel Plans**, as displayed in the following illustration.

☐ Show Quantity and Rate		☐ Show Percentage		
ITEM		EST AMT	PRIOR AMT	AMOUNT
01 Plans & Permits .:01.4 Remodel Plans		1,200.00		1,200.00

Note that once that selection is made, everything will fill into the Create Invoices window.

6. Choose **Due on receipt** as the Terms, and set the date to **1/22/2019**.

7. Click **Save & Close**.

8. Choose to not have the **Terms** permanently changed.

REINFORCE YOUR SKILLS 9-3

Collect a Customer Deposit

In this exercise, you will help Angela to collect a deposit from Tania Bates for $2,000 to begin the work. These funds will be held in a liability account until they are earned, at which time you will create a progress invoice to record the income. There is already a Customer Deposits account set up, so you will begin by creating two items.

1. Choose **Lists →Item List**.

2. Choose to create a new **Other Charge** item named `Cust Dep`.

3. Leave the Description blank so you can add it in to each invoice, change the **Tax Code** to **Non**, and then direct it to the **Customer Deposits** account.

4. Click **Next**, and choose to create a new **Payment** item called `Payment`.

5. Type `Customer Payment` as the Description, and then click **OK**.

6. Close the **Item List**.

Collect the Deposit

7. Choose **Customers→Create Invoices**, and then choose **Tania Bates: Remodel Kitchen** as the Customer:Job.

8. Click the **Cancel** in the **Available Estimates** window.

9. Ensure the date is set to **1/22/2019**, and then enter the deposit and payment using the following illustration.

ITEM	QUANTITY	DESCRIPTION	RATE	AMOUNT	TAX
Cust Dep			2,000.00	2,000.00	Non
Payment		Customer Payment	-2,000.00	-2,000.00	

10. Click **Save & New**.

Apply the Customer Deposit to a Progress Invoice

Angela has completed the kitchen remodel and will invoice Tania to record the earned income, utilizing the deposit. The Create Invoices window should still be open. If not, choose Customers→Create Invoices.

11. Choose **Tania Bates: Remodel Kitchen** as the Customer:Job.

12. Click the estimate for **1/7/2019** in the **Available Estimates** window, and then click **OK**.

13. Click **OK**, choosing to create an invoice for the remaining amounts of the estimate.

14. Click **OK** in the **Zero Amount Items** window, set the date of the invoice to **2/22/2019**.

15. Scroll down in the item area of the invoice, and then enter the customer deposit in the line below **25 Cleanup**, using the following illustration as a guide.

ITEM	DESCRIPTION	EST AMT	PRIO...	RATE	TOTAL %	AMOUNT	TAX
25 Cleanup	Cleanup & Restoration	450.00		45.00	100.0%	450.00	Non
Cust Dep	Customer Deposit Applied			-2,000.00		-2,000.00	Non

16. Click **Save & Close**.

Assess Finance Charges

In this exercise, you assess finance charges for customers with overdue invoices. The finance charge preferences have already been set up for the company, so you will not need to complete that step.

1. Choose **Customers→Assess Finance Charges**.

2. Type **013119** as the **Assessment Date**.
   Two invoices are selected to have finance charges assessed.

3. Click **Assess Charges**.

Enter Time Tracking Data and Produce a Paycheck

In this exercise, you will enter time spent on a job by Clark Mitchell and then create a paycheck for him.

1. Choose **Employees→Enter Time→Use Weekly Timesheet**.

2. Using the following illustration, enter the time worked for the week of **Jan 28 to Feb 3, 2019**.

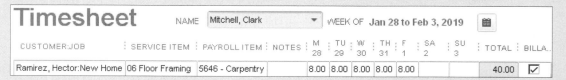

3. Click **Save & New**.

4. Use the following illustration to enter the time worked for the week of **Feb 4 to Feb 10, 2019**.

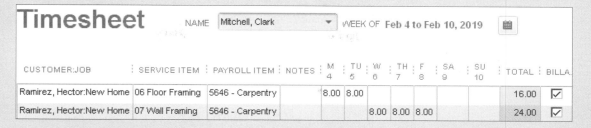

5. Click **Save & Close**.

6. Choose Employees→Pay Employees; use the following illustration to set the dates.

7. Click **Yes** in the **Pay Period Change** window.

8. Click to the left of **Mitchell, Clark**; click **Continue**.

9. Review the paycheck you are about to create using time data, and then click **Create Paychecks**.

10. Close the **Confirmation and Next Steps** window.

REINFORCE YOUR SKILLS 9-6

Display Reports for Estimates and Time Tracking

In this exercise, you will help Angela to create estimate and time tracking reports.

1. Choose **Lists→Chart of Accounts**.

2. Scroll down until you can see **4•Estimates,** and then right-click the account. Choose **QuickReport: 4•Estimates** from the pop-up menu.

3. Set the date range to **All,** and then close the **Account QuickReport** and the **Chart of Accounts** windows.

   Take a look at the report to view the estimates that have been created; the one you entered is at the bottom of the report.

View the Progress of Invoicing an Estimate

You will now run a report that will show you the percentage of the estimates that have been invoiced.

4. Choose **Reports→Jobs, Time & Mileage→Job Progress Invoices vs. Estimates**.

5. Tap $\boxed{a}$ to set the date range to All.

   Notice the estimate you created and the amount that has been invoiced.

6. Close the **Job Progress vs. Estimates** window, choosing not to memorize report.

Create a Time by Job Summary Report

Finally, you will create a report that shows time spent on Hector Ramirez' New Home job.

7. Choose **Reports→Jobs, Time & Mileage→Time by Job Summary**.

8. Tap a to set the date range to All.

   Scroll down to view the time data for the new home job for Hector Ramirez.

Premier Custom Homes, Chapter 9
Time by Job Summary
All Transactions

	⬧ Feb 22, 19 ⬧
▼ Ramirez, Hector:New Home	
06 Floor Framing	56.00
07 Wall Framing	24.00
Total Ramirez, Hector:New Home	80.00

9. Close the **Time by Job Summary** report, choosing to not memorize the report.

10. Choose the appropriate option for your situation:

    ■ If you are continuing on to the next chapter or the rest of the end-of-chapter exercises, leave QuickBooks open.

    ■ If you are finished working in QuickBooks for now, choose **File→Exit**.

Apply Your Skills

Before you begin the Apply Your Skills exercises, complete one of these options:

- Open **AYS_Chapter09** from your file storage location.
- Restore **AYS_Chapter09 (Portable)** from your file storage location. Make sure to place your last name and first initial at the end of the filename (e.g., AYS_Chapter09_JamesS).

APPLY YOUR SKILLS 9-1

Set the Preferences and Create a New Job

In this exercise, you will set the necessary preferences to be able to use QuickBooks' estimating and progress invoicing features. Then you will create a new "job" for Amy Ridgeway's new kitten, Autumn.

1. Open the **Preferences** window, and display the **Company Preferences** tab for the Jobs & Estimates category.
2. Choose to both create estimates and do progress invoicing.
3. Click **OK** in the **Preferences** window to save the changes.

Create a New Job

Now that the preferences have been set, you will create the job for Amy's new kitten.

4. Create a new job for Amy Ridgeway called `Cat-Autumn`.
5. Click **OK**.

   Dr. James has decided that it is not important for her to track "job status" for her customers, so you will leave the fields on the Job Info tab blank.

APPLY YOUR SKILLS 9-2

Create an Estimate for a Job

1. Create an estimate on 7/15/2014 for Amy Ridgeway: Cat-Autumn, using the items displayed in the illustration shown here.

   Amy knows that she needs to bring in her new kitten to be spayed, tested for FIV and feline leukemia, and vaccinated, but she is concerned about the total cost and needs to budget the services. In this exercise, you will create an estimate for her so she can see the full cost for all of the services.

   Remember that all service and non-inventory items are not taxable; only inventory items are taxable.

2. Click **Save & Close**.

ITEM	DESCRIPTION
New Patient	New Patient Exam
Vaccine	Vaccine Injection Fee
Pre-A Blood Wk	Pre-Anesthesia Blood Work
Spay Cat	Feline Spay Procedure
IV Fluids	Intravenous Fluids
Pain Meds	Pre- & Post-Surgical Pain Medication
FIV/FeLV	FIV/Feline Leukemia Test
F Leuk	Feline Leukemia Vaccine
Feline DHC	Feline DHC Vaccine
Rabies	Rabies Vaccine
Rev-Cat/Sm Dog	Revolution-Cat/Small Dog

Create an Invoice from the Estimate

Amy Ridgeway has decided to get Autumn the care she needs in phases. In this exercise, you will create a progress invoice for the first set of items.

1. Open the **Create Invoices** window, and choose **Amy Ridgeway: Cat-Autumn** as the Customer:Job.

2. Choose to create the invoice based on the estimate created on 7/15/2014, and then to create an invoice for selected items.

3. In the Specify Invoice Amount for Items on Estimate window, click in the Show Percentage checkbox, and then choose the following items to include on the invoice: New Patient, FIV/FeLV, Vaccine, and Rabies by typing **100%** in the Curr % column.

4. Click **OK** when you are finished.

Once you enter 100 in the Curr % column for the first item, you can use the ⬇ key to move down the column to enter the percentage for the other three items.

5. Read the warning message; click **OK** in the Zero Amount Items window.

6. Set the date to **7/19/14**, and the invoice # to 178.

7. Click **Save & Close** on the invoice.

   The invoice is created for the customer. The rest of the estimate will still be available, from which you can create future invoices.

Answer Questions with Reports

In this exercise, you will answer questions for Dr. James by running reports. You may wish to display the Report Center in List View to help you answer the questions. Ask your instructor if you should print the reports, print (save) them as PDF files, export them to Excel, or simply display them on the screen.

1. What are the details and what is the balance still outstanding on the estimate created for Amy Ridgeway?

2. How much does each customer currently owe?

3. Is it possible to see a pie chart that shows the income by account for May 2014?

4. Will you please create a report that shows all of the transactions for Amy Ridgeway's cat, Autumn?

5. Submit your reports based on the guidelines provided by your instructor.

6. Choose the appropriate option for your situation:

   ■ If you are continuing on to the next chapter or the Extend Your Skills exercises, leave QuickBooks open.

   ■ If you are finished working in QuickBooks for now, choose **File→Exit**.

Extend Your Skills

In the course of working through the following Extend Your Skills exercises, you will be utilizing various skills taught in this and previous chapter(s). Take your time and think carefully about the tasks presented to you. Turn back to the chapter content if you need assistance.

9-1 Sort Through the Stack

Before You Begin: Restore the **EYS1_Chapter09 (Portable)** file or open the **EYS1_Chapter09** company file from your storage location.

You have been hired by Arlaine Cervantes to help her with her organization's books. She is the founder of Niños del Lago, a nonprofit organization that provides impoverished Guatemalan children with an engaging educational camp experience. You have just sat down at your desk and opened a large envelope from her with a variety of documents and noticed that you have several emails from her as well. It is your job to sort through the papers and emails and make sense of what you find, entering information into QuickBooks whenever appropriate and answering any other questions in a word-processing document saved as **EYS1_Chapter09_ LastnameFirstinitial**. Remember, you are digging through papers on a desk, so it is up to you to determine the correct order in which to complete the tasks.

- Handwritten receipt: Dated 9/19/2014 for a $500.00 donation from Matthew Drill to purchase food for a camp to be offered in December 2014. Sticky note from Arlaine on the receipt: Can you please figure out a way to account for this donation since the food will not be purchased and consumed until December?

- Handwritten estimate for Expanding Opportunities Together: Dated 9/17/2014 for 50 scarves and 35 handbags. (Expanding Opportunities Together is another nonprofit that is looking to help us raise funds by purchasing and reselling the goods we get from the women in Guatemala.) Each of the products was on a separate line, and both at 25 percent off regular retail.

- Message from Arlaine: "We should probably think about what we should do if customers do not pay their bill on time…Can we assess finance charges in QuickBooks? If so, please set it up so we charge 12 percent interest on overdue invoices. I think we need to have a nice grace period, though, so please set that at 30 days. Don't worry about charging a minimum finance charge or charging interest on overdue finance charges."

- Printed email: Received the contract from Expanding Opportunities Together. Could you please bill them for 50 percent up front?

- Scribbled note from Arlaine: Is there a report you can create for me that will show how much of the estimate has been invoiced?

9-2 Be Your Own Boss

Before You Begin: You must complete Extend Your Skills 8-2 before you begin this exercise.

In this exercise, throughout the entire book, you will build on the company file that you outlined in previous chapters. If you have created a file for your actual business, then enter any estimates and progress invoices that your company has produced, set your file up for collecting unearned income and record any customer deposits and/or gift certificates, set up and assess any finance charges, and enter any time tracking data and create the appropriate time tracking paychecks. If you are creating a fictitious company, then turn it on to deal with estimates and progress invoicing, set it up to collect customer deposits, set up and assess any finance charges, enter time tracking hours for at least two employees, and create the paychecks for them. You will make up the names and information for this exercise.

Create an Employee Contact List report as well as a report showing how much was paid to each employee for the past month, submitting them to your instructor based on the instructions provided.

Open the company file you worked on in Extend Your Skills 8-2 and complete the tasks outlined above. When you are done, save it as a portable company file, naming it as **EYS2_Chapter09_ LastnameFirstinitial (Portable)** and submit it to your instructor based on the instructions provided.

9-3 Use the Web as a Learning Tool

Throughout this book, you will be provided with an opportunity to use the Internet as a learning tool by completing WebQuests. According to the original creators of WebQuests, as described on their website (http://WebQuest.org), a WebQuest is "an inquiry-oriented activity in which most or all of the information used by learners is drawn from the web." To complete the WebQuest projects in this book, navigate to the Student Resource Center and choose the WebQuest for the chapter on which you are working. The subject of each WebQuest will be relevant to the material found in the chapter.

WebQuest Subject: Working with gift certificates

Customizing and Integrating in QuickBooks

CHAPTER OBJECTIVES

After studying this chapter, you will be able to:

- Use Customer & Vendor Profile Lists
- Create and use custom fields
- Customize reports and graphs
- Create custom templates
- Integrate with Microsoft Office and mobile apps

Finally, the artist in you gets to have some fun! It's time to learn about customizing QuickBooks forms and reports to look good and work best for your company. In this chapter, you will learn to customize your reports to include pertinent information, to jazz them up, and to make them look more attractive. You will also learn about how to customize customer and vendor profile lists as well as how to create custom fields. Once you finish working with reports, you will create your own custom invoice template. In addition, you will learn how well QuickBooks integrates with Microsoft Office and the mobile apps available to help you manage your company's finances.

Average Guy Designs

With Guy and Allison both being designers, they really want to jazz up their QuickBooks forms and correspondence. Guy would also like to learn about how all of the lists and custom fields can be utilized for his business. He is also very interested in using Word and Excel seamlessly with QuickBooks. Allison will be in charge of adding some finesse to Average Guy Designs' company reports and templates.

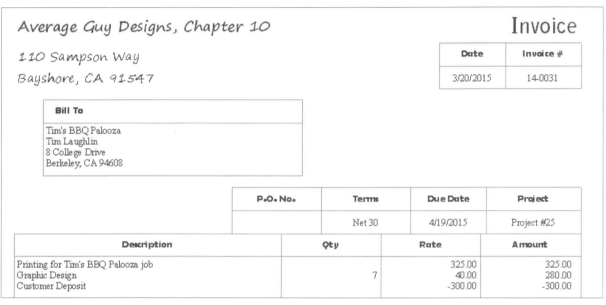

You can customize your templates to make them more appealing.

Working with Customer & Vendor Profile Lists

When you created your new QuickBooks company and chose a type of company on which to base it, QuickBooks gave you a generic Chart of Accounts and populated your Customer & Vendor Profile Lists with entries relevant to your chosen company type. You have already seen many of these profile lists in the forms and lists you will work with in this book.

Table of Customer & Vendor Profile Lists

Look at the profile lists that QuickBooks provides to track customer and vendor information, as well as the examples of forms and lists in which you may find them appearing as fields.

PROFILE LISTS AND WHERE THEY APPEAR	
Name of List	**You may find this list as a field on...**
Sales Rep List	Customer & Job List (Additional Info tab)
	Create Invoices form
Customer Type List	Customer & Job List (Additional Info tab)
Vendor Type List	Vendor List (Additional Info tab)
Job Type List	Customer & Job List (Job Info tab)
Terms List	Vendor List
	Create Invoices form
Customer Message List	Enter Sales Receipts form
Payment Method List	Receive Payments form
Ship Via List	Create Invoices form (product or custom template)
Vehicle List	Enter Vehicle Mileage window

Making the Lists Work for You

Using the Customer & Vendor Profile Lists can help you in many ways. You can even use a list for a purpose other than that for which it was intended. For instance, your company may not ship products, so you have no need for the Ship Via field. You can use this field to track an additional aspect of your company. You cannot create your own profile list, so you need to maximize the profile lists QuickBooks provides to track all information needed by your company.

The benefit of fully utilizing these lists is that they can be included on reports and custom form templates. This means that if you want to focus a marketing effort on your residential customers, you can create a report and filter out all customer types other than residential.

Task	Procedure
Open a profile list	■ Choose Lists→Customer & Vendor Profile Lists→[the name of the list you need].
Edit a profile list entry	■ Double-click the entry you need to edit. ■ Make any necessary changes; click OK.
Create a new profile list entry	■ Right-click within the list; choose New. ■ Enter all relevant information; click OK.
Delete a profile list entry	■ Click the entry to be deleted. ■ Use Ctrl+d to delete the entry, clicking OK to confirm the deletion.

DEVELOP YOUR SKILLS 10-1

Work with Customer & Vendor Profile Lists

In this exercise, you will work with the Customer Message, Vendor Type, and Customer Type Lists. You can use these procedures with any other profile list as well.

Intuit provides maintenance releases throughout the lifetime of the product. These updates may require you to update your student exercise files before you begin working with them. Please follow the prompts on the screen if you are asked to update your company file to the latest QuickBooks release.

1. Start **QuickBooks 2014**.

   If you downloaded the student exercise files in the portable company file *format, follow Option 1 below. If you downloaded the files in the* company file *format, follow Option 2 below.*

Option 1: Restore a Portable Company File

2. Choose **File→Open or Restore Company**.

3. Restore the **DYS_Chapter10 (Portable)** portable company file for this chapter from your file storage location, placing your last name and first initial at the end of the filename (e.g., DYS_Chapter10_MarshallG).

   It may take a few moments for the portable company file to open. Once it does, continue with step 5.

Option 2: Open a Company File

2. Choose **File→Open or Restore Company**, ensure that **Open a regular company file** is selected, and then open the **DYS_Chapter10** company file from your file storage location.

   The QuickBooks company file will open.

3. Click **OK** to close the QuickBooks Information window. Click **No** in the Set Up External Accountant User window, if necessary.

4. Close the **Reminders** window.

Edit a Profile List Entry

5. Choose **Lists→Customer & Vendor Profile Lists→Customer Message List**.

6. Double-click **Thank you for your business**.

7. Replace the current message with the following:

   We truly appreciate your business.

   When you open the message for editing, the current message is selected (highlighted); it will be replaced when you type the new message.

8. Click **OK** to save the new message.

   Now you can select this message on the Create Invoices and Enter Sales Receipt forms that you create for your customers.

9. Close the **Customer Message List** window.

Create a New Profile List Entry

You will now help Allison to add a new vehicle.

10. Choose **Lists→Customer & Vendor Profile Lists→Vehicle List**.

11. Click the **Vehicle** menu button, and then click **New**.

12. Follow these steps to complete the new list entry:

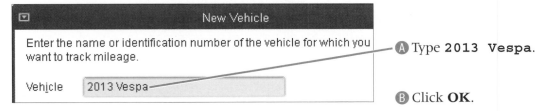

13. Close the **Vehicle List**.

Delete a Profile List Entry

Allison has decided that she doesn't want to have both Suppliers and Supplies on the Vendor Type List, so you will delete one for her.

14. Choose **Lists→Customer & Vendor Profile Lists→Vendor Type List**.

15. Single-click **Suppliers**.

16. Click the **Vendor Type** menu button and choose **Delete Vendor Type**; click **OK** to confirm the deletion.

17. Close the **Vendor Type List**.

Creating Custom Fields

You will work with many forms in QuickBooks, and you may choose to send some of these forms to customers and vendors. QuickBooks provides many standard forms (such as invoice, purchase order, and sales receipt), but you can also choose to create your own forms or modify the standard Intuit forms. In order to use custom fields on a form, you must create your own rather than use one of the standard forms provided by QuickBooks (you can also make a copy of a standard Intuit form and customize it).

Adding Custom Fields

Before you can use custom fields in reports, you must first set them up in the lists where they belong. You can set up custom fields for Customers:Jobs, Vendors, Employees, and Items. You can either populate custom fields in the lists or enter the information directly on the forms where they appear.

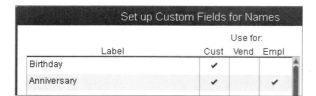

The Set up Custom Fields for Names window allows you to create custom fields for three lists: Customers & Jobs, Vendors, and Employees.

Custom fields are available for all types of items except for subtotals, sales tax items, and sales tax groups.

QUICK REFERENCE	WORKING WITH CUSTOM FIELDS
Task	**Procedure**
Create custom fields for customers, vendors, and employees	▪ Open the Vendor Center (this works the same for the other centers); double-click to open a vendor's record. ▪ Click the Additional Info tab; click the Define Fields button. ▪ Type the field names. ▪ Click in the column(s) below the list(s) where you want to see each field displayed; click OK. ▪ Enter the new field information into the vendor record; click OK.
Create custom fields for items	▪ Open the Item List; double-click to open an item for editing. ▪ Click the Custom Fields button; click the Define Fields button. ▪ Type the labels you wish to use. ▪ Click in the box to the left of each label that you want to activate; click OK. ▪ Enter any custom field information you want to see automatically appear on forms; click OK twice.

Create and Fill Custom Fields

In this exercise, you will help Allison to create custom fields to track additional information and for her to use on custom templates in the future.

1. Choose **Customers→Customer Center**.

2. Double-click **Chris Nelson** in the Customers & Jobs List at the left.

3. Click the **Additional Info** tab.

4. Click the **Define Fields** button in the Custom Fields section of the window.

5. Follow these steps to set up two custom fields:

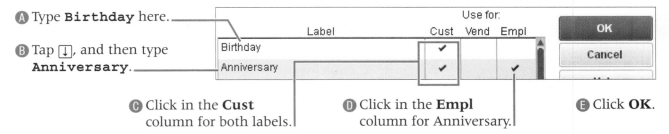

Ⓐ Type **Birthday** here.

Ⓑ Tap ⬇, and then type **Anniversary**.

Ⓒ Click in the **Cust** column for both labels.

Ⓓ Click in the **Empl** column for Anniversary.

Ⓔ Click **OK**.

QuickBooks may display an information window indicating that you can use the custom fields in templates.

6. Click **OK** to acknowledge the prompt, if necessary.

7. Click in the **Birthday** field and type **5/21/69**.

8. Click **OK** to accept the changes and close the Edit Customer window.

9. Close the **Customer Center** window.

Create and Fill an Item Custom Field

You will now add a custom field for items and use it on a non-inventory item.

10. Choose **Lists→Item List**.

11. Scroll down, and then double-click **Art Work**.

    The Edit Item window will open for Art Work.

12. Click the **Custom Fields** button. Click **OK** to continue to the **Custom Fields for Art Work** window if QuickBooks displays an Information window.

13. Click the **Define Fields** button.

14. Follow these steps to add the custom field:

    Ⓐ Type **Framed** in the Label column, tap Tab, and then tap Spacebar.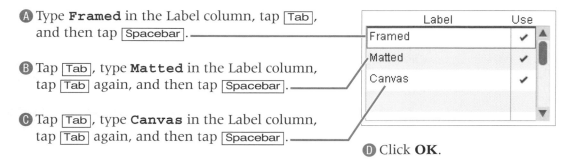

    Ⓑ Tap Tab, type **Matted** in the Label column, tap Tab again, and then tap Spacebar.

    Ⓒ Tap Tab, type **Canvas** in the Label column, tap Tab again, and then tap Spacebar.

    Ⓓ Click **OK**.

15. Click **OK** two more times.

    QuickBooks closes the Custom Fields for Art Work window. You did not type in any data here because you will add it to the individual forms instead. If you wish, you can type the custom field information into the Custom Fields for Art Work window and have it appear on each form or report you create that displays the field.

16. Click **OK** to close the Edit Item window.

17. Close the **Item List**.

Customizing Reports and Graphs

You have learned to create various reports throughout this book so far. Now you will customize the reports that you produce to make them work for you.

Customization takes place on many fronts. You may find yourself asking:

- Which accounts should I display?
- What information do I need to filter out?
- What header and footer information should I include?
- How do I want my fonts and numbers to look?

Display Properties

The Display tab of the Modify Report window allows you to change aspects of your report such as the dates it represents, your reporting basis (cash or accrual), the columns to display, and subcolumn preferences.

Report Date Range

Each preset report has a default date range displayed when the report is first created. The date can either be:

- When your reporting period ends, such as a balance sheet report created "As of June 30, 2014."
- For a range of days, such as a Profit & Loss report created for June 1-30, 2014.

The type of date is determined by the type of report you produce.

Accrual vs. Cash Basis Reporting

If you recall from Chapter 1, Introducing QuickBooks Pro, there are two methods of accounting from which you can choose for your company. You enter data into QuickBooks the same way regardless of whether you use the cash or accrual basis of accounting. When you create your reports, you can easily switch between cash and accrual basis. And when you first create a QuickBooks company, the default will be for the reports to be displayed as the accrual basis. Of course, you will want to set your company's default report basis in the report section of the Edit Preferences window. Take a look at a review of both methods.

Accrual Basis

In the accrual basis of accounting, income is recorded when a sale is made, and expenses are recorded when accrued. This method is used often by firms and businesses with large inventories; it's required for publicly traded companies.

Cash Basis

In the cash basis of accounting, income is recorded when cash is received and expenses are recorded when cash is paid. This method is commonly used by small businesses and professionals.

If you operate using the cash basis, you will not need to display Accounts Receivable and Accounts Payable on your financial statements because cash has yet to change hands.

Working with Report Columns

Each preset report displays certain default columns. You can change the columns to make your report much more useful. For instance, you can choose to display multiple months on a Profit & Loss report to compare income and expenses in different reporting periods. You can also specify subcolumns you want displayed if they are available for your specific report.

Subcolumns

Some reports allow you to add subcolumns to further analyze your data. Different subcolumns are available depending on the report you run. The entire list is shown in the following illustration.

The use of columns and subcolumns to stratify data can be a very valuable way to help you to analyze and scrutinize your company's financial data.

Filtering Reports

In order to have reports display only essential data, you have the ability to apply a filter in QuickBooks. A filter will let you choose what information to include in your report, thereby "filtering out" the rest of it. Filters can be applied to any report, and the specific information that can be filtered is determined by the report you run. You are also able to filter transaction reports for text that is contained in custom fields if the fields are on the forms for the transactions included in the report.

Formatting Fonts and Numbers

Formatting deals with the appearance of the report; it has nothing to do with the data contained within it. You can change the report's font(s) and the way numbers are displayed.

Fonts

QuickBooks displays its preset reports in the default font. You can make many choices as to the characteristics of the font in your report, such as the font name, style, color, and size.

Negative Numbers

When you have negative numbers in your report, they can be displayed in a variety of ways, as described in the illustration to the right.

All Numbers

You can also choose how QuickBooks will display all numbers in your report. The options available are displayed in the illustration to the right.

QUICK REFERENCE	CUSTOMIZING REPORTS
Task	**Procedure**
Change the default report basis	■ Choose Edit→Preferences.
	■ Choose the Reports & Graphs category, and then the Company Preferences tab.
	■ Choose Accrual or Cash in the Summary Report Basis section; click OK.
Apply a filter to a report	■ Create your report, and then click the Customize Report button.
	■ Click the Filters tab, apply the desired filter(s), and then click OK.
Change the font and number formatting on a report	■ Create your report; click the Customize Report button.
	■ Click the Fonts & Numbers tab.
	■ Select any number formatting changes.
	■ Click on the report element to change; click Change Font.
	■ Make your changes; click OK twice.

Customize Your Reports

In this exercise, you will help Allison to create and customize a Profit & Loss report. The QuickBooks default report basis is accrual. Guy spoke with his accountant and determined that Average Guy Designs would use the cash basis for reporting. You will begin by changing the default for the company file.

1. Choose **Edit→Preferences**.

2. Click the **Reports & Graphs** category on the left side of the window.

3. Click the **Company Preferences** tab, and then click in the circle to the left of **Cash** in the Summary Reports Basis section.

4. Click **OK** to save the new preference.

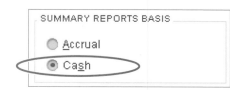

Add a Filter

Allison will first run the preset Profit & Loss Standard report. Then she will apply a filter to the report to show only income accounts.

5. Choose **Reports→Company & Financial→Profit & Loss Standard**.

6. Follow these steps to set a custom date range:

Ⓐ Tap [Tab], and then type **120114**.   Ⓑ Tap [Tab], and then type **123114**.

Ⓒ Click the **Refresh** button.

You will see the Profit & Loss report displayed for December 2014.

7. Click the **Customize Report** button on the report toolbar.

8. Follow these steps to apply a filter that will include only income accounts on the report:

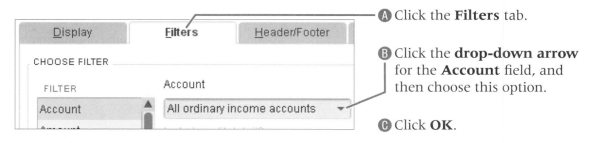

Ⓐ Click the **Filters** tab.

Ⓑ Click the **drop-down arrow** for the **Account** field, and then choose this option.

Ⓒ Click **OK**.

You will now see the report with no expense accounts shown.

Change the Font and Number Formatting

Allison wants to spruce up the report by changing the way the font and numbers appear.

9. Click the **Customize Report** button on the report toolbar.

10. Follow these steps to change the formatting:

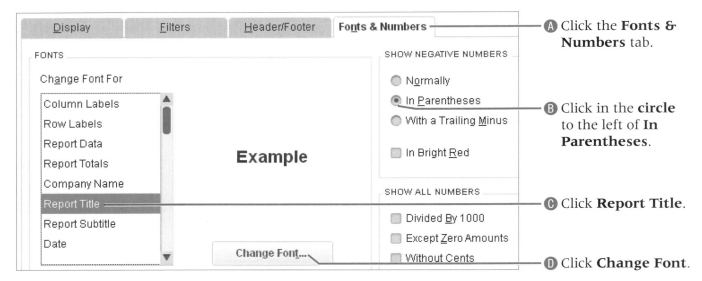

Ⓐ Click the **Fonts & Numbers** tab.

Ⓑ Click in the **circle** to the left of **In Parentheses**.

Ⓒ Click **Report Title**.

Ⓓ Click **Change Font**.

You will see a Report Title window similar to a Font dialog box that you may be familiar with from word-processing programs.

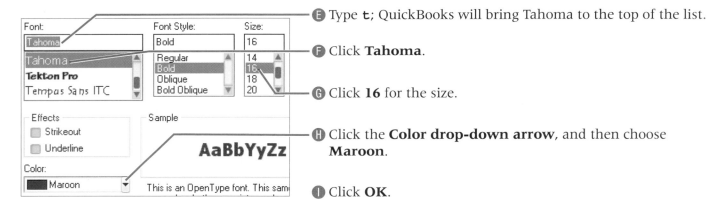

Ⓔ Type **t**; QuickBooks will bring Tahoma to the top of the list.

Ⓕ Click **Tahoma**.

Ⓖ Click **16** for the size.

Ⓗ Click the **Color drop-down arrow**, and then choose **Maroon**.

Ⓘ Click **OK**.

11. Click **Yes** to change all related fonts.

You will see the new font formatting displayed above the Change Font button.

12. Click **OK**.

You will see the font formatting changes that you just made. Leave the report open; you will continue to customize it in the next exercise.

Working with Additional Formatting Options

You have learned to choose many report customization options. Now you will learn to create a header and footer to your specifications and to memorize and recall a report.

Header and Footer Options

All preset QuickBooks reports have default headers and footers. You can change the information included and how it is formatted on the Header/Footer tab of the Modify Report window.

You have many options when it comes to customizing the header and footer of your report.

Page Layout

You can choose to use the default standard report layout or to use left, right, or centered alignment.

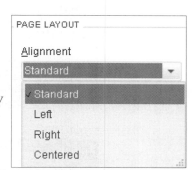

Memorizing Reports

Once you have created a report with your chosen settings, you may wish to save the report options so you can easily produce the same report again. The process of saving the settings of a report is called *memorizing* a report, and it is available for all reports. The memorizing feature memorizes the format of the report, not the data contained within it. This means that when you open a memorized report, it will contain your most recently entered data.

To recall the memorized report, you can choose it from the Memorized Report List.

Memorized Report Groups

QuickBooks allows you to organize your memorized reports into groups. There are six preset groups (accountant, banking, company, customers, employees, and vendors) for you to use, or you can choose to create your own. When you memorize a report, you can place it into a group immediately or later.

When you choose to memorize a report, you have the opportunity to save it in a memorized report group.

Batch Processing of Reports

If you have a group of reports that you run together on a regular basis, you may wish to process them as a batch to save time. You will first need to set the reports you wish to process together as a memorized report group, and then you will be able to process them all at once.

The Process Multiple Reports window allows you to choose which group of reports to process as a batch. You can set the date range in this window, too, if you need to change it from the range that was memorized.

QUICK REFERENCE	WORKING WITH AND MEMORIZING REPORTS
Task	**Procedure**
Change the report header/footer	■ Create your report; click the Customize Report button.
	■ Click the Header/Footer tab and make the desired changes; click OK.
Apply the % of row feature to a report	■ Create your report; click the Customize Report button.
	■ Click the Display tab and click in the box for % of row; click OK.
Create a memorized report group	■ Choose Reports→Memorized Report List.
	■ Click the Memorized Report menu button; choose New Group.
	■ Type the name of the group; click OK.

Task	Procedure
Place a report in the memorized report group	■ Create and modify a report to your liking; click Memorize. ■ Type the name of the report. ■ Click in the checkbox to the left of Save in Memorized Report Group. ■ Click the drop-down arrow to choose the group; click OK.
Batch process a group of reports	■ Choose Reports→Process Multiple Reports. ■ Choose the group from which you wish to process the reports. ■ Choose the reports you wish to process; click either Display or Print.

DEVELOP YOUR SKILLS 10-4
Make Additional Report Customization Changes

In this exercise, you will help Allison to make additional custom changes in the report and memorize the final product. The report that you were working on in the previous exercise should still be open. If not, repeat the steps in the previous exercise to produce the report needed to begin this exercise.

1. Click the **Customize Report** button on the report toolbar.

2. Follow these steps to make the changes to the header and footer:

Ⓐ Click the **Header/Footer** tab.

Ⓑ Replace the current Report Title with **Income Report**.

Ⓒ Click to uncheck the **Time Prepared** checkbox.

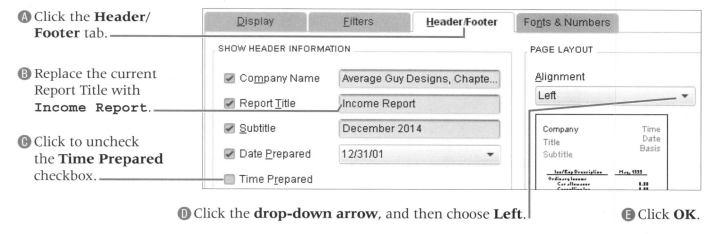

Ⓓ Click the **drop-down arrow**, and then choose **Left**.　　　　Ⓔ Click **OK**.

Look at the changes you have made to your report.

Change How Columns Are Displayed
Next you will help Allison modify the report so it separates the income by each two-week period.

3. Click the **Customize Report** button on the Report toolbar.

4. Click the **drop-down arrow** in the Columns section and choose **Two week**.

5. Click **OK**.

   QuickBooks displays the Income Report that Allison has customized.

Average Guy Designs, Chapter 10
Income Report
December 2014   **Cash Basis**

	Dec 1 - 13, 14	Dec 14 - 27, 14	Dec 28 - 31, 14	TOTAL
▼ Ordinary Income/Expense				
▼ Income				
42700 · Photography Income	0.00	200.00	0.00	200.00
43200 · Design Income ▶	1,340.00 ◀	865.00	230.00	2,435.00
Total Income	1,340.00	1,065.00	230.00	2,635.00
Gross Profit	1,340.00	1,065.00	230.00	2,635.00
Net Ordinary Income	1,340.00	1,065.00	230.00	2,635.00
Net Income	**1,340.00**	**1,065.00**	**230.00**	**2,635.00**

Memorize a Report
Now that Allison has the report just as she wants it, she will memorize it for easy recall.

6. Click the **Memorize** button on the report toolbar.

7. Follow these steps to memorize the report and place it in a group:

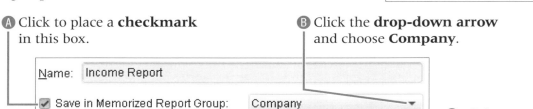

   Ⓐ Click to place a **checkmark** in this box.

   Ⓑ Click the **drop-down arrow** and choose **Company**.

   Name: Income Report

   ☑ Save in Memorized Report Group: Company

   Ⓒ Click **OK**.

8. Close the **Income Report**.

Process Multiple Reports
Allison will now process a batch of reports from the Company group.

9. Choose **Reports→Memorized Reports→Memorized Report List**.

10. **Scroll down** until you see the group header **Company**.

11. Right-click **Company**, and then choose **Process Group**.

    Take a look at the Process Multiple Reports window. You will see that the report that you just memorized, Income Report, is included in this group.

12. Click **Display** to process the batch of reports.

    QuickBooks will produce all of the reports in the Company group for the date ranges displayed.

13. Choose **Window→Close All**.

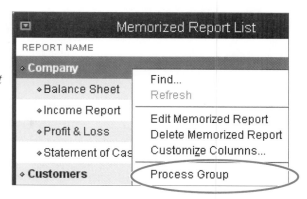

Creating Custom Forms

Before you customize your forms, think about what you want them to do for you:

■ Do you want to include custom fields?

■ Do you want to include a company logo?

■ What do you want the forms you will be sending out to your stakeholders to say about your company?

■ How much detail do you want to include?

■ What size fields will you need?

Templates

A template is a specific form format (with no data) on which you can base future forms. QuickBooks provides several templates, but you can also create custom templates to meet the needs of your unique company or create templates for preprinted forms. All of the templates available for a particular type of form are available from the drop-down list at the top of the form. Changing templates for a transaction that has already been entered will not change the information recorded in the transaction, even if the field is not visible on the new form.

Creating a Custom Template

When you choose to create a custom template, you begin by specifying information in the Basic Customization window. This window also provides a preview of how the template looks as you make changes to the various fields and information.

Adding a Company Logo to Templates

QuickBooks allows you to further personalize your templates by including your company logo. When you choose to add a logo to your template, the image file will be stored in the folder where your company file is located.

To add a logo or picture on a template, the company file must be located on the computer's hard drive or on a shared server. It will not work if your company file is located on a flash drive.

The Manage Templates Window

It is in the Manage Templates window where you will assign a name for your new template. You can also access additional templates online from this window. When you click the Download Templates button, QuickBooks launches a web browser and displays the QuickBooks website from which you can choose new templates.

Using Custom Fields in Forms and Reports

You need to create your own custom form template to utilize the custom fields you set up earlier in this chapter. You can choose to add the custom field information for customers, jobs, vendors, and employees on the Header tab of the Additional Customization window. To add the custom fields for items, you must use the Columns tab. It is up to you to determine whether the various fields will be displayed on the screen, on the printed form, on both, or in neither place.

If you wish to display custom fields on reports, you can choose to display them in the Columns box on the Display tab of the Modify Report window.

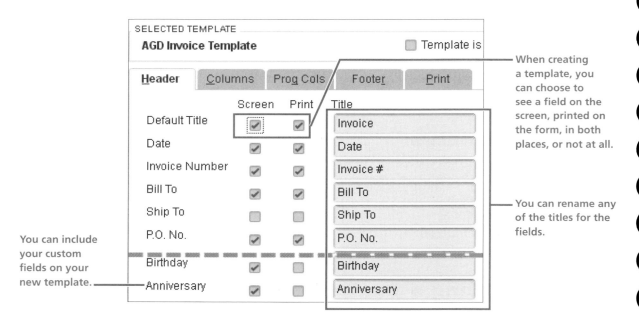

Working with the Layout Designer Window

QuickBooks allows you to determine not only what is included on a template, but also where it will be located. You can move fields and labels around your template and change the size of fields in the Layout Designer window. Each element on the template is termed an "object" in the Layout Designer window, and you can use some standard techniques to select, move, and resize all objects. The Snap to Grid feature ensures that all of your objects line up to a grid for which you can specify the spacing. In addition, you will see two shadows where the standard envelope windows are located so you can make sure to line up the addressees and return addresses properly.

QUICK REFERENCE	CREATING AND MODIFYING TEMPLATES
Task	**Procedure**
Create and name a new template	■ Choose Lists→Templates.
	■ Click the Templates menu button, choose New, and then choose the desired template type.
	■ Click the Manage Templates button; enter a name for the new template.
	■ Click OK twice to accept the new name and save the new template.
Modify a template	■ Choose Lists→Templates; single-click on the desired template.
	■ Click the Templates menu button; choose Edit.
	■ Make any desired changes; click OK.
Open layout designer for a template	■ Open the template you wish to modify further.
	■ Click the Layout Designer button.
	■ Make any necessary changes; click OK twice.

Set Up a New Template

In this exercise, you will help Allison to create a template for the company.

1. Choose **Lists→Templates**.

2. Click the **Templates** menu button, and then choose **New**.

3. Ensure Invoice is the type of template selected; click **OK**.

4. Click the **Manage Templates** button.

5. Replace the default Template Name with **AGD Invoice Template**, as shown at right.

6. Click **OK** to return to the Basic Customization window.

Change the Color Scheme of the Template

You will now help Allison to change the template and company name color.

7. Follow these steps to set a color scheme:

Ⓐ Click the drop-down arrow, and then choose **Green**.

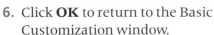

Ⓑ Click the **Apply Color Scheme** button.

You will now be able to view the new color in the preview area of the window to the right.

Add Customization

Now it is time to decide which customer and item fields you wish to include on the new template.

8. Click the **Additional Customization** button at the bottom of the window.

9. Click to place a checkmark in the **Due Date** checkbox in the **Print** column.

   A Layout Designer window appears to let you know how you can make changes to the way in which the new field will be laid out on the template.

10. Click in the box to the left of **Do not display this message in the future**; tap ⌨Enter.

11. Follow these steps to continue to customize your template:

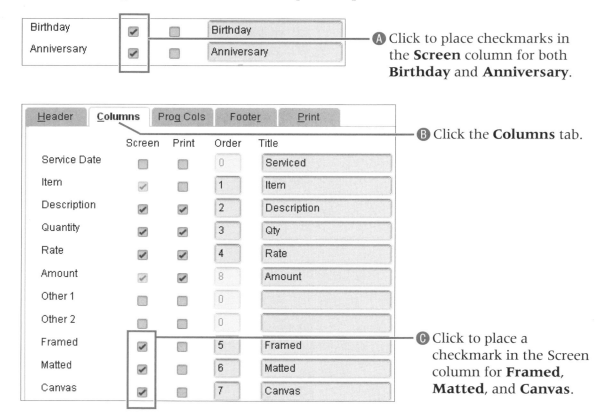

Ⓐ Click to place checkmarks in the **Screen** column for both **Birthday** and **Anniversary**.

Ⓑ Click the **Columns** tab.

Ⓒ Click to place a checkmark in the Screen column for **Framed**, **Matted**, and **Canvas**.

Notice the order column; it shows the order in which the columns will appear on the invoice from left to right.

12. Click **OK** in the Additional Customization window.

13. Feel free to play around and customize your template further, including using the Layout Designer!

14. When you are finished customizing your template, click **OK** in the Basic Customization window.

15. Close the **Templates** window.

Integrating with Microsoft Office and Mobile Apps

QuickBooks works very well with a variety of Microsoft Office Suite programs. For instance, you can import and export lists from Outlook, export reports to Excel, and merge data from QuickBooks with a Word document to produce letters for those with whom you work.

Sending Letters with Word

There are a large number of letter templates with which you can choose to work in Word, or you can customize your own. Once you have prepared your letter, QuickBooks will launch Word and merge your QuickBooks data into the letter for you.

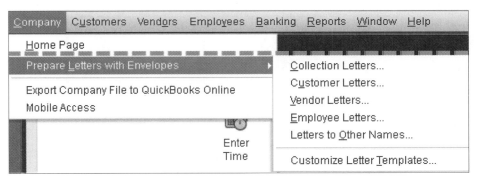

The option to create letters with Word is accessible from the Company menu.

Exporting QuickBooks Reports to Excel

While there are many reports provided for you in QuickBooks, even templates provided by other users, you may find that you would like more control over how you manage and display your QuickBooks data. To analyze your QuickBooks data more effectively, you may wish to export it to Microsoft Excel, a spreadsheet program, so you can use the advanced features available in it. QuickBooks makes it very easy to export and now update a report.

QuickBooks allows you to easily export a report or update an existing spreadsheet by clicking the Excel button on a report's toolbar.

Updating Excel Reports

One of the most exciting new features in QuickBooks 2012 was the ability for a user to update reports exported to Excel without having to reformat all of the data each time a new entry has been made in QuickBooks. What this means is that most of the formatting changes that you make to your QuickBooks data in Excel will be "memorized," so when you export that same report in the future, you will be able to update an existing worksheet rather than having to go in and change all of the formatting each time. Some of the formatting options that will be memorized for you are report titles, new formulas, row and column headers (both font changes and new header names), and inserted columns and rows.

You have two options for updating QuickBooks reports that have been exported to Excel. You can either initiate it from the report window in QuickBooks or from the Excel window while viewing the report.

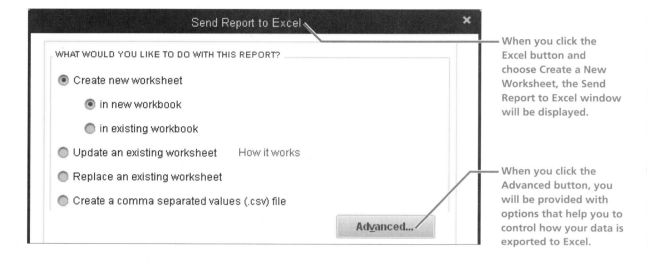

When you click the Excel button and choose Create a New Worksheet, the Send Report to Excel window will be displayed.

When you click the Advanced button, you will be provided with options that help you to control how your data is exported to Excel.

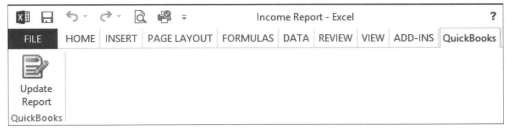

Advanced Excel Options ✕

QuickBooks Options:

Keep the following format options from QuickBooks:

- ☑ Fonts
- ☑ Space between columns
- ☑ Colors
- ☑ Row height

Excel Options:

Turn on the following Excel features:

- ☑ AutoFit (set column width to display all data)
- ☑ Freeze panes (keep headers and labels visible)
- ☑ Show Gridlines
- ☐ Auto Outline (allows collapsing / expanding)
- ☐ Auto Filtering (allows custom data filtering)
- ☑ Include QuickBooks Export Guide worksheet with helpful advice
- ☑ Create backup worksheet during update

Printing options:

Show report header:

- ◉ On printed report only
- ○ On printed report and screen
- ☑ Repeat row labels on each page

The Advanced Excel Options window lets you customize the report you will send to Excel.

Income Report - Excel

FILE | HOME | INSERT | PAGE LAYOUT | FORMULAS | DATA | REVIEW | VIEW | ADD-INS | QuickBooks

Update Report QuickBooks

When you are working in Excel with a spreadsheet containing data that has been exported from QuickBooks, you can update the spreadsheet using the QuickBooks tab from within Excel.

Advanced Skills

Accessing Your QuickBooks Data on a Mobile Device

QuickBooks provides an app for mobile devices, QuickBooks for Windows – Mobile Companion, that will allow you to access your information while you are on the go. You must purchase a subscription to utilize this service, and in order to learn more about it, see the Student Resource Center.

After you install the QuickBooks for Windows – Mobile Companion app on an Apple iPhone, you will see this screen when you click it, allowing you to log in to access your data or to learn more about the service.

QUICK REFERENCE	CREATING MICROSOFT WORD LETTERS THROUGH QUICKBOOKS
Task	**Procedure**
Create a letter for customers with QuickBooks data	■ Choose Company→Prepare Letters with Envelopes→Customer Letters. ■ Choose to copy the letter templates to your QuickBooks program folder, if necessary. ■ Follow the steps displayed to complete the letter(s).
Export a report to Excel	■ Create the report you wish to export. ■ Click the Export button on the report toolbar. ■ Choose the desired options; click Export.
Update an Excel spreadsheet with new QuickBooks data	■ Display the report you wish to update in QuickBooks. ■ Click the Excel button on the toolbar; choose Update Existing Worksheet. ■ Choose the worksheet you wish to update with new data; click Export. *or* ■ Display the Excel spreadsheet created from QuickBooks data. ■ Click the QuickBooks tab on the Excel Ribbon; click Update Report.

Work with Word and Excel in QuickBooks

In this exercise, you will produce letters for Olivia and Joanie to say Happy Birthday!

In order to complete this exercise, you must have a copy of Microsoft Word installed on your computer. If you do not have Word installed, skip this exercise and continue to the next topic.

1. Choose **Company→Prepare Letters with Envelopes→Customer Letters**.

2. Click **Copy** in order to place a copy of the QuickBooks letter templates in your default storage location, if necessary.

   The Letters and Envelopes window will appear, asking you to choose the recipients. By default, all customers are selected.

3. Follow these steps to select two customers:

Ⓐ Click **Unmark All**.

Ⓑ Click **Olivia York**.

Ⓒ Click **Dance a Little**.

4. Click **Next**.

   You will now have a chance to choose from a template or to create or edit your own template.

5. Scroll down, and then click to choose **Customer birthday**; click **Next**.

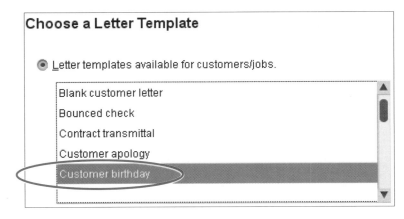

6. Follow these steps to set how you want to sign off on the letters:

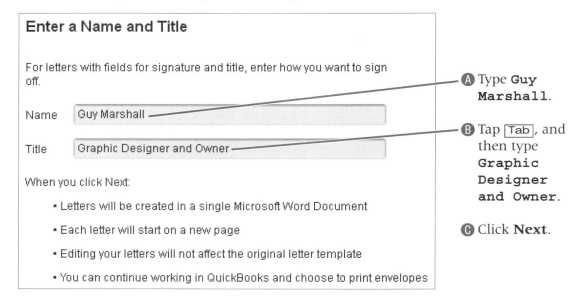

Enter a Name and Title

For letters with fields for signature and title, enter how you want to sign off.

Name   Guy Marshall

Title   Graphic Designer and Owner

When you click Next:

- Letters will be created in a single Microsoft Word Document
- Each letter will start on a new page
- Editing your letters will not affect the original letter template
- You can continue working in QuickBooks and choose to print envelopes

Ⓐ Type **Guy Marshall**.

Ⓑ Tap ⟨Tab⟩, and then type **Graphic Designer and Owner**.

Ⓒ Click **Next**.

QuickBooks will create the letter and launch Microsoft Word for you. If required information was missing from your customer record(s), you would see a "QuickBooks Information Is Missing" window explaining how to resolve the issue. Your letter will appear in a Microsoft Word window.

7. Follow these steps to modify the letter:

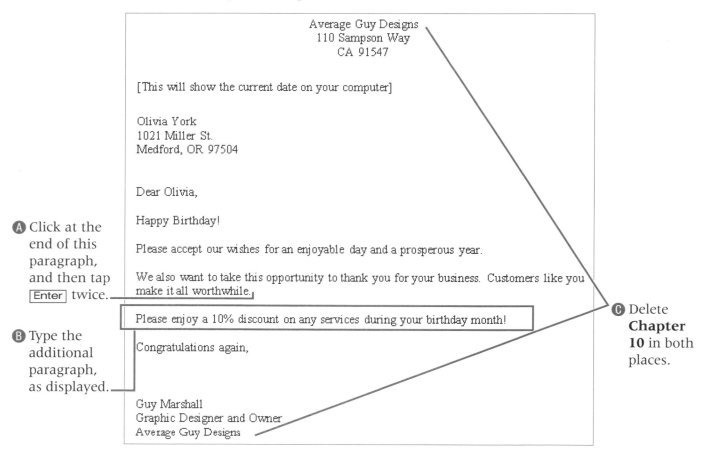

Average Guy Designs
110 Sampson Way
CA 91547

[This will show the current date on your computer]

Olivia York
1021 Miller St.
Medford, OR 97504

Dear Olivia,

Happy Birthday!

Please accept our wishes for an enjoyable day and a prosperous year.

We also want to take this opportunity to thank you for your business. Customers like you make it all worthwhile.

Please enjoy a 10% discount on any services during your birthday month!

Congratulations again,

Guy Marshall
Graphic Designer and Owner
Average Guy Designs

Ⓐ Click at the end of this paragraph, and then tap ⟨Enter⟩ twice.

Ⓑ Type the additional paragraph, as displayed.

Ⓒ Delete **Chapter 10** in both places.

8. Repeat the above steps to modify Joanie's letter as well.

9. Read the information presented regarding how to print the letters and envelopes, and then click **Next**.

Print Letters and Envelopes

Your options for printing letters and envelopes are:

- Print letters you've created by selecting Print in the Microsoft Word File menu

- Print envelopes in Microsoft Word by selecting Next on this screen

- Choose not to print envelopes by selecting Cancel on this screen

The Envelope Options window will appear.

10. Delete **Chapter 10** from the return address.

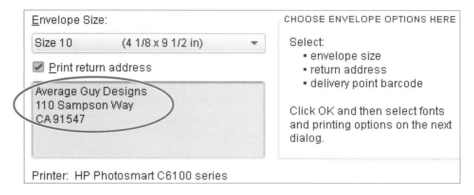

Envelope Size:

Size 10   (4 1/8 x 9 1/2 in)

☑ Print return address

Average Guy Designs
110 Sampson Way
CA 91547

CHOOSE ENVELOPE OPTIONS HERE

Select:
- envelope size
- return address
- delivery point barcode

Click OK and then select fonts and printing options on the next dialog.

Printer: HP Photosmart C6100 series

The envelope will appear in Word.

11. Click **OK** in the **Envelope Options** window in **Word** after making sure the printer options are correct.

12. Close all **Word** windows, and then close the **QuickBooks Letters and Envelopes** window.

Export a Report to Excel

Now you will export the report you memorized earlier to Excel. To complete this task, you will need to have Microsoft Excel 2003 or later installed on your computer.

13. Choose **Reports→Memorized Reports→Company→Income Report**.

14. Click the **Excel** button on the report toolbar, and then choose **Create New Worksheet**.

15. Ensure that your report data will be used to **create a new worksheet in a new workbook**.

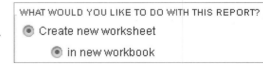

WHAT WOULD YOU LIKE TO DO WITH THIS REPORT?

◉ Create new worksheet

◉ in new workbook

16. Click **Export**.

17. Choose **File→Save As** from the Excel Ribbon.

18. Navigate to your file storage location, and then save the report as **Income Report**.

To learn more about how to work with your report in Excel, you may want to utilize a Labyrinth Learning Excel textbook for the version you are using (2013, 2010, 2007, etc.).

19. Close the **Microsoft Excel** window.

20. Close the **Income Report** window in QuickBooks.

Tackle the Tasks

Now is your chance to work a little more with Average Guy Designs and apply the skills that you have learned in this chapter to accomplish additional tasks. You will use the same company file you used in the Develop Your Skills exercises throughout this chapter. Enter the following tasks, referring back to the concepts in the chapter as necessary.

Delete Profile List Entries	Delete Retail and Wholesale from the Customer Type List.
Customize a report	Create a Balance Sheet Standard report and choose for it to display only assets. Set the date as of January 31, 2015. Customize it as you like, and then memorize it as `Assets Report`.
Create a custom form	Create a new template for sales receipts. Save it as `AGD Cash Sales`, and then customize it as you see fit.
Create a Letter in Word	Create a letter in Microsoft Word for Tim's BBQ Palooza, thanking him for the business and offering 10 percent off services through May 2015.
Export a Report to Excel	Open and then export the Assets Report to Excel. Save it in Excel as Assets Report.

Choose the appropriate option for your situation:

■ *If you are continuing on to the next chapter or to the end-of-chapter exercises, leave QuickBooks open.*

■ *If you are finished working in QuickBooks for now, choose* **File→Exit**.

Concepts Review

To check your knowledge of the key concepts introduced in this chapter, complete the Concepts Review quiz on the Student Resource Center or in your eLab course.

Reinforce Your Skills

Angela Stevens has just relocated her company, Quality-Built Construction, from California to Silverton, Oregon. You will be working with a QuickBooks Sample Company File in this exercise as it will allow you to run full payroll in a future chapter without having to purchase a payroll subscription.

Before you begin the Reinforce Your Skills exercises, complete one of these options:

■ Open **RYS_Chapter10** *from your file storage location.*

■ Restore **RYS_Chapter10 (Portable)** *from your file storage location. Make sure to place your last name and first initial at the end of the filename (e.g., RYS_Chapter10_StevensA).*

REINFORCE YOUR SKILLS 10-1
Create and Populate Custom Fields

In this exercise, you will create and populate a custom field.

1. Choose **Employees→Employee Center**.

2. Double-click to open **Mitchell, Clark** for editing.

3. Click the **Additional Info** tab, and then click the **Define Fields** button.

    Note that there are already three custom fields set up for customers and four for employees. You will create one more.

4. Type **Certification** as a label, and then place a check in the **Vend** and **Empl** columns to the right of the label.

5. Click **OK** twice to accept the new custom field.

6. Click in the **Certification** custom field for Clark Mitchell, and then type **Welding**.

7. Click **OK** to close the **Edit Employee** window.

8. Close the **Employee Center**.

    The custom field will now be available for all vendors and employees.

REINFORCE YOUR SKILLS 10-2
Add and Modify Profile List Entries

In this exercise, you will edit a profile list entry and then create a new one. Angela has just joined the local Chamber of Commerce, so she has decided to track new customers that come to her through her chamber participation.

1. Choose **Lists→Customer & Vendor Profile Lists→Customer Type List**.

2. Click the **Customer Type** button, and then choose **New**.

3. Type **From Chamber**, and then click **OK**.

4. Close the **Customer Type List** window.

Modify a Profile List Entry

5. Choose **Lists→Customer & Vendor Profile Lists→Customer Message List**.

6. Right-click **All work is complete!**, and then choose **Edit Customer Message**.

7. Type the message displayed in the following illustration.

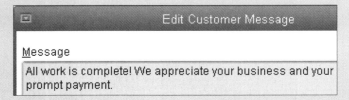

8. Click **OK**; close the **Customer Message List**.

REINFORCE YOUR SKILLS 10-3
Customize a Profit & Loss Report and Export to Excel

In this exercise, you will help Angela to create a customized Profit & Loss report for Quality-Built Construction.

1. Choose **Reports→Company & Financial→Profit & Loss Standard**.

2. Tap ⎡Tab⎤, type **010118**, tap ⎡Tab⎤ again, and then type **123118**.

3. Click the **Refresh** button on the Report toolbar.

Change the Columns Displayed

You will now display the columns by quarter across the top of the report.

4. Click the **Customize Report** button on the toolbar; choose the **Display** tab, if necessary.

5. Locate the **Columns** section of the window and choose to display the columns across the top by **Quarter**; click **OK**.

This report will allow you to compare the income and expenses from quarter to quarter.

Change the Formatting for the Header

You will now customize the formatting of the report for Angela.

6. Click the **Customize Report** button on the toolbar.

7. Display the **Header/Footer** tab.

8. Change the report title to **Profit & Loss by Quarter**.

9. Change the Alignment to **Left**.

10. Display the **Fonts & Numbers** tab.

11. Make any changes you like to the formatting of the fonts and numbers.

12. Click **OK** to save your changes.

13. Memorize the report, naming it **Profit & Loss by Quarter**; save it in the Company group.

14. Click the Excel button on the toolbar, and then choose **Create New Worksheet**.

15. Click **Export** in the **Send Report to Excel** window.

    Take a look at your customized report in Excel.

16. Save the report in **Excel** as **Profit & Loss by Quarter, 2018** in your file storage location.

17. Close **Excel** and the **Profit & Loss by Quarter** report.

REINFORCE YOUR SKILLS 10-4
Modify the Custom Estimate

In this exercise, you will create an appealing estimate template for Quality-Built Construction. You can make changes to a template directly from an open form, and that is the approach you will use to modify the estimate template.

1. Choose **Customers→Create Estimates**.

2. Ensure that **Custom Estimate** is the template displayed.

3. Click the **Formatting** tab of the Ribbon, and then click **Manage Templates**. Click **OK** in the Manage Templates window.

    The Basic Customization window displays.

4. In the **Company & Transaction** area of the window, choose to print the **Phone Number**.

5. Click **OK** in the **Layout Designer** window, choosing to not have it appear again in the future.

6. Choose to print the **Web Site Address**.

7. Change the font and color scheme of the template to your liking.

8. Click the **Additional Customization** button.

9. On the **Footer** tab, add a **Plain Text** that is to be printed:

    We stand behind all work that we do. Please let us know if you are not fully satisfied so that we can have a chance to make you happy.

Use Layout Designer

Finally, you will open the form in Layout Designer and make a few more changes.

10. Click the **Layout Designer** button.

11. Scroll down; select and move the **Phone #** and **Web Site** objects to the top of the form. (Hint: Select all four objects and move them simultaneously.)

12. Move and adjust any other objects around as you see fit.

13. When you have the template just right, click **OK** to save your changes.

14. Click **OK** in both the Additional Customization and the Basic Customization windows to save the changes to the template.

15. Close the **Create Estimates** window.

16. Choose the appropriate option for your situation:

    ■ If you are continuing on to the next chapter or the rest of the end-of-chapter exercises, leave QuickBooks open.

    ■ If you are finished working in QuickBooks for now, choose **File→Exit**.

Apply Your Skills

Before you begin the Apply Your Skills exercises, complete one of these options:

- *Open* **AYS_Chapter10** *from your file storage location.*
- *Restore* **AYS_Chapter10 (Portable)** *from your file storage location. Make sure to place your last name and first initial at the end of the filename (e.g., AYS_Chapter10_JamesS).*

APPLY YOUR SKILLS 10-1
Create Custom Fields

In this exercise, you will create a custom field and populate it for customers.

1. Open the **Customer Center**.
2. Double-click **Becky Karakash:Dog-Spencer**, and then click the **Additional Info** tab.
3. Click the **Define Fields** button.
4. Add the following **Labels** for Customers: `Species`, `Breed`, `Color`, and `Gender`.
5. Click **OK** twice to add the new custom fields.
6. Fill in the custom fields for Spencer using the following information:
   - Species: `Canine`
   - Breed: `Golden Retriever`
   - Color: `Light Brown`
   - Gender: `Male`
7. Click **OK** to close the Edit Job window.
8. Close the **Customer Center**.

APPLY YOUR SKILLS 10-2
Customize a Profit & Loss Report

In this exercise, you will help Sadie to create a customized Profit & Loss report.

1. Choose **Reports→Company & Financial→Profit & Loss Standard**.
2. Tap Tab, type `050114`, tap Tab again, and then type `053014`.
3. Click the **Refresh** button on the Report toolbar.

Change the Columns Displayed

You will now display the columns by week across the top of the report.

4. Click the **Customize Report** button on the toolbar.

5. Choose the **Display** tab, if necessary.

6. Locate the **Columns** section of the window and choose to display the columns across the **top by week**; click **OK**.

   This report will allow you to compare the income and expenses from week to week.

Change the Formatting for the Header

Sadie doesn't like the look of the default header, and she needs your help to get it just right.

7. Click the **Customize Report** button on the toolbar.

8. Display the **Header/Footer** tab.

9. Change the report title to **Profit & Loss by Week**.

10. Change the Alignment to **Left**.

11. Display the **Fonts & Numbers** tab.

12. Make any changes you like to the formatting of the fonts and numbers.

13. Click **OK** to save your changes.

14. Memorize the report, naming it **Profit & Loss by Week**; finally, close the report.

APPLY YOUR SKILLS 10-3

Modify the Custom Sales Receipt

In this exercise, you will create an appealing sales receipt for Wet Noses. You can make changes to a template directly from an open form, and that is the approach you will use to modify the sales receipt template.

1. Choose **Customers→Enter Sales Receipts**.

2. Click the **Formatting** tab of the Ribbon, and then click **Manage Templates**. Click **OK** in the Manage Templates window.

   The Basic Customization window displays.

3. In the **Company & Transaction** area of the window, choose to print the **company phone number**.

4. Close the **Layout Designer** window, choosing to not have it appear again in the future.

5. Choose to print the **company fax number**.

6. Change the font and color scheme of the template to your liking.

7. Click the **Additional Customization** button.

8. On the **Footer** tab, add a long text that is to be printed:

   We care about your pets! Please let us know if you see anything out of the ordinary for your pet so that we may help as early as possible.

Use Layout Designer

Finally, you will open the form in Layout Designer and make a few more changes.

9. Click the **Layout Designer** button.

10. Scroll down; select and move the **Phone #** and **Fax #** objects to the top of the form. *(Hint: Select all four objects and move them simultaneously.)*

11. Move any other objects around as you see fit.

12. When you have the template just right, click **OK** to save your changes.

13. Click **OK** in both the Additional Customization and the Basic Customization windows to save the changes to the template.

14. Close the **Enter Sales Receipt** window.

APPLY YOUR SKILLS 10-4

Answer Questions with Reports

In this exercise, you will answer questions for Dr. James by running reports. You may wish to display the Report Center in List View to help you answer the questions. Ask your instructor if you should print the reports, print (save) them as PDF files, export them to Excel, or simply display them on the screen.

1. Would you please print a Profit & Loss report that shows the income and expenses by month for the months of May and June 2014? Make sure to add some color to spice it up a bit.

2. Would you please create a summary balance sheet report that shows weekly columns for May 2014?

3. Is is possible to create a report that shows a summary of all expenses by vendor that are over $500 during June 2014?

4. Could you please create an inventory item price list that displays both the account that the sales are routed to and the quantity on hand? If you could name it "Inventory Price List" and align the title to the left it would be great!

5. Is it possible to create a "prettier" invoice for our customers? If so, could you please create a draft of one and print it for me to review?

6. Submit your reports based on the guidelines provided by your instructor.

7. Choose the appropriate option for your situation:

   - If you are continuing on to the next chapter or the Extend Your Skills exercises, leave QuickBooks open.

   - If you are finished working in QuickBooks for now, choose **File→Exit**.

Extend Your Skills

In the course of working through the following Extend Your Skills exercises, you will be utilizing various skills taught in this and previous chapter(s). Take your time and think carefully about the tasks presented to you. Turn back to the chapter content if you need assistance.

10-1 Sort Through the Stack

Before You Begin: Restore the **EYS1_Chapter10 (Portable)** file or open the **EYS1_Chapter10** company file from your storage location.

You have been hired by Arlaine Cervantes to help her with her organization's books. She is the founder of Niños del Lago, a nonprofit organization that provides impoverished Guatemalan children with an engaging educational camp experience. You have just sat down at your desk and opened a large envelope from her with a variety of documents and noticed that you have several emails from her as well. It is your job to sort through the papers and emails and make sense of what you find, entering information into QuickBooks whenever appropriate and answering any other questions in a word-processing document saved as **EYS1_Chapter10_LastnameFirstinitial**. Remember, you are digging through papers you just dumped out of an envelope and addressing random emails from Arlaine, so it is up to you to determine the correct order in which to complete the tasks.

- Note: The invoice that we send out is so boring looking...Would you please fancy it up a bit, add a picture (as a logo) that relates to the Guatemalan culture, and make it a bit more colorful? Also, please include our U.S. office phone number on the invoice.

- Printed copy of Balance Sheet report: A note on the report reads, "Please change the font on this report and make the title align to the right. Make the color of the heading match the color on the new invoice template. Memorize it or something so it will be easy for you to run it next time with the same look."

- Note from Arlaine: Please send letters to all of our donors thanking them for their support during 2014 and inviting them down to visit the camp.

- Note from Arlaine: I would like to indicate the color of the scarves that we sell on our sales forms. Is there a way to add this information? Can you make it appear on the new invoice template that you created?

10-2 Be Your Own Boss

Before You Begin: You must complete Extend Your Skills 9-2 before you begin this exercise.

In this exercise, throughout the entire book, you will build on the company file that you outlined in previous chapters. If you have created a file for your actual business, then create all of the new customer and vendor profile list entries that you have been or will be using, create any relevant custom fields for your business, create customized balance sheet and Profit & Loss reports and export them to Excel so that you can easily update them when you enter new data, and create a custom template for your company invoices. If you are creating a fictitious company, then create or modify at least seven customer and vendor profile list entries, create at least three custom fields for your inventory items, customize and memorize both a balance sheet and Profit & Loss report, and create a custom template for invoices. You will make up the names and information for this exercise.

Produce your customized balance sheet and Profit & Loss reports, submitting them to your instructor based on the instructions provided.

Open the company file you worked on in Extend Your Skills 9-2 and complete the tasks outlined above. When you are done, save it as a portable company file, naming it as **EYS2_Chapter10_ LastnameFirstinitial (Portable)** and submit it to your instructor based on the instructions provided.

10-3 Use the Web as a Learning Tool

Throughout this book, you will be provided with an opportunity to use the Internet as a learning tool by completing WebQuests. According to the original creators of WebQuests, as described on their website (http://WebQuest.org), a WebQuest is "an inquiry-oriented activity in which most or all of the information used by learners is drawn from the web." To complete the WebQuest projects in this book, navigate to the Student Resource Center and choose the WebQuest for the chapter on which you are working. The subject of each WebQuest will be relevant to the material found in the chapter.

WebQuest Subject: Shared reporting and custom templates

UNIT

3

Additional Skills

UNIT OUTLINE

Additional Skills

In this final unit, we'll cover all stages of the accounting cycle and review generally accepted accounting principles (GAAP) before taking on the use of classes in QuickBooks. You'll work through details of the accounting cycle steps, as well as how to use classes in QuickBooks, produce statements, make general and inventory adjusting journal entries, become familiar with the major end-of-period financial reports, and close the books in QuickBooks.

Introducing the Accounting Cycle and Using Classes

CHAPTER OUTLINE

CHAPTER OBJECTIVES

After studying this chapter, you will be able to:

- Work with the accounting cycle and GAAP
- Turn on class tracking
- Use classes in transactions
- Set price levels
- Create a Statement of Cash Flows

In this chapter, you will learn about the accounting cycle and review generally accepted accounting principles (GAAP) before taking on the use of classes in QuickBooks. Throughout this chapter, you will work in depth on the first three steps of the accounting cycle while exploring classes and how to use price levels in transactions. Using classes in QuickBooks allows you to classify transactions to give you more data with which to manage your business. Wrapping up this chapter, you will have the opportunity to learn about and produce a Statement of Cash Flows.

Average Guy Designs

In this chapter you will continue working with Average Guy Designs as you go a step past "behind the scenes" and look at the steps of the accounting cycle. You will have a chance to work closely with the first three steps as well as with classes and price levels. Finally, you will examine the cash flow for the business and the net income by class by using QuickBooks reports.

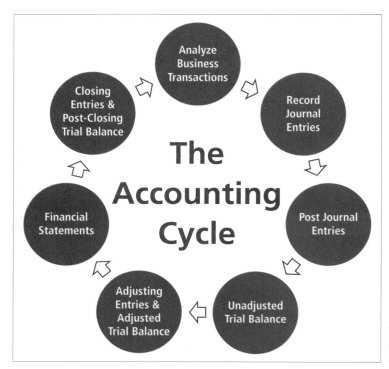

The Accounting Cycle is made up of seven separate steps. We will look at the first three in this chapter.

Average Guy Designs, Chapter 11
Statement of Cash Flows
December 2014 through January 2015

	Dec '14 - Jan 15
▼ OPERATING ACTIVITIES	
Net Income	3,340.43
▼ Adjustments to reconcile Net Income	
▼ to net cash provided by operations:	
11000 · Accounts Receivable	-3,571.07
12100 · Inventory Asset	-1,379.00
20000 · Accounts Payable	1,858.58
Net cash provided by Operating Activities	248.94
Net cash increase for period	248.94
Cash at beginning of period	12,815.02
Cash at end of period	**13,063.96**

The Statement of Cash Flows helps you to determine the "liquidity" of your company.

Exploring the Accounting Cycle and GAAP

Now we will dive deeper into what occurs behind the scenes in QuickBooks. So far you have had a glimpse of this through the Behind the Scenes and Flashback to the GAAP features of this book. Next we will look at how the accounting cycle and GAAP apply to QuickBooks users. If you are interested in a text that provides full coverage of these concepts and will help to you develop a strong understanding of accounting, you should check out Accounting Basics: An Introduction for Non-Accounting Majors published by Labyrinth Learning. Much of the following information is borrowed from this text, and it is a great supplementary text for any QuickBooks class.

Time to Review the Generally Accepted Accounting Principles (GAAP)

If you recall from Chapter 1, Introducing QuickBooks Pro, GAAP are rules used to prepare, present, and report financial statements for a wide variety of entities.

As GAAP attempts to achieve basic objectives, they have several basic assumptions, principles, and constraints. They are outlined in the following table.

GENERALLY ACCEPTED ACCOUNTING PRINCIPLES (GAAP)	
Principle	**Description**
Business entity principle	The business is separate from the owners and from other businesses. Revenues and expenses of the business should be kept separate from the personal expenses of the business owner.
The assumption of the going concern	The business will be in operation indefinitely.
Monetary unit principle	A stable currency is going to be the unit of record.
Time-period principle	The activities of the business can be divided into time periods.
Cost principle	When a company purchases assets, it should record them at cost, not fair market value. For example, an item worth $750 bought for $100 is recorded at $100.
Revenue principle	Publicly traded companies (sole proprietorships can operate using either basis) record when the revenue is realized and earned (accrual basis of accounting), not when cash is received (cash basis of accounting).
Matching principle	Expenses need to be matched with revenues. If a contractor buys a specific sink for a specific bathroom, it is matched to the cost of remodeling the bathroom. Otherwise, the cost may be charged as an expense to the project. This principle allows a better evaluation of the profitability and performance (how much did you spend to earn the revenue?).
Objectivity principle	The statements of a company should be based on objectivity.
Materiality principle	When an item is reported, its significance should be considered. An item is considered significant when it would affect the decision made regarding its use.
Consistency principle	The company uses the same accounting principles and methods from year to year.
Prudence principle	When choosing between two solutions, the one that will be least likely to overstate assets and income should be selected.

Introducing the Accounting Cycle

Accounting records are kept and used to produce financial information. The records are kept for a period of time called a *fiscal period*. A fiscal period can be any length of time. It may be a month or even a quarter of the year. Most businesses use a year as their fiscal period. A business does not need to use the dates January 1 through December 31 as its fiscal period. Many businesses start their fiscal period in February and end in January. Government and educational institutions often use a fiscal period that begins July 1 and ends June 30.

The Steps of the Accounting Cycle

The accounting cycle is a series of steps that help the business to keep its accounting records properly during the fiscal period. Prior to the steps outlined below, you should make sure to collect source documents and verify the financial information.

1. Analyze the business transactions.
2. Record the business transactions (both debit and credit parts) in a journal.
3. Post each journal entry to the ledger accounts.
4. Prepare the unadjusted trial balance.
5. Prepare adjusting entries and an adjusted trial balance.
6. Generate the financial statements.
7. Prepare closing entries and the post-closing trial balance.

Who uses this information? Many people do. Business owners need to know how the business is doing. Banks, when they consider lending money to a business owner, need to know what is happening. The government, when assessing taxes on small businesses, needs to know how much revenue the business is generating.

If you took a careful look at the steps of the accounting cycle, you probably saw that QuickBooks takes care of a lot it behind the scenes for you. But remember that if you leave too much to QuickBooks and don't exercise some common sense, you will be in trouble.

Throughout this chapter, we will look at the first three steps of the accounting cycle and how, together, you and QuickBooks can work as a team to ensure your books accurately document what is happening behind the scenes.

Collecting and Verifying Source Documents

In order to complete the first step in the accounting cycle and analyze transactions, you must first ensure that the information on source documents is recorded correctly in QuickBooks. Source documents take many forms. Whether it is a receipt, check stub, utility bill, memo documenting the transaction, or another document, it is up to you to verify the information on it because QuickBooks can't do it for you. But, as you learned in Chapter 5, Banking with QuickBooks, QuickBooks does make it easy for you to keep track of source documents through the Doc Center feature.

The QuickBooks Doc Center

The Doc Center feature provides you with the ability to store your source documents electronically, attaching them to the transactions or list entries to which they belong. QuickBooks allows you to enter documents into the Doc Center through a variety of methods, including:

- Drag and drop from Windows Explorer or Outlook
- From a scanner
- From another storage location accessible to your computer

While it is very convenient and affordable to utilize the Doc Center, the files contained within it are not secure, so you need to take additional precautions when storing documents with sensitive information. You may wish to consider a third-party secure document management service (such as SmartVault™) that interfaces well with the QuickBooks Doc Center and provides security features to protect sensitive information.

These buttons allow you to add documents by searching your computer or scanning.

You can drag and drop documents into the drop zone.

Note the documents that have been saved in the Doc Center.

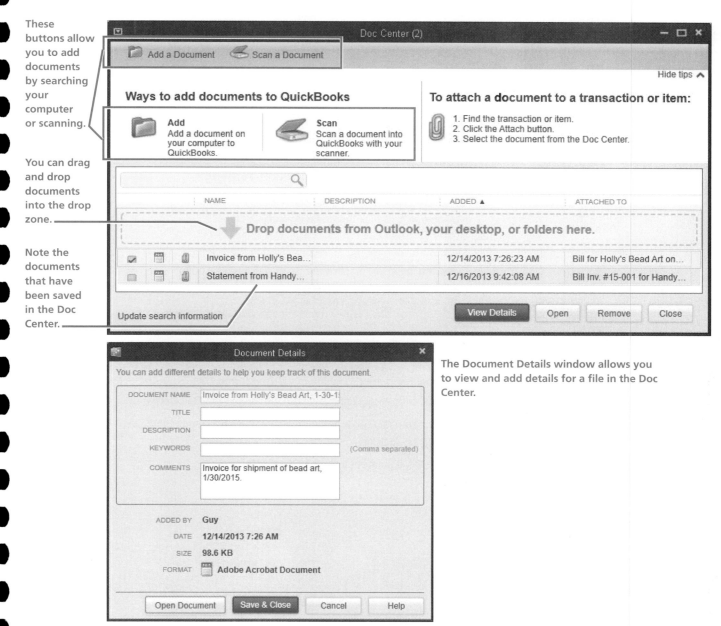

The Document Details window allows you to view and add details for a file in the Doc Center.

Additional Skills

The date that displays in your company file will be different as it is captured from your computer's clock when the document is added.

Cycle Step 1: Analyze Business Transactions

Once you have compiled and verified the source documents, you are ready to analyze the transaction, QuickBooks style. When you perform this analysis, you will need to answer the following questions from the perspective of *your business*:

- Which accounts are involved and what type are they?
- Is each account increased or decreased?
- Which account(s) is/are debited and for what amount?
- Which account(s) is/are credited and for what amount?
- What does the completed entry look like?

The good news here is that in the Behind the Scenes feature throughout this book, you have been seeing this analysis in action. You will just now have the opportunity to perform it for yourself!

QUICK REFERENCE	USING THE DOC CENTER
Task	**Procedure**
Open the Doc Center	▪ Choose Company→Documents→Doc Center.
Add a file located on your computer to the Doc Center	▪ Open the Doc Center; click the Add a Document button. ▪ Navigate to and click the desired file; click Open.
Add a file to the Doc Center by scanning	▪ Make sure your computer is connected to the scanner. ▪ Open the Doc Center; click the Scan a Document button. ▪ Choose a scan profile; click Scan.
Drag and drop a file from Outlook into the Doc Center	▪ Open Outlook and display the message with the attachment you wish to add to the Doc Center. ▪ Open the Doc Center. ▪ Move windows as needed to ensure that you can see both the Outlook attachment and the drop zone in the Doc Center. ▪ Drag and drop the attachment from Outlook to the Doc Center.
Attach a document to a transaction or item	▪ Open the transaction or item to which you wish to attach a document. ▪ Click the Attach button. ▪ Choose the document from the Doc Center.

Work with the Doc Center and Analyze Transactions

In this exercise, you will work with the Doc Center and analyze transactions. The first step is to open QuickBooks, and then either open a company file or restore a portable company file.

Intuit provides maintenance releases throughout the lifetime of the product. These updates may require you to update your student exercise files before you begin working with them. Please follow the prompts on the screen if you are asked to update your company file to the latest QuickBooks release.

1. Start **QuickBooks 2014**.

   If you downloaded the student exercise files in the portable company file *format, follow Option 1 below. If you downloaded the files in the* company file *format, follow Option 2 below.*

Option 1: Restore a Portable Company File

2. Choose **File→Open or Restore Company**.

3. Restore the **DYS_Chapter11 (Portable)** portable company file for this chapter from your file storage location, placing your last name and first initial at the end of the filename (e.g., DYS_Chapter11_MarshallG).

   It may take a few moments for the portable company file to open. Once it does, continue with step 5.

Option 2: Open a Company File

2. Choose **File→Open or Restore Company**, ensure that **Open a regular company file** is selected, and then open the **DYS_Chapter11** company file from your file storage location.

   The QuickBooks company file will open.

3. Click **OK** to close the QuickBooks Information window. Click **No** in the Set Up External Accountant User window, if necessary.

4. Close the **Reminders** window.

Explore and Use the Doc Center
You will copy a document from your file storage location into the Doc Center.

5. Choose **Company→Documents→Doc Center**.

   The Doc Center window will be displayed.

6. Click the **Add a Document** button.

   The Select Documents to add to Inbox window will be displayed.

7. Follow these steps to select the file to add:

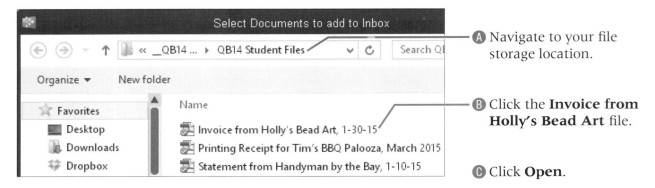

Ⓐ Navigate to your file storage location.

Ⓑ Click the **Invoice from Holly's Bead Art** file.

Ⓒ Click **Open**.

The Holly's Bead Art Invoice file will be displayed in the Doc Center.

View and Edit the Details of a File in the Doc Center

Now you will view the details for a file in the Doc Center and add a comment.

8. Follow these steps to open a file for viewing:

Ⓐ Click in the **checkbox** to select the invoice.

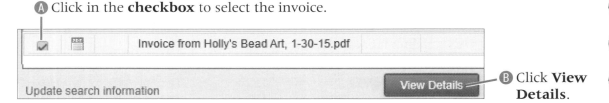

Ⓑ Click **View Details**.

The Document Details window will appear.

9. Click in the **Comments** field.

10. Type the comment as displayed in the figure below.

11. Click **Save & Close**.

The information will be added to the details for the document, and the Doc Center will be displayed.

12. Close the **Doc Center**.

Enter a Bill and Attach a Document

You will now open a transaction in QuickBooks and attach the source document to it.

13. Choose **Vendors→Vendor Center**.

14. Follow these steps to choose the vendor and transaction:

Ⓐ Single-click to select **Holly's Bead Art**. Ⓑ Double-click the **Bill** dated **01/30/2015**.

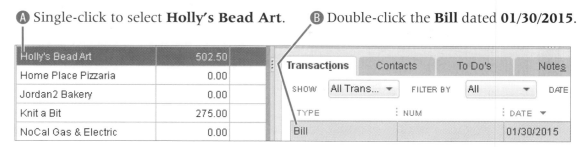

15. Click the **Attach File** button on the **Ribbon**.

16. Follow these steps to attach the document from the **Doc Center**:

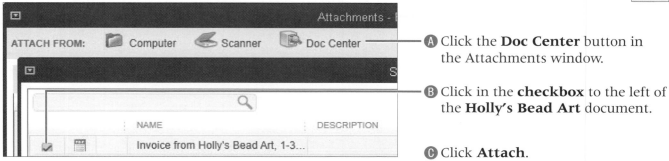

Ⓐ Click the **Doc Center** button in the Attachments window.

Ⓑ Click in the **checkbox** to the left of the **Holly's Bead Art** document.

Ⓒ Click **Attach**.

17. Click **Done**.

18. Look at the **Attach File** button on the **Ribbon**.

The button will change and will display the number of files attached to the transaction.

19. Click **Save & Close**; close the **Vendor Center**.

Analyze Business Transactions

You will now take a look at a variety of transactions and analyze each one in the table displayed below. You may print a copy of this table from the Student Resource Center if you do not wish to write in the book.

20. Complete the following table by answering the questions about each transaction in the space provided.

	Invoice #14-0024	Sales Receipt #1	Bill dated 1/16/15 for Knit a Bit, Ref. No. AGD-01-2015	Payment received on invoice #14-0024, dated 1/21/15	Deposit made to checking on 2/4/15
Which accounts are involved and what type are they?					
Is each account increased or decreased?					
Which account(s) is/are debited and for what amount?					
Which account(s) is/are credited and for what amount?					

The last question of "What does the completed entry look like?" is not included because you will be using the completed entry in order to answer the rest of the questions!

Working with Classes

Classes provide an additional way to track information about transactions. They allow you to keep an eye on particular segments of your business (such as new construction vs. remodel), tracking income and expenses for each. This way, if you wanted to evaluate which segment of the business was most profitable, it would be easy to do since your transactions contain class information that can easily be displayed on reports. Class tracking is a tool for you to use with your unique business, so you really need to think about what you want to see on your reports and base your class tracking on that.

What Are Classes?

You use classes to track income and expenses for different areas of your company; they classify transactions. Classes are not tied to any particular customer, vendor, or item. If you want to track types of customers, jobs, or vendors, use the profile lists QuickBooks provides. You use these "type" lists to classify customers, jobs, and vendors. An important rule to remember about classes is that you should use them to track only *one* particular aspect of your business. For instance, you should not use classes to track both locations and team performance; you will need to choose one aspect of your business and create classes only for that aspect.

Common Uses for Classes

There are many ways to use classes. The following table provides some examples of how classes are used by various types of companies or industries.

CLASS EXAMPLES FOR VARIOUS INDUSTRIES	
Industry	**Class Examples**
Construction	Crews of workers, locations of jobs
Design Firm	Individual employees, locations
Not-for-profit	Specific programs, administrative overhead
Restaurant	By business segment (bar, food, catering)
Retail	By department (accessories, ready to wear, shoes)
Consulting	Locations (North County, South County)

Do not use classes to track types of customers or vendors because QuickBooks already provides profile lists for these purposes. Since you can use classes to track only one aspect of your business, you will have eliminated this valuable tool if you use it to duplicate a specific list provided by QuickBooks.

A Class Example

Originally, Average Guy Designs considered using classes to track customers who were Chamber members and those who were not. Once this matter was discussed with the company's CPA, it was understood that QuickBooks already provides a list to track types of customers and that classes are meant to track an aspect of the business for which QuickBooks doesn't provide a list. It was then decided to use the class feature to track the work performed by individual employees (realize that one customer can have work done by multiple employees), with overhead as the class that is the "catch all" for income and expenses that are not easily attributed to one of the "main" classes. Guy had also thought about using classes to track jobs by location, but it was decided that it would be more meaningful to the business to use classes as shown in the following illustration.

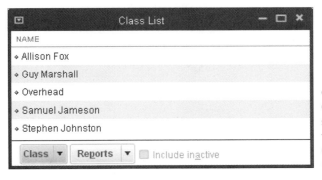

Classes are set up in the Class List in QuickBooks and are used to track a specific aspect of the business. They are flexible in that you can choose how to (and whether to) use the feature for your unique company.

Setting Up and Managing Classes

Before you can use class tracking in QuickBooks, you must turn on the preference. The Class List looks and functions similarly to some of the other lists you have worked with thus far. For example, QuickBooks won't allow you to delete a class that has been used in any transaction. Once you turn on this preference, class fields will appear on sales forms and in other locations. You can edit classes much the same way that you have edited other list entries.

Planning for Class Tracking

As you may recall from Chapter 2, Creating a Company, when you create a new company in QuickBooks, you should take time to plan what you need the company to do for you. Before you begin to track classes in QuickBooks, think about what type of reporting you need for your company and exactly what information you need to display on your reports.

When you are setting up classes for your own company, make sure to also create a class for any type of transaction that doesn't apply to one of your named classes (such as "Overhead" or "Administrative"). This is important because you want to make sure that you apply a class to every transaction involving an income and/or expense once you set up your company to track classes.

Using Classes for Profit Center Reporting

Many businesses use classes for profit center reporting. A profit center is a sector of a business for which income and expenses are tracked separately so that its individual profitability can be determined. One type of business that often relies on profit center reporting, in order to ensure that the entire business is operating efficiently, is farming.

Utilizing Subclasses

Even though you are only allowed to use classes to track a single aspect of your business, you can use subclasses to classify your data further. For instance, a restaurant can set up "main" classes to track income and expenses by location and then list food, bar, and catering as subclasses under each location (main class).

Some Examples of Subclasses in Action

The following table lists examples of subclasses that might be used with a class.

Industry	Class	Subclasses
Construction	Crews of workers	Location
Restaurant	Location	Bar, food, catering

Do *not* use classes to track more than one aspect of your business. If you need additional tracking, use subclasses. If you use classes to track more than one aspect, it will render the class data meaningless.

Task	Procedure
Turn on class tracking	■ Choose Edit→Preferences. ■ Click the Accounting category, and then the Company Preferences tab. ■ Click to check the Use Class Tracking box; click OK.
Create a new class	■ Choose Lists→Class List. ■ Click the Class menu button; choose New. ■ Type the name of the new class; click OK.
Edit a class	■ Choose Lists→Class List; click to select the class you wish to edit. ■ Click the Class menu button; choose Edit. ■ Make any desired changes; click OK.
Delete a class	■ Choose Lists→Class List. ■ Click to select the desired class, click the Class menu button, and then choose Delete. ■ Click OK to confirm the deletion.
Create a subclass	■ Choose Lists→Class List. ■ Click the Class menu button; choose New. ■ Type the name of the subclass; click to choose Subclass Of. ■ Choose the class to which you wish to assign it; click OK.

DEVELOP YOUR SKILLS 11-2

Turn On Class Tracking

In this exercise, you will turn on the class tracking feature of QuickBooks.

1. Choose **Edit→Preferences**.

2. Follow these steps to turn on the class tracking preference:

Ⓐ Click the **Accounting** category.

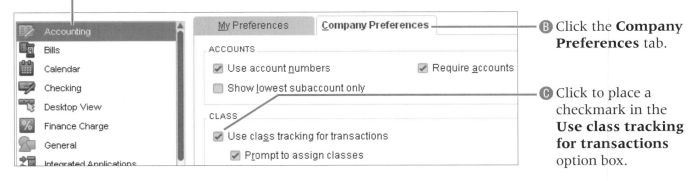

Ⓑ Click the **Company Preferences** tab.

Ⓒ Click to place a checkmark in the **Use class tracking for transactions** option box.

3. Click **OK** to activate the new preference.

Once you turn on this preference, QuickBooks will add class fields to many forms and registers such as the Create Invoices form, Enter Bills form, and customer Accounts Receivable reports. You can also run reports such as the Profit & Loss by Class now.

Additional Skills

Populate the Class List

You will now help Guy to enter the individual employees into the Class List.

4. Choose **Lists→Class List**.

5. Type **Guy Marshall**, and then click **Next**.

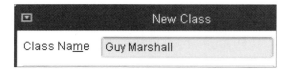

6. Using step 5 as an example, create a class for the remaining employees: **Stephen Johnston**, **Samuel Jameson**, and **Allison Fox**.

7. Click **OK** after creating the final class.

   Notice the classes are set up to track income and expenses based on employees.

8. Close the **Class List**.

Applying Classes to Transactions

You should apply classes to all transactions involving an income and/or expense account once the preference is set up. You can enter the class information on forms, registers, or journal entries. Once you have used classes in transactions, you can display them in reports and create budgets based on them. You can also apply classes to payroll transactions—either to a whole paycheck or to individual earning items.

Consistent Class Applications

Once you begin using class tracking, it is important to consistently apply a class to *every* transaction that deals with income and expense accounts so that your data, and therefore your reporting, is meaningful. If you apply classes to only some transactions and then create a report to show the profitability by class, the information will be skewed. This is why it is important to create a class (such as "Overhead") for transactions that don't fit one of your main classes.

Choosing Classes on Forms

Once you have set up your classes in QuickBooks, you can choose them on forms. You can find the class field in windows such as Create Invoices, Create Purchase Orders, and Pay Bills.

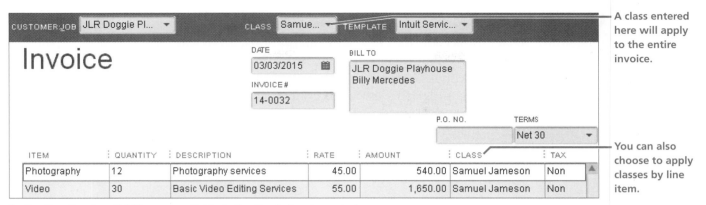

CUSTOMER:JOB JLR Doggie Pl... | CLASS Samue... | TEMPLATE Intuit Servic...

A class entered here will apply to the entire invoice.

Invoice

DATE 03/03/2015

INVOICE # 14-0032

BILL TO
JLR Doggie Playhouse
Billy Mercedes

P.O. NO. | TERMS Net 30

ITEM	QUANTITY	DESCRIPTION	RATE	AMOUNT	CLASS	TAX
Photography	12	Photography services	45.00	540.00	Samuel Jameson	Non
Video	30	Basic Video Editing Services	55.00	1,650.00	Samuel Jameson	Non

You can also choose to apply classes by line item.

Notice that the class field is now available in the Create Invoices window.

Cycle Step 2: Record Journal Entries

Since QuickBooks does the work behind the scenes for you, by entering a transaction in a QuickBooks form correctly, you will include the necessary general journal information. When entering any transaction, you must ensure that you are following GAAP. If you were doing this by hand, you would need to enter:

■ The date of the transaction

■ The account names and amounts of each of the debit and credit parts

■ A reference to the source document or a brief explanation

In QuickBooks, you need to ensure that your items are set up properly (i.e., routed to the right accounts) so the proper accounts will be debited and credited in the journal that is kept behind the scenes for you.

Average Guy Designs, Chapter 11
Journal
All Transactions

Trans #	Type	Date	Num	Adj	Name	Memo	Account	Debit	Credit
1	Transfer	11/30/2014				Funds Trans...	30000 · Opening B...		5,432.67
						Funds Trans...	10000 · Checking	5,432.67	
								5,432.67	5,432.67
2	Deposit	11/30/2014				Account Op...	10200 · Savings	7,382.35	
						Account Op...	30000 · Opening B...		7,382.35
								7,382.35	7,382.35
3	Invoice	12/01/2014	14-0...		Evelyn Huff:Projec...		11000 · Accounts...	105.00	
					Evelyn Huff:Projec...	T-shirt and i...	43200 · Design Inc...		105.00
								105.00	105.00
4	Invoice	12/03/2014	14-0...		Ashley Hakola:Pro...		11000 · Accounts...	120.00	
					Ashley Hakola:Pro...	Design of w...	43200 · Design Inc...		120.00
								120.00	120.00
5	Invoice	12/03/2014	14-0...		Lucy's Cupcake Fa...		11000 · Accounts...	400.00	
					Lucy's Cupcake Fa...	Branding for...	43200 · Design Inc...		400.00
								400.00	400.00

QuickBooks keeps a journal for you as you enter each transaction. Note the first five transactions that were entered into the Average Guy Designs company file.

Cycle Step 3: Post Journal Entries

In the third step of the accounting cycle, you find the entries that were entered into the general journal posted to the individual ledger accounts. This step is done entirely behind the scenes for you. (Thank you, QuickBooks!) If you recall in Chapter 5, Banking with QuickBooks, you can double-click to view a register for a balance sheet account and a QuickReport for any income or expense account to see the transactions affecting the account. When you view these registers and QuickReports, you will be able to see that the amounts have been properly posted from transactions to the underlying accounts.

DATE	NUMBER	CUSTOMER	ITEM	QTY	RATE	AMT CHRG	AMT PAID
	TYPE	DESCRIPTION		CLASS		BILLED DATE	DUE DATE
12/01/2014	14-0001	Evelyn Huff:Project #1					
	INV						Paid

11000 · Accounts Receivable

Go to... | Print... | Edit Transaction | QuickReport

Average Guy Designs, Chapter 11
Account QuickReport
December 2014

Accrual Basis

Type	Date	Num	Name	Memo	Split	Amount
43200 · Design Income						
Invoice	12/01/2014	14-0001	Evelyn Huff:Project #1	T-shirt and i...	11000 · Acco...	105.00
Invoice	12/03/2014	14-0002	Ashley Hakola:Project #2	Design of w...	11000 · Acco...	120.00

Notice that the third transaction entered in the journal can be found in both the Accounts Receivable register (there is no amount displayed as it has been paid) and on the Design Income Account QuickReport.

QUICK REFERENCE	ASSIGNING CLASSES TO TRANSACTIONS
Task	**Procedure**
Use a class on an invoice	■ Choose Customers→Create Invoices; enter all of the sales information.
	■ Enter the appropriate class for each line item or the entire invoice.
	■ Click Save & Close or Save & New.

DEVELOP YOUR SKILLS 11-3
Work with Classes in Transactions

In this exercise, you will help Allison to utilize classes in transactions beginning on March 1, 2015. First you will add a new job for JLR Doggie Playhouse, and then you will create an invoice for it with a class.

1. Choose **Customers→Customer Center.**

2. Scroll down the Customers & Jobs List, right-click **JLR Doggie Playhouse**, and then choose **Add Job.**

3. Type Project #26 as the **Job Name**, and then click **OK.**
   The Customer Center will be displayed with the new job selected.

Create an Invoice with Class

4. Click the **New Transactions** button, and then select **Invoices.**

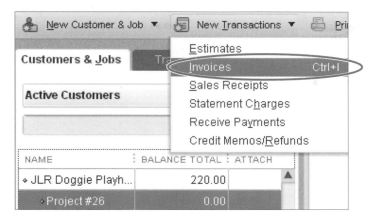

5. Follow these steps to create an invoice:

Ⓐ Click the **drop-down arrow**, and then click to choose **Samuel Jameson** as the **Class.**

Ⓑ Tap [Tab] twice, and then type **030315.**

Ⓒ Click in the **Item** column, and then type **ph.**

Ⓓ Tap [Tab], and then type **12.**

Ⓔ Tap [Tab] twice, and then type **45.**

Ⓕ Click in the **Item** column below Photography, and then type **vi.**

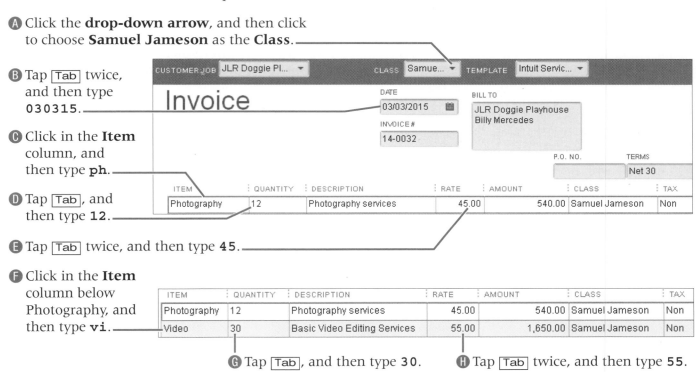

Ⓖ Tap [Tab], and then type **30.**   **Ⓗ** Tap [Tab] twice, and then type **55.**

BTS BRIEF

11000•Accounts Receivable DR 2,190.00; **42700•Photography Income CR <540.00>, 48900•Video Editing Services CR <1,650.00>**

6. Click **Save & Close**; close the **Customer Center** window.

Apply Classes to a Credit Card Charge

Allison needs to purchase some materials for the photo shoot for Samuel, so she will use the company credit card. While she is at the store, she will also purchase supplies for the office.

7. Click the **Enter Credit Card Charges** task icon in the **Banking** area of the Home page.

8. Ensure the **Sunriver Credit Union Visa** credit card account is chosen, and then follow these steps to complete the transaction:

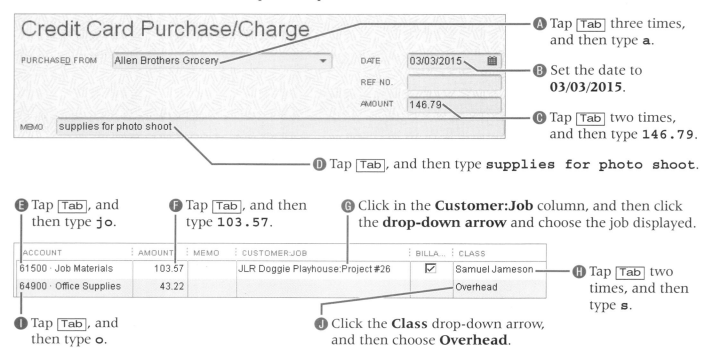

Ⓐ Tap ⌈Tab⌉ three times, and then type **a**.

Ⓑ Set the date to **03/03/2015**.

Ⓒ Tap ⌈Tab⌉ two times, and then type **146.79**.

Ⓓ Tap ⌈Tab⌉, and then type **supplies for photo shoot**.

Ⓔ Tap ⌈Tab⌉, and then type **jo**.

Ⓕ Tap ⌈Tab⌉, and then type **103.57**.

Ⓖ Click in the **Customer:Job** column, and then click the **drop-down arrow** and choose the job displayed.

Ⓗ Tap ⌈Tab⌉ two times, and then type **s**.

Ⓘ Tap ⌈Tab⌉, and then type **o**.

Ⓙ Click the **Class** drop-down arrow, and then choose **Overhead**.

The amount for the second line will fill in for you by subtracting the amount in the first line from the total.

> **BTS BRIEF**
>
> 54300•Job Materials DR 103.57; 63000•Office Supplies DR 43.22; **21000•Sunriver Credit Union Visa CR <146.79>**

9. Click **Save & Close**.

Running Class Reports

QuickBooks provides preset reports that help you to view your company data by class. For instance, the Profit & Loss by Class report shows you the net income or loss by class. If a column called "Unclassified" appears on your report, it will display all amounts that have not been assigned a class.

The Profit & Loss Unclassified Report

As you learned earlier in this chapter, once you begin to use class tracking, it is very important that you apply a class to each transaction. In order to ensure that you have done this, you can run the P&L Unclassified report, which will show you any amounts that do not have a class associated with them. It is then easy to use QuickBooks' QuickZoom feature to drill to the unclassified transactions and assign a class to them.

The Balance Sheet by Class Report

A new feature in QuickBooks 2011 was the Balance Sheet by Class Report. It is available for those who are using a Premier or Enterprise version of QuickBooks. In this report, each class appears as a column. This is not a basic report for novice users to use, as it may display unexpected results at times, and the ability to understand and fix these anomalies requires a solid accounting background.

QUICK REFERENCE	PRODUCING CLASS REPORTS
Task	**Procedure**
Run a Profit & Loss by Class report	▪ Choose Reports→Company & Financial→Profit & Loss by Class.
Run a Profit & Loss Unclassified report	▪ Choose Reports→Company & Financial→Profit & Loss Unclassified.
Run a Balance Sheet by Class report	▪ Choose Reports→Company & Financial→Balance Sheet by Class (only if you are using a Premier or Enterprise version of QuickBooks).

DEVELOP YOUR SKILLS 11-4
Create Class Reports

In this exercise, you will first create a report that will allow you to make sure that all transactions have been assigned a class. Then you will fix one that was entered without a class. Once you have cleared it up, you will produce a Profit & Loss by Class report for the month of March 2015.

1. Choose **Reports→Company & Financial→Profit & Loss Unclassified**.

2. Tap ⎡Tab⎤, type **030115**, tap ⎡Tab⎤ again, and then type **033115**.

Notice that there are income and expenses on the report that are not attributed to a class. You will now use QuickZoom to find the source of this amount.

3. Place your mouse pointer over the Design Income amount until you see the zoom pointer, and then double-click.

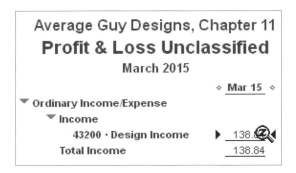

A Transaction Detail by Account report appears, on which you will see that the amount is from Invoice 14-0031.

4. Place your mouse pointer over the invoice line in the report until you see the zoom pointer, and then double-click.

◇	Type	◇	Date	◇	Num	◇	Name
43200 · Design Income							
	Invoice		03/20/2015		14-0031		Tim's BBQ Palooza...
Total 43200 · Design Income							

The source transaction will be displayed.

Add a Class to an Existing Transaction

Now that Allison has the unclassified transaction displayed, she will assign a class to it. You cannot assign a class to an entire transaction when you go back and edit it, so you will assign classes line by line.

5. Follow these steps to assign a class to the transaction:

A Choose **Guy Marshall** as the **Class** for the top two lines of the invoice.　　**B** Click **Save & Close**.

ITEM	QUANTITY	DESCRIPTION	RATE	AMOUNT	CLASS	TAX
		Printing for Tim's BBQ Palooza job	325.00	325.00	Guy Marshall	Non
Graphic Design	7	Graphic Design	40.00	280.00	Guy Marshall	Non
Cust Dep		Customer Deposit	-300.00	-300.00		Non

You must choose the class for each line item when you are applying a class to an existing transaction. You will not worry about applying a class in the Cust Dep line as it affects balance sheet accounts, not an income statement account.

6. Click **Yes** to confirm the changes and record the transaction; click **Save Anyway**.

7. Click **Yes** in the **Report needs to be refreshed** window.

The Transaction Detail by Account report will once again be displayed, but it will contain no data as there are no unclassified transactions affecting income statement accounts.

8. Close the **Transaction Detail by Account**, choosing not to memorize the report.

9. Using the steps outlined above, assign the following classes to the expenses still listed on the report:

Expense Account	Class
Job Materials	Guy Marshall
Insurance Expense	Overhead
Rent Expense	Overhead

You will need to right-click the transactions in the register windows for the Insurance Expense and Rent Expense transactions and choose to edit them in order to reach the Make General Journal Entries window where you will apply the class.

10. After classifying the last transaction, close the **Profit & Loss Unclassified** window, choosing not to memorize it.

Display a Profit & Loss by Class Report

Now that you know that all transactions have classes assigned to them, you will produce a report to show the net income (loss) by class and overall for March 2015.

11. Choose **Reports→Company & Financial→Profit & Loss by Class**.

The report will be displayed with the default date range of This Fiscal Year-to-date.

12. Tap Tab, type **030115**, tap Tab again, and then type **033115**.

You will now see the Profit & Loss by Class report for March 2015. Realize that there are not yet many transactions entered for the month, but you can see how the report is laid out.

13. Close the report window, choosing not to memorize it.

Working with Price Levels

There are many instances when a business may wish to charge different price levels for different customers or jobs. Once a price level is set and associated with a customer or job, it will automatically fill in for you in future transactions (although you can manually change what fills in, if needed). With all versions of QuickBooks, the price level can be set by a fixed percentage. If you are working with a Premier or higher version of QuickBooks, you can also set price levels per item. Before setting up price levels, you need to make sure that the preference is turned on in QuickBooks.

Types of Price Levels

There are two types of price levels from which you can choose in QuickBooks. The fixed percentage price level is available in QuickBooks Pro and higher editions, while the per item level requires that you are using at least the Premier version of the software.

Using Fixed Percentage Price Levels

The fixed percentage price level allows you to decrease or increase the items being charged to a customer or job by a specific percentage amount. For instance, you may wish to decrease all items charged to nonprofit agencies by 10 percent.

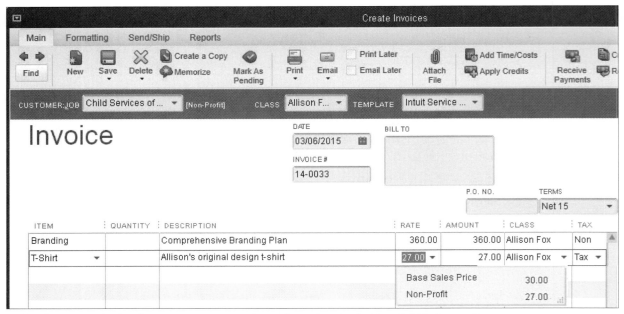

Notice that once price levels are set up, you can choose from them in the Rate field in transactions.

Using Per-Item Price Levels

If you use this Premier version or above option, you are able to create specific dollar amounts for items or groups of items that you can associate with selected customers or jobs. For instance, you may wish to charge Evelyn Huff $50 per hour for basic video editing services rather than the standard $55 per hour rate.

QUICK REFERENCE	WORKING WITH BILLABLE COSTS AND PRICE LEVELS
Task	**Procedure**
Turn on the price level preference in QuickBooks	■ Choose Edit→Preferences. ■ Choose the Sales & Customers category, and the Company Preferences tab. ■ Click to select the checkbox for Use price levels; click OK.
Create a price level in QuickBooks	■ Choose Lists→Price Level. ■ Click the Price Level menu button; choose New. ■ Enter the name and type of the new price level. ■ If you are creating a fixed percentage price level, enter whether it will be an increase or a decrease, and then enter the percentage. ■ If you are creating a price level by item(s), enter the custom price for the item(s) or group of items. ■ Click OK.

Set Price Levels and Enter Transactions Based on Them

In this exercise, you will first set a fixed percentage price level of 10 percent less than the "normal" price for nonprofit agencies. You will create a new customer, Child Services of Bayshore, for whom you will create an invoice utilizing the new price level.

1. Choose **Lists→Price Level List**.

2. Click the **Price Level** menu button, and then choose **New**.

The illustration and steps below are based on the Pro version of the software. If you are using a Premier version, you will need to ensure that Fixed % is the Price Level Type selected.

3. Follow these steps to set a new price level:

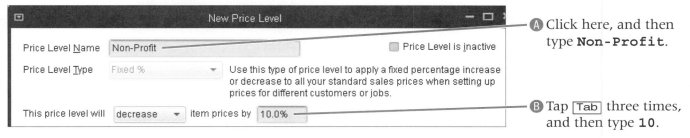

Ⓐ Click here, and then type **Non-Profit**.

Ⓑ Tap ⎡Tab⎤ three times, and then type **10**.

Ⓒ Click **OK**.

4. Close the **Price Level List**.

Assign a Price Level to a Customer

5. Choose **Customers→Customer Center**.

6. Tap ⎡Ctrl⎤ + ⎡n⎤.
   A New Customer window will open.

7. Type **Child Services of Bayshore**.

8. Click the **Payment Settings** tab, choose **Non-Profit** as the **Price Level**.

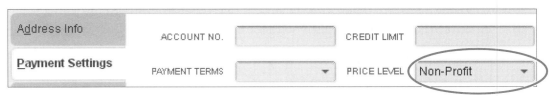

9. Click **OK**; right-click the new customer and choose **Add Job**.

10. Type **Project #27** as the **Job Name**, and then click **OK**.

11. Click **New Transactions**, and then choose **Invoices**.

12. Follow these steps to complete the invoice:

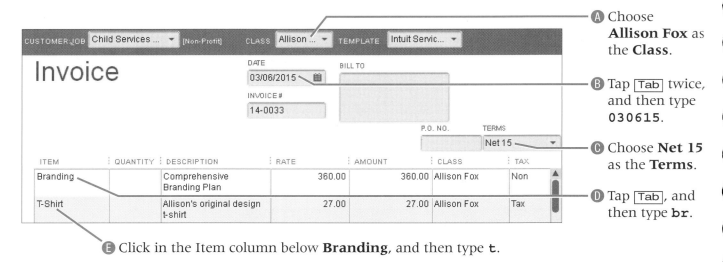

(A) Choose **Allison Fox** as the **Class**.

(B) Tap Tab twice, and then type **030615**.

(C) Choose **Net 15** as the **Terms**.

(D) Tap Tab, and then type **br**.

(E) Click in the Item column below **Branding**, and then type **t**.

BTS BRIEF
11000•Accounts Receivable DR 389.48; **43200•Design Income CR <360.00>; 41100•Clothing CR <27.00>, 25500•Sales Tax Payable CR <2.48>**

13. Click **Save & Close** to record the invoice; click **No** in the **Information Changed** window.

Producing a Statement of Cash Flows

The Statement of Cash Flows is a financial report that has been required under GAAP since 1987. You have already seen balance sheet and Profit & Loss reports, but this report plays an important part in showing how viable the company is in the short term. This helps a variety of stakeholders to see whether the company will be able to pay its bills, payroll, and other expenses. It also indicates the financial health of the company.

While the Profit & Loss report looks at the total amount of income coming in and the expenses going out, the Statement of Cash Flows specifically looks at the cash inflows and outflows during a period of time. If you remember from GAAP, corporations are required to use the accrual basis of accounting that records when income and expenses are accrued rather than when cash is exchanged. The Statement of Cash Flows essentially translates the company's data from accrual to cash basis so that an understanding of how the company is operating and how cash is being handled can be reached.

Method of Reporting

QuickBooks uses the indirect method when creating a Statement of Cash Flows. This means that net income is the starting point for the report; you make adjustments for the non-cash transactions from there. What basically happens is that you will take a net income generated using the accrual basis of accounting and convert it to the cash basis by adding increases to liability accounts and subtracting increases to asset accounts.

Sections of the Statement of Cash Flows Report

There are three sections of the Statement of Cash Flows that organize your company's financial information:

- **Operating:** In this section of the Statement of Cash Flows, you take the activities that result from the normal operation of the business and convert them to the cash basis. These types of activities may include such things as sales receipts, production costs, advertising, payroll, and expenses for services performed.

- **Investing:** In this section of the Statement of Cash Flows, you account for assets that are bought or sold, loans that you have issued, and other payments that are not related to the normal operation of the business (e.g., payments related to a merger).

- **Financing:** In this section of the Statement of Cash Flows, you take into account such items as cash from investors (company stock and bond transactions) and dividends that are paid.

Additional Skills

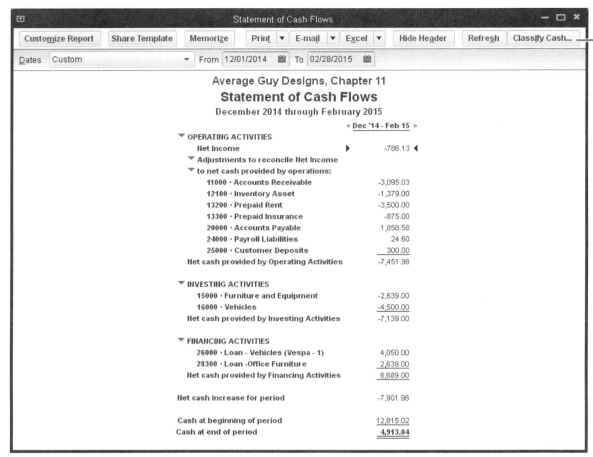

Clicking the Classify Cash button opens the Edit Preferences window with the Company Preferences tab of the Reports & Graphs category displayed.

The Statement of Cash Flows allows you to view the company financials "as if" you were using the cash basis of accounting. In QuickBooks, this report will be produced using the indirect method as shown above.

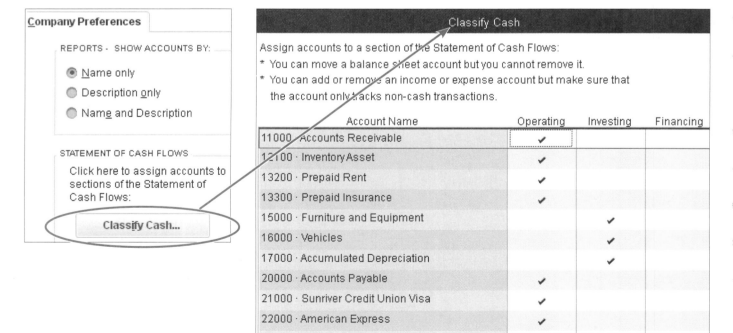

On the Company Preferences tab of the Reports & Graphs category, you will see a Statement of Cash Flows section. The Classify Cash window will launch if you click the button. The window allows you to assign accounts to different sections of the report.

Forecasting Cash Flow

As an average QuickBooks user, you may be wondering why this report is important. It is one of the main financial statements used to get approved for a loan, to attract shareholders, or to demonstrate the financial health of your company. You can also use it internally to help guide decisions that you have to make for your company by giving you a tool by which you can forecast the cash that is and will be flowing into and out of your company.

QuickBooks actually provides a separate report for you that will show you a forecast of cash flow, the Cash Flow Forecast report. The date range for this report will be in the immediate future.

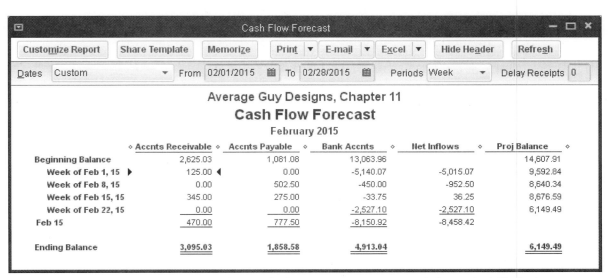

The Cash Flow Forecast report gives you a glimpse of what you can expect your cash flow to look like in the near future based on the data in your company file now.

QUICK REFERENCE	PRODUCING CASH FLOWS REPORTS
Task	**Procedure**
Produce a Statement Cash Flows report	■ Choose Reports→Company & Financial→Statement of Cash Flows.
Produce a Cash Flow Forecast report	■ Choose Reports→Company & Financial→Cash Flow Forecast.
Classify the accounts on a Statement of Cash Flows report	■ Choose Edit→Preferences. ■ Display the Reports & Graphs category and the Company Preferences tab. ■ Click the Classify Cash button in the Statement of Cash Flows section. ■ Make changes to any account classifications; click OK.

Additional Skills

Display Cash Flow Reports

In this exercise, you will help Allison to produce a Statement of Cash Flows for Guy. She will also create a report that will be used internally to make some decisions for the company.

1. Choose **Reports→Company & Financial→Statement of Cash Flows**.

   QuickBooks will display the Statement of Cash Flows report with a default date range of This Fiscal Year-to-date.

2. Set the date range of the report to be **12/01/2014-02/28/2015**.

3. Take a look at what the report tells you, and then close the report window, without memorizing it.

Run a Cash Flow Forecast Report

The next report will look at the cash flow forecast for the immediate future.

4. Choose **Reports→Company & Financial→Cash Flow Forecast**.

   QuickBooks will display the Cash Flow Forecast report with default date range of Next 4 Weeks.

5. Set the date range of the report to be **02/01/2015-02/28/2015**.

6. Take a look at what the report tells you, and then close the report window, without memorizing it.

Tackle the Tasks

Now is your chance to work a little more with Average Guy Designs and apply the skills that you have learned in this chapter to accomplish additional tasks. You will use the same company file you used in the Develop Your Skills exercises throughout this chapter. Enter the following tasks, referring back to the concepts in the chapter as necessary.

Add a document to the Doc Center	Add the Statement from Handyman by the Bay file from your storage location to the Doc Center. Attach it to the bill you have entered previously for Handyman by the Bay.
Analyze transactions	Answer the following questions on a separate sheet of paper about invoice 14-0033 that you produced in this chapter: ■ Which accounts are involved and what type are they? ■ Is each account increased or decreased? ■ Which account is debited and for what amount? ■ Which account is credited and for what amount?
Apply classes to transactions	Write a check on 3/17/15 to **East Bayshore Art & Supply**, using the next check number, for job materials that you need for the Project #28 for Grant Animal Rescue (a new customer) in the amount of **$56.29**. Choose to pass on the expense to the customer and indicate the class as Stephen Johnston.

Produce a class report	Produce a Profit & Loss by Class report for February 2015.
Enter an invoice with a price level	Create an invoice for `Child Services of Bayshore:Project #27` on 03/17/15 for eight hours of basic video editing. Use Stephen Johnston as the class, and ensure the price level is set as Nonprofit.
Create a Statement of Cash Flows	Create a Statement of Cash Flows for the date range of 1/1/15 through 3/31/15.

Choose the appropriate option for your situation:

■ *If you are continuing on to the next chapter or to the end-of-chapter exercises, leave QuickBooks open.*

■ *If you are finished working in QuickBooks for now, choose* **File→Exit**.

Concepts Review

To check your knowledge of the key concepts introduced in this chapter, complete the Concepts Review quiz on the Student Resource Center or in your eLab course.

Reinforce Your Skills

Angela Stevens has just relocated her company, Quality-Built Construction, from California to Silverton, Oregon. You will be working with a QuickBooks Sample Company File in this exercise as it will allow you to run full payroll in a future chapter without having to purchase a payroll subscription.

Before you begin the Reinforce Your Skills exercises, complete one of these options:

- Open **RYS_Chapter11** from your file storage location.
- Restore **RYS_Chapter11 (Portable)** from your file storage location. Make sure to place your last name and first initial at the end of the filename (e.g., RYS_Chapter11_StevensA).

REINFORCE YOUR SKILLS 11-1
Work with the Doc Center and Accounting Cycle

In this exercise, you will help Angela to add a file to the Doc Center (step 1 of the accounting cycle). Then you will classify accounting transactions (step 2 of the accounting cycle).

Angela realizes that she should be organizing the source documents for her business a bit better, so she has decided to store them electronically using QuickBooks. You will begin by helping Angela to add an invoice for some graphic design work to the Doc Center by attaching it to a bill.

1. Choose **Vendors→Enter Bills**.
2. Enter **Average Guy Designs** as the Vendor and **Quick Add** it to the Vendor List.
3. Set the date to **3/19/2019**, and then enter **$760.00** as the amount.
4. Set the **Terms** to **Net 15**, and then choose **6020•Advertising** as the expense account.
5. Click the **Attach File** button on the toolbar, and then click **Yes** to both record the transaction and save the new terms.
   The Attachments window for the bill will open.
6. Choose to attach from your computer, and then navigate to your file storage location.
   Notice that you don't have to add a document to the Doc Center before adding it to a transaction.
7. Click the **Invoice from Average Guy Designs** file, and then click **Open**.
   The file will be added to the Doc Center and attached to the bill.
8. Close the **Attachments** window, and then click **OK** in the Attachment Successful window.
9. Click **Save & Close**.

Classify Accounting Transactions

You will now take a look at a variety of transactions and analyze each one in the table displayed below. You may print a copy of this table from the Student Resource Center if you do not wish to write in the book.

10. Complete the following table by answering the questions about each transaction in the space provided.

	Invoice #FC 2	Sales Receipt dated 1/13/2019	Bill dated 3/19/19 for Average Guy Designs	Payment received on invoice #01-1051, dated 12/24/18	Deposit made to checking on 1/14/19
Which accounts are involved and what type are they?					
Is each account increased or decreased?					
Which account is debited and for what amount?					
Which account is credited and for what amount?					

Additional Skills

REINFORCE YOUR SKILLS 11-2

Track and Use Classes

In this exercise, you will turn on the class tracking feature and take a look at the classes that have been set up. Angela has decided to start tracking classes as of March 1, 2019.

1. Choose **Edit→Preferences**.
2. Choose the **Accounting** category, and then the **Company Preferences** tab.
3. Turn on **class tracking**, and then click **OK**.
4. Choose **Lists→Class List**.

Take a look at the classes that have already been set up for the company.

5. Close the **Class List** window.

Use Classes in Transactions

Now that class tracking is turned on for Quality-Built Construction, Angela will begin to use them in all transactions. In this section of the exercise, make sure to identify the correct class for each transaction.

6. Enter the following transactions, using the appropriate class(es) for each:

- On **3/3/19**, you purchased office supplies at **Priceco**. You paid the **$98.64** charge with your MasterCard. (Hint: Choose Banking→Enter Credit Card Charges.)

- On **3/5/19**, you received a bill from Supply Depot for **$349** for material costs for a job. The terms for the bill are Net 15. (Hint: Choose Vendors→Enter Bills.)

- On **3/6/19**, **Peggy Oceans** (new drywall subcontractor) submitted an invoice for you to pay for **$350**. The terms are Net 15. (Hint: Choose Customers→Enter Bills.)

- On **3/11/19**, **Rachel Geller** (new customer) came in and purchased a custom coffee table. She paid the entire amount with check number **1992**. (Hint: Choose Customers→Enter Sales Receipts.)

- On **3/17/19**, you rented a tractor from **Valley Rentals** for a job for **$300.00**. You used your Visa card for the purchase. (Hint: Choose Banking→Enter Credit Card Charges.)

- On **3/21/19**, you received a bill from **Marion County Gas & Electric** for **$200.13** for your gas and electric service. The terms for the bill are Net 15. (Hint: Choose Vendors→Enter Bills.)

REINFORCE YOUR SKILLS 11-3

Set Price Levels

In this exercise, you will create a price level to use for military customers. The first step is to set the preference.

1. Choose **Edit→Preferences**.

2. Click the **Sales & Customers** category, and then the **Company Preferences** tab.

3. Ensure that the **Enable Price Levels** checkbox is selected; click **OK**.

Create a New Fixed Percentage Price Level

Now that you have verified that QuickBooks is set to track price levels, you will create a new fixed percentage price level.

4. Choose **Lists→Price Level List**.

5. Click the **Price Level** menu button, and then click **New**.

6. Name the fixed % price level **Military Discount**.

7. Choose to decrease item prices by a fixed amount of **10 percent**.

8. Click **OK** to save the new price level, and then close the **Price Level List**.

Create an Invoice for a Military Customer

Angela has a new customer, Zoe Minch, who is a Captain in the Marine Corps Reserve. She has contracted with Angela to build a new house for her. While she was in the office, she saw the custom coffee tables and purchased one. Angela will create an invoice for her using the military price level.

9. Choose **Customers→Customer Center**.

10. Create a new customer, **Zoe Minch**. Set the price level as **Military Discount**.

11. Choose **Zoe Minch** as the Customer:Job, and then choose **Materials Cost – Job Related** as the Class.

12. Set the date as **3/25/2019**, and then choose **Coffee table** as the Item.

13. Click the **drop-down arrow** in the Rate column, verify that **Military Discount** is the rate for Karen, and then click **Save & Close**.

Create a Cash Flow Report

In this exercise, you will help Angela to look at how her company's cash flow has been for January – March 2019.

1. Choose **Reports→Company & Financial→Statement of Cash Flows**.

2. Tap Tab, type **010119**, tap Tab again, and then type **033119**.

3. Take a look at the cash flow for Quality-Built Construction for the period.

4. Close the **Statement of Cash Flows** window, choosing to not memorize the report.

5. Choose the appropriate option for your situation:

   ■ If you are continuing on to the next chapter or the rest of the end-of-chapter exercises, leave QuickBooks open.

   ■ If you are finished working in QuickBooks for now, choose **File→Exit**.

Additional Skills

Apply Your Skills

Before you begin the Apply Your Skills exercises, complete one of these options:

- Open **AYS_Chapter11** from your file storage location.
- Restore **AYS_Chapter11 (Portable)** from your file storage location. Make sure to place your last name and first initial at the end of the filename (e.g., AYS_Chapter11_JamesS).

APPLY YOUR SKILLS 11-1
Use the Doc Center and Analyze Transactions

In this exercise, you will help Dr. James to add a file to the Doc Center (step 1 of the accounting cycle). Then you will classify accounting transactions (step 2 of the accounting cycle).

1. Choose **Company→Documents→Doc Center**.
2. Add the **Bothell Pet Supply Co.-July 2014** invoice to the **Doc Center**.
3. Close the **Doc Center**.
4. Choose **Vendors→Enter Bills**.
5. Use the **Back** button to locate the **7/25/14** bill from **Bothell Pet Supply Co**.
6. Click the Attach button on the Ribbon, and choose to get the file from the **Doc Center**.
7. Select the invoice from **Bothell Pet Supply**, and then click **Attach**.
8. Verify the correct file is attached, and then click **Done**.
9. Click **Save & Close**.

Classify Accounting Transactions

You will now take a look at a variety of transactions and analyze each one in the table displayed below. You may print a copy of this table from the Student Resource Center if you do not wish to write in the book.

10. Complete the following table by answering the questions about each transaction in the space provided.

	Invoice #176	Sales Receipt #6, dated 6/4/2014	Bill dated 7/21/2014 for Wyland Broadband	Payment received on invoice #177, dated 7/22/2014	Deposit made to checking on 6/8/2014
Which accounts are involved and what type are they?					

Is each account increased or decreased?					
Which account is debited and for what amount?					
Which account is credited and for what amount?					

Use Classes to Track Why Customers Visit

Dr. James has decided that she wishes to know a bit more about what brings her customers through her doors. In this exercise, you will help her to use classes to track this aspect of her business.

1. Turn on the **class tracking** preference.

2. Set up four new classes: **Routine/Scheduled**, **Emergency**, **Product Sales**, and **Overhead**.

3. Enter the following transactions, using the new classes that have been established:

   - On **7/1/14**, enter a bill for the monthly rent for **$2,300** payable to Oberg Property Management.

   - On **7/1/14**, Chris Lorenzo brought in his cat, Jaguar, who was having a hard time breathing. Create invoice #179 for the visit and charge him for an Exam, a Venipuncture, and a CBC Chem.

   - On **7/2/14**, you received bill **#77-9-57** from Seattle Vet Supply for **$3,787.49** (**$1,946.72** for medical supplies, **$994.22** for medicines, and **$846.55** for vaccines). The terms for the bill are Net 15. All of these items are used in the practice for a variety of procedures and ailments.

   - On **7/2/14**, Krista Reinertson brought in her dog, Pansie, for her annual exam, a rabies shot, and a small dog dose of Revolution. She paid with check number **2627**.

   - On **7/5/14**, your received a bill from Brian's Pet Taxi for **$56** for transporting an injured dog to your office (you will need to create a new expense account called **Pet Transportation**). You will pass on this expense to the dog's owner, so you need to choose Steve Gaines:Dog-Jasper as the Customer:Job and indicate that the expense is billable.

   - On **7/5/14**, Toni Wagner brought in her dog, Arizona, for a checkup and to see if he can go off of his meds. Charge her for an Exam; she paid cash.

Set Price Levels

As QuickBooks is already set up to track price levels for Wet Noses, in this exercise you will create a new price level for the police dogs.

1. Open the **Price Level** List.

2. Create a new price level named **Police Dogs**.

3. Choose to decrease item prices by **10 percent**.

4. Click **OK** to save the new price level, and then close the **Price Level List**.

Use the Price Level in an Invoice

One of the Snohomish K-9 Unit handlers brought in Admiral for a scheduled exam because he has been limping a bit.

5. Open the **Create Invoices** window, and then choose **Snohomish County K-9 Unit:Dog-Admiral** as the Customer:Job.

6. Set the date to **7/8/2014**, and the Class to **Routine/Scheduled**.

7. Choose **Exam** as the first Item, and then **2 XRay films** as the second item.

8. Click the **Rate drop-down arrow** for both lines, and then choose the **Police Dogs** rate for each.

9. Click **Save & Close** for the invoice.

Answer Questions with Reports

In this exercise, you will answer questions for Dr. James by running reports. You may wish to display the Report Center in List View to help you to answer the questions. Ask your instructor if you should print the reports, print (save) them as PDF files, export them to Excel, or simply display them on the screen.

1. What is the forecasted cash flow for the month of July 2014, displayed in one-week periods?

2. What does a Profit & Loss by Class report look like? I would like to see an example of what to expect once we have more class data entered. Let's run it for July 2014.

3. Are there any unclassified transactions for the month of July 2014?

4. What is the per-item price for each item for the Police Dogs price level?

5. How much does each customer owe as of July 31, 2014?

6. What is our current balance with each vendor as of 7/31/2014?

7. Submit your reports based on the guidelines provided by your instructor.

8. Choose the appropriate option for your situation:
   - If you are continuing on to the next chapter or the Extend Your Skills exercises, leave QuickBooks open.
   - If you are finished working in QuickBooks for now, choose **File→Exit**.

Extend Your Skills

In the course of working through the following Extend Your Skills exercises, you will be utilizing various skills taught in this and previous chapter(s). Take your time and think carefully about the tasks presented to you. Turn back to the chapter content if you need assistance.

11-1 Sort Through the Stack

Before You Begin: Restore the **EYS1_Chapter11 (Portable)** file or open the **EYS1_Chapter11** company file from your storage location.

You have been hired by Arlaine Cervantes to help her with her organization's books. She is the founder of Niños del Lago, a nonprofit organization that provides impoverished Guatemalan children with an engaging educational camp experience. You have just sat down at your desk and opened a large envelope from her with a variety of documents and noticed that you have several emails from her as well. It is your job to sort through the papers and emails and make sense of what you find, entering information into QuickBooks whenever appropriate and answering any other questions in a word-processing document saved as **EYS1_Chapter11_ LastnameFirstinitial**. Remember, you are digging through papers you just dumped out of an envelope and addressing random emails from Arlaine, so it is up to you to determine the correct order in which to complete the tasks.

- Credit card receipt: From Crafters Supply Warehouse, dated 9/2/2014 in the amount of $1,200 for the purchase of supplies for the camp.
- Message from Arlaine: "Can you set up a way for us to easily give a 25 percent discount to resale customers on a per-invoice basis?"
- Note from accountant: "Please develop a system to keep better track of source documents. You can do it electronically or 'physically,' but we need the backup documentation organized."
- Scribbled on a scrap of paper: Can we keep track of the funds that come in and go out for different purposes? Is there some sort of feature that would let us track income and expense by, let's say, Food-Camp, Building-Camp, Supplies-Camp, General Use, Administrative Costs?
- Handwritten donation receipt dated 9/5/14: For camp supplies in the amount of $775 from Sharona Duke. Make sure you indicate that it is for camp supplies on the sales receipt.
- Scribbled note from Arlaine: "I would like to see what our cash flow is for July. Is there a report that will provide me with this information? What if I wanted to see what a prediction of cash flow for September 2014 might look like? Is there an easy way to do that in QuickBooks?"

11-2 Be Your Own Boss

Before You Begin: You must complete Extend Your Skills 10-2 before you begin this exercise.

In this exercise, throughout the entire book, you will build on the company file that you outlined in previous chapters. If you have created a file for your actual business, then determine if you wish to use class tracking for your business and if it does make sense, set up the classes and set a start date to begin tracking them, apply classes to any transactions created after the date determined in #1, set up price levels for any special customer groups, and enter any sales transactions (or edit previous ones) that require the special pricing. If you are creating a fictitious company, then set up class tracking for the company, set the start date for the class tracking to be in the past, update all transactions that have occurred since you began class tracking to reflect the appropriate class, and create price levels for at least three special categories of customers. You will make up the names and information for this exercise.

Create Profit & Loss by class and Statement of Cash Flows reports, submitting them to your instructor based on the instructions provided.

Open the company file you worked on in Extend Your Skills 10-2 and complete the tasks outlined above. When you are done, save it as a portable company file, naming it as **EYS2_ Chapter11_LastnameFirstinitial (Portable)** and submit it to your instructor based on the instructions provided.

11-3 Use the Web as a Learning Tool

Throughout this book, you will be provided with an opportunity to use the Internet as a learning tool by completing WebQuests. According to the original creators of WebQuests, as described on their website (http://WebQuest.org), a WebQuest is "an inquiry-oriented activity in which most or all of the information used by learners is drawn from the web." To complete the WebQuest projects in this book, navigate to the Student Resource Center and choose the WebQuest for the chapter on which you are working. The subject of each WebQuest will be relevant to the material found in the chapter.

WebQuest Subject: Diving into the accounting cycle

Reporting, Adjusting Entries, and Closing the Books

CHAPTER OUTLINE

CHAPTER OBJECTIVES

After studying this chapter, you will be able to:

- Prepare a Trial Balance report
- Make general journal entries
- Adjust inventory
- Create financial statements
- Close the books in QuickBooks

It is now time to wrap up all you have learned and finish out the accounting cycle. In this chapter, you will work through the last four steps of the cycle as you close out the fiscal period. You will have the opportunity to dive in and look a bit closer at what's behind the scenes by learning how to make general journal entries as well as inventory adjusting entries. You will also take a stroll through the major end-of-period financial reports—Trial Balance, Worksheet, Income Statement, Statement of Owner's Equity, and Balance Sheet. Finally, you will learn what closing the books looks like in QuickBooks.

Average Guy Designs

Guy has asked Allison to close Average Guy Designs' books for the first quarter of the 2015 fiscal year. She will begin the process by creating a Trial Balance report, which will tell her whether the debits and credits are equal and will display the balances of each account. Then it will be time to take a look at what a "pen-and-paper" worksheet includes and how the information flows from column to column through it.

Allison will next dive behind the scenes and take a look at the Make General Journal Entries window, where she will enter adjusting entries for depreciation and the Opening Balance Equity account. She will also make any necessary inventory adjustments.

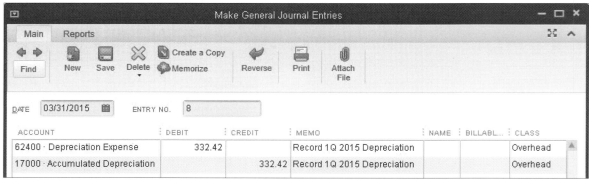

Adjusting entries are made in the Make General Journal Entries window.

Once the adjusting entries have been posted, it will be time for Allison to create Average Guy Designs' financial statements for the first quarter of 2015.

Average Guy Designs, Chapter 12
Summary Balance Sheet
All Transactions

	Mar 31, 15
▼ASSETS	
▼Current Assets	
Checking/Savings	▶ 7,628.68 ◀
Accounts Receivable	6,845.00
Other Current Assets	4,794.50
Total Current Assets	19,268.18
Fixed Assets	6,806.58
TOTAL ASSETS	**26,074.76**
▼LIABILITIES & EQUITY	
▼Liabilities	
▼Current Liabilities	
Credit Cards	471.79
Other Current Liabilities	27.08
Total Current Liabilities	498.87
Long Term Liabilities	6,689.00
Total Liabilities	7,187.87
Equity	18,886.89
TOTAL LIABILITIES & EQUITY	**26,074.76**

The Balance Sheet is one of the main financial statements. In this illustration you are viewing a summary balance sheet, which includes less detail.

Closing the Books in QuickBooks

The last four steps of the accounting cycle deal with "closing" the books at the end of a fiscal period. You have probably figured out by now that QuickBooks makes things easy for you in many ways by what it performs behind the scenes. The same is true when it comes to the end of the fiscal year. QuickBooks knows when your fiscal year has ended based on the information you entered when you first created your company or that is displayed in the Report Information tab of the Company Information window in QuickBooks.

The fiscal year information is set in the Report Information tab of the Company Information window.

Behind the Scenes with Closing the Books

You can set a closing date in QuickBooks, although QuickBooks will perform year-end adjustments automatically based on your fiscal year. You will learn how to set a closing date in QuickBooks at the end of this chapter, once you have explored the rest of the accounting cycle.

The Final Steps of the Accounting Cycle

This chapter will take you through the final four steps of the accounting cycle, which results in your company books being closed for the past fiscal period and made ready for the next one. For many companies, the last steps of the accounting cycle are carried out by an accountant. You will learn about the final steps, but it will be up to you to determine if it will be wiser for you to complete them yourself for your company or to trust them to your accountant. So far, in your path through the accounting cycle, you have ensured that source documents are available and organized before analyzing and recording transactions (QuickBooks posted them in a journal and to ledger accounts behind the scenes for you). Now you will prepare reports to show how your company performed for the fiscal period and close out temporary accounts. As you explore these final steps, you will be doing so "QuickBooks style" in that you will look at each step and how it is addressed in QuickBooks.

Permanent Accounts

Accounts for which the ending balance for one fiscal period is the opening balance for the next are called permanent accounts. These are also the balance sheet accounts. Think about it a bit… You don't zero out your checking account at the end of each year; it continues on from one accounting period to the next!

Temporary (a.k.a. Nominal) Accounts

No doubt you have figured out that not all accounts are permanent! The opposite of permanent accounts are temporary, or nominal, accounts. These accounts are zeroed out at the end of each fiscal period, with the amounts from them moving into an equity account as either a net income (if income was greater than expenses) or a net loss (if expenses exceeded income for the period).

The Income Summary Account

If you were doing paper-based accounting, you would use an Income Summary account to "clear out" the temporary account balances and move the lump sum to an equity account. QuickBooks doesn't actually create an Income Summary account, but it takes the net income or loss resulting from the balances in your income and expense accounts and moves them to the capital/equity account for you. You will learn more about this temporary capital/equity account as we progress through this chapter.

QuickBooks' Automatic Year-End Adjustments

As you learned earlier, QuickBooks performs adjustments automatically for you behind the scenes at the end of your fiscal year. Specifically, QuickBooks will:

- Close out the temporary accounts by moving the balances to a "virtual" income summary account
- Determine a net income or loss for the company to be displayed on the balance sheet for the last day of the fiscal year, after transferring the balances from the temporary accounts
- Automatically transfer the net income or loss from the last day of the fiscal period to the Retained Earnings account on the first day of the new fiscal period

The result of this behind the scenes action is that you will start off the new fiscal year with a net income of zero (and a zero balance in each of the temporary accounts).

QUICK REFERENCE	SETTING A COMPANY'S FISCAL YEAR IN QUICKBOOKS
Task	**Procedure**
Set the company's fiscal period in QuickBooks	■ Choose Company→Company Information. ■ In the Report Information area, click the Fiscal Year drop-down arrow to choose the correct first month of the company's fiscal year.

DEVELOP YOUR SKILLS 12-1
Verify Fiscal Period

In this exercise, you will verify that the correct month is set as the first month of the fiscal period for Average Guy Designs. The first step is to open QuickBooks, and then either open a company file or restore a portable company file.

Intuit provides maintenance releases throughout the lifetime of the product. These updates may require you to update your student exercise files before you begin working with them. Please follow the prompts on the screen if you are asked to update your company file to the latest QuickBooks release.

1. Start **QuickBooks 2014**.

   If you downloaded the student exercise files in the portable company file *format, follow Option 1 below. If you downloaded the files in the* company file *format, follow Option 2 below.*

Option 1: Restore a Portable Company File

2. Choose **File→Open or Restore Company**.

3. Restore the **DYS_Chapter12 (Portable)** portable company file for this chapter from your file storage location, placing your last name and first initial at the end of the filename (e.g., DYS_Chapter12_MarshallG).

   It may take a few moments for the portable company file to open. Once it does, continue with step 5.

Option 2: Open a Company File

2. Choose **File→Open or Restore Company**, ensure that **Open a regular company file** is selected, and then open the **DYS_Chapter12** company file from your file storage location.

   The QuickBooks company file will open.

3. Click **OK** to close the QuickBooks Information window. Click **No** in the Set Up External Accountant User window, if necessary.

4. Close the **Reminders** window.

Verify the Fiscal Period Information

Next you will verify that January is set up as the first month of the fiscal period for Average Guy Designs.

5. Choose **Company→My Company**.

6. Click the Edit button at the top-right corner of the My Company window.

7. Click the **Report Information** tab, and then verify that **January** is displayed as the first month in the company's fiscal year.

8. Click **OK** in the **Company Information** window; close the **My Company** window.

Preparing for Year-End Reporting

When you are doing pen-and-paper accounting, you must prepare a Trial Balance report to ensure that the debits and credits are equal. Preparing a Trial Balance report involves taking all of the ledger accounts and their balances and displaying them on one report to ensure debits equal credits. When you use QuickBooks, though, you cannot record a transaction if the debits and credits are not equal, so a more useful purpose for the Trial Balance report is to use it to prepare for adjusting entries.

QuickBooks Reporting Capabilities

QuickBooks provides users with a large number of reports organized into eleven categories. These reports can be used to tell the story about your business in many ways.

| Company & Financial |
| Customers & Receivables |
| Sales |
| Jobs, Time & Mileage |
| Vendors & Payables |
| Purchases |
| Inventory |
| Banking |
| Accountant & Taxes |
| Budgets |
| List |

Contributed Reports

As a QuickBooks user, you can use reports contributed by other users that may help you to better tell your company's story. You can sort for reports by report category and by industry sector. If you find a report that may be beneficial to you and your business, simply download it into your QuickBooks software.

The eleven categories into which QuickBooks reports are organized

Custom Reports

QuickBooks allows users to create custom summary and detail reports. The software provides a window that guides you through the decision of what custom report to create.

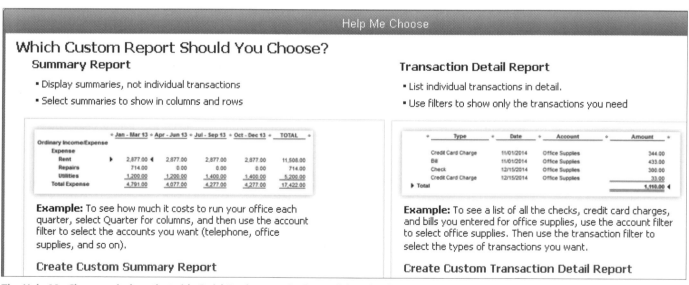

The Help Me Choose window that aids QuickBooks users in determining the desired custom report

Industry-Specific Reports

The industry-specific premiere editions of QuickBooks also provide reports that are specialized for industry sectors. You can access all of these reports through the Accountant edition of the software as well.

Contractor Reports
Manufacturing and Wholesale Reports
Professional Services Reports
Retail Reports
Nonprofit Reports

Industry-specific reports are available in these QuickBooks editions of QuickBooks Premiere, as well as in the Accountant edition.

Cycle Step 4: Unadjusted Trial Balance

In the third step of the accounting cycle, QuickBooks posted the amounts from the journal that documents all transactions to individual account ledgers behind the scenes for you. The next step of the accounting cycle involves creating a Trial Balance report. QuickBooks Pro allows you to create a Trial Balance report and if you have the Premier Accountant edition, you can create a Working Trial Balance report as well. This initial trial balance is termed an "unadjusted" trial balance as it is prior to the adjusting entries that you will complete later in this chapter.

In traditional accounting, a Trial Balance is a report that adds up all the debits and credits so mistakes can be traced if debits don't equal credits. Because QuickBooks always adds correctly, you do not need to do a trial balance. Nevertheless, QuickBooks provides a Trial Balance report if you want to see your data in this format.

What the Trial Balance Report Tells You

The Trial Balance report lets you look at the ending balance of every account in the Chart of Accounts for a chosen period of time. You can use it to help guide you as you create adjusting entries. If you are curious as to what transactions comprise a figure on the Trial Balance report, you can use the Quick Zoom feature to find the source of the amount.

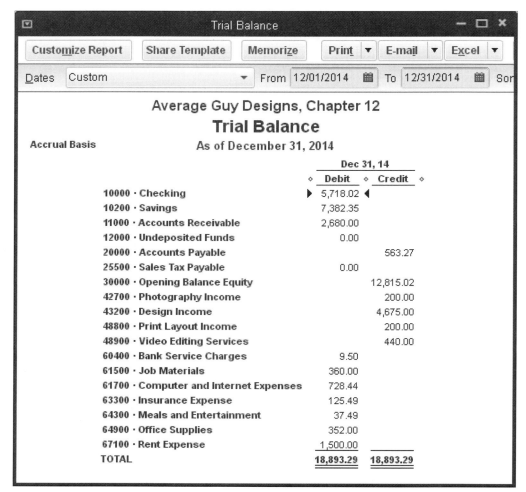

A Trial Balance report compiles all of the accounts in your ledger into a report that verifies that debits equal credits.

Preparing a Worksheet

In pen-and-paper accounting, a worksheet is a report that you create to assist you with preparing the year-end financial statements. The worksheet has five sets of debit and credit columns that represent the following sections (displayed from left to right):

- Trial Balance
- Adjustments
- Adjusted Trial Balance
- Income Statement
- Balance Sheet

The information from the Trial Balance report is displayed in the Trial Balance section. You would work across the worksheet as adjustments are made and then recorded in the Adjusted Trial Balance section. Finally, the amounts from the Adjusted Trial Balance would be transferred to the Income Statement and Balance Sheet sections, based on which accounts would be found on each one.

It is probably evident to you by now that QuickBooks does this behind the scenes for you, so there is no worksheet for you to physically produce in QuickBooks. Just realize that the steps performed in the preparation of a worksheet are being completed for you behind the scenes.

QUICK REFERENCE	PRODUCING A TRIAL BALANCE REPORT
Task	**Procedure**
Create a Trial Balance report	■ Choose Reports→Accountant & Taxes→Trial Balance. ■ Set the date range for the report.
Create a Working Trial Balance report (QuickBooks Premier Accountant Edition)	■ Choose Accountant→Working Trial Balance. ■ Set the date range for the report.

DEVELOP YOUR SKILLS 12-2

Run a Trial Balance Report

In this exercise, you will create a Trial Balance report for Average Guy Designs.

1. Choose **Reports→Accountant & Taxes→Trial Balance**.

2. Tap Tab, type **010115**, tap Tab again, and then type **033115**.

3. Click the **Refresh** button.

   Take a look at the information contained in this report. It displays all of the accounts in your Chart of Accounts and the current balance for each.

4. Close the **Trial Balance** report, choosing not to memorize it.

Additional Skills

Digging in "Behind the Scenes" with Adjusting Entries

Throughout this book, you have had the opportunity to take a glimpse at the accounting QuickBooks does behind the scenes. Now you will take a step further to see how QuickBooks records journal entries and how you can create your own journal entries.

Rule #1: Debits and Credits Must Always Be Equal

When you venture into the General Journal Entry window, you will see a debit column and a credit column. As you create your journal entries, you must make sure that the debits equal the credits. (Don't worry, though. QuickBooks will not let you record a transaction until you get this right!)

Depending on the version of QuickBooks you are using, the Make General Journal Entries window may look a bit different. The images in this text are from the Pro version.

Making Journal Entries

You already learned how to record a journal entry when you recorded the prepaid insurance transfer in the last chapter; you just used a register to accomplish the task rather than the Make General Journal Entries window. If you are familiar with pen-and-paper accounting, you will see that the Make General Journal Entries window looks like a journal you would use in manual accounting.

Average Guy Designs, Chapter 12
Journal
January 2015

Trans #	Type	Date	Num	Name	Memo	Account	Debit	Credit
59	Bill	01/02/2015	Inv. #...	Handyman by the ...	Inv. #15-001	20000 · Accounts...		239.44
				Handyman by the ...	Inv. #15-001	67200 · Repairs an...	239.44	
							239.44	239.44
60	Bill	01/02/2015	NGE ...	NoCal Gas & Electric	NGE Jan 2015	20000 · Accounts...		82.37
				NoCal Gas & Electric	NGE Jan 2015	68610 · Gas & Ele...	82.37	
							82.37	82.37
61	Bill	01/05/2015	BC In...	Bayshore City Wa...	BC Inv. #943...	20000 · Accounts...		48.22
				Bayshore City Wa...	BC Inv. #943...	68620 · Water	48.22	
							48.22	48.22

You can produce a report in QuickBooks that shows the entries as they would appear in a pen-and-paper journal.

Cycle Step 5: Adjusting Entries and Adjusted Trial Balance

Adjusting entries are made at the end of an accounting period in order to bring some of the general journal account balances up to date so they will be correct on the financial statements. Some examples of adjusting entries that are often made are:

- Updating the book value of fixed assets by recording depreciation for the fiscal period
- Updating prepaid accounts (other current assets) by transferring the amount used in the fiscal period to an expense account
- Transferring balances out of the Opening Balance Equity account to their correct "resting place"

Once the adjusting entries have been made, an adjusted trial balance is prepared. While you cannot produce this report in QuickBooks Pro, it can be created in the Premier Accountant edition, as displayed in the following illustration that shows the columns in the report.

Average Guy Designs, Chapter 12
Adjusted Trial Balance
Accrual Basis   All Transactions

	Unadjusted Balance		Adjustments		Adjusted Balance	
◇	Debit ◇	Credit ◇	Debit ◇	Credit ◇	Debit ◇	Credit ◇

Adjusting Inventory Quantity/Value on Hand

There may be times when you have inventory that is no longer in sellable condition. You should remove these items from inventory and expense the amount. Other times you may need to adjust the value of your inventory due to obsolescence or some other reason. Or, you may need to adjust both the quantity and the value of your inventory.

In the Adjust Quantity/Value on Hand window, you can choose the type of the adjustment via a drop-down list.

Adjusting the Quantity of Your Inventory

You can either enter the new quantity on hand (if you have just conducted an annual inventory, this may be the best choice) or the quantity difference (this option works well if you know how many items you have to remove). If you choose to enter the quantity difference, make sure to enter a minus sign in front of the number to show a decrease in the number of items.

Adjusting the Value of Your Inventory

If you don't need to adjust the quantity of your inventory but rather need to adjust the value of your inventory, you can use the same window. As was discussed earlier in this chapter, QuickBooks Pro and Premier use the average cost method of inventory valuation. You can adjust the average cost per inventory item by adjusting the total value of the inventory. Obsolescence or an incorrect beginning cost for inventory may require you to take this step.

The Adjust Quantity/Value on Hand window

Accounting for Depreciation

Previously, you learned about fixed assets and the fact that you don't expense them when purchased, but rather over the life of the asset. You should enter a depreciation transaction for your fixed assets for every fiscal period in which you produce financial statements. For small businesses, this is typically at the end of a fiscal year.

The depreciation adjusting entry can be made in the Make General Journal Entries window. It affects the expense account that tracks depreciation and the accumulated depreciation fixed asset contra account. When you make this transfer, the current book value of your fixed assets will be displayed correctly, meaning that the credit amount in the accumulated depreciation contra account will decrease the total value of the company's fixed assets (which have a debit normal balance).

Adjusted Trial Balance Report

If you are using the Premier Accountant edition of QuickBooks, once the adjusting entries have been entered into QuickBooks, you can create an Adjusted Trial Balance report if you wish. This report will show the beginning balance, the adjustments, and the ending balance for each account. It will be these final, ending balances that will be used for the financial statements. This report also represents one of the sections of the worksheet that illustrates the fifth step of the accounting cycle.

For those using the Pro version of QuickBooks, after adjusting entries are made, you can create another Trial Balance report, which reflects the adjusted amounts.

When making an adjusting entry for depreciation, you will debit the Depreciation Expense account and credit the Accumulated Depreciation account. Remember that Accumulated Depreciation is a fixed asset contra account. By crediting it, you are decreasing the value of the fixed assets.

62400-Depreciation Expense		17000-Accumulated Depreciation	
333.42			333.42

Behind the scenes in an inventory adjustment, you remove the items from the Inventory Asset account and enter them as an Inventory Adjustment to Cost of Goods Sold for the company.

64000-Inventory Adjustment		12100-Inventory Asset	
20.00			20.00

QUICK REFERENCE	WORKING WITH GENERAL JOURNAL ENTRIES
Task	**Procedure**
Adjust quantity or value of inventory items	▪ Choose Vendors→Inventory Activities→Adjust Quantity/Value on Hand. ▪ Choose the adjustment type and date. ▪ Choose Inventory Adjustment as the Adjustment Account; choose an adjustment class. ▪ Choose the desired items, indicate the new quantities and/or values, and type any memos. ▪ Click Save & Close or Save & New.
Make a general journal entry	▪ Choose Company→Make General Journal Entries. ▪ Set the correct date. ▪ Enter the first account, and then the debit or credit amount. ▪ Continue entering accounts and their debit or credit amounts as needed.
Create an Adjusting Journal Entries report	▪ Choose Reports→Accountant & Taxes→Adjusting Journal Entries. ▪ Set the date range.

Adjust Inventory and Make Adjusting Entries

Allison has completed a physical inventory count and needs to make sure that the items on hand match the count in QuickBooks. She will then make any necessary inventory adjustments. You will begin by creating an inventory report to assist you with your physical inventory count.

1. Choose **Reports→Inventory→Physical Inventory Worksheet**.

   Allison has used this report to conduct a physical inventory, the results of which are displayed in the following illustration.

Average Guy Designs, Chapter 12
Physical Inventory Worksheet

Item	Description	Preferred Vendor	Quantity On Hand	Physical Count
Coasters		Hartwell Designs	0	0
Earrings	Designer earrings	Holly's Bead Art	22	21
LS Shirt		Allison Fox Designs	20	18
Scarf		Knit a Bit	25	24
Sm Tiles		Hartwell Designs	0	0
T-Shirt	Allison's original design...	Allison Fox Designs	19	19

You will now use the information from the physical inventory count to adjust Average Guy Designs' inventory. In addition, Guy just told you that he created a gift basket for a local Chamber event to advertise the company's services. In the gift basket were a pair of earrings, a long-sleeve shirt, and a scarf.

2. Close the **Physical Inventory Worksheet** window.

3. Click the **Inventory Activities drop-down arrow** in the Company area of the Home page, and then choose **Adjust Quantity/Value On Hand**.

4. Follow these steps to make the first inventory adjustment:

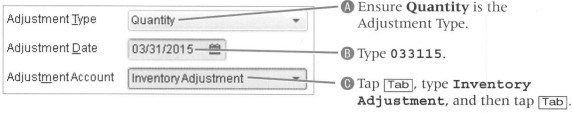

Ⓐ Ensure **Quantity** is the Adjustment Type.

Ⓑ Type **033115**.

Ⓒ Tap [Tab], type **Inventory Adjustment**, and then tap [Tab].

Inventory Adjustment is a new account, so QuickBooks will prompt you to set it up.

Ⓓ Click **Set Up**.

Ⓔ Choose **Expense** as the **Account Type**.　Ⓕ Type **64000** as the Number.

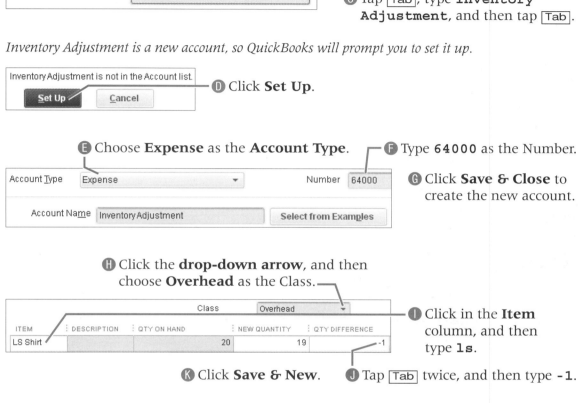

Ⓖ Click **Save & Close** to create the new account.

Ⓗ Click the **drop-down arrow**, and then choose **Overhead** as the Class.

Ⓘ Click in the **Item** column, and then type **ls**.

Ⓚ Click **Save & New**.　Ⓙ Tap [Tab] twice, and then type **-1**.

You will now mark out of inventory the three items that Guy included in the gift basket.

Additional Skills

5. Follow these steps to record the second inventory adjustment:

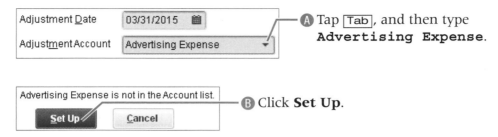

A Tap `Tab`, and then type **Advertising Expense**.

B Click **Set Up**.

C Choose **Expense** as the **Account Type**.

D Type **60100** as the Number.

E Click **Save & Close** to create the new account.

F Choose each of the **Items** displayed.

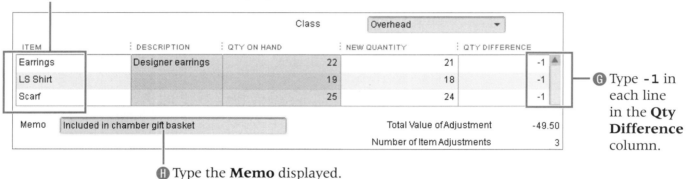

G Type **-1** in each line in the **Qty Difference** column.

H Type the **Memo** displayed.

6. Click **Save & Close** to record the inventory adjustment.

Make Adjusting Entries

Now you will help Allison to make two adjusting entries: one to transfer funds from the Opening Balance Equity account and another to account for the depreciation for the quarter.

The first general journal entry you will make will move $12,815.02 from the Opening Balance Equity account that was posted there when you entered the opening balance for the Checking and Savings accounts.

7. Choose **Company→Make General Journal Entries**. Click **OK** in the **Assigning Numbers to Journal Entries** window, if necessary.

8. Click the **Previous** button a few times to take a look at how transactions that you have entered are displayed in the general journal; click **Next** until you come to an empty window where no transaction is displayed.

9. Set the date to **03/31/2015**.

10. Follow these steps to record the journal entry:

Ⓐ Click in the top line of the **Account** column, and then type **3**.

Ⓑ Tap Tab, and then type **12815.02**.

Ⓒ Click below **Opening Balance Equity**, and then type **32**.

DATE 03/31/2015   ENTRY NO. 7

ACCOUNT	DEBIT	CREDIT
30000 · Opening Balance Equity	12,815.02	
32000 · Owners Equity		12,815.02

BTS BRIEF

30000•Opening Bal Equity DR 12,815.02; 32000•Owners Equity CR <12,815.02>

11. Click **Save & New** to record the journal entry.

12. Click **OK** to post to the Retained Earnings account; click Save Anyway in the Items Not Assigned Classes window.

The accounts affected are both balance sheet accounts, so you do not have to assign classes, since you are using those to track income and expense transactions.

Record the Depreciation Entry for the Quarter

The entry you are about to record will expense the depreciation for the year and decrease the book value of Average Guy Designs' fixed assets. Remember that there are a variety of ways to track depreciation, and the amount used in this exercise is just an example. You should use the value your accountant has provided to you for a transaction such as this.

The Make General Journal Entries window should still be displayed. If it is not, choose Company→Make General Journal Entries.

13. Ensure **03/31/2015** is the **Date**.

14. Follow these steps to record the journal entry for depreciation:

Ⓐ Click in the **Account** column, and then type **de**.

Ⓑ Tap Tab, and then type **332.42**.

Ⓒ Tap Tab two times, and then type **Record 1Q 2015 Depreciation**.

Ⓓ Tap Tab two times, and then type **o**.

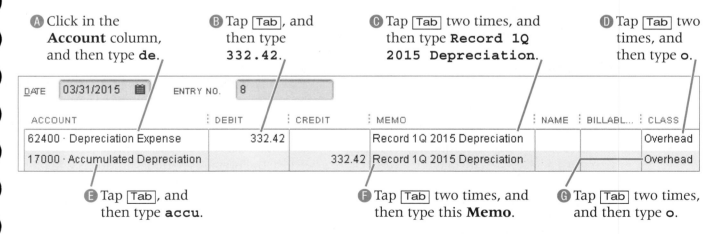

DATE 03/31/2015   ENTRY NO. 8

ACCOUNT	DEBIT	CREDIT	MEMO	NAME	BILLABL...	CLASS
62400 · Depreciation Expense	332.42		Record 1Q 2015 Depreciation			Overhead
17000 · Accumulated Depreciation		332.42	Record 1Q 2015 Depreciation			Overhead

Ⓔ Tap Tab, and then type **accu**.

Ⓕ Tap Tab two times, and then type this **Memo**.

Ⓖ Tap Tab two times, and then type **o**.

BTS BRIEF

62400•Depreciation Expense DR 332.42; 17000•Accumulated Depreciation CR <332.42>

15. Click **Save & Close**; click **OK** in the **Tracking Fixed Assets on Journal Entries** window.

Preparing Financial Statements

Once the adjusted entries have been made, it is time to move on to producing the financial statements for the company. Financial statements are very important in that they can be used both internally and externally to learn about the financial health of a company. Internally, reports are used by management to make decisions in regard to operations. It is beneficial to not only look at the current year's statements, but also compare them to the statements from the previous fiscal year. Externally, the financial statements are used in a variety of capacities such as to determine if money should be lent to a company, whether a business is profitable, and whether to purchase stock in a company.

> **FLASHBACK TO GAAP: OBJECTIVITY**
>
> Remember that the statements of a company should be based on objectivity.

Cycle Step 6: Financial Statements

The next step in the accounting cycle requires that financial statements be produced. The statements you must produce are the income statement, the statement of owner's equity, and the balance sheet. Some users of your company's financial data may also need a statement of cash flows, which you learned to produce in the previous chapter. You have seen two of these reports already in the first part of this book. Now you will look at them in more depth.

The Income Statement

The Income Statement (a.k.a the Profit & Loss report) is a report that displays the income and expenses generated over a specific period of time. In this case, the net income or net loss will tell a story about the financial health of the company. When using pen-and-paper accounting, the values to be displayed on the Income Statement will come from the Income Statement section of the worksheet.

The Income Statement will have either two or three sections, depending on whether the company deals with inventory or not. If inventory is involved, then a Cost of Goods Sold section will be displayed along with the Income and Expense sections.

> **FLASHBACK TO THE GAAP: MATCHING**
>
> Remember that you are to match the expenses to revenues within the same fiscal period. The Income Statement helps you to make sure this happens.

The Income Statement is made up of temporary accounts. Therefore, it will begin each fiscal year with all accounts displaying a zero balance because the previous period's amounts will have been transferred to the Retained Earnings account as either a net income or a net loss.

Analyzing the Income Statement

There are different measures used to analyze a company's health using the income statement, and the measure used will depend on the purpose of the analysis. As you learned in Chapter 11, Introducing the Accounting Cycle and Using Classes, the Statement of Cash

Flows is a more reliable report in many instances, but the Income Statement can still be a useful tool for analyzing aspects of the business such as:

- Ratios to measure profitability (gross margin %, net income %)
- Growth trend analysis (earnings vs. expenses)
- Comparison to similar businesses
- Return on investment

The Balance Sheet

The Balance Sheet is a report that displays the permanent accounts, which make up the elements of the accounting equation (Assets = Liabilities + Equity). It reflects the financial condition of a business on a particular date. In pen-and-paper accounting, the values for the Balance Sheet come from the Balance Sheet section of the worksheet.

FLASHBACK TO GAAP: TIME PERIOD
Remember that the activities of the business can be divided into time periods.

Analyzing the Balance Sheet

Just as the Income Statement is not a perfect tool for analyzing a business, the Balance Sheet is not always the right tool. It can, though, be useful for looking at:

- Ratios to measure profitability, liquidity, and financial strength in the long run (current ratio, quick ratio, return on assets, and return on equity)
- Comparison of assets to liabilities over time
- Working capital (current assets less current liabilities)
- Leverage (debt/worth)

The Statement of Owner's Equity

The Statement of Owner's Equity is a report that shows the capital at the beginning of the fiscal period, any additional investments as well as draws, the net income or loss, and the ending amount.

The amounts on the Statement of Owner's Equity come from two sections of the pen-and-paper worksheet. The net income or loss comes from the Income Statement section, and the beginning capital, investments, and draws come from the Balance Sheet section.

QuickBooks does not provide this as a report for you. One way to look at the change in owner's equity from one fiscal period to another is to customize a balance sheet previous year comparison report by filtering it to show only equity accounts.

Creating Reports to Compare Data from Previous Fiscal Periods

QuickBooks provides ready-made reports to help you compare company financial information from the current and previous fiscal periods easily. The Profit & Loss Previous Year Comparison and Balance Sheet Previous Year Comparison reports show the dollar values for each year and detail the change in amount and percentage.

In addition to the preset reports available in QuickBooks to compare data, you can also customize summary reports to show the same previous period information.

QUICK REFERENCE	PRODUCING FINANCIAL STATEMENTS AND EXPORTING TO EXCEL
Task	**Procedure**
Produce an Income Statement report	▪ Choose Reports→Company & Financial→Profit & Loss Standard. ▪ Set the date range for the report.
Produce a balance sheet report	▪ Choose Reports→Company & Financial→Balance Sheet Standard. ▪ Set the "as of" date for the report.
Produce a report showing the change in owner equity from one period to the next	▪ Choose Reports→Company & Financial→Balance Sheet Prev Year Comparison. ▪ Click the Modify Report button; set the date range for the report. ▪ Click the Filters tab, choose to filter by Account, and then choose All equity accounts. ▪ Click the Header/Footer tab, and then change the Report Title to `Equity Previous Year Comparison`.
Modify a summary report to show previous period comparison data	▪ Create a summary report with the data you wish to compare to a prior period. ▪ Click the Modify Report button on the toolbar; set the desired date range. ▪ Click to choose Add subcolumns for Previous Period and/or Previous Year. ▪ Choose if you want to see the % Change and/or $ Change for each subcolumn.

DEVELOP YOUR SKILLS 12-4
Create Financial Statements

In this exercise, you will help Allison to create financial statements for Average Guy Designs.

The first report you will create is the Income Statement for the first quarter of 2015.

1. Choose **Reports→Company & Financial→Profit & Loss Standard**.

2. Tap [Tab], type **010115**, tap [Tab] again, and then type **033115**.

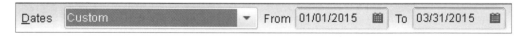

3. Click the **Customize Report** button on the toolbar; click the **Header/Footer** tab.

4. Tap ⌊Tab⌋ three times, and then type **Income Statement** as the new Report Title.

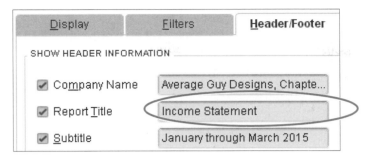

5. Click **OK** in the Modify Report window.

   You will now see the report that you have just modified.

6. Close the **Profit & Loss** window, choosing not to memorize it.

Run a Balance Sheet Report

The next financial statement to be produced is the Balance Sheet report for the period ending March 31, 2015.

7. Choose **Reports→Company & Financial→Balance Sheet Standard**.

8. Tap ⌊Tab⌋, and then type **033115**.

   You will now see a basic Balance Sheet report.

9. Close the **Balance Sheet** window, choosing not to memorize it.

Create a Report That Shows the Equity Account Information from Two Periods

Next, you will create a report that shows the change in equity information from one period to the next.

10. Choose **Reports→Company & Financial→Balance Sheet Prev Year Comparison**.

11. Click the **Customize Report** button.

12. Follow these steps to set the date and further modify the report:

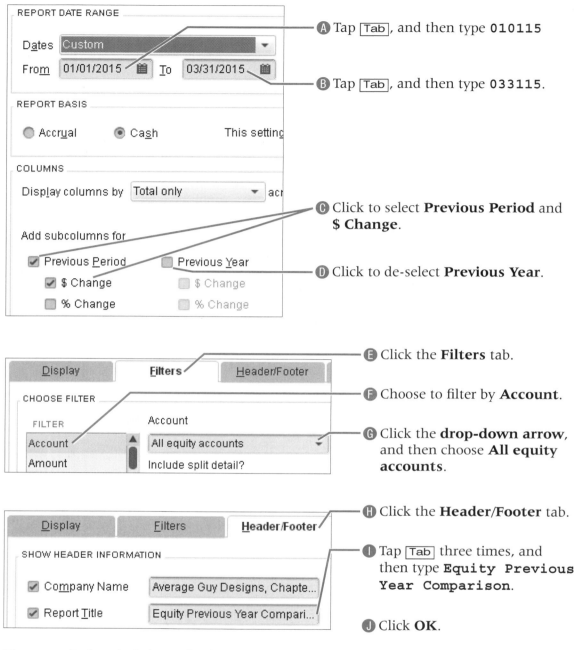

Ⓐ Tap ⟨Tab⟩, and then type **010115**

Ⓑ Tap ⟨Tab⟩, and then type **033115**.

Ⓒ Click to select **Previous Period** and **$ Change**.

Ⓓ Click to de-select **Previous Year**.

Ⓔ Click the **Filters** tab.

Ⓕ Choose to filter by **Account**.

Ⓖ Click the **drop-down arrow**, and then choose **All equity accounts**.

Ⓗ Click the **Header/Footer** tab.

Ⓘ Tap ⟨Tab⟩ three times, and then type **Equity Previous Year Comparison**.

Ⓙ Click **OK**.

The report displays the balances for the equity accounts on 12/31/2014 and 03/31/2015 as well as the dollar change.

13. Close the **Balance Sheet Prev Year Comparison** report window.

Wrapping Up the Accounting Cycle and Closing the Books

To wrap up the accounting cycle, you need to "zero out" the temporary accounts and move the resulting net income or net loss to a permanent account (specifically an equity account) to begin the next fiscal year. In addition to moving the net income or net loss to the equity account, you also need to bring the account that tracks owner's draw or shareholder distributions to zero.

Cycle Step 7: Closing Entries and Post-Closing Trial Balance

In pen-and-paper accounting, there are five tasks involved in the final step of the accounting cycle.

1. Transfer the ending amounts from all of the income accounts to the Income Summary account
2. Transfer the ending amounts from all of the expense accounts to the Income Summary account
3. Transfer the amount in the Income Summary account to the capital account
4. Transfer the amount in the owner's draw account to the capital account
5. Create a post-closing trial balance report

Each of these tasks results in journal transactions that close out the temporary accounts and move the amounts to Income Summary. Then a transaction is recorded that transfers the amount from Income Summary to the capital account. Take note of the following:

■ If the balance in the Income Summary account is a credit, then you will need to debit it and credit the capital account. This signifies that the company has experienced a net income.

■ If the balance in the Income Summary account is a debit, then you will need to credit it and debit the capital account. This signifies that the company has experienced a net loss.

In QuickBooks, all of this is done for you behind the scenes when you close the books. This step will result in either an increase or decrease in the capital account balance based on whether the company saw a net income or a net loss and the amount of funds the owner(s) drew from the company.

The final report that you will create is a Post-Closing Trial Balance that shows all of the temporary accounts with a zero balance. This report also allows you to check for one last time that debits and credits are equal. You should have only permanent accounts displayed in the Post-Closing Trial Balance.

Setting a Closing Date

As you know, you are not required to close the books in QuickBooks, but you can choose to if you like. When you close the books by setting a closing date, QuickBooks does the following for you:

- Transfers the net income or net loss to Retained Earnings
- Restricts access to transactions prior to the closing date by requiring a password
- Allows you to clean up your data

Only the company file administrator can set a closing date and allow or restrict access to prior-period transactions by user.

Pros and Cons of Setting a Closing Date

Since QuickBooks automatically performs some closing actions at the end of your fiscal year (as you learned about earlier in this chapter), you may wonder if you should set a closing date for your file. Take a look at the following pros and cons of setting a closing date in QuickBooks.

SETTING A CLOSING DATE IN QUICKBOOKS	
Pros	**Cons**
You can restrict access to prior-period transactions by setting a password.	You can't easily access all of the details from previous-period transactions
You can create a closing date exception report that displays any modified transactions that are dated on or before the closing date.	You can't create reports that compare transaction data from prior periods.

QUICK REFERENCE	SETTING THE CLOSING DATE
Task	**Procedure**
Set a company closing date	■ Choose Company→Set Closing Date. ■ Click the Set Date/Password button in the Closing Date area of the window. ■ Enter the closing date and password; click OK.

Following is an example of the final step of the accounting cycle in action. In this case, you can see that $100,000 of income will move into the Income Summary account as well as $50,000 of expenses. That results in a $50,000 credit balance that, when transferred to the capital account, will represent a net income of $50,000. In addition, you can see how the owner draw of $10,000 affects the capital account.

Income Summary			All Income Accounts	
	100,000		100,000	

Income Summary			All Expense Accounts	
50,000				50,000

Income Summary			Capital Account	
50,000				50,000

Owner Draw			Capital Account	
	10,000		10,000	

The net effect behind the scenes in this example is a zero balance in the Income Summary account, all the income accounts, all the expense accounts, and the owner draw account. There will be a net increase (credit) in the capital account of $40,000.

Additional Skills

Set the Closing Date in QuickBooks

In this exercise, you will set a closing date and password for the Average Guy Designs QuickBooks company file.

1. Choose **Company→Set Closing Date,** and then click the **Set Date/Password** button in the Preferences window.

   The Set Closing Date and Password window appears.

2. Follow these steps to set the closing date and password:

Ⓐ Click here to exclude some transactions.

Ⓑ Tap ⟨Tab⟩, and then type **123114.**

Ⓒ Tap ⟨Tab⟩, and then type **123.**

Ⓓ Tap ⟨Tab⟩, and then type **123.**

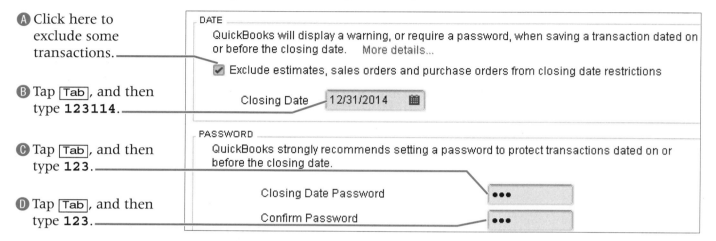

When closing the books, you can choose to not include transactions that do not affect what happens "behind the scenes" by excluding estimates, sales orders, and purchase orders. If you are not sure what decision to make for your own company, check with your accountant.

Also, remember that "123" is not a good password to use in your own company file. It is used here as a basic example.

3. Click **OK** in the **Set Closing Date and Password** window; click No in the **No Password Entered** window.

4. Close the **Preferences** window.

Working with a Company File After Closing

Once you have set a closing date, there is one additional step to the accounting cycle; it has to do with creating another Trial Balance report. You also may choose to clean up your company's data after you close the books.

Correcting Transactions from a Closed Period

As you learned in the last section, you can set a password when you set a closing date. If a password was set, you will need to enter it if you wish to change any of the transactions from the prior period.

The Closing Date Exception Report

If you are using the Premier Accountant edition of QuickBooks, you can choose to produce a report that shows any transactions dated on or before the closing date that were entered after you set the closing date.

The Audit Trail

The audit trail feature of QuickBooks allows you to track every entry, modification, or deletion to transactions in your file. The audit trail feature is always on to make sure that an accurate record of your QuickBooks data is kept. The audit trail does not track changes to lists, only to transactions. This can help you to research transaction history and determine whether certain types of fraudulent activity are occurring. To view the audit trail, you can run a QuickBooks report called "Audit Trail," which is available from the Accountant & Taxes category of the Report Center. In fact, the QuickBooks Audit Trail report has even been reported to have helped determine a fraud case in court!

Cleaning Up Your Data

Once you have closed the books, you have the opportunity to clean up your data. During this process, QuickBooks will delete transactions from before the company closing date that are no longer needed and create "summary" transactions to take their places. Types of transactions that will not be summarized are:

- Those with open balances or that are linked to others with open balances
- Any that have not been reconciled or cleared
- Any that are marked "to be printed"

QuickBooks will not remove any payroll transactions for the current calendar year because of payroll tax reporting requirements.

Cleaning up your company data has huge implications, so make sure you understand what you are doing before you perform this operation.

Preparing for Clean Up

Before QuickBooks begins the clean-up process, it will do three things.

1. Create a backup copy of your file so you can restore your company to its "before clean up" state if necessary.
2. Create an archive copy of your file that will allow you to examine the information that was cleaned up.
3. Verify the integrity of your company file.

Once these three steps are complete, QuickBooks will continue on with the clean-up process. Remember that transactions dated after your company closing date will not be affected by the clean-up process.

List Clean Up

An advantage to cleaning up your file is that you will be able to clean up your lists as well. As you know, when a list entry has been used in a transaction, you cannot delete it. After the clean-up process, if all of the transactions for a particular list entry have been deleted or summarized, you can then delete the list entry.

Make sure that you have completed all year-end activities before you clean up your company file, such as producing W-2s, W-3s, and 1099 MISC forms.

Working with an Accountant's Copy

If your accountant needs to make adjustments to your QuickBooks file but you do not want to lose access to it while it is being adjusted, you may want to create an accountant's copy file. Your accountant can make the needed adjustments, and you can at least keep up with your daily transactions.

However, there are some tasks that you *cannot* do while your accountant is working on your file, such as:

- Edit or delete accounts
- Add, edit, or delete transactions dated on or before the dividing date
- Reconcile an account

Just as with setting a closing date, only the company file administrator can create an accountant's copy.

The Dividing Date

When you create an accountant's copy, you must set a dividing date. The dividing date determines the point up to which your accountant can work on the file and the point from which you can work in your company file. Be careful when setting this date to ensure that your accountant will have the access needed and that you will still be able to modify recent transactions, if necessary. If your accountant is making adjusting entries, it makes sense to set the dividing date as the last day of the previous fiscal year.

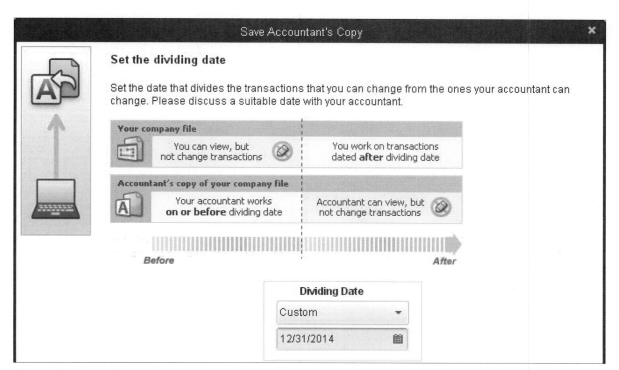

The dividing date will determine the date from which your accountant can make changes to your company file. It also dictates your own access to your company file.

Managing Accountant's Copies

There are four different tasks you will encounter when working with accountant's copies: saving, sending, importing, and removing restrictions. All of these are accessible through the File option on the menu:

- **Saving the file:** This task allows you to create a file, similar to a portable company or backup file, with which your accountant will be able to work while you continue with many of your daily tasks.

- **Sending the file:** You can email the file or save it to a CD or other storage media in order to provide your accountant with the file. Intuit also provides a service called Intuit's Accountant's Copy File Transfer service. This option, found under the File menu, is available if you have Internet access. It does not require that you save a copy of the file (it is done for you when you upload it to the Intuit web server). Your accountant will receive an email with a link that can be used to access your file for download.

- **Importing the file:** Once you receive the file back from your accountant, you must import it into your company file. When you import your accountant's changes, you will be prompted to create a backup copy of your file. This is important in case the import is not successful—you will still have a workable copy of your company file. During the import process, it will be up to you to accept all or none of the changes into your company file and to view the notes left for you from your accountant.

- **Removing restrictions on your file:** To cancel an accountant's copy, you must choose to remove restrictions. If you do this, though, you will not be able to import the accountant's copy changes. On the other hand, if you accidentally create an accountant's copy file, just cancel it to work with your file in normal mode.

Task	Procedure
Produce a closing date exception report (Premier Accountant edition)	■ Choose Reports→Accountant & Taxes→Closing Date Exception Report.
Run an audit trail report	■ Choose Reports→Accountant & Taxes→Audit Trail. ■ Set the desired date or date range.
Create an accountant's copy	■ Choose File→Accountant's Copy→Save File. ■ Choose Accountant's Copy; click Next. ■ Set the dividing date, click Next, and then click OK. ■ Choose the save location; click Save.
Import an accountant's copy	■ Choose File→Accountant's Copy→Import Accountant's Changes. ■ Locate the QuickBooks Accountant Change File; click Open. ■ Click Import; click OK to let QuickBooks close all windows. ■ Click OK to allow QuickBooks to create a backup file; set the location and complete the backup steps. ■ Once the backup is complete, click OK to acknowledge it; click Close in the Import Accountant's Changes window.
Cancel an accountant's copy	■ Choose File→Accountant's Copy→Remove Restrictions. ■ Click in box to the left of Yes, I want to remove the Accountant's Copy restrictions; click OK.
Send file via Intuit server	■ Choose File→Accountant's Copy→Send to Accountant. ■ Click Next to confirm; choose your dividing date. ■ Enter your and your accountant's email addresses and names. ■ Enter a password for your accountant's copy, enter any notes for your accountant (do not include the password here!), and then click Send.
Clean up a company file	■ Choose File→Utilities→Clean Up Company Data. ■ Choose whether to remove all transactions or those as of a certain date; click Next. ■ Select any additional criteria for removing transactions; click Next. ■ Choose whether you want unused list entries removed for you; click Next. ■ Click Begin Cleanup; follow the steps displayed. ■ Once the backup copy is created, QuickBooks will automatically continue with the archive copy, the data validation, and the clean-up process. When the cleanup is completed, click OK.

DEVELOP YOUR SKILLS 12-6

Correct a Transaction from a Closed Period and Run an Audit Trail Report

In this exercise, you will help Allison to correct a transaction from a closed period and produce an audit trail report.

Guy realized that invoice #14-0019, dated 12/18/2014, should have been dated 12/11/2014. You will first help Allison to make this change.

1. Choose **Edit→Find**, and then click the **Simple** tab.

2. Click in the **Invoice #** field, type **14-0019**, and then click **Find**.

3. Click the **Go To** button.

   Invoice #14-0019 was already selected, so when you clicked Go To, QuickBooks opened the Create Invoices window with it displayed.

4. Tap ⟦Tab⟧ three times, type **121114**, and then tap ⟦Tab⟧ again.

5. Choose San Tomas as the Tax Item.

   Once sales tax has been turned on for a company, you must choose a tax item, even if all items in the transaction are not taxable.

6. Click **Save & Close** to record the new date for the invoice; click **Yes** to make the change to the transaction.

   A QuickBooks window appears that lets you know that you are making a change to a transaction from a closed period. To bypass this window and make the change, you need to enter the closing date password.

7. Type **123**, and then click **OK**.

8. Click Save Anyway to save the transaction without a class.

   If you recall, Average Guy Designs did not begin tracking classes until March 2015.

9. Close the **Find** window.

Create an Audit Trail Report

You will now take a look at the Audit Trail report, which will show you the change that you just made to invoice #14-0019.

10. Choose **Reports→Accountant & Taxes→Audit Trail**.

11. Scroll down until you can see the documentation of the change that you just made to invoice **#14-0019**.

Average Guy Designs, Chapter 12
Audit Trail

Num	Entered/Last Modified	Last modified by	State	Date	Name	Memo	Account	Split	Amount
Invoice 14-0019									
14-0019	12/16/2013 13:09:11	Guy (Admin)	Latest	*12/11/2014*	Mary Jones		11000 · Accounts...	-SPLIT-	270.00
					Mary Jones	Production o...	43200 · Design Inc...	11000 · Acco...	-270.00
					State Board of E...	San Tomas...	25500 · Sales Tax...	11000 · Acco...	0.00
14-0019	11/04/2013 03:48:58	Guy (Admin)	Prior	12/18/2014	Mary Jones		11000 · Accounts...	43200 · Desig...	270.00
					Mary Jones	Production o...	43200 · Design Inc...	11000 · Acco...	-270.00

The Audit Trail report shows the prior and most current "version" of a transaction.

12. Close the **Audit Trail** report window.

Tackle the Tasks

Now is your chance to work a little more with Average Guy Designs and apply the skills that you have learned in this chapter to accomplish additional tasks. You will use the same company file you used in the Develop Your Skills exercises throughout this chapter. Enter the following tasks, referring back to the concepts in the chapter as necessary.

CREATE A BALANCE SHEET REPORT AS OF 03/31/2015	
Calculation	**Answer**
Quick ratio: (current assets – inventory)/current liabilities	
Return on assets: net income/total assets	
Working capital: current assets – current liabilities	

CREATE AN INCOME STATEMENT REPORT FOR THE PERIOD 1/1/2015–03/31/2015	
Calculation	**Answer**
Gross profit margin: (revenue – COGS)/revenue	
Operating profit margin: revenue – expenses related to day-to-day operations of the business	
Net profit margin: net income/revenue	

Choose the appropriate option for your situation:

■ *If you are continuing on to the end-of-chapter exercises, leave QuickBooks open.*

■ *If you are finished working in QuickBooks for now, choose* **File→Exit***.*

Concepts Review

To check your knowledge of the key concepts introduced in this chapter, complete the Concepts Review quiz on the Student Resource Center or in your eLab course.

Reinforce Your Skills

Angela Stevens has just relocated her company, Quality-Built Construction, from California to Silverton, Oregon. You will be working with a QuickBooks Sample Company File in this exercise as it will allow you to run full payroll in a future chapter without having to purchase a payroll subscription.

Before you begin the Reinforce Your Skills exercises, complete one of these options:

- Open **RYS_Chapter12** from your file storage location.
- Restore **RYS_Chapter12 (Portable)** from your file storage location. Make sure to place your last name and first initial at the end of the filename (e.g., RYS_Chapter12_StevensA).

REINFORCE YOUR SKILLS 12-1
Work with the Trial Balance Report

In this exercise, you will create a Trial Balance report for Quality-Built Construction.

1. Choose **Reports→Accountant & Taxes→Trial Balance**.
2. Tap Tab, type **010118**, tap Tab again, and then type **123118**.
3. Click the **Refresh** button.

   The trial balance report for the fiscal year displays.
4. Close the **Trial Balance** report, choosing not to memorize it.

REINFORCE YOUR SKILLS 12-2
Create an Adjusting Entry and Inventory Adjustment

Angela will need to make an adjusting entry to record depreciation for 2018. Then she will record an inventory adjustment to account for a coffee table that was damaged.

1. Choose **Company→Make General Journal Entry**; click **OK** in the Assigning Numbers to Journal Entries window.
2. Type **123118** as the date.
3. Debit Depreciation Expense for **$6,500**, typing **2018 Depreciation** as the Memo and **Overhead Costs** as the Class.
4. Credit Accumulated Depreciation for **$6,500**, typing **2018 Depreciation** as the Memo and **Overhead Costs** as the Class.
5. Click **Save & Close** to record the transaction.
6. Click in the checkbox to not display the message in the future; click **OK** in the Tracking Fixed Assets on Journal Entries window.

Make an Inventory Adjustment

Next you will help Angela to create an inventory adjustment to deduct the damaged coffee table from inventory.

7. Choose **Vendors→Inventory Activities→Adjust Quantity/Value on Hand**.

8. Type **013119** as the **Adjustment Date**, and then tap Tab.

9. Type **Inventory Adjustment** as the **Adjustment Account**, and then tap Tab.

10. Click **Set Up**.

11. Set the **Account Type** as **Expense** and the **Number** as **6220**; click **Save & Close**.

12. Choose **Material Costs - Job Related** as the **Class**.

13. Choose to reduce the number of **Coffee Tables** in inventory by one (**-1**).

14. Click **Save & Close**.

REINFORCE YOUR SKILLS 12-3
Produce Financial Statements

In this exercise, you will produce an Income Statement, Balance Sheet, and Statement of Owner's Equity for Quality-Built Construction.

1. Choose **Reports→Company & Financial→Profit & Loss Standard**.

2. Tap Tab, type **010118**, tap Tab again, and then type **123118**.

3. Click **Refresh**.

   The Profit & Loss report displays for 2018. You will now change the report title to Income Statement.

4. Click the **Customize Report** button, and then click the **Header/Footer** tab.

5. Change the Report Title to **Income Statement**, and then click **OK**.

6. Click the **Memorize** button on the toolbar, type **Income Statement 2018**, and then click **OK**.

7. Close the **report window**.

Create a Balance Sheet Report

8. Choose **Reports→Company & Financial→Balance Sheet Standard**.

9. Tap Tab, type **123118**, and then tap Tab again.

10. Click the **Memorize** button on the report toolbar, type **Balance Sheet, 12/31/18**, and then click **OK**.

11. Close the **report** window.

REINFORCE YOUR SKILLS 12-4

Close the Books

In this exercise, you will now help Angela to set a closing date for her QuickBooks company file. Because this is a sample company file, we will be setting the closing date to be 12/14/2018 so that we can do the next exercise.

1. Choose **Company→Set Closing Date**.

2. Click the **Set Date/Password** button.

   The Set Closing Date and Password window appears.

```
CLOSING DATE
Date through which books are closed:          (not set)

              Set Date/Password
```

3. Click in the checkbox to choose to exclude estimates, sales orders, and purchase orders from closing date restrictions.

4. Tap ⟨Tab⟩, and then type **121418**.

5. Tap ⟨Tab⟩, type **123**, tap ⟨Tab⟩ again, and then type **123**.

6. Click **OK** to set the closing date and password, click **No** in the No Password Entered window, and then click **OK** in the Preferences window.

REINFORCE YOUR SKILLS 12-5

Make a Correction to a Transaction from a Prior Period

In this exercise, you will make a correction to a transaction from a closed period. Angela realized that she needs to change the amount of the bill dated 12/12/2018 for Color-Brite Paint Company to $1,063.04. You will help her to make that change now.

1. Choose **Edit→Find**.

2. Choose **Bill** as the Transaction Type and choose **Color-Brite Paint Company** as the Vendor; click **Find**.

   You will see all of the bills for the vendor displayed at the bottom of the window.

3. Double-click the bill for **12/12/2018**.

   The Enter Bills window will open with the selected bill displayed.

4. Change the **Amount** on the bill to **$1063.04** (both in the top and bottom portion of the window) and click **Save & Close**; click **Yes** to record the transaction.

   A QuickBooks window appears, asking for you to enter the closing date password in order to make the change.

5. Type **123** and click **OK**; click **Yes** to permanently change the terms for the vendor.

6. Close the **Find** window.

7. Choose the appropriate option for your situation:
   - If you are continuing on to the rest of the end-of-chapter exercises, leave QuickBooks open.
   - If you are finished working in QuickBooks for now, choose **File→Exit**.

Apply Your Skills

Before you begin the Apply Your Skills exercises, complete one of these options:

- Open **AYS_Chapter12** from your file storage location.
- Restore **AYS_Chapter12 (Portable)** from your file storage location. Make sure to place your last name and first initial at the end of the filename (e.g., AYS_Chapter12_JamesS).

You will work with a one-month (May 2014) reporting period for Wet Noses Veterinary Clinic.

Create a Trial Balance Report

In this exercise, you will help Dr. James to create a Trial Balance report for Wet Noses.

1. Choose **Reports→Accountant & Taxes→Trial Balance**.

2. Set the date range to cover **May 2014**.

   The trial balance report for the one-month period of May 2014 displays.

3. Close the **Trial Balance report**, choosing not to memorize it.

Work with Journal Entries

In this exercise, you will create adjusting entries. Dr. James has realized that she needs to enter the equipment that she invested into the company. She will then need to enter the depreciation transaction for the fixed assets.

Record a Fixed Asset Investment

You will first help Sadie to enter a general journal entry to record the furniture and equipment that she provided to the company.

1. Open the **Make General Journal** Entries window.

2. Create a transaction dated **5/1/2014** that debits Furniture and Equipment and credits the Partner 1 Equity account for **$16,320**. Use **Overhead** as the class and **Record fixed asset investment** as the Memo.

Record a Depreciation Transaction

You will now help Sadie to record the depreciation for the month.

3. Create a transaction dated **5/31/2014** that debits Depreciation Expense and credits the Accumulated Depreciation account for **$128**. Use **Overhead** as the class and **Record May 2014 Depreciation** as the Memo.

4. Click **Save & Close** when you are finished to save the transaction and close the window.

Close the Books

In this exercise, you will close the books and create an Accountant's Copy of the file.

1. Open the **Preferences** window with the Accounting category and the Company Preferences tab displayed.

2. Choose to set the closing date and password; choose to exclude estimates, sales orders, and purchase order from closing date restrictions.

3. Enter **5/31/2014** as the Closing Date, and then use **123** as the Closing Date Password.

4. Choose to not add or edit users.

Create an Accountant's Copy

Next you will create an accountant's copy that your accountant can use to view your company data and make adjusting entries.

5. Choose **File→Accountant's Copy→Save File**.

   If using the Premier Accountant edition, the menu command will be File→Accountant's Copy→Client Activities→Save File.

6. Choose **Accountant's Copy**, and then click **Next**.

If you are completing this exercise prior to 5/31/2014, you will not be allowed to set the closing date (since it is in the future). In that case, click Cancel.

7. Set the dividing date as **5/31/2014**, click **Next**, and then click **OK**.

8. Choose your default file storage location, and then click **Save**.

   Now you have a file that you can send to your accountant.

Additional Skills

Answer Questions with Reports

In this exercise, you will answer questions for Dr. James by running reports. You may wish to display the Report Center in List View to help you to answer the questions. Ask your instructor if you should print the reports, print (save) them as PDF files, export them to Excel, or simply display them on the screen. This exercise requires you to create some basic formulas in Excel. If you do not have Excel on your computer, or do not know how to use it, you may skip this exercise.

1. Should we run something called a trial balance at the end of each month? Could you please run one for me for 5/31/14 so I can see what it looks like?

2. What is the net profit margin for the business during the month of May 2014? (Hint: Create a Profit & Loss Standard report and edit the report title to **Income Statement**. Export the report to Excel and then calculate the net profit margin by taking the net income and dividing it by the total income.) Memorize the report as **Income Statement, May 2014**. Type Net Profit Margin in cell I2, and right-align it. Enter the formula for the net profit margin in cell J2 and format it as a percentage.

3. What is the current ratio of the company as of May 31, 2014? (Hint: Create a Summary Balance Sheet report as of **5/31/2014**. Export the report to Excel and then calculate the current ratio by dividing the current assets by the current liabilities.) Memorize the report as **Balance Sheet, 5/31/2014**. Type Current Ratio in cell G2, and right-align it. Enter the formula for the current ratio in cell H2.

4. Create a report showing the change in owner's equity from **4/30/2014** to **5/31/2014**. Name and memorize it as Equity Previous Month Comparison.

5. Submit your reports based on the guidelines provided by your instructor.

6. Choose the option that is appropriate for your situation:
   - If you are continuing on to the Extend Your Skills exercises, leave QuickBooks open.
   - If you are finished working in QuickBooks for now, choose **File→Exit**.

Extend Your Skills

In the course of working through the following Extend Your Skills exercises, you will be utilizing various skills taught in this and previous chapter(s). Take your time and think carefully about the tasks presented to you. Turn back to the chapter content if you need assistance.

12-1 Sort Through the Stack

Before You Begin: Restore the **EYS1_Chapter12 (Portable)** file or open the **EYS1_Chapter12** company file from your storage location.

You have been hired by Arlaine Cervantes to help her with her organization's books. She is the founder of Niños del Lago, a nonprofit organization that provides impoverished Guatemalan children with an engaging educational camp experience. You have just sat down at your desk and opened a large envelope from her with a variety of documents and noticed that you have several emails from her as well. It is your job to sort through the papers and emails and make sense of what you find, entering information into QuickBooks whenever appropriate and answering any other questions in a word-processing document saved as **EYS1_Chapter12_ LastnameFirstinitial**. Remember, you are digging through papers on a desk, so it is up to you to determine the correct order in which to complete the tasks.

- Note from Arlaine: I know that the end-of-period accounting for not-for-profits is a bit different than what is done for "regular" for-profit businesses. Will you please go to http://labyrinthelab.com/qb14 and complete the WebQuest that will help you to learn more about what we need to know about not-for-profit accounting?

- Scribbled note from Arlaine: Please create a Balance Sheet report as of 8/31/2014, change the name of it to **Statement of Financial Position**, and export it to Excel. Save the Excel file as **SFP, 8-31-14**.

12-2 Be Your Own Boss

Before You Begin: You must complete Extend Your Skills 11-2 *before you begin this exercise.*

In this exercise, throughout the entire book, you will build on the company file that you outlined in previous chapters. If you have created a file for your actual business, then make all necessary adjusting entries, make any necessary inventory adjustments, and close the books in QuickBooks, if appropriate for you to do so at this time. If you are creating a fictitious company, then make an adjusting entry for depreciation (assume straight-line depreciation and calculate an estimated amount for the fixed assets you have entered), adjust at least one inventory item, and close the books in QuickBooks. You will make up the names and information for this exercise.

Create all of the main financial statements and submit them to your instructor based on the instructions provided.

Open the company file you worked on in Extend Your Skills 11-2 and complete the tasks outlined above. When you are done, save it as a portable company file, naming it as **EYS2_ Chapter12_LastnameFirstinitial (Portable)** and submit it to your instructor based on the instructions provided.

12-3 Use the Web as a Learning Tool

Throughout this book, you will be provided with an opportunity to use the Internet as a learning tool by completing WebQuests. According to the original creators of WebQuests, as described on their website (http://WebQuest.org), a WebQuest is "an inquiry-oriented activity in which most or all of the information used by learners is drawn from the web." To complete the WebQuest projects in this book, navigate to the Student Resource Center and choose the WebQuest for the chapter on which you are working. The subject of each WebQuest will be relevant to the material found in the chapter.

WebQuest Subject: End-of-period reporting

Need to Know Accounting

Even though QuickBooks does everything for you "behind the scenes," it is important that you have a basic understanding of what is happening to your books.

In this appendix, you will learn about the basic financial statements important to any business and the accounts that appear on these reports. You will also learn about the double-entry accounting system and the debits and credits that must always be equal.

Working with Financial Statements

There are two main reports that a company will produce periodically to illustrate its financial well-being.

- A **Balance Sheet** report displays all of the holdings of the company along with the debts as of a particular date.
- An **Income Statement**, otherwise known as a Profit & Loss Report, displays the income and expenses for a specified period of time.

Understanding the accounts that make up each of these reports is key to understanding your company's books.

The Accounting Equation and the Balance Sheet

The first equation you need to learn when it comes to accounting is simply termed the accounting equation:

$$\text{Assets} = \text{Liabilities} + \text{Equity}$$

This means that if you take all of your company's debt and add any investments (equity), you will have a value equal to all of the assets that your company owns.

A balance sheet is a financial statement that displays all asset, liability, and equity accounts (the balance sheet accounts). Take a look at the following illustrations to see how the accounting equation works and is represented in a balance sheet.

Average Guy Designs, Chapter 12
Balance Sheet
As of February 28, 2015

	◇ Feb 28, 15 ◇
▼ ASSETS	
▼ Current Assets	
▼ Checking/Savings	
10000 · Checking	1,269.38
10200 · Savings	3,382.35
10400 · Money Market	1,000.00
10500 · Petty Cash	247.76
Total Checking/Savings	5,899.49
▼ Accounts Receivable	
11000 · Accounts Receivable	250.00
Total Accounts Receivable	250.00
▼ Other Current Assets	
12100 · Inventory Asset	1,379.00
13200 · Prepaid Rent	3,500.00
13300 · Prepaid Insurance	875.00
Total Other Current Assets	5,754.00
Total Current Assets	11,903.49
▼ Fixed Assets	
15000 · Furniture and Equipment	2,639.00
16000 · Vehicles	4,500.00
Total Fixed Assets	7,139.00
TOTAL ASSETS	**19,042.49**

▼ LIABILITIES & EQUITY	
▼ Liabilities	
▼ Current Liabilities	
▼ Other Current Liabilities	
24000 · Payroll Liabilities	24.60
25000 · Customer Deposits	300.00
Total Other Current Liabilities	324.60
Total Current Liabilities	324.60
▼ Long Term Liabilities	
26000 · Loan - Vehicles (Vespa - 1)	4,050.00
28300 · Loan -Office Furniture	2,639.00
Total Long Term Liabilities	6,689.00
Total Liabilities	7,013.60
▼ Equity	
30000 · Opening Balance Equity	12,815.02
32000 · Owners Equity	2,402.08
Net Income	-3,188.21
Total Equity	12,028.89
TOTAL LIABILITIES & EQUITY	**19,042.49**

Notice that the amount for Total Liabilities & Equity is $19,042.49.

Notice that the amount for Total Assets is also $19,042.49.

The upper section (displayed here on the left) represents the left side of the accounting equation and displays all assets. The lower section (displayed here on the right) represents the right side of the accounting equation and displays all liability and equity accounts.

Appendix A

The Income Statement

The accounts that you find on the Income Statement (or Profit & Loss report) are income and expense. In the following illustration you can view an Income Statement and the accounts that appear on it.

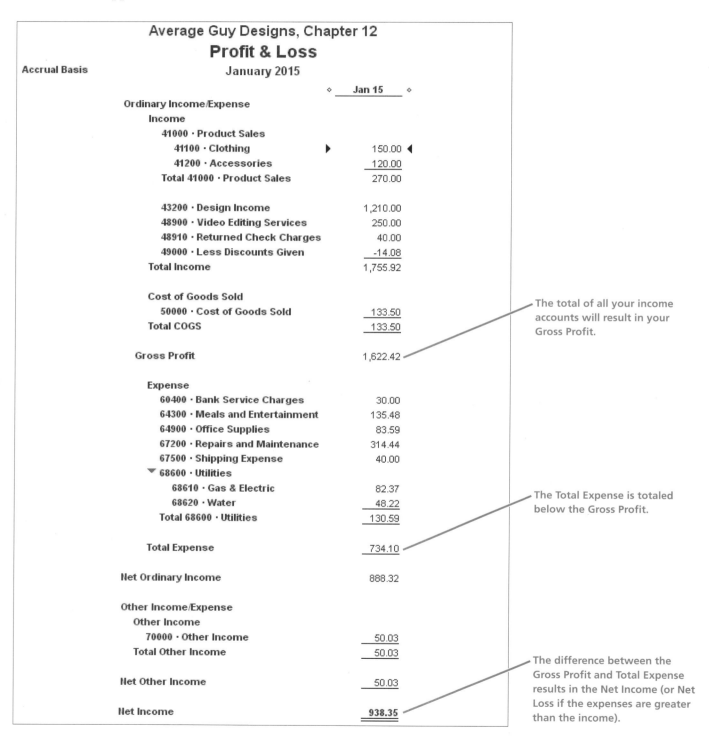

Average Guy Designs, Chapter 12
Profit & Loss
January 2015

Accrual Basis

	Jan 15
Ordinary Income/Expense	
Income	
41000 · Product Sales	
41100 · Clothing	150.00
41200 · Accessories	120.00
Total 41000 · Product Sales	270.00
43200 · Design Income	1,210.00
48900 · Video Editing Services	250.00
48910 · Returned Check Charges	40.00
49000 · Less Discounts Given	-14.08
Total Income	1,755.92
Cost of Goods Sold	
50000 · Cost of Goods Sold	133.50
Total COGS	133.50
Gross Profit	1,622.42
Expense	
60400 · Bank Service Charges	30.00
64300 · Meals and Entertainment	135.48
64900 · Office Supplies	83.59
67200 · Repairs and Maintenance	314.44
67500 · Shipping Expense	40.00
68600 · Utilities	
68610 · Gas & Electric	82.37
68620 · Water	48.22
Total 68600 · Utilities	130.59
Total Expense	734.10
Net Ordinary Income	888.32
Other Income/Expense	
Other Income	
70000 · Other Income	50.03
Total Other Income	50.03
Net Other Income	50.03
Net Income	**938.35**

The total of all your income accounts will result in your Gross Profit.

The Total Expense is totaled below the Gross Profit.

The difference between the Gross Profit and Total Expense results in the Net Income (or Net Loss if the expenses are greater than the income).

Debits and Credits: The Double-Entry Accounting System

There is another equation in accounting that is paramount for us to keep in mind: Debits must always equal credits! Most people who do not work in the accounting field are confused about debits and credits, though.

Accounts are often displayed in a "T" format in accounting (which you can see in all of the Behind the Scenes sections of this book). The T accounts allow you to place the name of the account on the top, account debits on the left side, and account credits on the right side. This means that the left side (debits) must always equal the right side (credits) when entering accounting transactions (hence the term "double-entry").

Account Name	
Debit Side	Credit Side

A simple way to view an account is to use the T format.

In order to understand debits and credits a bit better, we will now look at the types of accounts and their normal balances.

Types of Accounts and Normal Balances

We have looked at the two main financial statements and the types of accounts included in each. The balance sheet is composed of asset, liability, and equity accounts. The income statement is composed of income and expense accounts. Before we look deeper into each account type, it is important to understand normal balances.

Take a look at Chapter 2, Creating a Company, to view all of the account sub-types that you can create in QuickBooks.

About Normal Balances

Each type of account must have a normal balance of either a debit or a credit. The normal balance is the side that will increase the amount of the account. Assets and expenses both have debit normal balances and will increase when debited and decrease when credited. Liabilities, equity, and income all have credit normal balances and will increase when credited and decrease when debited.

The concept of normal balances makes sense if you think of the balance sheet. Assets with a debit normal balance must equal the sum of the liabilities and equity, which both have a credit normal balance. Think of this as the marriage of the accounting equation and the fact that debits must equal credits!

The following table describes the primary account types and their normal balances.

Account Type	Description
Assets	An asset is anything that a company owns or monies that are owed to the company. Examples of assets are checking accounts, accounts receivable, and autos. Assets have a debit normal balance.
Liabilities	A liability is something that a company owes such as an auto loan or a credit card balance. Liabilities have a credit normal balance.
Equity	Equity accounts are both investments into the company (Owner's Equity or Stockholder's Equity) and the net income or loss from the operation of a business (Retained Earnings). Equity accounts have a credit normal balance.
Income	Income accounts reflect the sales and fees earned during an accounting period. Income accounts have a credit normal balance.
Expenses	Expense accounts record the expenditures that a company accrues while conducting business. Expense accounts have a debit normal balance.

The Trial Balance Report

At the end of an accounting cycle a trial balance is prepared that shows all accounts affected during the cycle. The balance of each account is entered in the appropriate column based on its normal balance. The net income or net loss is the difference between income and expenses. If the income is greater than the expenses, an excess credit balance will result and will increase the equity account (a net income). If the expenses are greater than the income, an excess debit balance will result and will decrease the equity account (a net loss).

Average Guy Designs, Chapter 12
Trial Balance
As of February 28, 2015

	Feb 28, 15	
	Debit	Credit
10000 · Checking	1,269.38	
10200 · Savings	3,382.35	
10400 · Money Market	1,000.00	
10500 · Petty Cash	247.76	
11000 · Accounts Receivable	0.00	
12000 · Undeposited Funds	0.00	
12100 · Inventory Asset	1,379.00	
13200 · Prepaid Rent	3,500.00	
13300 · Prepaid Insurance	875.00	
15000 · Furniture and Equipment	2,639.00	
16000 · Vehicles	4,500.00	
20000 · Accounts Payable	0.00	
21000 · Sunriver Credit Union Visa	0.00	
24000 · Payroll Liabilities		24.60
25000 · Customer Deposits		300.00
25500 · Sales Tax Payable	0.00	
26000 · Loan - Vehicles (Vespa - 1)		4,050.00
28300 · Loan -Office Furniture		2,639.00
30000 · Opening Balance Equity		12,815.02
32000 · Owners Equity		85.35
41100 · Clothing		150.00
41200 · Accessories		120.00
43200 · Design Income		3,200.00
48800 · Print Layout Income		200.00
48900 · Video Editing Services		690.00
48910 · Returned Check Charges		40.00
49000 · Less Discounts Given	16.70	
50000 · Cost of Goods Sold	133.50	
60300 · Bad Debt Expense	345.00	
60400 · Bank Service Charges	30.00	
61700 · Computer and Internet Expenses	563.27	
63300 · Insurance Expense	175.00	
64300 · Meals and Entertainment	169.23	
64900 · Office Supplies	83.59	
66100 · Company-Paid Benefits	203.50	
66200 · Company-Paid Taxes	188.20	
66300 · Gross Wages	2,460.00	
67100 · Rent Expense	700.00	
67200 · Repairs and Maintenance	314.44	
67500 · Shipping Expense	58.49	
68610 · Gas & Electric	82.37	
68620 · Water	48.22	
70000 · Other Income		50.03
TOTAL	24,364.00	24,364.00

The debits and credits in a Trial Balance must be equal.

Finding Additional Accounting Resources

Want to learn more about what happens to your company's books behind the scenes in QuickBooks? Visit the student resource center to explore a variety of online learning resources or purchase a copy of *Accounting Basics: An Introduction for Non-Accounting Majors*, which is also published by Labyrinth Learning.

Appendix A

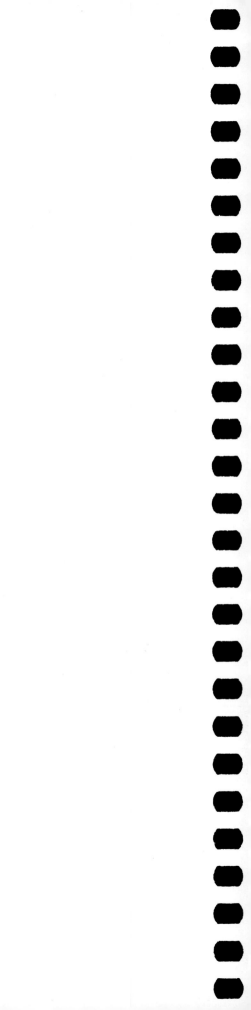

Glossary

accountant's copy   A special copy of your QuickBooks file that can be created if your accountant needs to make adjustments to your QuickBooks file, but you do not want to lose access to it while it is being adjusted

accounting cycle   A series of steps to help a business keep its accounting records properly during the fiscal period

accrual basis   In the accrual basis of accounting, income is recorded when the sale is made and expenses recorded when accrued; often used by firms or businesses with large inventories

activities   Affect what is happening behind the scenes; can be easily input into forms such as invoices or bills

administrator   QuickBooks user who controls the access of all users of a QuickBooks file; administrator also controls all company preferences in the Edit Preferences window

assets   Anything owned by a company or that is owed to a company; items such as a checking account, a building, a prepaid insurance account, or accounts receivable

audit trail   Allows you to track every entry, modification, or deletion to transactions in your file; accessed through the Accounting category in the Report Center or the Report option on the menu bar

Average Cost   A method of inventory tracking where the value of the inventory is determined by dividing the total value of the inventory by the total number of inventory items

backup   The process of creating a condensed copy of your QuickBooks file to ensure you don't lose your data or to allow yourself or another person the ability to view your company file on another computer

bad debt   Funds owed to you that are not collectable and need to be written off

balance sheet accounts   The asset, liability, and equity accounts, such as bank, credit card, current liabilities (sales tax payable and payroll liabilities), accounts receivable, accounts payable, and retained earnings

Balance Sheet by Class Report   Balance sheet report on which each class appears as a separate column; should be used only by expert users

balance sheet report   A report that displays all assets, liabilities, and equity as of a specific date

batch invoicing   Feature that lets a user create invoices that are basically the same for multiple customers at one time

batch timesheets   Feature that allows you to create timesheets for multiple employees who work the same hours on the same jobs and using the same payroll item(s)

behind the scenes   The accounting that QuickBooks performs for you when you enter transactions

bounced check   A check returned by the bank due to non-sufficient funds in the account; also called a "NSF" check

browser   A software application used to locate and display web pages, such as Netscape Navigator and Microsoft Internet Explorer

Budget   In QuickBooks, create a budget for your company either from scratch or based on actual values from a previous period

cash basis   In the cash basis of accounting, income is recorded when cash is received and expenses recorded when cash is paid; commonly used by small businesses and professionals

Cash Flow Forecast   A report that gives you a glimpse of what you can expect a company's cash flow to look like in the near future based on current data in the company file

centers   QuickBooks has four centers: Customer, Employee, Report, and Vendor; centers allow you to view the Customers & Jobs, Employee, and Vendor lists, access QuickBooks reports, and view snapshots of information (of an individual customer, vendor, or employee)

classes   Classes are used to rate; not tied to any particular customer, vendor, or item; used to track only one particular aspect of your business, such as location or individual programs

closing the books   During this process at the end of your fiscal year, QuickBooks transfers the net income or net loss to Retained Earnings, restricts access to transactions prior to the closing date (unless you know the password), and allows you to clean up your company data; you are not required to "close the books" in QuickBooks

company file   The QuickBooks file you use when working with your company's day-to-day operations

company setup   Takes you through the steps necessary to set up a new company in QuickBooks

Company Snapshot   A window that offers a quick view of your company's bottom line in one convenient place

Contributed reports   Feature that allows you to look for a report submitted by another user so you don't have to "reinvent the wheel"; you can also share your custom reports with this feature

Customers & Jobs List   A list in QuickBooks that stores all information related to your customers and the jobs associated with them

Customer & Vendor Profile Lists   Lists QuickBooks provides to track customer and vendor information

Depreciation   Provides a business with a way to match income to expenses; a fixed asset is used to produce income over a period of time, and depreciation allows you to record the appropriate expense for the same period; many small businesses record depreciation transactions just once a year, but they can be entered monthly or quarterly if the business produces financial statements for those periods

Doc Center   Feature that allows you to store your source documents electronically, attaching them to the transactions or list entries to which they belong

draw   An owner's withdrawal of funds from the company

edition   Intuit creates a multitude of editions of QuickBooks to choose from: QuickBooks Online, QuickBooks Pro, QuickBooks Premier, and QuickBooks Enterprise

electronic payments Some companies receive payments from customers electronically; they can be handled by using a new payment type called Electronic Payment

Employees List A list in QuickBooks that helps you to keep track of your employee data; can be used as a source of information to run payroll in QuickBooks; accessed through the Employee Center

equity accounts Reflect the owner's investment in the company and have a credit normal balance; in a Sole Proprietorship, equity is what the owner has invested in the company and in a corporation, the equity is what the shareholders have invested in the company

estimates Feature that allows a user to create a proposal for a customer or job

Express Start In this method of company creation, QuickBooks asks you for your basic company information, and it will be up to you to set up certain items such as payroll and inventory later

field A box into which data is entered

file storage location Location where you store files for this course (USB flash drive, the My Documents folder, or a network drive at a school or company)

filtering Filtering allows you to include only the essential data in your report; choose to filter out many types of data such as accounts, dollar amounts, and types of customers; allows you to closely examine and report on a specific group of data

finance charge A charge assessed to an overdue customer balance

Fixed Asset An asset you don't plan to use up or turn into cash within the next year; businesses use fixed assets in a productive capacity to promote the main operations of the company; are depreciable, which means that you don't expense the assets when you purchase them, but rather over the useful life of the asset

fixed asset account Type of account that tracks the activities associated with a fixed asset

fonts QuickBooks displays its preset reports in a default font; you can make many changes to the characteristics of the font in your report, such as the font name, style, color, and size

forecast A feature that allows you to make predictions about the future; they can be created based on actual figures from the last year or from scratch

Formatting Formatting deals with the appearance of the report; it has nothing to do with the data contained within it

Generally Accepted Accounting Principles (GAAP) Rules used to prepare, present, and report financial statements for a wide variety of entities

graphs Graphs in QuickBooks allow you to display your information in a more illustrative way

header and footer Default headers and footers appear on all preset QuickBooks reports; change the information included along with how it is formatted on the Header and Footer tabs of the Additional Customization window

Income Statement Financial report that can be found in the Company & Financial category of the Report Finder window; P&L reports reflect all transactions that have affected income and expense accounts within a specified time period; also called a Profit & Loss Report

Internet A collection of computers all over the world that send, receive, and store information; access is gained through an Internet Service Provider (ISP); the web is just a portion of the Internet

investment Occurs when an owner deposits funds into the company

job costing Allows a users to determine the profitability of each job for a customer

just in time Allows you to see summary information when entering a transaction for a customer or vendor

Layout Designer The Layout Designer window provides rulers to line up objects, and toolbar buttons to help manipulate your template objects

Lead Center Feature that allows you to track information about potential customers

link Also called hyperlink; provides navigation through a website; displayed on the QuickBooks Home page to provide navigation throughout the QuickBooks program

list (database) Allows you to store information about customers, vendors, employees, and other data important to your business

live community A place where a user can collaborate with other QuickBooks users to get advice or to provide insights

logo QuickBooks allows you to personalize your templates by including your company logo

Long Term Liabilities account A QuickBooks account that tracks a liability (loan) you do not plan to pay off within the next year

online backup QuickBooks offers an online backup option for a monthly fee that is determined based on the amount of room you wish to have available for your backup work

on the fly When you type a new entry into a field that draws from a list, QuickBooks gives you the opportunity to add the record to the list "on the fly" as you create the transaction

Opening Balance Equity account An equity account created by QuickBooks when you start your first balance sheet account; it allows you to have an accurate balance sheet from the start

other current assets An account that tracks the transactions related to an asset that you plan to either use up or convert to cash within one year

outside payroll service A service that runs payroll for a company outside of QuickBooks; the company inputs the information into QuickBooks without using the payroll features

Payroll Liabilities The account in which you hold payroll taxes and other deductions until you are required to pay them

payroll options Intuit provides a variety of options to run your payroll; to view and compare these options, visit the Student Resource Center

PDF file PDF stands for "portable document format;" it is a type of file that preserves formatting, data, and graphics; saves in a portable file

permanent account An account for which the ending balance for one fiscal period is the opening balance for the next

petty cash Cash kept by businesses for small expenditures; in QuickBooks, Petty Cash is set up as a bank account in the Chart of Accounts

portable company file A type of QuickBooks file that contains all company data in a compressed format; it must be restored to be utilized; it is much smaller in size than a company or backup file

preferences The way you interact with QuickBooks is controlled by the preferences you select; the Preferences window has 19 categories; company preferences are controlled by the administrator and determine how the entire company interacts with QuickBooks; personal preferences are controlled by individual users and dictate interactions between QuickBooks and only that one user

Price Level List Allows a user to set and charge different price levels for different customers or jobs

profit and loss (P&L) report A financial report that can be found in the Company & Financial category of the Report Finder window; P&L reports reflect all transactions that have affected income and expense accounts within a specified time period; also called an Income Statement

progress invoicing Allows you to invoice from an estimate in stages rather than for the entire estimate amount

purchase order A form utilized by many companies to enter items into inventory; it does not affect anything "behind the scenes"

Quick Reference tables Tables that summarize the tasks you have just learned. Use them as guidelines when you begin work on your own QuickBooks company file.

QuickReport A report that shows all the transactions recorded in QuickBooks for a particular list record, which can be run from the various list windows

QuickZoom A QuickBooks report and graph feature that allows you to zoom through underlying sub-reports until you reach the form where the data were originally entered; this can be extremely useful if you have questions about where a figure in a report or graph comes from

reconciliation The process of matching your QuickBooks accounts to the bank and credit card statements you receive. It is important to make sure that your account records in QuickBooks match those of the bank or credit card company

report A way to display your company information in various ways such as printed, onscreen, or as a PDF file

resize To change the height or width of an image, window, or object

restoring The process of decompressing a QuickBooks backup or portable company file; when you restore a file in the same location with the same name as another file, it will replace that file

sales orders Allows you to manage customer orders of both products and services; available in the Premier and Enterprise editions

search feature Allows a user to perform searches based on text entered throughout a company file and menu commands

Starter Chart of Accounts During the setup process, QuickBooks asks you to choose the business type that your company most closely resembles; QuickBooks uses your choice to create a Chart of Accounts close to what you need (it will take you less time to edit it to fit your unique business than to start from scratch); you cannot change the business type option later

Statement of Cash Flows Report that shows how viable a company is in the short term; demonstrates whether a company will be able to pay its bills, payroll, and other expenses; also indicates the financial health of the company

Statement of Owner's Equity Report that shows the capital at the beginning of the fiscal period, any additional investments, as well as draws, the net income or loss, and the ending amount

subaccounts Help you keep precise records; to track expenses more closely, you may want to have separate accounts for your office phone, office fax, cellular phone, etc.; subaccounts are a great way to track these separate expenses while keeping the number of expense accounts down

template A specific form format (with no data) on which you can base all of your future forms; QuickBooks provides several templates, but you can also create custom templates

temporary account Accounts are zeroed out at the end of each fiscal period, with the amounts from them moving into an equity account as either a net income (if income was greater than expenses) or a net loss (if expenses exceeded income for the period); also called a nominal account

Time Tracking Allows you to create weekly timesheets so you can break down the hours by customer/job or to record single activities for a customer/job

Trial Balance Report that adds up the debits and credits at the end of an accounting period so mistakes can be traced if debits don't equal credits

unearned income Funds received from a customer as a deposit or for a gift certificate; these funds should be held in a liability account until they are "earned"

units of measure Feature that allows you to convert units of measure; useful for companies that purchase and sell in different units of measure or need to indicate units on purchase or sales forms; available in the Premier and higher versions of QuickBooks

users You can set up an unlimited number of users for your QuickBooks company and assign a password for each person; users can only change their own personal preferences (the administrator controls the access each user has to the QuickBooks file)

Vendor Anyone (except employees) to whom you pay money; could be the electric company, the organization to which you pay taxes, a merchandise supplier, or subcontractors you pay to do work for your customers

Vendor List A list in QuickBooks that stores all information related to your vendors

version Intuit creates a new version of QuickBooks each year (such as QuickBooks 2011, 2012, or 2013) and each new version provides additional features that are new for that year

website Refers to a collection of related web pages and their supporting files and folders.

year-to-date amounts If you begin to use the QuickBooks payroll feature for existing employees who have received at least one paycheck from you (and it is not the first day of January), you must enter year-to-date amounts for them to ensure that QuickBooks calculates taxes with thresholds properly and you will be able to print accurate W-2s at the end of the year

Index

Index

Notes

Notes

Notes

Notes

Notes

Notes